MAJOR TUDOR AUTHORS

MAJOR TUDOR AUTHORS

A Bio-Bibliographical Critical Sourcebook

Edited by ALAN HAGER

Emmanuel S. Nelson, Advisory Editor

GREENWOOD PRESS
Westport, Connecticut • London

Library of Congress Cataloging-in-Publication Data

Major Tudor authors: a bio-bibliographical critical sourcebook /
edited by Alan Hager.
p. cm.
Includes bibliographical references and index.
ISBN 0–313–29436–4 (alk. paper)
1. English literature—Early modern, 1500–1700—Bio-bibliography—Dictionaries. 2. European literature—Renaissance, 1450–1600—Bio-bibliography—Dictionaries. 3. Authors, English—Early modern, 1500–1700—Biography—Dictionaries. 4. Authors, European—Renaissance, 1450–1600—Biography—Dictionaries. I. Hager, Alan, 1940– .
PR411.M25 1997
820.9'003—dc20
[B] 96–25008

British Library Cataloguing in Publication Data is available.

Library of Congress Catalog Card Number: 96–25008
ISBN: 0–313–29436–4

First published in 1997

Greenwood Press, 88 Post Road West, Westport, CT 06881
An imprint of Greenwood Publishing Group, Inc.

Printed in the United States of America

The paper used in this book complies with the Permanent Paper Standard issued by the National Information Standards Organization (Z39.48–1984).

10 9 8 7 6 5 4 3 2 1

Copyright Acknowledgment

The author and publisher gratefully acknowledge permission for use of the following material:

Excerpts from *Collected Works of Erasmus*. 86 vols., in progress. Toronto: University of Toronto Press, 1974. Reprinted by permission of University of Toronto Press.

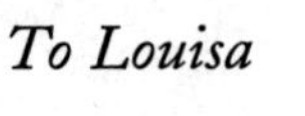

To Louisa

CONTENTS

PREFACE

In the late 1970s, sitting in his mother's home in Dallas, I asked my old friend, the meticulous and inventive scholar Norman Grabo, point-blank, ''What book would you like to beat?'' He said without pause, ''*English Literature in the Sixteenth Century, excluding Drama*,'' and I laughed because I had the same book in mind. I think my laughter and surprise convinced him I was not lying. C. S. Lewis' book, commissioned for Oxford out of the Clark Lectures, may have had the dullest title, but it was an *allegro*, brilliant, opinionated, erudite last-ditch effort to hold up the romantic notion of genius in the face of a groundswell of materialist rejection of any notion of the kind of human freedom that might allow new simple ideas and original works of art to exist. After all, we were being told of a sixteenth century that was totalized in terms of power configurations and by a Tudor consolidation of rule and courtly appointment that was leading England to revolution. Some of these determinist notions, however, have since come under attack even by their perpetrators. Since our conversation, Professor Grabo has given his hand to a gargantuan encyclopedic work of early North, Central, and South American writing, and I submit the following modest offering.

As in furniture design, architecture, and landscape gardening, the Tudor era (1485–1603) is often felt to be a unit in British literature, some feel the greatest era of any culture. Encompassing the advent of humanism, the Reformation, and the British Empire under three generations of Tudor rulers, literature in English evolved from brilliant late medieval (mostly in Scotland) to high Renaissance (mostly in England) in little over 100 years. Often thought of as the glory years of British civilization before the ''dark'' Stuart era and the English revolutions, its literature shows us a complexity of thought, genre, and response to political and other pressures unheard of in any comparable era. Thus, it is not surprising that the leading recent critical movement, new historicism, found its origins in studies of Tudor authors by Stephen Greenblatt, Louis Montrose, Annabel Patterson, Richard Helgerson, and others before spreading out to the ''American Renaissance'' and now other periods of British, American and Continental literature.

All critical reevaluations, however, run the risk of reflecting their own ages and obsessions in a kind of inadvertent narcissism in which the professor not only talks to his authors but becomes them. Even the most brilliant interpretations of the Renaissance have been plagued by anachronism from Jacob Burckhardt's looking at *quattrocento* Italy through the lens of Prussian mobilization of power to Stephen Greenblatt's post-Vietnam Tudor era. Walter Raleigh at the turn of this century tried to solve the problem of loaded interpretations of the sixteenth century by stating, ''The Renaissance is the name of a European movement so gradual, broad, manifold, and subtle, that any attempt to reduce it to a single expression is predestined to failure'' (Raleigh, vii). Thus, we must entertain many theories without conviction. Uncertainty and relativity, however, do not seem to reveal the age any better than anachronistic imposition. Relativism cannot go far in exegesis of an era obsessed with uncertainty and the relative and the proximity of opposites and opponents and what that relationship means. The age's best authors and artists grooved on ambiguity, contrariety, *concordia discors*, and other systems of looking at things two or more ways at once.

It is obvious that the Tudor era was rife with polemical and other strife. But one of its saving graces in intellectual and artistic accomplishment is a huge ground current of anticonflict and counterpolemicism that led to an extraordinary development of personal investigation and self-investigation in print. The fact that the book revolution created the platform for such a remarkable number of masterworks—holding opposing forces in dynamic symmetry and dazzling world-thought—goes without question. Can we now, beholding this new volume on an old subject, imagine how the Tudor author felt about the bound, printed book of, say, the Bible? I think not. It would have been geometrically greater than our present response to the most sophisticated computer hardware and software.

The Tudor era is a mysteriously creative epoch blessed by complexity and radical creativity, and as such it offers its students the greatest challenges and the most rewarding confrontations. As C. S. Lewis simply put it, ''I do not claim to know why there were many men of genius at that time'' (Lewis, 2). I might qualify his remark by saying ''men and women'' and perhaps exchange the phrase ''of genius'' for ''of such varied brilliance.'' However, we are left, willy-nilly, with an intellectual and artistic Leviathan that is rapidly regaining the audience it may have lost in another polemical age, the 1960s.

Perhaps because the new historians concentrated so much of their energy on examining the currents of power relationships and the possibility that a canon of Tudor authors might be merely the product of configurations of authority and censorship, considerable revision in notions of important authors and in literary history itself has been generated in the last forty or so years of scholarship following C. S. Lewis' astounding *English Literature in the Sixteenth Century, excluding Drama* (1954). Now I think we can remark on the importance of politics and political theory to our Tudor authors and how Tudor politics affected especially the authors who were marginalized. This new encyclopedic work significantly increases the number of women authors considered, and also, because they represent a significant minority in outlying areas of Tudor control, I have increased the number of authors from Ireland and, especially, Scotland. I also include certain writers who, though foreign-born and technically aliens, lived and wrote important works in Britain, such as Desiderius Erasmus among the intellectual lights of the court of Henry VIII and Giordano Bruno among the patrons of high art of the fin de siècle, Elizabeth, Leicester, and Sidney. Also imported into my collection are writers like Machiavelli, Calvin, Ariosto, and Tasso, who were immediately adopted, translated, or, indeed, naturalized in Tudor England. When I saw what I had, I was initially surprised by the number of Roman Catholic authors and the number of major works that were drastically incomplete, including Sidney's *Arcadia* and Spenser's *Faerie Queene*. My tentative conclusion about the latter was that, like American and European movies, English works at that time often had greater power than form. A violent, lame, or even nonexistent ending made little difference.

My volume provides, moreover, biographies and bibliographies of scientific writers, authors of music treatises, often marginalized, and some philosophical and mystical ones, as well. Furthermore, the articles emphasize, by means of the asterisk in the text, the remarkable interrelationship among those figures. Each entry reviews the writer's critical reception over the centuries and concludes with a statement on the author's relative significance in the Tudor era and in world literature. Each entry is followed by two bibliographies: one lists the authors' primary texts and manuscripts; the second includes the major critical studies of their works and biographies, all at my contributors' discretion.

The longer entries describe major figures such as Desiderius Erasmus, Thomas More, Edmund Spenser, and William Shakespeare; the shorter entries focus more on minor figures such as Catherine Parr, John Florio, and William Gilbert. All contributors were commissioned by the editor, but the backgrounds and approaches of those scholars are fairly broad, both ideologically and methodologically. In creating new groupings, I realize that I am not so much developing a new canon but am proposing a thesis that those Tudor authors who did not at least entertain both sides of various issues were neither the best nor the most influential figures of the era. That is, if, in looking at the ''American Renaissance,'' for every Thoreau, there are two Poes or Hawthornes, so in my era, for every Bale, there were two Mores or Elyots; for every Gosson, two Marlowes or Lodges. The British and American Renaissances have a good deal in common in that they preceded civil wars that became the central moments in their national histories. But my best authors attempted to contain future violence and sometimes, unlike Erasmus, succeeded.

Anticonflict and counterpolemicism appear in the form of dialogues and drama but also in what I call Platonic monologues in which opposite ideas can be contained within one text. If Castiglione can contain raging controversies within a dialogue with several adept speakers of both sexes and different ranks such as in *il Cortegiano*, or Shakespeare can do the same within a full-fledged drama such as *Julius Caesar* or *King Lear*, Erasmus can contain violently conflicting points of view in the supposed treatise *Encomium Moriae* (*Praise of Folly*) delivered by Stultitia's single voice. Machiavelli in *il Principe*, Montaigne in *Essais*, or Sidney in *Defence of Poesie* can, by a kind of ventriloquism, argue for both ideals and practical solutions, Platonic and Aristotelian positions, and other apparent contrarieties. This peculiar monolithic strain of yoked opposites in various texts has frustrated the more polemical readers of Tudor culture. Both to maintain my thesis about the relative importance of various authors and for considerations of space, I have excluded authors I determine to be excessively or narrowly argumentative in print and in the classroom or pulpit like Ascham, Gosson, or some of the churchmen of the early Tudor era, in favor of more sophisticated writers in Ireland, Scotland, and England. But though I commissioned my scholars, I never insisted they follow my lead, only my proposed subject and format.

Because spelling was not consistent in the Tudor Era (e.g., Shakespeare signed his own name several ways) and because my contributors chose different editions of the works discussed as definitive, at times the text refers to books and even authors in various old or foreign spellings rather than modern English. The index includes primarily modernized titles and names and, if deemed necessary, cross-references an old or foreign spelling to the modern English spelling or, vice versa, refers an English spelling to the foreign. For example, Castiglione's *il libro del Cortegiano* may appear in the text as *The Boke of the Cortyer* (an edition of Hoby's translation), but the index has only *Cortegiano, Il* to which *Book of the Courtier, The* is cross-referenced. I have allowed the contributors to choose between various editions of these works and to use period spellings or modernizations of words from this era. There are strong arguments for both.

Because they contributed time and energy on short notice to this huge project, I want to especially thank Andrew Weiner of the University of Wisconsin, Sarah Hilsman of the University of Chicago, and Terrence McGovern of SUNY Cortland for their help. I would also like to thank my readers and editors at Cortland and Greenwood, especially, Emmanuel Nelson, Norine Mudrick, and George Butler. I would also like to thank the University of Toronto Press for allowing me to quote extensively from their wonderful edition of Erasmus's works.

—*Alan Hager*

A

AGRIPPA VON NETTESHEIM (1486–1535)

BIOGRAPHY

Henricus Cornelius Agrippa von Nettesheim, a flamboyant and paradoxical German scholar and adventurer, was born near Cologne and was educated at the Universities of Cologne and Paris. Though he may have exaggerated his social standing and formal education to impress potential patrons, his extraordinary erudition in law, languages, medicine, and especially magic and the occult brought him international fame but only intermittent prosperity. A dynamic figure who gathered around him several secretive groups, his intellectual boldness and personal ambition provoked numerous confrontations in which, as Erasmus* once warned him, he was ill served by his short temper and sharp tongue.

Much of his life was spent as a wandering scholar, as well as a diplomat and soldier. His lectures at Dôle in 1509 on Reuchlin's cabalistic work netted him accusations of Judaizing heresy in an era when Hebrew studies were often eyed with suspicion and inaugurated a long career of hostility with religious conservatives. The year 1510 found him in England, possibly in the service of the Emperor Maximilian, studying the epistles of St. Paul with John Colet.* The fact that he was working on his most influential study of magic (*De occulta philosophia*) during the same year is an index of the strained and potentially heterodox mingling of esoterica and piety that marks much of his work.

From 1511 to 1518, Agrippa lived in Italy, where he married a "noble maiden'' (the first of three marriages). In addition to continuing his political and military pursuits, he came into closer contact with the culture of late Italian humanism, especially those elements influenced by the cabalistic and Hermetic studies of Ficino and Pico. A lucrative government post as orator and public advocate at Metz brought him back to Germany in 1518, where he found himself both sympathetic with, and deeply ambivalent about, the thought and practice of Martin Luther.* Agrippa's defense of a peasant woman accused of witchcraft, his participation in other theological controversies, and a general restlessness with what he perceived to be an intellectual backwater led to his resignation in 1520. Further travels seeking patronage and preferment met with varying degrees of success and frustration in Geneva, Fribourg, Lyons, Paris, Antwerp, Bonn, and elsewhere, and he served variously as physician, astrologer, lecturer, and historiographer.

Particularly painful were the years 1526–28, when, thanks in large measure to his remarkable tactlessness, he was stranded and impoverished in France after serving as personal physician to the Queen Mother, Louise of Savoy (mother of Francis I). During this period he wrote his most famous work, *De incertitudine et vanitate scientiarum declamatio inuectiua* (1526, pub. 1530), a skeptical and bitterly satirical attack on human learning and occupations that led, predictably, to further controversy including charges of heresy. His death in Grenoble gave rise to the notorious and widely repeated anecdote that on his deathbed he cursed his demonic black dog, after which his canine companion leaped into a river.

MAJOR WORKS AND THEMES

Agrippa's work is often preoccupied with the problem of knowledge, as he either hailed its power or despised its illusions, both attitudes courting rhetorical extremes. Its most optimistic mode focuses on the ways in which ancient and secret wisdom can transcend the limits of rational thought. The purified and enlightened soul of the magician achieves power over nature through his special understanding not only of the occult but also of Scripture and divine truth. This vision provokes at least three related questions for modern interpreters: (1) Is magic as consistent with religious orthodoxy as Agrippa tried to maintain? (2) Are his repeated warnings about the necessity of faith and grace ultimately only instrumental to, or a compensation for, an obsessive craving for intellectual power? (3) Can this demand for knowledge be reconciled with Agrippa's massive attack on the vanity of all learning, including magic? While these questions have been approached from several angles and answered variously (the first is usually answered in the negative; the others, with mixed responses), they remain crucial points of entry into the cultural maelstrom.

Agrippa's reputation rests primarily on two major works. *De occulta philosophia libri tres* (1510, rev. and partially pub. 1531, fully pub. 1533) surveys in its three books the harmoniously proportioned, ''three-fold'' hierarchical cosmos: the Elemental, the Celestial, and the Intellectual worlds. Power flows from above, but magic (uniting physics, mathematics, and theology) enables the magus to ascend through each world, from the sublunary to the stars, the angels, and the Creator. A spurious fourth book provides practical directions for conjuring and accounts for some of the book's popularity, but Agrippa's own sections were valued for their broad overview of Neoplatonic and sometimes heterodox themes: occult virtues; telepathy; the *spiritus* and *anima mundi*; astral influence; divination; talismans; word, letter, and number symbolism; the attracting of demons; the congruence between magical incantations and Christian prayer; and finally, mystical union with God.

Seemingly opposed to his optimism is the famous *De incertitudine et vanitate scientiarum declamatio inuectiua* (1526, pub. 1530; English trans. *Of the Vanitie and Vncertaintie of Artes and Sciences* by James Sandford* 1567, 1573). This work decries knowledge as the cause of the Fall and the continuing source of our ruin. All studies are surveyed and exposed as "hurtful and pestilent," though some are skewered more thoroughly than others—grammar, poetry, history, mathematics, dancing, stage plays, even his beloved cabala and several forms of magic. The best studies are polluted by superstition and misuse; most spring from, and perpetuate, uncertainty, error, and sin. Agrippa's invective expands to include satirical chapters on various offices and occupations: princes, courtiers, monks, merchants, physicians, prostitution, hunting, and so on. The work turns, finally, to the true blessedness that lies in simple piety, symbolized by the patient ass that outlives its persecutors.

Historians rightly note that *De vanitate* reflects a bitter period of Agrippa's life, when both philosophical and financial stays against confusion were crumbling around him. Some, however, while conceding this biographical context, have sought to close the gap between *De vanitate* and other works. Nauert, for example, shows that Agrippa had long been concerned about the abuses of learning, while *De vanitate* softens the blow on some redeemable studies. Although it ends denying mortal traditions and affirming Scripture, there remains the beguiling hint of enormous knowledge for the truly faithful. Others have argued that *De vanitate* is a "safety-device" to cover his dangerous enthusiasms (Yates); or, more cogently, that both sides of Agrippa's interest are focused on a similar goal, an ambiguously oriented spiritual regeneration and deification (Keefer); or that it is a mock vituperation, a rhetorically calculated satire mixing blame with praise to take ironic revenge on enemies while still affirming the value of knowledge (Korkowski). Agrippa was indeed known as a "playing wit" in the sixteenth century (the phrase is Sir Philip Sidney's*), and his tone veers from outraged to outrageous, but the sheer bulk and intensity of his railing suggest that his ironies are shot through with emotional as well as intellectual instability. I suspect, in addition, that Agrippa's multihued thought reflects to a greater degree than is sometimes acknowledged, his engagement with Nicholas of Cusa, his strange but important German predecessor whose theories of learned ignorance, conjectural knowledge, and longed-for but unattainable mystical solutions made for a volatile brew. The best summary of the Agrippan dilemma remains Nauert's, who sees in his "peculiar mixture of doubt . . . and absurd gullibility . . . a reflex of the intellectual anarchy which lay close to the heart of Renaissance culture" (241).

Of his numerous minor works, *De nobilitate et praecellentia foeminei sexus* (1509; translated into English three times in the sixteenth and seventeenth centuries) has received most attention in recent years from feminist critics and historians. This short work, mingling ethical earnestness and self-parody, courted the favor of Margaret of Austria by arguing for the superiority of the female sex with evidence drawn from Scripture, anatomy, history, and other sources. As with so many examples of Renaissance *serio ludere*, it is difficult to determine whether the praise is for the ostensible subject or the author's wit.

CRITICAL RECEPTION

The quality of Agrippa's thought has been challenged from his own day to the present, from Francis Bacon's* dismissal of him as a "trivial buffoon" to Richard Popkin's view of him, in his important history of skepticism, as the sponsor of a "fundamentalist anti-intellectualism" depending on condemnation rather than argument or analysis. While it is true that Agrippa lacks the subtle and probing imagination of Cusanus or Montaigne,* the energy and range of both his occult and skeptical writings had a broad, international appeal among philosophers, would-be magicians, artists, and writers: Albrecht Dürer, Giordano Bruno,* Michel de Montaigne, and others draw on him, sometimes extensively. In Tudor England, Sir Philip Sidney praises him with Erasmus as inspirations for his *Apology for Poetry*; he influenced John Dee* on mathematics and Reginald Scot on witchcraft; Christopher Marlowe's* Dr. Faustus aspires to be "as cunning as Agrippa was/Whose shadows made all Europe honor him"; Thomas Nashe* casts him as a conjurer in *The Unfortunate Traveller*, and his prose fiction may well have drawn energy from Agrippa's remorseless satire. His influence is felt as well in the poetry of John Davies, Fulke Greville,* possibly Edmund Spenser,* and in the work of the seventeenth-century twins, the poet Henry and the mystic Thomas Vaughan. His name continues to be associated with both skepticism and the occult long after the Renaissance. *De vanitate* had a profound effect on the young Goethe, and he was clearly influenced by Agrippa (and his dog) in *Faust*. When Mary Shelley traces the disastrous career of Victor Frankenstein, she begins with his chance discovery of "a volume of the works of Cornelius Agrippa," dismissed by his father as "sad trash" but later praised by a benevolent professor as the work of a misguided man of "genius."

BIBLIOGRAPHY

Works by Agrippa von Nettesheim

Female Pre-eminence or the Dignity and Excellency of that Sex above the Male. Trans. Henry Care (1670); rpt. *The Feminist Controversy of the Renaissance*, ed. Diane Bornstein. Delmar, NY: Scholars' Facsimiles and Reprints, 1980.

Of the Vanitie and Vncertaintie of Artes and Sciences. Ed. Catherine M. Dunn. Rpt. Northridge: California State University, Northridge Library, 1974.
Opera. Lyons, n.d. Ed. Richard Popkin, 2 vols. Hildesheim, 1970.
Three Books of Occult Philosophy, written by Henry Cornelius Agrippa, of Nettesheim. Trans. J. F. London, 1651.

Studies of Agrippa von Nettesheim

Hamilton, A. C. "Sidney and Agrippa." *Review of English Studies* n.s. 7 (1956): 151–57.
Keefer, Michael H. "Agrippa's Dilemma: Hermetic 'Rebirth' and the Ambivalences of *De vanitate* and *De occulta philosophia.*" *Renaissance Quarterly* 41 (1988): 614–53.
Korkowski, Eugene. "Agrippa as Ironist." *Neophilologus* 60 (1976): 594–607.
Levao, Ronald. *Renaissance Minds and Their Fictions: Cusanus, Sidney, Shakespeare.* Berkeley: University of California Press, 1985.
Nauert, Charles G., Jr. *Agrippa and the Crisis of Renaissance Thought.* Urbana: University of Illinois Press, 1965.
Popkin, Richard H. *The History of Skepticism from Erasmus to Descartes.* New York: Humanities Press, 1964.
Stadelmann, Rudolf. *Vom Geist des ausgehenden Mittelalters: Studien zur Geschichte der Weltanschauung von Nicolaus Cusanus bis Sebastian Franck.* Halle, 1929.
Walker, D. P. *Spiritual and Demonic Magic from Ficino to Campanella.* London: Warburg Institute, 1958.
Yates, Frances. *Giordano Bruno and the Hermetic Tradition.* Chicago: University of Chicago Press, 1964.
Zambelli, Paola. "Magic and Radical Reformation in Agrippa of Nettesheim." *Journal of the Warburg and Courtauld Institute* 39 (1976): 69–103.

RONALD LEVAO

WILLIAM ALABASTER
(1567/1568–1637)

BIOGRAPHY

William Alabaster lived at least two lives: he is known to us both as a recusant poet of the Elizabethan era and as an eccentric but avowedly Anglican chaplain to King James I.* His vacillation between his country's religion and that of Rome is summed up in the fact that he is the only English poet to be imprisoned both by officers of Queen Elizabeth* and by ministers of the Inquisition.

Alabaster's early life reads much like biographies of other budding young literary figures of his day. The oldest of six children born to a firmly Protestant merchant family on 27 January 1567/8 at Hadleigh Suffolk, he was guided and supported by his uncle John Still, master of Trinity College and later bishop of Bath and Wells. By 1584 he was elected a Queen's Scholar to Trinity and between 1588 and 1592 wrote in Latin an unfinished epic for Queen Elizabeth called *Elisaeis* and a tragedy, *Roxana*.

In 1596 Alabaster was engaged to be married and had made the conventional steps toward wealth and preferment by accepting the post of chaplain to Robert Devereux, earl of Essex. By Michaelmas of this same year, however, he began to experience feelings of inner turmoil that would both disrupt and characterize the rest of his life. He speaks in his autobiography of feeling ''a greater tendernes of harte towardes Christes Crosse and Passion than the protestants weare wont to feele'' and also describes having ''sweet visions or apprehensions in [his] sleepe.'' At Easter 1597, Alabaster debated privately with Father Thomas Wright, who was being held in ''light'' confinement at Westminster. After reading from a copy of *A Refutation of Sundry Reprehensions* (a defense of the Rheims version of the New Testament), Alabaster reports, ''I lept up from the place where I satt, and saide to my self 'Now I am a Catholique' and then fell down upon my knees and thanked God most hartely.''

Following this sudden conversion, Alabaster returned to Trinity and spent several months studying controversial theological writings and likely began writing his religious poems. As though to provoke his own capture, he wrote *Seven Motives*, about his conversion, and sent it to Essex in London, where it soon came into the hands of authorities, who then had him arrested. Intense but futile efforts were made by John Still and others to make the young man recant. By February 1597/8 he was deprived of Anglican orders. In April he escaped and took refuge with the Jesuit John Gerard, and in September he sailed to the Continent and was enrolled at the English College in Rome. By midsummer 1599 he returned to England, intending ''to give [his] life.'' He sought a public debate and was, by August, a prisoner at the Tower, where he remained until 1601, when he was removed to Framingham Castle, Suffolk, and kept prisoner for two years.

With the accession of James I in 1603, Alabaster was pardoned, but by 1606 he had fallen into new controversy and was imprisoned at the King's Bench in London. Though insistently Catholic, Alabaster proposed serving as a government spy against Catholic emigrés. He spent the next several years at Douay and Brussels, where he wrote *Apparatus in Revelation Jesu Christi*, which was not well received in Rome. In 1609 he returned to the English College in Rome, where, perhaps involved in some intrigue against his rector, Robert Persons, he was called before the Inquisition. In July he was imprisoned in Amsterdam, and by 1610 he had recanted and declared that he would live and die a Catholic. By 1613, however, this same Alabaster was again a Protestant, back in England, and in the service of King James. In 1614 John Donne* remarked, perhaps with a tinge of envy, that ''Mr. Alabaster hath got of the King the Deans best Living worth above £300, which the Dean had good hope to have held a while'' (*Letters*, 1651, 168). When he married in 1618, Alabaster became stepfather to the physician and alchemist Robert Fludd. He devoted his middle and declining years to mystical theology, kept acquaintance with Ben Jonson,* and died in April 1637.

MAJOR WORKS AND THEMES

Though William Alabaster may have written the conventional century of sonnets, only seventy-seven have survived. His essential innovation as an English poet is to have combined for the very first time three disparate ingredients: the Elizabethan sonnet sequence, religious devotional verse, and "metaphysical" poetry. Others before Alabaster had crafted religious devotional verse into otherwise conventional English sonnet cycles, but they had not shaped their sonnets out of peculiarly argued metaphors (tears, insects, spheres, vines, conduits and a full range of scriptural props), which would come to be called "metaphysical" conceits. Such conceits, though a conventional part of medieval mysticism, were, in sixteenth-century England, unique to Robert Southwell,* and in sonnet form unique to Alabaster.

Recognizing the first appearance of the metaphysical conceit in English poetry in the poems of Southwell and Alabaster is to acknowledge its essentially Catholic origins and qualities and hence the continuity of devotional verse in England from its medieval origins to the seventeenth century. Though no references are made to Alabaster's sonnets by seventeenth-century poets, I think it apparent that they were well acquainted with his work. Before Donne's* "I am a little world made cunningly," for example, was Alabaster's "My soul a world is by contraction, / The heavens therein is my internal sense, / Moved by my will as an intelligence." Before Crashaw's meditations upon physical ingredients in Scriptures were Alabaster's meditations upon the sponge and Crown. Before the personal outcries of Herbert's poems was Alabaster's "Lord, I have left all and myself behind, / My state, my hopes, my strength, and present ease."

The uneven quality of Alabaster's poems may be attributed in part to the difficult circumstances under which they were composed, though admittedly others composed better poetry under worse circumstances. At its worst, Alabaster's poetry drowns in its piety. At its best—that is, when the poetic vigor is sustained for a full fourteen lines without collapsing into a characteristically weak sestet or deplorable final couplet—it demonstrates not just the potential artistic beauty to be derived from Christian meditation but the poetic versatility of the sonnet in English.

CRITICAL RECEPTION

The first literary praise afforded William Alabaster comes from none other than Edmund Spenser* in *Colin Clout Comes Home Againe*, who proclaims "And there is *Alabaster* throughly taught, / In all his skill, though knowen yet to few, / Yet were he knowne to *Cynthia* as he ought, his Eliseïs would be redde anew. / Who liues that can match that heroick song?" (l. 400). Though the echo of "Who knows not Colin Clout?" in this hyperbolic rhetorical question may veil a not-so-subtle reference to Colin's own heroic song, Spenser clearly admired Alabaster's Latin work. Likewise, Samuel Johnson observed that

Alabaster's *Roxana* contained the best Latin verse by an English writer before John Milton.

During the seventeenth century Alabaster's Latin poems continue to receive mention. If seventeenth-century poets emulated Alabaster's metaphysical style, they did so without singing his praises. A few of his poems found their way into books in the nineteenth century, but he has remained ''knowen . . . to few.'' Alabaster's place as a Tudor poet was secured by two events in the twentieth century. The first was the publishing of *The Sonnets of William Alabaster* by G. M. Story and Helen Gardner (Oxford, 1959), which made his English works finally accessible as well as furnished readers with biographical context and some fundamental critical apparatus. Second, Louis Martz's inclusion of selected Alabaster sonnets in his anthology of metaphysical poets, *English Seventeenth-Century Verse* (1963), assured that any serious study of the ''metaphysical'' poets would properly begin in the sixteenth century. As an innovator in the sonnet tradition and a harbinger of what came to be called metaphysical poetry, Alabaster may be described as a minor English poet with a uniquely major contribution.

BIBLIOGRAPHY

Works by William Alabaster

Story, G. M., and Helen Gardner, eds. *The Sonnets of William Alabaster*. Oxford: Oxford University Press, 1959.

Studies of William Alabaster

Klawitter, George. ''Craft and Purpose in Alabaster's Incarnation Sonnets.'' *University of Hartford Studies in Literature* 15–16.3–1 (1983–84): 60–66.

O'Connell, Michael. ''The Elisaeis of William Alabaster.'' *Studies in Philology* 76.5 (1979): 1–12.

GARY M. BOUCHARD

ANN, LADY BACON (Anne Bacon, Anne Cooke) (1528–1610)

BIOGRAPHY

Ann, Lady Bacon was the second daughter of Sir Anthony Cooke and Lady Anne Fitzwilliam Cooke; she was the wife of Sir Nicholas Bacon and the mother of Sir Anthony Bacon and Francis Bacon,* Lord Verulam. She was sister to Mildred Cecil, wife of William Cecil, Lord Burghley, chief secretary under Queen Elizabeth,* and the sister of Elizabeth Hoby Russel, wife first to Sir Thomas Hoby* and afterward to Lord Russel. Her other sisters and brothers married less illustriously and, perhaps as a result, are less well known.

Lady Bacon is known to have been trained in the classical tongues, Greek and Latin (and possibly Hebrew), as well as in Italian and French, which, it is said, she spoke like a native. Her father was tutor to Edward VI, and it is believed by some that she may have served as a governess to Edward VI. Yet she was bred not only for a life at court but for a life of godliness as well, having been educated in the Scriptures and the church fathers, a fact for which Theodore Beza praised her in his dedication to his *Christian Meditation Upon Eight Psalms* (1582).

While still under her parents[1] supervision she translated out of the Italian *Fouretene Sermons of Barnardine Ochyne*, the head of the Capuchin Order, who had converted to Reformed Protestantism and fled Italy, coming to England during Edward's reign under the protection of Archbishop Cranmer.* These sermons were published c. 1550, then republished as *Certayne Sermons* c. 1550 and again c. 1570. Much has been made of her dedication to these sermons since she commends them to her mother in full courtly fashion, at the same time hoping that she has shown her time learning Italian was not spent in dilatory pleasures. Little, however, has been written about the sermons themselves or about her translation, although a considerable amount of attention has been given to C. S. Lewis' praise of her ability as a translator of the *Apology, or Answer, in Defence of the Churche of England* from Bishop Jewel's* Latin text. Her wit and acumen as a letter writer, particularly as demonstrated in her letters to her sons Anthony and Francis, are often commented upon, as is her facility at languages—she frequently punctuates her sentences with Latin and Greek phrases, the latter of which she seems often to have used as a kind of private language, using Greek for statements she clearly did not want read by anyone into whose hands their letters might come. It is, however, the translations and what they tell us about her interests as a learned woman and what they may foretell about her influence on her sons in which I am chiefly interested.

MAJOR WORKS AND THEMES

Lady Bacon's translations of Ochino's sermons show her complete understanding of the "necessity of believing we are elect," including the limitations on liberty that allow one to think one thing or another, to speak or not, to govern oneself, and to hear the words of God, but not to receive God's grace other than by his own election: "There are many that think that as men chose to serve a Prince, so we chose to serve God, but he himself in the contrary, when he said, you have not chosen me, but I you" (Thirteenth Sermon).

Throughout her life Lady Ann was a zealous adherent of the Reformed church. Although her letters to her sons show her maternal concern for their careers and their financial well-being, the primary argument of each of the letters is that they be true to the faith; this counsel she even extended to Essex, when in December 1596 she feared his negative influence over her sons: "This is the will of God, that ye should be Holy, and abstain from fornication, and every one know how to keep his own vessel in holiness and honour; and not in the lust of concupiscence, as do the Gentiles which know not God" (Birch, 218–19). That her sons recalled the model of service set forth in the passage is shown in Francis Bacon's letter to Elizabeth (20 July 1594) in which he acknowledges the will of God in preventing him from being in service to her (Spedding, I, 304–5).

Lady Ann may have felt that the will of God called her to respond to the need for a translation of Bishop Jewel's* *Apologia Ecclesiae Anglicanae*. Jewel himself was concerned that a proper response be made to the papal attack set forth at the Council of Trent lest England's failure to participate be seen as an opportunity to attack not only the English church but the queen and country as well. Following the publication in 1562 of an unsatisfactory translation, this need grew stronger. That a fine translation appeared from the hands of the wife and sister-in-law of Elizabeth's two foremost spokespersons on church matters should make Archbishop Parker's praise of it fully explicable, for the *Apology* shows not only that the English church was right in setting itself apart from the Roman church but, in copious detail, outlines the ways in which the Roman church had strayed from the "true church of Christ."

CRITICAL RECEPTION

As indicated before, Lady Ann reaped praise as a translator from Bishops Jewel and Parker as well as from Theodore Beza. Letters from Cecil and Essex, among others, show that her goodwill merited consideration. While Spedding takes her to task for attempting to maintain too much control over her sons' lives once they were adults, Birch clearly finds her to be a sympathetic character (although acknowledging her to have been difficult in her old age). Hughey says little about the quality of her translations, although she does find them superior to the Argentine translations of Ochino. As has already been noted, C. S. Lewis praised Lady Ann's ability as a translator, noting, "Latin prose has a flavour very hard to disguise in translation, but nearly every sentence in Lady Bacon's work sounds like an original. Again and again she finds the phrase which, once she has found it, we feel to be inevitable" (307). Her two recent commentators, Beilin and Lamb, both focus attention on the isolated position of the learned woman in the English Renaissance.

BIBLIOGRAPHY

Works by Ann, Lady Bacon

An Apologie, or answere in defence of the Churche of Englande, with a briefe and plaine declaration of the true Religion professed and used in the same. London, 1564. Rpt. the Parker Society. *The Works of John Jewel, Bishop of Salisbury*. Ed. John Ayre. Cambridge: University Press, 1863.

Certayne Sermons of the ryghte famous and excellente Clerk Master Barnardine Ochine. London, [1550?]; rpt. [1570?]. *Short Title Catalogue: 1475–1640* 18764; 18768.

Fouretene Sermons of Barnardine Ochyne, concernyng the predestinacion and eleccion of god: very expediente to the settynge forth of hys glorye among hys creatures. Translated out of Italian in to oure natyue tounge by A. B. [1550?] *STC* 18767.

Studies of Ann, Lady Bacon

Beilin, Elaine V. "Building the City: Women Writers of the Reformation." *Redeeming*

Eve: Women Writers of the English Renaissance. Princeton: Princeton University Press, 1987.

Birch, Thomas, ed. *Memoirs of the Reign of Queen Elizabeth from thee year 1581 till her Death . . . from the original papers of Anthony Bacon, esq.* 2 vols. London: A. Millar, 1754.

Hogrefe, Pearl. *Tudor Women: Commoners and Queens*. Ames: Iowa State University Press, 1975.

Hughey, Ruth. "Lady Ann Bacon's Translations." *Review of English Studies* 110 (1934): 211.

Lamb, Mary Ellen. "The Cooke Sisters: Attitudes toward Learned Women in the Renaissance." In *Silent But for the Word: Tudor Women as Patrons, Translators, and Writers of Religious Works*, ed. Margaret P. Hannay. Kent, OH: Kent State University Press, 1985.

Lewis, C. S. *English Literature in the Sixteenth Century excluding Drama*. New York: Oxford University Press, 1954.

Spedding, James, ed. *The Letters and the Life of Francis Bacon including All His Occasional Works*. 7 vols. London: Longman, Green, Longman, and Roberts, 1861.

SONJA HANSARD-WEINER

PIETRO ARETINO
(1492–1556)

BIOGRAPHY

Pietro, the son of Tita Bonci and a cobbler named Luca Del Tura, was born in Arezzo in the momentous year 1492. With typical disregard for propriety, he sometimes claimed to be the bastard of the nobleman Luigi Bacci, who kept his mother as a mistress. In all his publications, however, he adopted the *nom d'artiste* "Peter of Arezzo." "Born in a hospital, with the soul of a king," he would announce his presence in a room of courtiers by bellowing, "I AM PIETRO ARETINO." After a picaresque life in various employments he settled in Venice, "by the grace of God a free man" (except for periods as a fugitive from the law). Shimmering descriptions of that city, an urban Eden and "a living reproach to Rome," fill his famous correspondence.

By his death in 1556, Aretino had achieved perhaps the most monumental act of self-production in early modern history. Entirely without Latin and Greek education, he expanded the forces of the vernacular in thousands of letters that won him the friendship or hatred of patrons, intellectuals, and poets of the stature of Ariosto,* who gave him the sobriquet "Divine." His training as a painter led nowhere, but he became the closest friend of Titian and Sansovino, a major impresario and critic of art, and the conduit that led Italian painters to Fontainebleau. The cobbler's son wrote and conversed freely with the Emperor Charles V, François I of France, Henry VIII of England, and the princes of Italy, who rewarded him with pensions, commissions, and intangible marks of intimacy; "kings and emperors answer my letters," he warned Michelangelo. His most intimate transactions were openly published in these letters, the first to be collected and published in the vernacular within a few years of being written: Aretino wrote to Federigo Gonzaga, marquis of Mantua, on the most personal matters (e.g., the ruler's "lustful thoughts" about a statue of Venus by Sansovino), and in return Gonzaga declared him "a festival of joy . . . like being in a whole crowd"; he boasted that the doge was "his father" and that he himself "was father, brother, friend, and servant" to the *condottiere* Giovanni de' Medici. Just as he collected and displayed the gold chains given him by royalty, so he reveled in descriptive nicknames: the Terrible, the Divine, the Diabolic, the Scourge of Princes, the Fifth Evangelist, the Secretary of the World. His enemies called him sodomite, Lutheran, and *testa di cazzo*, but even these insults could be confidently brandished as compliments; two of his portrait medals carry on the obverse a head made of writhing phalluses, and some scholars believe that Aretino himself commissioned this image as a boast of his prowess as a "satyr." More portraits of Aretino circulated than of any other individual in his lifetime, including the pope and the emperor, when one counts the woodcut portraits that appeared on almost every publication. One edition of *The Humanity of Christ* merely shows him in silhouette, an instantly recognizable icon.

MAJOR WORKS AND THEMES

In addition to these letters, Aretino's varied and voluminous writings earned him the description "polygraph." His early and enduring reputation was for "scourging" satires and pasquinades, and his distinctive combination of cynical observation, salty topicality, and verbal exuberance generated successful comedies, including *La cortegiana* and *Il marescalco*. He published relatively conventional love poems to "La Sirena" (with a beautiful title page by Titian), and one manuscript in Venice contains sonnets to a Mantuan boy and to a woman who has converted him from a "born sodomite." Aretino also poured out devotional works—a retelling of Genesis and lushly emotive biographies of Jesus and the saints—that in his opinion qualified him for a cardinal's hat. Here, as throughout his work, he tries to find the verbal equivalent of the paintings that proliferated around him; his description of Mary Magdalene, for example, clearly sets out to emulate Titian.

As far as his reputation in England is concerned, however, Aretino's definitive works are his two ventures into pornography. The sonnets he wrote to accompany the erotic engravings of Marcantonio Raimondi after Giulio Romano, published and prosecuted in 1524, gave him a reputation as the original expert in "postures"—ironically, since these sonnets have a complex and tense relationship to Giulio's images; they act out the conflict of aesthetic appreciation, naturalistic hedonism, and transgressive violence, often seeming hostile to the bodies and pleasures they ostensibly celebrate. The famous letter that accompanies the sonnets likewise pursues two contradictory arguments. Aretino's naturalistic assault on false propriety—"What is wrong with seeing a man mount a woman? Should the animals have more freedom than we do?"—with its paradoxical encomium of the phallus, which anticipates Montaigne,* is hard to reconcile with the claim to re-create the artistic license of a classical elite, especially when his main example is a strikingly "unnatural" statue of a satyr raping a boy.

In the prose dialogues known as *Ragionamenti* or *Sei giornate*, Aretino sometimes maintains the naturalistic, sex-positive stance that he used to justify the sonnets; the praise of the phallus in his letter, for example, appears almost verbatim in the final dialogue, recited by a wet nurse and a midwife. Nevertheless, such voluptuary set pieces are increasingly isolated in a sea of satire against the tricks and extortions of the prostitute and the brutality of her customers. Erotic spectacles, pictures, and "modi" continue to feature in the *Ragionamenti*, but punitive associations compromise any celebratory impulse they might express. The cosmic whore-figure (Rojas' Celestina, Aretino's Nanna) elaborates most fully the paradox more tightly expressed in the sonnets, where sexual vocabulary stands for the greatest pleasure and the commonest insult. Within her pleasure-world she reigns as "mistress of inchantment"; in the social-political universe she stands for the whore of Babylon, chief witness and symbol of abjection.

CRITICAL RECEPTION

Just as England's fascination with Italian politics created the composite figure of "Machiavel,"* so Elizabethan and Stuart culture amplified the mythic Aretino. This sole progenitor supposedly invented, codified, and performed the "postures" themselves, designed the engravings and paintings, and composed all the associated texts. Educated circles could have developed a more discriminating knowledge of Aretino through contact with exiles like Giordano Bruno,* whose *Spaccio della Bestia Trionfante*, which calls the *Ragionamenti* fit reading for the gods, first appeared in London. Indeed, the first full version of those pornographic dialogues was published in London (John Wolfe 1584), and a copy found its way into the library of that great Machiavellian William Cecil, Lord Burghley. But for the most part England preferred its imaginary polymath of perversity, who conveniently defined the outer limits of sexual discourse. "Posture" became a code word for pornographic display in scandalous locations, and "Aretino" lost its status as a proper noun, grammatically as well as morally. We might find Thomas Nashe's* *Choice of Valentines* closer to Chaucer than to Aretino, but when Nashe's enemy Gabriel Harvey* chose to denounce this venture into protolibertine discourse, the word he coined to express his loathing was a verb: to "Aretinize." By the time of Jonson's* *Volpone*, the Falstaffian figure of Aretino had become familiar enough to use in satires against pretention: Lady Politick rattles off a list of Italian classics that culminates in the "desperate wit" of Aretino, conceding only as an afterthought that "his pictures are a little obscene" (3.4); the city husband justifies prostituting his wife to the decrepit Volpone by contrasting him to some young lecher who "had read ARETINE, conn'd all his printes, / Knew every quirke within lusts laborinth'' (3.7); Sir Epicure Mammon raves on about the ''oval roome'' he will purchase with alchemical gold, filled with original erotic artworks of the kind that ''dull ARETINE / But coldly imitated'' (2.2).

BIBLIOGRAPHY

Works by Pietro Aretino

Aretino's Dialogues (1971). Trans. Raymond Rosenthal. Reissued with epilogue by Margaret Rosenthal. New York: Marsilio, 1995.

I Modi. The Sixteen Pleasures: An Erotic Album of the Italian Renaissance. Ed. Lynne Lawner. Evanston, IL: Northwestern University Press, 1988.

Lettere sull'arte di Pietro Aretino. Ed. Fidenzio Pertile and Ettore Camesaca. Milan: Del Milione, 1957–60.

The Marescalco (Il marescalco). Trans. and ed. Leonard G. Sbrocchi and J. Douglas Campbell. Ottowa: Dovehouse, 1986.

Poesie varie. Ed. Giovanni Aquilecchia and Angelo Romano. Rome: Salerno, 1992. (Part of the ongoing ''Edizione nazionale delle opere di Pietro Aretino.'')

Sei giornate (originally *Ragionamento della Nanna e della Antonia* [1534] and *Dialogo nel quale la Nanna . . . insegna a la Pippa* [1536]). Ed. Giovanni Aquilecchia. Bari: Laterza, 1969.

Selected Letters. Trans. George Bull. New York: Viking, 1977.

The Letters of Pietro Aretino. Ed. Thomas Caldecot Chubb. New Haven, CT: Archon, 1967.

Tutto il teatro. Ed. Antonio Pinchera. Rome: Newton Compton, 1974.

Studies of Pietro Aretino (16th-Century Apocrypha and Responses)

Delle rime di M. Nicolo Franco contra Pietro Aretino, e de la Priapea del medesimo. ''3rd edn.'' 1548; repr. London: Privately printed, 1887.

Il Piacevol Ragionamento de l'Aretino. Dialogo di Giulia e di Madalena. Ed. Claudio Galderisi. Intro. Enrico Rufi. Foreword by Giovanni Aquilecchia. Rome: Salerno, 1987.

Roskill, Mark. *Dolce's ''Aretino'' and Venetian Art Theory of the Cinquecento*. New York: New York University Press, 1968.

Critical Works

Ferroni, Giulio. *Le voci dell'istrione: Pietro Aretino e la dissoluzione del teatro*. Naples: Liguori, 1977.

Frantz, David O. *Festum Voluptatis: A Study of Renaissance Erotica*. Columbus: Ohio State University Press, 1989.

Innamorati, Giuliano. *Tradizione e invenzione in Pietro Aretino*. Messina: D'Anna, 1957.

Land, Norman E. ''Ekphrasis and Imagination: Some Observations on Pietro Aretino's Art Criticism.'' *Art Bulletin* 58 (1986): 107–17.

Larivaille, Paul. *Pietro Aretino fra rinascimento e manierismo*. Rome: Bulzoni, 1980.

McPherson, David C. ''Aretino and the Harvey-Nashe Quarrel.'' *PMLA* 84 (1969): 1551–58.

Waddington, Raymond B. ''A Satirist's *Impresa*: The Medals of Pietro Aretino.'' *Renaissance Quarterly* 42 (1989): 655–81.

Woods-Marsden, Joanna. ''Toward a History of Art Patronage in the Renaissance: The

Case of Pietro Aretino.'' *Journal of Medieval and Renaissance Studies* 24 (1994): 275–99.

JAMES GRANTHAM TURNER

LUDOVICO ARIOSTO
(1474–1533)

BIOGRAPHY

Although born in Reggio Emilia on 8 September 1474, Ludovico Ariosto's life and fame are intimately connected to the city of Ferrara, where he grew up from his thirteenth year. There, in one of the great Renaissance cities of Italy, Ariosto studied Latin under the humanist Gregorio da Spoleto and then law for five years at the university. He also worked as one of the *familiari* of the Estensi, first for Cardinal Ippolito d'Este—until 1517, when he broke with his patron because Ariosto refused to move to Hungary—and then for Duke Alfonso I, who ruled the city and presided over one of the most splendid courts in the world. At Ferrara and as part of the Estense court, Ariosto came into contact with an extraordinarily diverse and cultured group of men and women, some of whom are recorded with affection in the last canto of his masterpiece, the *Orlando furioso*. There they applaud the completion of his poetic labors. He participated as well in the theatrical activities encouraged and supported by the Estensi, and he had access to the large and rich Estense library, which was particularly well stocked in romances and contained some of the earliest Ptolemaic maps, both of which Ariosto consulted in writing his *Furioso*. At Ferrara he also fell in love with Alessandra Benucci, to whom he remained devoted throughout his life and whom he finally married in secret sometime between 1526 and 1530. He died on 6 July 1533, the author of a number of important works in the vernacular: in particular, seven satires in tercets (often credited with reviving in form and style Horace's *Epistolae* as a form of subtle self-reflection and social critique); four completed comedies (*La Lena, Il Negromante, La Cassaria*, and *I Suppositi*), as well as a translation of Terence's *Phormio*, all of which helped shape Italian comedy in its infancy and further helped bring about a revival of interest in classical Latin drama in the Renaissance; the *Cinque canti*, a dark and despondent work left unfinished; and the *Orlando furioso*, a sprawling yet remarkably learned and complex romance that Ariosto began in 1504. The *Orlando furioso*, the work to which Ariosto dedicated his greatest poetic labors, went through three different versions (1516, 1521, and 1532) and in time won him more than a modicum of fame. In this poem he claimed that he would sing of things ''non detta in prosa mai nè in rima'' (never said before in prose or poetry) (1.2).

MAJOR WORKS AND THEMES

Ariosto constructed his *Furioso*, a romance composed of forty-six cantos in the final 1532 version, as generically mixed narrative—a ''varied tapestry,'' as the narrator describes it at one point. This flair for change, typical of romances, is visible in the myriad stories intricately woven into the length of the narrative, as well as in the numerous stories that remain compact, self-contained units. The variety of the *Furioso* is also conspicuously evident in the poet's multiple alterations of tone, style, and genre as he passes, for example, from an epic battlefield in which two friends reveal their love for one another in a moment of extreme danger, to a pastoral landscape in which two lovers carve their names on trees. The variety of the *Furioso* is further present in the plethora of literary sources, both classical and contemporary, that underpin the text, beginning with Boiardo's *Orlando innamorato*, to which the *Furioso* is an obvious continuation and its formal completion, and extending to the works of Dante, Boccaccio, Petrarch, Ovid, Catullus, Virgil, Statius, and Seneca—to name but a few of its Italic progenitors. Moreover, in borrowing from, and alluding to, these and a host of other works, Ariosto significantly sets up literary authorities and genres over and against one another in dialectical interplay, privileging the many over the one. There is, to be sure, no single underlying narrative authority to this poem, which begins with a title that evokes Seneca's *Hercules Furens*, opens with verses that echo Dante's *Purgatorio*, soon passes through episodes that repeatedly imitate and emulate Ovid's *Metamorphoses* and Petrarch's *Canzoniere*, and ends with a conspicuous allusion to the last verse of the most revered classical epic of the Middle Ages and the early Renaissance, Virgil's *Aeneid.*

Variety, an essential part of Boiardo's poem, was also central to early cinquecento aesthetics and rhetoric, which privileged richness and copiousness in disposition, invention, and elocution. Perhaps Ariosto's *Furioso* not only represents this variety but seeks to embrace it as a totality within a harmonious—though by no means always felicitous—vision. For unlike the *Orlando innamorato*, amid the multiple voices that make up the strands of this narrative, there are unifying forces at work in this highly structured and sophisticated romance. In particular, Ariosto unifies his romance by often enforcing connections between characters through the conspicuous juxtaposition of parallel episodes, as when he has both Ruggiero and Orlando free naked women—respectively, Angelica and Olimpia—from a sea monster or when both Ruggiero and Orlando discard weapons—respectively, a blinding shield and the harquebus—in order to rely on their valor alone. Ariosto further gives the impression that his rapid shifts in focus are not arbitrary but consistently the product of an extraordinary mastery of the typical romance structure of interlacement (*entrelacement*), a poetic strategy that creates suspense, complexity, and narrative depth as one story line is suddenly dropped or carefully woven into another in the formation of an intricate textual web. But above all the most pervasive unifying force in the *Furioso* is the poet's celebrated irony, which allows him to hold together conflicting points of view in a sort of "discordant concord" or *discordia concors* and assert absolute control over all events and characters.

The highly self-conscious and discursive poet of the *Furioso*, however, does not exercise narrative control with complete emotional and cognitive detachment. One striking characteristic of the poet of the *Furioso* is his ability to use irony to separate himself from, yet identify with, the characters whom he controls in his poem. Like his characters, the poet of the *Furioso* is a subject with an object of desire, though throughout he remains the subject who always oversees the actions he describes, from Angelica fleeing the grasps of her alternately lusty and loving suitors, to a knight-errant chasing after his own horse, to Astolfo descending into the first circle of hell and then voyaging to the moon. Hence, at one moment the poet of the *Furioso* can be (or feign to be) a lover on the verge of insanity; at another instant he can seem to be a distant, almost indifferent god controlling the threads of his multiple and varied tapestry; and at yet another instant he emerges as the poet who self-consciously reflects on the linguistic errancy of his own text and, in general, the truth value of all literature since Homer. Repeatedly, he can ridicule his characters and then become a mocked character within his own field of vision as he goes about composing his poem, as he puts it, in a "lucid interval." At the same time, he can gaze serenely at the slaughter of millions in his text but then reflect bitterly upon his own society and the erosion of its "*bel viver*" (beautiful way of life) (34.2) ever since foreigners invaded Italy in 1494.

Typical of romances, characters in the *Furioso* often wander in search of adventure in a world ruled by Fortune, traveling through cities and forests, over sea and land as they relentlessly crisscross the globe. In the process, they customarily quest after, as well as engage in staged or spontaneous contests over, an object of desire, whether it be a helmet, a fabulous horse, a sword, or an elusive loved one. Nevertheless, what distinguishes Ariosto's romance from so many others of the Middle Ages and Renaissance is the extraordinary nature of the quest in the *Furioso* as an expression of a desire for an absolute, an impossible plenitude. This desire animates Orlando's quest for Angelica, which ends in his madness at the center of the poem, as he recognizes—with an almost heroic capacity for self-delusion—that the woman he has persistently loved and held up as the image of perfection and completion has finally chosen and married another man. Orlando's love, like his madness, is a "furor," an overwhelming passion that consumes his entire existence from the moment he sets out on his quest to the moment when his wits are finally restored to him, at which point he immediately begins to operate once more as an agent of the community engaged in an epic war. Similarly, the desire for a totality instills in Ruggiero and Astolfo a longing to circle the entire globe upon the hippogriff, though neither wanderlust hero manages to complete his circumnavigation. In much the same way, the desire for an impossible plenitude imprisons heroes and heroines within Atlante's labyrinthine castle as they wander about endlessly seeking what they have most longed for in their lives. Objects of desire in the *Furioso* are thus often abstractions, symbolic end points for desire itself.

Though the poem takes its title from an event placed in the near structural center of the poem—Orlando's madness and "furor"—a significant narrative strand running throughout the *Furioso* tells the story of Ruggiero's and Bradamante's love for one another and their eventual marriage, once they have successfully overcome a number of obstacles. At one level, the Ruggiero–Bradamante narrative functions as a complement and counterpoint to Orlando's single-minded desire for Angelica. A woman, Bradamante, steadfastly quests after a man, Ruggiero, who inversely proves throughout much of the romance to be an elusive object of desire, as well as a knight easily distracted from his goal of locating his beloved. Moreover, through the figure of Bradamante, a virtuous warrior who unsaddles a number of male heroes, Ariosto explores a number of central issues in the Renaissance regarding the normative conceptions of a woman's role in society and the ways in which those roles were then being culturally debated and redefined. At yet another level, the story of Bradamante and Ruggiero's love allows Ariosto to inscribe into his poem a developmental narrative—a sort of bildungsroman—in which a pagan hero eventually converts to Christianity and learns through his adventures to place his individual passion at the service of Charlemagne's greater victorious community. Unlike the older, wiser Orlando who has lost his wits, Ruggiero, a young man from the outset driven by passion rather than reason, gradually matures over the course of the narrative and becomes the hero who rightfully wins Bradamante's hand. As predicted in a number of places in the poem, the marriage of Ruggiero and Bradamante further marks, within the fiction of the *Furioso*, the origins of the Este dynasty. Hence, through Ruggiero's maturation into a hero and Bradamante's devotion to her future husband, along with her extraordinary perseverance and strength, Ariosto introduces into his poem a number of passages in praise of his patrons and their family line. This was by no means an insignificant aspect to Ariosto's romance. The fashioning of Ruggiero's identity allowed for the refashioning of the Este dynasty; it also permitted Ariosto to present himself, in typical humanist fashion, as the poet who would immortalize his patrons in the very moment that he would win everlasting fame for himself through his poem.

CRITICAL RECEPTION

Ariosto's fortune as a writer is mostly linked to his *Furioso*, which attracted some attention after the 1516 edition. By the final version of 1532 the *Furioso* had become one of the most widely read and influential poems of its time. Its fame accrued rapidly, but not everyone shared a high opinion of the poem. With the rise of Aristotelian poetics in the cinquecento and the shift in interest from the errant structures of romance to the linear, teleological structure of epic, the *Furioso* was often criticized for being shapeless, digressive, and not verisimilar.

Rhetorically, it was often deemed to lack decorum, and its popularity became for many an indication that it lacked proper seriousness or *gravitas*. The merits and demerits of the poem in turn sparked a debate in the Italian Renaissance, of which Torquato Tasso* himself was a part (see the indispensable work of Bernard Weinberg, *The History of Literary Criticism in the Italian Renaissance*, 2 vols. [Chicago: University of Chicago Press, 1961] and Daniel Javitch, *Proclaiming a Classic: The Canonization of the ''Orlando furioso''* [Princeton: Princeton University Press, 1991]). Nevertheless, even poets such as Tasso,* who criticized the *Furioso*, found themselves incorporating Ariostan themes and narrative strategies into their poems in an effort to ''overgo'' them. Ariosto's episodes were often appropriated and reworked by writers of the English Renaissance, including William Shakespeare,* Edmund Spenser,* and John Milton.

BIBLIOGRAPHY

Works by Ludovico Ariosto

I Suppositi. Bologna: A. Forni, 1976.

La Cassaria. Bologna: A. Forni, 1976.

Orlando furioso. Milano: Rizzoli, 1974.

Scolastica. Bologna: A. Forni, 1980.

Studies of Ludovico Ariosto

Ascoli, Albert R. *Ariosto's Bitter Harmony: Crisis and Evasion in the Italian Renaissance*. Princeton: Princeton University Press, 1987.

Brand, Charles P. *Ludovico Ariosto: A Preface to the ''Orlando Furioso.''* Edinburgh: Edinburgh University Press, 1974. (The bibliography on Ariosto is extensive.)

Caretti, Lanfranco. *Ariosto e Tasso*. 2d ed. Turin: Einaudi, 1967.

Carne-Ross, D. S. ''The One and the Many: A Reading of the *Orlando furioso*, Cantos 1 and 8.'' *Arion* 5 (1966): 195–234.

Croce, Benedetto. *Ariosto, Shakespeare, Corneille*. Bari: Laterza, 1920.

Donato, Eugenio. '' 'Per Selve e Boscherecci Labirinti': Desire and Narrative Structure in Ariosto's *Orlando furioso*.'' *Barroco* 4 (1972): 17–34.

Durling, Robert. *The Figure of the Poet in Renaissance Epic*. Cambridge: Harvard University Press, 1965.

Fichter, Andrew. *Poetics Historical: Dynastic Epic in the Renaissance*. New Haven, CT: Yale University Press, 1982.

Giamatti, A. Bartlett. *The Earthly Paradise and the Renaissance Epic*. Princeton: Princeton University Press, 1966.

Greene, Thomas. *The Descent from Heaven: A Study in Epic Continuity*. New Haven, CT: Yale University Press, 1963.

Javitch, Daniel. ''*Cantus Interruptus* in the *Orlando furioso*.'' *Modern Language Notes* 95 (1980): 66–80.

———. ''The Imitation of Imitation in *Orlando furioso*.'' *Renaissance Quarterly* 38 (1985): 215–39.

Kennedy, William. ''Ariosto's Ironic Allegory.'' *Modern Language Notes* 88 (1973): 44–67.

Marinelli, Peter V. *Ariosto and Boiardo: The Origins of ''Orlando furioso.''* Columbia: University of Missouri Press, 1987.

Momigliano, Attilio. *Saggio sull'Orlando furioso*. Bari: Laterza, 1928.
Parker, Patricia. *Inescapable Romances: Studies in the Poetics of a Mode*. New Haven, CT: Yale University Press, 1979.
Quint, David. "The Figure of Atlante: Ariosto and Boiardo's Poem." *Modern Language Notes* 94 (1979): 77–91.
———. *Origins and Originality in Renaissance Literature: Versions of the Source*. New Haven, CT: Yale University Press, 1983.
Rajna, Pio. *Le fonti del "Orlando furioso."* 2d ed. Ed. Francesco Mazzoni. Florence: Sansoni, 1975.
Saccone, Eduardo. *Il "soggetto" del Furioso e altri saggi tra '400 e '500*. Naples: Liguori, 1989.
Scaglione, Aldo, ed. *Ariosto 1974 in America*. Ravenna: Longo, 1976.
Segre, Cesare. *Esperienze ariostesche*. Pisa: Nistri-Lischi, 1966.
Shapiro, Marianne. *The Poetics of Ariosto*. Detroit: Wayne State University Press, 1988.
Weaver, Elissa. "Lettura dell'intreccio dell'*Orlando furioso*: Il caso delle tre pazzie d'amore." *Strumenti critici* 11 (1977): 384–406.
Wiggins, Peter DeSa. *Figures in Ariosto's Tapestry: Character and Design in the "Orlando furioso."* Baltimore: Johns Hopkins University Press, 1986.

Gender Issues

Bellamy, Elizabeth. *Translations of Power: Narcissism and the Unconscious in Epic History*. Ithaca, NY: Cornell University Press, 1992.
Finucci, Valeria. *The Lady Vanishes: Subjectivity and Representation in Castiglione and Ariosto*. Stanford, CA: Stanford University Press, 1992.
Marcus, Millicent. "Angelica's Loveknots: The Poetics of Requited Desire in *Orlando furioso*." *Philological Quarterly* 72 (1993): 33–52.
Shemek, Deanna. "That Elusive Object of Desire: Angelica in the *Orlando furioso*." *Annali d'italianistica* 7 (1989): 116–141.

DOUGLAS BIOW

ANNE ASKEW (Anne Askewe, Anne Ascough, Anne Kyme) (1521–1546)

BIOGRAPHY

Anne Askew, whose martyrdom in the last days of the reign of Henry VIII raised her from the ranks of the lesser gentry to at least historical immortality, was the second daughter of Sir William Askew, Lincolnshire landowner and courtier to Henry VIII, and his wife, Elizabeth Wrottesley. Reasonably well educated, she was a fervent student of the Scriptures and might have lived her days in relative anonymity had not her elder sister, betrothed to Thomas Kyme, an uneducated landowner and staunch Roman Catholic, died. Deeming the match too good to pass up, Sir William insisted on his younger daughter's marriage to Kyme, thus setting in motion the events that would lead to her martyrdom.

While Askew bore her husband two children, the two became increasingly disaffected as her study of the Scriptures fired her Protestant sympathies. Encouraged by his priests at Lincolnshire, with whom Askew had debated successfully, Kyme cast her out of his house as a heretic; Askew, on similar grounds, appealed to the king for a divorce. Although the divorce was never granted, Askew apparently did secure a position in the retinue of Queen Catherine Parr.* During the time that she is known to have been in the queen's circle she was arraigned as a heretic, examined, imprisoned, released, reexamined, and eventually burned at the stake. The history of these events we have in her own words, published after her death by Bishop Bale as *The First Examination of the Worthy Servant of God, Mistress Anne Askewe* and as *The Latter Examination of Anne Askewe, Lately Martyred in Smythfield by the Wicked Synagogue of Antichrist.*

MAJOR WORKS AND THEMES

Although Askew was outspoken in her religious beliefs and had gained a reputation as a "gospeller," the testimonies of her two examinations and one "Ballad which Anne Askewe Made and Sang when she was in Newgate" (believed to have been written by her but possibly apochryphal) are the sum of her written works. The quality of these works, not the quantity, thrust Askew into the spotlight of her own times and makes her a figure worthy of continued consideration. To understand the attention given to her beliefs and to her testimonials, it is important to reflect briefly on both the position of women and the controversy surrounding the Eucharist in the 1540s.

While there is still contention about the degree to which women's lives and position changed during the early Tudor years, it is generally accepted that, as a result of the dual influences of humanism and Protestantism, women were more apt to be trained so that they could read the Scriptures. It is equally clear that by the latter years of Henry VIII's reign the marriages that resulted from his concern for securing a male heir to the throne had actually emphasized the importance of his last queen, Catherine Parr, as well as his two daughters, Mary and Elizabeth, and a host of additional possible female claimants to the throne. At the same time, although the marriage question had occasioned Henry's break with Rome, it also had fired the hopes of the Reformers. While Queen Catherine of all Henry's wives was the strongest adherent of the Reform movement, many of Henry's bishops and counselors were equally zealous defenders of the Roman catechism. Henry himself, we may recall, had been awarded the title "Defender of the Faith" as a result of Thomas More's* response to Luther, and Reformers and Romanists alike debated the nature of the "true catholic church" throughout much of Henry's reign.

If the soul of this debate was over the question of justification by faith or works, at the heart of it stood the Eucharistic controversy, a debate that reached particularly heated dimensions in the 1540s. On the Roman side of the debate stood the believers in transubstantiation, the belief that at the moment of consecration the bread and wine of the Eucharist physically as well as spiritually were transformed into the body and blood of Christ. On the other side of the debate stood an array of differing beliefs ranging from the consubstantiationists (the Lutheran position) through the ''memorialists'' (Zwingli's position) to the ''virtualists'' (associated with Calvin,* Bucer, Bullinger, and others). While women's position in the church, especially regarding reading the Scripture and preaching, was at issue in Askew's examinations, without the question of the Eucharist it is not clear that the heresy charge would have been made or could have been proven, so adroitly did Askew defend herself against all other charges. The question of whether Askew believed ''that the sacrament hanging over the altar was the very body of Christ really'' was the first asked of her at her first examination and is the only issue in the second. Askew's varying responses to the question mark not only the two examinations but the two outcomes of the examinations.

In the *First Examination*, Askew makes clear to her questioner from the very beginning that she has no intention of sharing with him the contents of her beliefs, nor does she find him adequate to interpret her responses. Throughout, her conscious tactic is to parry her accusers' questions by reference to a greater scriptural knowledge than they possess, always, as Elaine Beilin has pointed out, managing to have the last word without adding to her offenses. As Bishop Bale remarks, ''Courteous enough is her answer'' when the bishop's chancellor rebuked her and said that she ''was much to blame for uttering the scriptures.'' In like manner did Askew hold her examiners off during her entire imprisonment (a period of not less than thirteen days) until at last bail was allowed and, upon her cousin's entreaties to ''take [her] as a woman, and not to set [her] weak woman's wit to his lordship's great wisdom,'' she was at last released.

While she consistently parried her examiners' questions regarding the Eucharist in her *First Examination*, accusing a number of priests of being papists and challenging the lord mayor of London regarding the ''true catholic church,'' Askew's responses to the Eucharistic questions in the *Latter Examination* are markedly different. Whether she had read Ridley's 1545 treatise, ''On the Body and Blood of Christ,'' in the fifteen months separating the two examinations or had other reasons, from her first words in prison to her ''dear friend in the Lord'' she maintained ''the truth concerning the Lord's supper.'' Each day of her imprisonment, in fact, her assertions of the spiritual nature of the Sacrament and her utter rejection of the Roman doctrine of transubstantiation grow more direct: ''I find in the scriptures (saith she) that Christ took the bread, and gave it to his disciples, saying, 'Eat, this is my body, which shall be broken for you;' meaning in substance his own body, the bread being thereof only a sign, or sacrament. . . . So that the bread is but a remembrance of his death, or a sacrament of thanksgiving for it, whereby we are knit unto him by a communion of christian love.'' Throughout the period of her imprisonment and torture, she remained steadfast, never wavering from her belief: ''Lo, this is the heresy I hold, and for it must suffer the death.'' At the end, she prayed that the Lord forgive the violence done her and ''[o]pen also their blind hearts, that they may hereafter do that thing in thy sight which is only acceptable before thee, and to set forth thy verity aright, without all vain fantasies of sinful men. So be it. O Lord, so be it.''

CRITICAL RECEPTION

Given the evidence of her own testimony, it is little wonder that Bishop Bale should acclaim Mistress Anne's sanctity above that of ''the old canonized martyrs, which in the pope's English church have had so many solemnities, services, and censings.'' Those martyrs, Bale argued at length, died for worldly causes, while Anne and her companions died for Christ. John Fox declared her a ''singular example of Christian constancy for all men to follow'' and noted that more than a thousand came to the faith because of her. That Archbishop Cranmer's* 1549 rite and 1550 treatise effectively made orthodox the position for which Askew was burned at the stake no doubt fanned the early flames of belief. Today her *Examinations* are looked at as the records of ''an effort to attack more influential and powerful figures with whom she was associated'' (Travitsky 1981) as a means of developing a woman's voice that ''fulfills the role she recognized she was to have for the Reformers, but [that functions so that] she also becomes an autobiographer who composes the woman, Anne Askew'' (Beilin 1985), and as a document of ''a woman's comprehension of patriarchy and her courageous attack against its power'' (Beilin 1991). Whether Askew would have welcomed these interpretations, it is nonetheless likely that in the end she would have affirmed, ''So be it.'' Thus, so be it.

BIBLIOGRAPHY

Works by Ann, Lady Bacon

The First Examinacyon of Anne Askewe, lately martyred in Smythfelde, by the Romysh Popes upholders, with the Elucydacyon of John Bale (1545).

The Lattre Examinacyon of Anne Askewe, lately martyred in Smythfelde, by the wicked Synagogue of Antichrist, with the Elucydacyon of John Bale (1546). In *Select Works of John Bale*, ed. Henry Christmas. Cambridge: University Press for the Parker Society, 1849.

Studies of Anne Askew

Beilin, Elaine V. ''Anne Askew's Dialogue with Authority.'' In *Contending Kingdoms: Historical, Psychological, and Feminist Approaches to the Literature of Sixteenth-Century England and France*. Ed. Marie-Rose Logan and Peter L. Rudnytsky. Detroit: Wayne State University Press, 1991.

———. ''Anne Askew's Self-Portrait in the Examinations.'' In *Silent but for the Word: Tudor Women as Patrons, Translators, and Writers of Religious Works*. Ed. Margaret P. Hannay. Kent: Kent State University Press, 1985.

———. *Redeeming Eve: Women Writers of the English Renaissance*. Princeton: Princeton University Press, 1987.

Fox, John. *Actes and monuments of these latter and perillous dayes, touching matters of the church, wherein ar comprehended and described the great persecutions & horrible troubles that have been wrought and practised by the Romishe prelates, speciallye in this realme of England and Scotlande, from the yeare of Our Lorde a thousande, unto the tyme nowe present.* London: Iohn Daye, 1563.

Hannay, Margaret P., ed. *Silent but for the Word: Tudor Women as Patrons, Translators, and Writers of Religious Works.* Kent: Kent State University Press, 1985.

Hogrefe, Pearl. *Tudor Women: Commoners and Queens.* Ames: Iowa State University Press, 1975.

King, Margaret L. *Women of the Renaissance.* Chicago: University of Chicago Press, 1991.

Logan, Marie-Rose, and Peter L. Rudnytsky, eds. *Contending Kingdoms: Historical, Psychological, and Feminist Approaches to the Literature of Sixteenth-Century England and France.* Detroit: Wayne State University Press, 1991.

Travitsky, Betty, ed. *The Paradise of Women: Writing by Englishwomen of the Renaissance.* Westport, CT: Greenwood Press, 1981.

Travitsky, Betty S., and Adele F. Seeff, eds. *Attending to Women in Early Modern England.* Newark: University of Delaware Press, 1994.

Warnicke, Retha M. *Women of the English Renaissance and Reformation.* Westport, CT: Greenwood Press, 1983.

SONJA HANSARD-WEINER

B

FRANCIS BACON
(1561–1626)

BIOGRAPHY

Born in 1561, Francis Bacon was the youngest son of Sir Nicholas Bacon, the lord keeper of the seal under Queen Elizabeth* from 1559 until his death in 1579, and Lady Ann Bacon,* one of the famously learned daughters of Sir Anthony Cooke. He entered Trinity College, Cambridge, at the age—then unremarkable—of thirteen and left in 1576 without taking a degree. Later that year he traveled to France in the ambassadorial retinue of Sir Amias Paulet, a trip that was to give Bacon an education in foreign courts and culture and thus prepare him for a career, like his father's, in Elizabeth's government. Sir Nicholas' death in 1579 brought Bacon back to England, where he took up residence at Gray's Inn and studied law. Helped along the way by his uncle Sir William Cecil (who had married Lady Bacon's sister, Mildred), he was admitted to the bar in 1582.

Though Bacon won several parliamentary seats from 1584 to 1593, his political career under Elizabeth was otherwise unprecocious. Despite strong lobbying on his behalf by his friend Essex, Bacon was passed over for the job of queen's attorney when it fell vacant in 1593, probably because he had spoken against one of Elizabeth's tax proposals. The job went instead to Sir Edward Coke,* who would be Bacon's bitter rival for the next three decades. With the accession of James I* Bacon's political fortunes changed dramatically: knighted in 1603, he went on to hold posts as solicitor-general (1607), attorney general (1613), lord keeper of the great seal (1617), and lord chancellor (1618). But in the same year that he was made Viscount St. Albans (1621) he was imprisoned for bribery. Released three days later, he was fined some £40,000 and forbidden to hold public office. He died on 9 April 1626.

MAJOR WORKS AND THEMES

Though Bacon's earliest writings aimed at reforming English law, we know him best for his *Essays* and for his writings on the reformation of natural science—the three most prominent being *The Advancement of Learning [AL]* (1605), *The New Organon [NO]* (1620), and *New Atlantis* (c. 1624). Throughout these works, Bacon plays the scornful Thracian maid to the Schoolman's skyward-looking philosopher whose ethereal abstractions land him in a ditch. Bacon's was not, however, the Socratic call ''to leave natural philosophy behind, and apply knowledge only to morality and policy'' (*AL* 23), but the suggestion that the philosopher ''look down'' to particulars, to nature, and to the remarkable lack of progress in man's understanding the physical world. As his book titles indicate, in suggesting how to overcome this stagnation, Bacon thought of himself as offering something new—not a new theory or a new school, but a new way of proceeding, such that the mind would be governed by something other than its own ''anticipations,'' Bacon's name for the prejudice of current opinion. As articulated in *The New Organon*, this new inductive approach encourages a fierce attention to the ''things themselves'' and a disciplined reluctance to jump to conclusions, a program exactly antithetical, in Bacon's view, to the Scholastic tradition of looking first to authoritative texts. For all of its newness, then, Baconian induction aimed to uncover something he considered respectably old: man's original proximity to a natural world as yet unobscured by layer upon layer of mental fabrications and inherited distortions.

The novel aim of this renewed proximity to nature was not contemplative wonder but practical control. Bacon wanted to do for science what Machiavelli* had done for politics—to encourage an attentiveness to the actual operations of the world so as to be in a better position to derive benefits from them. Unlike Machiavelli, however, Bacon meant for these benefits to accrue to mankind as a whole. ''For the benefits inventors confer extend to the whole human race,'' he writes in *Cogitata et Visa* (c. 1607), ''while those of civil heroes are confined to particular regions and narrower circles of human settlement.'' In this insistence on practicality, Bacon was preceded in various and complicated ways by John Dee,* Giordano Bruno,* and Cornelius Agrippa,* among others. But Bacon was unimpressed with the magical speculation favored by Dee and Agrippa and was straightforwardly hostile to the idea of the elevated illuminati, ruminating alone in single cells. For Bacon, science was to be a corporate enterprise, an activity of men working together for the betterment of the species. He sketched a society so inclined in his *New Atlantis*.

His emphasis on practical progress made Bacon vulnerable to the charge of profane, if not Faustian, ambition, and as a preemptive strike against such a charge, I suspect, Bacon's critique of intellectual stagnation had its force. There is greater humility in the search for new scientific knowledge, Bacon suggests, than in being indolently satisfied with what little has been obtained. Man's overvaluation of ancient authority[1] he attributes to an idolatrous attraction to the orderly works of the mind and a prideful revulsion at the (apparently) disorderly phenomena of nature. But just as Erasmus'* Folly encourages our humility by directing our attention toward the unlovely—our genitals, our illogical obsessions, our foibles and faults—Bacon counseled an attention to what he called in *Advancement of Learning* ''trite and vulgar matters, which are neither subtle enough for dispute or eminent enough for ornament.'' Attention to such matters, he hoped, would serve as a prophylactic against the human tendency to traffic with words rather than things.

The aphorism, which flowers fully in the *New Organon*, is the stylistic correlative of ''vulgar matter.'' Bacon was remarkably suspicious of language and thought that words, given half a chance, tended to run away with themselves, fabricating a world, Pygmalion-like, according to their own specifications. The aphorism was his hobble. It was his stylistic answer to the question of how one combats abstraction without reproducing that abstraction in the process. Moreover, with a series of short, pithy statements Bacon could conduct guerrilla warfare on a tradition with which no extended argument was possible, since ''we agree neither upon principles nor upon demonstrations'' (*NO* 58). Bacon construed his program, then, as nothing less than a paradigm shift, a break so decisive as to preclude any judgment by the accepted canons of rationality, ''since I cannot be called on to abide by the sentence of a tribunal which is itself on trial'' (*NO* 46).

CRITICAL RECEPTION

Bacon's iconoclastic desire to restore an immediacy to man's perception of nature made it possible for Shelley to quote him admiringly in his ''A Defence of Poetry,'' but the majority of Bacon's eighteenth- and nineteenth-century readers associated him unreservedly with the Enlightenment and the Industrial Revolution. Their estimation of the man has often reflected little more than their estimation of those developments. For every William Blake, who subtitled his copy of Bacon's *Essays* with the phrase ''Good advice from Satan's kingdom,'' there was a Lord Macaulay, who celebrated with equal enthusiasm the superiority of British industry and the prodigious talents of Lord Bacon, the man he thought most responsible for it.

Though that dichotomy has often been replicated among twentieth-century readers, on a variety of fronts Bacon's connection to modern science and technology has been made less obvious than it once seemed. Karl Popper, for example, has suggested that Baconian induction has, to its discredit, little or nothing to do with the way science, in fact, proceeds, while other critics, such as John Dewey and Hans Blumenberg, have de-emphasized Bacon's methodological program and pointed instead to his revolutionary promotion of a pragmatic science that eschewed, in their view, metaphysical foundationalism.

NOTE

1. Perhaps the exception that proves the rule to Bacon's rejection of abject adherence to ancient authority is his curious Plutarchian *Wisdom of the Ancients* (*De sapientia vetorum*), which seems to glean all his own knowledge from certain abstrusities of olympian myth, often ones contemplated by Natalis Comes.

BIBLIOGRAPHY

Works by Francis Bacon

The Works of Francis Bacon. 7 vols. *The Letters and Life of Francis Bacon.* 7 vols. Ed. James Spedding, R. L. Ellis, and D. D. Heath. London, 1857–74; rpt., New York: Garrett Press, 1968.

Studies of Francis Bacon

Bowen, Catherine Drinker. *Francis Bacon: The Temper of a Man.* Boston: Little, Brown, 1963.

Briggs, John C. *Francis Bacon and the Rhetoric of Nature.* Cambridge: Harvard University Press, 1989.

Farrington, Benjamin. *The Philosophy of Francis Bacon.* Liverpool: Liverpool University Press, 1964.

Fish, Stanley. "Georgics of the Mind: The Experience of Bacon's Essays." In *Self-Consuming Artifacts.* Berkeley: University of California Press, 1972, 78–155.

Jardine, Lisa. *Francis Bacon: Discovery and the Art of Discourse.* Cambridge: Cambridge University Press, 1974.

Knights, L. C. "Bacon and the Seventeenth-Century Dissociation of Sensibility." *Scrutiny* 11 (1942): 268–85.

Macaulay, Thomas B. "Essay on Bacon." In *Historical Essays.* 2 vols. London, 1961.

Pérez-Ramos, Antonio. *Francis Bacon's Idea of Science and the Maker's Knowledge Tradition.* Oxford: Clarendon Press, 1988.

Rossi, Paolo. *Francis Bacon: From Magic to Science.* Trans. Sacha Rabinovitch. Chicago: University of Chicago Press, 1968.

Urbach, Peter. *Francis Bacon's Philosophy of Science: An Account and Reappraisal.* La Salle, IL: Open Court, 1987.

Vickers, Brian. *Essential Articles for the Study of Francis Bacon.* Hamden, CT: Archon, 1968.

———. *Francis Bacon and Renaissance Prose.* Cambridge: Cambridge University Press, 1968.

Weinberger, Jerry. *Science, Faith, and Politics: Francis Bacon and the Utopian Roots of the Modern Age.* Ithaca, NY: Cornell University Press, 1985.

Whitaker, Virgil K. *Francis Bacon's Intellectual Milieu.* Los Angeles: William Andrews Clark Memorial Library, University of California, 1962.

Whitney, Charles. *Francis Bacon and Modernity.* New Haven, CT: Yale University Press, 1986.

Zeitlin, Jacob. "The Development of Bacon's *Essays*—with Special Reference to the Question of Montaigne's Influence upon Them." *Journal of English and Germanic Philology* 27 (1928): 496–512.

LYELL ASHER

FRANCIS BEAUMONT
(c. 1585–1616)

BIOGRAPHY

Perhaps the most memorable description of Francis Beaumont's life is related in Aubrey's *Brief Lives*; Beaumont and his dramatic collaborator, John Fletcher, "lived together on the Banke side, not far from the Play-house, both batchelors: lay together; had one wench in the house betweene them, which they did so admire; the same cloathes and cloake, &c., betweene them." Their celebrated partnership lasted less than a decade, after which Beaumont forsook both the shared wench and house, as well as the writing of plays, for marriage to Ursula Isley in 1613. At his death three years later, he joined Chaucer and Spenser* as the third to be buried in Poet's Corner, Westminster Abbey. The considerable prestige as poet and playwright that he enjoyed in his adult life continued throughout the seventeenth century, although it diminished after unsympathetic treatment by more recent critics.

Beaumont was the third son born to one branch of a prominent Leicestershire family, and he was related both to the earls of Huntington as well as to the Villiers, the family of King James'* later favorite, the duke of Buckingham. Beaumont's family was also well established at the Inner Temple, which Francis entered in 1600 after a short residency at Broadgates Hall (Pembroke College), Oxford. His first known poem, "Salmacis and Hermaphroditus," was published at age seventeen. Contemporary recollections and another poem attributed to Beaumont refer to his membership in a group of London's men of letters, including Fletcher* and Jonson,* who frequented the Mermaid tavern. Scholarly consensus now ascribes *The Knight of the Burning Pestle* to Beaumont as his first play, which was unpopularly received at its premiere in 1607. Shortly after, however, he was teamed with John Fletcher, with whom he wrote several highly successful plays. At the height of their popularity, they were celebrated by contemporary poets as Olympians of the London stage, compared favorably with Shakespeare* and frequently performed at court. Beaumont's early retirement from dramatic success has traditionally been ascribed to his marriage to an heiress, but new research by Philip J. Finkelpearl has demonstrated that in the same year, 1613, Beaumont suffered a stroke, which prevented him from writing and eventually claimed his life.

MAJOR WORKS AND THEMES

Beaumont's position in London society during his productive years, 1602–13, as the younger son of a well-connected but penalized, recusant family; his continuation of the family tradition at the Inns of Court; his poetic accomplishments as a younger colleague of Shakespeare in the King's Men; and the importance of his literary circle naturally focus examination upon how these might have influenced his choice of themes. Beaumont's elegies are unconventional if not offensive in the extreme; the four dedicated to women display a sometimes perverse or morbid view of female sexuality, which can also be found in women characters in his plays. Issues of female chastity (or the appearance of it) figure frequently and somewhat cynically in his work. By extension, men's relationships with women are troubled and often violent. These turbulent domestic or sexual relationships in the plays find parallels with a political reality of courtly corruption and self-delusion. Many critics have highlighted the consequent unease between tone and genre that characterizes his poetry. In drama, this has led to consideration of Beaumont and Fletcher's particular use of tragicomedy, where the troubled romance between a heterosexual couple is finally resolved in conjunction with a promise of political renewal. The sense of decadence, which has been fully explored elsewhere in Jacobean tragedy, pervades Beaumont and Fletcher's comedies as well, evoking a seriocomic, dark view of noble character tainted by social and political imperatives.

CRITICAL RECEPTION

The critical fortunes of Beaumont have been inextricably linked with those of Fletcher. Indeed, in many cases the precise assignment of authorship of several passages is still disputed. Together and separately, Beaumont and his collaborator have traditionally been regarded as courtier-poets, inferior to Shakespeare. Critics see their works as so popular because they reflect the concerns of wealthy and powerful court interests. As John Danby says, their "work is brilliantly opportunistic. They are quick to catch and reflect back the lights of their social and literary environment" (161). This majority view has been challenged recently by Philip J. Finkelpearl, who explores the phenomenon of the dramatists' "precipitous" decline in popularity and argues that their work reveals "that political criticism of court and king was a central urge in the most important plays of Beaumont and Fletcher" (*Court and Country Politics*, 7) and that their "plays dramatize a moral vacuum and a hollow center. . . . They are plays that comment on the decadence of the age" (6).

Beaumont's share in the collaboration and his individual works, then, are frequently part of the analysis of the partnership. Danby finds Beaumont's unaided work adolescent: "Beaumont's plays, in fact, have no developing revelations, crowded as they are with surprises and fresh turns . . . a curious sense, typical of decadence, of something at once more primitive and more sophisticated than normal'' (172). Lee Bliss also finds adolescent concerns but sees their psychological weight: ''Beaumont and Fletcher's subject is idealistic adolescence, trembling on the brink of adult commitment and decisive action and youth's first confrontation with experience and disillusionment'' (153). Finkelpearl finds Beaumont more attractive, especially in his verse epistle on the Mermaid Tavern: ''Technically, the tension between the seeming freedom and formal control is masterful. Through it Beaumont conveys another kind of wit that appears in his best dramatic poetry'' (*Court*, 46).

BIBLIOGRAPHY

Works by Francis Beaumont

Beaumont and Fletcher. 10 vols. Ed. Arnold Glover and A. R. Waller. Cambridge: Cambridge University Press, 1905–12.

The Dramatic Works in the Beaumont and Fletcher Canon. 10 vols. Gen. ed. Fredson Bowers. Cambridge: Cambridge University Press, 1966– .

The Knight of the Burning Pestle. Ed. J. W. Lever. London: 1962.

The Knight of the Burning Pestle. Ed. Benjamin W. Griffith Jr. Great Neck, NY: Barron's, 1964.

The Knight of the Burning Pestle. Ed. Andrew Gurr. Berkeley: University of California Press, 1968.

The Knight of the Burning Pestle. Ed. Brian Gibbons. Menston: Scolar Press, 1973.

The Knight of the Burning Pestle. Ed. Sheldon P. Zitner. Manchester: Manchester University Press, 1984.

''The Masque of the Inner Temple and Gray's Inn.'' *A Book of Masques: In Honour of Allardyce Nichol*. Ed. T.J.B. Spencer and Stanley Wells. Intro. G. E. Bentley. Cambridge: Cambridge University Press, 1967.

''Salmacis and Hermaphroditus.'' *Elizabethan Minor Epics*. Ed. Elizabeth Storey Donno. London: Routledge and Kegan Paul, 1963.

''Salmacis and Hermaphroditus.'' *Elizabethan Narrative Verse*. Ed. N. Alexander. 1968.

Studies of Francis Beaumont

Bald, R. C. *Bibliographical Studies in the Beaumont and Fletcher Folio of 1647*. Oxford: Oxford University Press, 1938.

Bentley, Gerald Eades. *The Jacobean and Caroline Stage*. 7 vols. Oxford: Clarendon Press, 1962.

Bliss, Lee. *Francis Beaumont*. Boston: Twayne, 1987.

———. '' 'Plot mee no plots': The Life of Drama and the Drama of Life in *The Knight of the Burning Pestle*.'' *Modern Language Quarterly* 45 (1984): 3–21.

Danby, John, F. *Poets on Fortune's Hill*. London: Faber and Faber, 1962.

Doebler, John. ''Beaumont's *The Knight of the Burning Pestle* and the Prodigal Son Plays.'' *Studies in English Literature* 5 (1965): 333–44.

———. ''The Tone of the Jasper and Luce Scenes in Beaumont's *The Knight of the Burning Pestle*.'' *English Studies* 56 (1975): 108–13.

Ellis-Fermor, Una. *The Jacobean Drama*. London: Methuen, 1936.

Farley-Hills, David. *Jacobean Drama: A Critical Study of the Professional Drama, 1600–1625*. New York: St. Martin's Press, 1988.

Finkelpearl, Philip J. ''Beaumont, Fletcher and 'Beaumont and Fletcher': Some Distinctions.'' *English Literary Renaissance* 1 (1972): 144–64.

———. " 'The Comedian's Liberty': Censorship of the Jacobean Stage Reconsidered." *English Literary Renaissance* 16 (1986): 123–38.

———. *Court and Country Politics in the Plays of Beaumont and Fletcher*. Princeton: Princeton University Press, 1990.

———. "The Role of the Court in the Development of Jacobean Drama." *Criticism* 24 (1982): 138–58.

———. " 'Wit' in Francis Beaumont's Poems." *Modern Language Quarterly* 28 (1967): 33–44.

Hammersmith, James P. "The Printer's Copy of Francis Beaumont's Poems, 1653." *Papers of the Bibliographic Society of America* 72 (1978): 74–88.

Hoy, Cyrus. "The Shares of Fletcher and His Collaborators in the Beaumont and Fletcher Canon." *Studies in Bibliography* 8–15 (1956–62).

Kirsch, Arthur. *Jacobean Dramatic Perspectives*. Charlottesville: University of Virginia Press, 1972.

Krier, Theresa M. "Sappho's Apples: The Allusiveness of Blushes in Ovid and Beaumont." *Comparative Literature Studies* 25 (1988): 1–22.

Miller, Ronald F. "Dramatic Form and Dramatic Imagination in Beaumont's *The Knight of the Burning Pestle*." *English Literary Renaissance* 8 (1978): 67–84.

Pennel, Charles A., and William Williams, comps. *Elizabethan Bibliographies Supplements VIII*. London: Nether Press, 1968.

Samuelson, David A. "The Order in Beaumont's *Knight of the Burning Pestle*." *English Literary Renaissance* 9 (1979): 302–48.

Shapiro, I. A. "The Mermaid Club." *Modern Language Review* 45 (1950): 14–22.

Smith, Denzell S. "Francis Beaumont and John Fletcher." In *Later Jacobean and Caroline Dramatists: A Survey and Bibliography of Recent Studies in English Renaissance Drama*, ed. Terence P. Logan and Denzell S. Smith. Lincoln: University of Nebraska Press, 1978, 3–89.

Thompson, Ann. "Death by Water: The Originality of 'Salmacis and Hermaphroditus.' " *Modern Language Quarterly* 40 (1979): 99–114.

Waith, Eugene. *The Pattern of Tragicomedy in Beaumont and Fletcher*. New Haven, CT: Yale University Press, 1952.

Willson, Robert F., Jr. "Francis Beaumont and *The Noble Gentleman*." *English Studies* 49 (1968): 523–29.

SUSANNE COLLIER

THOMAS BECON
(1512–1567)

BIOGRAPHY

Thomas Becon is one of those writers whom students of English history and literature invariably see, when they look at the writers at all, as examples of the "incipient Puritanism" of the mid-Tudor dynasty. One of the most prolific of the first generation of English Protestant divines, Becon wrote dozens of works aimed initially at providing devotional guides to the new faith during the 1540s but later added explicitly catechetical and polemical strands to his bow as monarchs and circumstances changed. His collected edition published in the 1560s runs to three long folio volumes. By the time of his death in 1567, he had written over thirty works, not including various collections of prayers and sermons, and several of his more fortunate pieces ran to multiple editions.

Born around 1512 near Thetford, Norfolk, Becon entered Cambridge in 1527 at a time when the university was known for its Lutheran leanings. He appears to have been turned to the new learning by Hugh Latimer, with whom he is often compared, with some justification: both were homilists rather than theologians, and both were tremendously popular. After he left Cambridge with his B.A. in 1531, he joined the community of religious scholars at the College of St. John Evangelist in Rushworth, close to his home, and was there ordained priest in 1533. He seems to have left before the house ascribed to the oath acknowledging the royal supremacy in 1534, for his signature is not among the members who affirmed the schism. By 1538 Becon had attracted the patronage of Thomas Lord Wentworth of Nettlestead (who helped bring John Bale into the Protestant fold) and was plying the circuit between Norwich and London as an intinerant preacher. The conservative backlash in 1540 forced him into the first of his two recantations, and he retreated to the relative security of layman's clothing and pseudonymous publication, which he left only when Henry VIII died. Three years before his books were officially condemned in 1546, he was forced to cut them up in his second recantation at Paul's Cross. From that time until Edward VI's accession, Becon once again became itinerant—this time drifting among households of Protestant gentry in the Midlands, educating children and servants and writing.

After Edward's accession, Becon attracted the patronage of Edward Seymour, the lord protector, and left his rural retreats for St. Stephen's Walbrook in London. His theology, which formerly had been Lutheran and rather circumspect concerning the Eucharist, calcified into Zwinglianism—perhaps as a result of his exposure to the daunting intellectual household of the protector whose chaplain he had become. His writings, now under his real name, make explicit and predictable connections between Reformed theology and the acute social problems then current. Perhaps as a result of his many years on foot among the rural laborers, Becon's Edwardine works voice a guarded but laudable sympathy for the poor.

Under Mary, Becon spent some time in the Tower, then fled abroad. He adopted a moderate stance in the theological tussles between Cox's moderation and the Calvinism of John Knox* that divided the English exiles on the Continent. Eventually, in 1556, Becon found himself in a familiar position as domestic tutor to the household of Philip, Langrave of Hesse. He continued to write exhortatory works for an English audience as well as undistinguished Latin polemics for a Continental readership, but his pen was sharpened by the company he kept—notably John Foxe and John Bale. Convinced that Mary's persecutions were proof of God's direct and unmistakable punishment for the failure of the Reformation under Edward, Becon was ready to join the chorus of her champions in proclaiming Elizabeth* as the English Deborah. While many of the more rigorous former exiles were led to Calvinist nonconformism and even active opposition to the Elizabethan settlement, Becon lived out his days after her accession as a minor prebendary in Canterbury, patronized by Matthew Parker, collecting income as a nonresident pastor from his several cures in London and elsewhere.

MAJOR WORKS AND THEMES

Becon's works fall most easily into two groups—the homiletic or devotional and the polemical, both of whose margins bristle with scriptural references. He also compiled and published lists of Protestant proof-texts and "common-places," translated Continental Protestant authors into English, and composed lengthy prayers and sermons, many of which are found in the various official formularies of Edward VI and Elizabeth. His early devotional pieces include a sequence of dialogues superficially modeled after Erasmus'* *Colloquies*. The similarities are strictly formal—in his *A Christmas Banquet* (1542) he draws the setting, the sequence, and even many of the names of the interlocutors from Erasmus' *A Godly Feast* (1522). Unfortunately, he passes over the irony, the complexity, the verbal dexterity and, of course, the humanist leaning of his model in favor of a prolix and transparent Protestant catechesis whose rhetorical simplicity and signal distrust of figurative speech are its most prominent features. Becon's forte as a popularizer perhaps resulted from his homiletic style, and many of his works are really little more than sermons in print.

By the time it became necessary to educate the second generation of English Protestants, distrust in the virtues of a classical curriculum was widespread among the more evangelical. The impact of Becon's efforts under Elizabeth in shaping the emerging generation has yet to be assessed, but his views on the utility of non-Christian authors are unmistakable. His educational works, such as the later *New Catechism* (c. 1560), bring the genre of the humanist dialogue to its knees: in it, a father expounds on the repugnance of Ovid and other pagan authors while his six-year-old son cites approvingly (if somewhat hypocritically) Plato's expulsion of "poets" from his ideal commonwealth. Lucian, whose ironies and ambiguities delighted both More* and Erasmus only a generation earlier, is delated as especially wicked. Becon's antihumanist attitude is seen most clearly in the introduction to his collected works, published in 1560, where he chastises English schools for teaching "the profane and strange letters of the wanton poets, lying historiographers, prattling sophisters, babbling orators, vain philosophers" (Ayre, vol. 1, p. 10) instead of an exclusive focus on sacred Christian texts as they once did in the golden apostolic age and now do in Germany.

Becon's polemics, such as his *The Monstrous Merchandise of the Romish Bishops* and his *Displaying of the Popish Mass*, reflect the chiliastic theology then popular among returning exiles and draw from the common stock of Protestant diatribe. But they were never as popular as his devotional pieces or his prayers. An inventory of Tudor-Stuart private libraries reveals quite a few works by Becon, including his best-selling contribution to the *ars moriendi* genre, *The Sick Man's Salve*.

CRITICAL RECEPTION

Perhaps the soporific effect of his prose is responsible for the relative absence of scholarly attention to this quintessentially Tudor writer. Yet Becon's acknowledged popularity suggests we can learn much from a study of his works and the ironies of his career. A creature of the new technology of print, Becon owes his popularity to a medium he exploits yet repeatedly condemns. He imitates writers whose works he censures and whose rhetorical forms he laments but imitates. Like those of his colleagues Bale and Foxe,* Becon's writings helped shape generations of English piety. Ayre's edition of his collected works is the only one available, and it deliberately omits several polemical pieces offensive to nineteenth-century decorum. Only one study—a biography—treats his theology in any depth, and it is now badly out of date. With the rising interest in the history of print and its relationship to the popular culture of the English Reformation, attention to Becon's works promises to be rewarding.

BIBLIOGRAPHY

Works by Thomas Becon

The Works of Thomas Becon. 3 vols. Ed. John Ayre. Parker Society, 1843–44.

Biography and Bibliographies

Bailey, Derek. *Thomas Becon and the Reformation of the Church in England.* Edinburgh: Boyd, 1952.

House, Seymour. "Thomas Becon." *Dictionary of Literary Biography*. Ed. David Richardson. Second series, vol. 136. Columbia, SC: Bruccoli Clark Layman, 1994.

Studies of Thomas Becon

Beaty, Nancy Lee. *The Craft of Dying: A Study in the Literary Tradition of the* Ars Moriendi. New Haven, CT: Yale University Press, 1970, 108–56.

Bond, Ronald. " 'Dark Deeds Darkley Answered': Thomas Becon's Homily against Whoredom and Adultery, and Its Affiliations with Three Shakespearean Plays." *Sixteenth-Century Journal* 16 (1985): 191–205.

Pineas, Ranier. "Polemical Technique in the Works of Thomas Becon." *Moreana* 5 (1968): 49–55.

———. "Thomas Becon as a Religious Controversialist." *Nederlands Archief voor Kerkgeschiedenis* 46 (1965): 206–20.

SEYMOUR BAKER HOUSE

PIETRO BEMBO
(1470–1547)

BIOGRAPHY

Descended from a noble family, Bembo was born in Venice, but as a boy he accompanied his father, the diplomat Bernardo Bembo, on embassies to Florence and later to Rome and Bergamo. As a young man, he studied Greek with Constantine Lascaris (1492–94) at Messina and philosophy with Niccolò Leoniceno (1497) at Ferrara. For about a decade, Bembo alternated residence between Ferrara and Venice, where his fruitful collaboration with Aldo Manuzio (Aldus Manutius)—as editor, author, colleague—commenced in 1494. According to Erasmus,* Bembo gave Aldus a Roman coin, the reverse of which inspired the famous anchor-and-dolphin mark of the Aldine Press.

Bembo's activities, however, were not exclusively literary; he fell in love three times. About the mysterious "M. G." nothing is known; but the love letters he exchanged with Maria Savorgnan (1500–1) and with Lucrezia Borgia (primarily 1503–5), the wife of Alfonso d'Este, soon to be duke of Ferrara, have been preserved. The letters to Lucrezia seem intense beyond courtly love games, doubtless spiced for both by the *frisson* of danger, but it is difficult to judge the character of the relationship. Bembo's first major work, *Gli Asolani*, was published by Aldus in 1505 with a dedication to Lucrezia. As Castiglione* memorably recorded, he then lived at the court of Urbino (1506–12), before moving to the papal court at Rome (1512–21). When Giuliano de' Medici was elected Pope Leo X (1513), Bembo and Jacopo Sadoleto were appointed to share the office of papal secretary, in which role he continued until Leo's death, whereupon he retired to his villa near Padua. Untroubled by having taken Holy Orders, he there produced three children by a common-law wife, Morosina. He also produced his second major work, *Prose della volgar lingua* (1525), his collected *Rime*, and was appointed official historian of Venice (both 1530). Paul III made Bembo a cardinal in 1539; thereafter he spent most of his time in Rome, being appointed bishop of Gubbio and of Bergamo before his death at the grand age of seventy-six.

Bembo was the leading man of letters and arbiter of literary taste for his generation. His contemporary celebrity is indicated by numerous portraits, including medals by Valerio Belli and Cellini and paintings by Bellini and Titian. Looking back from the end of the century, Justus Lipsius described Bembo as "easily the prince of the learned men of Italy in our times."

MAJOR WORKS AND THEMES

Bembo was preeminently a humanist: devoted to the *studia humanitatis*, a philologist and rhetorician, student of Latin and Greek, a stylist concerned to express wisdom through eloquence. Living during the ascendance of vernacular languages, however, made Bembo a liminal figure with a foot in both camps; he wrote voluminously in Latin and Italian, particularly favoring the humanist genres of letter and dialogue. Erasmus praised Bembo's Latin style as the best kind of Ciceronianism. In an exchange of letters on literary imitation (1512), Bembo agreed with Gianfrancesco Pico della Mirandola in distinguishing emulation from imitation; one should attempt to outdo one's models. But, in contrast to Pico's eclecticism, he maintained it was necessary to follow a single model, in poetry Virgil and in prose Cicero. When preparing to write his history of the republic, Bembo studied not the Venetian archives but Caesar's prose style.

In his editorial activities and his own writings, however, Bembo was concerned to establish Trecento authors and the Tuscan dialect as the ''classical'' standards of Italian literature. For Aldus, Bembo edited the texts of Petrarch (1501) and Dante (1502). These were issued in the same octavo format and italic type as the Aldine classical texts; and, in his reliance on manuscripts and his linguistic scrupulousness, Bembo set new editorial standards. Bembo's fullest consideration of the vernacular occurs in the *Prose della volgar lingua*, a Ciceronian dialogue set in Venice in December 1502 on three successive days. The speakers are Federigo Fregoso, Giulano de' Medici (both, like Bembo himself, speakers in Castiglione's* *Il Cortegiano*), his friend Ercole Strozzi, and his brother Carlo Bembo. Through Carlo emerges the argument that the Tuscan of an earlier age should be the foundation of a vernacular literary style, with Boccaccio as the model for prose and Petrarch for poetry. Bembo's authority as Petrarch's foremost advocate was reinforced by the example of his own *Rime*, sonnets and canzoni that often are Petrarchan to a fault. Indeed, Bembo's conscious emulation of Petrarch is foreshadowed by his first publication, the dialogue *De Aetna* (1496), which describes his exploration of Mount Etna in Sicily, evoking Petrarch's ascent of Mount Ventoux.

Spending nearly five impressionable years in Florence undoubtedly germinated Bembo's veneration of Tuscan and his attachment to the Medici family. It also would have brought him into the milieu of Florentine Neoplatonism; and we know that he met Angelo Poliziano in Venice (1491). Bembo's most notable literary accomplishment was *Gli Asolani*, translating Marsilio Ficino's commentary on the *Symposium, De Amore*, from philosophic to imaginative literature. Set in the garden of the palazzo at Asolo, the dialogue occupies three days and three books. Ciceronian in style and Tuscan in language, it consists of long monologues by three speakers, Perottino, a passionate and disillusioned lover; Gismondo, who argues that human love, rightly conceived, can be happy and is indeed necessary to society; and Lavinello, who recounts the lessons he learned from a hermit about the ascent to divine love. The structure of the dialogue itself embodies the ascent pattern by its progression through speakers who exemplify the three kinds of love—sensual, rational, and spiritual. *Gli Asolani* went through at least twenty-two editions by 1600 and was translated into both French and Spanish.

None of Bembo's major works were translated into English during the Tudor age. His direct influence would have been limited to humanists engaged in their own skirmishes over the vexed topics of Ciceronianism, imitation, and use of the vernacular. In shades from direct to oblique his championing of Petrarch affected the phenomenon of English Petrarchism; at the direct end, Wyatt* paraphrased one of Bembo's poems. Later, Bembo's learning made a literal entrance to England when Sir Henry Wotton, the ambassador to Venice, purchased a large portion of his library (1617–20), now mostly at Eton College. For ordinary Englishmen, however, undoubtedly the most vivid impression of Bembo comes from *The Book of the Courtier* in Hoby's* translation, asserting the superiority of letters to arms and discoursing on platonic love even more eloquently than the real man had done. Thus, Sidney, in his *Defence of Poetry*, extols the poet who was also a cardinal and sheds doubt on his idea that poets "were the first bringers-in of all civility."

CRITICAL RECEPTION

In the twentieth century, attention has centered on Bembo's place and influence in the humanist debates over theories of imitation, the *questione della lingua*, the Ciceronian movement, and on his role in the reform of an extravagant Petrarchan poetic style. More recently, several translations of his Latin poetry and his dialogues have indicated a responsiveness to his writings for their own merits. Criticism of *Gli Asolani* in particular has advanced its claim to be accepted as an elegantly conceived and sophisticated literary work. General readers still are most likely to connect his name with that of an elegant typeface, deriving from his association with Aldus.

BIBLIOGRAPHY

Works by Pietro Bembo

Petri Bembi De Aetna. Venice, 1496.

[Editor]. *Le Cose volgari di Messer Francesco Petrarcha*. Venice, 1501.

[Editor]. *Le Terze rime di Dante*. Venice, 1502.

Gli Asolani di Messer Pietro Bembo. Venice, 1505. Rev. ed. 1530.

Prose di M. Pietro Bembo nelle quali si ragiona della volgar lingua. Venice, 1525.

Rime di M. Pietro Bembo. Venice, 1530.

Petri Bembi cardinalis Historiae venetae libri XII. Venice, 1551. Italian trans. 1552.

Petri Bembi Carminum libellus. Venice, 1552/53.

Opere del Cardinale Pietro Bembo. 4 vols. Ed. Francesco Hertzhauser. Venice, 1729. (Most complete edition.)

Pietro Bembo's Gli Asolani. Trans. Rudolf B. Gottfried. Bloomington, 1954.

Prose e rime di Pietro Bembo. 2d. ed. Ed. Carlo Dionisotti. Turin, 1966. (Standard modern edition.)

Benacus. In *An Anthology of Neo-Latin Poetry*. Ed. and trans. Fred J. Nichols. New Haven; CT: Yale University Press, 1979.

Salemi Joseph S. trans. " 'Priapus' by Pietro Bembo." *Allegorica* 5.1 (1980): 81–94.

———. "The Faunus Poems of Pietro Bembo." *Allegorica* 7.2 (1982): 31–57.

Kilpatrick, Ross. "The *De Aetna* of Pietro Bembo: A Translation." *Studies in Philology* 83 (1986): 331–58.

The Prettiest Love Letters in the World: Letters between Lucrezia Borgia and Pietro Bembo, 1503 to 1519. Trans. Hugh Shankland. London, 1987.

Studies of Pietro Bembo

Clough, Cecil. *Pietro Bembo's Library as Represented Particularly in the British Museum*. Rev. ed. London: British Museum, 1971.

Cochrane, Eric. *Historians and Historiography in the Italian Renaissance*. Chicago: University of Chicago Press, 1981.

Cox, Virginia. *The Renaissance Dialogue: Literary Dialogue in Its Social and Political Contexts, Castiglione to Galileo*. Cambridge: Cambridge University Press, 1992.

D'Amico, John F. *Renaissance Humanism in Papal Rome*. Baltimore: Johns Hopkins University Press, 1983.

Della Terza, Dante. ''*Imitatio*: Theory and Practice. The Example of Bembo the Poet.'' *Yearbook of Italian Studies* 1 (1971): 119–41.

Dionisotti, Carlo. ''Pietro Bembo.'' *Dizionario biografico degli italiani* 8 (Rome, 1966): 133–51.

Greene, Thomas M. *The Light in Troy: Imitation and Discovery in Renaissance Poetry*. New Haven, CT: Yale University Press, 1982, 172–77.

Hager, Alan. ''Castiglione's Bembo: Yoking Eros and Thanatos by Containment in Book Four of 'Il Libro del cortegiano.' '' *Canadian Journal of Italian Studies* 16.46 (1993): 33–47.

Kennedy, William J. *Authorizing Petrarch*. Ithaca, NY: Cornell University Press, 1994, 82–113.

Marinelli, Peter V. *Ariosto and Boiardo: The Origins of 'Orlando Furioso'*. Columbia: University of Missouri Press, 1987.

Nelson, John Charles. *Renaissance Theory of Love*. New York: Columbia University Press, 1958, 102–7.

Richardson, Brian. *Print Culture in Renaissance Italy: The Editor and the Vernacular Text, 1470–1600*. Cambridge: Cambridge University Press, 1994, 48–63.

Wilson, Kenneth J. *Incomplete Fictions: The Formation of English Renaissance Dialogue*. Washington, DC: Catholic University of America Press, 1985.

RAYMOND BRUCE WADDINGTON, JR.

GIORDANO BRUNO
(1548–1600)

BIOGRAPHY

Born at Nola, Italy, the son of a military officer in the Spanish vice-regency of Naples, Giordano Bruno entered a Dominican monastery at the age of fifteen. After renouncing Aristotelian Scholasticism and leaving the order in 1576, he settled first in Geneva, then in Toulouse (1579), and finally in Paris (1581), where he lectured on systems of memory derived from the fourteenth-century mnemonics of Ramón Lull. His reputation caught the attention of the king of France, Henry III, to whom he dedicated his *Ars memoriae* (Art of Memory) and *De umbris idearum* (On the Shadows of Ideas) along with his (unperformed) Italian comedy *Il Candelaio* (The Candle Bearer) (1582).

To pursue the king's patronage Bruno cultivated the friendship of Michel de Castelnau, the French ambassador to England, whom he accompanied to Elizabeth's* court in 1583. There he sought the patronage of Elizabeth's favorite, the earl of Leicester, his nephew Philip Sidney,* and the latter's friend Fulke

Greville* (for intriguing complications see Bossy). At London he published his major philosophical dialogues, all in Italian, at the press of John Charlewood, though bearing the fictitious imprints of Venice or Paris to enhance their prestige on the Continent. They consist of three "Venetian" works on cosmology and metaphysics: *La cena de li ceneri* (The Ash Wednesday Supper), *De la causa, principio et uno* (Concerning the Cause, Principle, and One), and *De l'infinito universo et mondi* (Concerning the Infinite Universe and Worlds), all in 1584; and three "Parisian" works on ethics and morals: *Spaccio della Bestia Trionfante* (The Expulsion of the Triumphant Beast) (1584), *Cabala del cavallo Pegaseo* (The Cabal of the Horse Pegasus) (1585), and *De gli eroici furori* (The Heroic Frenzies) (1585).

When de Castelnau was recalled to Paris in 1585, Bruno went with him, unsuccessful in his bid for English patronage. Henry III likewise denied him support, prompting Bruno to emigrate to Wittenberg, Prague, Helmstadt, and finally Frankfurt, where in 1591 he published in Latin three long didactic poems summarizing his cosmology and epistemology. In 1592 a potential benefactor invited him to Venice but then denounced him to the Inquisition. Imprisoned in the Castel Sant'Angelo at Rome in February 1593, he underwent repeated examinations on murky charges and was finally burned at the stake on 17 February 1600.

MAJOR WORKS AND THEMES

Bruno's early interest in the organizational and combinatory schemes of memory forecasts his lifelong obsession with defining a unity amid moral, metaphysical, scientific, and epistemological diversity. From Copernicus'* premise that the earth occupies no privileged position in the material world, Bruno deduces that our solar system belongs to a multitude of possible systems in limitless space. To this vision he applies metaphysical insights of Plato and Plotinus as mediated by Nicholas of Cusa and medieval mysticism. If the universe is limitless, then divinity must be immanent within it instead of transcendent apart from it. Humankind strives toward a state of divinity without fully achieving divine autonomy, so that the process of becoming extends indefinitely to all matter and spirit.

Among Bruno's "cosmological" dialogues, *The Ash Wednesday Supper* presents a wide-ranging discussion about the Copernican system at a dinner party in the home of Fulke Greville. Alternately festive and serious, it spares no opportunity to parody, satirize, spoof, and deflate opposing Aristotelian theories that Bruno found uncouth. *Concerning the Cause, Principle, and One* and *On the Infinite Universe and Worlds* argue that the infinity of the universe derives from God's infinite omnipotence, in which humankind possesses a share. As the chief interlocutor of the latter dialogue, the eminent poet/scientist Girolamo Fracastoro, declares, everything seeks perfection in this best of all possible worlds.

Bruno's three "moral" dialogues question whether everything moves toward perfection in a continuous, undeviating fashion. The Lucianic discussion of *The Expulsion of the Triumphant Beast* occurs among Greco-Roman gods who have grown weary and dissatisfied with their own incompetence. Momus urges Jove to expel the Beast of Ignorance and Superstition and to replace it with a constellation of forty-eight virtues. Jove instead decides to reinstate Egyptian nature worship because ''Nature (as you must know) is none other than God in things'' (trans. Imerti, 235). Far from proposing a serious return to ancient cult practices as some scholars (notably, Yates) have argued, Bruno is here imagining Egyptian beliefs as precursors of Greek and Hebrew ideas that have merged with Christian ones. Bruno is challenging complacent readers to reexamine familiar Christian topoi in the light of new scientific understandings about the expanded universe. He encourages a similar reevaluation in the Lucianic fantasy of *The Cabal of the Horse Pegasus*, whose speakers investigate the place of asininity in a reformed heaven. The sardonic humor evident in these texts also dominates the carnivalesque satire of *The Candle Bearer*. The prologue of this play about misers, pedants, alchemists, and foolish lovers warns that ''here you will see nothing certain, but much action, much weakness, little that is fine and nothing that is good'' (trans. Hale, 209–10).

Bruno's most complex dialogue is *The Heroic Frenzies*. Here five sets of interlocutors discuss the workings of love, human and divine, in a universe energized with godlike power. Eighty-two Petrarchan poems, four by the Neapolitan poet Luigi Tansillo and the rest by Bruno, prompt the speakers to articulate their ideas as a commentary on the poetry. Fifteen sonnets at the end of part 1 and another fifteen at the beginning of part 2 appear with verbal ''emblems'' and Latin mottos that deepen their philosophical import. The final dialogue narrates the plight of nine young men. Blinded by Circe, they travel to the banks of the Thames, where their sight is restored, a parable of transformation that may plausibly evoke the author's bid for patronage in the land of Elizabeth Tudor.

CRITICAL RECEPTION

The extraordinary intertextuality of Bruno's writing with its syncretic echoes from, among others, Pseudo Dionysius, the Cabbala, Lucian, Lucretius, Dante, Petrarch, Ficino, Erasmus,* and Fracastoro, belies Bruno's marginality in early modern science, philosophy, and literary discourse. Bruno's imaginative insights vaguely anticipate Spinoza's theory of world substance and Leibnitz's theory of monads, and they casually inform James Joyce's fantasy about ''the firm of Bruno and Nolan'' in *Finnegan's Wake*, but they exert no direct influence on these writers nor on the author's contemporaries (see Kristeller, Copenhaver, and Schmitt). Bruno dedicated *The Expulsion of the Triumphant Beast* and *The Heroic Frenzies* to Philip Sidney, and he represented Fulke Greville as a character in *The Ash Wednesday Supper*, but there is only internal proof that he ever met them or that they read his work. Sidney, in any case, had drafted most of his own literary corpus before Bruno's arrival in London and had left England for the Low Countries just after Bruno's dedication. Bruno befriended John Florio,* whose English and Italian phrase books (1578, 1591) and translation of Montaigne's* *Essays* (1603) touched Shakespeare's* imagination. Still, one cannot argue for Bruno's definitive influence on, say, the characterization of the eccentric Berowne in *Love's Labor's Lost* or on the skepticism of *Hamlet* or the cosmology of *King Lear* (see Gatti). Evidence of his local impact on Walter Ralegh's* School of Night, Marlowe's* *Doctor Faustus*, or Donne's* *Anniversaries* is gossamer at best. But for various causes, the case is not closed.

For students of sixteenth-century poetry, Bruno's dialogues may provide a foil against which to read flights of Neoplatonic fancy in various sonnet sequences. The interlocutors of *The Heroic Frenzies* appear to offer a practical demonstration of Renaissance literary criticism when they explicate versified portions of that dialogue. Their allegorical interpretations recall procedures governing marginal commentaries in early printed editions of Petrarch's poetry (see Roche, Kennedy). Whereas these commentaries increasingly secularize and biographize Petrarch's experience as a model for the obsessive lover or ambitious poet to imitate, Bruno reads into his own figures and tropes the signs and symbols of an extravagant, largely inimitable imagination. Eight sonnets in 2.3, for example, dramatize a debate between the speaker's heart and eyes, a topic explored in the sonnet sequences of Sidney, Spenser, and Shakespeare, where it registers a conflict between the lover's perception and emotion. For Bruno's glossators, however, the debate reveals ''according to a certain similitude, how the highest good must be infinite, and how the impulse of the affection toward it must also be infinite'' (trans. Memmo, 237). This exegesis epitomizes an associative style of reading and interpreting Petrarchan poetry as Hermetic allegory that was passing out of currency in Elizabethan England, to be replaced by more literal text-bound strategies of reading and interpretation. In this regard, as in his preoccupation with discovering Neoplatonic order and unity at the expense of empirical science, Bruno looks more to the past than to the future of literary, cultural, and intellectual history.

BIBLIOGRAPHY

Works by Giordano Bruno

Italian and Latin Editions

Dialoghi italiani. 3d ed. Ed. Giovanni Gentile and Giovanni Aquilecchia. Florence: Sansoni, 1958.

Il Candelaio. Ed. G. Barberi Squarotti. Turin: Einaudi, 1964.

Opere latine. Ed. Carlo Monti. Turin: Einaudi, 1980.

English Translations

The Ash Wednesday Supper. Trans. Stanley L. Jaki. The Hague: Mouton, 1975.

The Ash Wednesday Supper. Trans. Edward A. Gosselin and L. Lerner. Hamden: Shoestring Press, 1977.

The Candle Bearer. Trans. J. R. Hale. In *The Genius of the Italian Theater*, ed. Eric Bentley. New York: New American Library, 1964.

Cause, Principle, and Unity: Five Dialogues. Trans. Jack Lindsay. New York: International, 1962.

The Expulsion of the Triumphant Beast. Trans. Arthur D. Imerti. New Brunswick, NJ: Rutgers University Press, 1964.

The Heroic Frenzies. Trans. Paul Eugene Memmo, Jr. Chapel Hill: University of North Carolina Press, 1964.

On the Composition of Images, Signs, and Ideas. Trans. Dick Higgins. New York: Willis, Locker, and Owens, 1991.

Singer, Dorothea Waley. *Giordano Bruno: His Life and Thought, with an Annotated Translation of His Work "On the Infinite Universe and Worlds."* New York: Henry Schuman, 1950.

Studies of Giordano Bruno

Bossy, John. *Giordano Bruno and the Embassy Affair*. New Haven, CT: Yale University Press, 1991.

Cavallo, Jo Ann. "The *Candelaio*: A Hermetic Puzzle." *Canadian Journal of Italian Studies* 15 (1992): 47–55.

Copenhaver, Brian P., and Charles B. Schmitt. *Renaissance Philosophy*. New York: Oxford University Press, 1992.

Farley-Hills, David. "The 'argomento' of Bruno's *De gli eroici furori* and Sidney's *Astrophil and Stella*." *Modern Language Review* 87 (1992): 1–17.

Gatti, Hilary. *The Renaissance Drama of Knowledge: Giordano Bruno in England*. London: Routledge, 1989.

Gentile, Giovanni. *Giordano Bruno e il pensiero del Rinascimento*. Florence: Vallecchi, 1925.

Gosselin, Edward A. "Fra Giordano Bruno's Catholic Passion." In *Supplementum Festivum: Studies in Honor of Paul Oskar Kristeller*, ed. James Hankins, John Monfasani, and F. Purnell Jr. Binghamton, NY: Medieval and Renaissance Studies and Texts, 1987, 537–61.

Greenberg, Sidney. *The Infinite in Giordano Bruno*. New York: Columbia University King's Crown Press, 1950.

Kennedy, William J. *Authorizing Petrarch*. Ithaca, NY: Cornell University Press, 1994.

Kristeller, Paul Oscar. *Eight Philosophers of the Italian Renaissance*. Stanford, CA: Stanford University Press, 1964.

Roche, Thomas P., Jr. *Petrarch and the English Sonnet Sequences*. New York: AMS Press, 1989.

Schmitt, Charles B., and Quentin Skinner, eds. *The Cambridge History of Renaissance Philosophy*. Cambridge: Cambridge University Press, 1988.

Spampanato, Vincenzo. *Vita di Giordano Bruno*. Messina: Principato, 1921.

Yates, Frances. *Giordano Bruno and the Hermetic Tradition*. Chicago: University of Chicago Press, 1964.

WILLIAM J. KENNEDY

WILLIAM BYRD
(c. 1543–1623)

BIOGRAPHY

William Byrd, the greatest musician of his age, was probably born in the year 1543, but nothing certain is known about his parentage or early life. In light of his subsequent career, his father is commonly presumed to be one Thomas Byrd, a member of the Chapel Royal during the reigns of Edward VI and Queen Mary, compositions by whom appear in manuscript with others by Thomas Tallis, a distinguished member of the chapel.

Byrd was certainly associated with Tallis and the Chapel Royal from an early period. Anthony à Wood, the Oxford antiquary, affirmed that Byrd had been ''bred up under Tallis,'' a remark borne out by comments in 1575 from a fellow student. Whatever his parentage, then, Byrd quite probably received his musical training in the Chapel Royal under one of England's leading musicians.

In 1563, at about twenty years of age, Byrd began serving as organist and master of the choristers at Lincoln Cathedral, appointments he retained for nearly a decade. He may have been responsible for the general schooling of the choirboys in addition to their musical education. Much of his music in English for the Anglican rite, including the Short Service, may have been written at this time, as was much of his early instrumental music. In 1568 he married Juliana Birley at St. Margaret's-in-the-Close, where his first two children were baptized, circumstances suggesting that Byrd was a conforming recusant at this period of his life.

In February 1570 Byrd was sworn in as a gentleman of the Chapel Royal, but he did not relinquish his position at Lincoln Cathedral. Instead he seems to have traveled between the two locations for three years, not leaving Lincoln for London until December 1572, after which time he shared the duties of organist in the chapel with Tallis. There he remained for the next two decades, serving the queen and gaining highly influential patrons. It was a time of extraordinary accomplishment, and most of Byrd's surviving instrumental music comes from this period.

In 1575, in recognition of the high esteem in which she held them, the queen granted Tallis and Byrd a license giving them a monopoly on the printing of all part-music. The composers responded by publishing *Cantiones sacrae*, a collection of thirty-four compositions, seventeen each, quite probably, as Denis Stevens suggested, in recognition of the seventeenth year of the queen's reign. Elizabeth* had doubtless heard some of the anthems performed earlier in the chapel. Byrd's prominent position in the chapel despite his known Catholicism and his continued composition in Latin is explicable only in terms of the queen's favor and in light of her personal interest in maintaining Latin for divine services.

Byrd's Catholicism, moreover, became more pronounced throughout the period. By the late 1570s he had moved to the parish of Harlington, where he and his wife are repeatedly cited for recusancy from 1577 on. His house is cited as a suspected site for recusant gatherings as early as 1580. Byrd seems, in fact, to have been drawn to the underground Jesuit priests. His moving lamentation upon the martyrdom of Edmund Campion, executed in 1581, is an early sign of that allegiance, and over the next few years he is associated with Father Garnet, Robert Southwell,* and Father Weston. Aware of such associations, authorities searched his house and annually saddled Byrd and his wife with stiff fines, but Byrd's patrons offered protection, and he does not seem to have suffered for his recusancy.

In 1586 Byrd lost his wife, who had borne him at least five children. In 1593 he retired from London (perhaps with his second wife, Ellen) to an estate at Stondon Massey in Essex. He may have been persuaded to undertake such a move by the increased persecution of Catholics on the part of English authorities, which may have made his continued presence in London more than awkward. He retired near his patrons, the Petres, who are associated with many of his later projects. In the dedication of the second volume of the *Gradualia* to Lord Petre of Writtle, Byrd reports that the compositions have "mostly proceded from your house" and were "plucked as it were from your gardens."

Byrd was thus apparently found in London less frequently, and he is absent from the records of the Chapel Royal from 1592 to 1623 (apart from two official lists). He may well have served as a gentleman retainer in the Petre family, for he is known to have had a room in the Petres' house at West Thorndon. Even so, Byrd was still to be found in London on occasion. Certain details point to his active participation in the publication of *Parthenia*, published during the winter of 1612–13, which contained eight of his keyboard compositions, and his will mentions his apartments in the London house of the earl of Worcester. Byrd may thus have served in his final years as a private musician in more than one household.

Byrd died at Stondon Massey on 4 July 1623. He was presumably buried there in the churchyard, although this is not certain. His will reveals that he died in comfortable circumstances.

MAJOR WORKS AND THEMES

Byrd was an exceptionally versatile and prolific composer, exploring virtually every form of interest to Elizabethan and Jacobean composers (with the notable exception of lute music and music for mixed consort with plucked instruments). Whatever he touched, moreover, he enhanced, leaving a remarkable legacy in form after form. One of the greatest composers of sacred music in Latin—over 200 works in Latin survive—he also made striking contributions to the Anglican rite, inventing the form of the English verse anthem. He devoted considerable energy to consort music and the consort song, a form he made very much his own, and to the English part-song (not madrigals in the Italian sense, but a form better described as "polyphonic song").

His greatest achievements lie in the realm of instrumental music, but the lack of a sure chronology here makes it difficult to reliably chart his development. He explored instrumental forms, however, with unsurpassed intensity, imagination, and range—dozens of keyboard dances, groups of preludes, fantasias, "grounds," organ hymns and antiphons, and elaborate sets of variations flowed from his pen, a body of instrumental works dwarfing the accomplishments of his predecessors. Almost single-handedly, he established a vigorous native tradition of keyboard music. Equally important, in their expressive range, technical complexity, and cumulative power, the finest instrumental compositions are fully equal to his celebrated compositions for voice.

Overall, Byrd's development lies in increasing sophistication. In his first publication, the prestigious *Cantiones sacrae* with Thomas Tallis, he demonstrates his virtuosity by presenting an enviable technical mastery of numerous forms of vocal composition, tenaciously confronted one at a time. As he matures, Byrd displays greater interest in modifying and combining techniques and styles for more flexible and powerful effects. From the beginning, moreover, Byrd is captivated by problems of abstract form. He possesses an extraordinary architectonic sensibility, and music of his maturity persistently weaves melodic, harmonic, phrasal, and rhythmic materials into brilliantly expressive combinations. In instrumental as well as vocal compositions, he is driven to discover ways of creating denser and more comprehensive designs, and he insists increasingly upon elements of highly diverse and contrastive character. As Oliver Neighbour has pointed out, too, Byrd characteristically refuses to repeat himself. He approaches each composition in light of fresh technical and expressive problems, and he returns to a form only out of a sense of earlier failure. His fundamental musical grammar is that of imitative polyphony, in common with every major composer of the period, but he can abandon it at will for the sake of other expressive and technical interests.

For students of Elizabethan and Jacobean culture, Byrd's compositions for choir possess the greatest interest, for Byrd's life as a composer here was greatly conditioned by activities and patterns within the English Catholic community.

In the earliest vocal compositions, those in *Cantiones sacrae* (1575), Byrd is generally conservative, composing in light of older traditions within the Chapel Royal. Particularly notable is Byrd's interest in the old votive antiphons and hymns to the Virgin Mary, and if some early doubtful compositions are indeed his, Byrd has the distinction of being the last major composer to participate in the native tradition of the Sarum Rite. Traces of the Sarum liturgy appear, in fact, throughout his compositions. In two respects, however, Byrd evinces the spirit of a new age—in his interest in *cantus firmus* composition and in his disrespect for the integrity of chant. Even in his earliest period, Byrd treats chant freely, omitting notes and sections at will, even transposing sections for special effects. Although many of the compositions here are stiff and pedantic, two in particular, *Emendemus in melius* and *Attollite portas*, hint at the greatness to come.

Queen Elizabeth's interest in retaining Latin as a language for religious services allowed Byrd to perfect his mastery of the Latin motet while lending his considerable talents to the development of a new repertory for the nascent Anglican service. The worsening situation for English Catholics in the 1570s and 1580s, however, altered Byrd's compositional interests. He abandoned liturgical composition, redirecting his talents toward creating music for private devotional use.

The majority of the new compositions appeared in two additional collections of *Cantiones sacrae* in 1589 and 1591. Byrd marked his independence as a religious composer here in his selection of texts, most of which have no set liturgical function. He chose texts, however, expressing great anxiety and despair, and a striking number of the new compositions allude to the Babylonian captivity and to the coming of God. The highly emotional character of the texts is matched, furthermore, by a widened range of expressive techniques, many deriving from Italian modes of composition increasingly popular in English circles. Byrd was particularly influenced by Alfonso Ferrabosco, an Italian musician employed by the queen since 1562. But examination of his texts reveals that Byrd had also studied works by great Franco-Flemish masters, such as Willaert and Lassus. Byrd was clearly writing for the oppressed recusant community, in both personal and communal terms (as evidenced by his use of plural pronouns in a number of pieces), and the collections contain many of his most celebrated compositions, among them *Laudibus in sanctis, Vide Domine, Haec dicit Dominus, Infelix ego, Tristitia et anxietis, Ne irascaris, Domine, non sum dignus*, and *Haec dies*.

Byrd's retirement from London about 1593 led to a final phase of liturgical composition for the Catholic community. He seems to have revived the ambitious program begun in the 1550s under Queen Mary to create a complete cycle of musical settings for all texts for the major feasts of the church year in the Roman rite. The first stages of that project appeared with the publication of three exquisite settings of the Ordinary of the Mass, issued variously without a title page between 1592 and 1595. Byrd's settings are austere and intended for use by amateur choirs, yet they are replete with sections of extraordinary beauty and poetic power and are justly famous.

The remaining compositions in the project appeared in two volumes entitled *Gradualia*, issued in 1605 and 1607. Publication of these volumes was the most defiant expression of Byrd's Catholicism, and some critics associate the project with Byrd's connections to the Jesuits and their militant programs. Byrd was fully aware, moreover, of their political implications. In the aftermath of the Gunpowder Plot in 1605, he suppressed the first collection (of which only one copy survives). But he reissued the volume, together with the second, in 1610. With these publications Byrd offered music to sustain recusant families in their forbidden worship throughout the year.

Nothing like this had appeared since Isaac's massive cycles earlier in the century. Byrd devised, furthermore, a remarkably flexible system, so that various compositions could serve in more than one liturgical context. Certain compositions, consequently, are not meant to be performed in full as printed, and interpretation demands an understanding of liturgical contexts. There is also a significant shift in Byrd's style. As in the masses, Byrd writes with an exceptional economy of means. Gone are the chromatic and exuberant, madrigalian passages of the earlier volumes. Byrd composes, nonetheless, with a sure hand, each composition revealing an absolute mastery of form and an exceptional pacing of materials. Despite their relative severity, the two collections display a stunning emotional range, and the volumes contain some of his finest compositions, among them *Justorum animae, Diffusa est gratia, O magnum misterium, Plorans plorabit, Gaudeamus omnes*, and *Ave verum corpus*.

CRITICAL RECEPTION

No English composer was more cherished in his lifetime. Thomas Morley deemed Byrd a "great master" in 1597, one "never without reverence to be named of the musicians." When he died, a unique entry in the Cheque Book of the Chapel Royal referred to him as "a Father of Musick." By the end of the seventeenth century, however, Byrd's reputation was already in decline.

So ignored were his accomplishments that the industrious musicologist Edmund Fellowes felt that even those in musical circles at the beginning of the century were unaware of his existence. The 300th anniversary of his death in 1923 led to the performance of much of his music, much of it unheard for centuries.

Since then the work of industrious scholars, most notably Edmund Fellowes, Thurston Dart, Joseph Kerman, Philip Brett, Oliver Neighbour, and Alan Brown, has led to the thorough study and publication of most of Byrd's works, many formerly unavailable or in manuscript, and Byrd has regained the position in which he was held by his contemporaries.

BIBLIOGRAPHY

Works by William Byrd

Cantiones, quae ab argumento sacrae vocantur (with Thomas Tallis). London, 1575.

Psalmes, Sonets and Songs. London, 1588.

Liber primus sacrarum cantionum [Cantiones sacrae]. London, 1589.

Songs of Sundrie Natures. London, 1589.

Liber secundus sacrarum cantionum [Cantiones sacrae]. London, 1591.

Mass, 4vv. c. 1592–93.

Mass, 3vv. c. 1593–94.

Mass, 5vv. c. 1595.

Gradualia ac cantiones sacrae. London, 1605.

Gradualia seu cantionum sacrarum, liber secundus. London, 1607.

Psalmes, Songs and Sonnets . . . fit for Voyces or Viols. London, 1611.

Parthenia (with John Bull and Orlando Gibbons). London, 1612.

Modern Editions

The Byrd Edition. Ed. Philip Brett. 17 vols. projected. London, 1970–.

The Collected Works of William Byrd. 20 vols. Ed. Edmund H. Fellowes. London, 1937–50; rev. Thurston Dart, Philip Brett, and Kenneth Elliott. London, 1962–.

William Byrd: Keyboard Music I and II. Ed. Alan Brown. Musica Brittanica, xxvii and xxviii. 1969 and 1971; rev. ed., 1976.

Studies of William Byrd

Andrews, H. K. *The Technique of Byrd's Vocal Polyphony*. London, 1966.

Brett, Philip. "Homage to Taverner in Byrd's Masses." *Early Music* 9 (1981): 169–76.

———. "The English Consort Song, 1570–1625." *Proceedings of the Royal Musical Association* 88 (1961–62): 73–88.

Brown, Alan, and Richard Turbet, eds. *Byrd Studies*. Cambridge: Cambridge University Press, 1992.

Caldwell, John. *English Keyboard Music before the Nineteenth Century*. New York: Praeger, 1973.

Clulow, Peter. "Publication Dates for Byrd's Latin Masses." *Music and Letters* 47 (1966): 1–9.

Dart, Thurston, and Philip Brett. "Songs by William Byrd in Manuscripts at Harvard." *Harvard Library Bulletin* 14 (1960): 343–46.

Fellowes, E. H. *William Byrd*. 2d ed. London: Oxford University Press, 1948.

Huray, Peter Le. *Music and the Reformation in England, 1549–1660*. 1967; rpt. Cambridge: Cambridge University Press, 1978.

Jackman, James L. "Liturgical Aspects of Byrd's *Gradualia.*" *Musical Quarterly* 49 (1963): 17–37.

Kerman, Joseph. "The Elizabethan Motet: A Study of Texts for Music." *Studies in the Renaissance* 9 (1962): 273–305.

———. *The Masses and Motets of William Byrd*. Berkeley: University of California Press, 1981.

———. "Old and New in Byrd's Cantiones Sacrae." In *Essays on Opera and English Music in Honour of Sir Jack Westrup*. Oxford, 1975, 25–43.

Neighbour, Oliver. *The Consort and Keyboard Music of William Byrd*. London: Faber and Faber, 1978.

Shaw, Watkins. "William Byrd of Lincoln." *Music and Letters* 48 (1967): 52–59.

Wulstan, David. *Tudor Music*. Iowa City: University of Iowa Press, 1986.

CLAYTON D. LEIN

C

JOHN CALVIN
(1509–1564)

BIOGRAPHY

John Calvin, humanist, biblical theologian, and Reformer, was born 10 July 1509 at Noyon, France, to Gerard Cauvin (French form of the family name) and Jeanne Lefranc. Since Calvin spoke very little of himself, knowledge of his early life is limited to documentary evidence. Sent by his father to Paris to prepare for an ecclesiastical career, Calvin enrolled in the College de Montaigu to study the arts, a prerequisite for entry into the faculty of theology, and studied Latin with Mathurin Cordier. Upon Calvin's completion of the master of arts, his father decided that the law would be more lucrative than theology and sent Calvin to study law at Orleans. Although Calvin obeyed the wishes of his father by earning a law degree, the young man's real interests were in the literary and intellectual currents of the day. In addition to his legal studies, he pursued the study of Greek under the tutelage of Melchior Wolmar. Probably during his years at Orleans he came into contact with the Reform movement. With the death of his father in 1531, Calvin returned to Paris, where he pursued his interest in humanist studies, began studying Hebrew, and completed his commentary on Seneca's *De Clementia*, which he published in April 1532 at his own expense. By 1533 Calvin had converted to the Reformed faith, although he is silent on the circumstances that led to his conversion. Evidence of his public identification with the Reform movement was Calvin's departure from

Paris following the inaugural address on 1 November 1533 by Nicolas Cop, the newly appointed rector of the University of Paris. The speech created an uproar, as it contained several ideas central to the evangelical movement, most notably that of justification by faith, not by works. Whether Calvin contributed directly or indirectly to the address is still the object of scholarly debate. In any case, Calvin apparently thought it prudent to leave Paris, but he returned there in December. As a consequence of the Affair of the Placards in October 1534, Calvin left Paris for Basel. During this initial period of exile, he wrote the first edition of the *Institutes*, completing it in August 1535, and made contact with French-speaking Reformers, including Guillaume Farel and Pierre Viret. After a brief sojourn at the court of the duchess of Ferrara, Calvin returned to France to settle family affairs. Since the political climate continued to be hostile to the Reform movement, Calvin left for Strasbourg on 15 July 1536. Because of a troop movement on the direct road to Strasbourg, Calvin traveled south, stopping on the way in Geneva, a stop that was to change the direction of his life. Geneva had recently become a Protestant city, with Guillaume Farel as one of its principal pastors. Farel urged Calvin to become his coworker in promoting and consolidating the Reformed church in that city. Yielding to Farel's request, Calvin gave up the life of a scholar to become a teacher and preacher in the Reformed church of Geneva and in time its chief pastor. At the beginning of 1537 the city's leaders were friends of Farel and open to his and Calvin's attempts to establish a separate church discipline. However, there was a growing resentment by the populace against being forced to swear to a confession of faith, which culminated in Calvin and Farel's opponents gaining control of the city's leadership. In April 1538, the struggle came to a head when, in an argument over liturgical practices, Calvin and Farel refused to celebrate the communion service. As a result, Calvin and Farel were expelled from the city. Calvin went on to Strasbourg, where he was invited by Martin Bucer to become the pastor of the French congregation.

For the next three years, Calvin lived a generally happy and productive life. Although at the beginning of his exile, he had some self-doubts about his call to the ministry, these were quickly resolved. In addition to his parochial duties, he completed the second edition of the *Institutes* (1539), the *Reply to Sadoleto* (1539), *Commentary on the Romans* (1540), a French translation of the *Institutes* (1541), and *The Short Treatise on the Lord's Supper* (1541). In August 1540, at the urging of Bucer, a reluctant Calvin married one of his parishioners, Idelette de Bure, a widow with two children.

Meanwhile in Geneva, the pro-Calvin faction had regained control. Farel and Calvin were invited to return as pastors. Farel chose to remain in Neuchatel but urged Calvin to accept the invitation. On 13 September 1541, Calvin returned to Geneva. Although the *Ecclesiastical Ordinances* of 1541 clearly established the sphere of church authority, Calvin once again found himself in a power struggle with the city council over church discipline, especially the power of excommunication. By the summer of 1553 the situation became so tense that

Calvin offered to resign. The council refused his resignation. At the height of this battle, an event occurred that was to tarnish Calvin's reputation not only in his own lifetime but up to our own day, namely, the execution of Michael Servetus. Although Calvin was not directly involved in the trial and passing of sentence, he had been involved in the infamous accusation and arrest of the anti-Trinitarian Michael Servetus. Several weeks after Servetus' death, the Council of the Two Hundred voted in favor of the city council's right to have the ultimate jurisdiction regarding excommunication, further frustrating Calvin's attempt to establish control over the spiritual life of the Genevans.

In 1555, the tide of battle turned in favor of Calvin. His supporters gained control of city government, and he was able to implement his vision of the church and state, each in its own sphere serving God. In spite of his increasingly poor health, Calvin continued to maintain a heavy preaching schedule, revise the *Institutes*, and write his biblical commentaries. After bidding farewell to his ministers in April, Calvin died 27 May 1564 and was buried, at his request, in an unmarked grave. Although he spent most of his ministry in Geneva, his reputation and influence went far beyond the city limits. John Knox* and other Reformers visited Calvin to seek his advice. Keenly interested in the Reform movement in England, Calvin maintained correspondence with Cranmer* and the duke of Somerset, offering counsel and encouragement. Richard Hooker* knew and commented on Calvin's ideas on church polity in Geneva.

MAJOR WORKS AND THEMES

Three major issues were at the center of the controversy between the Reformers and the Roman church: salvation, Scripture, and the nature and role of the church. Calvin's main themes reflect his views on these distinct but interrelated topics.

For Calvin the starting point of theology is knowledge of God together with knowledge of self, which are closely linked and lead to an acknowledgment of the sovereignty of God. God has created the world and continues to be intimately involved in its affairs. All blessings enjoyed by mankind are freely given gifts by the Creator; what are perceived as disasters or sorrows are often chastisements for sin. Although mankind is God's greatest act of creation, the sin of Adam has broken that original union with the Creator. The human race as Adam's descendants thereby inherits and shares in his sin, the consequence of which is the total depravity of mankind. In the spiritual realm, the human race cannot of itself restore this original union with God. Neither good works nor pilgrimages nor any devotional practices can procure salvation. Through a sovereign act of mercy, God sent Christ, whose life, death, and resurrection are the means by which sinful man is restored to union with the Creator. This restoration is effected when an individual is united to Christ through faith. This saving faith, which is the work of the Holy Spirit, is a free gift. It is neither deserved nor earned. However, some upon hearing the gospel preached, accept the message; others do not. Within that context, Calvin posits the idea of double predestination: God has from before the creation of the world chosen those who would be saved (the elect) and those who would be damned (the reprobate).

Knowledge of God's saving act in Christ through the power of the Holy Spirit is made known through the church's preaching and administration of the Sacraments. Membership in the church is necessary for the remission of sins and salvation. Cognizant of the church's need for structure and discipline, Calvin developed his idea of church polity and the necessity of the church to be free from civil jurisdiction and control in spiritual matters. At the same time civil authority originates with God, and all rulers and magistrates are thereby ministers of God in civil affairs who must be obeyed. In addition to maintaining public order, civil officials are responsible for the protection and support of the true worship of God.

Sacred Scripture informs and sustains the notion of salvation and the church, and *sola scriptura* is an operating principle of Calvin's theology. The Scriptures are not only the source of knowledge of God and of ourselves, but they are also the sole basis of all Christian doctrine, liturgy, and church polity.

These principal themes are found throughout Calvin's vast corpus. However, they received their fullest expression in the 1559 edition of the *Institutes of the Christian Religion*, the "most influential theological work of the Protestant Reformation, eclipsing in importance the rival works of Luther, Melanchthon, and Zwingli" (McGrath, 139). As early as 1561, Thomas Norton, coauthor of *The Tragedy of Gorboduc*, translated it into English. The first edition of the *Institutes*, published in March 1536, consisted of only six chapters, which discussed the Decalogue, the Apostles' Creed, faith, the law, prayer, Sacraments and false Sacraments, and Christian liberty. The text was preceded by a prefatory address to Francis I of France. The second edition (1539), written during his exile in Strasbourg, was enlarged to seventeen chapters and contained many citations of the church fathers (Greek and Latin) as well as classical writers—Plato, Cicero, Seneca. In this edition, Calvin expanded his discussion on the Trinity, predestination, and justification by faith. In 1541, Calvin produced a French translation of the *Institutes*, which became not only an important tool for the spread of the Reformed faith in France but also a literary work included in anthologies of French literature. In the third edition (1543) he added four more chapters, with a major section on ecclesiology. The fourth edition was published in 1550. The fifth and final edition (1559) is divided into four books, each book further subdivided into chapters.

Book I begins with the basic premise that knowledge of God and of self are inseparable concepts. Knowledge of God leads to knowledge of self; knowledge of self leads to knowledge of God, the latter being the "final goal of the blessed life" (I, v, 1). God places in every person an awareness of himself in addition to which he makes himself continually known through the created universe. The latter knowledge is available to all regardless of educational level. At this point, Calvin speaks favorably of medicine, astronomy, the natural sciences, and the liberal arts as means to a deeper knowledge of God and his absolute sovereignty. The beauty and wonder of creation together with the innate awareness of the divine have as their goal the worship of God and the hope of future life. Sin, however, prevents mankind from achieving these goals. The saving knowledge of God comes through the Scriptures, where God reveals himself as both creator and redeemer. Calvin then discusses at some length the authority and divine inspiration of the Scriptures. Writing about the true worship of God, Calvin turns to a consideration of idolatry, which manifests itself in his time in the worship of images (icons and statues). Images have no place in Christian churches, and he rejects the Catholic position that images help the uneducated. He blames the Roman church for that ignorance, as it had been negligent in its duty to teach the gospel. Following the diatribe against idolatry is an analysis of the Trinity and a refutation of anti-Trinitarian heresies, with a special emphasis on Servetus' teaching and the role of angels. In the final chapters Calvin speaks about the biblical notion of man created in God's image and reprises the theme of the interrelatedness of the knowledge of God and of self. He concludes with an exposition of God's providence and its application to the believer.

In Book II Calvin focuses on the notion of God the Redeemer in the person of Christ. Before discussing his Christology, Calvin details the reasons that necessitate the mediatorship of Christ: total depravity of human nature due to sin, hence the inability of mankind to achieve union with God without divine assistance. Calvin then turns to a consideration of the law as a preparation for the advent of Christ. Although the judicial and ceremonial aspects of the law have no relevance to the gospel, Christians are still bound to the moral law given in the Decalogue. For Calvin, the principal use of the law is that through the work of the Holy Spirit believers gain knowledge of God's will and conform to it. Within this context Calvin then examines the similarities and differences between the Old and New Testaments. The remaining chapters focus on the person and work of Christ. Calvin's Christology is founded on the knowledge of God and of mankind's sinful nature. The chasm that exists between God and mankind can be bridged only by a mediator who is both divine and human. This qualification is achieved by Christ through the hypostatic union, that is, the union of the human and divine natures in the person of Jesus. Through his human obedience to God's will, Christ removed the debt of sin exacted by mankind's disobedience. The best way to know the purpose of Christ's work is through the three Old Testament offices of prophet, king, and priest. In his prophetic office, Jesus is the "herald and witness of His Father's grace" (II, xv, 2); in his kingly office, he guards and protects the believers; in his priestly office, he offers his death as the expiation for mankind's sin and remains an eternal intercessor with the Father.

Book III focuses on how the redemptive act of Christ becomes operative in each individual. Apart from Christ there is no salvation, for it requires union with Christ, obtained through faith. Faith comes through the work of the Holy Spirit. Calvin defines faith as "a firm and certain knowledge of God's benevolence toward us, founded upon the truth of the freely given promise in Christ, both revealed to our minds and sealed upon our hearts through the Holy Spirit'' (III, ii, 7). Justification is God's free gift, which cannot be acquired by good works. Justification for Calvin is, in a word, God's acceptance of the individual through union in Christ. Sins are forgiven through the mediatorship of Christ's righteousness. The believer is called to a life of holiness and obedience to God's will as revealed in the Scriptures through the inspiration of the Holy Spirit. Calvin goes on to address what he calls the *decretum horrible*, the frightening decree that states that some will gain eternal life; others, eternal death. He defends his views against those who have a more universalist notion of God's gift of salvation. The book ends with analysis and defense of the doctrine of the final resurrection of the body.

The nature and role of the church is the focus of Book IV. The church is a divine institution within which God continues the work of salvation. In the opening chapter Calvin outlines the principal ideas that he will address: the nature of the church, its government, its orders, power, and civil power. Acknowledging that the church is both invisible and visible whose head is Christ, Calvin concentrates on the visible church. The visible church contains both the elect and the reprobate. Outside this church there is neither forgiveness of sin nor salvation. What are the signs of an authentic church? For Calvin, they are the reading and preaching of the Word of God and the correct administration of the Sacraments. Based on these two signs, he argues that the Roman church cannot claim to be the true church. Church polity has its foundation and authority in Scripture. According to Calvin there are four offices sanctioned and prescribed by Scripture: teacher, pastor, elder, and deacon. The office of teacher consists of the interpretation of Scripture; the office of pastor, preaching, teaching, exercising discipline, and administering the Sacraments; the office of elder, ensuring, together with the pastors, discipline and proper moral behavior; the office of deacon, taking care of the poor. Ministers of the church should be duly called, authorized, and ordained. After a lengthy discussion on the history of church polity from the ancient church to the Roman church of his day, Calvin discusses the areas that come under ecclesiastical power—doctrine, discipline, church laws.

After addressing the issues of fasting, public penance, clerical marriage, celibacy, vows, and monasticism, Calvin addresses the second mark of the true church, namely, the administration of the Sacraments. Along with the other Reformers, Calvin rejects the traditional seven Sacraments and accepts only Baptism and the Eucharist as divinely instituted. For Calvin Sacraments are outward signs ''by which the Lord seals on our consciences the promises of His good will toward us in order to sustain the weakness of our faith'' (IV, xiv, 1). For the Sacrament to be efficacious the power of the Holy Spirit is necessary. In Calvin's view neither Baptism nor the Eucharist is necessary for salvation. Baptism is a rite of initiation of adults and children into the church and a sign of their being cleansed from sin and reborn in Christ. As for the Lord's Supper,

Calvin enters into the debate of Christ's presence or absence in the bread and wine after the words of institution. He rejects Luther's theory of consubstantiation and Zwingli's notion that the elements are only symbols. For Calvin, the bread and wine that nourish the body are by analogy the symbols of the spiritual nourishment of Christ's body and blood received by the individual through faith. Calvin dedicates the final chapter to the topic of civil government and makes a clear distinction between ecclesiastical and civil power. The former is confined to the spiritual realm; the latter, to the body politic. Among the various forms of governments in the world, Calvin opts for a combination of aristocracy and democracy while at the same time acknowledging that God decides what kind of government is established for a given people. Obedience is due all rulers, even those who are unjust, since the latter are often sent by God as a punishment for the sins of the people. However, there is one exception to this precept. Commands given by rulers that are against the laws of God do not have to be obeyed.

CRITICAL RECEPTION

Studies of Calvin have grown considerably during the past two decades. Much of this recent scholarship reflects an attempt to recast the popular (and at times scholarly) image of Calvin as the cold, harsh, and inflexible theocrat who ruled Geneva. Recent biographies, as Klempa points out, attempt to get "behind the myth [Calvin as the religious dictator] to the man" (343). Calvin's reluctance to speak about himself makes this task quite difficult. However, in a recent biography, Bouwsma argues that we can get behind the received image of the Reformer by paying attention to his "oblique modes of communication . . . manner, tone and imagery . . . remarks that in context seem unexpected, gratuitous or even irrelevant" (5). Establishing the date and circumstances of Calvin's conversion continues to be a debated topic. That debate is "largely a reaction to the work of Alexandre Gangoczy, *Le jeune Calvin, Genèse et évolution de sa vocation réformatrice*" (Wolters, 356). Calvin's influence not only on his own time but on the centuries following his death is also a favored topic for research, with a special emphasis on distinguishing what Calvin actually thought, as evidenced in his writings, as opposed to the teachings of his disciples otherwise known as Calvinism. McGrath's recent life of Calvin subtitled *A Study in the Shaping of Western Culture* underlines the impact of Calvin on European history. Other critics have focused on Calvin's importance in specific countries—France, England, Scotland, among others. Scholarly inquiry includes studies on Calvin's sources. Of particular interest in this regard is an emphasis on the influence of the humanist tradition on Calvin's thought, especially the use of rhetoric, not in the sense of "rendering the speaker effective, but rather upon rendering the truth effective" (Demson, 368). Critical studies have examined Calvin's debt to classical writers such as Seneca and Cicero as well as to other Reformers such as Bucer, Bullinger, and Zwingli. Calvin's theology is being studied within the context that he "did not construct his theology around one pivotal idea, such as predestination, justification . . . but he preferred instead to draw together a number of biblical and theological concepts" (Klempa, 346). The social and political views of the "worldly Calvin" (Graham, 361)—for example, the separation of church and state, the ideal form of government, the family, social welfare—continue to be debated. Max Weber's thesis of the Protestant work ethic thesis vis-à-vis Calvin is also being critically reexamined and challenged. In keeping with trends in other disciplines scholars are reexamining Calvin's attitudes toward women. Although Calvin's biblically based attitude views women as subordinate to men, Blaisdell points out that Calvin does stress women's "spiritual equality" (22) and that his view on marriage is "extremely original and affirmative" (23). That view is echoed by Douglass, who states that "Calvin's intent . . . was to affirm that women as well as men are fully created in the image of God" (194). Calvin's letters to women have also received critical analysis. Research also focuses on Calvin's attitude toward the Jews, an attitude that can be gleaned only indirectly, since "his teachings on the Jews are so well integrated into his theological system that they are concealed" (Robinson, 25). Calvin's criticism of the Jews was "most often limited to the Jews mentioned in the Scriptures" (Robinson, 92), a view challenged by some other critics.

Calvin's prose, both Latin and French, receives praise from literary critics. He wrote in a "refined and elegant Ciceronian Latinity" (Payton, 101). His French style has earned him the reputation as one of the great prose writers of French literature, the foundation of that reputation being his "simplicity of syntax and precision of vocabulary" (Higman, 36) together with a "particular talent for the rhythmic control of his sentences" (Higman, 30).

Students of the Renaissance and Reformation will find an invaluable resource in Calvin's sermons, biblical commentaries, polemical treatises, letters, and the *Institutes*. His importance remains undiminished, for he is "a seminal figure in European history, changing the outlook of individuals, and institutions at the dawn of the modern period, as western civilization began to assume its characteristic form" (McGrath, xi).

BIBLIOGRAPHY

Works by John Calvin

Calvin's New Testament Commentaries. Ed. David W. Torrance and Thomas F. Torrance. 12 vols. Grand Rapids: Eerdmans, 1960–72.

Institutes of the Christian Religion. 26 vols. Ed. John T. McNeil. Trans. Ford Lewis Battles. Vol. 20 of *The Library of Christian Classics*. Philadelphia: Westminster Press, 1960.

Ioannis Calvini Opera Supersunt Omnia. 59 vols. Ed. G. Baum, E. Cunitz, and E. Reuss. Brunswick: C. A. Schwetschlke and Son, 1863–1900.

John Calvin's Sermons on the Ten Commandments. Ed. and trans. Benjamin W. Farley. Grand Rapids: Baker Book House, 1980.

Selected Works of John Calvin: Tracts and Letters. 7 vols. Ed. and trans. Henry Beveridge. Grand Rapids: Baker Book House, 1983.

Three French Treatises. Ed. Francis M. Higman. London: Athlone Press, 1970.

Studies of John Calvin

Baldwin, Claude-Marie. "Marriage In Calvin's Sermons." In *Calviniana: Ideas and Influences of John Calvin,* ed. Robert V. Schnucker. Kirksville, MO: Sixteenth Century Journal Publications, 1988, 121–30.

Battles, Ford Lewis. "The Future of Calviniana." In *Renaissance, Reformation, Resurgence: Papers and Responses Presented at the Colloquium on Calvin and Calvin Studies,* ed. Peter De Klerk. Grand Rapids: Calvin Theological Seminary, 1976, 133–73.

Blaisdell, Charmarie J. "Calvin and Loyola's Letters to Women: Politics and Spiritual Counsel in the Sixteenth Century." In *Calviniana: Ideas and Influence of Jean Calvin,* ed. Robert V. Schnucker. Kirksville, MO: Sixteenth Century Journal Publications, 1988, 234–54.

———. "Response to the Role and Status of Women in the Writings of John Calvin." In *Renaissance, Reformation, Resurgence: Papers and Responses Presented at the Colloquium on Calvin and Calvin Studies,* ed. Peter De Klerk. Grand Rapids: Calvin Theological Seminary, 1976, 21–32.

Bouwsma, William J. *John Calvin: A Sixteenth Century Portrait.* New York: Oxford University Press, 1988.

Bratt, John H., ed. *The Heritage of John Calvin: Heritage Hall Lectures 1960–1970.* Grand Rapids: William B. Eerdmans, 1973.

———. "The Role and Status of Women in the Writings of John Calvin." In *Renaissance, Reformation, Resurgence: Papers and Responses Presented at the Colloquium on Calvin and Calvin Studies,* ed. Peter De Klerk. Grand Rapids: Calvin Theological Seminary, 1976, 1–17.

Büsser, Fritz. "Elements of Zwingli's Thought In Calvin's Institutes." In *In Honor of John Calvin, 1509–1564: Papers from the 1986 International Calvin Symposium McGill University,* ed. E. J. Furcha. Montreal: McGill University, 1987, 1–27.

De Klerk, Peter. "Calvin Bibliography 1991." *Calvin Theological Journal* 26.2 (1991): 341–89.

Demson, David E. "The Image of Calvin in Recent Research." In *In Honor of John Calvin, 1509–1564,: Papers from the 1986 International Calvin Symposium McGill University,* ed. E. J. Furcha. Montreal: McGill University, 1987, 367–83.

Douglas, J. D. "Calvinism's Contribution to Scotland." In *John Calvin: His Influence in the Western World,* ed. W. Stanford Reid. Grand Rapids: Zondervan Publishing House, 1982, 217–37.

Douglass, Jane Dempsey. "The Image of God in Humanity: A Comparison of Calvin's Teaching in 1536 and 1559." In *In Honor of John Calvin, 1509–1564: Papers from the 1986 International Calvin Symposium McGill University,* ed. E. J. Furcha. Montreal: McGill University, 1987, 175–203.

Gerrish, B. A., ed. *Reformatio Perennis: Essays on Calvin and the Reformation in Honor of Ford Lewis Battles.* Pittsburgh: Pickwick Press, 1981.

Graham, W. Fred. *The Constructive Revolutionary: John Calvin and His Socio-Economic Impact.* Richmond: John Knox Press, 1971.

———. "Recent Studies in Calvin's Political, Economic and Social Thought and Impact." In *In Honor of John Calvin, 1509–1564: Papers from the 1986 Interna-*

tional Calvin Symposium McGill University, ed. E. J. Furcha. Montreal: McGill University, 1987, 361–66.

Grislis, Egil. ''Seneca and Cicero as Possible Sources of John Calvin's View of Double Predestination: An Inquiry in the History of Ideas.'' In *In Honor of John Calvin, 1509–1564: Papers from the 1986 International Calvin Symposium McGill University*, ed. E. J. Furcha. Montreal: McGill University, 1987, 28–63.

Higman, Francis M. *The Style of John Calvin in His French Polemical Treatises*. Oxford: Oxford University Press, 1967.

Hughes, Philip Edgcumbe. ''Calvin and the Church of England.'' In *John Calvin: His Influence in the Western World*, ed. W. Stanford Reid. Grand Rapids: Zondervan Publishing House, 1982, 217–37.

Kendall, R. T. *Calvin and English Calvinism to 1649*. Oxford: Oxford University Press, 1979.

Klempa, William. ''Introduction.'' In *In Honor of John Calvin, 1509–1564: Papers from the 1986 International Calvin Symposium McGill University*, ed. E. J. Furcha. Montreal: McGill University, 1987, 343–48.

McGrath, Allister E. *A Life of John Calvin: A Study in the Shaping of Western Culture*. Oxford: Basil Blackwell, 1990.

McLelland, Joseph C. ''Renaissance in Theology: Calvin's 1536 Institutio—Fresh Start or False.'' In *In Honor of John Calvin, 1509–1564: Papers from the 1986 International Calvin Symposium McGill University*, ed. E. J. Furcha. Montreal: McGill University, 1987, 154–74.

Parker, T.H.L. *John Calvin: A Biography*. Philadelphia: Westminster Press, 1975.

Pater, Calvin Augustine. ''Calvin, the Jews, and the Judaic Legacy.'' In *In Honor of John Calvin, 1509–1564: Papers from the 1986 International Calvin Symposium McGill University*, ed. E. J. Furcha. Montreal: McGill University, 1987, 256–95.

Payton, James R. ''History as Rhetorical Weapon: Christian Humanism in Calvin's Reply to Sadoleto 1539.'' In *In Honor of John Calvin, 1509–1564: Papers from the 1986 International Calvin Symposium McGill University*, ed. E. J. Furcha. Montreal: McGill University, 1987, 96–132.

Robinson, Jack Hughes. *John Calvin and the Jews*. New York: Peter Lang, 1992.

Thompson, John Lee. ''John Calvin and the Daughters of Sarah: Women in Regular and Exception Roles in the Exegesis of Calvin, His Predecessors, and His Contemporaries.'' Diss., Duke University, 1989.

Wolters, A. ''Recent Biographical Studies of Calvin.'' In *In Honor of John Calvin, 1509–1564: Papers from the 1986 International Calvin Symposium McGill University*, ed. E. J. Furcha. Montreal: McGill University, 1987, 349–60.

TERRENCE J. McGOVERN

ELIZABETH CARY
(1586/1587–1639)

BIOGRAPHY

Elizabeth Tanfield Cary, most famously the author of *The Tragedy of Mariam*, was born at the Priory of Burford in Oxfordshire in 1586 or 1587. Many of the details of her life currently known are drawn from *The Lady Falkland, Her Life*, which was no doubt written by one of her four daughters in the 1640s. This narrative provides the major dates and events in Cary's life, but the account relies heavily upon hagiographic anecdotes. Consequently, although we have much more information available to us about Cary than about many other female writers from this era, the individual stories about her may not be reliable. A subsequent biography, *The Life of Elisabeth Lady Falkland, 1585–1639*, published by Lady Georgiana Fullerton in 1883, draws most of its material from the daughter's text. Barry Weller and Margaret W. Ferguson include a copy of *The Lady Falkland, Her Life* with their edition of *The Tragedy of Mariam*; thus, it is now widely accessible.

The young Elizabeth Tanfield was apparently a voracious reader and talented linguist, despite the opposition of her mother. She reputedly convinced her servants to provide her with candles for reading, thereby running up a large debt to them, which she repaid upon her marriage. At the age of fifteen, she was married to Sir Henry Cary, later Lord Falkland. All indications suggest that this match grew solely from a financial arrangement between the families. Elizabeth and Henry had eleven children together, but their marriage seems to have been predominantly characterized by physical and emotional distance. The couple initially lived apart for several years, while Henry was engaged in military service, and Elizabeth spent much of this time unhappily with her mother-in-law. It is presumed that *The Tragedy of Mariam* was written during this period, c. 1602–8. The play was licensed at the Stationer's Register in 1612, then published in quarto the following year. Also during this period Elizabeth secretly converted to Catholicism, although she did not make her conversion public until 1625.

Lord Falkland was appointed lord deputy of Ireland in 1622, a post he held until 1629. Elizabeth Cary remained in Ireland only until 1625, but she devoted much of her time to the Irish population, an unusual decision for an English resident in Ireland during this period. While there, she studied the Irish language and attempted, largely unsuccessfully, to provide schooling for the locals (Lewalski, 184). It is not clear whether Elizabeth Cary was sent back to England to get away from growing rebellion in Ireland or in response to her increasingly evident Catholic sympathies, but we know that she remained estranged from her husband until his death in 1633. The couple fought bitterly over finances during this final separation, with Elizabeth reportedly living on the brink of starvation.

Her religious problems continued even after her husband's death, however. Although she successfully converted six of her children to Catholicism and helped them move to the Continent, where they joined religious orders, she continued to face the religious opposition of her eldest son, Lucius, the second Lord Falkland, who coincidentally was a friend of Ben Jonson,* another famous convert to Catholicism. Elizabeth Tanfield Cary died in 1639.

MAJOR WORKS AND THEMES

Cary's extant works include *The Tragedy of Mariam* (1613) and the *History of the life, reign and death of Edward II* (1627). Until the twentieth century, *Edward II* was attributed to her husband and still often appears under his name in libraries, since the correct author was identified only after publication. Barry Weller and Margaret W. Ferguson discuss the textual questions about this piece that still trouble critics (12–13). Elizabeth Cary also wrote several saints' lives and a life of Tamberlaine, which do not survive, and a translation of Jacques Davy du Perron's *The reply of the most illustrious cardinal of Perron* (1630), a text that was suppressed shortly after publication.

The Tragedy of Mariam is a Senecan closet drama that retells the story of Herod and Mariam. Cary seems to rely most directly on Josephus' account of this tale, a version of which was published by Thomas Lodge in 1602. Since *The Tragedy of Mariam* presents Cary's revision of Mariam's history, however, it remains uncertain whether Cary encountered Josephus' narrative through Lodge, in the original, or through another source. In any case, Cary's drama was published in 1613, possibly without her consent, then withdrawn from publication immediately (Foster, 160).

Cary's *Tragedy of Mariam* often receives autobiographical readings since it offers the story of a woman's unhappy marriage and her crises of conscience. In the play, Mariam falsely receives word of her husband's death and learns that he has left word that her own death should follow upon his. Furthermore, her love for her husband is compromised by the knowledge that he earlier ordered the deaths of her brother and grandfather.

The play focuses upon Mariam's struggle to choose between speaking her mind or silence. In this regard, it is notable that she adds a character not found in Josephus' narrative: Graphina, a woman who models more conventional female verbal discretion. In addition, Cary's play presents the figure of Salome as a woman who openly defies traditional constraints against women. Although the drama does not directly offer support for Salome's views, it allows her space to make a case in favor of female-initiated divorce.

The play is particularly noteworthy for its presentation of the Herod and Mariam story from a female perspective and for compelling insights into early modern concepts of race. It is also probable that the drama is offering a commentary upon the marital practices of Henry VIII.

Cary's *Edward II* provides further evidence of the author's interest in revising traditional histories as more sympathetic to female concerns. It also suggests Cary's thinking about marriage may have been influenced by her time in Ireland. She does not speak directly about her experiences there; nevertheless, the difference between her portrayals of marriage in *The Tragedy of Mariam* and in *Edward II*, as well as the variation between her depiction of Queen Isabel and depictions found in her sources, suggests that her exposure to Irish marriage practices may have combined with her own marital dissatisfactions to produce an unusually sympathetic account of a woman's nontraditional choices.

Ireland provided a range of subversive behavioral models for women—something that would undoubtedly appear attractive to the Elizabeth Cary we know through the *Life*. In Irish law, for example, divorce was comparatively easy, and unions were formed and dissolved with relative impunity. Women, particularly those of high birth, had a stronger voice in creating or changing their marital allegiances than most Englishwomen enjoyed.

As others have noted, Cary's representation of Isabel in her *Edward II* differs significantly from the image of the queen proffered in Holinshed,* Marlowe,* and elsewhere. Cary's Isabel demonstrates more agency and less unquestioned culpability than other accounts allow. Although the specifically political aspects of Edward's story receive more extended treatment, Cary's account of a savvy and active Isabel stands in sharp contrast to her earlier portrait of the more resigned Mariam. While both the drama and the history present intelligent, articulate women, Isabel evinces the kind of forceful ingenuity that characterized renowned early modern Irishwomen. Mariam, on the other hand, responds verbally to events and situations but impacts her fate less actively. Read together, this pair and Cary's other female characters offer commentary on a range of roles and choices available to women during the author's lifetime.

CRITICAL RECEPTION

Critical responses to Elizabeth Cary reflect the concerns that dominate in the study of early modern women generally. Current scholarship is devoted in part to the dissemination and expansion of historical and textual knowledge about Elizabeth Cary and her writings. At the same time, critics are working to illuminate the significant issues represented in her works. Consequently, scholarship on Elizabeth Cary is found both in texts discussing women writers during this period and in books and essays that focus on literary subjects.

Many readings of Cary's works posit intersections between the author's life and her literary concerns. Tina Krontiris, for instance, uses examples both from *Mariam* and from *Edward II* to suggest that "Cary's reluctance to support openly rebellious behaviour in her life carries over into her literary work" (81). Similarly, Betty Travitsky notes that while critics need to look at more than connections between authors' lives and their texts, "one surely adds a dimension of interest and meaning to the reading of Cary's play by remembering that it was written when her own efforts to subordinate herself to her husband were presumably at their height" (192). Margaret W. Ferguson separates most of her biographical treatment of Cary from her discussion of *Mariam* in her essay "The Spectre of Resistance" but remarks that the dramatic text probably included for Cary and her initial readers "something we might call the woman author's *signature*" (Ferguson, "The Spectre," 239).

Less biographical treatments of Cary's work include Catherine Belsey's discussion of the character of Mariam as "the subjectivity which precedes and undergoes the conflict" (172) in a play that displays a "consistent unease about its heroine's right to speak" (173) and Dympna Callaghan's essay on *The Tragedy of Mariam*, which demonstrates that the "discourse of race" in the drama is "a vital mechanism for the construction and negotiation of difference" (177).

Since Weller and Ferguson's modern edition of *The Tragedy of Mariam* has made Cary's work and the details of her life readily available, it is likely that future scholarship will focus more on the literary and cultural implications of the drama and less upon issues of biographical concern.

BIBLIOGRAPHY

Works by Elizabeth Cary

Cary, Elizabeth, Lady. "Elizabeth Cary's The History of the Life, Reign, and Death of Edward II: A Critical Edition." Ed. Jesse G. Swan. Diss., Arizona State University, 1993.

———. *The Tragedy of Mariam, the Fair Queen of Jewry*. Ed. Barry Weller and Margaret W. Ferguson. Berkeley: University of California Press, 1994.

Purkiss, Diane, ed. *Renaissance Women: The Plays of Elizabeth Cary: The Poems of Aemilia Lanyer*. London: Pickering, 1994.

Studies of Elizabeth Cary

Beilin, Elaine V. *Redeeming Eve: Women Writers of the English Renaissance*. Princeton: Princeton University Press, 1987, 151–76.

Callaghan, Dympna. "Re-Reading Elizabeth Cary's *The Tragedie of Mariam, Faire Queene of Jewry*." In *Women, Race, and Writing in the Early Modern Period*, ed. Margo Hendricks and Patricia Parker. New York: Routledge, 1994, 163–77.

Ferguson, Margaret W. "Running On with Almost Public Voice: The Case of E.C." In *Tradition and the Talents of Woman*, ed. Florence Howe. Urbana: University of Illinois Press, 1991, 37–67.

———. "The Spectre of Resistance: *The Tragedy of Mariam* (1613)." In *Staging the Renaissance: Reinterpretations of Elizabethan and Jacobean Drama*, ed. David Scott Kastan and Peter Stallybrass. New York: Routledge, 1991, 235–50.

Fischer, Sandra K. "Elizabeth Cary and Tyranny, Domestic and Religious." In *Silent But for the Word: Tudor Women as Patrons, Translators and Writers of Religious Works*, ed. Margaret Patterson Hannay. Kent, OH: Kent State University Press, 1985, 225–37.

Foster, Donald. "Resurrecting the Author: Elizabeth Tanfield Cary." In *Privileging Gender in Early Modern England*, ed. Jean R. Brink. Kirksville, MO: Sixteenth Century Studies Journal, 1993, 141–73.

Fullerton, Georgiana. *The Life of Elisabeth, Lady Falkland, 1585–1639*. London: Burns and Oates, 1883.

Gutierrez, Nancy. "Valuing *Mariam*: Genre Study and Feminist Analysis." *Tulsa Studies in Women's Literature* (Fall 1991): 233–51.

Krontiris, Tina. *Oppositional Voices: Women as Writers and Translators of Literature in the English Renaissance*. New York: Routledge, 1992.

———. "Style and Gender in Elizabeth Cary's *Edward II*." In *The Renaissance Englishwoman in Print: Counterbalancing the Canon*, ed. Anne M. Haselkorn and Betty S. Travitsky. Amherst: University of Massachusetts Press, 1990, 137–53.

Lewalski, Barbara Kiefer. *Writing Women in Jacobean England.* Cambridge: Harvard University Press, 1993.

Pearse, Nancy Cotton. "Elizabeth Cary, Renaissance Playwright." *Texas Studies in Literature and Language* (1977): 601–8.

Travitsky, Betty S. "The *Feme Covert* in Elizabeth Cary's *Mariam.*" In *Ambiguous Realities: Women in the Middle Ages and Renaissance*, ed. Carole Levin and Jeanie Watson. Detroit: Wayne State University Press, 1987, 184–96.

SHEILA T. CAVANAGH

BALDASSARE CASTIGLIONE
(1478–1529)

BIOGRAPHY

Born at Casàtico, near Mantua, Castiglione studied at Milan, then, after the death of his father in 1499, returned to Mantua and entered the service of Francesco Gonzaga, to whose family the Castigliones were connected. With Francesco he witnessed the occupation of Milan by the French troops of Louis XII, inaugurating the long era of foreign domination for the Italian peninsula. Castiglione's relationship with Francesco never was easy; and in 1504 he welcomed the opportunity to shift his allegiance to the more congenial service of Guidobaldo da Montefeltro, duke of Urbino. Castiglione's duties for both Francesco and Guidobaldo were, at least in part, military. After Guidobaldo was appointed *gonfaloniere*—captain of the papal forces—Henry VII elected him to membership in the Order of the Garter. Guidobaldo's chronic ill health prevented him from journeying to England for the installation ceremony, so he knighted Castiglione and sent him as his proxy. The image of Castiglione disembarking in 1506 with gifts for Henry VII—a pair of fine horses, hunting hawks, and, in grateful tribute to the patron saint of the order, a painting of St. George and the Dragon by an Urbino artist, Raphael—suggests the physical arrival of the Italian Renaissance in England.

This memorable journey signaled an increasing shift to diplomatic activities, such as a 1507 mission to Louis XII in Milan. To Castiglione's distress, Guidobaldo died in 1508, to be succeeded by his nephew, Francesco Maria della Rovere, whom Castiglione continued to serve from 1513 to 1516 as envoy to the papal court. In 1516 Pope Leo X deprived Francesco Maria of Urbino, giving the duchy to his own nephew. The exiled Urbino court took refuge in Mantua, where Castiglione married and passed three quiet years. *Il libro del cortegiano* was begun some time after Guidobaldo's death, but largely written during this period in Mantua. With the death of Francesco, Federico II Gonzaga succeeded as marquis of Mantua in 1519, sending Castiglione to Rome as his emissary. This position provided Castiglione with some much-needed financial security and influence at the papal court, which endured and increased over the death of Leo X and the brief tenure of Adrian VI; in 1524 Clement VII sent him to

Spain as papal nuncio to the imperial court. Despite the difficulties of defending the pope's policies, Castiglione gained the esteem of Charles V, which he retained through the trauma of the 1527 sack of Rome by imperial armies. Although the *Cortegiano* had been finished effectively years earlier, the threat that a pirated manuscript copy would appear induced Castiglione to issue an authorized version, edited by Pietro Bembo* and published in Venice by the Aldine Press in April 1528. Castiglione's diplomacy helped reestablish normal relations between the empire and the papacy; and he seems to have been disposed to accept Charles' offer of the bishopric of Avila, when he died from a fever on 7 February 1529. Charles mourned the loss of one of the greatest knights in the world. In a discarded preface to the *Cortegiano*, Castiglione wrote that "only recently has a profession been made of this court service, if we can call it that, only recently has it been refined to an art and a discipline" (Woodhouse, 189). This was the profession to which Castiglione devoted his life.

MAJOR WORKS AND THEMES

The quite extraordinary success and influence of the *Cortegiano* have so indelibly stamped Castiglione as a one-book author that it can come as a surprise to learn that he first gained a reputation for his Italian and Latin poetry. This includes his *Rime*, sonnets and canzoni heavily derivative from Petrarch; the *Tirsi*, a dramatic eclogue, composed with Cesare Gonzaga, for the 1506 Urbino carnival; Latin *carmina*, elegies, and a Virgilian eclogue, *Alcon*, which Milton read attentively. His *Epistola* on the life of Guidobaldo da Montefeltro was dedicated to Henry VII. In retrospect, this work retains an interest only because it comes from Castiglione's hand.

Il libro del cortegiano is a dialogue in four books with connecting narrative. It is set in Urbino, at the duke's palace, in March 1507. Four women and nineteen men, all real persons, are the participants; these are both regular members of the court and known visitors, some plausibly remaining from a visit by the pope (I.6). Although Castiglione was present at this time, in the fictive frame he professes to have been absent on his journey to England, instead relying on a report from a participant. It is the custom for the gentlemen to gather after supper in the presence of the duchess, Elisabetta Gonzaga; Guidobaldo, the victim of illness in fiction as in life, does not appear in the dialogue. On this occasion the group agrees that their game shall be "to fashion in words a perfect courtier, setting forth all the conditions and particular qualities requisite for a man deserving of his name, everyone being allowed to contradict anything thought to be appropriate" (I.12). So challenging a task does this prove that it occupies four consecutive evenings, with the promise of continuation beyond the frame of the dialogue.

Emilia Pia, who acts as mistress of ceremonies throughout, assigns the first speech to Count Ludovico da Canossa, who sensibly begins with nature and nurture as prerequisites: the courtier's innate qualities and his education. The ideal courtier should be noble by birth, intelligent, sound in character, attractive in appearance, behavior, and disposition. Because Canossa postulates that the courtier's true profession is in arms, his education requires skill with weapons, horsemanship, training in combat, dueling, and physical sports. He should be graceful in all his actions, including speech—both writing and oratory—and knowledgeable about literature and the arts. Toward the end of Book I it is agreed that the continuation should explain how the courtier puts into effect his good qualities.

Book II, the longest and most miscellaneous, therefore, addresses a variety of practical considerations. Federico Fregoso guides the discussion through games, music, conversation, dress, friendships, and behavior, arguing for moderation in all things and the avoidance of affectation. The latter part of the evening is devoted to the examination of wit and humor, with Bernardo da Bibbiena, himself author of a comedy, appropriately serving as principal speaker.

Book III complements Book I in posing as its subject the definition of the ideal lady, *la donna di palazzo*. The protofeminist Giuliano de' Medici leads the discussion through her qualities (e.g., beauty, modesty, a virtuous character, affability) and education, her role in relation to the courtier, the relative nobility of each, and how she spurs him to achievement.

Book IV parallels II in again having two principal speakers. Ottaviano Fregoso defines the political role of the courtier, maintaining that the perfection he should seek is not an end in itself but to better serve his prince. This moves the discussion to the qualities of the ideal prince and to consideration of the ideal state, debating the merits of principality versus republic. Pietro Bembo* turns the focus inward, presenting the spiritual aspirations of the courtier through a definition of love and its proper end. Adapting from his own *Gli Asolani* and, beyond it, Marsilio Ficino's exposition of platonic love, Bembo postulates love as the desire for beauty and asserts that beauty in any individual is a manifestation of divine beauty emanating from God. In contrast to the sensual love that gets stuck on the physical plane, true love leads through the perception of spiritual beauty in the individual to the desire for union with the source of divine beauty in God. At the end of a rapture in which Bembo seems transported by the force of his own vision, Emilia Pia gently tugs him back to earth. Noticing the light of dawn, the people realize they have talked all night and adjourn the discussion.

In fashioning his book, Castiglione draws on two types of dialogue, Ciceronian and Platonic. The *Cortegiano* broadly follows the model of the Ciceronian "documentary" dialogue in its historicity of setting, the realistic delineation of personalities, the subject (matching Cicero's perfect orator), even the inclusion of subsidiary topics on Cicero's authority. Nonetheless, Plato's "philosophic" dialogue is evoked by the quest to define ideals and by the symposium structure and conventions (e.g., the choice of a topic; and the Alcibiades-like, late entrance of a guest at I.54 and IV.3). This becomes most insistent in Book IV with the overt Platonism of both speakers. Ottavanio's epistemology, his conviction that evil and wrong choice result from ignorance, and his projection of the ideal prince as a philosopher king point, through whatever intermediaries, to the *Republic*, just as Bembo's account of love, beauty, and the spiritual ascent up the scale or ladder of love derives from *De Amore*, Ficino's commentary on the *Symposium*. In its generic inclusiveness, as the *Courtier* is the best of the century's courtesy books, so it also incorporates the most readable of the many love treatises.

Some of the themes that occupied Castiglione—the *questione della lingua* and the *querelle des femmes*, for example—have not outlived their own age. Other aspects of the dialogue have seemingly inexhaustible interest. Any short list would include the key terms in defining the courtier's behavior—*grazia, sprezzatura*, and its opposite, *affettazione*. So insistently does Canossa characterize the perfect courtier's actions as graceful that he is pressed to explain how one acquires grace. He does this by advising the practice in all things of *sprezzatura* (nonchalance or, in Hoby's* translation, recklessness): the true art consists in seeming artlessness. The courtier's manner projects casualness and effortlessness; he appears to do everything well without laboring at it, avoiding the display of specialized training or knowledge that is dismissed as affectation.

The dynamic of the dialogue frame itself needs to be understood through laughter and games. The presentation of the activity as a game with mutually understood rules (disruptive speakers repeatedly are warned not to exceed the bounds) has been analyzed through anthropological constructs, such as Clifford Geertz's "deep play," but the Renaissance concept of serious play, *serio ludere*, would be apposite historically. Repeatedly, too, speakers are described as laughing, *ridendo*, reminding us that, although the extended section on jokes has its immediate source in Cicero, the *Symposium*, as amiable a gathering as the one in Urbino, has Aristophanes deliver a crucial speech.

The impact of Castiglione's book was immediate, enormous, and international. It was known in England as early as 1530, when Edmund Bonner begged Thomas Cromwell* to lend him Petrarch's *Triumphs* "and especially, if it please you, the book called *Cortegiano* in Italian." Following on the Spanish translation by Juan Boscán (1534) and French by Jacques Colin (1537), Sir Thomas Hoby began his English version in 1552 but delayed its publication until 1561, apparently fearing that Mary Tudor's reign would be intolerant of its anticlerical aspects. His printer, William Serres, specialized in Protestant theology; and Hoby dedicated the translation to Henry Hastings—later to be earl of Huntingdon, Elizabeth's* "Puritan Earl"—nicely reminding Hastings that, as his ancestors had entertained and honored "Castilio the maker," so he should receive "this his handywoorke." The xenophobic Roger Ascham offered Castiglione the equivocal praise that it was better to read the book than visit Italy, but he commended Hoby's translation. In 1571 Bartholomew Clerke published a Latin translation that, judging by the number of editions, was more popular than Hoby's English.

Two special circumstances, the author's status as an "honorary Englishman" and the Protestant baptism the book underwent with Hoby's translation, help account for the commanding influence *The Courtier* held during Elizabeth's reign. Further, given her anomalous situation as a regnant queen, Castiglione's description of how her namesake Elisabetta Gonzaga ruled a male court through Platonized–Petrarchist adoration must have been read as a behaviorial handbook for both Elizabeth and her courtiers. Certainly, as the preeminent account of Renaissance self-fashioning and the most articulate statement of "the art of dissimulation," *The Courtier* has provided valuable paradigms for analyzing Elizabethan court culture.

Because the mainstream of Elizabethan poetry flowed through the court, written either by courtiers or by aspirants seeking patronage, this especially has been true for literature. Puttenham's* *The Art of English Poesie* (1589) translates Castiglione's courtly aesthetic directly into poetics; but, even earlier, Sidney* and Gascoigne* had done this for themselves. Spenser's* vast epic absorbed Castiglione among many other models; Donne's* *sprezzatura* in his poetry might have been blueprinted from *The Courtier*; and Jonson's* "A Celebration of Charis" enters into oblique debate with Castiglione. Even England's belated responsiveness to the visual arts, evidenced by seventeenth-century collecting and patronage, appears to have taken impetus from Castiglione's unconventional insistence that gentlemen need to be knowledgeable about such matters.

CRITICAL RECEPTION

Life may not follow art, but criticism has a way of assuming the form of its subject. Appropriately, therefore, discussion of *The Courtier* in recent years has taken the form of dialogue or debate on a number of recurrent topics. Readings that emphasize the idealistic, escapist, and nostalgic elements have been challenged or modified by those pointing to the political realism, some even finding Machiavellian* qualities. In fact, both aspects are in the text; the genuine question is one of establishing proportions. A related debate arises in judging the morality of the courtier's dissimulation, with a split between those who find any equivocation reprehensible and those who allow that human society could not exist without polite deceptions. Still another argument concerns the relationship of Book IV, apparently composed later, to the body of the dialogue, with some critics finding discontinuity, and others seeing it as carefully anticipated and entirely integral to the larger structure. Feminist scholars have introduced new issues. Although they concede that overtly the text treats women very positively, they either dismiss this by contrasting the status of women in contemporary society or by arguing that Castiglione's fictive strategies nonetheless silence and disempower the women characters. The one argument seems to ignore the limits of the society portrayed, and the other, the actual power wielded by the duchess and Emilia Pia. Gender criticism has provided a more rewarding analytical method, suggesting that the process of aestheticizing the courtier has the effect of "feminizing" him. The critical dialogue is as resistant to closure as was the fictive dialogue in Urbino; but studies of dialogue as a literary form, of Renaissance rhetoric, and of the political and cultural contexts of Castiglione's life continue to refine our positions in these critical debates and to help us understand why *The Courtier* was such a remarkably resonant text for its own time and remains so in ours.

BIBLIOGRAPHY

Works by Baldassare Castiglione

Il libro del Cortegiano del Conte Baldesar Castiglione. 1st ed. Venice, 1528.

The Courtyer of Count Baldessar Castilio. Trans. Thomas Hoby. London, 1561. Later editions: 1577, 1588 (Italian, French, and English in parallel columns), and 1603.

Balthasaris Castilionis Comitis de curiale. Trans. Bartholomew Clerke. London, 1571. Latin. Later editions: 1577, 1585, 1603, 1612.

The Book of the Courtier. Trans. Charles S. Singleton. Garden City, NY: Doubleday, 1959. (Modern English.)

Il Libro del Cortegiano con una scelta delle Opere minori. Ed. Bruno Maier. 2d ed., Turin; 1964. (Standard scholarly edition.)

Studies of Baldassare Castiglione

Anglo, Sydney. "The Courtier: The Renaissance and Changing Ideals." In *The Courts of Europe: Politics, Patronage and Royalty, 1400–1800*, ed. A. G. Dickens. New York: Greenwich House, 1984, 33–53.

Burke, Kenneth. *A Rhetoric of Motives.* New York: George Braziller, 1955, 221–33.

Cartwright, Julia. *Baldassare Castiglione, The Perfect Courtier: His Life and Letters, 1478–1529.* 2 vols. London, 1908.

Clough, Cecil H. *The Duchy of Urbino in the Renaissance.* London: Variorum Reprints, 1981.

Cox, Virginia. *The Renaissance Dialogue: Literary Dialogue in Its Social and Political Contexts, Castiglione to Galileo.* Cambridge: Cambridge University Press, 1992.

Finucci, Valeria. *The Lady Vanishes: Subjectivity and Representation in Castiglione and Ariosto.* Stanford: Stanford University Press, 1992.

Hager, Alan. " 'Castiglione's Bembo: Yoking Eros and Thanatos by Containment,' in Book Four of *Il Libro del Cortegiano.*" *Canadian Journal of Italian Studies* 16: 46 (1993): 33–47.

Hanning Robert W., and David Rosand, eds. *Castiglione: The Ideal and the Real in Renaissance Culture.* New Haven, CT: Yale University Press, 1983.

Javitch, Daniel. *Poetry and Courtliness in Renaissance England.* Princeton: Princeton University Press, 1978.

Kelly, Joan. "Did Women Have a Renaissance?" In *Women, History, and Theory: The Essays of Joan Kelly.* Chicago: University of Chicago Press, 1984, 19–50.

Kinney, Arthur F. *Continental Humanist Poetics.* Amherst: University of Massachusetts Press, 1989, 87–134.

Mazzeo, Joseph A. "Castiglione's *Courtier*: The Self as a Work of Art." In his *Renaissance and Revolution.* New York: Pantheon, 1965, 131–60.

Rebhorn, Wayne A. *Courtly Performances: Masking and Festivity in Castiglione's* Book of the Courtier. Detroit: Wayne State University Press, 1978.

Trafton, Dain A. "Politics and the Praise of Women: Political Doctrine in *The Courtier*'s Third Book." In *Castiglione: The Ideal and the Real in Renaissance Culture*. New Haven, CT: Yale University Press, 1983, 27–44.

———. "Structure and Meaning in *The Courtier*." *English Literary Renaissance* 2 (1972): 283–97.

Waddington, Raymond B. "Elizabeth I and the Order of the Garter." *Sixteenth Century Journal* 24 (1993): 97–113.

Whigham, Frank. *Ambition and Privilege: The Social Tropes of Elizabethan Courtesy Theory*. Berkeley: University of California Press, 1984.

Woodhouse, J. R. *Baldesar Castiglione: A Reassessment of* The Courtier. Edinburgh: Edinburgh University Press, 1978.

RAYMOND BRUCE WADDINGTON, JR.

GEORGE CAVENDISH
(1499–c. 1562)

BIOGRAPHY

George Cavendish was born in Suffolk around 1499. An official of the Exchequer under both Henry VII and Henry VIII, his father, Thomas, acquired substantial land holdings. Little is known of George's early years, but it is certain that he attended Cambridge in 1510, although he seems to have left before taking a degree. Although he appears to have married sometime shortly after the death of his mother, Alice, in 1515, there is no record of his first wife's name nor of the date of their marriage. She appears to have died young. Between 1520 and 1525 he married Margery Kemp, with whom he had two children. Margery was the daughter of William Kemp and Mary Colt of Spains Hall, Essex, and the niece of Thomas More* through his first wife, Jane Colt. Once George entered Wolsey's service, by 1522, glimpses of his life are more plentiful insofar as they are recorded in his *Life of Wolsey*. Cavendish served Wolsey for at least seven years as a gentleman usher, and when Wolsey died in the winter of 1530, he retired to his native Suffolk, abandoning a career of royal service that lay open before him. He remained at his estate of Cavendish Overhall, while his brother William (1505?–57) busily prosecuted a career with Thomas Cromwell* that led to a "sizable fortune" (Sylvester, xxii) built on the proceeds of confiscated monastic land. Between 1530 and his death in c. 1562, George played the part of a country gentleman, serving in minor capacities and on various commissions. At some point during Mary's reign he moved to Spains Hall in Essex, where he finished his *Life of Wolsey* as well as his *Metrical Visions*. The date of his death is not known, but it is almost certain that he died sometime in late 1561 or 1562.

MAJOR WORKS AND THEMES

Cavendish wrote two works: a *Life of Wolsey* and a collection of poems on various notable figures in the reigns of Henry VIII, Edward VI, and Mary I, which have come down to us as his *Metrical Visions*. These poems were largely completed between 1552 and 1554, but he does add an epitaph to Mary, who died in November 1558. In 1554 he appears to have begun work on the *Life* whose *terminus ad quem* of June 1558 is provided by his autograph manuscript.

The *Metrical Visions* is a collection of poems in the *de casibus* tradition of medieval tragedy relating the fall of various Tudor notables, beginning with Thomas Wolsey and ending with Lady Jane Grey. Mirroring the structure of Lydgate's *Fall of Princes* (from which Cavendish borrows some 200 lines), the poems present a "chronological progression of historical figures loosely linked by a narrator in the framework of a dream or reverie" (Edwards, 10). His subjects, little more than moral exempla, are invariably those who fell victim to fortune—Anne Boleyn, Thomas Cromwell, the earl of Surrey,* the duke of Somerset. With the notable exception of Wolsey, all were executed. Cavendish labors to connect their political reversal with some inner fault or failure of perception, which probably explains the omission of Sir Thomas More's voluntary ride down fortune's wheel. The common themes are intrigue and understanding, not religious conviction and stoic acceptance. So rigorously does Cavendish adhere to his formulaic reductions that Wolsey himself is presented as an example of deceitful ambition outmaneuvered by his own machinations—which portrait is at odds with the complexities his *Life of Wolsey* convincingly constructs.

A different picture of both Cavendish and the relationship between historical and biographical truth is presented in the *Life of Wolsey*. Unprinted in the sixteenth-century, it enjoyed widespread circulation in manuscript and was incorporated into the major Tudor chronicles of Stow and Holinshed,* although Cavendish's criticisms of Anne Boleyn were regularly omitted until the end of the Tudor dynasty. Various seventeenth-century writers used Cavendish to substantiate Henry VIII's culpability in Wolsey's fall (Wiley 134), which all but overturns the portrait of an overreaching minister found in Tudor accounts, including Cavendish's own *Metrical Visions*.

The *Life* is structurally symmetrical, neatly divided in half by Wolsey's rapid rise and equally rapid fall. By compressing all but the last year of Wolsey's life in the first half, Cavendish emphasizes the cardinal's precipitous ascent. The tempo is slowed considerably in the second half, which narrates the final year of Wolsey's disgrace. Cavendish constructs explicit and implicit parallels between the two sections, amounting to a "structural metaphor" (Sylvester, 52): scenes from Wolsey's rise are echoed, often inverted, in his fall. But Cavendish avoids the formulaic sterility of his *Metrical Visions* by retaining a tight focus on Wolsey's character, which he presents with sympathy and an admirable, even ironic awareness of his own "interpretive presence" (Anderson, 14). In a sense, the *Life* is as much about Cavendish's own growing awareness of the nature of political service as it is about Wolsey. The author re-creates his own presence and perceptions as a young man, giving us, in effect, two narrating personae; the two voices merge only in the final scene, where Cavendish refuses to enter the service of Henry VIII after Wolsey's death—a refusal based on his then inarticulate comprehension of the price one pays for access to power. The *Life*, written as reflection, gives voice to that decision. The result is ''one of the most effective, revealing, and bitterly ironic glimpses of Henry and his Court available in descriptions of the period'' (Anderson, 27). Through Wolsey's life, Cavendish articulates his own.

CRITICAL RECEPTION

Cavendish's *Life of Wolsey* has naturally drawn the attention of scholars more interested in its subject than its literary merits. In 1641 it received its first (but bowdlerized) printing when a Puritan faction tried to tar Archbishop Laud with Wolsey's brush. In 1810 it received a more or less complete printing in Wordsworth's *Ecclesiastical Biography*, but the true merits of the work awaited publication of Pollard's *Wolsey* (1929). Pollard has limited use for its allegedly verbatim speeches and often inaccurate detail but frequently employs its colorful idiom, while noting carefully its partisan spirit. The widespread acclaim that surrounded Pollard's study sparked a new appreciation for the literary merits of the *Life* as an example of the several notable Tudor attempts in biography. Sylvester notes that many of Cavendish's supposed errors are related to the genre in which he was writing—the depiction of Wolsey's growing insight into the nature and limits of ''policy'' and his awareness that by serving his king absolutely, he has necessarily neglected God (Sylvester, 58–61). Wolsey's most recent biographer has a considerably deeper appreciation for the generic concerns and the rhetorical complexities of the *Life* than did Pollard—Gwyn (*The King's Cardinal*, 1990) uses Cavendish's testimony with all its factual inaccuracies to rewrite the relationship between Henry and Wolsey and calls his description of Wolsey's last days ''one of the great passages of English prose'' (Gwyn, 599).

Several literary studies of Cavendish's *Life* are notable: Wiley's dated but reliable tracking of the *Life* in the works of English Renaissance writers, Sylvester's analysis of its structure and language (1960), and Anderson's excellent investigation of Cavendish's concept of biographical truth and the generic constraints of contemporaneous biography (1984). Crewe's (1988) curious critique lamentably pays more attention to Anderson than to Cavendish as it attempts to construct a paradigm shift on which Cavendish wove his biography. Yet the Tudor years pioneered several notable biographies in English—several on Sir Thomas More, one of Wolsey, More's own darkly ironic attempt in *Richard III*, Foxe's sketches of Thomas Cranmer* and others, and John Bale's polemical descriptions of Anne Askew* and Sir John Oldcastle (to say nothing of his self-congratulatory autobiography). Each attempts to set right the record, but only Anderson has firmly linked Cavendish with a few of his literary colleagues.

BIBLIOGRAPHY

Works by George Cavendish

Cavendish's *Life of Wolsey* is widely available, published with Roper's *Life of More* in a single volume entitled *Two Early Tudor Lives*, ed. Richard Sylvester and Davis Harding (New Haven, CT: Yale University Press, 1962); the fullest edition of it remains *The Life and Death of Cardinal Wolsey*, ed. R. S. Sylvester, Early English Text Society, o.s. 243 (London: Oxford University Press, 1959); his verse sketches of other Tudor figures is available as *Metrical Visions*, ed. A.S.G. Edwards (Columbia: University of South Carolina Press, 1980).

Studies of George Cavendish

Anderson, Judith. *Biographical Truth: The Representation of Historical Persons in Tudor-Stuart Writing*. New Haven, CT: Yale University Press, 1984, 27–39.

Crewe, Jonathan. "The Wolsey Paradigm?" *Criticism* 30 (1988): 153–69.

Gwyn, Peter. *The King's Cardinal: The Rise and Fall of Thomas Wolsey*. London: Barrie & Jenkins, 1990.

Pollard, A. F. *Wolsey*. London: Longmans, Green, 1929.

Sylvester, Richard S. "Cavendish's *Life of Wolsey*: The Artistry of a Tudor Biographer." *Studies in Philology* 57 (1960): 44–71.

Wiley, Paul. "Renaissance Exploitation of Cavendish's *Life of Wolsey*." *Studies in Philology* 43 (1946): 121–46.

SEYMOUR BAKER HOUSE

WILLIAM CAXTON
(1422/1423–1491)

BIOGRAPHY

William Caxton described himself as a "simple person," but his influence on English culture was complex. Not only did he introduce printing with movable type into England, but he established precedents in English translation and editorial practice.

Caxton was born in Kent (as he tells us) likely sometime during 1422 or 1423. In 1438, Caxton was apprenticed to Robert Large of the Mercers Company. At some time during his apprenticeship Caxton left England for Bruges, a bustling commercial hub with a rich cultural tradition. Robert Large died in 1441, and it appears likely that Caxton was released from his apprenticeship at that date.

Caxton's life in Bruges was only one part of a lengthy sojourn abroad. In the prologue to *The Recuyell of the Historyes of Troye* he tells us that he was "for the most parte in the contres of Brabant, Flandres, Holand, and Zeland" for "the space of xxx [30] yere." In 1464–65, passports were issued to Caxton and his servants to go to Utrecht. His political prominence is indicated by the fact that he was assigned by Edward IV to negotiate a new treaty with Philip the Good on 20 October 1464. Clearly, his role abroad also included the duties of a diplomat. On 19 September 1471, he went to Cologne. There has been some debate about precisely what he did during that particular sojourn abroad. Edmund Childs suggests that he may have become familiar with the newly established printing press in Cologne and even have learned the art of printing in a religious establishment. William Blades, Caxton's nineteenth-century biographer, strongly argues that he did not learn printing in Cologne but learned it in Bruges. In any case, Caxton left Cologne at the end of 1472 to return to Bruges. There he collaborated with Colard Mansion, who had just established a press. The collaboration produced at least six different editions prior to Caxton's return to England.

When he returned to England in 1476, Caxton established his own press at Westminster, adjacent to the Chapter House at Westminster Abbey. His first dated publication was an indulgence of 13 December 1476. A vital flow of major English cultural documents was to follow. In England Caxton's associations with "persons of quality" continued. He knew Elizabeth Woodville, the wife of Edward IV, and her brother, Earl Rivers. Indeed, one of his earlier publications was a translation by Earl Rivers. Under such royal patronage, Caxton's efforts thrived. Not only did he maintain a press, but he carried on his own activities in editing and translation, often at a frenetic pace. He also maintained a bookstore. Nonetheless, despite his connection to the household of Edward IV, he also managed to thrive under Richard III and Henry VII, with the output of his press undiminished. Indeed, he presented a copy of *Eneydos* to Prince Arthur, the elder son of King Henry VII. His later patrons include Margaret Beaufort, King Henry VII's mother. During his later years, Caxton was assisted by Wynkyn de Worde, who ultimately took over the press. Caxton died in 1491.

MAJOR WORKS AND THEMES

Besides providing a major contribution to English technology by introducing printing with movable type into the country, Caxton also made a contribution in belles lettres, English translation, and editorial practices. Most of Caxton's contribution in the area of belles lettres is to be found in his prologues and epilogues. In these works, he provides details about his editorial practice and the authors he published. For instance, his prologue to his edition of Trevisa's *Polychronicon* makes clear that he has updated the English somewhat and added a selection to make the material current. He also provides tantalizing tidbits about a given work. He notes that the *Lyf of our Lady* was written at the request of "king harry the fifth." He also inserts information about his personal life. The mixture of anecdotal, personal, and authorial information enlivens his discussions of editorial practice.

Caxton's editorial procedures, as described in his prologues and epilogues, have raised several questions. N. F. Blake and others have suggested he did not tell his readers the whole truth. Blake and Eugène Vinaver particularly indicate that, in his editing of Thomas Malory's* *Le Morte Darthur*, Caxton deceived his reader by omitting crucial details about his editorial procedure. However, as other studies have shown, Caxton tends to be meticulous in describing what has happened. This vignette from the preface to the 1484 edition of *The Canterbury Tales* illustrates his sensitivity to his readers and feelings of obligation to his authors:

> one gentylman cam to me / and said that this book was not accordyng in many places vnto the book that Gefferey Chaucer had made / To whom I answerd that I had made it accordyng to my copye / and by me was nothyng added ne mynusshyd / Thenne he sayd he knewe a book whyche hys fader has and movhe louyd That was very trewe / and accordyng vnto hys owen first book by hym made / and sayd more yf I wold enprynte it agayn he wold gete me the same book for a copye / how be it he wyst wel / that hys fader wold not gladly departe fro it / To whom I said / in caas that he coude gete me suche a book trewe and correcte / yet I wold ones endeuoyre me to enprynte it agayn / for to satysfye thauctour.

Providing fifteenth-century audiences the "best text" available made both good editorial sense and good business sense from Caxton's point of view. It is therefore logical to believe that the practices described in the prologues and epilogues reflect his concerted effort to meet the expectations of his market. In any case, these interesting essays (sometimes employing poetry) extend beyond the realm of mere "literary curiosity." As methodological statements of the earliest printer in England, they shed an interesting light both on his editorial practices and on information available to him (and of potential interest to his audience) with regard to the authors he printed. The fact that he occasionally inserts personal information establishes a tone that helps to make Caxton a living presence to modern audiences.

CRITICAL RECEPTION

Caxton's efforts as a translator have drawn mixed reviews. N. F. Blake in *Caxton and His World* notes that Caxton's pursuit of a "high style" led him to formulaic writing and at times even bombast. There is no doubt that the style of Caxton's translations, like that of his prologues and epilogues, tends to the florid end of the spectrum. Unfortunately, it also lacks at times the Ciceronian balance of later florid stylists, perhaps because of constraints imposed by the material he translated. Another concern often raised with regard to Caxton's role as a translator includes his literary taste. His translations include *Caton, Charles the Great, Curial, The Doctrinal of Sapience, Eneydos, The Boke of the Fayte of Armes, The Game of Chess, The Golden Legend, The Recuyell of the Histo-ryes of Troye*, and *The Order of Chivalry*, among others. In many ways, his inventory of translations is similar to the output of his press. While classical titles are included, Caxton clearly valued books from the later Middle Ages in vernacular tongues, which he demonstrated by including later works such as

Reynard the Fox, which he translated from the Dutch. Some of the choices irritated early modern critics, who believed that Caxton did not give enough attention to classical titles in his press list. Yet it is perhaps remarkable that in his translations he gave them much attention at all, for much of the literate population of London in the fifteenth century could read Latin. Such critics also charge that Caxton perpetuated a taste for medieval material. That assertion may be true, but, given Caxton's attention to the demands of his audience, it appears that those titles constituted what he felt to be "marketable." The fact that in the fifteenth century England was participating in a revival of chivalric values (whether serious or ironic) presented Caxton with ready buyers for his medieval treatises on arms and chivalry. Given the fact as well that he updated the language in some of these texts (as he did in the *Polychronicon*), it is apparent that he had a serious dedication to the culture of the later Middle Ages. That dedication was shared by his reading public. No matter how prolix his style might have been or how much one may quarrel with his choice of items for translation, there is no doubt that Caxton served the needs of the late medieval and early modern culture in England.

Even earlier critics felt an obligation to "take a stand" on Caxton. John Bale made the ambiguous observation that Caxton was "vir non omnino stupidus aut ignavia torpens" (a man not entirely foolish nor stiffening from sloth). Gavin Douglas* attacked his translation of the *Aeneid* by saying, "I reid his werk with harmes at my hert" and suggested that Caxton had no idea of Virgil's intent. R. Braman (1555) said that Caxton's translation of the *History of Troy* was "a long, tedious, and brayneles bablyng." Caxton also had a series of important defenders, including John Leland and Thomas Fuller. Fuller's summary comment was that Caxton "deserved well of Posterity." The interest in Caxton in the nineteenth century coincided with a revival of interest in the Middle Ages. In general, he was recognized for his contribution to English culture, but that contribution was often linked to the perception of his character. Blades sets the tone when he observes that Caxton "attracted the love and respect of his associates" and possessed a character "on which history has chronicled no stain" (92). This tone has persisted into the twentieth century. Curt Bühler, for instance, notes that Caxton's nature "was a gentle one, utterly devoid of the slightest trace of venom" (15). These observations were not gratuitous flattery—they were based instead on more detailed attention to Caxton's texts and a broader understanding of his historical setting.

The outpouring of modern criticism on Caxton around 1976, the 500th anniversary of the introduction of printing into England, was, for the most part, laudatory. Childs, Deacon, Blake, Hellinga, and others all made an effort to put Caxton in focus. In general, his editorial practices are now understood in the context of his role as a commercial printer and the parameters of acquiring accurate manuscripts in the fifteenth century. There is considerably more acceptance of his "Burgundian taste," the materials that he printed, and his prose style. While there are still the occasional cries of denigration, Caxton is generally praised for printing and preserving some of the documents that he selected, most notably Malory's* *Le Morte Darthur*. He is still not praised as a master stylist. Much of his English prose sounds awkward to modern readers who do not derive the enjoyment from it that they find in Malory or other fifteenth-century prose. Nonetheless, studies remain to be done on the *reasons* behind his prose style. Given Caxton's business orientation and his desire to please his audience, he must have felt that his prose style would have a sympathetic audience. More comparisons with public documents and private letters (which are now becoming available in greater quantity) may demonstrate additional intrinsic interest in his prose style.

Caxton's reputation waxes and wanes along with current literary taste. He was neither textual scholar in the modern sense nor merely venal businessman. Making money was likely his overriding concern, but, within the limits of the materials available to him and the practices of his day, he did indeed strive for excellence, and he always made an effort to print the "best text" out of respect to his authors and his audience.

BIBLIOGRAPHY

Works by William Caxton

Blake, N. F., ed. *Caxton's Own Prose*. London: Andre Deutsch, 1973.

———. *Selections from William Caxton*. Oxford: Clarendon Press, 1973.

Crotch, W.J.B., ed. *The Prologues and Epilogues of William Caxton*. London: Oxford University Press, 1928.

Vinaver, Eugène. *Works*. 2nd edition. London: Oxford University Press, 1971.

Studies of William Caxton

Blades, William. *The Life and Typography of William Caxton*. 2 vols. London: Trubner, 1861–63.

Blake, N. F. *Caxton and His World*. London: Andre Deutsch, 1969.

———. *Caxton, England's First Publisher*. London: Osprey, 1976.

———. *William Caxton and English Literary Culture*. London: Hambledon Press, 1991.

———. *William Caxton: A Bibliographical Guide*. New York: Garland, 1985. (Contains a bibliography of all printed editions.)

Bühler, Curt. *William Caxton and His Critics*. Syracuse, NY: Syracuse University Press, 1960.

Childs, Edmund. *William Caxton: The First English Editor*. London: Frederick Muller, 1976.

Hellinga, Lotte. *Caxton in Focus*. London: British Library, 1982.

Painter, George D. *William Caxton*. London: Chatto and Williams, 1976.

Wilson, Robert H. "Malory and Caxton." In *A Manual of the Writings in Middle English*, ed. Albert E. Hartung. New Haven, CT: Connecticut Academy of Arts and Sciences, 1972, 909–60.

ROBERT L. KINDRICK AND RUTH E. HAMILTON

GEORGE CHAPMAN
(1559–1631)

BIOGRAPHY

We know little about George Chapman's early life. He seems to have sought a loan to buy clothes to attend upon Sir Ralph Sadler in 1585, and he may have spent time fighting in the Netherlands around 1591, but not until the beginning of 1594, at what seems for a serious writer the comparatively late age of thirty-four, did he appear on the literary scene. Yet within four years he was being mentioned as an important dramatist by the always enthusiastic Francis Meres and as a significant literary figure by Gabriel Harvey.* In the last seven years of Elizabeth's reign and the decade after James's ascension Chapman produced a cluster of much-praised comedies and some successful tragedies, most of which were based on recent or contemporary French history. In 1598 he also began to publish in parts a verse translation of Homer, which was encouraged and supported by Henry, the Prince of Wales, after Queen Elizabeth's death. The prince's own early death left Chapman without a patron, but he remained in favor at court. In the second decade of the century he was entrusted with one of the central masques for the 1611 marriage of Princess Elizabeth, and to honor the scandalous marriage in 1613 of the earl of Somerset, one of King James'* favorites, and the notorious Lady Frances, he wrote an ambitious epithalamion, *Andromeda Liberata*, for which he quickly had to issue an apologetic defense. Chapman himself never married, though he is the putative author of some letters wooing a wealthy widow that appear in a collection of letters now owned by the Folger Library. At various times in his life he was harassed by creditors, some of them notorious cheats, and he spent time in prison for debt and for offending the king. If his career was always a struggle, nevertheless he seems to have been friends with important dramatists, poets, and intellectuals. In the later 1590s he was associated with Thomas Harriot, the scientist and mathematician patronized by Ralegh,* and in the first part of the seventeenth century he was much involved with Ben Jonson.* In the 1620s Michael Drayton wrote of him admiringly, and in 1642 Henry Reynolds invoked him posthumously in a belated attempt to defend the reading of classical verse for its hidden mysteries.

MAJOR WORKS AND THEMES

Chapman was one of an ambitious age's most ambitious poets, not in quantity so much as in the seriousness and difficulty of his verse. His first book of poems, the deeply enigmatic *The Shadow of Night* (1594), consists of two very obscure "Orphic Hymns" "to Night" and "to Cynthia." A year later he published *Ovid's Banquet of Sence*, an elegant little book with four poems: the title work, whose interpretation has in the last few decades come into debate, is a long, difficult, apparently allegorical verse narrative about the uses of the senses to achieve philosophic ecstasy. It is accompanied by a set of ten linked sonnets, ''A Coronet for his Mistresse, Philosophie,'' which can be taken as either a recantation of, or a complement to, the first poem. The book concludes with two pastoral poems open to philosophic interpretation and probably not by Chapman. These first publications have generally been understood as Neoplatonic statements of some kind, but their obscurity, about which Chapman boasted in his two introductory letters to fellow poet Matthew Roydon, continues to thwart convincing readings.

In 1598 Chapman published his most popular and still most widely read poem, his completion of Christopher Marlowe's *Hero and Leander*. Chapman's part of the poem was twice as long as Marlowe's. He divided the poem into six ''Sestiads'' (named after Sestos, the scene of the tragedy, on the model of Homer's naming *The Iliad* after Ilium). Chapman's poem announces itself as ''[m]ore dark, / At least more grave and high'' than Marlowe's. It treats Hero's sexual indulgence more seriously than does Marlowe, tracing the psychology of being ''Venus' nun'' and worrying about the possibilities for hypocrisy. It also takes her world more seriously, seeing the lovers as the victims of a competition between hypocritical goddesses, and it concludes with a moving lament about the wretchedness of all human life. The poem lacks some of Marlowe's Ovidian wit and lightness, but it has compensating values that some modern critics have appreciated. The poem was popular in the seventeenth century and was frequently reprinted, though after the first edition Chapman's name does not appear on the title page.

One other early poem deserves special mention: a 164-line poem to Thomas Harriot, which Chapman published in 1598 with the translation of ''Achilles' Shield.'' While not an easy poem, it states as clearly as one can find anywhere in Chapman his sense of the high philosophical mission of poetry and the difficulties the world poses for the intellectual.

Chapman's major later poems, *Euthymiae Raptus; or the Tears of Peace* (1609), a translation of Petrarch's *Penitential Psalms* and Virgil's *Epigrams* (1612), and *Eugenia* (1614), an elegy for Lord Russell, are immensely learned and often consist of versified passages from Neo-Latin writers. These poems are not much read, but they have certainly contributed to Chapman's reputation as a moralist and a pedant.

For modern readers and critics, Chapman is most important for his plays, though none of them have become part of the modern repertory. His earliest plays were comedies: *The Blind Beggar of Alexandria* (1595) (which we know only in a very mutilated version), *An Humorous Day's Mirth* (1597), *The Gentleman Usher* (1605), *Monsieur D'Olive* (1604–5), *All Fools* (1605), *The Widow's Tears* (1605), and *May Day* (1609) were all produced at the private theaters by the famous London boys' companies. Chapman also collaborated with Ben Jonson and John Marston on *Eastward Hoe* (1605). Insults in this comedy to some members of the court—usually understood as slighting references to James' selling of knighthoods to his Scottish followers—landed Jonson and Chapman in the Tower for a month, but the anger of the king seems to have been short-lived, for both of them had later successes at court. Chapman's comedies tend to be dark, cynical, and satiric, and they can have serious philosophical moments and characters, as in the case of the stoic Lord Strozza in *The Gentleman Usher*, but they are also often startlingly comic and open to unphilosophic and unstoic enjoyments and foolery.

Chapman's tragedies have attracted the most serious modern attention—T. S. Eliot even planned an essay on Chapman's drama—and of those, *Bussy D'Ambois* (1604?) has been considered much the most interesting. *The Tragedy of Caesar and Pompey* (1612–13?) is exceptional among the tragedies for its Roman setting; it seems to want to be paired with Jonson's *Sejanus*. All the other tragedies derive from recent French history. The production of *The Conspiracy and Tragedy of Charles Duke of Byron* (1608) was suspended in April 1608 because the depiction of the living queen of France on stage (in a scene that appears to have been censored from the play that has come down to us) offended the French ambassador. *The Tragedy of Chabot Admiral of France* cannot be accurately dated but belongs to a period after 1611. In *The Revenge of Bussy D'Ambois* (1610?), the tragedy least indebted to the facts of French history, the protagonist, Clermont D'Ambois, Bussy's brother, is a fictional creation. The *Revenge* depicts a stoic hero remarkable for his refusal of the passion of revenge, and it might be argued that the play is not a sequel but a retraction of its precursor.

Of all these plays, *Bussy D'Ambois* is the most theatrical: though drawn into courtly life, Bussy, a moral but impecunious soldier, is clearly his own man, insulting the notorious duke of Guise, defeating three courtiers in a duel, winning the forgiveness and admiration of King Henry, and becoming the paramour of Tamyra, the countess of Montsurry. When he is no longer of use to the duke, Bussy is ambushed in an elaborate and sinister plot involving devils and a friar. When he dies standing up, declining the help of Tamyra, leaning on his sword, Bussy is eulogized by the ghost of the friar as the "brave relics of a complete man." It is a play with powerful speeches, but of such intellectual and moral complexity that modern critics have disagreed whether Bussy is a hero or a villain.

For the twenty years that Chapman was publishing poems and having plays produced he also devoted himself to the translation of Homer. In 1598 the first fragments were printed: seven early books of the *Iliad* in one small volume and the description of Achilles' Shield from Book 18 in another. In 1614 *The Whole Works of Homer* appeared in a magnificent folio. Keats' famous praise of Chapman's Homer is well justified. The translation may want something by the standards of modern scholarship, but nonetheless it radiates immense energy and intelligence. Written in rhymed hexameters, the *Iliad* is much the liveliest translation of the period. Chapman's Homer is not neoclassic, and by comparison to later translations this *Iliad* is full of barbaric angers and insults. Menelaus is a figure to be derided, and Agamemnon is at times a tyrant. Chapman dedicates his earliest translations to the earl of Essex for his "Achillean Virtues." Such a dignifying of Achilles strains the Renaissance idea that an epic poem should present a civic moral *exemplum*, and recent critics find Chapman experiencing some confusion as he nears the end of the translation. But the final effect is one of a political and moral complexity not often found in such a poem. Chapman himself was proud of the translation, and at the conclusion of it he declared, "The work that I was born to do is done."

CRITICAL RECEPTION

In his lifetime Chapman was respected, admired, even envied (he is a plausible candidate for Shakespeare's rival poet), but his reputation has not fared well. Immediately after his death publishers sometimes advertised undistinguished plays by attributing them to him (*Alfonsus, Emperor of Germany*, and *Revenge for Honour*), but by the Restoration Dryden found *Bussy* bombastic nonsense. Though he was always recognized as of historical importance, and though the *Homer* always has had admirers, Chapman came to represent the archaic and awkward aspects of the Renaissance golden age. Arnold quoted his prose as an example of the barbarism that Dryden would reform, and Swinburne, in his important essay prefacing the first complete edition in 1874, found his difficulty a sign of confusion, in contrast to Browning's powerful intellectuality. The later enthusiasm of T. S. Eliot and of Havelock Ellis (who published a book of selections of Chapman in 1934) has not been generally shared by the more academic critics of the last half-century. In 1926 F. L. Schoell showed that Chapman often translated Continental humanists (such as Ficino, Politiano, and Erasmus*) into verse without acknowledging his debt. In the late 1930s Chapman began to be read as a scholarly and pedantic moralist.

Interest in Chapman's poetry and in the whole issue of his moral stance was brilliantly stimulated by Frank Kermode's essay of 1957, arguing that "Ovid's Banquet of Sence" is not a description of rapturous insight, as had generally been assumed, but a cautionary poem warning about the dangers of an "Ovidian" philosophy of the senses. Though a number of critics defended Kermode's reading, the issue is by no means settled. Kermode's reading was received with skepticism by Millar MacLure and Raymond Waddington, who emphasized Chapman's learning over his moralism. Recently, Gerald Snare has argued that Chapman's aims should be understood in aesthetic rather than moral or philosophical terms.

At about the same time Kermode was challenging the traditional reading of the early poetry, Ennis Rees was overturning the traditional interpretation of *Bussy D'Ambois* by arguing that the play, which had generally been read as an awkward heroic tragedy, was in fact holding Bussy up as an example of a misguided and sensuous man. Unlike Kermode's, Rees' revisionary interpretation has not found support, but the fact that such an inversion could be proposed suggests the difficulty of interpreting the play. In the work of Richard Ide, A. R. Braunmuller, and others the play has been read as a study of heroic behavior in an ambiguous and complex social and political world not unlike Chapman's own. If fifty years ago the critical tendency was to turn Chapman into a lonely and stern moralist, more recent critics have tended to see him as a lively intellectual poet engaged in putting together a career. Chapman may have painted himself as a man of learned and removed integrity, somewhat like his friend Ben Jonson, but criticism is now more aware of how, like his friend, he was also competing vigorously in a number of very realistic and practical markets: seeking support from traditional aristocratic patrons, selling scripts to theatrical producers, and even, in the monumental project of the *Homer*, hoping to profit in the comparatively new commerce in printed books.

BIBLIOGRAPHY

Works by George Chapman (Modern Editions)

Chapman's Homer. 2 vols. Ed. Allardyce Nicoll. New York: Pantheon Books, 1956.

The Comedies and Tragedies of George Chapman. 2 vols. Ed. Thomas March Parrott. London: Routledge, 1910.

The Comedies of George Chapman. Gen. ed. Allan Holaday. Urbana: University of Illinois, 1970.

The Poems of George Chapman. Ed. Phyllis Bartlett. 1942. Rpt. New York: Russell and Russell, 1962.

The Tragedies of George Chapman. Gen. ed. Allan Holaday. Cambridge: D. S. Brewer, 1987.

Studies of George Chapman

Bradbrook, Muriel. *The School of Night: A Study of Ralegh and His Circle*. Cambridge: Cambridge University Press, 1936.

Braunmuller, A. R. *Natural Fictions: George Chapman's Major Tragedies*. Newark: University of Delaware Press, 1992.

Huntington, John. "Condemnation and Pity in Chapman's Hero and Leander." *English Literary Renaissance* 7 (1977): 307–23.

———. "Philosophical Seduction in Chapman, Davies, and Donne." *ELH* 44 (1977): 40–59.

———. "The Serious Trifle: Aphorisms in Chapman's Hero and Leander." *Studies in the Literary Imagination* 11.1 (1978): 107–13.

Ide, Richard. *Possessed with Greatness: The Heroic Tragedies of Shakespeare and Chapman*. Chapel Hill: University of North Carolina Press, 1980.

Jacquot, Jean. *George Chapman (1559–1634): sa vie, sa poésie, sa théâtre, sa pensée*. Paris: Société d'Édition Les Belles Lettres: 1951.

Kermode, Frank. "The Banquet of Sense." *Journal of the John Rylands Library*. 1957. Rpt. Frank Kermode. *Shakespeare, Spenser, Donne*. New York: Viking Press, 1971.

MacLure, Millar. *George Chapman: A Critical Study*. Toronto: University of Toronto Press, 1966.

Rees, Ennis. *The Tragedies of George Chapman*. Cambridge: Harvard University Press, 1954.

Schoell, Frank L. *Études sur l'humanisme continental en Angleterre à la fin de la Renaissance*. Paris, 1926.

Snare, Gerald. *The Mystification of George Chapman*. Durham: Duke University Press, 1989.

Waddington, Raymond. *The Mind's Empire: Myth and Form in George Chapman's Narrative Poems*. Baltimore: Johns Hopkins University Press, 1974.

JOHN W. HUNTINGTON

JOHN COLET
(1467–1519)

BIOGRAPHY

The persistent claims of John Colet to a place at the head table in the English Reformation rest on slender props that now appear to have been carefully placed by his Victorian admirers. One was his sermon to the Convocation, formerly seen as the ''overture'' to the Reformation (Trapp, 130). Others were his interest in education, his peripheral contact with Renaissance humanism through Erasmus* and his trip to Italy, and perhaps most convincing, his troubles with his bishop over the question of images. Erasmus himself describes, in a fictionalized account, Colet's disdain for relics on a trip to Becket's shrine. In fact it was claimed that Erasmus was set on his own course of biblical scholarship by Colet's Oxford lectures on St. Paul and their new type of critical exegesis that emphasized the literal meaning of Scripture over the far-flung allegorical preferences of the scholastics.

Yet something vital was missing from this portrait of Colet as a radical Reformer. Other critics of the church urged a return to the biblical languages where a more vigorous gospel awaited, shorn of the accumulated smoke and grime of the Latin overlay and the institution that supported it. Nearly all clamored, too, for an English Bible and criticized the sacramental system built around an authoritarian magisterium couched in a language no layman understood. Many questioned pluralism and other common practices. Colet did none of these. The denunciation of pluralism in his ''Sermon to the Convocation'' is conventional hypocrisy since he had three prebends, three churches with cure of souls, and a free chapel all before he received deacon's orders and retained multiple benefices even as dean of St. Paul's. As for biblical or vernacular languages, Colet was satisfied that acquisition of Greek was unnecessary, and he published nothing in English. Instead, he devoted his time to writing Latin commentaries on the Neoplatonic tangles he found in the works of Dionysius, whom he wrongly believed to have been St. Paul's companion. His was not an activist's stance.

Colet's interest in Neoplatonism has been seen as the link between his Christianity reforms and pagan philosophy—a link strengthened by the traditional view that Dionysius was an early Greek Christian. His trip to Italy had been, in part, a quest to meet Ficino, who called Dionysius ''the Supreme Platonist.''

Other scholarly Englishmen of Colet's generation were interested in Renaissance philosophers and were openly critical of contemporary church praxis. Yet when Thomas More* focused on the Italian Neoplatonist Pico della Mirandola, he did so not on account of his philosophy but because he had rejected philosophy and the intellectual spirit whence it sprang in favor of a life dedicated to Christian good works and conventional piety. If anything, here was the reforming spirit that would link up with Tyndale* and Luther.

The biographical details of his life are relatively well known: Colet's family was prominent enough to leave substantial traces in the records. Born in 1467, by the time he was in his early teens his father was prominent among the Mercers' Company, and around John's twentieth birthday Colet's father was elected lord mayor of London and knighted. John attended Cambridge, where he received his B.A in 1485 and his M.A. in 1488. By 1504 Colet was a D.D. of Oxford. From 1492 until 1495 he traveled in Italy, but exactly what he did and whom he met there are the subject of much debate. Erasmus claims he went there to study sacred texts and to work on his preaching. Some have him meeting with Ficino, Pico, and others in Florence. He may have heard Savonarola preach. In Rome, where he stayed for the first year, he may have met humanists in the Curia. What is known about his Italian sojourn is that he became acquainted with Piccolomini's sympathetic account of the Czech heretic Jan Hus and that he expressed a deep interest in the works of Marsilio Ficino.

Colet may have spent some time in Orléans studying law after leaving Italy, but by 1497 he was immersed in his theological studies at Oxford. Sometime around then he began his series of lectures on St. Paul's epistles that reputedly introduced his novel method of exegesis. The texts for these lectures have not survived. In 1499 he met Erasmus, who heard at least some of the lectures and corresponded with him on matters of scriptural interpretation, so on the remains of their epistolary relationship much of the debate around Colet's exegetical techniques is centered.

As one would expect from the scion of an established London family, Colet's career prospered. He garnered more ecclesiastical offices in 1502, completed his doctorate in 1504, and was elected dean of St. Paul's in 1505—a significant achievement for a man still in his thirties. That same year, as Sir Henry's sole heir, Colet inherited one of the more substantial fortunes in London, part of which was used to found his famous St. Paul's school begun in 1508. In 1510 Colet delivered the now-famous convocation speech to the clergy. The speech contains some stinging rebukes to England's clergy and is held at least partially responsible for the friction between Colet and some of England's clerical establishment, including his own bishop, between 1514 and 1516. Yet Colet found favor at the hands of his king and a rising young archbishop named Wolsey, and the charges against him had no effect. Erasmus anticipated a glowing future for the dean—the bishop of London was quite old, and it would be only natural for Colet to succeed him. But after repeated bouts of the English sweat, Colet died in 1519.

MAJOR WORKS AND THEMES

This outline of Colet's life has become inseparable from the assessment of his contribution to the English Reformation. Recent scholarship has revised the earlier chronology of his writings and significantly altered the interpretation of his exegetical method as well as his position with respect to the ecclesiastical hierarchy and his allegedly heterodox beliefs. New evidence shows Colet as an active judge of heretics, not a sympathetic and well-placed spokesman for reform. Colet the man appears now as an energetic, even zealous champion of moral integrity among the clergy whose troubles with his cathedral chapter stem more from misplaced attempts to enforce his own personal austerity on his colleagues than heterodox beliefs.

Colet's writings focus almost single-mindedly on an attempt to elucidate the true—and often hidden—meaning of Scripture, primarily the letters of Paul to the Romans and First Corinthians. Because he believed, as did many in the West, that the fifth-century writer known as Dionysius was actually Dionysius the Areopagite, the companion of Paul and various disciples, Colet was led into an investigation of his Neoplatonic writings in his attempt to get at the true wisdom in Paul's work. His interests in Hermeticism (and it should be noted that he hosted Cornelius Agrippa* in 1510) led him to believe not only in the existence of a parallel and unwritten revelation, guarded by the church and vouchsafed only to those empowered by the Spirit, but in "still other channels less authoritative and more diffuse" (Gleason, 144). Colet published none of his commentaries, nor is there much evidence that they circulated in manuscript, although a revised chronology of his extant papers suggests he may have been preparing them for publication shortly before he died.

Colet had an unusual view of the nature of the literal sense of Scripture that denied the full play of figurative language. Rather, the ordinary figures of human speech (i.e., the historical or contextual sense) were somehow meant to convey literal truth. He distrusted the ability of everyday language to carry the weight of revelation: "What the words 'literally' mean is therefore simply what they mean to men and women, a meaning at an indeterminate remove from the intention of the divine author" (Gleason, 137). Therefore their spiritual truth—the meaning intended by God—could be elucidated only through something akin to direct revelation, not philology. Fasting and prayer were more conducive to proper exegesis than language study. Colet's indifference, if not hostility, to classical and humanistic rhetoric and to Greek in particular underlines the distance between his approach and Erasmus'. The statutes he drew up for St. Paul's school so eviscerated the corpus of acceptable pagan authors that his dedication to humanist studies is certainly questionable. In his own words, "No one reads pagan books except out of distrust or scorn of the Scripture'' (Gleason, 139).

CRITICAL RECEPTION

Two developments have helped recapture the sense of what Colet's famous Oxford lectures contained and explain their undoubted popularity: redating his surviving manuscripts on Paul, which earlier commentators had believed contained the texts of these, and a closer analysis of the exegetical methods, which found a contemporaneous account. By removing the manuscripts to a later date closer to the end of his career—which Gleason has done plausibly if laboriously—we come to the study of his views on Scripture in a long account by a young priest who came seeking guidance. In this account of Colet's handling of the very texts he was engaged in lecturing on—Paul's letter to the Romans—we see an accumulation of scriptural *sententiae*, wrenched from their literary and historical context, isolated from the rest of the letter as a whole. In short, Colet extracted for the priest a glittering but inconsequential set of moral and theological topoi digested and recombined to illustrate a preconceived truth. This, it seems, was Colet's method. Compelling, vigorous, and pithy it may have been—Erasmus goes so far as to say he could easily work himself into a ''holy frenzy'' in discussion over Scripture (Lochman, 83). But a new type of exegesis it was not.

We can now understand Colet's notoriety. The widespread fame of his austerity, the moral and hortatory *exempla* he drew from Paul, and his energetic, if sometimes overbearing, manner all point to an effective speaker and tireless moral conscience. But his pursuit of the arcane and esoteric brought him to the brink of heterodoxy, not Protestant reform.

BIBLIOGRAPHY

Works by John Colet

''Oratio ad Clerum in Convocatione.'' In *The Life of Dr. John Colet, Dean of St. Pauls*, by Samuel Knight. Oxford, 1823, 238–50.

Super Opera Dionysii. Ed. and trans. J. H. Lupton. London: Bell, 1869.

Enarration in Epistolam S. Pauli ad Romanos. Ed. and trans. J. H. Lupton. London: Bell, 1873.

Opuscula quaedam Theologica. Ed. and trans. J. H. Lupton. London: Bell, 1876.

Commentary on First Corinthians. Ed. and trans. Bernard O'Kelly and Catherine Jarrott. Binghamton, NY: Medieval and Renaissance Texts and Studies, 1985.

On the Sacraments. Ed. and trans. John Gleason in his *John Colet*. Berkeley: University of California Press, 1989, 270–333.

Studies of John Colet

Erasmus, Desiderius. *Les Vies de Jean Vitrier et de John Colet*, ed. A. Godin. Angers: Editions Moreana, 1982.

Gleason, John. *John Colet*. Berkeley: University of California Press, 1989.

Jayne, Sears. *John Colet and Marsilio Ficino*. Oxford: Oxford University Press, 1963.

Kaufman, Peter Iver. ''John Colet's *Opus de sacramentis* and Clerical Anticlericalism: The Limitations of 'Ordinary Wayes.' '' *Journal of British Studies* 22 (1982): 1–22.

Lochman, Daniel. ''John Colet.'' *Dictionary of Literary Biography*, ed. David Richardson. First series, vol. 132. Columbia, SC: Bruccoli Clark Layman, 1993.

Miles, Leland. *John Colet and the Platonic Tradition*. La Salle, IL: Open Court, 1961.

Trapp, J. B. ''John Colet and the *Hierarchies* of the Pseudo-Dionysius.'' In *Religion and Humanism*, ed. Keith Robbins. Oxford: Blackwell, 1981, 127–48.

SEYMOUR BAKER HOUSE

NICOLAUS COPERNICUS
(1473–1543)

BIOGRAPHY

Given that we have only nineteen of Copernicus' letters—all of a rather formal nature—it is unlikely that a twentieth-century playwright like Berthold Brecht would base an epic drama on his personal and intellectual struggles. In this respect, Copernicus and Galileo seem polar opposites. In fact, study of the development of Copernicus' thought provides us with a number of puzzles. He had something of a poetic temperament. The greatest sixteenth-century astronomer, best known by his Latin name, Nicolaus Copernicus, was born Mikolaj Kopernik to a prominent family in Prussian Poland at Thorn (Torun on the Vistula) on 19 February 1473.

Copernicus' first intellectual home was the University of Cracow—in some ferment over the ''new learning''—which he probably attended from 1491 to 1494. He then went to the University of Bologna, where he studied Greek and Latin literature, mathematics, and astronomy. Elected, at the young age of fourteen, canon of Frauenburg (Frombork), he lectured on mathematics in Rome for the jubilee celebration in 1500 and continued his studies at the great University of Padua in law, theology, and medicine with occasional trips home, where he practiced as a physician among the poor almost up to the time of his death. He also took a special interest in problems of currency in Poland and circulated a work on money reform that was not published until 1816. He died in Frauenburg on 24 May 1543.

MAJOR WORKS AND THEMES

In several ways, Copernicus was an exemplary Renaissance man, a man for all seasons. He had remarkably varied accomplishments as mathematician, expert in canon law, astronomer, theorist of currency exchanges, and medical doctor. Like the careers of many authors of the era, his success was filled with ambiguity. Although his central impact resulted from *De revolutionibus orbium coelestium* (1543), published just before his death, professionally he remained a superb instructor of mathematics, an in-depth reader of Greek philosophy, especially of the "literary philosopher," Plato, and, as we have seen, a practicing physician in the area of north Poland, where he was church canon.

His first published work is a peculiar creative mistranslation of the pseudoletters of an antipolemicist and historian of high Byzantine era, Theophylactus Simocotta. Dedicated to his maternal uncle, the bishop of Ermeland, the translator's work was apparently a self-devised Greek exercise based on Aldo Manuzio's Venice edition of the letters of that well-known Egyptian author (fl. 610–29), a onetime mayor of Byzantium. Necessarily, Copernicus toned down Theophylactus' emphasis on earthly love. That Copernicus' masterpiece *De Revolutionibus* opens with the grim caveat in Greek "Let no one enter here who lacks expertise in geometry" hardly expresses any excessive mathematical rigor, since it was the motto over the door of Plato's Academy in Athens, as well as the subject of a humorous anecdote in Aristoxenus' *Harmonics*, where Plato loses, one by one, all his students in a lecture on the nature of the good—except, of course, Aristotle—by opening up with a discussion of geometric axioms and correlatives.

Perhaps the most memorable early moment in Copernicus' masterpiece helps explain why earthlings do not experience any sensation of the movement of spinning around the sun; he does so by use of a notable quote from Virgil's *Aeneid* (3.72), where Aeneas describes his ship's departure from the cursed land of Thrace: "While we were carried forward from the harbor, both the land and cities receded into the distance." Quotation of this passage raises perhaps the two most traditional questions about Copernicus' thought, which, however, I think can be easily answered. One, what is his relationship to classical thought, especially the heliocentric astronomical theory of Aristarchus of Samos (310–230 B.C.)? In this very work he admits he is merely borrowing a theory that was fairly current in antiquity. That the second edition did not contain this remark cannot be held at his door.

Second and more important, since Aeneas' boat is seen in two ways in relation to the shore, is Copernicus essentially a relativist, saying that his heliocentric theory is only a means of explaining data according to Ockham's razor, that is, of the most efficient and economical explanation, as suggested by the preface to his masterpiece? The answer is no. Copernicus shows lively interest in relativity, but his whole work makes clear that he believes—and even feels he has proven—that the planets revolve around the sun, and the moons around the planets. Whether or not the sun moves or that the universe is infinite, he does not say. Those issues would have to wait for Giordano Bruno,* Galileo, and others to theorize.

There is some evidence that Copernicus, like William Harvey,* delayed the publication of his masterpiece in order to avoid the perpetual controversy that would ensue. He is famous for having received his first copy of the printed book on his deathbed on the very day he died. Oddly, when he circulated an earlier version of his findings, *Commentariolus* (1514), in manuscript and later planned to publish the full work in Nuremburg in 1540, he and his student and sole living disciple Georg Rhaticus came under the criticism of Luther and Melanchthon, not the Roman Catholic authorities, and the work was finally published in Leipzig.

CRITICAL RECEPTION

That Copernicus' sole disciple Rhaticus' great work was in the form of pure calculations in the form of manuals of sines, cosines, and tangents—essentially the book of trigonometry that led to so many practical results from astronomical measurements to survey—may suggest that the disciple was making up for the failings of his master. In Copernicus' case, that would be the absence of adequate proof of his heliocentric theory in *De Revolutionibus* in the form of unfudged astronomical readings. Luckily, Copernicus avoided—in the tense era of the Inquisition—suffering immediate controversy over an innovation that gradually gained general scientific acceptance. Throughout his lifetime his astronomical findings found more support from Roman Catholic authorities than Protestants. He was excoriated by Luther in his *Table Talk* yet received unusual support from Pope Clement VII. The first vernacular versions of passages of *De Revolutionibus* were developed in Thomas Digges' *Commentaries upon the Revolutions of Copernicus* toward the end of the sixteenth century in England. William Gilbert* was a convert.

BIBLIOGRAPHY

Works by Nicolaus Copernicus

Complete Works. 3 vols. Ed. Pawel Czartoryski, supervised by Edward Rosen. London: Macmillan, 1972, 1985.

Three Copernican Treatises: The Commentariolus of Copernicus, The Letter against Werner, The Narratio Prima of Rheticus. 2d ed. Ed. and trans. Edward Rosen. New York: Dover, 1959.

Studies of Nicolaus Copernicus

Adamczewski, Jan, and Edward J. Piszek. *Nicolaus Copernicus and His Epoch*. New York: Copernicus Society of America, 1970.

Armitage, Angus. *Copernicus: The Founder of Modern Astronomy*. New York: Dorset Press, 1990 (orig. 1938).

Bienkowska, Barbara. *The Scientific Work of Copernicus on the Occasion of the Five Hundredth Anniversary of His Birth (1473–1973)*. Boston: D. Reidel, 1973.

The Copernican Achievement. Ed. Robert S. Westman. Berkeley: University of California Press, 1973.

Rosen, Edward. *Copernicus and the Scientific Revolution*. Malabar, FL: Robert E. Krieger, 1984.

ALAN HAGER

THOMAS CRANMER
(1489–1556)

BIOGRAPHY

The second son of Thomas Cranmer and Agnes (née Hatfield), Cranmer was born in Nottinghamshire. Because his father had only enough property to endow his eldest son, Cranmer pursued a career in the church. To this end, he went to Cambridge in 1503, where he received a fellowship at Jesus College in 1510 or 1511. When he married his first wife, his fellowship was revoked; it was restored soon afterward when his wife died in childbirth. Through dedicated study, Cranmer became a learned, if not thoroughly original, theologian who maintained throughout his life his scholarly drive to reexamine his beliefs.

Cranmer's early beliefs were already leaning away from Catholic orthodoxy. Around 1520 he participated in discussions with a group of Cambridge scholars concerning theological problems arising from Luther's challenges to Catholicism; by 1525, Cranmer was praying for the abolition of papal power in England. Thanks to Henry VIII's desire to divorce Catherine of Aragon, those prayers were inadvertently realized. In 1529, Cranmer privately suggested to two of Henry's councillors that the king ought to rely upon English theologians in the matter of his divorce. Acting quickly upon this suggestion, Henry instructed Cranmer himself to work toward a divorce. Cranmer wrote a treatise arguing the king's case and ultimately was dispatched to Rome in 1530, along with other diplomats, to argue Henry's cause. In 1532 he was sent to Germany in order to serve as ambassador to Charles V and to establish contact with Lutheran princes. There, he met Andreas Osiander, whose moderate theological position between Lutheran and Catholic beliefs appealed to Cranmer and whose niece he secretly married. This second marriage suggests that Cranmer did not expect nor seek high promotion in the church, for in the event of promotion, his marriage, if discovered, would spell trouble; as events proceeded, in fact, Cranmer was unable to acknowledge his wife publicly until 1548.

Cranmer's high promotion, in fact, came quickly; in 1532, William Warham, archbishop of Canterbury, died, and the king appointed Cranmer to the position. By March 1533, when Cranmer was consecrated, Anne Boleyn's pregnancy made the divorce a matter of pressing importance. Cranmer took the obligatory oath to the pope but first declared that he did not consider the oath binding if it were against the laws of God or England. He then ruled the king's marriage to Catherine of Aragon void and validated the marriage to Anne Boleyn. Cranmer's continued obedience to Henry put him in awkward positions in the future. In 1536, Cranmer reversed his earlier decision and deemed the marriage to Anne Boleyn invalid. Continuing to assist Henry, in 1540, he helped free his king from his fourth wife, Anne of Cleves, and in 1542 he participated in the proceedings against Catherine Howard that led to her execution.

While maintaining obedience to Henry, however, Cranmer was able to advance a moderate Reformation in England despite the king's general resistance to change. Together with Cromwell,* for example, he promoted the publication of an English Bible. During his long tenure as archbishop, his theology developed along increasingly Protestant lines; he gradually abandoned his belief in transubstantiation, though retaining his belief in the real presence, and by 1545 he had composed a reformed litany for the Church of England. After the Act of Six Articles (1539), however, his position was endangered by the country's increasingly conservative religious climate. His enemies tried several times to convict him of heresy but were prevented by Henry's persistent, lifelong attachment to his archbishop; as Cromwell once remarked to Cranmer, ''[D]o or say what you will, the King will always well take it at your hand.''

Upon the young Edward VI's accession, the government advanced the Reformation of the English church considerably. Cranmer assisted the Protestant cause through his interests in educating the laity and promoting Protestant doctrine. In 1547 he was responsible for the publication of a Book of Homilies designed to aid inadequate ministers in their preaching, and in 1548 he was involved in the English adaptation and publication of a Latin catechism. His first, moderate prayer book was published in 1549, followed by a more definitely Protestant revision in 1552. In 1553 Cranmer produced the English church's first doctrinal formulary, the Forty-two Articles, to which all clergy, schoolmasters, and university degree candidates were required to subscribe and which served as the basis for the Thirty-nine Articles of 1571. During 1550, he published his *Defense of the True and Catholic Doctrine of the Sacrament*, a work defending a decidedly sacramentarian view of the Eucharist. Cranmer also desired to revise the canon law of the English church; his proposal, never enacted, was published, fifteen years after his death, in 1571 as the *Reformatio Legum Ecclesiasticarum*. His contributions to the Church of England's liturgy and doctrine have influenced the liturgical and theological debates of that church to the present day.

Just before Edward VI's death, the obedient Cranmer swore against his better judgment to join the king in supporting Northumberland's attempt to settle the Crown not on the Catholic princess Mary, but on Henry's great-niece, the Lady Jane Grey. Proclaimed queen, Grey was deposed nine days later. Upon Mary I's accession Cranmer was accused of treason; this charge was soon superseded, however, by charges of heresy. Indeed, Cranmer probably preferred a charge of heresy, for to a man who had devoted his life to obedient service a charge of treason was unconscionable; to die for Christ was infinitely more acceptable. Cranmer underwent a heresy trial in September 1555, the verdict of which was never in doubt. On 14 February 1556, he was degraded from his episcopal and sacerdotal offices in preparation for execution. Following his trial, Cranmer was put under intense pressure to recant. Desperately lonely and broken, Cranmer at last signed a series of six recantations, the last of which rejected his entire theological development. Although the more traditional practice was to impose a lesser sentence on recanted heretics, Mary maintained that Cranmer should burn. On 21 March 1556, Cranmer was to recant publicly, using a speech that had been endorsed by the government before suffering his punishment. Instead, he stunned the authorities and the gathered crowd by recanting not his earlier theological positions but the recantations themselves. He then ran to the stake and steadfastly held his right hand, the hand that had signed the recantations, in the fire. His heroic end undid much of the government's planned propaganda against him and his Protestant cause and earned him an honored place in Foxe's catalog of Protestant martyrs.

MAJOR WORKS AND THEMES

As is evident from his biography, Cranmer considered obedience to one's sovereign a doctrinal tenet. Yet he was no mere time-server; in Cranmer's writings, the progress of the Reformation is linked to, and indeed can only be achieved through, such peaceful accommodation. In response to the 1549 uprisings, Cranmer made notes toward a sermon on rebellion that link rebellion with resistance to the Reformation itself; he writes that the devil is the source of sedition because he ''can abide no right reformation in religion.'' He characterizes the current civil unrest as a punishment visited upon the English for not reforming both public religion and individual lives. For Cranmer, even if magistrates are enemies to religion, subjects must still obey in all worldly things; yet the elucidation of this boundary between submission in worldly and submission in spiritual things haunted Cranmer throughout his life. In his letter offering tepid support for the cause of Anne Boleyn, for example, Cranmer cautiously defends the woman whose cause elevated him to the archbishopric and to whom, he admits, he owes the most next to Henry himself. Although ''clean amazed'' at her reputed crimes, he quickly suggests that ''your Highness would not have gone so far, except she had surely been culpable.'' While guarded in his remarks about Anne, he boldly urges Henry that her demise ought not to threaten the Reformation: ''I trust that your grace will bear no less entire favor unto the truth of the Gospel than you did before; forsomuch as your Grace's favor to the Gospel was not led by affection unto her, but by zeal unto the truth.'' As Ridley notes, the letter is not a proper defense of Anne, although Cranmer did say more for her than other courtiers (104); rather, his concern is to obey his sovereign's will even in this dubious undertaking and thus secure the progress of the Reformation. Later in his life, simultaneous support for the reigning monarch and the Reformation became not just difficult but impossible; forced to choose between his two highest principles, Cranmer performed his most straightforward act of political resistance and all but ensured his martyrdom. Shortly after Mary's accession, Cranmer wrote a *Declaration* in which he decried the mass as full of errors, asserted that he would have nothing to do with its reintroduction, and offered to engage in a scholarly dispute over the theological issues at stake. Cranmer intended to post this notice on church doors throughout London; the piece was printed and distributed widely before he got the chance. Although the mass was still technically illegal, since much legislation of the previous two reigns had yet to be repealed, Cranmer's *Declaration* suggests that he was not incapable of protest when he felt that the Reformation itself was at stake.

Cranmer's other writings also maintain a link between proper Reformation and political obedience; for example, his preface to the 1540 edition of the *Great Bible* connects proper biblical study to a peaceful and politically obedient Reformation. Indeed, the preface argues for the importance of Bible reading through reference to Henry's endorsement of the vernacular Bible, which ought to be enough for "obedient subjects." In colloquial language, oddly reflecting some of the language in Plato's *Phaedrus*, Cranmer expresses a desire for moderation between extreme Protestant and conservative positions: "For truly some there are, that be too slow and need the spur; some other seem too quick and need more of the bridle. Some lose their game by short shooting; some by overshooting." Both the proper pace of Reformation and proper scriptural interpretation can be achieved by humble reading: "I would advise you all that cometh to the reading or hearing of this book . . . that ye bring with you the fear of God, and that ye do it with all reverence, and use your knowledge thereof not to vainglory of frivolous disputation, but to the honor of God, increase of virtue, and edification both of yourselves and other." This avoidance of disputation through properly deferential reading yields spiritual and social learning for people in every walk of life: "all manner of persons . . . of what estate or condition soever they be, may in this book learn all things what they ought to believe, what they ought to do, and what they should not do, as well concerning Almighty God, as also concerning themselves and all other." Proper learning extends beyond an intellectual assent to the reformation of lives; Cranmer later blamed the lack of such reformation, as noted previously, for instances of rebellion. Cranmer's linking of deferential reading and individual reformation results in a continually educational process spreading throughout the realm: "every man that cometh to the reading of this holy book ought to bring with him first and foremost this fear of Almighty God; and then next, a firm and stable purpose to reform his own self according thereunto. . . . Which if he do, he shall prove at length well able to teach, though not with his mouth, yet with his living and good example; which is sure the most lively and effectuous form and manner of teaching."

Cranmer's desire for lay education is evident again in both versions of the *Book of Common Prayer*, upon which his was the principal influence; here, Cranmer sets forward a plan for Scripture reading in the churches that covers the Old Testament once and the New Testament three times each year. Cranmer continues his emphasis upon humble learning and self-reformation in his instructive homilies on salvation, faith, and good works. These homilies were written as a set to proclaim the basic tenets of Reformation theology in a manner that he claims is as "plain" as possible. His first homily, concerning salvation, stresses that justification comes through God's gift of faith alone, not by works. His second sermon, on faith, reiterates the previous lesson of justification through faith alone but begins to define a "quick or lively faith" that manifests itself through good works against an unfruitful faith. His final homily opens with summaries of main points from the previous two and argues the converse of his earlier proposition: that works are no good without faith. Cranmer develops his points with examples of flawed works-centered theologies, including a generous list of Catholic abuses. As in his preface to the Bible, Cranmer links proper works and self-reformation with Protestantism's insistence upon man's helplessness before God. The Forty-two Articles of 1553, upon which Cranmer was the primary influence, continue his practice of defining proper Reformation doctrine against what he considers religious extremes. The articles condemn Anabaptist and other radical sectarian beliefs, as in those articles entitled "All men are bound to keep the Moral commandments of the Law" and "Heretics called Millenarii." Roman Catholic doctrines are similarly dismissed throughout; the title of the thirty-first article proclaims, "The state of single life is commanded to no man by the word of God," while the article on the Lord's Supper asserts that transubstantiation is "repugnant to the plain words of scripture." Alongside this condemnation of those who, in the language of the preface, need bridles or spurs, the articles illuminate the familiar Reformation tenets of justification by faith and the conception of mankind as incapable of meriting his own salvation. The articles also affirm the recent standardization of Church of England practice through a solid endorsement of the 1547 *Book of Homilies* and the *Book of Common Prayer*. Throughout his homilies and the articles, Cranmer emphasizes the need to standardize Church of England doctrine and educate both laity and clergy about basic Reformation theology.

Familiar Reformation doctrinal themes figure prominently throughout documents that Cranmer authored and that bear his influence. Yet those themes became more explicitly Reformed (that is, Swiss-influenced) as Cranmer's theology developed, a shift that is most apparent in Cranmer's changing views on the Eucharist, the most divisive issue amongst Protestant Reformers. Cranmer, who had maintained a belief in the real presence despite his early rejection of transubstantiation, changed his view sometime between 1547 and 1549, partly due to the influence of Reformers such as Ridley, Hooper, Peter Martyr, and Bucer. His *Defense of the True and Catholic Doctrine of the Sacrament* (1550) exhibits this Reformed influence; here, Cranmer defines the Sacrament as a "perpetual memory" of Christ's sacrifice. He writes that humanity, too focused on the material, has often misinterpreted the Sacrament, and his very language reflects an erring and materialistic literalism: "[C]arnal man . . . when he heareth the Holy Ghost speak of meat and drink, his mind is by and by in the kitchen and buttery, and he thinketh upon his dishes and pots, his mouth and his belly." Cranmer argues for a more figurative reading: just as meat and drink satisfy the body, Scripture labels that which satisfies the soul as meat and drink. Based upon this central principle linking corporal and spiritual nourishment, Cranmer argues that the Sacrament was established to use visible signs as a confirmation of the elect's "inward faith." Thus, the Sacrament does not have an efficacy independent of the faith of the recipient, a faith that, in turn, is dependent on God's election. The differences between the 1549 and 1552 prayer books underscore the liturgical ramifications of this more sacramentarian theology. Both versions assert that the Eucharist is a "remembrance" of Christ's sacrifice; the 1552 version of the communion service, however, undergoes considerable rewriting and rearrangement to reflect more accurately its proclaimed theology. For example, the priest's reading of the decalogue is inserted as the service's third element in order that the people might "ask God's mercy for their transgression of the same"; as more sacramentarian views stressed that proper reception of the Sacrament was dictated by one's inward, spiritual state, the decalogue serves to prepare worshipers for a worthy, spiritual reception. Cranmer's significant influence upon the articles' Eucharistic doctrine is apparent in the article on the Lord's Supper, which claims that "to such as rightly, worthily, and with faith receive the same, the bread which we break is a communion of the body of Christ: likewise the Cup of blessing is a Communion of the blood of Christ." This dependence of the Sacrament on the spiritual state of its receiver significantly influenced later doctrinal formularies of the Church of England and marked its sixteenth-century doctrinal affinity with Continental Reformed churches.

CRITICAL RECEPTION

Predictably, critical reception of Cranmer's works from the sixteenth century forward has varied with the religious sympathies of the recipients. The Marian government, for example, found Cranmer's doctrine of the Eucharist particularly repugnant; in the fullest recantations, the government ensured that all of Cranmer's writings against transubstantiation were revoked. His doctrinal stances, mediated through his influence upon the Thirty-nine Articles and later versions of the prayer book, have influenced Anglican debates from the sixteenth century to the present day. In the seventeenth century, controversy developed between Charles and his Parliament over the issue of predestination as outlined in the seventeenth of the 1571 Articles, an article whose differences from Cranmer's are slight. In 1628 Charles issued a proclamation against Puritans' understanding of the article, urging them to interpret the articles according to a "plain and literal sense"; Parliament's Puritans angrily responded that they had constantly affirmed the originally intended meaning of the doctrines in the Thirty-nine Articles. This struggle over the location of the articles' "plain" meaning continued with their first modern historian, Charles Hardwick. Writing in the mid-nineteenth century, Hardwick argues that the articles are essentially Lutheran and therefore, for him, moderate. Following in his steps, other Anglican historians have occasionally de-emphasized Reformed influence on the articles. On issues where Lutheran and Reformed views diverge, however, the articles, due to Cranmer's theological influence, take the Reformed position, thus meriting their inclusion in the 1581 Geneva volume *A Harmony of the Confessions of the Faith of the Orthodox and Reformed Churches*. Recent controversies over subscription to the articles and adherence to the prayer book evaluate Cranmer's doctrinal positions in order to debate the relevance of his theology's official incarnations to current Anglican thought. The Anglican theologian Oliver O'Donovan, for example, acknowledges Cranmer and his articles as embracing a Reformed position not always consistent with current Anglican theology, thus recognizing both similarities and differences between twentieth- and sixteenth-century incarnations of the Church of England. The still unrepealed 1662 *Book of Common Prayer*, significantly influenced by Cranmer's 1552 version, is also a point of debate. Endorsing Cranmer's theology, Samuel Leuenberger claims that the changes made to the 1552 version have no other purpose but to "return to the pure word of God" (123) and warns that recent attempts to alter Anglican liturgy may contribute to a separation of the close relationship between theology and liturgical practice that Cranmer established. Cranmer's theological positions, alternatively seen as essentially Anglican and as one of many historical incarnations of Anglican thought, continue to provoke reevaluations and unresolved controversy.

In terms of historical assessment, Cranmer is similarly a controversial figure. To many Catholic historians over the four centuries since Cranmer's death, Cranmer is not only a heretic but an opportunist who readily adapted his theological views to current tastes in order to advance his career. In the sixteenth century, the pro-Catholic author of *Bishop Cranmer's Recantacyons* lambasted Cranmer for theological vacillation, such as his submission under the Six Articles. Later writers voiced similar reserve; Sanders in *The Rise and Growth of the Anglican Schism* (1877) mocks Cranmer for shifting his theological views from Henrician to Lutheran to Calvinist depending, presumably, upon the current political climate. Most Protestant historians, on the other hand, see Cranmer as a genuinely devout man upon whom the truth gradually dawned; his recantations are largely forgiven him because of his martyrdom. Foxe advances this view most strongly in his *Actes and Monuments*; for Foxe, Cranmer is a mild and forgiving man whose character, though not perfect, cannot be easily superseded. In the twentieth century, this Protestant line continues in Pollard's *Thomas Cranmer and the English Reformation* (1904), which, although offering a spirited defense of his subject, is marred by the author's bias. Ridley's is the most authoritative and balanced recent biography of the archbishop. After an opening chapter that details these persistent biographical controversies, Ridley finds an ironic consistency in the archbishop's actions. Ridley argues that Cranmer, like many of his contemporaries, believed in royal absolutism and felt that the Christian's principal duty was to serve his king unless ordered to sin. Thus, Ridley finds that Cranmer repeatedly struggles over whether to submit or resist when faced with religious policies with which he disagreed; this struggle between obedience to God and obedience to monarch is consistent, though the actions resulting from that struggle may not be. Ridley notes that "Cranmer . . . was obviously aware that obedience meant continued residence at Lambeth, and that resistance would bring him to the stake. But this is not the same thing as deliberate time-serving; and when in 1553 the issue was too plain for mental evasion, Cranmer was prepared to choose the hard road" (12). Indeed, Cranmer's final choice has argued most strongly for more sympathetic assessments of his life and actions. Participation in Tudor government meant that Cranmer knew only too well the costs of religious resistance; in his homily *Of Faith*, however, he also acknowledges the power of martyrdom, noting with admiration that "some [have been] brent without mercy, and would not be delivered, because they looked to rise again to a better state." Strype, Cranmer's seventeenth-century chronicler, is inspired with a similar admiration by Cranmer's own death:

> His body was not carried to the grave in state, nor buried, as many of his predecessors were, in his own cathedral church, nor enclosed in a monument of marble or touchstone. Nor had he any inscription to set forth his praises to posterity: no shrine to be visited by devout pilgrims. . . . Cranmer's martyrdom is his monument, and his name will outlast an epitaph or a shrine.

BIBLIOGRAPHY

Works by Thomas Cranmer (including reports of his conduct)

A Catechism set forth by Thomas Cranmer. Ed. and with an introduction by D. G. Selwyn. Oxford: Sutton Courtenay Press, 1978.

Certaine Sermons or Homilies Appointed to be Read in Churches in the Time of Queen Elizabeth I (1547–1571). Facsimile of 1623 Edition. Introduction by Mary Ellen Rickey and Thomas B. Stroup. Gainesville: Scholars' Facsimiles and Reprints, 1968.

Foxe, John. *Actes and Monuments.* London, 1563.

Jenkyns, H. *The Remains of Thomas Cranmer.* Oxford: Oxford University Press, 1833.

Strype, J. *Memorials of the Most Reverend father in God, Thomas Cranmer.* London, 1694.

Two Liturgies, A.D. 1549 and A.D. 1552: with other documents set forth by authority in the reign of King Edward VI. Ed. Joseph Ketley for the Parker Society. Cambridge: Cambridge University Press, 1844.

Studies of Thomas Cranmer

Brooks, Peter N. *Cranmer in Context.* Cambridge: Cambridge University Press, 1989.

———. *Thomas Cranmer's Doctrine of the Eucharist.* 2d ed. Hampshire: Macmillan, 1992. (Still the best work on this issue.)

Leuenberger, Samuel. *Archbishop Cranmer's Immortal Bequest—The Book of Common Prayer of the Church of England: An Evangelistic Liturgy.* Trans. Samuel Leuenberger and Lewis J. Gorin Jr. Grand Rapids: William B. Eerdmans, 1990.

O'Donovan, Oliver. *On the Thirty-nine Articles: A Conversation with Tudor Christianity.* Oxford: Latimer House, 1986. (Addresses Cranmer's role as principal influence upon, and source of, the Thirty-nine Articles, as well as his theology's relevance to current Anglican thought.)

Ridley, Jasper. *Thomas Cranmer*. Oxford: Clarendon Press, 1962. (Still the best biography.)

Thomas Cranmer: Churchman and Scholar. Ed. Paul Ayris and David Selwyn. Rochester, NY: Boydell Press, 1993. (Contains an extremely useful bibliography.)

SUSANNAH BRIETZ MONTA

THOMAS CROMWELL, EARL OF ESSEX (1485–1540)

BIOGRAPHY

Other than the fact of Cromwell's birth at Putney, little is known about his early life. He apparently went abroad at a young age and lived for a time in Italy. While in Italy, his detractors charge, Cromwell learned the tools of unscrupulous politics; it is more fair to say, however, that Cromwell gained a valuable education that prepared him for his role in government. After 1510, he resided in the Low Countries for a year or two before returning to England around 1512. By 1520 he had entered Cardinal Wolsey's service as his solicitor and had developed a reputation as a successful lawyer. When Wolsey fell from power in 1529, Cromwell became a member of Parliament, where his talent attracted the attention of the king. He entered Henry's service early in 1530, was sworn into the council at the end of that year, and reached Henry VIII's circle of top advisers one year later. He soon achieved several high offices: in 1532 he obtained the office of master of the jewels, in 1534 he became principal secretary and master of the rolls, and in 1536 he received the office of lord privy seal. Indeed, he had so many governmental and administrative responsibilities that at the end of his life he wrote to Henry, "I have meddled in so many matters under your Highness, that I am not able to answer them all."

Cromwell quickly and decisively made an impact on the Henrician government. In 1532, Cromwell employed his well-honed executive and parliamentary skills in the service of Henry's most pressing matter: his divorce from Catherine of Aragon. He saw to the drafting and passage of legislation that legally enacted Henry's claims of sovereign power by replacing Roman authority with the monarch's supreme headship over church and state. The 1533 Act in Restraint of Appeals to Rome cleared a legal pathway for Henry to obtain his divorce from the Church of England, of which he was now the head, and from that point forward Cromwell saw to the passing of other legislation to complete the construction of the royal supremacy. This legislation enacted in law what monarchs had often claimed—the sovereignty of the English state.

Cromwell's practice of enacting the king's policies through parliamentary statute, furthermore, resulted in greater government efficiency and greater activity in Parliament; the collection *Statutes of the Realm* allows 1,092 pages for legislation passed during the 294 years from Magna Carta till Henry's accession, while the laws of Henry's thirty-seven-year reign fill 1,032 pages alone. Cromwell's other important legislative and administrative efforts include the initiation of laws for the incorporation of Wales, the abolition of abuses of sanctuary, and the creation of a smaller and more powerful Privy Council. Since Henry was notoriously uninterested in legislative and administrative details, Cromwell alone was responsible for these actions.

Cromwell's responsibilities and influence also loom large in the area of religious policy. In January 1535, Cromwell was appointed vice-regent, vicar general, and special commissary, offices that allowed him to administer the powers granted to Henry as supreme head of the Church of England. Perhaps Cromwell's most notorious and controversial work in this capacity was his supervision of the dissolution of the monasteries. During 1536–40 Cromwell suppressed monastic houses through pressure and persuasion. Despite considerable opposition, by 1540 all monastic institutions were dissolved, and their property had been absorbed by the Crown. Although the nature and strength of Cromwell's personal religious beliefs are subject to much debate, he came to be associated with pro-Reform policies. It was largely due to Cromwell's support that the Bible was made available in English; thanks to his persuasive efforts, Henry required that a Bible be placed in every church in the realm, though this requirement was not always met.

To a certain extent, Cromwell's pro-Reform policies also guided his diplomatic efforts. To safeguard England against Continental powers, he desired an alliance between England and the German Lutheran princes. The prospect of this alliance was not always pleasing to Henry, who preferred to claim Catholic orthodoxy for himself and his nation. In 1539 Cromwell attempted to force such an alliance by convincing the king to take as his fourth wife Anne of Cleves, whose family was closely tied to the Lutheran duke of Saxony. The king found his new wife distasteful, and by February 1540 the international situation was such that the German alliance that the marriage represented was no longer necessary. Cromwell's fall came quickly due both to the failure of the Cleves marriage and to the successful maneuverings of his enemies. He struggled to retain power, being created earl of Essex and lord great chamberlain as late as April 1540, but early in June his enemies persuaded Henry that he was both a heretic and a traitor. He was arrested on 10 June and condemned without a hearing; his arrest was kept secret, and his scaffold was carefully guarded because the government feared his popularity in London. His pleas to Henry, which recounted the "labors, pains, and travails" taken for a king whom he labeled "more like a dear father . . . than a master," obtained for him no mercy, and he was executed on 28 July. His death marked the end of efficient government during Henry's reign.

MAJOR WORKS AND THEMES

Cromwell's major legislative achievements were based upon two political principles: the idea that England was a sovereign nation-state subject to no outside authority and the concept of the legislative supremacy of the king in Parliament, best understood as an absolute monarchy working through statute and limited only by the need for parliamentary assent. Cromwell's ideas about government and the proper relationship between church and state are most clearly laid out in the Henrician statutes upon which he exerted his influence. The Act of Appeals of 1533 was an important landmark in bringing about the break from Rome; more constitutionally significant, however, is its declaration that England is a sovereign nation-state, an assertion that is revolutionary not for its novelty but because its legal ramifications were acknowledged. Legislating the claims to national sovereignty that Henry had made from time to time, the preamble to this act asserts that England is "governed by one supreme head and King" who holds "plenary, whole and entire power . . . to render and yield justice and final determination to all manner of folk residents or subjects within this realm, in all causes, matters, debates and contentions happening to occur . . . without restraint or provocation to any foreign princes or potentates of the world." The preamble clearly asserts that the king need appeal to no outside authority regarding matters in his realm. The authority for this assertion of national sovereignty resides in history ("divers sundry old authentic histories and chronicles") as well as divine institution ("[sovereignty] being . . . institute . . . by the goodness and sufferance of Almighty God"); Parliament need only affirm the theoretical consensus of these authorities. This legislative enactment of Henry's claims to sovereign rule is also apparent in the statutes that completed the separation of England from Rome. The Dispensation Act of 1534, for example, recognizes that the authority of the papacy in England had been a "usurpation" of monarchical authority. In similar language, the Act against Papal Authority of 1536 reflected the work of the previous four years by rejecting utterly the "pretended power and usurped authority of the bishop of Rome" and the papacy's "pretended monarchy." The act forbids anyone to support the authority of Rome and its jurisdiction within the realm, making it treason to reject the royal supremacy. This language characterizing papal authority in England as political usurpation sums up the earlier decrees about England's status as a sovereign nation-state and extends the subsequent break with Rome to its logical political conclusions. It also consolidated Tudor power within the realm.

Cromwell's legislative work also defines how the sovereignty of the king is to be realized in terms of practical legal enforcement. The statutes that he influenced uphold the legislative supremacy of the king in Parliament by recognizing a supreme monarchy restrained only by the need for parliamentary acknowledgement and enforcement of its claims and policies. The Act of Supremacy of 1534, for example, affirms the king as head of the church, an honor that is divinely bestowed and that Parliament therefore cannot grant but merely confirm:

> Albeit the King's majesty justly and rightfully is . . . the supreme head of the Church of England, and so is recognized by the clergy of this realm in their convocations; yet

nevertheless for corroboration and confirmation thereof . . . be it enacted by authority of this present Parliament that the King our sovereign lord, his heirs and successors, kings of this realm, shall be taken, accepted and reputed the only supreme head in earth of the Church of England.

Parliament exists to confirm what it claims has already been established as fact: the king's headship of the church. Yet the act further implies that Parliament has the subordinate but necessary role of enforcing the king's headship, as it legislates the practical judicial and administrative actions deriving from the theoretical fact of that supreme headship:

Our said sovereign lord, his heirs and successors, Kings of this realm, shall have full power and authority from time to time to visit, repress, redress, reform, order, correct, restrain and amend all such errors, heresies, abuses, offenses, contempts and enormities, whatsoever they be, which by any manner spiritual authority or jurisdiction ought or may lawfully be reformed, repressed, ordered, redressed, corrected, restrained or amended.

Similarly, on one hand, the Act against Papal Authority merely confirms Henry's declarations of a divinely instituted supreme headship. Yet, on the other hand, the legislation of that claim is crucial if those who challenge the supreme headship are to be prosecuted under charges of treason, as the act decrees; since only Parliament can rule certain actions criminal and decree punishments for those actions, Parliament's legislative enactment of Henry's claims becomes necessary for their practical and legal enforcement. Through these statutes, Cromwell did not seek to put the king above the law, as he realized that the Crown needed Parliament and its legislation to put its concepts, theories, and policies into practice. Conversely, Cromwell and the Cromwellian Parliament certainly did not legislate policy independent of the Crown's wishes. Rather, Cromwell sought to make his monarch's policy more effective by working through statute; thus, the partnership that he labored to establish between Crown and Parliament created both a more powerful and a more efficient government.

In matters of religion, Cromwell exhibited a similar drive toward efficiency as well as an affinity with pro-Reform policies. He was responsible, for example, for the institution of parish registers, a typical manifestation of Cromwellian order. In a March 1538 letter to Bishop Salisbury he establishes himself as an orderly executor of reform: "I do not cease to give thanks that it has pleased His goodness to use me as an instrument and to work somewhat by me." Cromwell was instrumental—as I have noted—in one of the Reformers' major efforts: the publication of an official English translation of the Bible. In 1535, for example, the biblical printer Nicholson procured Cromwell's help in obtaining permission for the printing of Coverdale's 1535 translation. In 1537 a translation edited by John Rogers known as the Matthew Bible emerged; upon receiving a copy Cromwell persuaded Henry to permit its sale. For this act, Archbishop

Cranmer* praised Cromwell in a letter dated 13 August 1537: ''[I]t shall well appear hereafter, what high and acceptable service you have done unto God and the King.'' Early in 1538, Cromwell entrusted the revision of the English Bible to a grateful Coverdale, who on 23 June wrote that he had ''no other refuge,'' next to God and king, than Cromwell. The first edition of this new translation, known as the Great Bible, was printed in 1539 and achieved official status as Cromwell granted its printer a monopoly. Cromwell also sought to enforce the reading of these biblical translations. In 1538, he reissued the 1536 order that a Bible must be placed in every church and went beyond the 1536 order to demand that clergy ''expressly provoke, stir and exhort every person to read the . . . very lively word of God.'' Cromwell's 1538 injunctions to the clergy also encourage basic education of the laity in Christian fundamentals, such as the Paternoster.

Cromwell's religious policies yielded more equivocal results. His 1538 injunctions ordered the removal of images that were ''abused'' by superstitious activities such as pilgrimages or offerings. These injunctions contributed to the destruction of many images, which, despite their inspiring of superstition, were valuable works of art, as well as the 1538 government dismantling of the shrine of Thomas Becket. The most controversial manifestation of Cromwell's ostensibly pro-Reform policies was, as I have said, the suppression of the monasteries. The first Act of Suppression (1536) couches its project in the language of indignant reform, claiming that the suppression is prompted by the ''vicious, carnal, and abominable living'' practiced in ''little and small'' houses. The act asserts that ''the possessions of such spiritual religious houses, now being spent, spoiled and wasted for increase and maintenance of sin, should be . . . converted to better uses''—that is, to the use of the Crown. According to this statute, only houses with an income of £200 or less were to be suppressed; in actuality, however, many larger houses capitulated to increasing governmental pressure, and by 1540 monastic life no longer existed in England. Ironically, monastic suppression brought no lasting source of income to the Crown, as revenue generated from the suppression was squandered after Cromwell's death.

CRITICAL RECEPTION

Cromwell is one of the more controversial figures of Henry's reign, and the controversy begins in his own day. He was bitterly attacked by conservative rivals such as Gardiner and Norfolk. The Act of Attainder that they brought against him frequently asserted the fact of his comparatively low birth; it accused Cromwell of heresy and of pretending to have power over the king. On the other hand, Cromwell's pro-Reform policies earned him a place among Foxe's martyrs. Foxe attributes to Cromwell ''such a dexterity of wit as England shall scarcely have again.'' Because Cromwell resisted attempts to restore papal authority in England, Foxe terms him ''a mighty . . . wall and defense of the church'' and rather extravagantly pronounces him a ''valiant soldier and captain of Christ.'' Merriman, Cromwell's earliest twentieth-century biographer, is more equivocal in his assessment. He finds Cromwell unscrupulous though patriotic and remarks that Cromwell's goal was "the elevation of the crown to absolute power on the ruins of every other institution which had ever been its rival" (164). Among recent historians who decry either a decrease in the church's power or the English break from Rome or both, Cromwell has received little praise. Maynard, himself a Roman Catholic, is revolted by Cromwell, remarking that "his cold-bloodedness is more appalling than the fierce animosity of the King he served" (1). Maynard proposes that Cromwell held a cynic's indifference toward religion, that his politics were driven by a similarly cynical opportunism, and that he manipulated the king into effecting a break from Rome that the conservative king would never have determined on his own.

Other historians have resisted excessive praise or condemnation of Cromwell and have, I argue, presented a more evenhanded picture. Dickens provides a balanced evaluation of his impact on the English Reformation. While acknowledging unfair practices in the suppression of the monasteries, Dickens nevertheless gives Cromwell due credit for implementing many basic reforms under Henry as well as for overseeing the publication of an official English Bible. Elton, among others, has rehabilitated Cromwell in the political arena. At times, Elton may go too far in asserting the revolutionary nature of Cromwell's actions and ideas, yet by emphasizing the governing role that Cromwell gave Parliament as the necessary executor of the king's policies, Elton substantiates his claim that Cromwell was England's first parliamentary statesman. Beckingsale, Cromwell's recent biographer, writes a balanced assessment of his subject. He notes as a matter of course that Cromwell's principal aim was to please the king by enacting his policies. He stresses, however, that Cromwell was not a mere agent of the king because he used Henry's aspirations, which were most often personal and dynastic, as a means to transform the nation. This transformation came about through Cromwell's transposition of Henry's marital issues into issues of common law, political theory, and theology. In sum, Cromwell must not be judged by the standards of any age but his own. Those involved in Tudor government were often harsh and arbitrary in their exercise of power, and Cromwell is no exception. However, he showed the highest respect for the letter of the law and thus did not encourage despotism. His political contributions—the necessary, if unequal, partnership between Crown and Parliament as well as the ushering of Protestantism's voice onto the English political stage—shaped the future of the nation. As he acknowledged in a letter to Henry at the end of his life, he had not yet fulfilled all of his duties; further political and religious developments that built upon the foundations he had laid were reserved for future generations.

BIBLIOGRAPHY

Works by Thomas Cromwell, Earl of Essex (including reports of his conduct)

Foxe, John. *Actes and Monuments*. London, 1563.

Letters to Cromwell on the Suppression of the Monasteries. Ed. G. H. Cook. London: John Baker, 1965.

Merriman, Roger Bigelow. *Life and Letters of Thomas Cromwell.* Oxford: Clarendon Press, 1902. (Contains most of the extant letters.)

State Papers. Vols. 1–8. London, 1834–49.

Statutes of the Realm. 11 vols. London, 1810–28.

Studies of Thomas Cromwell, Earl of Essex

Beckingsale, B. W. *Thomas Cromwell, Tudor Minister.* New York: Macmillan, 1978.

Dickens, A. G. *Thomas Cromwell and the English Reformation.* London: English Universities Press, 1959.

Elton, G. R. *England under the Tudors.* 3d ed. London: Routledge, 1991.

———. *Policy and Police.* Cambridge: Cambridge University Press, 1972.

———. *Reform and Renewal: Thomas Cromwell and the CommonWeal.* Cambridge: Cambridge University Press, 1973.

———. *The Tudor Revolution in Government.* Cambridge: Cambridge University Press, 1953.

Maynard, Theodore. *The Crown and the Cross: A Biography of Thomas Cromwell.* New York: McGraw-Hill, 1950.

Williams, Neville. *The Cardinal and the Secretary.* London: Weidenfeld and Nicholson, 1975.

SUSANNAH BRIETZ MONTA

D

SAMUEL DANIEL
(1562–1619)

BIOGRAPHY

Samuel Daniel's biography, beyond a recitation of his published works and political connections, offers an essential context for studying his writings. Daniel exemplifies the writer indebted to a system of patronage, who was shaped by, and helped to perpetuate, the literary system of Tudor and Stuart England.

Daniel was born in 1562. His father was John Daniel, a music master, and his brother John was a musician; some would say that heredity and environment contributed to the lyrical quality of Daniel's own poetry. The young Daniel, like other aspiring statesmen of his day, notably Sir Philip Sidney,* followed a course of learning, travel, and political apprenticeship. He attended Magdalen College, Oxford, as a commoner but left without taking a degree. His first published work was a translation of a tract on impresa or devices, *The Worthy Tract of Paulus Jovius* (1585); dedicated to Sir Edward Dymoke, the queen's champion, this was Daniel's first attempt to please a patron. He gained notoriety not with a political appointment, however, but with the publication of twenty-eight of his poems with the unauthorized edition of Sidney's *Astrophil and Stella* in 1591. The following year Daniel issued his own sonnet sequence, *Delia*, with *The Complaint of Rosamond.* With apologies and praises, this work was dedicated to the countess of Pembroke,* Sidney's* sister. Around this time, Daniel entered Pembroke's household as a tutor to her son, William Herbert. With these two publication events, Daniel worked the literary system to his advantage. Despite his protest in the dedication of *Delia* that he was "betraide by the indiscretion of a greedie Printer" and "forced to appeare so rawly in publique," I suspect he was complicit in the publication of the "unauthorized" 1591 volume. After all, he had nothing to lose and everything to gain by an association with Sidney, famous since his untimely demise in 1586. Daniel's careful revisions in the 1592 volume, together with his modified Petrarchism, suggest to me a poet intent on pleasing his reader and convincing her that he is worthy to be Sidney's poetic heir. While promoting himself, Daniel affirms the powerful system of patronage that Pembroke represents and on which he depends.

Daniel continued to mount the ladder of literary achievement, charting a Virgilian progression from lyric poetry, tragic complaints, and drama to epic history in verse. While associated with Pembroke, Daniel published the Senecan drama *The Tragedie of Cleopatra* (1594), a companion to her own translation of Garnier's *Antonie*. His sympathetic and complex portrayal of Cleopatra's heroism most surely pleased her. Between 1595 and 1609, he published installments of *The Civil Wars of England*, completing eight volumes and bringing the history as far as the marriage of Edward IV to Lady Grey (he never fulfilled his intention to bring the work to the eve of the Tudor dynasty). By this time he had moved on to new patrons, Fulke Greville* and Lord Mountjoy, through whom he became an acquaintance and admirer of the earl of Essex. Abandoning his *Civil Wars*, he turned his back on poetry, to write, in prose, *The Collection of the History of England* (1618). Like so many grand Elizabethan projects, this one, too, remained unfinished, ending with the death of Edward III. With the accession of the new monarch, Daniel sought favor at James'* court. His *Panegyricke Congratulatorie to His Majestie* was printed with *A Defence of Ryme* in 1603, the volume sporting six additional dedicatory epistles to various noblemen and noblewomen. With the patronage of the countess of Bedford, Daniel became a prominent figure in court festivities, authoring the masques *The Vision of the Twelve Goddesses* (1604), *The Queens Arcadia* (1605), *Tethys Festival* (1610), and *Hymens Triumph* (1615). In 1604, he was appointed licenser of the Children of the Queen's Revels, a post he held briefly. About this time, he encountered problems with censorship of his own play, *Philotas* (1605). The play was suspected of containing sympathetic commentary on Essex in his trial and execution in 1601. Daniel was called before the Privy Council but was able to extricate himself from trouble with a written apology. He continued in the queen's favor as one of the grooms of her privy chamber, receiving an annual salary of sixty pounds. He retired to Wiltshire and there he died in 1619. An oft-published poet and accomplished courtier, secure in his patronage connections, he nonetheless failed to produce the successful epic work that would have earned him a more esteemed place in literary history.

MAJOR WORKS AND THEMES

Delia is perhaps Daniel's best-known work of poetry, admired for its pleasant lyricism, its textbook examples of Petrarchism, and its employment of the "eternizing conceit," the celebration of the poet's ability to immortalize the beloved in his poetry. In Sonnet XXX, the speaker imagines an aged Delia and offers his timeless poetry:

> When if she grieve to gaze her in her glas,
> Which then presents her winter-withered hew;
> Goe you my verse, goe tell her what she was;
> For what she was she best shall finde in you.
> Your firie heate lets not her glorie passe,
> But Phenix-like shall make her live anew.

These borrowed themes Daniel uses to a new purpose: to present himself to the countess of Pembroke as a skillful and ambitious poet. He also refashions commonplaces of Petrarchism to reflect and effect a mutually sustaining patronage relationship; the poet/lover is not the conventional bitter captive but a worshiping lover whose pleas for reciprocity lack the erotic charge of Sidney's Astrophil. *The Complaint of Rosamond*, published with the 1592 *Delia*, contributes to this purpose; it presents Daniel as no callow lover, but a morally serious poet condemning adultery while raising sympathy for the wronged Rosamond, paramour of Henry II. He also frames the tale with an image of a patron–client relationship, where the ghost of Rosamond asks Delia (the Countess) to grace the poet and thus enable her distressed soul to find rest. Daniel's 1592 volume apparently succeeded in establishing him in Pembroke's graces; the dedication of the 1594 *Delia* calls her "Great Patroness of these my humble Rymes. . . . Begotten by thy hand, and my desire."

Daniel's confidence in poetry's personal and cultural efficacy does not last, however. Even while he defends poetry and learning in *Musophilus* (1599) and *A Defence of Ryme* (1603), he meditates upon human frailty and the limitations of poetry in a world of change and devolution. The dialogue between the learned Musophilus and the worldly Philocosmos addresses the familiar humanist dilemma, the struggle to reconcile the often conflicting values of scholarship and action. Daniel's solution is to promote the man of learning as most fit for public governance. The *Defence of Ryme* also gives a humanist emphasis to its subject. It is most often read for its progressive views on language, as Daniel rejects "the authoritie of Antiquitie" and proposes as criteria of judgment "Custome that is before all Law, Nature that is above all Arte." As I read it, however, the work expresses anxiety about various authorities, as Daniel challenges Thomas Campion (who favored ancient Latin meters), establishes his own poetic authority, and, importantly, engages political issues. The *Defence*, after all, appeared with the *Panegyricke*, which praises and admonishes King James* to maintain the commonwealth and avoid tyranny. In the *Defence*, abandoning custom is linked to the dangers of tyranny; what is customary and common, whether in government or literary practice, is seen as the source of strength and stability (this dedication to preserving the commonwealth and the rights of knighthood is, according to Richard McCoy, also an important theme of the *Civil Wars*). Natural and customary rhyme, employed in formal verse, orders and stabilizes language. Ironically, Daniel's emphasis on naturalness of language eventually leads him away from poetry and rhyming to prose, which he calls the "common tongue of the world."

The problem, as Daniel and his contemporaries, including Francis Bacon,* realized, is that custom is an ever-shifting criterion. Social and poetic values are changing and relative, and certitude is thus hard to come by. Accordingly, Daniel found insoluble difficulties in the writing of history. Initially, he claimed that his *Civil Wars* would unfold events "Unintermixt with fictions fantasies. / I versifie the troth, not Poetize." In the 1609 dedication, however, he is less confident: "I have carefully followed that truth . . . without adding to, or subtracting from, the general receiv'd opinion." He feels obliged to report "popular bruites, and opinions, which run according to the time & the bias of mens affections." The search for certainty and fact has run aground on the rocks of opinion and individual bias, not to mention conflicting evidence, which he elsewhere bemoans. Furthermore, like Sidney, Daniel is aware that the historian cannot escape poetic feigning, as he defends his "poeticall licence, of framing speaches" to historical figures by claiming they are drawn "according to the portraiture of Nature." Daniel arrived early at the awareness (now shared by some of today's historians) that history can never retrieve the "truth" of the past, that historians regularly construct fictions of their own.

CRITICAL RECEPTION

Daniel has been praised primarily as a lyric poet, hailed in his own time as "well-languaged" and admired for "sweetness of ryming." In our time, C. S. Lewis remarks of *Delia* that it "offers no ideas, no psychology, and of course no story: it is simply a masterpiece of phrasing and melody." Following Lewis, modern critics have devoted themselves to appreciating the sonnets' lyrical qualities. But the case is not closed. Daniel's historical verse has, however, been judged a failure, although the *Civil Wars* has received close attention as a source for Shakespeare's first tetralogy. *Delia* has likewise been counted among Shakespeare's reading and always, of course, pales in critical comparison to his *Sonnets*. Studying mainly the *Civil Wars* and *Collection of the History of England*, historians have placed Daniel at the forefront of an emergent historiography in the late sixteenth century, conflicted in its relation to poetry and shifting from a providential view of history to one emphasizing human actions and their consequences (see Ferguson and Levy). For these writers and for most readers of *Musophilus* and the *Defence of Ryme*, Daniel is appreciated for his ideas rather than his poetic expression. In sum, Daniel has been seen as a pleasant but decidedly second-tier poet, a literary ''professional'' rather than a laureate, to use Richard Helgerson's distinctions. These terms are useful to new historicists seeking to reevaluate Daniel's career in terms of the patronage system, with its shifting power relations that both impede and enable poetic self-fashioning. Appreciation of his poetry per se may come with time.

BIBLIOGRAPHY

Works by Samuel Daniel

The Complete Works in Verse and Prose of Samuel Daniel. 5 vols. Ed. Alexander Grosart. London, 1885–96; rpt. 1963.

An edition by John Pitcher is forthcoming from Clarendon Press.

Studies of Samuel Daniel

Clark, Ira. ''Samuel Daniel's 'Complaint of Rosamond.' '' *Renaissance Quarterly* 23 (1970): 152–62.

Ferguson, Arthur B. ''The Historical Thought of Samuel Daniel: A Study in Renaissance Ambivalence.'' *Journal of the History of Ideas* 32 (1971): 185–202.

Gill, R. B. ''Moral History and Daniel's *The Civil Wars.*'' *Journal of English and Germanic Philology* 76 (1977): 334–45.

Godshalk, W. L. ''Recent Studies in Samuel Daniel (1975–1990).'' *English Literary Renaissance* 24 (1994): 489–502.

Hulse, Clark. ''Samuel Daniel: The Poet as Literary Historian.'' *Studies in English Literature 1599–1900* 19 (1979): 55–69.

Levy, F. J. ''Hayward, Daniel, and the Beginnings of Political History in England.'' *Huntington Library Quarterly* 53 (1987): 1–34.

Lewis, C. S. *English Literature in the Sixteenth Century, excluding Drama.* Oxford: Clarendon Press, 1954.

McCoy, Richard. *The Rites of Knighthood: The Literature and Politics of Elizabethan Chivalry.* Berkeley: University of California Press, 1989.

Primeau, Ronald. ''Daniel and the *Mirror* Tradition: Dramatic Irony in *The Complaint of Rosamond.*'' *Studies in English Literature* 15 (1975): 21–36.

Rees, Joan. *Samuel Daniel: A Critical and Biographical Study.* Liverpool: Liverpool University Press, 1964.

Roche, Thomas P. *Petrarch and the English Sonnet Sequences.* New York: AMS Press, 1989, Chapter 7.

Seronsy, Cecil. *Samuel Daniel.* New York: Twayne, 1967.

Svensson, Lars-Haken. *Silent Art: Rhetorical and Thematic Patterns in Samuel Daniel's* Delia. Lund Studies in English, 1980.

Williamson, C. F. ''The Design of Daniel's *Delia.*'' *Review of English Studies* 19 (1968): 251–60.

Woolf, D. R. ''Community, Law and State: Samuel Daniel's Historical Thought Revisited.'' *Journal of the History of Ideas* 49 (1988): 61–83.

LISA MARY KLEIN

JOHN DEE
(1527–1608)

BIOGRAPHY

John Dee was one of the few Elizabethans to write about his own youth. Here he describes one of its most formative events:

I was out of St. John's Colledge chosen to be Fellow of Trinity Colledge, at the first erection thereof by King Henry the Eight. I was assigned there to be the Under-Reader of the Greeke tongue, Mr. Pember being the chiefe Greeke Reader then in Trinity Colledge. Hereupon I did sett forth (and it was seene of the University) a Greeke comedy of Aristophanes, named in Greek *Eirene*, in Latin, *Pax*; with the performance of the *Scarabeus* his flying up to Jupiter's pallace, with a man and his basket of victualls on her back: whereat was great wondering, and many vaine reportes spread abroad of the meanes how that was effected. (*Autobiographical Tracts*, 5f.)

The "vaine reports" were that Dee was conversant with the black arts. Gossip of this sort led to a mob's looting of his Mortlake house in 1583 and ultimately to King James'* refusal, in 1604, to allow him a trial to clear his name. Yet throughout his life Dee would stubbornly proclaim his innocence:

I take the same God, to be my witnesse; that, with all my hart, with all my soule, with all my strength, power and understanding . . . for the most part of my time, from my youth hitherto, I have used, and still use, good, lawful, honest, christian, and divinely prescribed meanes, to attain to the knowledge of those truthes, which are meete and necessarily for me to know. (*Autobiographical Tracts*, 79)

Two points are especially worth noting here: first, that in defending his reputation, Dee implicitly makes the distinction between the Renaissance magus, whose marvelous arts were "Naturally, Mathematically and Mechanically wrought and contrived" (*A Mathematical Preface*), and the wicked conjurer, who used evil powers; second, that by qualifying his defense chronologically ("*for the most part of my time*"), Dee admits to having slipped at least once.

In all probability Dee's veiled admission concerns his activities over the period 1581–89 in the company of the alchemist and confidence-man Edward Kelly. Kelly, a young Worcestershireman whose perpetual black skullcap concealed the fact that his ears had been lopped off in a Lancaster pillory, convinced Dee that they could talk to spirits. A series of absurd seances followed (see Casaubon), and Dee was not cured of Kelly until the latter convinced him that they should hold both of their wives in common, an arrangement that resulted in destructive quarrels.

MAJOR WORKS AND THEMES

Dee's career was otherwise not only respectable but distinguished. Early on he achieved international celebrity by lecturing in Paris about Euclid; and his reputation for broad learning, though sullied by the Kelly episode, remained strong throughout his life.

CRITICAL RECEPTION

Queen Elizabeth* honored Dee with visits and (though belatedly) largesse, and he was cultivated by such notables as Sir Francis Walsingham, Peter Ramus, Sir Edward Dyer,* Sir Philip Sidney,* the earl of Leicester, and John Stow. Dee was a celebrated Hermetic philosopher and astrologer; he made notable contributions to mathematics, theory of science, geography, navigation, and astronomy; he was a bold philosophical apologist for British imperialism; he was an energetic advocate for reform in the calendar and in the preservation of British antiquities.

BIBLIOGRAPHY

Works by John Dee

For Dee's own listing of his published and manuscript writings, see Dee, 73–77. For major bibliography up to 1970, see French, 210–29.

Dee, John. *Autobiographical Tracts*. In *Remains Historical and Literary Connected with the Palatine Counties of Lancaster and Chester*. Vol. 24. The Chetham Society, 1851.

Suster, Gerald, ed. *John Dee: Essential Readings*. Wellingborough: Crucible, 1986.

Studies of John Dee

Casaubon, Meric, ed. *A True and Faithful Relation of what Passed for Many Years between Dr. John Dee and Some Spirits*. 1659; rpt. Glasgow: Antonine, 1974.

Clulee, Nicholas H. ''At the Crossroads of Magic and Science: John Dee's Archemastrie.'' In *Occult and Scientific Mentalities in the Renaissance*, ed. Brian Vickers. Cambridge: Cambridge University Press, 1984, 57–71.

French, Peter. *John Dee*. London: Routledge and Kegan Paul, 1972.

Sherman, William H. ''John Dee's *Brytannicae Reipublicae Synopsis*: A Reader's Guide to the Elizabethan Commonwealth.'' *Journal of Medieval and Renaissance Studies* 20.2 (Fall 1990): 293–315.

ROBERT GRUDIN

THOMAS DEKKER
(c. 1572–1632)

BIOGRAPHY

Thomas Dekker was, by his own account, born in London, probably in 1572, probably of Dutch descent. Nothing is known of his early life, but he may have seen military service in Holland. He first appears in the public record in Henslowe's* *Diary* in 1598, but his name is also mentioned in Frances Meres' *Palladis Tamia* as among "our best for Tragedy" in 1598, so he was probably a known writer before that. Between 1598 and his death in 1632, he wrote seven original plays and collaborated on fifty-one others. His collaborators were Chettle, Drayton, Wilson, Shakespeare,* Webster, Jonson,* Marston, Haughton, Day, Munday, Hathaway, Middleton, Smith, Massinger, Ford, and Rowley. In addition to the plays, he wrote pageants for public events like King James' coronation and Lord Mayors' Feasts and published nondramatic pamphlets on a variety of subjects and in a variety of media: prose, poetry, and prose fiction. He made a living entirely by his writing—when he could, that is. He was imprisoned for debt three times, once for seven years from 1612 to 1619. Late in life, he was twice arrested for recusancy for not attending church. I suspect this reversal may come less from religious conviction than fear of arrest for debt if he left his home, but we can hardly say for sure. His first wife died in 1616 while he was in prison, and he left a widow at his death in 1632. There are baptismal records for three children.

MAJOR WORKS AND THEMES

The titles of the lost plays Dekker wrote during the reign of Elizabeth give us some indication of the range of his subjects and genres: European and Continental history, biblical and classical legend, exotic and domestic tragedy and comedy. His four most important extant plays of that period (three original and one a collaboration) also show an amazing variety: a citizen comedy firmly grounded in middle-class city life and values, a darkly pessimistic morality play, a literary satire, and a medieval folktale that is usually interpreted as a moral *exemplum.*

Dekker's most famous play is *Shoemakers' Holiday*. The title derives from one of its plots: the rise to the position of lord mayor of the main character, the shoemaker Simon Eyre, a larger-than-life craftsman and entrepreneur whose signature line is "prince am I none, yet am I princely born." In the multiplot mode, Dekker deftly weaves Eyre's story among two others: the romance of the aristocratic Lacy and wealthy Rose, daughter of the previous lord mayor, both of whose elders disapprove of the match, and the marriage between Ralph, one of Eyre's apprentices, and Jane, the seamstress. Ralph has to leave his new wife when he is drafted into Lacy's regiment and returns from France wounded. The three plots converge at a number of points: Lacy deserts his regiment and disguises himself as a Dutch shoemaker seeking work in Eyre's shop. Hammon, a wealthy bourgeois, woos first Rose, from the aristocratic plot, and then Jane, from the lower-class plot. Simon Eyre brings all the characters together in a more-or-less harmonious conclusion as he intercedes with the king for Lacy's pardon and mollifies the tyrannical parents blocking Lacy and Rose's marriage and as his apprentices prevent the marriage of Hammon and Jane and celebrate the reunion of Ralph and Jane.

Dekker's gift for character creation is seen in this play. Eyre—jovial, exuberant, expansive, generous, and warmhearted—resembles a workaholic Falstaff in epitomizing the comic spirit and having the most colorful and memorable dialogue in the play. Lacy is redeemed from the colorlessness of the typical romantic hero by his disguise, his phony Dutch accent, and his willingness to work alongside Eyre's journeymen. He is able to be all things to all men, endearing himself to the apprentices by buying beers for the rest of the shop and using his influence to help Eyre make the shrewd investment that puts him over the top in competition for the sheriff of London post. The women are finely drawn: the nagging and social-climbing but affectionate Marjory, hardworking Jane, bawdy Sybil. Even the villain Hammon, who lies to Jane about Ralph's death and offers Ralph money for his wife, is humanized by a speech reminiscent of Shakespeare's "How happy some o'er other some can be." The hapless Ralph energizes himself to work and to chase over London on crutches to find his wife and prevent her from unknowingly committing bigamy. Only the tyrannical parent and guardian seem clichéd, and one of them, Rose's father, is, ironically, based on a real person of Dekker's day who was arrested for mistreating his disobedient daughter.

The twentieth-century reader and audience member whose knowledge of Elizabethan drama is limited to Shakespeare is most immediately struck by Dekker's controlling interest in the lower and middle classes. The focus of the play is on the citizens. The scene in Eyre's shop at the dawn of a working day has been compared to a Dutch genre painting. Lacy is a much more interesting character when he becomes a Dutch shoemaker than when he is an aristocratic lover. Hammon, for all his despicable qualities, is not a snob. When Rose, the wealthy daughter of the lord mayor, rejects him, he turns right around and woos a hardworking seamstress who is supporting herself while her soldier/husband is at the front.

The work ethic is not merely idealized; it is glorified. When Ralph returns from the war missing a leg and discovers that his wife has disappeared, the solution proposed by foreman Hodge is work:

> Limbs? Hast thou not hands, man? Thou shalt never see a shoemaker want bread, though he have but three fingers on a hand.

The working classes help one another: Eyre and his family and employees try to stop the newly wedded Ralph from being drafted and promise to look after his wife. The journeymen all work together at the end of the play to save Jane from a bigamous marriage. The moral of Simon Eyre's story is obvious: work as hard as he, and you too can become lord mayor. There are jockeying among the workers for precedence and some sleepy-eyed grumbling at having to begin a workday, but all animosities are smoothed over, and Eyre cajoles everyone out of laziness.

The comedy is democratic and inclusive. The wealthy middle-class lord mayor hates the aristocratic earl of Lincoln as much as the earl hates him, and both characters are judged severely. Sunny and celebrative as the play is, however, it is not without shadows. After refusing to release Ralph from conscription, Lacy promises to look after him, knowing full well that he plans to desert his troops and sneak back to London and his love, Rose. Lacy is forgiven by the king at the end of the play, but Ralph, who stays in the army, loses a leg and very nearly loses his wife. Money and status help.

At first glance, it seems incredible that Dekker could have written both *Shoemakers' Holiday* and *Old Fortunatus* and at about the same time (the composition date of *Old Fortunatus* is unknown, but it was performed in 1599). *Old Fortunatus* is based on a German folktale about a poor man who is visited by Fortune and offered a choice of wisdom, strength, health, beauty, long life, or riches. He chooses riches. Where *Shoemaker* seems very modern in its democratic outlook and its journalistic detail about workaday life that anticipates nothing less than the modern novel, *Old Fortunatus* is a medieval allegory, a *de casibus* tragedy. *Shoemaker* celebrates life; *Old Fortunatus* is a grimly moral, cautionary tale. *Shoemaker* ends happily; *Old Fortunatus* kills off the title character by the end of Act II, and his sons die gruesomely in Act V. *Shoemaker* celebrates the middle classes; *Old Fortunatus* begins and ends with unabashed celebration of Queen Elizabeth.* *Shoemaker* is realistic; *Old Fortunatus* has a magic purse and hat and includes among its characters Fortune, the Parcae, Tamberlaine, and Bajazeth. *Shoemaker* takes place in London; the protagonists of *Old Fortunatus*, with the help of the magic wishing hat, travel instantaneously among Cyprus, Babylon, and London.

However, the two plays do have similarities. Old Fortunatus is a common man, a very poor one at the play's beginning. The play is democratic in its criticism of all classes—rich and poor alike are greedy and lacking in common sense. Both plays are wonderfully theatrical, especially in the modulations of tone. The scene in *Shoemaker* in which Margery's vulgar and self-absorbed gloating over her husband's success is interrupted by the appearance of Ralph on one leg is a showstopper; comparable is the scene in which Fortunatus returns in triumph from visiting the world's courts and is interrupted by Fortune and the Parcae coming to announce his death.

Finally, both plays deal with riches and their use and abuse. Eyre shows hospitality to foreigners by accepting Lacy in his shop, and Lacy lends Eyre the money to make a profitable investment. In turn, Eyre reciprocates at the end of the play by interceding with the king on Lacy's behalf. Eyre uses his wealth to feast all London apprentices in the festive conclusion. *Shoemaker* illustrates, mainly, the right use of riches, with Hammon's warped values (thinking he can buy a wife) and Ralph's plight serving as reminders of the effects of greed and poverty. Dekker makes clear right from the beginning of *Old Fortunatus* that

Fortunatus has made the wrong choice but allows us to share the initial reaction of Fortunatus and his son that a purse that can never be emptied is a very nice thing to have. As remote and steeped in the morality play tradition as *Old Fortunatus* is, it is probably the more biographical in revealing the deepest longings of the playwright, who was imprisoned for debt the same year it was written. In both plays, Dekker anticipates Dickens in his treatment of the ambiguity of riches.

Because *Patient Grissel* (1600) was a three-way collaboration with Chettle and Haughton, it's uncertain which parts of the play Dekker wrote, but the scenes of Grissel's family—her father, starving-scholar brother, and comic servant—are thought to be his. These characters illustrate Dekker's gift for giving the human touch to all his portraits. The brother and servant are the truth-tellers of the play, objecting to the marquis' treatment of his wife. Their criticism, the fact that the marquis tells the audience he is testing his sycophantic courtiers as well as testing Grissel, and the presence of two comic subplots with untamable women all undermine the notion that Grissel and her legend are an *exemplum* of human patience under adversity.

Satiromastix (1601) is Dekker's response to Jonson's attack on Dekker and Marston in *Cynthia's Revels* and *Poetaster*. Funny scenes satirizing Jonson's* purported colossal ego and developing a second plot about the wooing of a widow are loosely tacked on to a third plot, a tragicomic romance involving a newly married couple, a tyrannical king demanding his *droit de seigneur*, and a sleeping potion. By Swiftian or even Jonsonian standards, the attack on Jonson is more comic than satiric, but modern critics give the prize to Dekker in his war with Jonson, and Dekker does seem to have had the last word; Jonson did not reply with a counterblast.

Dissimilar as these four plays are, they show Dekker's moral earnestness and his gift for creating vivid, sympathetic, memorable, and psychologically interesting characters in dramatically powerful situations. His view of the damage human beings are capable of inflicting upon others and upon themselves is honest and unsparing, but he is ultimately hopeful and gives us this view in genial and compassionate comedy.

CRITICAL RECEPTION

Aphra Behn wrote an adaptation of the 1600 Dekker collaboration, *Lust's Dominion* as *Abdelezar* in 1676, but there was little interest in Dekker until Charles Lamb's 1808 evaluation that Dekker had "poetry enough for anything." The Dekker revival in the nineteenth century coincided with the awakening of interest in anything remotely Shakespearean, as typified by Collier's forgeries added to Henslowe's* *Diary*, some of which pertain to Dekker.

Because so much of Dekker's dramatic work was collaborative, establishing the canon remains a major problem. This has been partially resolved in the twentieth century with a number of scholarly editions and book-length critical studies. Also making assessment of his early work difficult is lost plays. That so many different playwrights were willing to work with him both early and late in his career suggests the esteem in which he was held by his contemporaries. Jonson accused Dekker of being a hack writer, but given the circumstances of composition, it is remarkable that some of the collaborations are as seamless as they are. Dekker never repeated the critical success of *The Shoemaker's Holiday*, but it is agreed that the much later *Witch of Edmunton*, a 1621 collaboration with Ford and Rowley, shows that he was, even after several breaks from playwriting, capable of greatness.

In the latter nineteenth-century, Swinburne admired Dekker's humor and pathos but criticized his supposed carelessness. The books listed in the bibliography have echoed Swinburne in finding a combination of comic absurdity and compassionate sympathy in Dekker's works and have largely absolved him of lack of form. All agree on Dekker's moral seriousness, and most recently, Julia Gasper has made a case for taking Dekker seriously as a polemical writer by examining the political, topical, and religious themes in his work.

Dekker is of special appeal to modern readers and audiences for his sympathy for marginalized groups like the poor and women, for his interest in the urban milieu, and for his contempt for class snobbery.

Shoemaker's Holiday has received the most critical attention and praise and is the play most likely to receive a modern production. A vibrant one was mounted by the Stratford (Ontario) Festival in 1990.

BIBLIOGRAPHY

Works by Thomas Dekker

Dramatic Works of Thomas Dekker. 4 vols. Ed. Fredson Bowers. Cambridge: Cambridge University Press, 1953–61.

Non-Dramatic Works of Thomas Dekker. 5 vols. Ed. A. B. Grosart. London, 1884–86.

Plague Pamphlets of Thomas Dekker. Ed. F. P. Wilson. Oxford: Clarendon Press, 1925.

Selected Prose Works. Ed. E. D. Pendry. London, 1968.

Shoemakers' Holiday. Ed. Paul C. Davies. Berkeley: University of California Press, 1968.

Shoemakers' Holiday. Ed. R. L. Smallwood and Stanley Wells. Baltimore: Johns Hopkins University Press, 1979.

Thomas Dekker: Best Plays. Ed. Ernest Rhys. New York: A. A. Wyn, 1949.

Studies of Thomas Dekker

Adler, Doris Ray. *Thomas Dekker: A Reference Guide*. Boston: G. K. Hall, 1983.

Champion, L. S. *Thomas Dekker and the Tradition of English Drama*. New York: Peter Lang, 1985.

Conover, James Harrington. *Thomas Dekker: An Analysis of Dramatic Structure*. The Hague: Mouton, 1969.

Gasper, Julia. *The Dragon and the Dove: The Plays of Thomas Dekker*. Oxford: Clarendon Press, 1990.

Hoy, Cyrus. *Introductions, Notes, and Commentaries to Texts in ''The Dramatic Works of Thomas Dekker.''* 4 vols. Cambridge: Cambridge University Press, 1980–81.

Hunt, Mary Leland. *Thomas Dekker: A Study*. New York: Russell and Russell, 1964.

Jones-Davies, Marie Therese. *Un Peintre de la Vie Londonienne: Thomas Dekker*. Collection des Etudes Anglaises, No. 6. Paris: Didier, 1958.
Price, George R. *Thomas Dekker*. New York: Twayne, 1969.

JANET WOLF

THOMAS DELONEY
(156?–1600)

BIOGRAPHY

The life of Thomas Deloney remains largely unknown. With no birth record and no university records, he left no convenient benchmarks by which to judge his date of birth. His first known work was his translation of *A Declaration made by the archbishop of Collen* in 1583, so scholars range widely as they use it to make a guess based on how mature they judge him to have been when he translated it. Deloney may have been born in Norwich; editor F. O. Mann guessed so, misquoting Thomas Nashe* as evidence. The only real evidence for Norwich is that Deloney's first known published ballad was printed there in 1586, which I find unconvincing given that we can establish him in London that same year: the St. Giles, Cripplegate, Parish Register for 1586 lists the birth of a son, Richard, to a Thomas Delonie silk weaver on 16 October (Wright, 17). Certainly, once in London (if not from there originally), he was increasingly prominent for his ballads, succeeding William Elderton as the dominant balladeer by the early 1590s.

His title of silk weaver does tell us that Deloney was somewhat unusual for a writer of his time, in that he had a day job: he was a yeoman member of the liveried London Company of Weavers. He continued a double life as weaver and writer at least until 1595, when he was arrested and imprisoned for writing and printing a letter, "To the Ministers and Elders of the French Church in London" (Consitt, 312–18). This incident reveals intriguing details about his status in his craft, as the letter unsuccessfully requests the ministers to force alien weavers to conform to the ordinances of the Company of Weavers. Deloney's legal problems continued after this incident (he was released from jail by the aldermen and the Privy Council), because a year later in 1596 he was sought by the lord mayor for the penning of a ballad, "On the Want of Corn" (Wright, 18), now lost. The mayor never caught him, and after writing all four of his novels in his final years, Deloney died of causes unknown in 1600 (Wright, 19).

MAJOR WORKS AND THEMES

Deloney's literary endeavors fall primarily into three categories: Protestant polemic, street ballads, and prose fictions, that I call novels for lack of a better term. In the first category, he published translations, *A Declaration Made by the Archbishop of Collen upon the Deede of his Mariage* and *The Proclamation and Edict of the Archbishop and Prince Elector of Culleyn*, which are reasonably clear, but primarily of interest to scholars of the English Reformation. Perhaps a similar impulse inspired Deloney's serious poetic work, *Canaans Calamitie*, which follows Nashe's *Christes Teares Over Ierusalem* in its use of the fall of Jerusalem as an allegory for a purported fall of London. While he makes great use of the grotesque, I must admit that in *Canaans Calamitie* Deloney demonstrates the extent to which he was not a great poet. His verse is not the worst of the period but cannot match the energy and intensity of his prose works.

Similarly, the ballads that were the foundation of Deloney's Elizabethan reputation are not great poetry, although they often show signs of the vivid dialogue and characterization that would make his novels the cornerstone for his later reputation. Appearing in *The Garland of Good Will* (from which volume the term "garland" for a collection of ballads is derived) and *Strange Histories*, along with innumerable broadsides, the ballads range in subject from the romantic tales of the nobility to patriotic and domestic journalism of his time. Deloney was at his best when presenting the voices and lives of his fellow commoners and tradespeople; he was possibly the first English author to use dialect effectively in *A pleasant Dialogue betweene plaine Truth, and blind Ignorance* (Mann, 351). The chronicle ballads and journalistic ballads, like his song on Elizabeth's* speech at Tilbury, reflect the popular taste of his time, while his ballads, like "A Song in praise of Women," show his interest in the concerns of common people.

Deloney finally hit his stride after 1596, with the publication of four novels, *Iacke of Newberie, The Gentle Craft I* (the source for Thomas Dekker's* *Shoemaker's Holiday*), *The Gentle Craft II*, and *Thomas of Reading*. All four detail the lives of tradespeople, shoemakers in *The Gentle Craft* and Deloney's fellow weavers in *Iacke* and *Thomas*. All four novels lack unified narrative lines, but they share an insight into the lives of real people that is not to be found in the other prose writers of the time, like Nashe, Robert Greene,* or John Lyly.* While Deloney has his euphuistic moments when trying to create high speech for his noble characters, he in general favors a realistic and conversational style, and the novels are like plays in their reliance on characters' speech (Lawlis, xiff.). Deloney's novels are polemical, glorifying the virtues of the guild class, but along the way he presciently creates a sort of prose narrative, unlike those of any of his contemporaries, that predicts the novel to come.

CRITICAL RECEPTION

In his own time, Deloney was largely regarded as a very successful practitioner of the debased form, the ballad. In particular, Nashe invoked Deloney to defend Elderton from an attack by Gabriel Harvey,* and Harvey in turn told Nashe to spend less time with Deloney and more with Thomas More* (*Pierce's*

Supererogation). In a similar vein, Greene* (the same fellow who called Shakespeare* an upstart crow) accused Deloney of "yarking up" (jerking up) ballads (*Defense of Conny-Catching*). On the other hand, there remain no first editions of any of Deloney's novels or garlands, suggesting that they were read out of existence, and the novels remained in print for centuries (Wright, 120).

In our own century, the reception of Deloney has been a long string of missed opportunities. There have been two good editions, F. O. Mann's *Works* and Merritt Lawlis' *Novels*, but there have been only a few book-length studies of Deloney. He appears in histories of the novel, and he spawns an article or two every few years, but few critics have risen above the level of noticing his existence. There is an excellent body of source study on Deloney, but there remains a scarcity of insightful readings. I remain mystified in particular that more historical or Marxist readings have not been done, given the balance of Deloney's involvement with his guild and his focus on guild-dominated trades. Because he wrote novels in an age preceding the invention of the novel, he has, by and large, fallen through the cracks of the academy.

BIBLIOGRAPHY

Works by Thomas Deloney

Consitt, Frances. *The London Weavers Company*. Vol. 1. Oxford: Clarendon Press, 1931.

Deloney, Thomas. *Novels*. Ed. Merritt E. Lawlis. Bloomington: Indiana University Press, 1961.

———. *Works*. Ed. F[rancis] O[scar] Mann. Oxford: Clarendon Press, 1912.

Studies of Thomas Deloney

Chevalley, Abel. *Thomas Deloney: le Roman des Métiers au temps de Shakespeare*. Paris: Librairie Gallimard, 1926.

Davis, Walter R. *Idea and Art in Elizabethan Fiction*. Princeton: Princeton University Press, 1969.

Devine, Paul. "Unity and Meaning in Thomas Deloney's *Thomas of Reading*." *Neuphilologische Mitteilungen* 87 (1986): 578–93.

Dorsinville, Max. "Design in Deloney's *Jack of Newbery*." *PMLA* 88 (1973): 233–39.

Jordan, Constance. "The Art of Clothing: Role-Playing in Deloney's Fiction." *English Literary Renaissance* 11 (1981): 183–93.

Kuehn, G. W. "Thomas Deloney: Two Notes." *Modern Language Notes* 52 (1937): 103–5.

Lawlis, Merritt. *Apology for the Middle Class: The Dramatic Novels of Thomas Deloney*. Bloomington: Indiana University Press, 1960.

Linton, Joan Pong. "Jack of Newbury and Drake in California: Domestic and Colonial Narratives of English Cloth and Manhood." *ELH* 59 (1992): 23–51.

Mustazza, Leonard. "Thomas Deloney's *Jacke of Newbery*: A Horatio Alger Story for the Sixteenth Century." *Journal of Popular Culture* 23 (1989): 165–77.

Pätzold, Kurt Michael. "Thomas Deloney and the English Jest-book Tradition." *English Studies* 53 (1972): 313–28.

Reuter, Ole. "Some Aspects of Thomas Deloney's Prose Style." *Neuphilologische Mitteilungen* 49 (1939): 23–72.

Rollins, Hyder. "Thomas Deloney's Euphuistic Learning and *The Forest.*" *PMLA* 50 (1935): 679–87.

Wright, Eugene P. *Thomas Deloney*. Boston: Twayne, 1981.

ROGER A. LADD

JOHN DONNE
(1572–1631)

BIOGRAPHY

John Donne was born in London in the first half of 1572 to Catholic parents. Whether or not one agrees with John Carey's assessment that Donne's Catholicism and his subsequent "apostasy" constitute the primary facts of his biography, Donne's childhood as a member of a persecuted religion certainly had lifelong consequences. His mother and other members of his family were forced to flee to the Continent to avoid persecution, and his younger brother Henry, with whom Donne had entered Oxford and presumably spent much time, was arrested for harboring a priest and died in prison in 1593 at the age of nineteen or twenty. It is impossible to know why or even when Donne shifted allegiance from the Catholic Church to the Anglican Church, but it is clear that much of his young adulthood was spent immersed in the literature of religious controversy, and he later contributed to it on behalf of the Protestant position in his prose works *Pseudo-Martyr* and *Ignatius His Conclave*.

Nevertheless, there were other formative influences in Donne's life besides the complications of religion. His father's death when Donne was four and his mother's prompt remarriage (although there is no evidence that her second husband was anything but an adequate father) may have contributed to the most obsessive theme in Donne's poetry—the faithlessness of women (assuming that there is any biographical content in Donne's poetry at all). Donne's tenure at Lincoln's Inn (1592–95) was crucial to his career as a poet because there he wrote at least the first two satires, most of the elegies, and some of the poems in *Songs and Sonnets*. There he also formed lifelong friendships with some of the men for whom he composed his verse epistles. Among the men he met there was Thomas Egerton, son of the Lord Keeper Egerton, into whose service Donne entered as secretary in late 1596 or early 1597.

While he was in Egerton's employ Donne met Ann More, Lady Egerton's niece. In late 1601 Donne secretly married the young Ann without her father's consent. When Sir George More finally heard of the marriage, he had Donne imprisoned briefly because Ann was still a minor. He also tried unsuccessfully to have the marriage annulled, refused to provide Ann with a dowry, and persuaded Lord Egerton to dismiss Donne from his service. Whatever emotional consolations his marriage to Ann provided (and there is reason to believe they were considerable), Donne's marriage was an unmitigated disaster for his career in public service.

The first significant break in Donne's political exile came in 1611, when he entered the service of Sir Robert Drury, for whom he composed the two *Anniversaries* in honor of his deceased daughter Elizabeth. Only after much resistance did Donne finally acquiesce in King James'* advice to seek a career in the Anglican Church, and Donne was ordained 23 January 1615 and almost immediately appointed royal chaplain. On 15 August 1617, Ann Donne died at the age of thirty-three, in part, apparently worn out by continuous childbearing. Donne's biographer R. C. Bald sees her death as "a turning point in Donne's life," deepening his religious vocation (328). Donne apparently took his ministerial duties very seriously during the next few years and was finally elected dean of St. Paul's 22 November 1621, a position he held until his death 31 March 1631.

MAJOR WORKS AND THEMES

Because Donne published virtually none of his poetry during his lifetime, the first task involved in an assessment of the "Tudor" Donne is to identify the works composed before 1603. The satires and elegies are almost certainly pre-1603, and the unfinished "Progress of the Soul" (or "Metempsychosis") is dated 1601, but the works for which Donne is best known today, the lyrics published posthumously in 1633 as *Songs and Sonnets*, are generally impossible to date. Many of them were written before 1603, but there is no consensus on which ones they are. For the sake of convenience, I treat the entire *Songs and Sonnets* as Tudor poetry.

Donne's earliest poetry was forged in the competitively witty environment of the Inns of Court. They are performances by a young man displaying mental agility for the entertainment of other young men. Perhaps the quintessential works of this period are Donne's "paradoxes," because they most clearly display the values implicit in the poetry—irony, distance, wit in service to nothing but its own demonstration. These qualities characterize all of Donne's early poetry. Even the satires, which pretend to be criticizing faults and which include the powerful passages on religious truth in "Satire III" (which no doubt had serious relevance for Donne himself at the time), are generally tongue-in-cheek. The objects of his scorn—the dandy in "Satire I," the lawyer/poet in "Satire II," and the courtiers and the court in "Satires III and IV"—are simultaneously objects of serious pursuit by Donne and his contemporaries at the Inns of Court, so much of the effect is light self-mockery (despite the edge of bitterness in "Satire V" lacking in the earlier ones).

It would, of course, be equally inappropriate to take Donne's elegies at face value. The often cynical, ribald, even obscene qualities of the poems say little if anything about Donne himself. They are inconsequential *jeux d'esprit* delivered with a wink and a nudge to other young men aspiring to worldliness. Like much else in Donne's early work, the humor of the elegies lies in their deliberate unconventionality and their frequent deployment of paradox (''Until I labour, I in labour lye''—''Elegy 19''). The paradoxical quality of Donne's early poetry does reflect one autobiographical fact, however. The central paradox of Donne's life and work is the contrast between the powerful self-assuredness of the poetry and the frustrated powerlessness of his actual circumstances. As John Carey and Arthur Marotti have argued at length, much (if not all) of Donne's early poetry is compensatory in nature—the cavalier misogynist of the elegies and the self-assured lover of the songs and sonnets are smoke screens for Donne's inescapable sense of failure in the larger political world.

Such an insight has particular force in my reading of the *Songs and Sonnets*. Despite Helen Gardner's enthusiasm for Donne's ''rapture'' and ''bliss'' in the love poems, I find them curiously lacking in passion or emotion of any kind. The almost universal appreciation of Donne's cleverness or ''wit'' is perhaps an unconscious acknowledgment of this phenomenon. The poems are engaging in many ways—they are dramatic, energetic, verbally and intellectually exciting—but they are not love poems. To Gardner's claim that Donne is ''our greatest love-poet'' (xvii), I would respond with Carey, ''In some respects, Donne isn't a love poet at all'' (9).

For all the critical admiration of Donne's ''dramatic voice,'' it remains a fact that the drama in the poems is *staged*. Donne was characterized by a contemporary as ''a great frequenter of Playes,'' and it is clear that Donne was a good student of theatrical art. When Donne opens ''The Canonization'' with ''For God's sake, hold your tongue,'' it is powerful, effective poetry, but it is not the voice of John Donne, lover, revealing his love for Ann More or any other woman; it is the voice of an actor declaiming from the stage, a persona, a well-wrought mask. I am convinced, as Carey and Marotti both argue, that Donne's audience remained his male friends from the Inns of Court, even when he was writing love poems, not his wife or any other woman.

To acknowledge the ''staged'' quality of Donne's dramatic voice is not to deny its poetic power. We do not, after all, reject the great dramatic literature of the age because it was written for actors on the stage. Nevertheless, there is a vague disappointment in reading the love poems because the voice finally sounds a little hollow. The different generic expectations of dramatic and lyric poetry encourage us to locate an authorial presence in lyric poetry, and, for all the power of the persona's voice in Donne's love poems, no one is really there. The voice, for all its specificity, for all its individuality, is ultimately disembodied.

That is perhaps why I find John Carey's account of Donne's life and art so satisfying. He locates the cause of Donne's emotional distance in his struggle with the ''anguish'' resulting from his ''apostasy.'' Describing Donne's treatment of religious themes in his poetry as an attempt ''to cauterize himself,'' Carey sees the elegies in particular as ''the record of a soul trying to coarsen itself'' (41). In order to explain the absence of passion in Donne's love poetry,

Carey postulates a repressed passion, conferring on Donne's interior spiritual and emotional life an anguish that, while not unreasonable, given the historical circumstances, remains nowhere evident in the poems themselves. Still, such a speculative passion is preferable to no passion at all. (In Donne's later poetry and sermons, especially *The Holy Sonnets*, there is, as it were, a passionate clamor for passion, figured both as Christ's Passion and the poet's desire for passionate experience, but the cry remains finally unanswered.) There is evidence in Donne's poetry that he himself saw his poetry as a way to escape the burden of emotion. In "The Triple Fool," for instance, the speaker says,

> I thought, if I could draw my paines,
> Through Rimes vexation, I should them allay,
> Griefe brought to numbers cannot be so fierce,
> For, he tames it, that fetters it in verse.

For all its brilliance and wit, there is something decidedly "tame" about Donne's love poetry.

The most obvious mechanism Donne uses to maintain an emotional distance from the putative subject of his love poetry is, in fact, his famous wit. Poems like "The Flea," "A Valediction: forbidding Mourning," and "A Valediction: of my Name in the Window," for all their occasional power, finally draw the reader's attention away from the relationship being described and focus it exclusively on the poet's demonstration of his own cleverness. Wit is not the only distancing effect in Donne's love poetry, however. Perhaps the most frequent method of denying the value of lyric romanticism is a sometimes flippant, occasionally bitter cynicism. "Song (Goe, and catche a falling starre)," "The Indifferent," "Woman's Constancy," "Loves Usury," and "Loves Diet," to name some of the most obvious, insist upon a universal faithlessness in order to recommend an essentially anonymous sexuality as the basis for male–female relations.

Interestingly, one of the most thoroughly lyrical of *The Songs and Sonnets* is spoken by a woman. In spite of the slight undercutting effect of the final image of the "maryed man" wooing, "Breake of Day" achieves a sustained sense of desire and even vulnerability (which perhaps explains the use of the female voice). It is instructive to compare "A Feaver," which opens with a very moving *cri de coeur*: "Oh doe not die, for I shall hate / All women so, when thou art gone," but the sense of impending loss, of vulnerability, dissolves in the speaker's confident mastery of complex metaphors, as the mistress' fever becomes alternately apocalyptic fires and meteors.

The use of metaphors, of course, is not inevitably debilitating to love poetry; the issue is whether they deepen the mood of the poem or simply distract the reader. In many of Donne's poems the self-referentiality of his cleverness is distracting, but in a poem like "A Nocturnall upon S. Lucies Day," the familiar images drawn from alchemy, philosophy, and natural history provide a powerful reinforcement for the themes of darkness and loss. Such an effect, however, seems all the more powerful because of its infrequence among Donne's love poems. Far more commonly, the final line or final image undercuts the initial tone of a poem, as if mocking the reader for being taken in. ''A Nocturnall'' is unique among Donne's love poems in ending where it began, the final line offering a resonant variation on the opening line.

Like the disembodied voice of the poems that generally directs our attention to the presence of the poet behind the poem, the lovers who are the ostensible subject of the poems are rarely actually ''there.'' They are dead or disembodied as ghosts or shadows or angels, or they are reduced metonymically to a name scratched on glass or a bracelet of hair. Paradoxically, the one thing the love poems often explicitly claim to exclude—the ''real world'' of politics and mercantilism—is frequently the most persuasive presence in the poem. This is obviously no accident. Whatever Donne's relationship to his wife (or other women) was, the absence his poetry most lamented and sought to fill during his most productive years as a poet was his lack of a public career. The famous exclusionary gestures in such poems as ''The Sunne Rising'' and ''The Canonization,'' therefore, are not to be taken literally as invoking the world-well-lost-for-love motif. They should instead be seen as the self-advertisements of a frustrated courtier/statesman. Given the recent emphasis on the political subtext of Renaissance love poetry, Donne seems like a good candidate for critical reassessment.

CRITICAL RECEPTION

John Donne himself initiated the perception of a self-division in his life and works when he drew a distinction between ''Jack Donne'' and ''Doctor Donne.'' Since then the critical response to his works has negotiated the tensions, contradictions, and paradoxes of that self-division, either to assert it as the defining element of the works or to try to heal it by discovering a more unifying vision. In his famous formulation regarding metaphysical poetry—''the most heterogeneous ideas are yoked by violence together''—Samuel Johnson saw the contradictions as unresolvable. In his equally famous formulation—''there is a direct sensuous apprehension of thought, or a recreation of thought into feeling''—T. S. Eliot embraces the paradox, seeing it as evidence of a unified ''sensibility'' (though in appropriately paradoxical fashion, he reverses himself in a later essay—''in Donne there is a manifest fissure between thought and sensibility'').

In an early essay, C. S. Lewis saw Donne's self-dividedness as a ''limitation''—''Donne's real limitation is not that he writes *about*, but that he writes *in*, a chaos of violent and transitory passions''—while Cleanth Brooks, writing at nearly the same time, saw Donne's paradoxes as the necessary language of poetry—''Donne's imagination seems obsessed with the problem of unity . . . that fusion is not logical; it apparently violates science and common sense; it welds together the discordant and the contradictory.'' This discordant and contradictory quality is, of course, the source of the notorious "difficulty" of Donne's poetry, which inspired Ben Jonson* to declare that "Donne himself for not being understood would perish." However, as Richard Halpern has observed, "Literary history has ironically reversed Ben Jonson's prediction. . . . For the difficulty of Donne and the other metaphysical poets was what attracted figures such as Cleanth Brooks and T. S. Eliot, who saw in Donne an important precursor of the modernist aesthetic."

More recently, however, a renewed emphasis on history and biography has sought the more unitary springs beneath the surface contradictions in Donne's poetry. For Carey, the surface tensions, contradictions, and paradoxes in the poetry are all manifestations of the single, profound dislocation originating in Donne's "apostasy." For Marotti, on the other hand, what unifies the apparently competing voices of Donne's poetry is the fact of a single, homogeneous audience of like-minded male friends. C. S. Lewis' question of "what any sensible woman would make of such a wooing" is rendered immaterial if one concedes that there was never any wooing going on, that the poetry was self-display, a rhetorical performance. In that case the paradoxes and contradictions cease to need defense or explanation, because it is no longer an issue of what position the speaker holds but how well the speaker can hold simultaneously competing and contradictory positions. We simply learn to appreciate the performance, presumably as the original audience did.

BIBLIOGRAPHY

Works by John Donne

The Elegies and the Songs and Sonnets. Ed. Helen Gardner. Oxford: Clarendon Press, 1965.

Paradoxes and Problems. Ed. Helen Peters. Oxford: Clarendon Press, 1980.

The Poems of John Donne. 2 vols. Ed. Herbert J. C. Grierson. Oxford: Clarendon Press, 1912.

The Satires, Epigrams and Verse Letters. Ed. W. Milgate. Oxford: Clarendon Press, 1967.

Studies of John Donne

Bald, R. C. *John Donne: A Life*. Oxford: Oxford University Press, 1970.

Carey, John. *John Donne: Life, Mind and Art*. Oxford: Oxford University Press, 1981.

Docherty, Thomas. *John Donne, Undone*. New York: Methuen, 1986.

Halpern, Richard. "The Lyric in the Field of Information: Autopoiesis and History in Donne's 'Songs and Sonnets.' " In *Critical Essays on John Donne*. Ed. Arthur Marotti. New York: G. W. Hall, 1994.

Leishman, J. B. *The Monarch of Wit*. London: 1951.

Marotti, Arthur. *John Donne: Coterie Poet*. Madison: University of Wisconsin Press, 1986.

———, ed. *Critical Essays on John Donne*. New York: G. W. Hall, 1994.

Summers, Claude, and Ted-Larry Pebworth, eds. *The Eagle and the Dove: Reassessing John Donne*. Columbia: University of Missouri Press, 1986.

DEREK ALWES

GAVIN DOUGLAS
(c. 1475–1522)

BIOGRAPHY

Gavin Douglas' life is more fully documented than any other poet's up to his time with the possible exception of Geoffrey Chaucer. In Chaucer's case, however, the records of the public career presumably follow the course of another, less documented one. Douglas' public life after 22 July 1513 completely overshadowed his life as poet. On that day, just three months before Flodden and its disastrous losses for the Scottish and for his immediate family, Douglas concluded his translation of Virgil's *Aeneid* and announced the end of his poetic career. The evidence suggests that he kept his promise to follow a more solitary muse: there is no poetry after this date. But the man who emerges from the extant poetry and the official records is nonetheless of a piece: he is worldly, intellectually up-to-date, and outspoken.

Gavin Douglas attended St. Andrews University, where he is listed as a *Determinantes* in 1493 and a *Licentiati* in 1494. He may have earned an advanced degree in either theology or law; the study of law was commonly associated with advancement in the church. The Cambridge manuscript of the *Eneados* mentions three church positions, two simultaneous: provost of the wealthy church of St. Giles' in Edinburgh *and* parson of Linton in East Lothian, after which he was bishop of Dunkeld. The earliest reference to a church appointment is on 28 January 1497, when Douglas, acting as witness to an indenture, is referred to as "dene of Dunkeldene." The documentation of Douglas' activities is primarily civic and, in the period before Flodden, included meetings of the Lords of Council in 1505 and 1509 and twice assisting the rector of St. Andrews University. Son of one earl of Angus and uncle to another, Douglas was variously active in Edinburgh on behalf of members of his large and powerful family.

Douglas' intellectual contacts included lively ties to Paris, though it is not certain that he actually studied there. John Major wrote that he enjoyed Douglas' friendship both in Scotland and in Paris. His Commentary on the first book of Peter Lombard's Sentences (29 April 1510) has attached to it a *Dialogue* between David Cranston and Gavin Douglas in which these two "*famatos viros magistrum*" converse on subjects they regard as "fitting to be treated by a theologian." The *Dialogue* casts Douglas as critical of scholastic philosophy, quoting Lorenzo Valla and expressing ideas current in humanist thought, especially in the teaching and writing of Erasmus* and Jacques Lefevre (Bawcutt, 27–30). His friends included the Italian Polydore Vergil,* author of *Historia Anglica*, and Robert Cockburn. Douglas' learning and his extensive contact with Italian humanism are undisputed (see Bawcutt).

After September 1513 and the death of James IV at Flodden Field, Douglas' activities were increasingly political. He was appointed one of the Lords of Council on 19 September 1513 and a month later "ordanit to remane daily with the quenys graice to gif hir consell in all materis concerning the wele of the realme." This proximity to the queen and to the regency was more firmly fixed less than a year later, when the widowed queen was married to Douglas' nephew, the sixth earl of Angus. Until his death in 1522, Douglas' life reflected not only the worldliness of the church in the late fifteenth and early sixteenth centuries but the bitter factional strife in Scotland.

The last years of his life included prison, a bitter trial, and exile. Letter exchanges between Douglas and powerful contemporaries suggest the political advantages and the perils of Douglas' position, recording at once mind-boggling schemes and bitter emotion. Thus, for example, Margaret, his most significant supporter and ally in the years immediately after Flodden, writes to her brother, Henry VIII, on 6 January 1522:

> I pray his Grace richt effectuoslie that he help not the said Dunkeld, considdering the gret evill that he has don to this Realm be his evill counsall, for he has bene the caus of all the dissention and trobill of this Realme, and has maid fals and evill raport of me baitht in Ingland and Scotland . . . and sen I helpit to get hyme the benefice of Dunkeld I sall help hyme to want the samyn.

On 21 February the Lords of Council decreed Douglas guilty of high treason, ordering that his Dunkeld estates be confiscated. The decree claimed that he had entered and stayed in England even after that country had declared war against Scotland. Though isolated pieces of the public record, including letters, have been used to portray a self-interested and litigious man, a more realistic reading suggests a man fully engaged, in a period of Scottish history when a person of obvious talent and boldness of opinion would surely offend someone. Gavin Douglas died in September 1522.

MAJOR WORKS AND THEMES

The *Eneados*, the translation of Virgil's *Aeneid* and a thirteenth book by Maffeo Vegio, completed on 22 July 1513, is Douglas' last and most significant literary achievement. In what is surely an elegant echo of Book V of the *Aeneid*, in which an aging boxer gives up his gloves—"Here, as champion, I lay aside my gauntlets and my art"—Douglas declares: "Thus vp my pen and instrumentis full zor / On Virgilis post I fix for evirmor." He asserts that the contemplative muse will hereafter be solitary, like the bird in the cage ("Conclusio," 1–17). Douglas' work, in addition to the *Eneados* and the innovative and various poetry that constitutes its framing material, includes "Conscience," a clever short poem that breaks down the syllables of its title to describe the degeneration of the clergy; the *Palice of Honour* (1501), an extended dream vision that explores the idea of honor; and *King Hart*. Though there has recently been some debate about the attribution to Gavin Douglas of this allegorical poem, C. S. Lewis, for one, singled it out, remarking that ''it is an admirably ordered little work'' (*Allegory of Love*, 287).

The prologues and epilogues of the *Eneados* include theoretical commentary that is highly deserving of critical attention. Douglas is outspoken, for example, about the ways in which his translation of the *Aeneid* into ''the language of Scottis natioun'' (Prologue I, 103) differs from the purported carelessness of earlier attempts, especially Caxton's* *Aeneas*. He is particularly contemptuous of Caxton's treatment of the Dido episode, pointing out that it occupies about half of Caxton's work to Virgil's one–twelfth. He charges Caxton with jumbling gods and geography (I, 159–62), clumsily ''huddling togetherr'' the final six books, and shamefully perverting the story (I, 145). Neither does Chaucer escape criticism. In words that call attention to the elegance of classical Latin and echo contemporary humanist discussions of language, he describes the challenges facing the translator from Latin. Chaucer, in describing Aeneas as a false traitor, misrepresents Virgil's aims and renders his twelve years of labors ''nocht worth a myte'' (424).

The poet's extended rhetorical tribute to ''my maister Chauser'' in the first prologue pales somewhat in the context of Douglas' loyalty to Virgil's text, a loyalty that places him in the forefront of Renaissance humanism and reminds us that he is, indeed, a contemporary of Erasmus,* Castiglione,* and Machiavelli.* His attention to the political implications of Virgil's epic, especially as embodied in Aeneas, is apparent in the translation, as well as in the framework of prologues and epilogues and other poetic commentary that accompanies it. The Cambridge manuscript includes an explanatory note, generally thought to be in Douglas' hand, that spells out the lines of family and power that motivate Virgil's praise of the Romans: ''Bot ye sall knaw that the principall entent of Virgill was to extoll the Romanys, and in specyal the famyllye or clan Julyan, that commin from this Ascanyus, son to Eneas and Crevsa, otherwais callyt Iulus: because the empryour August Octauyan, quhamto he direkkit this wark, was of that hows and blud, and sisyr son to Cesar Julyus.'' The parallels to the political situation in Scotland, to the factionalism never absent in Douglas' lifetime, are surely not far to seek: Aeneas portrays precisely the leadership that Scotland lacks. Gavin Douglas is the earliest of the Renaissance translators, like Barclay (c. 1520), John Brende (1553), and Sir Anthony Cope (1554), whose translations from the Latin either implicitly or explicitly urge a political example. By his own account he shared with them an interest in the wider reception of classical texts:

> Go, wlgar Virgill, to euery churlych wight
> Say, I avow thou art translatit rycht . . .
> Now salt thou with euery gentill Scot be kend,
> And to onletterrit folk be red on hight,
> That erst was bot with clerkis comprehend.

(Exclamatioun, 37ff.)

CRITICAL RECEPTION

The immediate success of Douglas' *Eneados* is suggested by the number of manuscripts from the first half of the sixteenth century that survive; of the six, five are complete. Now in the Library of Trinity College, Cambridge, the earliest of these (No. 1184 in M. R. James' Catalogue) was copied shortly after 1513 by Douglas' chaplain, Mathew Geddes. On the basis of variant readings in the extant manuscripts, J.A.W. Bennett suggests that there were intermediate texts and that we can assume that "at least ten copies of this long work (Douglas has two lines for each line of Virgil's) were made in less than forty years" (Bennett, 84). Copland's Black Letter Quarto of 1553 was the first printed edition of Douglas' *Eneados.* Thomas Ruddiman's 1710 edition of *The Threttene Bukes of Eneados* is surprising considering the Jacobite sympathies of Ruddiman and his circle; Dearing avers that they "managed to overlook Gavin Douglas' somewhat unsavory intrigues for ecclesiastical preferment as a protege of Henry VIII," and he suggests that these intrigues "evidently alienated many of his nineteenth-century critics" (848).

The "entirely curious history of Gavin Douglas' literary reputation" was the impetus of Bruce Dearing's "reinterpretation" of the *Eneados* in his 1952 *PMLA* essay. He pointed out "that most scholars seem to have been content to accept G. Gregory Smith's disparagement in *Cambridge History of English Literature* of Gavin Douglas as the 'last and the least' of the poets of one of Scotland's golden ages." Dearing stressed the importance of avoiding "some of the biases, patriotic, sentimental, philological, and biographical," that have rendered invalid most criticism of the *Eneados* and observed that "as poet and as politician Douglas was steadfastly on the side that advocated peace with England and the suppression of the turbulent noblemen at home" (Dearing, 846, 849, 861). The bias Dearing observed is indeed part of the critical legacy. Thus, C. S. Lewis remarked that the "problem" of the *Palice of Honour,* " 'Where does true Honour lie?' was one that probably had more than literary interest for the poet; and if his own political career after Flodden does not suggest that he solved it very well in practice, we need not thence assume that he did not ask it in good faith" (*English Literature in the Sixteenth Century, excluding Drama* 77). C. S. Lewis, however, elsewhere admired *King Hart* and the *Palice of Honour* for their "artistic control," "disciplined splendour of style," and "proportion and balance," qualities, Lewis added, in which the Scottish writers often excel the English (*Allegory of Love*, 287).

The bias that Dearing mentions still pertains in 1964, when David Coldwell's edition of Douglas' *Aeneid* asserts that Douglas' "life as a poet ended in 1513, not so much perhaps because his time was filled with activities and occupations, or because he chose to resign poetry to younger emotions, as because his poetic philosophy was deliberately repressed in favour of a career he could not intellectually defend." Coldwell describes Douglas' *Aeneid* as "an affirmation of the political convictions of the Renaissance," but he sees Douglas' life as proclaiming "the aristocratic right to be selfish" and asserts he was "acquiescent to the advantages of the hour" (Coldwell, *Virgil's Aeneid*, 37–38). Recent studies (see especially Bawcutt) pave the way for a more canny appreciation of historical context and the particular mix of poet, politician, and churchman that Douglas brings to the sixteenth-century Scottish court.

BIBLIOGRAPHY

Works by Gavin Douglas

The Poetical Works of Gavin Douglas. 4 vols. Ed. John Small. Edinburgh, 1874.

Virgil's Aeneid Translated into Scottish Verse by Gavin Douglas. 4 vols. Ed. D.F.C. Coldwell. Edinburgh: William Blackwood and Sons, 1964.

The Shorter Poems of Gavin Douglas. Ed. Priscilla J. Bawcutt. Edinburgh: William Blackwood and Sons, 1967.

Studies of Gavin Douglas

Bawcutt, Priscilla. *Gavin Douglas: A Critical Study*. Edinburgh: Edinburgh University Press, 1976.

Bennett, J.A.W. "The Early Fame of Gavin Douglas's *Eneados*." *Modern Language Notes* 61 (1946): 83–88.

Dearing, Bruce. "Gavin Douglas' *Eneados*: A Reinterpretation." *PMLA* 67 (1952): 845–62.

Hager, Alan. "British Virgil: Four Renaissance Disguises of the Laocöon passage of Book 2 of the *Aeneid*." *Studies in English Literature* 22.1 (1982): 21–38.

Lewis, C. S. *The Allegory of Love: A Study in Medieval Tradition*. Oxford: Oxford University Press, 1958.

Ridley, Florence H. "Did Gawin Douglas Write *King Hart?*" *Speculum* 34 (1959): 402–12.

Note: The editor has chosen to add the following works to the bibliography. Their absence was not an oversight on the author's part:

Pound, Ezra. *ABC of Reading*. New York: New Directions, c. 1951.

———. *Literary Essays*. New York: New Directions, c. 1954.

MICHAELA PAASCHE GRUDIN

JOHN DOWLAND
(c. 1563–1626)

BIOGRAPHY

John Dowland, composer and lutenist, was one of the most highly regarded and widely traveled musicians of his time. He was probably born in London, and comments in his works place his birth around 1563. Nothing is known of his early life and education. In 1580, Dowland traveled to Paris in the retinue of the queen's ambassador, where he came in contact with currents of musical thought and practice sweeping across Europe. He also converted to the Catholic faith, a decision that would have a pronounced effect upon his career.

Dowland returned to England in 1584 and received the B.Mus. degree from

Christ Church College, Oxford, in 1588. In 1590 some of his compositions to lyrics by his patron, Sir Henry Lee, were performed at court. In 1592, he performed on the lute before the queen at Sudeley Castle. Dowland seems to have married during this period, but nothing has been discovered about his wife. He also broke into print; harmonizations of six psalm tunes bearing his name appear in Thomas East's *The Whole Booke of Psalmes* (1592).

Dowland had his heart set on a court appointment. When one of the queen's lutenists died in 1594, he applied for the position. Despite powerful patronage, however, he was rejected. Convinced he had been refused on the basis of his Catholicism, he determined to go abroad.

Dowland's travels took him through Holland and Germany to various courts, where he was warmly welcomed. At some point he decided to travel to Rome to meet Luca Marenzio, but he was in no hurry, for his journey took him to Venice, Padua, Genoa, Ferrara, and finally Florence, where he took up with a group of exiled English Catholics. When Dowland discovered the group was planning to assassinate the queen, he panicked and fled to Nuremberg, where he wrote to Robert Cecil describing the plot and protesting his innocence.

Dowland spent the next year with the Landgrave of Hesse, at the end of which time a patron, Henry Noel, persuaded him to return home. By the time Dowland finally arrived in England, however, his patron had died, and Dowland again found himself unable to obtain a court position. He utilized his time, however, by compiling a collection of twenty-one songs, published in 1597 as *The First Booke of Songes or Ayres* and presented in a format to be sung either by four singers or by solo voice and lute. Dowland's volume was the first printed book of English lute songs, and it spurred a new fashion. Despite the competition, moreover, Dowland's publication remained a favorite, being reprinted at least five times over the next sixteen years. Dowland's double format was a shrewd concession to the fad of singing madrigals, but careful scrutiny of his textual underlay demonstrates that the solo format was the one he favored. Dowland announced himself on the title page as "Bacheler of Musick in both the Universities," the only surviving indication of his connection to Cambridge.

Again Dowland sought foreign employment, and in 1598 he began service as lutenist at the court of Christian IV of Denmark, who enjoyed Dowland's talents and treated him with marked generosity. Intent upon keeping his works before the English public, Dowland sent the manuscript of a second book of songs to his wife for publication. It appeared in 1600 in a run of 1,000 copies, a figure providing some measure of Dowland's popularity. A third volume of songs appeared in 1603.

In 1603 Dowland returned to England "on his own commitments." During his protracted stay he supervised the publication of *Lachrimae or Seaven Teares* (1604), his most important volume of instrumental music, which presented the English public for the first time with music specifically written for five viols and lute. The prefatory material discloses that his family had moved to Fetter Lane in London and that he had been in contact with Queen Anne, his employer's sister, to whom *Lachrimae* was dedicated. No appointment, however, was forthcoming. Dowland had returned to Denmark by July 1605, but from that point there is a record of perpetual indebtedness. In 1606, he was dismissed.

Virtually nothing is known of Dowland's personal life in the period immediately following. In 1609 he published a translation of a musicological treatise, disclosing in the preface that he was still living in Fetter Lane; and he may about that time have entered the service of Theophilus Howard, Lord Walden (a son of the king's Lord Chamberlain). Throughout the period, he appears to have been sensitive to every perceived slight and to have considered himself wholly neglected and scorned. "Heere, *Philomel*, in silence sits alone,/In depth of winter, on the bared brier," Henry Peacham wrote of his friend in 1611, showing he shared the same opinion. The view had justification. Tobias Hume, for one, had cast doubts upon Dowland's talent, suggesting he could not compose in a "modern" manner, and interest in the lute song was fading.

Such challenges, however, provoked Dowland to greater effort, and from 1609 to 1612 he is connected with three additional publications. In 1610 came two excellent anthologies of works by English and Continental composers, *A Musicall Banquet* and *Varietie of Lute-Lessons*. Dowland's son Robert appears as editor on the title pages, but many critics assign the volumes to Dowland himself. He certainly played a significant role in their publication, for he contributed excellent work to both collections, most notably "In darkness let me dwell," one of the finest songs in the English language. Then in 1612 Dowland published his fourth book of songs, *A Pilgrimes Solace*, where his bitterness appears in the dedication to Lord Walden as "the onely and alone Supporter of goodnes and excellencie." The presence of pieces by Caccini in *A Musicall Banquet* and of compositions such as "Go nightly, cares," "Lasso vita mia," and "From silent night" in this collection show Dowland responding to Hume's jibes and demonstrating his knowledge and command of the "modern" manner.

In 1612, Dowland finally achieved his cherished ambition, receiving an appointment as lutenist to the King James.* The appointment led, ironically, to a virtual cessation of creative activity. Dowland had been slowing down, in fact, for some time. Little of his solo music for lute dates from after 1600, and few compositions can be assigned to his later years. He continued, however, to appear before the public through commendatory poems before the works of friends, such as Sir William Leighton and Thomas Ravenscroft. In 1621 he signed a harmonization of Psalm 100 in Ravenscroft's *Whole Booke of Psalmes* as "Dr." John Dowland. Documents from the court confirm that one of the universities had granted him the degree, but all other record is lost.

Dowland's last documented activity is of performance during the funeral ceremonies for King James I, in May 1625. On 20 February 1626 Dowland was buried at St. Anne, Blackfriars. Robert received the final payment for his services and succeeded his father as court lutenist.

MAJOR WORKS AND THEMES

Dowland's achievement is brilliant, if limited in compass. He is unusual among the composers of his generation, in fact, in offering neither church music nor madrigals nor music for the keyboard among his compositions. Instead, Dowland concentrated upon instrumental work for consort and the lute and upon the accompanied song.

In the realm of song, Dowland is one of the supreme composers in the English tradition, with a range, subtlety, and power of expression exceeding those of all of his contemporaries. He became acquainted with the Continental tradition of the accompanied song as a young man in France, a medium that had, at best, a limited vogue in England, and much has been made of French influences upon his work. In truth, however, Dowland's songs display a unique blend of foreign and native influences. There are distinct developments within the four books of songs, but in general Dowland kept to the tradition of the contrapuntal accompanied song. Each volume, moreover, contains songs of enduring value, among the most famous, "Come away, come sweet love," "Sleep, wayward thoughts," "Come heavy sleep," "I saw my Lady weep," "Sorrow, sorrow stay," "Fine knacks for Ladies," "Flow not so fast ye fountains," "What if I never speed," and "Weep you no more sad fountains."

Dowland fashioned for himself within his corpus, moreover, a distinctive personality—that of a deeply melancholic spirit. Such an image was something of a literary affectation, but it reflected a dominant strain within his personality. Dowland insisted, moreover, upon his melancholy from an early stage, in such pieces as the "Melancholy Galliard" and the early "Lachrimae," his signature composition. In 1596, he signed himself "Infoelice Inglese"; "Unquiet thoughts" is the first composition in the *First Booke of Songs*; melancholy likewise dominates the opening sequences of the second and third books of airs; and the eighth composition within the *Lachrimae*, following seven variations upon "tears," is entitled "Semper Dowland semper Dolens" (Ever Dowland, ever doleful).

Too much, however, can be made of the melancholy. For one thing, Dowland was the greatest lutenist of his age, and his compositions for lute present a far more buoyant personality in their many lively tunes, compositions lending support to Thomas Fuller's depiction of Dowland as a "cheerful person . . . passing his days in lawful merriment."

Dowland composed in each of the chief instrumental forms for his instrument, and he wrote memorably in them all. His greatest and most original composition is the *Lachrimae*, or "seaven teares," a brilliant set of variations upon his personal theme. Each of the famous pavans begins with a statement of the theme in one of the voices, then develops an independent set of themes (also shared from composition to composition), the entire set gaining exceptional cumulative power from the dense interweaving of themes and textures. Here and here alone Dowland matches Byrd* at his best in intensity and structural sophistication.

CRITICAL RECEPTION

Dowland enjoyed an exceptional reputation both in England and on the Continent, where his solo compositions are found in virtually every significant collection of music for the instrument. As early as the 1590s, Thomas Campion and Richard Barnfield both pay tribute to his abilities, and references to his works appear regularly in dramatic works throughout the early seventeenth century. Dowland's reputation, moreover, outlasted that of most of his contemporaries: Fuller praised him in 1662 as "the *rarest Musician* that his age did behold," and Dowland's songs were still found in London bookstores in the 1680s.

Thereafter, Dowland's reputation took a dive. Charles Burney scorned Dowland's "scanty abilities in counterpoint." Awareness of his music grew with the renewed interest in early music, but even in 1929 Edmund Fellowes wrote that "apart from singers, a large section of the English musical world still remains in complete ignorance as to the value of his work." The reappearance of gifted lutenists, coupled to the publication in modern editions of both his songs and his works for lute, much of which had remained in manuscript, has restored Dowland to fame. He is now universally recognized as one of England's supremely gifted writers of songs and one of the most brilliant instrumentalists in musical history.

BIBLIOGRAPHY

Works by John Dowland

Andreas Ornithoparcus his Micrologus. Trans. Dowland. London, 1609.

Ayres for Four Voices. Ed. Thurston Dart and Nigel Fortune. Musica Britannica, vi. 1955; rev., 1963.

The Collected Lute Music of John Dowland. Ed. Diana Poulton and Basil Lam. London, 1974.

The Firste Booke of Songes. London, 1597; rpt. 1600, 1603, 1606, 1608, 1613; ed. E. H. Fellowes. 1920; rev. Thurston Dart, London, 1965.

Lachrimae or Seaven Teares. London, 1604. Ed. Peter Warlock. London, 1927.

"Other Necessary Obseruations." In *Varietie of Lute-Lessons*, ed. Robert Dowland. London, 1610.

A Pilgrimes Solace. London, 1612; ed. E. H. Fellowes. 1924; rev. Thurston Dart, London, 1969.

The Second Booke of Songs. London, 1600; ed. E. H. Fellowes 1922; rev. Thurston Dart, London, 1969.

The Third and Last Booke of Songs. London, 1603; ed. E. H. Fellowes. 1923; rev. Thurston Dart, London, 1970.

Studies of John Dowland

Davis, Walter R. "Melodic and Poetic Structure: The Examples of Campion and Dowland." *Criticism* 4 (1962): 89–107.

Fellowes, Edmund H. "The Songs of Dowland." *Proceedings of the Musical Association* 56 (1929–30): 1–26.
Leech-Wilkinson, Daniel. "My Lady's Tears: A Pair of Songs by John Dowland." *Early Music* 19 (1991): 227–33.
Pattison, Bruce. *Music and Poetry of the English Renaissance*. 2d ed. London: Methuen, 1970.
Pilkington, Michael. *Campion, Dowland, and the Lutenist Songwriters*. Bloomington: Indiana University Press, 1989.
Poulton, Diana. *John Dowland*. 2d ed. Berkeley: University of California Press, 1982.
Rooley, Anthony. "New Light on John Dowland's Songs of Darkness." *Early Music* 11 (1983): 6–21.
Sparr, Kenneth. "Some Unobserved Information about John Dowland, Thomas Campion, and Philip Rosseter." *The Lute* 27 (1987): 35–37.
Spink, Ian. *English Song: Dowland to Purcell*. Rev. ed. London: B. T. Batsford, 1984.
Toft, Robert. "Musicke a Sister to Poetrie: Rhetorical Artifice in the Passionate Airs of John Dowland." *Early Music* 12 (1984): 191–99.
Wells, Robin Headlam. "John Dowland and Elizabethan Melancholy." *Early Music* 13 (1985): 514–28.
———. "The Ladder of Love: Verbal and Musical Rhetoric in the Elizabethan Lute-Song." *Early Music* 12 (1984): 173–89.
Wulstan, David. *Tudor Music*. Iowa City: University of Iowa Press, 1986.

CLAYTON D. LEIN

WILLIAM DUNBAR
(c. 1460–c. 1514)

BIOGRAPHY

Much has been written about Dunbar's life, largely on evidence from his poems, but most is conjectural. *The Flyting of Dunbar and Kennedie* contains references to an eclipse that justifies the date of birth and to wide travel that indicates Dunbar may have been in the king's service, analogous to Chaucer's role abroad as messenger. *How Dumbar wes Desyrd to be Ane Freir* has led to a case that Dunbar was a Franciscan who preached in England. *Dunbar at Oxinfurde* suggests residence, if not study there. It is likely that the "William Dunbar" who took a bachelor of arts degree at St. Andrews in 1477 and a master of arts in 1479 is the poet. The poems reveal a man not so learned as Henryson* but well read and knowledgeable about vernacular poetry. This included Highland Gaelic traditions, but Dunbar favored French and English, especially "The noble Chaucer, of makaris flour." Biographical evidence is solid for Dunbar's service to King James IV: in 1500 he received an annual "pension" of ten pounds for life; subsequent records show increases and gifts of clothing, with a last note of the pension on 14 May 1513, followed by a gap in the record; Dunbar likely died about 1514. Some have conjectured that he fought at the Battle of Flodden (September 1513), a disastrous defeat of the Scots by the English. Dunbar's poems are often connected with the king. A poem *To the City of London* was written on the occasion of an embassy to arrange the marriage of James IV (1488–1513) and Margaret Tudor; Dunbar may have been the "Rhymer of Scotland" who received a gift from Henry VII. Some of his most beautiful lyrics honor this Englishwoman who became Scotland's queen. James IV's offering for the first mass of Dunbar, March 1503, confirms that the poet was in orders. Many poems of "petition" indicate little success in securing preferment. Those named and the topicality of Dunbar's poems suggest that his audience is the Scots court.

MAJOR WORKS AND THEMES

The more than eighty poems attributed to Dunbar show a remarkable variety of interests. A modern editor (Mackenzie) has arranged them in nine categories that are used by the standard reference work (Ridley). The topics and numbers in each section suggest the scope of Dunbar's themes: Personal (10), Petitions (15), Court Life (16), Town Life (3), Women (8), Allegories and Addresses (13), Moralisings (12), Religious (7), Some Attributions (9). Since a chronology has not been easy to establish, a noting of ideas is a helpful way to approach Dunbar, even though many of the poems could as easily be placed in several sections. The Bannatyne Manuscript has a five-part scheme: devotional, moral, witty and humorous, erotic and countererotic, narrative. One point is immediately apparent: Dunbar is a lyric poet. This is unusual for the time he was writing, as a comparison with Henryson, who was essentially a storyteller and moralizer, makes clear. Dunbar's choice of poetic form links him to the achievement of the sixteenth century as an age of lyric. His "I" occurs more frequently than in medieval lyrics, and an intensity of sentiments gives an immediacy and suggests a persona that provokes autobiographical interpretation of one who was an ecclesiastic and part of a court circle.

The range of themes in Dunbar's "ballats" demands many voices, which are not easy to evaluate, so that the surest initial approach is to note the variety of subject and treatment, beginning with the court, which was more central than the city, while the country does not appear. Several lyrics are directed to James IV. *A New Year's Gift to the King* is a conventional but very elegant address: "My Prince, in God gif the guid grace," joy, comfort, prudent and generous governance, virtue, play, many French crowns (the common coinage), and so on. The five stanzas are linked both by a refrain about the gift of a good New Year and by reiteration of prayerful "God gif" in the first line of four of the stanzas, as well as alliteration in such lines as "Fair fortoun and felicitie." This confident and gentle attitude appears in *Aganis the Solistaris in Court*, which identifies those seeking gains at court and casts the poet as humble, content with the wealth of seeing the king's countenance.

Sharply contrasted to these sentiments are several petitions in which Dunbar seeks patronage and resents being ignored. Three poems—*Of Discretioun In*

Asking, In Geving, and *In Taking*—present abuses of privilege, discrepancies between worth and reward, in somewhat restrained tones. In contrast, *Remonstance to the King* attacks the parasites whom the king rewards while he is denied. The poet cries ''Fy!'' and threatens that unless he is soon rewarded, ''with my pen I man we wreik'' and ''lat the vennim ische all out.'' There is a profusion of this substance. Dunbar's daring is not limited to petitioning. *The Wowing of the King Quhen He Was in Dunfermline* is a beast fable usually glossed as a comment on James IV's amorous indulgences and includes obscenity in its sexual description; *To the Quene* describes the prevalence of veneral disease at court, albeit concluding with a warning against behavior that results in the ''pockis.''

An entirely different poetic manner characterizes *The Thrissil and the Rois*, which is an aureate allegory, written to mark the marriage of James IV and Margaret Tudor. Here rich descriptions of spring, a garden of flowers, gathering of birds and beasts, heraldic imagery, dream vision, figures of May and Nature—all commonplaces of medieval convention—recall *The Roman de la Rose*, Chaucer (''Quhen Merche wes with variand windis past, / And Appryll had, with his silver schouris''), and countless imitators. The argument is for the king's faithfulness to the Rose, Queen Margaret, to whom Dunbar's poems show genuine devotion. *To Aberdeen* describes her visit to the city and welcome by the burgesses, a magnificent procession of scenes combining biblical events with Scots history, tapestry-bedecked streets, lively music, playing of pageants, a shout of ''Welcum, our Quein!'' from the commons, free-flowing wine, the gift of a cup of gold. This poem is notable for its evocation of the city—a positive image that contrasts with the negative representation in *To the Merchantis of Edinburgh*. Through precise description conventional praise becomes memorable, offering a companion to the courtly qualities of *The Thrissil and the Rois* or *The Golden Targe*.

The latter is another compendium of courtly commonplaces in which echoes of Chaucer, Douglas*, Henryson, *The King's Quhair*, as well as *The Roman de la Rose*, have been suggested. The theme is the experience of the poet, and the form is a dream vision in which he meets Nature, Venus and her cohorts, and an ineffective Reason so that he wakens in fright at the sound of guns as the company sails away. Most interesting is Dunbar's noting of literary tradition. The last three stanzas are apostrophes: first, ''O reverend Chaucere, rose of rhetoris all, / As in our tong ane flour imperiall,'' then ''O morall Gower, and Ludgate laureate, / Your sugurit lippis and tongis aureate, / Bene to our eris cause of grete delyte;'' and finally his own ''lytill Quhair, be evir obedient, / Humble, subject, and symple of entent.'' Dunbar identifies and effectively imitates the aureate style, acknowledging its significance in the development of English poetry, but he also shows the way to an alternative, simple style: ''Rude is thy wede, disteynit, bare, and rent'' that restores unencumbered language and appears in a poet like Wyatt.* Another example of change comes with the satiric humor deployed in *Of Sir Thomas Norny*, which resembles Chaucer's parody of romance in *Sir Thopas* but also includes scatological detail and finishes with the renowned knight needing only the fool's bells. Such breaking down of the old form makes clear why chivalric romance is an antiquarian interest in Spenser's* *The Faerie Queene.*

Dunbar's seeking of a poetic voice is seldom more distinctive than in his imitation of an earlier form of verbal combat in the *Flyting of Dunbar and Kennedie*, an aggressive argument that has many antecedents from Ovid, through French, Italian, Anglo-Saxon, Celtic, and Scandinavian. Highland traditions and close ties with Norway suggest the cogency of the last two. The poem is written in irregular iambic pentameter, and its sixty-nine stanzas are divided into speeches—*Quod Dumbar to Kennedy* and *Quod Kennedy to Dumbar*—of varying length but unchanging abuse. Kennedy is a poet, but the theme is less literary qualities than comprehensive denunciation of each's lineage, physical appearance, intelligence, morality, beliefs, and behavior. The language is scurrilous and obscene, always vigorous, often made resonant through alliteration—"Turk, trumpour, traitour, tyran intemperate; . . . Devill, dampnit dog." Such lines give the lie to Dunbar's early disclaimer—"Flyting to use richt gritly I eschame"—or they force recognition of his self-mockery. Skelton* is a subsequent writer of such scoldings.

The 552 lines of *Flyting* are almost the same number as the 530 of *The Tretis of the Tua Mariit Wemen and the Wedo.* These are the longest of Dunbar's poems but keep a feeling of lyric because they are presented as lively dialogue. *The Tretis* is mostly the arguments of three women who, on Midsummer's Eve, denounce men and urge their own self-indulgence. Their often crude language and sentiments are set in aureate descriptions, another example of Dunbar's changing tones. The poem's theme is similarly open to debate, whether conventional antifeminism indebted to La Vielle and the Wife of Bath, or protofeminism of survival, final exploitation of men, and a case for female sexuality. Dunbar acknowledges the conventions with a débat conclusion: "auditoris most honorable," which would you choose for wife?

Nevertheless, some of Dunbar's finest lyrics are serious treatments of well-established medieval themes that do not pose questions. *I that in heill wes* (Lament for the Makaris) is notable for its references to writers, but it is also a brilliant Dance of Death, punctuated by the refrain "Timor mortis conturbat me," taken from the Office of the Dead. Such somber statements about the transcience of earthly life are balanced by the brilliance of *On the Resurrection of Christ*, which has as refrain "Surrexit Dominus de sepulchro," from Easter matins and begins "Done is a battell on the dragon blak, / Our campioun Chryst confountet hes his force." The exultation is palpable in a powerful deployment of the imagery of bestiary and warrior to proclaim salvation. It follows from the agony painfully detailed in *Of the Passioun of Christ*, which is a late medieval confrontation with the sufferings of Christ as man that were relentlessly presented in visual art and enacted in plays, a popular entertainment that Dunbar refers to in other poems. *The Dance of the sevin deidly Synnis* is a gloss for pageants in Marlowe* and Spenser.

CRITICAL RECEPTION

Dunbar's many petitions for tangible support suggest a rather slow acceptance, and the survival of a fragment from one edition by Chepman and Myllar in 1508 adds to this impression. The poems survive in three sixteenth-century manuscript collections (National Library of Scotland Acc. 4233 [Asloan], Nat Libr Scot 1.16 [Bannatyne], and Magdalen College Cambridge 2553 [Pepys Library Maitland Folio], respectively, almost contemporary with the poet, 1568 and 1570–86) and a copy of the last in 1623. Early readers knew Dunbar through circulation of manuscripts, which is how Dunbar knew Chaucer. David Lindsay* noted a significant career by 1530. Poems appear in several early collections of Scots poetry, David Laing published the first collected edition in the early nineteenth century, and at the end of the century there were editions in Vienna and by the Scottish Text Society. In the twentieth century Dunbar's work has been edited, richly discussed, and widely praised.

His lyric vigor and characteristic satirical incisiveness make him appealing to modern readers less at ease with the impersonal detachment of the Middle Ages. Incisive social commentary, especially that exploring tensions between opposing values (secular clergy and friars, gender, high and low style), make him relevant to modern interests, as is the art of his contemporary Hieronymous Bosch. The many lyrics that are medieval in their interests and attitude, often thoroughly traditional, are usually less highly praised or apologized for as outbursts of the piety of old age. It is more accurate to focus on contrasts, tensions, to see that much of Dunbar's importance is that he illustrates the process of transformation of older materials through addition of a sense of an individual who records his responses, typically comic, often indignant and derisive, frequently eschatological, but sometimes conventionally praising and pious. Moreover, his extraordinary technical accomplishment—a variety of lines and stanza forms, alliteration, refrains, macaronic verse, and a Scots language that is often difficult, very colloquial, but flexible—shows a poet who moves easily from aureate to popular styles and constantly proves his commitment to being a ''makar,'' a craftsman.

BIBLIOGRAPHY

Works by William Dunbar

The Poems of William Dunbar. 2 vols. Ed. David Laing. Edinburgh: Laing and Forbes, 1834.

The Poems of William Dunbar. 3 vols. Ed. John Small et al. Edinburgh: S.T.S., 1884–93.

The Poems of William Dunbar. Ed. W. Mackay Mackenzie. London: Faber and Faber, 1932; rpt. 1950.

The Poems of William Dunbar. Ed. James Kinsley. Oxford: Clarendon Press, 1979.

Studies of William Dunbar

Bawcutt, Priscilla. *Dunbar the Makar*. Oxford: Clarendon Press, 1992.

———. ''William Dunbar and Gavin Douglas.'' In *The History of Scottish Literature*, ed. R.D.J. Jack. Vol. 1. Aberdeen: Aberdeen University Press, 1988, 73–89.

Fox, Denton. ''The Scottish Chaucerians.'' In *Chaucer and the Chaucerians*, ed. D. S. Brewer. London: Thomas Nelson and Sons, 1966, 164–200.

Reiss, Edmund. *William Dunbar*. Boston: Twayne, 1979.

Ross, Ian. *William Dunbar*. Leiden: E. J. Brill, 1981.

Scott, Tom. *Dunbar: A Critical Exposition of the Poems*. Edinburgh: Oliver and Boyd, 1966.

VELMA BOURGEOIS RICHMOND

SIR EDWARD DYER
(1543–1607)

BIOGRAPHY

Edward Dyer was born sometime in October 1543, in the manor of Weston, Somerset. His father, Thomas Dyer, having risen as a ''gentleman steward'' in Henry VIII's household and gaining estates in Somerset after the dissolution of the monasteries, named his first son and heir in honor of Prince Edward. It is important to remember what this fact says about Dyer's age, for Dyer—perhaps the most talented English poet between Surrey* and Spenser*—would forge a living link between the era of *Tottel's Miscellany* (1557) and the generation of poets responsible for the golden verse of the 1580s and 1590s. Dyer studied at Oxford (probably at Broadgates Hall) without taking a degree and after 1561 traveled on the Continent, returning to England in 1564 upon his father's death. He soon became a courtier in the service of Robert Dudley, earl of Leicester, and by 1570 had so risen in Elizabeth's eyes that he was granted the stewardship of Woodstock. During the next few years, however, he fell into disfavor with the queen, and in a letter of 1572 giving advice to Christopher Hatton he paints a moving portrait of what it was to be a courtier under that most peevish of monarchs. In September 1575, still lacking Elizabeth's* good graces, Dyer engineered an encounter with the queen during the celebrated entertainments at Woodstock; perched in an oak with an instrument, Dyer sang a trenchant complaint, since titled ''The Song in the Oak'' (''The man whose thoughts against him do conspire''). Successful in restoring him to Elizabeth's favor, this incident suggests a hopeful, risk-taking aspect of Dyer's character and would be only the first of many schemes through which Dyer would seek the wherewithal—real and symbolic alike—necessary to sustain the life of an Elizabethan courtier. In the next decade Dyer would be a frequent guest at Leicester House, solidifying friendships with Philip Sidney,* Fulke Greville,* and Edmund Spenser, writers whose literary creations often advanced the Protestant politics of the Leicester faction. Spenser and Gabriel Harvey* would refer (perhaps only half-seriously) to this literary circle as the ''Areopagus,'' after the Athenian council of elders. As the oldest by a decade, Dyer must have had something like a senior and leading voice in this group. He may appear, in fact, as ''Cuddie'' in Spenser's *The Shepheardes Calendar* (1579) and as ''Coridens'' in the manuscript of Sidney's *Arcadia*. These names have struck some scholars as, respectively, abbreviations and anagrams of various forms of ''Cousin Dier.''

Dyer joined Sidney and Spenser in experimenting with quantitative, rhymeless verse in English—precisely the kind of failed speculative endeavor in poetry that later marked Dyer's financial affairs. Indeed, during this period in the later 1570s Dyer began his feverish promotion of Martin Frobisher's expeditions to find a Northwest Passage. After it became clear to him that this scheme would not produce the wealth he needed to meet his mounting debts, Dyer pleaded with Burghley and the queen to grant him a patent of ''concealment,'' that is, the right to search out illegitimate and lapsed titles to land of which, after paying the Crown a certain sum, he would assume ownership. After extensive pleading, Dyer was granted this right in 1588, though with disappointingly limited scope. Like all the schemes Dyer subscribed to, this one repaid neither the labor nor hope he invested in it. Then Dyer came, with many others, under the spell of Edward Kelley, the alchemical confidence-man associated with John Dee.* For some years Kelley had tantalized various European leaders with his promises of converting base matter to gold. Journeying as government agent to woo Kelley from the court of Rudolph II in Prague, Dyer ironically experienced a form of success when, after being placed under house arrest by that monarch, Elizabeth quickly interceded on his behalf; failing to bring home Kelley—whom neither Dyer, Burghley, nor Elizabeth apparently suspected of charlatanism—Dyer simultaneously escaped future embarrassment, displayed his dedication to Elizabeth, and earned a show of her concern.

Yet this trip to the Continent had not been Dyer's first serious travel. A youthful tour had given him a familiarity with the Continent that stood him in good stead during diplomatic missions not only to Bohemia but to the prince of Orange, the court of Denmark, and throughout the Low Countries. Dyer also served as knight of the shire for Somerset in the Parliaments of 1589 and 1593 and, in 1596, saw nominal reward for his longtime allegiance by being knighted and made chancellor of the Order of the Garter.

With the passing of Elizabeth, Dyer's standing at court dissolved. He died in London in 1607 at the age of sixty-four, having lived under five English monarchs and having associated with the most preeminent writers and nobles of the Elizabethan era. His death went unnoticed. Dyer never married, and what little remained of his estate after his debts were settled was left to his sister Margaret; one of his brother's descendants would later complain to John Aubrey that Dyer had squandered the family fortune.

MAJOR WORKS AND THEMES

Although Dyer published none of his verse, many of his poems appeared in such miscellanies as *The Phoenix Nest* (1593), *England's Helicon* (1600), and *A Poetical Rhapsody* (1602). While we now believe only a dozen poems can be safely assumed his, nearly as many more were associated with his name during and after his lifetime. A later, spurious attribution to his pen was the prose pamphlet *The Praise of Nothing* by "E. D." (1585), ascribed to him in the nineteenth century, perhaps the high tide of attribution of works to him. Following Ralph Sargent's critical biography in 1935, however, the corpus of Dyer's works has steadily contracted. Steven May publishes definitive versions of Dyer's poems in *The Elizabethan Courtier Poets*. One poem that May doubts is Dyer's is "My Mind to Me a Kingdom Is," a lyric that enjoyed immense popularity during the early modern era as well as later. May demonstrates that it is more likely that this poem was written by the earl of Oxford. One could add to May's already convincing argument the observation made by Paul McLane that the sentiments of this lyric run counter to Dyer's philosophy in other poems. Among Dyer's best poems are "I would it were not as it is," "Prometheus when first from heaven high," "The lowest trees have tops," and "Bewailing his exile he singeth thus" ("He that his mirth hath lost"), an elegy widely imitated and responded to (by Greville,* Robert Southwell,* and King James,* among others). A poet's poet, Dyer's works were almost invariably couched as complaint; woeful and bittersweet, they resemble the efforts of Ralegh* and Greville, though lacking the sharp cynicism of the former and the cool profundity of the latter. Dyer's favorite subject is his own mindset, and he sees the world through its melancholic filter. Sargent points out that all Dyer's verse reads as easily today as it must have in his own time, so clear and direct was his diction. Dyer's persistent use of native English words, in fact, may have influenced Spenser's poetic vocabulary—although the effect is entirely different.

CRITICAL RECEPTION

Dyer was lauded by all who knew his verse—especially in the 1580s, when his poems enjoyed greatest attention from his younger contemporaries. As late as the second half of the 1590s, however, a verse-loving admirer at Cambridge would record Dyer's "Fancy Farewell" in the company of like extracts from Shakespeare's* *Venus and Adonis* and Sidney's *Astrophil and Stella*. Besides Sidney, Spenser, and Harvey,* writers like Thomas Nashe,* Geoffrey Whitney, George Puttenham,* and Francis Meres praised Dyer's works, the last two his skill in elegy. Lacking a collection of his poems, however, writers in the next generation such as Edmund Bolton and William Drummond would be forced to confess that they had seen little of his work. Since Dyer's lifetime, his poems have been mentioned primarily in studies of Sidney and Spenser.

BIBLIOGRAPHY

Works by Sir Edward Dyer

May, Steven W. *The Elizabethan Courtier Poets: The Poems and Their Contexts.* Columbia: University of Missouri, 1991, 287–316. (Careful reediting of poems.)

Sargent, Ralph M. *The Life and Lyrics of Sir Edward Dyer.* Oxford, 1968; formerly titled *At the Court of Queen Elizabeth,* 1935, 24–26, 83, 86–87. (Selected letters.)

Studies of Sir Edward Dyer

Kelliher, Hilton. "Unrecorded Extracts from Shakespeare, Sidney and Dyer." *English Manuscript Studies 1100–1700* 2 (1990): 163–87.

McLane, Paul E. "Spenser's Cuddie: Edward Dyer." *Journal of English and Germanic Philology* 54 (1955): 230–409.

May, Steven W. "The Authorship of 'My mind to me a kingdom is.' " *Review of English Studies* n.s. 26 (1975): 385–94.

———. *The Elizabethan Courtier Poets: The Poems and Their Contexts.* Columbia: University of Missouri Press, 1991.

Sargent, Ralph M. *The Life and Lyrics of Sir Edward Dyer.* Oxford, 1968; formerly titled *At the Court of Queen Elizabeth,* 1935; Appendix: "On the Poetry of Dyer," 165–73.

DOUGLAS BRUSTER

E

QUEEN ELIZABETH I
(1533–1603)

BIOGRAPHY

Daughter of a king and herself one of the longest reigning monarchs of England, Queen Elizabeth's life is well documented, recorded not only in her own speeches and letters but in the writings of contemporaries who chronicled her life even before its end. Yet even as documentation of events exists, little evidence of Elizabeth's personal passions remains, and the desire to construct private emotions from public action remains strong for biographers eager to find motivation and intention in her royal activities.

Born in Greenwich on 7 September 1533 to Henry VIII and his second wife Anne Boleyn, Elizabeth spent her first years as a princess living in the royal household. At the age of three, however, her circumstances changed dramatically with her mother's execution on charges of treason and adultery. Deemed illegitimate, Elizabeth moved from the royal household, joining her half-sister Mary. Despite the ill treatment of his wives, Henry nevertheless proved a decent father. While exiled from her father's residence, Elizabeth continued to attend royal functions as her father's daughter, and indeed some biographers read her as her father's favorite.

In 1543, Henry married the last of his wives, Catherine Parr,* a woman who acted as mother to Elizabeth and her half-brother Edward, moving them into her household. Elizabeth's years with Parr proved fundamental to the girl's intellectual development. During this time, she received her education under the Protestant humanists Roger Ascham, Sir John Cheke, and William Grindal. As he records in *The Schoolmaster* (1570), Ascham tutored Elizabeth in classical and modern languages, as well as in humanist philosophy and theology, claiming of Elizabeth that "her mind has no womanly weakness." Thomas Heywood mentions her devotion to study as well. In his account of her childhood with Catherine Parr, he writes of her and her brother Edward that "[t]heir *horae matutinae* were so welcome, that they seemed to prevent the nights sleeping for the entertainment of the morrows schooling." Two hallmarks of the later queen, her linguistic competence and her religious moderation, both originate in these early years.

With her father's death in 1547 and Catherine Parr's death the following year, Elizabeth found herself in a more vulnerable political position. Courted by her stepmother's second husband, the ambitious Thomas Seymour, she suffered under the investigation that followed Seymour's arrest for plotting to marry her as a means to the Crown. Showing characteristic self-possession, Elizabeth successfully braved the interrogations into her own conduct with Seymour. She found herself again under suspicion in 1554, this time for her alleged role in Sir Thomas Wyatt's* rebellion against the Catholic Queen Mary. For a short time following the Wyatt rebellion, she lived in confinement first in the Tower of London and subsequently at the manor Woodstock, where Elizabeth composed two of her six extant poems. One poem, scratched on the window, taunts "[m]uch suspected by me, / Nothing proved can be." Both poems protest her innocence, although during the reign of her Catholic half-sister Mary, the Protestant Elizabeth was never free from suspicion.

Queen Mary died in 1558. Two months later, at age twenty-five, Elizabeth rode through London for her coronation. While records of the coronation note the celebrations greeting the queen as she rode through London, her ascension to the Crown was greeted with suspicion as well. First, Mary's Catholic supporters vilified the Protestant Elizabeth, supporting her rival, Mary, Queen of Scots.* In addition, detractors of female rule, who found a voice in John Knox's* *The Blast of the Trumpet Against the Monstrous Regiment of Women*, continued to protest a female sovereign. Yet Elizabeth's rule proved a contrast to the instability marking the reigns of Edward VI and Mary I. With her fiscal conservatism and her moderate Protestantism, Elizabeth shaped a government reluctant to persecute subjects for religious beliefs or to involve them in foreign wars.

Attempts to gain stability in fiscal and foreign policy were counterbalanced by the unsettled state of Elizabeth's marital affairs. Her famous flirtations and engagements, well documented in her own letters and in biographies, often allowed her to stabilize her European alliances. Yet Elizabeth remained elusive, reluctant to settle the ever-present question of succession. Parliament became increasingly demanding about her marital negotiations in the 1580s, provoking a series of well-known speeches from Elizabeth, who powerfully asserted her own control over the questions of marriage and succession. Twice addressing Parliament in 1563 on the question of marriage, Elizabeth again spoke on the issue in 1566, concluding, "I am your anointed queen. I will never be by violence constrained to do anything. I thank God I am endued with such qualities that if I were turned out of the realm in my petticoat, I were able to live in any place in Christendom." Elizabeth vehemently asserts her self-sufficiency even when faced with Parliament's demands. Yet Parliament's demands were justified: at stake in the question of marriage was the religious fate of the country. Without an heir, the Catholic Mary, Queen of Scots would inherit the throne, as supporters of both Protestant Elizabeth and Catholic Mary knew. Yet, despite the obvious security threat that Mary posed, Elizabeth refused to execute her, reluctant to shed royal blood. Only after the discovery of Mary's role in the infamous Rudolfi plot against her life did Elizabeth give the "answer-answerless," a famously ambiguous phrase that allowed Elizabeth to appear equivocal even as Mary was executed in 1587.

Most foreign monarchs maintained amicable relations with the English queen, the notable exception being Spain. Despite all of Elizabeth's efforts to stall, war erupted on the Continent, with England's invading the Spanish Netherlands in 1585. Three years later, Spain attacked England. The Spanish Armada's surprising defeat at the hands of the much smaller English navy proved the occasion for Elizabeth's famous speech at Tilbury. The period of triumph immediately following the 1588 defeat is seen as the peak of Elizabeth's reign in terms of national pride directed affectionately toward "the Virgin Queen." In the decade following, Elizabeth continued to control her courtiers through a mixture of flirtation and domination, which had become her hallmark. At this point due to age, the question of succession that had dominated the early part of her reign was no longer an issue. On 24 March, Elizabeth I died, succeeded by James VI* of Scotland, James I.*

MAJOR WORKS AND THEMES

Remembered primarily for her statecraft, Elizabeth was also an accomplished author. She wrote and translated poetry in addition to composing most of her own letters and speeches. Of the various poems attributed to her, two were etched into the house at Woodstock, where she was confined as a child. These poems deal with the themes of fortune and entrapment, which reappear in another poem, written nearly thirty years later on the subject of love. This poem, "On Monsieur's Departure," perhaps grew out of the prolonged marital negotiations with François of Valois, duke of Alençon, which Elizabeth terminated in 1582. Most likely written by Elizabeth, the poem uses Petrarchan language to express the conventional sentiments of disappointed love.

Admired for her knowledge of French, Italian, Spanish, Flemish, German, Latin, and Greek, Elizabeth displayed her talent for languages in her own translations of Horace's *De Arte Poetica*, Petrarch's "Trionfo dell'Eternita," and

Boethius' *De Consolatione Philosophiae*. At the age of eleven, Elizabeth translated Marguerite de Navarre's *The Mirror of the Sinful Soul*, sending her text in a case embroidered by her own hand to Catherine Parr. This early gesture typifies much of Elizabeth's later work. In its careful presentation and pious content, the translation shares with Elizabeth's other writings attention to occasion and a thematic focus on her own devotion. Indeed, Elizabeth's second book after the early Navarre translation was a compilation of prayers entitled *A Book of Devotions*. Elizabeth translated this collection of her own private prayers into French, Italian, Latin, and Greek.

While her poetry and translations reveal her literary and linguistic accomplishment, the bulk of Elizabeth's authorial accomplishment lies in her speeches and letters. In these writings the typically Elizabethan theme of devotion emerges most strongly. Her devotion is twofold: to her country and to God. Nearly every speech highlights this devotion, emphasizing the personal risks she took to maintain it. Well known for her physical bravery, Elizabeth displays her courage in the delivery of one of her most famous speeches "To the Troops at Tilbury, 1588." Disregarding her advisers' warnings, Elizabeth risked injury to stand among the troops at Tilbury just after the Armada's defeat. There Elizabeth uttered the now famous lines, "I know I have the body but of a weak and feeble woman; but I have the heart and stomach of a king, and of a king of England too." Nowhere is Elizabeth's ability to move a crowd and to speak to the occasion more obvious than in these lines. Elizabeth's pride is at once personal and national, a combination quite typical of the queen who wore a marital ring from the time of her coronation to signify her marriage to her country. Elizabeth juxtaposes her own courage with her awareness of her physical presence as a female sovereign speaking before men. Using a savvy awareness of her physical vulnerability, noted by her detractors, Elizabeth highlights her own courage in disregarding this weakness to defend the nation. As many recent critics have noted, Elizabeth charts a course that claims both male power and female virtue. Chaste and strong, she stands in her speeches, as she does in the poetry dedicated to her, as a Diana figure, from Ralegh's* Cynthia, to Spenser's* Belphoebe, to Shakespeare's* Titania, to countless others.

Elizabeth's love for her subjects offered a rhetoric appropriate at once for a sovereign speaking publicly to subjects and for a devoted woman expressing herself intimately to her family. Evoking Diana and the Virgin Mary in her chastity, Elizabeth presents herself as the devoted spouse of England as well. Yet the tone of vulnerability and intimacy of certain speeches often masks Elizabeth's savvy reticence. Particularly in her speeches regarding marriage, succession, and the future of Mary, Queen of Scots, Elizabeth adopts a candid tone while refusing to commit herself. This indecision allowed her to reassess continually her political returns in a given situation. Critics speak of Elizabeth's last years as a less successful balancing of the ambiguous roles of sovereign and mistress, ruler and object of devotion, because her famous indecision by that point seemed less a matter of sophisticated politics than of fearful stagnation. Yet Elizabeth's own letters and speeches from the last years of her reign reveal the same assertion of strength seen throughout her tenure, as in these lines from her famous ''Golden Speech'' of 1601: ''[T]hough you have had and may have many princes more mighty and wise sitting in this seat, yet you never had or shall have any that will be more careful and loving. Should I ascribe anything to myself and my sexly weakness, I were not worthy to live then, and of all most unworthy of the mercies I have had from God, Who hath ever yet given me a heart which never yet feared foreign or home enemies.''

CRITICAL RECEPTION

As Christopher Haigh notes in his recent biography, ''It is almost impossible to write a balanced study of Elizabeth I. The historiographical tradition is so laudatory that it is hard to avoid either floating with the current of applauding opinion or creating an unseemly splash by swimming too energetically against it'' (175). The majority of Elizabeth scholarship insists on her brilliant managing of the unstable state she inherited. William Camden's *Annales* (1610) began this long tradition of representing Elizabeth's reign as a golden age of progress. In the proliferation of studies of Elizabeth in the last fifteen years, however, scholars steer between unqualified praise and overexuberant critique. These scholars praise her statecraft, while often focusing on the latter decade of her reign as a time when her performance no longer enchants. Wallace MacCaffrey's 1994 biography, for example, chronicles the queen's frustrating oscillation between anger and indifference in her latter years. Feminist new historicist scholars point to the gender expectations that constrained Elizabeth, particularly during her latter years as her representation as the ever-youthful ''Virgin Queen'' increasingly contrasted with the reality of her age.

Given Elizabeth's position as sovereign, balanced assessment of her poetry and translations could not begin until well after her death. In addition, her fame as a subject of literature generally overshadows her fame as an author. In the proliferation of recent studies, more scholars are turning to the queen's own work, yet studying Elizabeth's writings presents a singular challenge, for her own writings rarely expose her interior life or beliefs. As G. B. Harrison writes in his volume of the queen's letters, ''[t]hough few rulers have on occasion written better letters, she was not a good correspondent, for the famous letter writers are those who record intimate experiences and share secrets and observations. . . . The Queen wrote to command, to exhort, to censure, to persuade, and sometimes to prevaricate: but she had no familiar confidant, man or woman.'' Because Elizabeth remains the sovereign even in her private letters, the preponderance of historical rather than literary studies of her writings should not be surprising. Yet with the recent flowering of Elizabeth scholarship has come a new interest in her role as author, and the next decade may well result in a deeper understanding of Elizabeth in both historical and literary terms.

BIBLIOGRAPHY

Works by Queen Elizabeth I

A Book of Devotions Composed by Her Majesty Elizabeth R. Trans. A. Fox and intro. J. Hodges. Gerrards Cross, U.K., 1970.

The Letters of Queen Elizabeth I. Ed. G. B. Harrison. New York: Funk and Wagnalls, 1968.

Mirror of the Sinful Soul. Ed. P. Ames. London: 1897.

The Poems of Queen Elizabeth I. Ed. Leicester Bradner. Providence: Brown University Press, 1964.

The Public Speaking of Queen Elizabeth: Selections from Her Official Addresses. Ed. George P. Rice Jr. New York: Columbia University Press, 1951.

Translations

Navarre, Margaret of. *A Godly Meditacyon of the Christen Sowle, Concerninge a Love towardes God and Hys Christe.* Ed. John Bale. Wesel: Printed by Derick van der Straten, 1548.

———. *The Mirror of the Sinful soul: A Prose Translation from the French of a Poem by Queen Margaret of Navarre, Made in 1544 by the Princess (Afterwards Queen) Elizabeth.* Ed. Percy Willoughby Ames. London: Royal Society of Literature, 1897.

Queen Elizabeth's Englishings of Boethius . . . Plutarch . . . Horace. Ed. Caroline Pemberton. London: Printed for the Early English Text Society by K. Paul, Trench, Trubner, 1899.

Studies of Queen Elizabeth I

Bassnette, Susan. *Elizabeth I: A Feminist Perspective.* Oxford: Berg, 1988.

Brennan, Michael G. "Two Private Prayers by Queen Elizabeth I." *Notes and Queries* 32 (1985): 26–28.

Crane, Mary Thomas. " 'Video et Taceo': Elizabeth I and the Rhetoric of Counsel." *Studies in English Literature* 28 (1988): 1–15.

Frye, Susan. *Elizabeth I: The Competition for Representation.* Oxford: Oxford University Press, 1993.

Haigh, Christopher. *Elizabeth I.* New York: Longman, 1988.

Heisch, Alison. "Queen Elizabeth I: Parliamentary Rhetoric and the Exercise of Power." *Signs* 1 (1975).

King, John N. "Queen Elizabeth I: Representations of the Virgin Queen." *Renaissance Quarterly* 43 (1990).

Levin, Carol. *The Heart and Stomach of a King: Elizabeth I and the Politics of Sex and Power.* Philadelphia: University of Pennsylvania Press, 1994.

MacCaffrey, Wallace. *Elizabeth I.* London: Edward Arnold, 1994.

Neale, J. *Queen Elizabeth.* New York: Harcourt, Brace, 1934.

Perry, Maria. *The Word of a Prince: A Life of Elizabeth I from Contemporary Documents.* Woodbridge, England: Boydell Press, 1990.

Ridley, Jasper. *Elizabeth I: The Shrewdness of Virtue.* New York: Viking, 1988.

Somerset, Anne. *Elizabeth I.* New York: Knopf, 1991.

Teague, Frances. "Editing Elizabeth's Speeches." Ed. Suzanne Gossett. *Renaissance English Text Society Proceedings* (1987): 15–19.

REBECCA LEMON

THOMAS ELYOT
(c. 1490–1546)

BIOGRAPHY

The Book of the Governor by Sir Thomas Elyot, humanist and courtier, was one of the most popular publications of sixteenth-century England. A guidebook written in English on how to become a virtuous, sophisticated, and accomplished member of the ruling class, it was reprinted at least eight times during the Tudor period. More's* *Utopia*, by contrast, was not translated into English during the author's life. *The Governor* was considered useful by members of the gentry class for several generations beyond Elyot's time. Thomas Jefferson owned a copy, as did another prestigious member of the eighteenth-century Virginia planter aristocracy, William Byrd II. In other books, Elyot was a political commentator whose views ran counter to Henrician Reformation policies, yet he still managed to die of natural causes.

Thomas Elyot was born in or just prior to 1490. His father, Richard, was a lawyer and instructor at the Inns of Court who owned two manors in Wiltshire. Thomas developed an avid interest in medicine early in life, a pursuit that would later be reflected in his *Castle of Health*. But by 1511 he had started on a path of public service as clerk of the assize on the western circuit, where his father was judge. Thomas was a friend and pupil of Thomas More, studying Latin, Greek, logic, philosophy, theology, mathematics, and astronomy in More's home (Lehmberg, 6). He went on to study at Oxford, and in 1522 he married Margaret Abarrow of Hampshire in a union that would prove childless. The deaths of his father and a cousin put him into a considerable inheritance in 1523, including three sizable estates, of which he chose Combe in Oxfordshire as his main residence.

It is unclear how Elyot attracted the attention of Cardinal Wolsey, but by the mid-1520s he served as chief clerk of the king's Privy Council, a post with considerably more political influence than its title might sound to the modern reader. Elyot was also "pricked" (compulsory royal nomination) as sheriff of Oxford and Berkshire in 1527, and the two counties were joined for that purpose, remaining so until the reign of Henry VIII's daughter, Elizabeth.* Elyot's swift rise met an even swifter fall, as he was summarily dismissed from the King's Council in 1530 without compensation and with no clear explanation extant.

His *Book of the Governor* appeared in print in 1531, the impressiveness of which most likely accounts for his appointment as ambassador to the imperial court, where he was charged with a mission to persuade Charles V, king of Spain and Holy Roman Emperor, to cooperate with Henry VIII's divorce from Queen Catherine of Aragon. Charles was Catherine's nephew, and Elyot's diplomatic predicament was made all the more difficult by his sympathy for the queen's cause. Elyot doubtless shared with Thomas More and other humanists the belief that since truth is singular in nature, the possibility of more than one Christian church is logically untenable and spiritually disastrous, with civil and social devastations to ensue. Elyot thought that Henry's unhealthy struggles with the papacy were primarily the fault of court flatterers who fanned the flames of the king's considerable inherent passions. He thus found himself in a hopeless position of urging the English court to maintain cordial relations with Spain, all the while aware that Charles was unlikely to assent to Henry's heretical actions, some of which asserted that his marriage to Queen Catherine was sinful and unlawful. Some scholars have suggested that there is sufficient evidence to conclude that Elyot acted as a secret agent for Charles V, cooperating with the Spanish ambassador, Chapuys, to work for Roman Catholicism and giving clandestine assistance to the victims of the Protestant Reformation in England. If he did so, he did not state his reasons directly in his writings. At any rate, Elyot never made overt affronts against Henry's religious changes and was careful to distance himself from his old tutor, More, as he sank deeper into trouble.

Meanwhile, Elyot had formed, ironically in retrospect, a friendship with Thomas Cromwell,* who became the king's secretary, most influential adviser, and chief engineer of the Henrician Reformation. Elyot's correspondence with Cromwell dates from at least 1528. Elyot attempted to withdraw from politics following his first diplomatic mission to Charles V and devote himself to his literary works. In 1532 he attempted to relinquish his local posts as well, pleading with Cromwell to release him from his duties as sheriff of Cambridgeshire. The office of sheriff carried diminished authority since the late Middle Ages but retained considerable and costly obligations. Cromwell insisted he stay on as sheriff.

Rumors of Elyot's Catholicism led to an investigation by Cromwell and eight members of the Privy Council from 1534 to 1537. Elyot admitted that his library contained a copy of Richard Pace's* translation of Bishop Fisher's sermon against Luther but that he was unable to locate it. Perhaps to quell further suspicions of his sympathy with the cloistered clergy, he participated in a commission to survey monastic property in preparation for their dissolution.

Elyot returned to international politics in 1535, once again as ambassador to the court of Charles V, at that time located in Naples. Here he learned the news of More's execution, which had taken place on 6 June 1535. Elyot's friendship with More increased royal suspicions regarding his religion, despite his protestations of having accepted Henry's arrangements as the best hope of reforming church corruption. Perhaps in part to put aside the memory of More's martyrdom among humanists, Henry warmly encouraged Elyot to take up the useful project of compiling a Latin–English dictionary in 1536. Elyot's public renunciation of the old religion appears to have been complete by 1540, as he attended the reception of Henry's new Protestant bride, Anne of Cleves, at Blackheath. He even dedicated his new book, *The Defense of Good Women*, to Anne. Elyot weathered Cromwell's fall and execution successfully, though he had purchased property from Cromwell shortly before his imprisonment. He served as member of Parliament from Cambridgeshire in 1539 and 1542. He died in 1546, writing and publishing, with the concurrence of Roger Ascham, almost to the end. A monument was erected to his memory, which has since been destroyed. The location of his burial site in Cambridgeshire has been lost.

MAJOR WORKS AND THEMES

Elyot meant for the *Book of the Governor*, which went to press in 1531, to be a practical handbook whose advice could be put into place by government officials on the local and national levels. Its popularity as a reference work is undoubted. Nevertheless, at least three factors mitigated against Elyot's goal of practical application of his advice in toto. First, *The Governor* is platonically idealistic in the sense that the author believed a perfect state can result from leaders becoming wise and virtuous. *The Governor* like an earlier work by Erasmus,* *Education of a Christian Prince*, attempted to mollify political ruthlessness and selfishness by inculcating good character in leaders. Elyot went beyond Erasmus' preoccupation with the abstract or ideal by exploring the concrete traits of the ruling class, an approach most likely inspired by Castiglione's *Book of the Courtier*. Second, Elyot's proposed educational curriculum was highly involved and so costly in terms of duration and money that few in England possessed the leisure time and income to complete it. Finally, *The Governor* is more a long treatise than a how-to manual. Henry H. S. Croft's 1883 edition, which retains sixteenth-century spelling and syntax, was published in two large volumes consisting of just over 1,000 pages, including editorial notes.

Thomas Elyot wrote his books in English, doubtless to increase their accessibility as well as to expand the expressive power of the language by introducing new words. The following is a partial list of words and phrases that, to date, appear to have occurred for the first time in English in the *Book of the Governor*, indicating that Elyot either invented them or adapted them from another language, usually Latin or French: *involve, exactly, articulate, emulation, aggravate, activity, audacity, beneficence, clemency, education, frugality, imprudence, liberty of speech, loyalty, magistrate, mediocrity, society, encyclopedia, chaos, democracy, maturity* (Major, 17; Kinghorn, 92). Elyot often included lengthy etymological definitions of his new words as he introduced them in *The Governor*, along with illuminating examples from classical texts as well as from contemporary Italian writers.

The Book of the Governor seeks to present a formula for political success within moralistic boundaries. Advice on classical education, physical development, government service training, courtly etiquette, religious and ethical standards, and artistic and musical skills was included. Chapters 1–3 of Book I treated political theory in a ''public weal,'' which Elyot believed worked to the benefit of all when hierarchical and monarchical. Elyot asserted that elites form in every society, and since hierarchies tend to build upward to an apex, monarchy is the most natural form of government. This appeal to nature as an authority predicts similar theories in later writings by Hobbes and Locke, as well as the French philosophers of the eighteenth century. Elyot's preference for the natural over the contrived in this instance does not appear to have been inspired by an interest in the new science, however. He occasionally made humorous references in his writings to the Copernican* theory as baffling and seemingly absurd to commonsense reckoning. The rest of Book I, through Chapter 27, consisted of Elyot's plan for an ideal mental and physical education. His educational program terminated when the pupil reached the age of twenty-one. Books II and III concerned themselves with how to cultivate virtue and wisdom in leaders, replete with classical and biblical examples—tales that were almost exclusively about kings. A shorter Book II emphasized personal qualities, and a lengthier Book III emphasized moral philosophy, introduced by an exploration of the meaning and nature of justice. His interest in justice and advocation of philosopher-kings help connect him closely with the neoplatonism of the Renaissance. According to Elyot, a good leader must, among other qualities, possess mercy, benevolence, liberality, fortitude, patience, magnanimity, temperance, sapience, and nobility.

Elyot believed in a natural nobility insomuch as genetic traits required to make effective and admirable leaders are not distributed equally in a population and as these same traits tend to be passed down from generation to generation among certain families. But he also believed that, occasionally, common people inherit qualities needed for good leadership. His educational scheme argued in favor of a "nurture over nature" perspective. An indolent nobleman could squander away his inherited talents as well as property, whereas a talented commoner could become a good leader if brought up in a suitable learning environment that inculcated true nobility derived from knowledge and virtue. Elyot gave chivalric principles a diminished role.

The training for a future governor began in a nursery that admitted only adult women as caretakers of the child, guarding him from unsuitable associates, "pestiferous dew of vice to pierce . . . infect and corrupt the soft and tender buds" (*Governor*, I, 30). The child's cognitive development emphasized primarily the study of history, especially Livy, up to age seventeen. At that point students were sufficiently mature to study and absorb philosophy and morals. Each ingredient of education had a specific purpose. In Elyot's chapters on dancing, for example, specific dance steps symbolized such aspects of the virtue of prudence as honor, modesty, industry, and maturity, thereby transforming an aesthetic recreation of emotional release into an exercise designed to hone and reinforce virtues. As was typical during the Renaissance, Elyot's curriculum throughout stressed the classics, including the mastery of Greek and Latin, seldom questioning the validity of ancient authorities as repositories of virtue and wisdom. Sound ethical values had to be internalized before the young man took up the study of law, a profession inclined to decay the practitioner's morals despite the fact that, according to Elyot, the laws of England were beneficent results of an evolution of refined reason. Therefore, Elyot's ideal student commenced his training in law as an essential tool in the art of governing, not as an education in itself, at twenty-one years or older (*Governor*, I, 141).

In one sense, *The Governor* represents an attempt to counteract a European political world that was becoming increasingly Machiavellian in early modern Europe by retaining, even expanding, moralistic expectations in leaders. Like many others before and since, Elyot yearned for a return to traditional values, especially amid political and religious changes he found frightening. The book can also be seen as a secular example of the lay Pietistic movement of the northern Renaissance, which Erasmus vigorously espoused as a benign purgative of church corruption. Of course, Elyot was unwilling to go as far as Luther in insisting that all true believers are priests. But if piety were no longer the exclusive property of the clergy, then why not expect a functional version of it from an erudite political elite? Elyot's conception of political success, unlike Machiavelli's,* depicted a harmonious interplay among the various elements of the commonwealth, with justice as the guiding principle that prevents leaders from exploiting the common people and inspires loyalty to, and respect for, the governing classes. Elyot thereby implicitly denied the Machiavellian assumption that success or gain by one person or group requires failure or loss on the part of others—an attitude very close to the medieval social ideal.

Pasquil the Plain appeared in 1533. It was a satire presented in dialogue form. Three characters, Pasquil, Gnatho, and Harpocrates—representing sincerity, flattery, and silence, respectively—discussed the best method of giving counsel. The point of argument is initiated by Aeschylus' advice "Hold your tongue when it behooves you and speak in time which is convenient." Elyot's voice was that of the plain-speaking Pasquil, who insisted upon expressing the truth as you see it regardless of how your words are received (*Pasquil*, 98). The Epicurean withdrawal from confrontation as advocated by Harpocrates was presented as a denial of the essential duty of a counselor. A king's adviser is just as responsible to warn the sovereign of dangerous consequences of his own actions as of imminent dangers to his physical person. In this Elyot maintained that royal advisers share responsibility with the monarch in protecting the best interests of the subject, even if this means curbing or blocking the king's intentions.

Of the Knowledge Which Maketh a Wise Man quickly followed *Pasquil* to press in 1533. Another Socratic dialogue, *Knowledge* was ostensibly about the benefits of classical learning. Its real subject was, again, the nature of good counsel. Plato's argument with Aristippus centered on whether Plato's unwelcome advice to the tyrant, King Dionysus of Syracuse, was wise, considering the resulting banishment and foreign enslavement by royal command. Hence, a definition of wisdom was required before the issue could be settled between Plato and Aristippus. The conclusions in *Knowledge* indicate Elyot's agreement with Aristotle that awareness of truth is insufficient unless acted upon. Plato insisted that kings who are motivated by selfishness rather than by the "public weal'' are tyrants. By courageously acting upon his knowledge as he understood it despite the antagonism of Dionysus, Plato revealed himself to be a wise man.

The original publication date of *The Castle of Health* is uncertain, with 1536 as the best estimate. It was the first health manual written in English, and by 1610 it had undergone fourteen printings. It consisted of four books: the nature and functions of the four bodily fluids and the use of complexion as a diagnostic tool; nutrition and exercise; medicines; digestion. Elyot's research for *Castle of Health* was exhaustive, and he incorporated many ancient and contemporary medical theories. Another first of its kind was a Latin–English dictionary entitled *The Dictionary of Sir Thomas Elyot* (1538), also reprinted several times. He used a Latin dictionary, first published in 1502 by the Italian Ambrose Calepine, as his major source.

The Defense of Good Women appeared in 1540, and a second edition was printed in 1545. Elyot's impatience with the antifeminism of his day was sufficiently pronounced to put one of his heroes, Aristotle, in a category with perverse ancient poets due to his lowly opinion of women. Elyot argued that true philosophers praised women; physical weakness relative to men did not imply inferiority of women, since physical strength is not their purpose. He believed women to be more gifted in using reason than men and more likely to resort to reason to solve problems. His admonitions promoting female education were perhaps partly due to his having known More's well-educated and intellectual daughters.

CRITICAL RECEPTION

The Book of the Governor appears to have approached the level of required reading for the sixteenth-century English gentleman. Two centuries later in Britain's American colonies, continuing interest in the book can be seen in the lives of such aristocrats as William Byrd II of Virginia, who busied himself making a conscious attempt to put Elyot's advice into practice (Lockridge, 22–25, 49–50, 142). The educational theory in *The Governor* also became the ideal for members of the gentry class. Just as government-sponsored education is supposed to produce good citizens today, a classically educated elite in Elyot's day and for long thereafter was meant to produce enlightened ''governors'' whose wisdom and largesse protected the best interests of the people, enabling them to enjoy traditional rights while enjoining them to volunteer to perform traditional obligations in a harmoniously functioning organism aptly named a commonwealth. Elyot believed that class distinctions should be upheld but that the elite should be trained in such a way as to preclude social exploitation, persistently maintaining a gentle and familiar ''visage'' to their inferiors to make them more approachable.

The main point of controversy among some recent scholars of Elyot's literary works is whether or not he intended his books to send disapproving messages about Henry VIII. Scholarship is undivided on the abundance of evidence of

Elyot's religious conservatism (e.g., *Governor*, II, 210–11) and of his reluctance to concede to the king and Cromwell's solution for church reform. But Elyot's criticism of typical political behavior as contrasted to his arguments in favor of the ideal in *The Governor* can easily be seen as his underscorings of the shoddy and unethical environment of high politics in England. Henry's apparent approval and enjoyment of *The Governor* when it first came into print in 1531 seem inconsistent unless explained away by positing that the king certainly thought of himself as principled, a conclusion based more on contemplating his inner self than by analyzing his actions (Caspari, 89).

Elyot's withdrawal from politics in 1532, followed by his writing *Pasquil the Plain* and *Of the Knowledge Which Maketh a Wise Man* in 1532–33, has led to interpretations of these books as vindications of Thomas More (Major, 102–3). Elyot shared the belief of Erasmus and most humanists that the need for friendship sets us apart from animals and accentuates our special quality as divine creations. Furthermore, Elyot repeated the Greek notion in *Image of Governance* (1541) that Eros is present in friendship bonds. It would be hard to doubt that Elyot suffered for More's predicament, perhaps all the more so because he lacked the stubborn substance of saints. The thesis that Elyot used his books against Henry can be expanded by reading Catherine of Aragon as the "good woman" in his *Defense of Good Women* (Lehmberg, 212). *Sir Thomas Elyot and Renaissance Humanism* presents two similarly worded quotations—one from Elyot and another from More's son-in-law, Roper—as conclusive evidence that *Of the Knowledge Which Maketh a Wise Man* was "veiled commentary on More's resignation from the chancellorship" (Major, 103), without considering Roper's likely familiarity with *Knowledge*, perhaps finding its lament that good counselors are more valuable than cities an apt metaphor to apply to his martyred father-in-law.

Other scholars have found conceptual leaps based on juxtaposing texts implausible (Hogrefe, 310–11). The likelihood that Elyot's works were clandestine criticism of the establishment is further diminished by a lack of corroborating contemporary perceptions of his books as seditious works. If Elyot indeed intended to exonerate More and Catherine, among others, the point was missed by his readers, including the king, during the Reformation crisis.

On more solid evidential ground are modern investigations showing Shakespeare's* use of Elyot's political theory in his plays (Phillips). Shakespeare lifted phrases verbatim from *The Governor* in writing *Troilus and Cressida* and *Coriolanus* (Starnes), indicating that perhaps Elyot's perceptions passed into conventional wisdom.

Etiquette books have a way of enduring beyond the normal life expectancy of how-to books of advice, though few people succeed in internalizing their precepts and rules. The durability of *The Book of the Governor*, a book of political etiquette, is likewise remarkable, all the more so considering how few leaders turned out as bearing the qualities Elyot so plainly described.

Thomas Elyot likely did more to spread the popularity of humanism than any writer in England. Nonetheless, because of his lack of literary brilliance and relatively uneventful life, his memory has dissolved into obscurity outside the world of specialized scholarship.

BIBLIOGRAPHY

Works by Thomas Elyot

The Book of the Governor. 1531; 1537; 1544; 1546; 1553; 1557; 1565; 1580; ed. A. T. Eliot, Newcastle upon Tyne, 1834; ed. H.H.S. Croft, 2 vols., London, 1883; ed. F. Watson, Everyman's Library, New York, 1907, 1937; German translation, H. Studniczka. Leipzig, 1931; ed. J. M. Major, Columbia University Classics in Education Series, New York, 1969.

The Doctrinal of Princes. 1533?; 1548?

Pasquil the Plain. 1533; 1540.

Of the Knowledge Which Maketh a Wise Man. 1533; 1534; 1548?; 1552?; ed. E. J. Howard. Oxford, OH: Richard S. Barnes, & Co. 1942.

The Castle of Health. 1536?; 1539; 1541; 1544?; 1549?; 1559?; 1560?; 1561; 1572; 1580; 1587; 1595; 1610; ed. S. A. Tannenbaum. New York, 1937.

The Dictionary of Sir Thomas Elyot. 1538; 1542; 1548; 1552; 1559.

The Defense of Good Women. 1540; 1545; ed. E. J. Howard. Oxford, OH: Richard S. Barnes, & Co. 1940.

The Image of Governance. 1541; 1544; 1549; 1556.

Studies of Thomas Elyot

Caspari, Fritz. *Humanism and the Social Order in Tudor England.* Chicago: University of Chicago Press, 1954.

Dees, Jerome S. *Sir Thomas Elyot and Roger Ascham, A Reference Guide.* Boston: G. K. Hall, 1981.

Hogrefe, Pearl. *The Life and Times of Sir Thomas Elyot.* Ames: Iowa State University Press, 1967.

Kinghorn, Alexander. *The Chorus of History: Literary-Historical Relations in Renaissance Britain, 1485–1558.* New York: Barnes and Noble, 1971.

Lehmberg, Stanford E. *Sir Thomas Elyot, Tudor Humanist.* New York: Greenwood Press, 1969.

Lockridge, Kenneth A. *The Diary, and Life, of William Byrd II of Virginia, 1674–1744.* Chapel Hill, NC: University of North Carolina Press, 1987.

Major, John M. *Sir Thomas Elyot and Renaissance Humanism.* Lincoln: University of Nebraska Press, 1964.

McConica, James K. *English Humanists and Reformation Politics under Henry VIII and Edward VI.* Oxford: Clarendon Press, 1965.

Phillips, J. E., Jr. *The State in Shakespeare's Greek and Roman Plays.* New York, 1940.

Simon, Joan. *Education and Society in Tudor England.* Cambridge: Cambridge University Press, 1966.

Starnes, D. T. "Shakespeare and Elyot's *Governor.*" *University of Texas Studies of English* 7 (1927): 112–35.

JOHN A. SHEDD

DESIDERIUS ERASMUS
(1466/1469–1536)

BIOGRAPHY

Erasmus was born in Rotterdam on 28 October of either 1466 or 1469. About his early life we know nothing save what we are told in *A Brief Account of the Life of Erasmus of Rotterdam*, a short biographical compendium almost certainly written by Erasmus himself and sent to Conradus Glocenius on 2 April 1524, according to which his father, Gerard, ''lay with Margaret [his mother] secretly, in the expectation of marrying her. Some say they were already betrothed'' (*Collected Works of Erasmus* [*CWE*] 4, 403). Meeting with the intense disapproval of his family, who wanted him to become a priest, Gerard ran off to Rome, where he earned his living as a copyist until his family wrote that Margaret had died. ''In his grief he became a priest, and devoted his whole mind to religion. Upon returning home, he discovered this was a fraud. But she was never after willing to marry, nor did he ever touch her.'' Erasmus' account does not mention his older brother Pieter, born three years earlier and, while conceding his unfortunate illegitimacy, carefully places his birth before his father became a priest. Had his father already been a priest at the time of his conception, Erasmus would have been forbidden entry into the priesthood unless he had first taken monastic vows; since Erasmus had gone to some lengths to get a papal dispensation from his monastic vows and from wearing the robes of his order under condition that he always wore his priestly garb, he may have felt that this version of his conception and birth made his life less complicated than otherwise.

Erasmus (and his brother) were sent by their parents to be educated by the Brothers of the Common Life at Deventer, an education about which Erasmus later said that ''the school there was at that time in a state of barbarism . . . except that Alexander Hegius and Synthen had begun to introduce something of a higher standard of literature'' (*CWE* 4, 404–5). However, his schooling was interrupted by the plague, which carried off first his mother and then his father. Erasmus, who was then thirteen, wanted to go to the university at 'sHertogenbosch, but his guardians ''had already decided to bring the boy up for the life of a religious'' (*CWE* 4, 405) and sent him to spend (''or rather waste'' [*CWE* 4, 406]) three years in a house of the brothers. Following another outbreak of the plague, Erasmus, ill, returned home, where he found one of his three guardians dead, and the other two, eager to end their responsibilities (and having ''not managed their [fiscal] responsibilities very skillfully'' [*CWE* 4, 406]), pressured him to enter ''a monastery of regular canons.'' As Erasmus described it, he was betrayed by a friend, who painted a picture of life in his monastery at Steyn as ''a very saintly way of life, with plenty of books, leisure, tranquillity, and a society like that of the angels. . . . The young man was lured on by some people and driven forward by others; the fever lay heavy on him. So he chose this place . . . and of the moment all was made pleasant for him, until he should take the habit. . . . Though he made preparations to leave before his profession, he was restrained partly by natural shyness, partly by threats, and partly by necessity'' (*CWE* 4, 407). Although the young Erasmus had come to realize ''how far the place was from true religion,'' he notes nonetheless that ''he inspired the whole community to study harder'' (*CWE* 4, 407).

Erasmus' account of his early years takes up more space than the next thirty years of his life and clearly suggests that he became the great scholar he had come to be not because of his schooling but despite it and that it was not hatred of true religion but love of it that made him flee it (with the consent of his superiors) when the opportunity came to serve as secretary to the bishop of Cambrai, who was hoping for a cardinal's hat (''and would have had one had he not been short of ready money'' [*CWE* 4, 408–9]) and ''needed a good Latin scholar'' (*CWE* 4, 409). The notion that piety is not to be found in a place but by one's inner efforts, beginning with a good Latin education, can easily be found in many of Erasmus' works, including most especially his *Life of Saint Jerome* (1516). In this work, he holds up St. Jerome's life and early upbringing—in many ways so drastically opposed to the picture he paints of his own in his *Brief Account*—as a model: ''He was carefully educated at home by his parents, and in an atmosphere of parental love and domestic affection . . . he drank in the knowledge of Christ from the very beginning. Then imbued with the rudiments of Christian piety and at the same time with a liberal education commensurate with his age, while still a child he was sent to Rome, the most distinguished teacher, as it were, in that era of both religious and secular learning, to be instructed in the liberal arts'' (*CWE* 61, 25). Unlike the moderns—at least those who had his education in their charge—the ancients were conscious that ''Christian piety and . . . a liberal education'' were the foundation of the ideal Christian life: ''The wisest parents, it seems, understood that it was very important among whom and by whom a child was first taught. . . . And so just as if they already understood at that time that this child of theirs had been born not for themselves but for the world at large, they saw to it that he was educated for the service of mankind and not for their own private concerns'' (*CWE* 61, 25).

Unlike St. Jerome, however, Erasmus was sent by the bishop to Paris to study theology. Although the bishop had promised an annual subvention, nothing was sent (as Erasmus observed, ''Great men are like that'' [*CWE* 4, 408]); sick, in poverty, ''repelled'' by modern theology, ''for he felt himself not disposed to undermine all its foundations with the prospect of being branded as a heretic'' (*CWE* 4, 408), Erasmus accepted an invitation to England from Lord Mountjoy, ''who was at that time his pupil and later his Maecenas, though more of a friend than a benefactor.'' During 1499–1500, Erasmus spent time in England with Thomas More* and John Colet,* beginning lifelong friendships with both. On his return, English customs seized all of the gold he had been given by his

English friends, and he arrived home as poor as when he left. In 1500 he published the first versions of the *Adages*; in 1501, he published an edition of Cicero's *De Officiis.* These two works attracted the attention of European humanists, and Erasmus' reputation as one devoted to, and expert in, *bonae litterae* began to grow. In 1504 Erasmus responded to an invitation to become a counselor to Philip with his *Panegyric for Archduke Philip of Austria,* which he described in the preface to the printed edition of 1504 as less a eulogy than an admonition, urging peace rather than war upon Philip; he also published the first edition of his *Enchiridion (The Handbook of the Christian Soldier).* In 1505, he returned to England, where he became friendly with William Warham, archbishop of Canterbury, to whom he would dedicate translations of two plays of Euripides in 1506 and his edition of St. Jerome in 1516. The years 1506–8 found him in Italy, where he received his doctorate in theology, became fluent in Greek, and published a second enlarged edition of the *Adages* in 1508 while staying at the home of Aldus Manutius in Venice. Apparently, forthcoming preferment in Rome was put off by the death of Henry VII, the ascension of Henry VIII to the English throne, and Erasmus' summons to return to England yet again. *The Praise of Folly* (first published in 1511) was conceived on his journey across the Alps and written at the house of Thomas More, to whom Erasmus dedicated it.

From 1509 to 1514 Erasmus was based in England and published a number of educational treatises and textbooks at the request of John Colet, the dean of St. Paul's, who had reendowed the St. Paul's Cathedral School in 1510; the most famous of these, the *Copia: Foundations of the Abundant Style* (written in 1512, dedicated to Colet, and first published in Paris in 1514), went through more than fifty editions during Erasmus' lifetime. During these years he also wrote the *De ratione studii* for Colet's school, revised the *Adages*, collaborated with Thomas More on Latin translations of Lucian's dialogues, translated works by Plutarch, and prepared editions of St. Basil and St. John Chrysostom. Except for financial insecurity, this stay was one of his happiest times; as he tells us in the *Brief Account*, "In England he had decided to spend the rest of his life" (409), but when the generous promises of his friends were not fulfilled, he traveled to Brabant, having been named one of the counselors of the future emperor Charles V, but hoping rather for funds to consider his editing and publishing enterprises; in *The Education of a Christian Prince* (published 1516) and, though less openly, in the *Julius Exclusis* (written c. 1513, published c. 1517 after circulating widely in manuscript), Erasmus continued to enlarge upon his picture of the ideal and far-from-ideal rulers. The war-making Pope Julius is refused entry to heaven by St. Peter; the ideal king must learn that he holds authority from the Prince of Peace. The unsuitability of war as an activity for Christians is developed at some length in a number of essays in the third edition of the *Adages*, culminating in the adage *Dulce bellum inexpertis* (War is sweet to those who have not experienced it) and published by Johann Froben of Basel in 1515.

In 1514, the new prior of Erasmus' monastery at Steyn, his old friend Servatius Rogerus, demanded that Erasmus return to his monastery. Instead, Erasmus began efforts to receive a papal dispensation of his monastic vows, which would call him back to England in 1516 and 1517 to press for, and finally to receive, his desired dispensation from Pope Leo X's agent, Andrea Ammonio. Erasmus' refusal to return to Steyn coincided with the beginning of a series of attacks upon his life and work, first by Martin Dorp, a former friend who attacked Erasmus on the behalf of the theology faculty at Louvain, who professed to regard his attacks upon theologians in *The Praise of Folly* as directed at them and who regarded his intention to produce a Greek edition of the New Testament as an attack upon the founding text of Christianity, the Vulgate Bible. Happily joining in the subsequent fray were Edward Lee, afterward archbishop of York, and an anonymous English monk. Erasmus wrote a lengthy apologia to Dorp (1515) and published (1520) a bitter attack on Lee; Thomas More wrote an even lengthier response to Dorp (1516) and savage attacks on Lee and the monk, the latter two published at Antwerp in 1520 as part of a volume defending Erasmus, *Epistolae aliquot eruditorum.* Dorp repented, conditioned on the promise that More's attack not be published, and later published an Erasmian lecture on the Pauline epistles in 1519, complete with laudatory comments from More. But the rising swell of attacks on Erasmus both from conservative Catholic theologians deeply suspicious of his Greek New Testament, his Latin Paraphrases of the New Testament (both dedicated to Pope Leo X), and his edition of the works of St. Jerome (all 1516) and later from Lutherans deeply resentful that Erasmus would not openly endorse Luther's program continued. To make things worse, Erasmus, who agreed with many of Luther's criticisms of Catholic ritual and the cult of ceremonies, was also attacked by the conservatives for not openly attacking Luther. Not even a letter of papal approval published with the second edition of the New Testament (1518) could silence the attacks of Catholic conservatives; and only the death of Erasmus' former friend, Ulrich von Hutten, who had become a fervent Lutheran and attacked Erasmus for his fearfulness in not publicly acknowledging Luther, could even slightly stem the attacks from the left upon one whom many had regarded as their inspiration.

The Louvain theologians, angered anew that Erasmus had undertaken to find masters in Hebrew, Greek, and Latin for a new Collegium Trilingue at the University of Louvain created by a bequest from Jerome Busleiden, recently deceased counselor of Prince Charles, still angered by his jests at "modern" theology, and rightly seeing in the new college an attempt to create an alternative kind of theology similar to that for which Erasmus had praised St. Jerome and to that which Erasmus had prayed in the *Paraclesis*, took advantage of the controversies raised by Luther's attacks on the abuses of the church to damn Erasmus as Luther's inspiration (if not indeed his ghostwriter!). Soon Erasmus was lamenting that instead of studying the philosophy of Christ, all too many found themselves disputing "about instances, relations, quiddities, and formalities with an obscure and irksome confusion of words" (*Paraclesis*, 101). Even when Erasmus initially supported Luther's gospel-based theology and his attacks on worldly corruption in the church, he lamented their intemperateness and feared that they would draw down the wrath of those who already hated ''human studies—for which they have a burning hatred, as likely to stand in the way of her majesty queen Theology, whom they value much more than they do Christ—and myself at the same time. . . . As for me, I keep myself uncommitted, so far as I can, in hopes of being able to do more for the revival of good literature. And I think that one goes further by courtesy and moderation than by clamour'' (Letter to Luther, 30 May 1519, *CWE* 6, 391). In a letter to Cardinal Albrecht of Brandenburg, Erasmus again blamed the quarrel on those who, ''for gain and despotic power, deliberately ensnare the consciences of men,'' those who would weigh the world ''with ordinances made by man,'' burden it with ''the opinion and dogmas of the schools,'' and allow it to be oppressed by ''the tyranny of mendicant friars'' who preach, ''to the exclusion of Christ, nothing save their own new and increasingly more shameless dogmas'' (15 October 1919, *CWE* 7, 112). Although Erasmus insists that he neither defends Luther nor is answerable for him, it is clear that the rhetorical weight of Erasmus' condemnation falls far more heavily on those whom Luther opposes than on Luther.

In November 1520, after the coronation of Charles as emperor and the issuance of the papal bull *Exsurge Domine* excommunicating Luther, Erasmus was asked by Elector Frederick the Wise how to respond to the papal official who conveyed the bull. Erasmus prepared a list of points in favor of defending Luther, which, though meant to be private, were almost immediately published under Erasmus' name in Leipzig. The *Axiomata* or the *Brief Notes of Erasmus of Rotterdam for the Cause of the Theologian Martin Luther* begin with the statement that the ''matter has sprung from a tainted source, the hatred of literature and the claim for spiritual domination'' and assert that the ''means by which it has been pursued are in keeping with this source—wrangling, conspiracies, bitter passions and poisonous libels.'' Noting that the ''persons by whom it is being pursued are suspect,'' Erasmus insists that ''the best authorities and those closest to the doctrine of the Gospels are least offended by Luther'' and that the ''world is thirsting for the gospel truth, and it seems to be borne on its way by some supernatural desire.'' He concludes his brief notes by suggesting that this desire ''should perhaps not be resisted by such hateful means'' (*CWE* 71, 106–7). Although Erasmus notes that Luther has said he is willing to submit to ''a public disputation before unbiased arbitrators,'' his enemies' refusal to agree casts their insistence upon using ''arguments which no Christian audience can tolerate'' into doubt that they are ''trying to forward their own interests'' rather than those of Christ or Christendom.

By 1522, Erasmus, who had earlier evaded a request from Pope Leo X to controvert Luther, was being pressed by his old friend Pope Adrian VI to write against Luther, to ''employ in an attack on these new heresies the literary skill with which a generous providence has endowed you so effectually. . . . You have great intellectual powers, extensive learning, and a readiness in writing such as in living memory has fallen to the lot of few or none, and in addition the greatest influence and popularity among those nations whence this evil took its rise'' (Halkin, 151), but Erasmus resisted, and not until 1524, provoked by Luther's attack on free will in his *Assertio* (1520), did Erasmus respond with his *On the Freedom of the Will.* Although, as late as 1523, when Erasmus wrote his *Inquisitio de Fide* (published in March 1524), he finds that Luther, though already excommunicated, believes in the same things that all Christians do, as expressed by Luther's assent in the colloquy to the articles of the Apostles' Creed, there were matters of substance as well as of style to which he objected in Luther's works. When Erasmus finally did break his public neutrality and write against Luther, the eyes of Europe were upon him, and the issue upon which he chose to focus was, at least for him, essential. The will's freedom is almost the sine qua non for anyone who has adopted an aesthetic based upon rhetorical persuasion, for there is hardly any point in trying to persuade readers to change their minds if, in fact, either they cannot or it is irrelevant even if they do.

Although the *Freedom of the Will* plunged Erasmus into a prolonged controversy with Luther, who responded with his *De servo arbitrio* (1525), to which in turn Erasmus responded in 1528 with his massive *Hyperaspistes* (published in two volumes in 1526 and 1527), it neither freed him from attacks by Catholics nor kept him from continuing both to attack the abuses of the modern theologians and to try to find a formula that would appease both Catholics and Lutherans and heal the widening schism. In *Concerning the Immense Mercy of God* (1524), Erasmus had argued that there are ''two main evils . . . of which the pious soul must beware if he wants to share in God's happiness. They are self-reliance and despair'' (*The Essential Works of Erasmus* [*EE*], 227). The cure for the first, clearly aimed at those whose confidence in human wisdom made all else superfluous, was to remind them that ''we are called by faith, that is to say by readiness, to believe'' and that ''faith is a free gift of God'' (239); the cure for the second, clearly aimed at those who believe that there is no place left for human efforts and whose consciousness of their sins outweighs their faith in God's promises, is to remember that God's mercy is always available: ''Mention has been made of prayers, tears, fasting, sackcloth, and ashes. These things do indeed obtain His mercy for us: but kindness for our neighbor actually, if I may use the expression, wrests it from Him'' (*EE*, 265). Erasmus envisioned a middle way between the arrogance of the theologians so forward in their attacks on the Gospels and the philosophy of Christ and the Lutherans, left totally dependent upon the will of God for salvation and helpless to do anything but wait for it.

Again, in *On Mending the Peace of the Church* (1533), Erasmus tried to bring the opposing sides together. Speaking to those who embrace ''the wisdom of this world, which rejects faith and investigates the things of God with human reasoning'' (*EE*, 349), Erasmus paints a picture of how failure can turn into success: ''Since . . . the entire man . . . is not capable of receiving heavenly gifts, what is left except that he becomes entirely deficient in himself and falls (to the point) whence, renewed and raised up by the spirit of God, he sees by faith the greatness of the gifts bestowed upon us by the goodness of God through his Son and worthily draws near his tabernacles'' (*EE*, 350). While Lutherans would reject the notion of desert that Erasmus' ''worthily'' implies, they could be happy with his description of the rhythms of a Christian life: ''Thus, to fail is to advance; thus, to lose one's life is to be vivified; to fail oneself is to be returned to oneself; to fall is to be raised up; to lose one's strength is to become strong in Christ; to die is to be transformed into God. For unless that which is animal dies, that which is spiritual does not begin to live'' (*EE*, 350). Yet it is hardly a peace offering to conservatives, and when, later, Erasmus turns to the question of the freedom of the will, his offered compromise will satisfy neither of the warring parties: ''Let us agree that we are justified by faith, i.e., the hearts of the faithful are thereby purified, provided we admit that the works of charity are necessary for salvation'' (*EE*, 379). Though for Erasmus both of these are essentials, Catholic conservatives and Lutherans would insist upon their mutual irreconcilability: the peace of the church was not to be mended.

Despite the controversies raging around him and his active role in them, Erasmus kept busy on works more to his liking as well. In the years following the publication of the first edition of the Greek New Testament, Erasmus published Paraphrases on Romans (1517), Galatians and Corinthians (1519), Ephesians, Philippians, Colossians, Thessalonians, Timothy, Titus, Philemon (1520), and Hebrews (1521). He completed the set with Paraphrases of Matthew (1522), Mark, Luke, and John (1523), dedicated respectively to Charles V, Francis I, Henry VIII, and Ferdinand, adding a Paraphrase of Acts dedicated to Pope Clement VII in 1524. The 1520s also saw the publication of a series of educational works: *Colloquies* and *De conscribendis epistolis* (1522), *Ciceronianus* and *De recta latini graecique sermonis pronuntiatione dialogus* (1528), and *De pueris statim ac liberaliter instituendis* (based primarily on Plutarch's *On the Education of Children* and Quintilian's *Institutio oratoria*) and *De civilitate morum puerilium* in 1529. During the 1520s, Erasmus also saw his editions of the works of St. Augustine and other church fathers published by Johann Froben at his press in Basel, but the winds of change were blowing too strong for him. In 1528, the University of Basel closed, and, after rioting, the mass was abolished, and evangelical services were made compulsory. In 1529 Erasmus accepted King Ferdinand's invitation to settle in Catholic Freiberg, where he stayed until 1535. He returned to Basel, completed *On Preaching*, and died on the night of 11 or 12 July 1536, the prince of humanists in a world where they were no longer welcome.

MAJOR WORKS AND THEMES

In the light of later events—occasionally at least partially caused by Erasmus' writings—it is clear that we can no longer see Erasmus' theological and literary works entirely as he intended us to see them. *The Praise of Folly* has probably had a greater impact than he might have dreamed; the works upon which he thought his reputation would rest—his Greek New Testament with its accompanying Latin translation, his edition of the works of St. Jerome with accompanying *Life of St. Jerome*, his defense of free will against Luther, and his attempts to find common ground between Catholics eager to purge the church of abuses and Lutherans prepared to damn it for its sins—are far less often read. His New Testament and Works of St. Jerome have been superseded by better texts. Yet attending to them will let us better understand Erasmus' centrality in the intellectual life of the early sixteenth century.

In *The Praise of Folly* (1511 and later editions), we can see the main Erasmian themes clearly laid out. Folly, Erasmus' speaker throughout the work, offers a realist view of human nature: "By Stoic definition wisdom means nothing else but being ruled by reason; and folly, by contrast, is being swayed by the dictates of the passions. So Jupiter, not wanting man's life to be wholly gloomy and grim, has bestowed far more passion than reason—you could reckon the ratio as twenty-four to one. . . . Then he set up two raging tyrants in opposition to reason's solitary power: anger . . . and lust, whose empire spreads far and wide, right down to the genitals. How far reason can prevail against the combined forces of these two the common life of man makes quite clear. She does the only thing she can, and shouts herself hoarse repeating formulas of virtue, while the other two bid her go hang herself and are increasingly noisy and offensive until at last their ruler is exhausted, gives up, and surrenders" (*CWE*, 27, 95). Folly's standard—the common life of man—allows her to mock the claims of those who would ignore such inconvenient realities, and throughout the work, she periodically returns to this standard in her commentary on her role in human life. She reserves her greatest wonder for those who seek an unobtainable wisdom: "Now I believe I can hear the philosophers protesting that it can only be misery to live in folly, illusion, deception, and ignorance. But it isn't—it's human. I don't see why they call it a misery when you're all born, formed, and fashioned in this pattern, and it's the common lot of all mankind" (*CWE*, 27, 106).

Not to be content with what we are is for Folly almost a sign of impiety: "[T]he innocent folk of the Golden Age had no learning to provide for them and lived under the guidance of nothing but natural instinct. . . . They were also too pious in their beliefs to develop an irreverent curiosity for probing the secrets of nature, measuring the stars, calculating their movements and influence, and seeking the hidden causes of the universe. They thought it sacrilege for mortal man to attempt to acquire knowledge outside his allotted portion. The madness of inquiring into what is beyond the heavens never even entered their heads. But as the innocence of the Golden Age gradually fell away, the branches of learning were invented by those evil spirits ["the 'demons' who were given their name because it means 'those who know' in Greek"], as I said" (*CWE*, 27, 107). Yet this impiety reigns not merely in the philosophical world but in the theological as well. In the case of the philosophers, Folly seems more amused than anything: ''[T]he philosophers . . . insist that they alone have wisdom and all other mortals are but fleeting shadows. Theirs is certainly a pleasant form of madness, which sets them building countless universes and measuring the sun, moon, stars, and planets by rule of thumb or a bit of string, and producing reasons for thunderbolts, winds, eclipses, and other inexplicable phenomena. They never pause for a moment, as if they were private secretaries to Nature, architect of the universe, or had come to us straight from the council of the gods. Meanwhile Nature has a fine laugh at them and their conjectures, for their total lack of certainty is obvious enough from the endless contention amongst themselves on every single point. They know nothing at all, yet they claim to know everything. Though ignorant even of themselves and sometimes not able to see the ditch or stone lying in their path, either because most of them are half-blind or because their minds are far away, they still boast that they can see ideas, universals, separate forms, prime matters, quiddities, ecceities'' (*CWE*, 27, 125–26).

Folly's attitude shifts, however, when she comes to the theologians, ''a remarkably supercilious and touchy lot'' (*CWE*, 27, 126), who are ingrates as well, ''none so unwilling to recognize my good services to them, and yet they're under obligation to me on several important counts, notably for their happiness in their self-love, which enables them to dwell in a sort of third heaven, looking down from aloft, almost with pity, on all the rest of mankind as so many cattle crawling on the face of the earth'' (*CWE*, 27, 126). Like the scientists, they claim mastery over the physical universe (they ''interpret hidden mysteries to suit themselves: how the world was created and designed; through what channels the stain of sin filtered down to posterity; by what means, in what measure, and how long Christ was formed in the Virgin's womb; how, in the Eucharist, accidents can subsist without a domicile'' (*CWE*, 27, 126). But their delusions are less harmless than those of the philosophers, because the theologians claim the power to make them the only basis for talking about God. Though their questions are silly (''What was the exact moment of divine generation? Are there several filiations in Christ? Is it a possible proposition that God the Father could hate his Son? Could God have taken on the form of a woman, a devil, a donkey, a gourd, or a flintstone? If so, how could a gourd have preached sermons, performed miracles, and been nailed to the cross? And what would Peter have consecrated if he had consecrated when the body of Christ still hung on the cross? Furthermore, at that same time could Christ have been called a man?'' [*CWE*, 27, 127]), they have successfully monopolized Christian discourse to the point that they have silenced the Apostles: ''Such is the erudition and complexity they all display that I fancy the apostles themselves would need the help of another Holy Spirit if they were obliged to join issue on these topics with our new breed of theologian. Paul could provide a living example of faith, but when he says 'Faith is the substance of things hoped for, the evidence of things not seen,' his definition is quite unscholastic. And though he provides the finest example of charity, in his first letter to the Corinthians, chapter 13, he neither divides nor defines it according to the rules of dialectic. The apostles consecrated the Eucharist with due piety, but had they been questioned about the *terminus a quo* and the *terminus ad quem*, about transubstantiation, and how the same body can be in different places, about the difference between the body of Christ in heaven, on the cross, and at the sacrament of the Eucharist, about the exact moment when transubstantiation takes place, seeing that the prayer which effects it is a distinct quantity extended in time, they wouldn't, in my opinion, have shown the same subtlety in their reply as the Scotists do'' (*CWE*, 27, 127).

While the theologians fight about these unknowable trifles, the work of the church goes undone: ''The apostles baptized wherever they went, yet nowhere did they teach the formal, material, efficient, and final cause of baptism, nor did they ever mention the delible and indelible marks of the sacraments. They worshipped, that is true, but in spirit, in accordance only with the words of the Gospel, 'God is a spirit: and they that worship him must worship in spirit and in truth.' Apparently it had never been revealed to them that a mediocre drawing sketched in charcoal on a wall should be worshipped in the same manner as Christ himself, provided that it had two fingers outstretched, long hair, and three rays sticking out from the halo fastened to the back of its head. Who could understand all this unless he has frittered away thirty-six whole years over the physics and metaphysics of Aristotle and Scotus? Similarly, the apostles repeatedly teach grace, but nowhere do they draw the distinction between grace *gratis data* and grace *gratificans*. They encourage good works without distinguishing between *opus operans and opus operatum*. Everywhere they teach charity, but fail to separate infused charity from what is acquired. Nor do they explain whether it is accident or substance, a thing created or uncreated. They detest sin, but on my life I'll swear they couldn't offer a scientific definition of what we call sin unless they'd been trained in the Scotist spirit'' (*CWE*, 27, 128). Folly takes pains to suggest the seriousness of her critique and insists that the theologians be treated not with the reverence they demand but with the contempt they truly deserve: ''You may suppose that I'm saying all this by way of a joke, and that's not surprising, seeing that amongst the theologians themselves there are some with superior education who are sickened by these theological minutiae, which they look upon as frivolous. Others too think it a damnable form of sacrilege and the worst sort of impiety for anyone to speak of matters so holy, which call for reverence rather than explanation, with a profane tongue, or to argue with the pagan subtlety of the heathen, presume to offer definitions, and pollute the majesty of divine theology with words and sentiments which are so trivial and even squalid'' (*CWE*, 129).

In passages like these, however, we note some slippage. No longer is Folly's standard ''the common life of man,'' but it is that of ''some with superior education''; the second perspective Folly has always shunned is here accepted as valid in order to critique the theologians of the ''trivial.'' Normally, Folly will recognize this view only to reject it, as she does in the midst of her discussion of prudence, when, having suggested that life is like a play, which is "all a sort of pretence, but it's the only way to act out this farce" (*CWE*, 27, 103), she considers and dismisses the appropriateness of a theater critic: "At this point let us suppose some wise man dropped from heaven confronts me and insists that the man whom all look up to as god and master is not even human, as he is ruled by his passions, like an animal. . . . If he had the same sort of thing to say about everyone else, what would happen? We should think him a crazy madman. Nothing is so foolish as mistimed wisdom, and nothing less sensible than misplaced sense. A man's conduct is misplaced if he doesn't adapt himself to things as they are . . . and asks for the play to stop being a play. On the other hand, it's a true sign of prudence not to want wisdom which extends beyond your share as an ordinary mortal, to be willing to overlook things along with the rest of the world or to wear your illusions with a good grace. People say that this is really a sign of folly, and I'm not setting out to deny it—so long as they'll admit on their side that this is the way to play the comedy of life" (*CWE*, 27, 103–4).

The Praise of Folly represents Erasmus both at his most playful and at his bitterest, and the way to see the relationship is to consider the metaphor of the Sileni Alcibiades that Folly introduces in this same discussion of prudence. Folly insists that "all human affairs are like the figures of Silenus described by Alcibiades and have two completely opposite faces, so that what is death at first sight . . . is life if you look within, and vice versa, life is death. The same applies to beauty and ugliness, riches and poverty, obscurity and fame, learning and ignorance, strength and weakness, the noble and the baseborn, happy and sad, good and bad fortune, friend and foe, healthy and harmful—in fact you'll find everything suddenly reversed if you open the Silenus" (*CWE*, 27, 102–3). In the adage of the same name (expanded to over 100 times its original length in the 1515 edition), Erasmus, in his own person, opens up this image for us: "The Sileni are said to have been a kind of small figure of carved wood, so made that they could be divided and opened. Thus, though when closed they looked like a caricature of a hideous flute-player, when opened they suddenly displayed a deity, so that this humorous surprise made the carver's skill all the more admirable" (*CWE*, 34, 264). Erasmus goes on to compare first Socrates and then Antisthenes, Diogenes, and Epictetus to one of the Sileni, but Christ turns out to be the ultimate example: "Observe the outside surface of this Silenus: to judge by ordinary standards, what could be humbler or more worthy of disdain? Parents of modest means and lowly station, and a humble home; poor Himself and with few and poor disciples. . . . And then His way of life: what a stranger He was to all physical comforts as He pursued through hunger and weariness, through insults and mockery the way that led to the cross! . . . And now, if one has the good fortune to have a nearer view of this Silenus, open . . . in heaven's name what a treasure you will find, in that cheap setting what a pearl, in that lowliness what grandeur, in that poverty what riches, in that weakness what unimaginable valour, in that disgrace what glory, in all those labours what perfect refreshment, and in that bitter death, in short, a never-failing spring of immortality!'' (*CWE*, 34, 264).

The problem, Erasmus argues, is twofold: our world contains mostly inside-out Sileni who wear their ''deity'' on the outside and have nothing precious within, while most beholders settle for the surface view, which they find attractive, and cannot fathom what lies hidden within: ''In this world there are, as it were, two worlds, which fight against each other in every way, one gross and corporeal, the other heavenly and already practising with all its might to become what it will one day be. In one of these, first place is taken by him who is as far as possible removed from what is truly good and burdened with what is falsely so called'' (*CWE*, 34, 276). What Erasmus has done in *The Praise of Folly* is to employ both views, sometimes sequentially, sometimes simultaneously, sometimes indiscriminately, and leave it to readers to sort out as well as they may when they are seeing only grossly or only spiritually, when they are seeing the two as they exist in simultaneous tension with each other, for at those times the ''carver's skill'' is ''all the more admirable.''

The problem can be seen most clearly if we consider Folly at the beginning of the work, where she presents herself as the ''true bestower of good things'' (*CWE*, 27, 87), ''the Alpha of all gods, when I dispense every benefit to all alike'' (*CWE*, 27, 90), and Christ at the end of the work, the Alpha and Omega, from whom, according to the canon of the mass, all good things come. Folly's promise—one that she does not keep at least while we are reading her words, which continuously make us see precisely how bleak our lives are—is that she brings relief from the human condition: ''Now suppose someone could look down on the life of a man from a great height, . . . how many disasters would he see in store for it! Man's birth is painful and sordid, his upbringing wearisome, his childhood fraught with dangers, and his youth hard-won with toil. Old age is a burden and death a harsh necessity; armies of disease close their ranks around him, misfortunes lie in wait, ill luck is always ready to attack. There's nothing without its tinge of acute bitterness, quite apart from all the evil things man does to man, such as the infliction of poverty, imprisonment, slander, dishonour, torture, treachery, betrayal, insult, litigation, and fraud'' (*CWE*, 27, 105). Folly claims that she alone can come to our aid when faced with this sordid reality: ''However, I am here, and with a mixture of ignorance and thoughtlessness, often with forgetfulness when things are bad, or sometimes hope of better things, with a sprinkling too of honeyed pleasures, I bring help in miseries like these'' (*CWE*, 27, 105). Wisdom would teach us that the lives of humans are like ''a swarm of flies or gnats quarreling amongst themselves, fighting, plotting, stealing, playing, making love, being born, growing old, and dying. It's hard to believe how much trouble and tragedy this tiny little creature can stir up'' (*CWE*, 27, 122); Folly does not deny that this is true, but she helps us find distraction from our troubles and tragedies.

Christ, on the other hand, takes a different approach, according to Folly. Because Christ became man in order to save man, Folly asserts, Christ became a fool for man's sake and refuses to have any interest in those not content to show themselves as he did: ''Christ too, though he is the wisdom of the Father, was made something of a fool himself in order to help the folly of mankind, when he assumed the nature of man and was seen in man's form; just as he was made sin so that he could redeem sinners. Nor did he wish them to be redeemed in any other way save by the folly of the cross and through his simple, ignorant apostles, to whom he unfailingly preached folly'' (*CWE*, 27, 148). Consequently, ''Christ always loathes and condemns those wiseacres who put their trust in their own intelligence; as Paul bears witness in no uncertain words when he says 'God has chosen the foolish things of the world,' and again 'God chose to save the world through folly,' since it could not be redeemed by wisdom. God himself makes this clear enough when he proclaims through the mouth of the prophet, 'I will destroy the wisdom of the wise and reject the intelligence of the intelligent.' So does Christ, when he gives thanks because the mystery of salvation had been hidden from the wise but revealed to little children, that is, to fools'' (*CWE*, 27, 147). Like Folly, Christ believes all to be fools, but unlike Folly, Christ cares for his fools and intends to save those who put their faith in Him and not in their own wisdom: ''So Paul openly condemns knowledge for building up conceit and doing harm, and I believe St. Bernard had him in mind when he interpreted the mountain on which Lucifer set up his seat as the mount of knowledge'' (*CWE*, 27, 148). In a sense, given their shared attitudes toward wisdom and the theologians puffed up with it, one could say that Folly and Christ differ as the exterior of the Sileni differ from the god within, as the corporeal differs from the spiritual; Folly's relief, however, is momentary, and Christ's is eternal. For Erasmus, the Folly of Christ, not the wisdom of the philosophers and the theologians, is ''the one and only way to achieve what others pursue by differing means, that is, true felicity'' (*CWE*, 34, 264–65).

In the light of the attacks evoked from those who thought themselves attacked by *The Praise of Folly*, it is not difficult to see Erasmus reflecting upon his own life and presenting an implicit defense of himself at this time in his *Life of Saint Jerome*, published 1516 in the first volume of his edition of the *Works* of St. Jerome. According to Erasmus, after completing the first phase of his education, St. Jerome ''began to think about choosing a way of life and about a suitable place, because he was not unaware that human happiness depends above all on the assumption of a mode of life suited to a person's natural disposition and chosen by careful reflection and not by chance. For some plunge headlong into a way of life before they know themselves'' (*CWE*, 61, 28). Like Erasmus, St. Jerome became a monk; unlike Erasmus, however, he was not compelled to do so but did so freely. Furthermore, the monastic life St. Jerome chose looks very much like the life Erasmus had been leading since he left his monastery: ''I must say, on the chance that the reader may labour under a misapprehension, that the life of a monk was far different at that time from what we see today, trammeled as it is by ceremonial formality. On the contrary, those for whom freedom especially was dear made their profession as monks. For first of all that freedom remained inviolate once the decision had been made, the power to come and go as one wished remained, and so did the most delightful and unrestricted opportunities for literary pursuits'' (*CWE*, 61, 29). To be a monk in St. Jerome's time was to be ''excused from public activities and from service and duties at the imperial court. Lastly they were free from the tyranny of some bishops, who even then became overbearing'' (*CWE*, 61, 29). For Erasmus, the model of St. Jerome could very well serve as a justification of his own way of life as well as of his own activities. Like St. Jerome, he had ''occupied himself with rhetoric more diligently'' than with other arts; like St. Jerome, he too believed that ''theology in the Latin world was practically incapable of effective speech, a situation, he felt, that turned many away from reading theological works''; like St. Jerome, he ''hoped more would take pleasure in sacred literature if theologians were to match the majesty of their discipline with dignity of style'' (*CWE*, 61, 27). Erasmus' argument in the *Life* was implicit but nonetheless quite clear: to demand that he return to the servitude and empty ritual of the monastery, to dismiss him as a mere rhetorician because he preferred St. Jerome's mode of theology to the triflings of the scholastic theologians of his own time—this was to deny not simply Erasmus' goals and accomplishments but St. Jerome's as well.

Those goals are spelled out openly in the *Paraclesis*, the Preface to Erasmus' 1516 Greek and Latin New Testament, where Erasmus prays that ''an eloquence far different than Cicero's be given me. . . . an eloquence which not only captivates the ear with its fleeting delight but which leaves a lasting sting in the minds of its hearers, which grips, which transforms, which sends away a far different listener than it had received'' (93). In the *Paraclesis*, Erasmus offers us a full statement of the program that he and More and their other friends have been supporting over the years. In place of the arid disputations of the Scholastics, Erasmus calls for a return to the study of the basic texts in which the philosophy of Christ is expressed, the New Testament and the works of the fathers, and urges that all Christians ''investigate, examine, explore each tenet. . . . Especially since this kind of wisdom, so extraordinary that it renders foolish once and for all the entire wisdom of this world, may be drawn from its few books as from the most limpid springs with far less labor than Aristotle's doctrine is extracted from so many obscure volumes, from those huge commentaries of the interpreters at odds with one another'' (96). What Erasmus is calling for is the end of the theologians' monopoly upon theology; what he wants is for all to take in as much as they are capable of being taught.

The Erasmian theologian is much closer to the Apostles than to the contemporary doctors of the church; love, not wisdom, must be the goal of a true teacher of the philosophy of Christ: ''To me he is truly a theologian who teaches not by skill with intricate syllogisms but by a disposition of mind, by the very expression and by the eyes, by his very life that riches should be disdained, that the Christian should not put his trust in the supports of this world but must rely entirely on heaven, that a wrong should not be avenged . . . that all good men should be loved and cherished equally as members of the same body, that the evil should be tolerated if they cannot be corrected. . . . And if anyone under the inspiration of the spirit of Christ preaches this kind doctrine, inculcates it, exhorts, incites, and encourages men to it, he indeed is truly a theologian, even if he should be a common laborer or weaver. And if anyone exemplifies this doctrine in his life itself, he is in fact a great doctor'' (98). Erasmus believed that if everyone would abandon the quibbles of the modern theologians and instead turn to the philosophy of Christ, then the world would be transformed: ''If princes in the execution of their duties would manifest what I have referred to as a vulgar doctrine, if priests would inculcate it in sermons, if schoolmasters would instill it in students rather than that erudition which they draw from the fonts of Aristotle and Averroes, Christendom would not be so disturbed on all sides by almost continuous war, everything would not be boiling over with such a mad desire to heap up riches by fair means or foul, every subject, sacred as well as profane, would not be made to resound everywhere with so much noisy disputation, and, finally, we would not differ from those who do not profess the philosophy of Christ merely in name and ceremonial. . . . If it should happen that [princes and magistrates, bishops and their delegated priests, and teachers] . . . having laid aside their own affairs, should sincerely cooperate in Christ, we would certainly see in not so many years a true and . . . genuine race of Christians everywhere emerge, a people who would restore the philosophy of Christ not in ceremonies alone and in syllogistic propositions but in the heart itself and in the whole life'' (99).

Erasmus' hopes, as we have seen, were dashed both by the emergence of Luther and by the conservative attacks Luther occasioned not simply on his own positions but also on Erasmus' attempts to bring theology back to the teachings of the church fathers, the Apostles, and Christ in the Gospels. What Erasmus had hoped to do was to offer the world those ''writings that bring you the living image of His holy mind and the speaking, healing, dying, rising Christ himself, and thus . . . render Him so present that you would see less than if you gazed upon Him with your very eyes'' (*Paraclesis*, 106). What he was forced to do was become a controversialist. In *The Freedom of the Will*, what is at stake is the whole Erasmian program. For Erasmus, the freedom of the will is so basic an axiom that he begins by saying that he sees almost no point in talking about the question since all the fathers of the church teach not only that the will is free but also that even if it were not, public morality demands that one act as if it were in any case. For Erasmus, the thought of man without free will (which he defines as ''the power of the human will whereby man can apply to or turn away from that which leads unto eternal salvation'' [*Freedom*, 20]) creates such unbearable strains that, given his choice of heresies, he would prefer Manichaeus to Wycliffe (from whom he feels Luther derived his teaching), for ''[T]he former explains good and evil by the two natures in man, but in such a way that we owe the good acts to God on account of his creation, and because we can, despite the power of darkness, implore the creator for help. This can help us to sin less and to do good more readily. If everything reduces itself to pure necessity, where does Wycliffe leave us any room for prayer or our own striving?'' (15).

Two main themes can be seen in this passage, ready to emerge at more length later on in the argument. First, Erasmus, while as willing as Luther to attribute man's good acts to God, also wants to insist that human ''striving'' for goodness is not fruitless. Second and equally important, the concept of a God who could damn men for the sins he compels them to commit is anathema to Erasmus. ''Who could love with all his heart a God who fires a hell with eternal pain, in order to punish there poor mankind for his own evil deeds, as if God enjoyed human distress?'' (12). Underlying these positions are some very basic assumptions on Erasmus' part about the nature of both man and God. Erasmus, like the Reformers, insists that man has fallen far from that ''image and likeness of God'' in which he was first created: ''Our will, considered as ability to choose or to avoid, had thus been weakened to a degree, so that it could not improve itself by its own natural means; it had lost its freedom and was obliged to serve the sin to which it willingly assented'' (22–23). Their insistence upon this point, in fact, set the Christian humanists apart from the Scholastics, who conceded the fall in theory but often acted as though it were but an inconvenience. In turn, however, what set the Reformers apart from the humanists was the Reformers' sense of the greater depths to which man had fallen. For Erasmus, ''Our power of judgment . . . has only been obscured by sin, and not extinguished'' (22), and, thanks to God's grace, ''which forgives sin, the freedom of the will has been restored. . . . This happens in such a manner that, first, one owes his salvation to the will of God, who both created and restored free will; and according to the orthodox, because of the help of divine grace, which always aids his effort, man can persevere in the right state without, however, being freed of his propensity to evil, which stems from the remains of sin once committed'' (23). Thanks to this universal restoration through Christ of a free will once lost to sin, man can once again play a role in the drama of his own salvation (see 29). Although Erasmus affirms that ''we owe salvation solely to God without whose grace the will of man could not be *effectively* free to achieve good'' (26; emphasis added), his faith in man, founded on his faith in a God whose love for his creatures would reach out and save them all if they would only cooperate with his grace, leads him to emphasize man's potential for goodness—especially if to God's grace is added the spur to man's intent of ''an eloquence which not only captivates the ear with its fleeting delight but which leaves a lasting sting in the minds of its hearers, which grips, which transforms, which sends away a far different listener than it received'' (*Paraclesis*, 93).

No sooner, however, does Erasmus conclude that ''[m]an is able to accomplish all things if God's grace aids him. Therefore it is possible that all works of man be good'' (78), than his fear of thereby encouraging ''man's trust in his own prowess and merits'' and his fear of the ''unbearable . . . arrogance of certain persons who boast of their good works and sell them to others according to measurement and weight like selling oil and soap'' (79) cause him to profess his understanding of the motives of those who have tried to diminish the freedom of the will in order to remind man of his dependence upon God. Indeed he might, for this is one of the main themes of *The Praise of Folly* and of many of the essays Erasmus added to the *Adages* during the second decade of the sixteenth century. Yet despite his fear of human pride, Erasmus rebukes the Reformers for their immoderation in seeking a remedy in assertions that ''[m]an is unable to accomplish anything unless God's grace helps him. Therefore there are no good works of man'' (78). He does so because such formulations imperil his conception of God, according to which ''[i]t is incompatible with the infinite love of God for man that a man's striving with all his might for grace should be frustrated'' (29).

In place of their extreme rejection of man's striving, he suggests a more ''balanced'' view: ''According to this moderation man can do a good, albeit imperfect work; man should not boast about it; there will be some merit, but man owes it completely to God. . . . But we do not assume that even a justified man is capable of nothing but sin'' (93). Although Erasmus, for the sake of combating pride, would be willing to deprive man of the ''merit'' to be gained by his ''imperfect'' works, he could do so only at a price far greater than he is willing to pay, for to attribute everything to God is to deprive man not only of pride but of hope. It is also to call into question his justice: ''Why, you ask, is anything attributed to the freedom of the will, then? It is in order to justify blaming the godless ones who resist spitefully the grace of God; to prevent calumnies attributing cruelty and injustice to God; to prevent despair in us; to prevent a false sense of security; to stimulate our efforts. For these reasons the freedom of the will is asserted by all. Yet it is, however, ineffectual without the continuous grace of God, in order not to arrogate anything to ourselves. Someone says, what's the good of the freedom of the will, if it does not effect anything? I answer, what's the good of the entire man, if God treats him like the potter his clay, or as he can deal with a pebble'' (93). Clearly, for Erasmus, ''effectual'' freedom for the will takes second place to God's grace, but it cannot disappear altogether without calling that very grace into question. Although Erasmus would very much like to leave man enough free will to give him more dignity than clay or pebbles, he will settle for leaving him only enough free will to be able obstinately to reject offered grace if he so chooses. Thus, God is not guilty of damning man; rather man is guilty of damning himself. A place remains for man's strivings toward charity, but God is still so much needed that man's wisdom and pride are humbled, and the philosophy of Christ is more necessary than the philosophies of men.

CRITICAL RECEPTION

The story of the rise, decline, fall, and recovery of Erasmus' critical reception is an immense one and has been told elsewhere (see Mansfield and Devereux). Beatus Rhenanus' *Life of Erasmus* (1540), commissioned to introduce Froben's nine-volume *Opera Omnia* (1538–40), dedicated to Charles V, attributes to him a revival of learning and theology: "In Germany and France letters lay cold and lifeless; hardly anyone knew Latin, no one Greek. And behold, immediately when the *Adagiorum chiliades* and the *De copia verborum et rerum* were published, the knowledge of languages began to come forth, like the sun breaking through the clouds." To the Council of Trent, however, Erasmus' works were too dangerous to be read. In the 1559 *Index of Forbidden Books*, all of Erasmus' works were banned, and in the revised version of 1564, some were to be allowed in expurgated form, but others (including *The Praise of Folly* and *The Colloquies*) were forbidden. This did not stop either the printing or the reading of Erasmus' works, and hundreds of editions poured off the presses (John Milton remarked that everyone was reading *The Praise of Folly* while he was a student at Cambridge University, and Sir Philip Sidney* and Shakespeare's* Hamlet have been suggested as careful readers of it as well), but it did mean that Erasmus was more likely to be found chained in the Protestant churches of England than he was in the libraries of the church to whose reform he had dedicated so much of his life. In the latter half of the twentieth century, Erasmus can again be seen as he was in the sixteenth, when Rabelais enthusiastically hailed him as one who had "so nurtured me with the pure breasts of your holy teaching that whatever I am and can do, if I do not owe to you alone what I have received, I should be the most ungrateful of all men today and in times to come. Therefore keep well perpetually, most beloved father, father and honour of your homeland, defender of literature, invincible champion of truth." Looking back over the nearly 500 years separating us from the beginnings of Erasmus' career, it is impossible to imagine what the sixteenth century would have been like had Erasmus never emerged from his monastery.

BIBLIOGRAPHY

Works by Desiderius Erasmus

Collected Works of Erasmus. 86 vols., in progress. Toronto: University of Toronto Press, 1974.

Colloquies of Erasmus. Trans. Craig R. Thompson. Chicago: University of Chicago Press, 1965.

Erasmus-Luther. *Discourse on Free Will*. Ed. and trans. Ernst F. Winter. New York: Frederick Ungar, 1961.

The Essential Works of Erasmus. Trans. John P. Dolan. New York: New American Library, 1964.

Paraclesis (1516). Erasmus. *Christian Humanism and the Reformation: Selected Writings*. Ed. John C. Olin. New York: Harper and Row, 1965.

Studies of Desiderius Erasmus

Bainton, Roland H. *Erasmus of Christendom.* New York: Scribners, 1969.

Bouwsma, William J. "The Two Faces of Humanism." In *Itinerarium Italicum: The Profile of the Italian Renaissance in the Mirror of Its European Transformations*, ed. Heiko A. Oberman. Leiden: E. J. Brill, 1975, 3–60.

Boyle, Marjourie O'Rourke. *Christening Pagan Mysteries: Erasmus in Pursuit of Wisdom.* Toronto: University of Toronto Press, 1981.

———. *Erasmus on Language and Method in Theology.* Toronto: University of Toronto Press, 1977.

Christian, Lynda Gregorian. "The Metamorphoses of Erasmus' 'Folly.' " *Journal of the History of Ideas* 32 (1971): 289–94.

Devereux, E. J. *Renaissance English Translations of Erasmus: A Bibliography to 1700.* Toronto: University of Toronto Press, 1983.

Halkin, Leon E. *Erasmus: A Critical Biography.* Trans. John Tonkin. Oxford: Blackwell, 1993.

Kaiser, Walter. *Praisers of Folly: Erasmus, Rabelais, Shakespeare.* London: Gollancz, 1964.

Mansfield, Bruce. *Interpretations of Erasmus c. 1750–1920: Man on His Own.* Toronto: University of Toronto Press, 1992.

———. *Phoenix of His Age: Interpretations of Erasmus c. 1550–1750.* Toronto: University of Toronto Press, 1979.

Markish, Shinon. *Erasmus and the Jews.* Trans. Anthony Olcott. Chicago: University of Chicago Press, 1986.

Rebhorn, Wayne. "The Metamorphoses of Moria: Structure and Meaning in *The Praises of Folly.*" *PMLA* 89 (1974): 463–76.

Rummel, Erika. *Erasmus' Annotations in the New Testament: From Philologist to Theologian.* Toronto: University of Toronto Press, 1986.

———. *Erasmus as a Translator of the Classics.* Toronto: University of Toronto Press, 1985.

Screech, M. A. *Ecstasy and the Praise of Folly.* London: Duckworth, 1980.

Sylvester, Richard. "The Problem of Unity in *The Praise of Folly.*" *English Literary Renaissance* 6 (1976): 125–39.

Thompson, Geraldine. *Under Pretext of Praise: Satiric Mode in Erasmus' Fiction.* Toronto: University of Toronto Press, 1973.

Tracy, James. D. *The Politics of Erasmus.* Toronto: University of Toronto Press, 1977.

Weiner, Andrew D. "Erasmus, More, and the Shape of Persuasion." *Moreana* 17 (1980): 87–98.

———. "Raphael's Eutopia and More's *Utopia*: Christian Humanism and the Limits of Reason." *Huntington Library Quarterly* 39 (1975): 1–27.

ANDREW D. WEINER

F

EDWARD FAIRFAX
(c. 1575–1635)

BIOGRAPHY

Edward Fairfax was born in Leeds about 1575. The second (and possibly illegitimate) son of an important Yorkshire gentleman, Fairfax shunned the active life, choosing rather to live in retirement with his family near the small Yorkshire town of Fewston. There he devoted himself to studies and to the leisurely literary life of a country squire, producing little and publishing less. Indeed, Fairfax would have been almost completely unknown in his time (and would be forgotten today) if it were not for his youthful translation of Torquato Tasso's* *Jerusalem Delivered.* Entitled *Godfrey of Boulloigne, or the Recoverie of Ierusalem,* it appeared in print in 1600 and immediately became an enormous success.

As far as we know, however, Fairfax made no effort to capitalize on this success. Although the translation is said to have been a favorite of both James I* and Charles I, Fairfax, in sharp contrast with Tasso, not only stayed away from court but also never even bothered to publish his other works. Of his twelve pastoral eclogues, for example, only three survive, and none appeared in print until the eighteenth century. His only other known work, a *Discourse of Witchcraft,* in which Fairfax describes what he believed to be the bewitchment of two of his own children, remained in manuscript until the nineteenth century despite the fact that the general topic was of great interest in the 1620s, when the work was written. He died and was buried in Fewston in 1635.

MAJOR WORKS AND THEMES

Fairfax's extant eclogues are charming, sophisticated exercises in a conventional, mainly Spenserian, pastoral manner. Equally conventional—and less charming—is the learning of the *Discourse on Witchcraft*, although the work has some special interest that derives from the intimate family circumstances that prompted its writing; Fairfax seems to have had no doubts about the power of the black arts. None of these works, however, provide anything but the remotest glimpse of the brilliance that he displays as a poetic translator in his *Godfrey of Boulloigne*.

Sparkling with the language and rhythms of Elizabethan narrative poetry at its best—reminiscent especially of Spenser's* *Faerie Queene—Godfrey of Boulloigne* is still the best way for the English reader with no Italian to get a sense of the *Jerusalem Delivered*. Fairfax follows Tasso very closely, rendering each ottava rima stanza in the original by one of his own, giving an accurate sense of action and character, and rarely falling into the awkwardness that is so often the affliction of translators forced to follow a genius that is not their own. Occasionally, it is true, Fairfax's knowledge of Italian appears to let him down, and sometimes he alters the tone, making Tasso's generalized descriptions more concrete, simplifying ambiguities, moralizing explicitly where Tasso—even in the *Jerusalem Conquered*—refrains from comment. Anyone who wishes to understand Tasso thoroughly cannot rely on Fairfax. Nevertheless, the virtues of his translation far outweigh its limitations, and it remains, nearly four centuries after its publication, a genuine pleasure to read.

CRITICAL RECEPTION

As previously mentioned, the poem's success was immediate and general. Besides the first two Stuart kings, its admirers included John Dryden, who reports in the preface to the *Fables* that he had heard Edmund Waller say that he learned his metrical skill from Fairfax's translation. This was high praise, because Dryden and later Augustans attributed to Waller a seminal role in the development of the polished style that they considered the standard of poetic taste. Since the Romantics, that standard has fallen from favor, of course, but Fairfax's translation has never really lost its preeminence despite the competition of later versions that might claim to be more literal or more up-to-date. It has been republished at least once in every century since it appeared and is still available.

BIBLIOGRAPHY

Works by Edward Fairfax

Daemonologia: A Discourse on Witchcraft. Ed. William Grainge. London: F. Mueller, 1970. (Repr. of 1882 ed.)

Godfrey of Bulloigne: A Critical Edition of Edward Fairfax's Translation of Torquato Tasso's Gerusalemme liberata, together with Fairfax's original poems. Ed. Kathleem M. Lea and T. M. Gang. Oxford: Oxford University Press, 1981.

Jerusalem Delivered. The Edward Fairfax Translation. Ed. Roberto Weiss. London: Centaur Press, 1962.

Studies of Edward Fairfax

Knutson, Roslyn L. "Henslowe's Naming of Parts: Entries in the Diary for Tamar Cham, 1592–3, and Godfrey of Bulloigne, 1594–5." *Notes and Queries* 30.2 (1983): 157–60.

Warren, Roger. " 'Now Folds the Lily All Her Sweetness Up': Tennyson and Edward Fairfax." *Tennyson Research Bulletin* 4.1 (1982): 28.

DAIN A. TRAFTON

GILES FLETCHER, THE ELDER
(1546–1611)

BIOGRAPHY

Giles Fletcher was born in November 1546, the second son to Richard Fletcher, who, four years later, was ordained in the Church of England. In 1561 Giles entered Eton College, where we see his young promise in the eleven Latin epigrams included in the collection of verses presented to the queen upon her visit. In 1565 Fletcher entered King's College, where he would stay for the next sixteen years. His academic career served as a fitting prelude to his later political posts. He received acclaim as a scholar, the customary progression of degrees, and the accompanying preferments. Along the way to becoming dean of arts and earning his doctor of civil laws degree, Fletcher served his college as lecturer of Greek, deputy orator, steward, and bursar and took part in, but avoided the lasting bruises of, religious controversies. All the while he dabbled in poetry seriously enough to contribute the customary Latin verses to commendatory collections. So—albeit in more powerful circles and with higher stakes and more severe consequences—would go the rest of Fletcher's professional life. A man of commanding intellect, political astuteness, and able diplomacy, he served his queen in a rich variety of ways, finding himself never far from a controversy, either officiating others' disputes or rescuing himself from his own, and amid it all he wrote a sonnet cycle worthy enough to keep his small place in a crowded canon of Tudor poets.

Fletcher left Cambridge in 1581 and was married, by his father, to Joan Sheafe. His eldest son, Phineas, was born in 1582, and in that same year Giles was made chancellor of the diocese of Sussex. In 1584 he was elected to Parliament and in 1585 was recommended by the queen and confirmed as the remembrancer of the city of London, an office he would hold until 1605. His duties included writing letters for the city and making copies of all letters sent to, and received by, the city, as well as attending upon the mayor and the aldermen for any variety of services or messages they might require. Fletcher likely subsisted at this time under the patronage of Sir Thomas Randolph and Sir Francis Walsingham. In 1586 he traveled to Scotland with Randolph as part of the negotiating team from Elizabeth* to James VI.* In the same year he traveled as a special agent of the queen to partake in messy trade negotiations with the senate of Hamburg. He returned, having secured a successful treaty, and in 1588 was sent by Elizabeth to Russia, where, after being received coldly, he withstood slights patiently and returned with the best treaty for the English since 1569.

In the autumn of 1590 Fletcher turned his attention to literary endeavors, intending to write a Latin history of the queen's time. However, failing to gain the patronage of Lord Burghley for this work, Fletcher turned to revising and expanding *Of the Rus Commonwealth*, which he published in 1591. In 1593 his *Licia or Poems of Love* was published anonymously "where unto is added the Rising to the Crowne of Richard the third." If there can be found any calm in Fletcher's life after leaving Cambridge, it would be these few years during which his English poetry, for which he is remembered, was produced. In the year 1596 any calm soon vanished when his brother Richard died, leaving behind eight children and a £1,400 debt to the queen. Fletcher took his brother's children into his own household, though he had nine children of his own by now. After persistent appeals he managed in 1597 to have his brother's debt discharged, though arguments over the estate would persist in future years in the form of suits against Giles from Richard's eldest son, Nathaniel.

In 1600 Cambridge University granted Fletcher a ten-year lease of Ringwood Parsonage, and if he did not yet yearn to retreat to his quieter days as a lecturer of Greek, the events of the next year would certainly spur such longing. The earl of Essex had become Fletcher's patron in 1596, and this support nearly proved his ruin after the Essex Rebellion in February 1601. Fletcher himself, though protesting his innocence, was brought in for questioning and held in custody for over a month. In 1605 he resigned his post of remembrancer. The final extant letter from him in 1609 indicates that he had never recouped financially and was still enduring the consequences of the crimes of his former patron. Giles Fletcher died on 11 March 1611 and is recalled in his eldest son's *Eclogs* as "Thelgon, poorest, but the worthiest swain, / That ever grac't unworthy povertie!"

MAJOR WORKS AND THEMES

When one weighs Fletcher's political service, particularly the successful trade agreements that he negotiated, with his relatively meager literary output, it seems clear that his most significant, if not lasting, contributions to his age were non-poetical. It is characteristic of the Tudor era that one of its most astute international political negotiators would likewise have some traffic with the Muses. Giles Fletcher's works include a significant amount of Latin verse, most of which was published during his Cambridge years: *Of the Rus Commonwealth*, "the most important book on Russia by an Englishmen in the sixteenth century" (Berry, 149); *The Rising To the Crowne of Richard the third. Written by him selfe*, a novel idea, but an unfortunately dull poem; and *Licia*, a cycle of fifty-two sonnets, an ode, a dialogue, three elegies, and one longer poem. Upon *Licia* Fletcher's literary reputation rests.

A work of unabashed imitation, *Licia* sports both learning and wit. Each sonnet owes something to the Latin poetry of Italian or French writers, to Watson or Daniel* or Sidney,* or to some combination of some or all of these sources. Fletcher is interested not in literal translations of his Continental sources, but in innovative adaptations. While Cupid makes a cameo appearance in every Elizabethan sonnet cycle, in *Licia* he is a central figure. No mere motif or convention, he is the energy and player in a number of the sonnets, with the interesting effect of deflecting attention away from both Licia and the poems' narrator and placing it upon Love him/itself.

Sidneyesque in his layering of narrative ironies, Fletcher produces in sonnet 33 the ultimate self-consuming artifact. Licia, the poet's invention, scolds the sonnet, "False Scrawle, untrue thou art, / To faine those sighes, that no where can be found," condemning it to the very fire with which the poet says he burns: "Thus at her word we ashes both became." Such inherent and only loosely veiled commentary upon the art of Love and the art of art in *Licia* holds, I believe, the central interest for contemporary readers.

CRITICAL RECEPTION

Interestingly, the words of Giles Fletcher that have garnered the most attention from literary critics over the years come not from his poetry, but from his brief introductory remarks to his sonnets dated 4 September 1593. Here, in much witty and postured defense of this idle enterprise, he observes at the very height of the sonnet-writing tradition what critics long afterward continue to preach: "[A] man may write of love, and not bee in love, as well as of husbandrie, and not goe to plough." Addressing the question of whether Fletcher's poetry might record an actual love affair, C. S. Lewis proclaims, "What he actually does is to poke fun at critics who ask such irrelevant questions" (*Oxford History of English Literature*, Cambridge, 1944, 493). More recently, Thomas Roche in his study *Petrarch and English Sonnet Cycles* (*AMS*, 1989) cautions, "We ignore at our peril the enigmatic statements of Giles Fletcher in the preface to his *Licia*" (335). Limiting the metaphorical possibilities to "the boy-meets-girl syndrome,'' Roche argues, is not something Fletcher and his contemporaries had any interest in doing.

Fletcher's chief patron in the twentieth century—and perhaps since the death of Phineas Fletcher—is Lloyd E. Berry, who published five Latin poems by Fletcher in 1961 and whose 1964 edition, *The English Works of Giles Fletcher the Elder*, offers access to the texts, a thorough biography, excellent introductory material, and elaborate explanatory notes. While Berry's edition cannot rescue Fletcher's ''Richard III'' from the obscurity I feel it well deserves, it does allow modern readers access to *Licia*, which has earned some attention despite its damnation by faint praise from Lewis: ''There is some feeling for nature in *Licia*, and some graceful fancy: no pathos and no exaltation'' (494). While they do not champion the pathos and exaltation of *Licia*, both Prescott (1978) and Røstvig (1991) bring more recent and more elaborate observations to bear upon Fletcher's poems.

BIBLIOGRAPHY

Works by Giles Fletcher, the Elder

Berry, Lloyd E., ed. *The English Works of Giles Fletcher the Elder*. Madison: University of Wisconsin Press, 1964.

———. ''Five Latin Poems by Giles Fletcher, the Elder.'' *Anglica Zeischrift fur Englische Philologie* 79 (1961): 338–77.

Schmidt, Albert J., ed. *Of the Rus Commonwealth*. Ithaca: Cornell University Press, 1966.

Studies of Giles Fletcher, the Elder

Prescott, Anne Lake. ''Licia's Temple: Giles Fletcher the Elder and Number Symbolism.'' *Renaissance and Reformation* 2 (1978): 170–81.

Røstvig, Maren-Sofie. ''Golden Phrases: The Poetics of Giles Fletcher.'' *Studies in Philology* 88.2 (1991): 169–200.

GARY M. BOUCHARD

JOHN FLORIO
(c. 1553–1625)

BIOGRAPHY

John, or Giovanni, Florio, was born about 1553 in London, the son of an expatriate Italian clergyman. His father, Michael Angelo Florio, had left his Franciscan friary in Italy and had been arrested in 1548 by the Inquisition in Rome. In 1550 he fled Rome and arrived at last in London, where for a short time he held a pastorate for Protestant Italian refugees and was patronized by William Cecil. He was later deprived of this pastorate. The elder Florio then turned to teaching Italian to support himself and his little family and became Lady Jane Grey's Italian master. This connection was later to lead Michael Angelo Florio to write a semihagiographical work about her. Upon the accession of Mary

Tudor, Michael left London, taking his family with him and settling as the pastor of the Reformed church in Soglio, in the Grisons canton of Switzerland. John Florio spent his first few years here, presumably instructed by his fiery and religiously unorthodox father, and was placed in 1563 at school in Tübingen.

It is unclear when Florio emigrated to England. He may have spent some time in France, as his mastery of that language certainly suggests personal contact. Ironically, the one place in Europe he may never have visited is Italy, given his and his father's devout Protestantism. Yet he was to be heavily responsible for the spreading of Italian culture and letters in educated English society. In *Queen Anna's New World of Words*, published in 1611, John Florio indicated that he had been teaching Italian for thirty-five years, which would set the date of his emigration at 1576 or before. He published his first book, appropriately enough called *Florio his First Fruits*, in London in 1578, and made the acquaintance of the puritanical Stephen Gosson, whose name appears on the title page. He later went to Oxford, matriculating at Magdalen, the Puritan college, in 1581. At this time he seems to have become friendly with Samuel Daniel* and married Daniel's sister. Sometimes it has been maintained that this woman was named "Rosa" Daniel and was the model for Edmund Spenser's* Rosalind, and Florio for Menalcas in *The Shepheardes Calendar* (1579), but there is no objective evidence for this. In 1580 Florio translated Cartier's voyages out of Italian into English. From 1583 to 1585, he worked at the French Embassy for Michel Castelnau, lord of Mauvissière, until the latter's hasty departure from England, and seems to have stayed on to work for the latter's successor, during which time he became acquainted with Giordano Bruno.* It has been suggested that Florio was employed by the efficient Elizabethan spy system under Sir Frances Walsingham, and certainly his linguistic versatility and loyal Protestantism would have made him an excellent candidate for this sort of work. Mauvissière asked him to present his respects to a number of highly influential people in the English court, including Robert Dudley, earl of Leicester, and his nephew, Sir Philip Sidney,* in whose literary circle he became active. He was later patronized by Henry Wriothesley, earl of Southhampton, to whom he dedicated his *Worlde of Wordes* in 1598 and through whom he probably became acquainted with William Shakespeare.* The year 1603 saw the publication of perhaps his most famous work, the translation of Montaigne's* *Essays*, which he dedicated to Lucy, countess of Bedford, Lady Anne Harington, Lady Penelope Rich, the countess of Rutland, and two of his pupils, Lady Elizabeth Grey and Lady Mary Neville.

Upon the accession of James* in 1603, Florio became Italian reader to Queen Anne, acting as her secretary and as Italian tutor to the Princess Elizabeth and probably to Prince Henry, a position of artistic and political influence. He held this position until Queen Anne's death in 1619. At this time he lost his position at court and died in debt in 1625. His literary colleagues and associates included, in addition to Shakespeare and Daniel, Ben Jonson,* Thomas Nashe,* and John

Donne.* Signing himself ''Risoluto'' or ''Resolute,'' and using the motto ''che si contenta gode'' (''who contents himself, enjoys''), Florio held a small but secure position in the world of English Renaissance letters.

MAJOR WORKS AND THEMES

Florio's work can be divided into three major areas, all of which involved his polyglot ability: his Italian–English dialogue books (the *First* and *Second Fruits*), his dictionaries (*Worlde of Wordes, Queen Anna's World of Words*), and his translation of Montaigne.

The *First Fruits* (1578) is a self-teaching guide to Italian. It is obvious upon a perusal of this and the *Second Fruits* that Florio considers himself to be an instructor not merely in language but in classical Italian culture and good taste. It is clear that in the xenophobic English atmosphere of the 1570s Florio has to make a case for studying other languages, and he makes it by pointing out the limited utility of English: ''[W]hat think you of this English tongue, tel me, I pray you?'' ''It is a language that wyl do you good in England, but passe Dover, it is worth nothing.'' He criticizes English theater as well, both from the social standpoint: ''I beleeve there is much knaverie used at those Comodies; what think you? So beleeve I also'' and from the neo-Aristotelian viewpoint: ''[B]ut they are neither right comedies, nor right tragedies.'' The *First Fruits* contains a long section on proverbs, one of Florio's weaknesses, and Shakespeare put his ''Venetia, chi non ti vede, non ti prese'' (''Venice, only those who do not see you, do not prize you''), into Holofernes mouth in *Love's Labor's Lost*, a fact that has led many scholars to conclude that Holofernes is, in part, a parody of Florio. In any event, the *First Fruits* and its companion the *Second Fruits*, with their dialogues and phrase lists, may well be what Shakespeare had in mind when he had Sir Toby Belch make the preposterous remark of Sir Andrew Aguecheek that ''he knows three or four languages word for word without book,'' when his French does not include a knowledge of the word ''*pourquoi*.''

Florio delighted in collecting words, and in his dictionaries (*Worlde of Wordes, Queen Anna's World of Words*) he continually updated and augmented his collection. Verbosity is much in evidence in his translation of Montaigne. Florio was the first translator of Montaigne in English and an inventive one, but his euphuistic style is very unlike Montaigne's succinct rumination—he often doubles words and whole phrases. Unlike Montaigne, he was a staunch Protestant, and this led him to alter and add to statements that supported Montaigne's Catholicism. Yet the same Protestantism is his justification for translation itself in his preface: ''[H]old we ignorance the mother of devotion, praying and preaching in an unknowne tongue.'' Perhaps his own challenge stands as the best reply to his critics: ''[I]f any thinke he could do better, let him trie; then will he better thinke of what is done. . . . If this doone it may please you, as I wish it may, and I hope it shall, I with you shall be pleased: though not, yet still I am the same resolute IHON FLORIO.''

CRITICAL RECEPTION

During his lifetime, Florio had a number of influential Italian students and literary patrons and was much respected and indeed copied. He has been credited with promoting the literary prose fashions of euphuism, proverbs, and Arcadianism. He was the subject of admiring poetry by his brother-in-law Daniel and probably assisted Ben Jonson, especially with the Italianisms of *Volpone*. He was also the subject of attacks by Gabriel Harvey* and of probable satires by Shakespeare and John Donne, among others.

The *Essays* have been continuously successful and have largely fulfilled Florio's wish to the countess of Bedford: "[I]t may not onely serve you . . . to repeate in true English what you reade in fine French, but many thousands more, to tell them in their owne, what they would be taught in an other language." His translation has been criticized as wordy and overly artistic, what Frances Yates called "Florio's Montaigne," an entirely different work. Recently, post-structuralist criticism has redeemed Florio's translation, suggesting that his usage of multiple words and thereby refusing to choose is more faithful to the open spirit of translation, eluding as it does the concept of a "right translation."

Finally, Florio has been numbered among the candidates for anti-Stratfordian authorship of Shakepeare's works. This idea rests largely upon the grounds of the rather limited unknowns of Shakespeare's life but also upon the incidence of Montaigne (especially in *Hamlet* and *The Tempest*) and the Italianate content of Shakespeare's plays. It does not, however, satisfactorily explain why he might wish to satirize himself.

BIBLIOGRAPHY

Works by John Florio

The Essays, or Moral, Politic and Military Discourses of Lord Michel de Montaigne. London, 1603, 1613, 1632.

Florio his first Fruits . . . Also a perfect Induction to the Italian. London, 1578.

Florios Second Fruits. London, 1591.

Giardino di Ricreatione. London, 1591.

A Letter lately written from Rome, by an Italian gentleman. London, 1585.

The New Found Politic. Disclosing the secret natures and dispositions as well of private persons as of Statesmen and Courtiers . . . By Traiano Boccalini. London, 1626.

Queen Anna's New World of Words. London, 1611, 1611, 1638. (New edition of *Worlde of Wordes.*)

A short and brief narration of the two navigations and discoveries to the Northwest parts called New France . . . London, 1580.

A Worlde of Wordes, or Most Copious, and exact Dictionarie in Italian and English. London, 1598.

Studies of John Florio

Ashley, Leonard R. N. "Floreat Florio: A Fruitful Area for Shakespeare Scholarship." *Shakespeare Newsletter* 30.6 (December 1980): 49.

Conley, Tom. "Institutionalizing Translation: On Florio's Montaigne." In *Demarcating the Discipline: Philosophy, Literature, Art*, ed. Samuel Weber. Minneapolis: University of Minnesota Press, 1986.

Frantz, David O. "Florio's Use of Contemporary Italian Literature in *A Worlde of Wordes*." *Dictionaries: Journal of the Dictionary Society of North America* 1 (1979): 47–56.

Murray, Timothy. "Translating Montaigne's Crypts: Melancholic Relations and the Sites of Altarbiography." *Bucknell Review* 35.2 (1992): 121–49.

Yates, Frances. *John Florio: The Life of an Italian in Shakespeare's England*. Cambridge: Cambridge University Press, 1934.

MELISSA D. AARON

ABRAHAM FRAUNCE
(c. 1558–1593/1633)

BIOGRAPHY

Abraham Fraunce was born in Shrewsbury and educated first at the famous Shrewsbury School (1571/72), which Sir Philip Sidney* and Fulke Greville* attended, and later went on to St. John's College, Cambridge, matriculating in 1576, and, supported by Sidney, himself, Fraunce received from there a B.A. in 1579–80 and M.A. in 1583. While at Cambridge he acted in the anonymous *Hymenaeus* (1578/79) and again in the college's 1579 production of *Ricardus Tertius*. Writing of his Cambridge days, Fraunce noted in his preface to *The Lawiers Logike* that, though he experienced in full the "perpetuall vexation of Spirite, and continuall consumption of body, incident to euery scholler," such pain of study was offset by the "delicate and pleasant a kinde of learning," and "I do not repent that I was a Vniuersitie man." Fraunce thereafter became a student at Gray's Inn until he was admitted to the bar in 1588, and he went on to practice law in the court of the marches of Wales. After the death of Sir Philip Sidney in 1586, Mary, Countess of Pembroke,* became his patroness, and Fraunce dedicated nearly all of his literary productions to her. After failing to obtain the office of queen's solicitor in 1590, Fraunce soon after entered the service of Sir John Egerton, first earl of Bridgewater, with whom, it is assumed, he remained until his own death. Fraunce's death has conventionally been set in the year 1633; but recently this has been challenged. Victor Skretkowicz, in a piece of literary detective work, has convincingly argued that nothing definitive is known of Fraunce's life after 1592 and that the evidence for the traditional dating of Fraunce's death was an error made by the nineteenth-century antiquarian Joseph Hunter, who confused Abraham Fraunce and Abraham Darcie. The case, however, is not closed.

MAJOR WORKS AND THEMES

During years spanning roughly 1585 through 1592, virtually everything literary for which Fraunce is known was published: *The Lamentations of Amyntas for the Death of Phillis* (1587), *The Arcadian Rhetorike* (1588), *The Lawiers Logike* (1588), *The Countess of Pembroke's Emanuel* (1591), and *The Countess of Pembroke's Ivychurch* (1591), which was republished and expanded in 1592 with the inclusion of *Amyntas Dale*. Other works by Fraunce consist of his unpublished Cambridge-days compositions, including three treatises on Ramistic rhetoric (one of which, *The Shepheardes Logike*, was published in 1969) and an insufferable Latin drama, *Victoria*, which will probably never be translated and, if so, scarcely ever read and certainly never acted. Finally, in many ways standing apart from his poetic and rhetorical works, there is his *Insignium, Armorum, Emblematum, Hieroglyphicorum et Symbolorm Explicatio* (1588), a treatise in Latin prose on the nature of symbolism.

CRITICAL RECEPTION

Though Fraunce is seen today as a minor literary figure at best, he was well received by the literati of his day. In his "Honour of the Garter," George Peele* described Fraunce as "the peerless sweet translator of our times"; Francis Meres named Fraunce with Sidney and Spenser* for "the best for pastoral"; Thomas Lodge,* Thomas Nashe,* Gabriel Harvey,* and Spenser all wrote highly of him; and his connections with Sir Philip Sidney and the Sidney circle endured throughout his life.

Though Fraunce was, like many of his contemporaries, versatile in his literary endeavors, both in his rhetorical work and in his poetry, he is best described as a translator rather than an innovator. His *Amyntas* is a translation of Thomas Watson's poem, itself a translation from Tasso,* and Fraunce offered nary a word in acknowledgment to his source until Watson gently (though publicly) objected. Fraunce's principal contribution as poet/translator was his most egregious failure: all of his poetical works in English are in hexameters, rendering him (and Thomas Campion) virtually the lone versifiers of the period to write quantitative English verse. Fraunce's poetic shortcomings did not go unnoticed by Ben Jonson,* whose harsh assessment of Fraunce's verse offers at once the only negative contemporary comment made regarding Fraunce and the prevailing view of Fraunce's place in English poetry today. "Abram Francis in his English Hexameters was a Foole."

In the realm of rhetoric, Fraunce has enjoyed a more favorable view from posterity. Fraunce was a Ramist, and most of his rhetorical treatises echo ideas found in Ramus—(*The Lawiers Logike* is largely a paraphrase of Ramus' *Dialectique*)—or Ramus' principal disciple, Talaeus (*The Arcadian Rhetorike* being a virtual translation of the 1567 version of Talaeus' *Rhétorique*). The title *The Arcadian Rhetorike* is illustrative regarding what renders it, at least from a literary standpoint, unique: *The Arcadian Rhetorike* (or, the *Praecepts of Rhetorike Made Plaine by examples*). Though fellow Ramist Dudley Fenner had used examples to illustrate Ramistic rhetorical principles, rather than drawing illustrative extracts from Scripture as did Fenner, Fraunce turned to secular literary sources, drawing passages from an array of languages, ancient and modern, featuring Homer, Virgil, Tasso, Du Bartas, Boscan, Garcilaso, and Sidney. The result is a veritable anthology of literary passages gleaned to illustrate Ramist precepts—prompting Richard Schoeck to dub Fraunce "that most romantic of Ramists." Furthermore, in the inclusion of Sidney—and, though to a lesser extent, Spenser—Fraunce offers what can be accurately termed a vernacular poetic, with English authors taking the place of honor after Homer and Virgil. *The Lawiers Logike*, on the other hand, is, as Wilbur Howell points out, "the first systematic attempt in English to adapt logical theory to legal learning and to interpret Ramism to lawyers" (223). In his preface, Fraunce both defends Ramus and objects to detractors who seek "to locke vp Logike in secreate corners"; *The Lawiers Logike* was an attempt to remedy that neglect by making logic accessible even to carters and cobblers. Despite Fraunce's avowed hope of disseminating logic and rhetoric to a wider, nonprofessional audience, his rhetorical works never reached beyond a small coterie, both *The Arcadian Rhetorike* and *The Lawiers Logike* being published only once.

BIBLIOGRAPHY

Works by Abraham Fraunce

The Arcadian Rhetorike. 1588. Ed. Ethel Seaton. London, 1950.

The Countess of Pembrokes Emanuel. 1591.

The Countess of Pembrokes Ivychurch. 1591.

Insignium, Armorm, Emblematum, Hieroglyphicorum et Symbolorm Explicatio. 1588.

The Lamentations of Amyntas for the Death of Phillis. 1587, 1588, 1589, 1591 (and in *Ivychurch*, 1596).

The Lawiers Logike. 1588.

Renaissance Latin Drama in England. 2d series 13. Ed. Horst-Dieter Blume. Hildesheim: Georg Olms Verlag, 1991.

The Shepheardes Logike.

The Third Part of the Countess of Pembrokes Ivychurch/Amyntas Dale. 1592.

Victoria. Ed. G. C. Moore Smith. (Bang's *Materialien*, 1906, xiv).

Studies of Abraham Faunce

Attridge, Derek. *Well-weighed Syllables: Elizabethan Verse in Classical Metres*. Cambridge: Cambridge University Press, 1975.

Buxton, John. *Sir Philip Sidney and the English Renaissance*. London, 1954.

Dunn, Catherine. "A Survey of Experiments in Quantitative Verse in the English Renaissance." Diss., UCLA, 1967.

Howell, Wilbur S. *Logic and Rhetoric in England, 1500–1700*. Princeton: Princeton University Press, 1956.

Koller, Kathrine. "Abraham Fraunce and Edmund Spenser." *ELH* 7 (1940): 108–20.

Morris, Harry. "Richard Bamfield's *Amyntas*, and the Sidney Circle." *PMLA* 74.2 (September 1959): 318–24.

Orr, David. *Italian Renaissance Drama in England before 1625*. Chapel Hill: University of North Carolina Press, 1970.

Pomeroy, Ralph S. "The Ramist as Fallacy-Hunter: Abraham Fraunce and *The Lawiers Logike*." *Renaissance Quarterly* 40.2 (Summer 1987): 224–46.

Schoeck, Richard. ''Rhetoric and Law in 16th Century England.'' *Studies in Philology* 50 (1953): 110–27.

Skretkowicz, V. ''Abraham Fraunce and Abraham Darcie.'' *The Library* 31.3 (1976): series 5, 239–42.

Staton, Walter F., Jr., and Harry Morris. ''Thomas Watson and Abraham Fraunce.'' *PMLA* 76.1 (March 1961): 150–53.

Taylor, Anthony B. ''Abraham Fraunce's Debts to Arthur Golding in *Amintas Dale*.'' *Notes and Queries* 231 (September 1986): series 3, 333–36.

JOHN WILSON

G

GEORGE GASCOIGNE
(c. 1539–1577)

BIOGRAPHY

George Gascoigne was born c. 1539 to Sir John Gascoigne and his wife, Margaret Scargell Gascoigne. The son of well-off country gentry, Gascoigne attended Cambridge and went to Grey's Inn to study law in 1555. He stood for Parliament in 1557, but with the arrival of the new queen at court, he left Grey's Inn for life as a courtier in 1558. During this period Gascoigne was thought to have written much of his early poetry. In addition, he translated two plays from the Italian, *Jocasta* and *Supposes*. Despite this promising beginning, young Gascoigne never reached his full promise, partly due to his litigious and squabbling nature; in fact, even his own father reportedly tried to disinherit him.

These problems were exacerbated by his marriage to Elizabeth Bacon Bretton Boyes in 1562. Although his wife had been widowed once by William Bretton—she was the mother of the writer Nicholas Bretton—she had also married a man named Edward Boyes after Bretton's death. Unfortunately, her divorce from Boyes was evidently not legitimate, causing numerous legal and financial problems for the couple. Between the lawsuits surrounding his family and the dissipations of court life, Gascoigne was quickly on the road to bankruptcy and, over the course of ten years, retired to the country, returned to Grey's Inn, and then finally retired to the country again. Eventually his downward spiral landed him in debtor's prison in 1570.

Disheartened by his spectacular lack of success in law, land-ownership, and courtiership, Gascoigne thought to redeem his fortunes by soldiering in the Low Country Wars. However, as he recounts in his long poem ''Dulce Bellum Inexpertis,'' waging war under conditions of mismanagement and ineptitude was not really the path to riches and fame either. In 1574, when he returned from the Continent, he found out that *A Hundreth Sundrie Flowres*, a book of his erotic poetry and prose published a year earlier, had been censored and withdrawn. After this point, Gascoigne decided to write in the moralizing vein, and after brushing up *A Hundreth Sundrie Flowres* and rereleasing it as the *Posies*—which was also banned—he wrote several texts promoting the virtuous life, including *The Steele Glas, The Complaint of Phylomene, The Glasse of Government, The Droome of Doomes day, A Delicate Diet for daintie-mouthde Droonkardes*, and *The Grief of Joye*. Fortuitously, his worldly fortunes also took an upswing during the last few years of his life. In 1575, Gascoigne was asked to write an entertainment for the Queen's Progress at Kenilworth and, under Burghley's aegis, was sent to the Low Country as an observer for the court in 1576. From this mission came his description of the bloody Spanish sack of Antwerp, ''The Spoyle of Antwerp,'' which he published upon his return. In 1577, he died of a lingering illness while visiting a friend in Lincolnshire. Gascoigne was ultimately an unfortunate figure; in a less forgiving vein, Gabriel Harvey* described him as having ''want of resolution & constancy, [which] marred his witt & undid himself.'' But his real accomplishment as a precursor to the golden poets is unquestioned.

MAJOR WORKS AND THEMES

George Gascoigne worked in a variety of genres and formats that were unique for his period. His three dramatic pieces, *Supposes, Jocasta*, and *The Glasse of Government*, were, respectively, the first translation of an Italian prose comedy, the first performed translation of a Greek tragedy, and the first English original blank-verse drama. His ''Adventures of Master F. J.'' was one of the first important pieces of English prose fiction, and *A Hundreth Sundrie Flowres* contained a loosely connected group of sonnets that was arguably the first sonnet sequence. Despite this unique variety and influence, Gascoigne's writing was rarely celebrated during his lifetime or after.

Much of his work was paradoxically connected, as he chose to write of the dangers of ambition and desire at court and in love, while at the same time writing works deliberately designed to get him notice and preferment. His love poetry uses conventional Petrarchan methods of expressing unfulfilled desire; an unusually fine aspect of some of his poetry is his examination of the effects of aging on his public ambitions and his private loves in such poems as ''Gascoignes Lullabie'' and ''Gascoignes Recantation.'' These poems, as well as others such as ''Gascoignes Wodmanship,'' reflect a sadness at misspent youth that is more than a mere conventionality. As Gascoigne points out in the ''Wodmanship,'' his ''youthfull yeares myspente'' reflect an inability to hit the mark that would grant him the fulfillment of his ambitions and desires. Armed with this realization, with regret we see him repeatedly musing on the vanity of his early life that led him to pursue a sequence of futile courses of endeavor.

This undercurrent emerges when we consider his later works, where he asks for favor from patrons during his period of worldly renunciation. He wrote and performed in key entertainment for Queen Elizabeth* at Kenilworth, as I have suggested, and wrote a masque in honor of the marriage of the Viscount Montague's children. These pieces have all the fawning one could wish from a good courtier, including Gascoigne in the guise of the character Sylvanus trotting beside the queen's horse, reciting his lines. These later pieces, written during Gascoigne's period of repentance after the dual banning of his book of poetry for its lascivious and immoral nature, reflect Gascoigne's better judgment about what will help him in the world.

Aside from his own lack of ability to succeed in the attainment of worldly fortune, Gascoigne seems to be trying to use his literature to make up for the literary and political mistake that was part of the publication of his first book, *A Hundreth Sundrie Flowres*. After its initial censorship, apparently because of lascivious and scandalous content, Gascoigne made a few changes in order and in content, but once again the renamed *Posies* was censored by the queen's commissioners. Given the evidence of his changes, much of the problems seemed to stem from his ribald and engaging prose romance, ''The Adventures of Master F. J.'' Interspersed with the occasional love poem, this prose piece describes F. J.'s affair with the married Lady Elinor, who eventually grows tired of him. The plot is made more complicated by the crush that a virtuous Lady Fraunces has on F. J. at the same time. Some supposed the plot of this work to be a roman à clef. When Gascoigne rewrote the piece, he changed the venue from northern England to Italy and tried to make it appear as though it were written originally by an Italian author. This attempt to attribute the book's lewdness to Continental lapses in morality did not succeed.

In his later writings, Gascoigne seems anxious to establish himself both as a moralist and as a seasoned traveler. Particularly in his latter role, he provides us with a fascinating look at what one Englishman thought of the troubles on the Continent and the futility of the religious/economic war being fought there. As Gascoigne points out in ''Dulce Bellum Inexpertis,'' ''warre seemes sweete to such as little knowe / What commes therby, what frutes it bringeth forth'' (35.3–4). In his ''Spoyle of Antwerp,'' he readily describes the savagery and veniality of the Spaniards during their invasion as well as the corrupt and cowardly Dutch. Even taking into account sometime English xenophobia, his description of a city laid to waste and repeatedly ravished is affecting and moving.

The ending of his description of the sacking of Antwerp by the Spaniards asks God to continue protecting the English while punishing the unrighteous. This moralistic tone became even stronger in his following works. *The Glasse of Government* is a prodigal-son play that rewards the plodding, dutiful sons over the quick-witted, independent sons. Those who learn the simplicity of virtue best get the rewards in this play. In such works as *The Steele Glas* and *The Complaint of Phylomene*, he talks vividly about the fruitlessness of worldly ambitions and desires by his satire on courtly behavior and through his rewriting of Ovid's story of Philomela. The overtly moralistic tracts, *The Droome of Doomes day* and *A Delicate Diet for daintie-mouthde Droonkardes*, use the works of church fathers such as Pope Innocent and St. Augustine to discuss the inevitability of death and destruction in the face of sin.

CRITICAL RECEPTION

Despite the size of his literary output, Gascoigne is often ignored by critics except in passing. Part of this slighting stems from his time; he is a little too early to be considered part of the literary boom of the late sixteenth century. His "plain style," a combination, in some estimations, of Chaucer and Petrarch, also makes him difficult to classify. However, as I stated earlier, the wide variety of his writings, as well as the representative failures of his careers, makes him an important figure for study. Yvor Winters, in a well-known critical essay, saw Gascoigne as a master of his craft who in his "Woodmanship" wrote "one of the greatest passages in English lyrical poetry" (101). Despite this high praise, current critics tend to view Gascoigne as little more than a transitional figure.

Many of Gascoigne's critics who do treat him fully tend to take a biographical approach. Influenced mainly by C. T. Prouty's treatment in his definitive biography of Gascoigne, this type of criticism feeds off the self-referentiality of Gascoigne's works and his ambivalence about his successes and failures. Given Gascoigne's status as the prototypical Renaissance failure at "self-fashioning," his poems of remorse as well as the false lures of court life ring only too true. The large variety of Gascoigne's experiences have lent themselves to such new historicist treatments as McCoy's "Gascoigne's 'Poemata castrata': The Wages of Courtly Success," where he examines the cutting off of Gascoigne's poetic authority in the service of state authority.

This type of approach also influences another current critical strain that looks at Gascoigne's interactions with poetry, language, and the role of the poet as maker. Some critics prefer to examine Gascoigne's classical and medieval antecedents, such as Roy T. Eriksen, who discusses the influence of Augustinian and Christian thought on the work, or Nancy Williams, who looks at the influence of classical studies on Gascoigne's moral literature. Other critics have chosen to look at the issues of writing in Gascoigne's work based on his own musings on rhetoric. Concerned, like other writers of his day, about the role of the literature in England, Gascoigne wrote a short essay, "Certayne Notes of Instruction," as well as frontispieces and introductions on writerly intention and technique. Rowe and Staub have pointed out in their studies that Gascoigne's work is very tied up with the issues of authority and the relationship of words to the truth. They both use the highly self-conscious "Adventures of Master

F. J.'' to explore Gascoigne's ''[concern] with reading and interpretation—with, in other words, the creation of a capable literary audience—and with the relationship between literature and empirical reality'' (Rowe, 272). These critics fruitfully explore the mid-to-late sixteenth-century literary obsession with the uses, purposes, and formats of fictional literature.

Much work remains to be done on Gascoigne's collections of prose and poetry. Given his status as one always on the periphery of success, his literature provides the perfect picture of the aspiring early modern courtier. In addition, his time on the Continent and his writings about those experiences provide a fascinating picture of the perceptions of an astute yet representative Englishman, about the developments of his day. His best works, as Winters aptly pointed out over fifty-five years ago, still await adequate attention.

BIBLIOGRAPHY

Works by George Gascoigne

The Complete Works of George Gascoigne in Two Volumes. Ed. John W. Cunliffe. Cambridge: Cambridge University Press, 1907, 1910.

A Hundreth Sundrie Flowres. Ed. C. T. Prouty. *The University of Missouri Studies* 17.2 (1942): 1–304.

The Steele Glas and The Complainte of Phylomene. Ed. William L. Wallace. Salzburg, Austria: Institut für Englische Sprache und Literatur, 1975.

Studies of George Gascoigne

Eriksen, Roy T. ''Two into One: The Unity of George Gascoigne's Companion Poems.'' *Studies in Philology* 81 (1984): 275–98.

Haynes, Evelyn. ''George Gascoigne: A Bibliography of Secondary Sources.'' *Bulletin of Bibliography* 49.3 (1992): 209–14.

Hedley, Jane. ''Allegoria: Gascoigne's Master Trope.'' *English Literary Renaissance* 11 (1981): 148–64.

Johnson, Ronald C. *George Gascoigne*. New York: Twayne, 1972.

McCoy, Richard C. ''Gascoigne's 'Poëmata castrata': The Wages of Courtly Success.'' *Criticism* 27 (1985): 29–55.

Mills, Jerry Leath. ''Recent Studies in Gascoigne.'' *English Literary Renaissance* 3 (1973): 322–27.

Prouty, C. T. *George Gascoigne: Elizabethan Courtier, Soldier, and Poet*. New York: Columbia University Press, 1942.

Rowe, George E. ''Interpretation, Sixteenth-Century Readers, and George Gascoigne's 'The Adventures of Master F. J.' '' *ELH* 48 (1981): 271–89.

Staub, Susan C. '' 'According to My Source': Fictionality in 'The Adventures of Master F. J.' '' *Studies in Philology* 87 (1990): 111–19.

Williams, Nancy. ''The Eight Parts of a Theme in 'Gascoigne's Memories: III.' '' *Studies in Philology* 83 (1986): 117–37.

Winters, Yvor. ''The 16th Century Lyric in England: A Critical and Historical Reinterpretation.'' In *Elizabethan Poetry: Modern Essays in Criticism*, ed. Paul J. Alpers. New York: Oxford University Press, 1967, 93–125.

IRENE S. BURGESS

WILLIAM GILBERT
(1544–1603)

BIOGRAPHY

William Gilbert's reputation rests upon his research into magnetism, seemingly a far remove from his original field of medicine. Gilbert was born 24 May 1544 in Colchester, Essex, and died on 10 December (30 November, old style) 1603. After receiving the B.A., M.A., and M.D. from Cambridge, he began to practice medicine in London in 1573. Like William Harvey,* he became a fellow of the College of Physicians, eventually donating all of his books and instruments to that institution. Twenty-seven years later appeared his work on magnets, magnetism, and the earth as a magnet. Here he outlines the research methods he used to conclude that the earth operates as a magnet. Almost immediately afterward he was appointed physician to Elizabeth. James I renewed the appointment, but Gilbert died within the year.

MAJOR WORKS AND THEMES

Gilbert's masterpiece, *De Magnete* (1600), probably the greatest treatise on physics first published in England, argues, with full scientific demonstration and even a section on etymology, that the earth is a huge ball-like magnet. Thus, he is the father of magnetic and electrical science, for which he coined several essential terms such as ''electrical attraction,'' ''electrical force,'' and ''magnetic pole.'' He also demonstrated practical uses of this theory in relation to the compass needle and navigation without stars. A second work on the *New Philosophy of Our Sublunar World* was published posthumously in 1651. Here he argues that the magnetism of the earth is generated by its rotation and that magnetism is the force that holds the planets in their orbits. Without an examination of the manuscripts from which the work was published, it would be difficult to say how much of this was original to Gilbert and how much was influenced by the scientific work of Kepler and Galileo. Copernicus'* influence is duly noted.

CRITICAL RECEPTION

Gilbert must have had contacts with the powerful (he seems heavily influenced by Bacon*), but he earned little mention among his contemporaries, except for praise from Galileo and Bacon. His theory, however, came into scientific currency almost immediately, causing Dryden in the next age to remark, ''Gilbert shall live till loadstones cease to draw.'' With William Harvey he can be seen as the founder of modern science. There is no recent biographical work on

Gilbert. His work on magnetism is available in a late Victorian translation (1893).

BIBLIOGRAPHY

Works by William Gilbert

De Mundo Nostro Sublunari Philosophia Nova. Ed. Suzanne Kelly. Amsterdam: Hertzberger, 1965.

On the Loadstone and Magnetic Bodies. Trans. P. Fleury Mottelay. Chicago: Encyclopedia Brittanica, 1955 (orig. 1893).

Studies of William Gilbert

Benham, Charles Edwin. *William Gilbert of Colchester: A Sketch of His Magnetic Philosophy.* Colchester: Benham, 1902.

Cooke, Conrad William. *William Gilbert of Colchester.* London: Bedford Press, 1890.

Thompson, Silvanus Phillips. *Gilbert of Colchester: An Elizabethan Magnetizer.* London: Chiswick Press, 1891.

FRANCIS R. CZERWINSKI

ROBERT GREENE
(c. 1558–1592)

BIOGRAPHY

Robert Greene was one of the earliest English writers to realize the potential of printed works as commodities; he was, as Theophilus Cibber said in 1753, "amongst the first of our poets who writ for bread" (in Crupi, 17). Greene even marketed future works, specifically his Conny-catching (confidence game) pamphlets, through prefatory "teasers" about information to be revealed in later works, presumably to entice prospective buyers. For the same reason, he went so far as to let stand a reputation, probably unmerited, that he had committed crimes similar to those he describes in the Conny-catching pamphlets. By using "probably," we intend to indicate how few certainties there are surrounding Robert Greene's life.

The sources we have for biographic data on Greene are his own works—the repentances and the semiautobiographical *A Groatsworth of Wit*—and the occasional mention of him in friends' writings, most notably in Thomas Nashe* and in Gabriel Harvey's* *Four Letters.* But the value of the autobiographical data is lessened somewhat because Greene always had an eye on the marketplace and because his publisher, Henry Chettle, may have written both Greene's deathbed repentance and his *A Groatsworth of Wit.* Also, because the *Four Letters* is a castigation of Greene by a Harvey who was furious over insults aimed at himself and his family in Greene's *A Quip for an Upstart Courtier*, Harvey's descriptions of Greene's lifestyle are suspect as well. With the preceding cautions in mind, we can present what is thought to be known about Robert Greene's life.

Greene seems to have been torn between a desire for respectability and a lust for physical pleasure. While his reputation bespeaks a man in almost constant rebellion against conservative values, the many dedications of his works to members of the nobility hint at a wish for the traditional and respectable position of an author who has a patron. He was a flamboyantly dissolute character who produced copious works, perhaps as many as forty-one but certainly more than thirty-five and with a rapidity that astounded his friends. According to Nashe, ''in a night & a day would he haue yarkt vp a Pamphlet as well as in seauen yeare'' (1:287), and Nashe hardly exaggerates, considering Greene wrote all but one of his works between 1583 and 1592. But Nashe, in nearly his next breath, diminishes Greene's achievements—and adds to the Greene myth—by implying Greene wrote only to maintain his licentious existence: ''He made no account of winning credit by his workes . . . his only care was to have a spel in his purse to coniure vp a good cuppe of wine with at all times'' (1:287).

Greene was born in Norwich, probably in 1558, and attended Saint John's College as a sizar (a poor student who performed various tasks to pay his way). He was an undistinguished scholar yet received his M.A. from Clare Hall in Cambridge in 1583 and in 1588 an honorary M.A. from Oxford. During his college years, possibly under the influence of the wealthier students he served, Greene developed a taste for wild living. Also during his college period, perhaps as early as 1579, he married a Norwich gentleman's daughter, who would bear him a son. Greene apparently stayed with his wife for about as long as it took him to spend her dowry; then he made for London. In his *Repentance*, Greene says he left her to escape her pleas that he abandon his profligate lifestyle. The date for this desertion, from a reference in the *Repentance* to a separation of six years, places it in 1586. But considering the number of works Greene published before 1586 (eight) and the unlikelihood of his wife's dowry lasting more than a few years, it seems reasonable to place Greene in London by 1583, the year the second part of the romance *Mamillia* was entered with the stationer's register.

Once in London, Greene engaged in a flurry of production. He developed the reputation of an incorrigible reveler but was never accused of any serious crime. He was, however, supposed to have had a friendship with a criminal named Cutting Ball, later hanged, and a relationship with Ball's sister, a prostitute, which produced a son named Fortunatus (dubbed ''Infortunatus'' by Harvey). It is reasonable to surmise that Greene's association with this segment of London society formed the basis for his Conny-catching pamphlets.

Greene's death in 1592 at only thirty-four can be seen as a manifestation of the tensions of living in a small community of driven writers. Of the five other writers in Greene's circle between the ages of twenty-five and thirty-five in 1590—Thomas Nashe, Christopher Marlowe,* Thomas Watson, George Peele,* and Thomas Lodge*—all were dead by 1595 except Nashe, who was also thirty-four when he died in 1601, and Lodge (d. 1625), who took up the full-time profession of medicine. This group of writers, with Nashe the most caustic and

Greene a close second, lived hard and exacerbated the pressures upon themselves by both competing with each other and offending those in power. Greene's attack on the social status of Gabriel Harvey's family so incensed Harvey that he not only wrote the well-known *Four Letters* but continued to compose pamphlets vilifying Greene for years after Greene's death, stopped only by an edict from the authorities forbidding him and Nashe (who defended Greene) from any further publications on the subject.

Despite his popularity as a writer, Greene died alone, in poverty, having been dependent on the good graces of a shoemaker's wife, one Mrs. Isam, for a roof over his head. The story, from Harvey, is that Greene became ill with the sickness that would lead to his death from an excess of pickled herring and Rhenish wine during a revel with Nashe. Nashe would later deny being present. One of Greene's last visitors (perhaps only visitor, for it seems that all Greene's friends, including Nashe, abandoned him) was Cutting Ball's prostitute sister, Greene's mistress. If Chettle is to be believed, then Greene's final act before death was to write a note to his long-estranged wife asking her forgiveness and requesting she pay the shoemaker "tenne pound, and but for him I had perished in the streetes" (32).

MAJOR WORKS AND THEMES

As a dramatist, Greene was, for the most part, unsuccessful, yet powerful and influential. Of the five plays definitely attributable to him, none were published before his death. Two of the plays, *Alphonsus, King of Aragon* and *The Scottish Historie of James the fourth* are not known to have been performed; and the remaining three, *Orlando Furioso, A Looking Glass . . .*, and *Friar Bacon and Friar Bungay*, had one, four, and ten performances, respectively, all of which occurred during 1592 and 1593, except for one performance of *Friar Bacon and Friar Bungay* in 1602 by the queen's players. *Alphonsus* is the story of the peasant Alphonsus, rising above his humble beginnings to fulfill a heroic destiny. He defeats the Great Turk in battle and marries his daughter, Iphigina. The play is considered by many to be an awkward and hyperbolic imitation of Marlowe's* *Tamburlaine*, an assessment with which we have no pointed disagreement.

A similar heroic rise occurs in Greene's *Orlando Furioso*. Greene's main alteration of Ariosto's* plot is to have his Angelica remain faithful to Orlando, though Orlando's suspicions of her faithlessness provide the driving conflict of the play. Because *Orlando* also imitates Marlowe, though less so than *Alphonsus* but with even more awkwardness of language, some have said that this play is a parody of *Tamburlaine*. However, it is more likely that the text we have is a corrupt version published from playbooks with little editing; so it is more useful, suggests Charles W. Crupi, if we attempt to examine the play's larger structures for evidence of Greene's intentions, one of which is to display "the victory of love over war and madness" (108). There is no difficulty, though, involved in determining the intentions behind *A Lookinge Glasse for London and England.* Coauthored with Thomas Lodge, *A Lookinge Glasse* is a didactic play in the morality tradition with a hint of Puritan repentance. It relates the story of Jonah and Nineveh and is obviously asking London and England to examine their sins as if they were Nineveh and Assyria.

The remaining two plays, *James IV* and *Friar Bacon and Friar Bungay*, are clearly Greene's best. *James IV* is based not on historical chronicle but on a tale found in Cinthio's novellas. It is a romantic comedy in which the benefits of a strong monarchy and the perils of parasitic courtiers constitute two of the major themes. Though the play has little to do with historical fact, it is valuable for its thematic content. Through the characters of Bohan and Oberon, Greene develops an argument between a Jaques-like cynicism and an optimism based on the realization that all is merely "seeming." If others might handle these themes more adeptly, Greene must at least be given credit for influence on their writings, perhaps extending to Shakespeare's* *As You Like It* and *A Midsummer Night's Dream*, if not to *The Tempest*.

Friar Bacon and Friar Bungay is said by J. Churton Collins to stand "in the same relation to Marlowe's *Faustus* as *Alphonsus* stood to his *Tamburlaine*, not indeed in the sense of borrowing from it, but in the fact that it was intended to rival it" (2). But to say only that and nothing more would diminish the significance of the play as one of the first in English to have a double plot and its function of providing the groundwork for the development of romantic comedy by Shakespeare and others.

The play concerns the friars' magic creation of a brazen head, which will philosophize as well as shield England, and the resolution of a love triangle involving Edward, Prince of Wales (Edward I), Margaret (daughter of a game keeper), and Lord Lacy. The plots intertwine when Friar Bacon agrees to use magic to help Edward woo Margaret, who is really in love with Lacy. The broad complications are Bacon's growing and losing struggle to keep his magical abilities from being manipulated by demons and Edward's disruption of the social order by attempting to marry someone of lower station. Near the play's end, Bacon renounces his powers as evil, promising to spend the remainder of his days "in pure deuotion, praying to my God" (4.3.1851), and Edward realizes his duty to the realm and agrees to marry Elinor of Castile. The play ends with order restored and England improved as the final line, Henry III's, shows: "Thus glories *England* over all the West"(5.3.2101).

Greene's nineteen romances, too numerous to discuss in sufficient detail here, are all what might be called "patterned fiction." That is, into whatever areas of thought the romances may move, they take as their starting point conflicts surrounding love, then expand on those conflicts to debate moral and social positions (Barker, 76–77). For example, in *Gwydonius, the Carde of Fancie*, Greene has Gwydonius, the son of the duke of Metelyne and (at first) a typical prodigal, not return home, as expected, after squandering his money. Instead, Gwydonius travels to the dukedom of his father's rival, Orlanio, where he marries Orlanio's daughter, Castania, and ends up serving in the army his father-in-law is sending against his father. When it is discovered whose son he is, Gwydonius is imprisoned, but Orlanio's son, Thersandro, releases him upon the promise that Gwydonius will put in a good word for him with his sister, Lewcippa, who represents the good child who remained at home. So with a young man pursuing the object of his love for its guiding frame, *Gwydonius* moves to examine love between parent and child, loyalty and to whom one owes it, and the parents' role during their children's courtships and after their marriages.

Though Greene's best-known romance *Pandosto, or the Triumph of Time*, has been important mainly as the source for Shakespeare's *The Winter's Tale*, it was highly popular in its own time. *Pandosto* went through seven editions before *The Winter's Tale* was ever performed and went on to have eighteen more editions in the seventeenth century and sixteen in the eighteenth century. Most recently, Lori Humphrey Newcomb has found an investigation into the popular reception of *Pandosto* an excellent tool for examining the culture of its time. According to Newcomb, works like *Pandosto*, popular with the common people, engendered both derision and a discussion about limiting access to them by the elite.

Even more useful than *Pandosto* for examining the culture are the pulp non-fiction works Greene produced at the end of his career, the cony-catching pamphlets. Written and published between 1590 and the time of his death, they comprise six tracts describing a wide variety of swindles. The pamphlets demonstrate Greene's adoption of a plainer voice than the elevated, euphuistic style—popularized by John Lyly*—that typified his earlier prose works. At the same time, he embarked on a copious vernacular exploration of the seamy underbelly of urban London and the characters who peopled it—cardsharps, cutpurses, horse thieves, and prostitutes—ostensibly with the intent of offering some form of moral edification and encouragement to the criminals to repent. The sincerity of that purported intention has been the subject of debate virtually since the pamphlets began to appear, but one thing is certain: Greene carefully sidesteps passing absolute moral judgment on the conniving individuals who populate *The Defence of Conny Catching, A Notable Discovery of Coosnage*, and the like. Instead, he assiduously marries admirable and less-than-admirable qualities in his subjects, not creating the flat characters one might find in a morality play (and in some of Greene's plays and romances), but rather realistically representing them as complex, very human individuals who populate a world with which he himself was familiar.

CRITICAL RECEPTION

The level of Greene's familiarity with the lifestyle he at once glamorizes and deplores in the pamphlets is, of course, a matter of debate as well, and Greene contributes to the enigma in no small way by inserting himself as a character in his work. Throughout these tracts, Greene posits himself as a collaborator-cum-informer, knowledgeable of highly detailed aspects of criminal life and willing to share just enough with his readers to ensure that they are "conned" into buying his next publication. Indeed, Greene tantalizes his audience, on one hand, with narrative definitions of the illicit vocabulary of thieves and, on the other, intrigues with promises to reveal names and dangerous techniques the next time around. Supposedly, in the *Blacke Booke*, which *The Blacke Bookes Messenger* promised would be out soon, Greene actually did give the names and addresses of some of the criminals, but after his death, according to Chettle, cony-catchers stole the manuscript. In *The Second Part of Conny-Catching*, Greene goes so far as to suggest that these villains had threatened to "cut off [his] right hand for penning downe their abhominable practises" (6), so it is possible the theft is not a fabrication.

To Henry Chettle, then, and Greene's final two pamphlets we turn before closing. These two pamphlets are *Greens Groatsworth of Wit, bought with a Million of Repentance*, the story of Roberto, a prodigal who leads his brother astray; and *The Repentance of Robert Greene, Maister of Artes*, wherein, as mentioned, Greene, on the verge of death, repents of his wasteful life. *Groatsworth* contains Greene's apparent criticism of Shakespeare (for plagiarism?) and the famous "upstart Crow" remark, but as these remarks have been discussed at length, they need not be dealt with here.

In *Groatsworth*, Greene interrupts the work—"Here (Gentlemen) breake I off *Robertoes* speach; whose life in most parts agreeing with mine" (Carroll, 75)—to give another deathbed repentance. Both of these repentances provide much of the information included in biographies of Robert Greene, but it is likely neither was written by Greene. Henry Chettle, "a printer of limited means who occasionally turned his hand to writing" (1), published the pamphlets, and almost at once he was accused by Nashe and others of writing them. Chettle admitted to making a copy of *Groatsworth* because "it was il written, as sometimes *Greenes* hand was none of the best" (2), and the debate over authorship began. It has continued now for 400 years, for as late as 1994 D. Allen Carroll published a full-length book arguing that Chettle had a far greater hand in *Groatsworth* than has been thought. Whether or not Carroll is right, it somehow seems fitting that Robert Greene, a pioneer in self-promotion, should have his name used after death to increase the sales of a product.

BIBLIOGRAPHY

Works by Robert Greene

The Dramatic and Poetical Works of Robert Greene and George Peele. London: Routledge, 1861.

Life and Complete Works in Prose and Verse of Robert Greene. Ed. Alexander B. Grosart. London, 1881–86.

Plays and Poems of Robert Greene. Ed. J. Churton Collins. Oxford: Clarendon Press, 1905.

Studies of Robert Greene

Baldwin, Anna. "From the *Clerk's Tale* to *The Winter's Tale*." In *Chaucer Traditions: Studies in Honour of Derek Brewer*, ed. Ruth Morse and Barry Windeatt. Cambridge: Cambridge University Press, 1990, 199–212.

Barker, W. W. ''Rhetorical Romance: The 'Frivolous Toyes' of Robert Greene.'' In *Unfolded Tales: Essays on Renaissance Romance*, ed. George M. Logan and Gordon Teskey. Ithaca, NY: Cornell University Press, 1989, 74–97.

Carroll, D. Allen, ed. *Greene's Groatsworth of Wit*. Binghamton, NY: Medieval and Renaissance Texts and Studies, 1994.

———. ''The Player-Patron in *Greene's Groatsworth of Wit (1592)*.'' *Studies in Philology* 91 (1994): 301–12.

Crupi, Charles W. *Robert Greene*. Boston: Twayne, 1986

Dean, James Seay. *Robert Greene: A Reference Guide*. Boston: G. K. Hall, 1984.

Grantley, Darryll. ''*The Winter's Tale* and Early Religious Drama.'' *Comparative Drama* 20 (1986): 17–37.

Harvey, Gabriel. *Foure Letters and certeine Sonnets, especially touching Robert Greene and other parties by him abused*. Ed. G. B. Harrison, Bodley Head quartos. London: John Lane, Bodley Head, 1922.

Heilman, Robert B. ''Greene's Euphuism and Some Congeneric Styles.'' In *Unfolded Tales: Essays on Renaissance Romance*, ed. George M. Logan and Gordon Teskey. Ithaca, NY: Cornell University Press, 1989, 49–73.

Newcomb, Lori Humphrey. '' 'Social Things': The Production of Popular Culture in the Reception of Robert Greene's *Pandosto*.'' *ELH* 61 (1994): 753–81.

Peterson, Douglas L. ''Lyly, Greene, and Shakespeare and the Recreations of Princes.'' In *Shakespeare Studies*, ed. J. Leeds Barrol. New York: Burt Franklin, 1988, 67–88.

Relihan, Constance. ''The Narrative Strategies of Robert Greene's Cony-catching Pamphlets.'' *Cahiers Elisabethains* 37 (April 1990): 9–15.

Woods, Paula M. ''Greene's Conny-Catching Courtesans: The Moral Ambiguity of Prostitution.'' *Explorations in Renaissance Culture* 18 (1992): 111–24.

THE OREGON MANNERISTS
(Monica Durant, Mary A. Peters, and Kenneth R. Wright)

FULKE GREVILLE
(1554–1628)

BIOGRAPHY

Fulke Greville's long life encompassed the reigns of both Queen Elizabeth* and King James.* Born to a wealthy Warwickshire family in 1554, five years before Elizabeth ascended the throne, he died at the hands of a knife-wielding servant some seventy-four years later, in the third year of the reign of Charles I. His longevity was nowhere more impressive than in the realm of politics, where a decade-long exile from James' government ended in 1614 with his being made chancellor and undertreasurer of the Exchequer, an appointment that began a late, second career in public service. He wrote steadily all his life but avoided the stigma of print: nothing save a few poems and a pirated edition of his *Mustapha* was published in his lifetime. He superintended the publication of an incomplete version of Sidney's* *Arcadia* (Ponsonby's 1590 edition) only after he learned that a bookseller had applied to the London censors for permission to do the same.

Greville's life exemplifies the virtues of being second-best. Growing up in the shadow of his illustrious friend Sidney, with whom he shared a birth year, a grammar school education at Shrewsbury, and, according to Giordano Bruno's* *Spaccio della Bestia Trionfante* (1584), "interior and exterior perfections," Greville entered the service of the queen's court in the mid-1570s as a follower of Sidney's uncle, Robert Dudley, the earl of Leicester. The queen considered Leicester's Protestant politics extreme and consequently kept a tight leash on his faction, which meant that advancement for Greville and his peers would be slow and painstaking. There is little doubt that Greville occasionally chafed at the queen's restraints. But unlike Sidney, whose visceral impatience at the queen's caution may have led indirectly to his quixotic death on the battlefield at Zutphen, Greville learned to adapt himself to political necessity. Moving steadily up the ladder of Elizabeth's government, he occupied a number of smaller offices before finally being made treasurer of the navy in 1598, the position he held at the queen's death in 1603. That he still held the office despite his close association with the treasonous earl of Essex suggests the extent of Elizabeth's confidence in both his ability and loyalty.

Robert Cecil was disinclined to be so generous toward members of the Essex circle and, when James acceded to the throne, made short work of Greville's political ambitions by forcing him to give up his position as treasurer of the navy; Greville retained his Welsh offices—granted him in 1590—only after paying the king's new appointee to those offices some £500. The Greville family had always been particularly acquisitive where Warwickshire property was concerned, and in 1604 Fulke succeeded where his father had failed by securing from the Crown a grant of the dilapidated Warwick Castle. To this castle Greville retired for the next decade, which time he spent working on both his estate and his writing. In the early years of his exile he attempted to ingratiate himself with Cecil, plying him with entertainments and flattery in hopes of resuming his public life, but to no avail. His energies were more fruitful on the home front. By 1614, when Greville's political career was resuscitated, Warwick Castle and its grounds had become a remarkable showplace, and Greville's writing included an additional thirty sonnets in the *Caelica* cycle, revisions of the plays *Alaham* and *Mustapha*, and the so-called *Life of Sir Philip Sidney*.

Cecil's death in 1612 made it possible at long last for Greville to insinuate himself in James' court, and he did so with considerable success, gaining the chancellorship of the Exchequer in 1614. Greville held that post for the next seven years, during which time he sat on a variety of councils and commissions that were integral, if not decisive, to the functioning of the government. Pressured to retire from office in 1621 because of a weakening physical condition, Greville was given a barony as compensation. For the next few years he continued to be a presence at court, exerting subtle pressure against the pro-Spanish tendencies in James government. Serving briefly as a privy councillor under

Charles I, Greville suffered an illness in August 1625 that further diminished his public life. He was fatally stabbed three years later by a servant, Ralph Hayward. Though Hayward's motives will probably never be known, it has been plausibly suggested that he felt he had been shortchanged in Greville's will.

MAJOR WORKS AND THEMES

Greville's earliest works were the first seventy or so poems of *Caelica*, a sequence ultimately composed of 109 loosely connected lyrics, most of them in the Petrarchan vein. Greville wrote the bulk of these poems between 1577 and 1588—perhaps in friendly competition with Sidney and Dyer—but, like Petrarch himself, he was an inveterate reviser and seems to have tinkered with the sequence until the day he died. The trials of love are the inevitable subject of the cycle, and Greville's poet/lover runs the conventional gamut between high compliment and bitter complaint. Among the distinctive features of these poems, however, is Greville's pervasive sense of love as a covert form of pride, as an illusion of future felicity designed to shield man from his actual, which is to say fallen, condition. The view is hardly unprecedented, but Greville arrives at it earlier in his sequence and returns to it more often than do any of his peers. Though he engages its conventions, Petrarchan love is for him what Scholastic philosophy is for Bacon*: yet another symptom of man's prideful tendency to retreat from the world of dross into the gilded interiors of the imagination. Vision for Greville is less often a means of passively receiving the world than actively transforming it. As early as poem 6, the lover chastises those most cherished of Petrarchan highways, the eyes, for bringing "unto me those graces, / Grac'd to yield wonder out of her true measure," and nowhere in the sequence are we ever more than a poem or two away from a Calvinist* critique of idolatrous fancy. In the last, roughly two dozen poems Greville turns from appraisals—mostly ironic—of erotic love, to explicitly moral and religious meditation.

The truth is that he had little or no faith in the edifying capacity of art. If Sidney cheered the poet's power to transcend nature's brazen world and "deliver a golden," Greville suspected all such gilt of prideful presumption. In his *Life of Sidney*, written probably in 1610, Greville tended to minimize the difference between himself and Sidney on this score, partly because his admiration for Sidney would brook no qualification but also because the decadence and immodesty of the Jacobean nobility, the central, if oblique, focus of criticism in the *Life*, tended to make such differences seem minuscule by comparison. The vices he attaches to James' regime are visible in the virtues ascribed to Elizabeth's—her disinclination to "enlarge her royal prerogative," for example, or her refusal to let "any aristocratical cloud . . . shadow forth any superstitious or false lights between her and her people." The portrait of a heroically selfless Sidney is likewise conceived both as a tribute to his old friend and as a reproach to Greville's own present enemies.

To a woman whose husband had taken a mistress, Greville wrote, in the 1590s

Letter to an Honourable Lady, a formal epistle in the *consolatio* tradition, recommending an alloy of humility, forbearance, and lowered expectations as the proper response to her husband's abuse. The identity of the addressee is uncertain, but the letter's counsel radiates outward, in any case, to those of "us inferiors" who are on the receiving end of authority's excesses. Greville's condemnation of the husband's dalliance is unmitigated and, for readers of *Caelica*, familiar, invoking as it does the insatiable human appetite for novel excitement and idolatrous fantasy. Indeed, the *Letter* consoles, at least in part, by situating the husband's dereliction in the larger context of humanity's decline from a golden age of equality and reciprocal love. But consolations do not come cheaply for Greville. Even if the mistress denies the husband her body, "yet is that no advantage to you," he says. For here, as in *Caelica*, there is greater danger in a contrived chastity than in sex: "For unsatisfied desire is too earnest for counsel, too confident for mistrust, too omnipotent for remorse." To the wronged wife, Greville encourages neither hope nor fear, but a noble and implacable endurance.

Such endurance will be required of any modern reader who tackles Greville's plays, *Alaham* and *Mustapha*. Written to be read rather than performed ("I have made these Tragedies, no Plaies for the Stage," he remarks in *Life of Sidney*), these dramas are Greville's experiments in Senecan tragedy, a form also taken up by Thomas Kyd,* Samuel Daniel,* and the countess of Pembroke,* among others. A third play, *Antonie and Cleopatra*, Greville consigned to the fire for fear that it would be construed as "a personating of vices in the present governors and government" (*Life of Sidney* 93). But the vices of government generally are the central focus of the two surviving plays, both of which Greville offers as navigational guides, *via negativa*, to the safe water between the Scylla of a weak tyrant (*Alaham*) and the Charybdis of a strong one (*Mustapha*). Greville's verse treatise, *Monarchy*, was in all likelihood written at about the same time as these two plays (1595–1605) and constructs a similar dichotomy. In all three works, Greville's politics share the least common denominator of Machiavelli* and Calvin.* He is dryly pragmatic about the techniques of maintaining power—"Only let faction multiply her seed, / Twoe bodies headles seldome danger breed"—and simultaneously suspicious of the motives leading men toward it: "Pow'r making men vainely, by offering more, / Hope to redeeme that state they had before."

On the level of style, there is not as much separating the verse treatise from the two plays as one might wish. Greville's dramatic characters are often little more than mouthpieces for some poetical vice or virtue and are rarely more than a step or two away from summary *sententia*. This being so, it is not surprising that Greville should have taken up the verse treatise as the form for his last four works: *Fame and Honour, Wars, Human Learning*, and *Religion*. The subjects of these works Greville approaches with characteristic double vision: fame is at once a spur to virtue and an invitation to vanity; war, a symptom of human pride and an instrument of divine purgation; human learning, a vain idol and a potentially useful enterprise; religion, a degradation of divinity and an index of man's spiritual longing.

CRITICAL RECEPTION

In 1934, T. S. Eliot lamented the fact that ''Fulke Greville has never received quite his due.'' Within five years of Eliot's making that statement, however, the situation showed signs of changing, for 1939 was the year that Geoffrey Bullough published his two-volume *Poems and Dramas of Fulke Greville*, and Ivor Winters began to articulate the terms of taste through which Greville's talent, he hoped, could be seen to rival Shakespeare's, Jonson's,* and Donne's.* The early 1970s marked an even more impressive watershed in Greville studies with the publication of biographies by R. A. Rebholz and Joan Rees and a book-length study of Greville's lyric poetry by Richard Waswo. These came on the heels of G. A. Wilkes' 1965 edition of *A Treatise of Monarchy* and *A Treatise of Religion*, works not included in Bullough's collection, and Thom Gunn's edition of *Caelica*, published in 1968.

Though Greville's literary stock has not—to most minds at least—been raised by this scholarly attention to the level of Donne's or Jonson's, his talents are more likely than ever to be judged on something like their own terms. That likelihood we owe primarily to Ivor Winters, who, in articles first published in *Poetry* in 1939 (later revised and published as Chapter 1 of *Forms of Discovery*), described a seam of sixteenth-century poetic temperament—a temperament shared, according to Winters, by Wyatt* and Gascoigne* especially—marked by restraint of feeling and economy of expression, virtues antithetical to the more flamboyant Petrarchan school. Winters considered many of the *Caelica* lyrics to be perfect examples of what he dubbed ''the plain style,'' and his essays made it possible to see Greville's intellectual density and rhetorical spareness as a feat rather than failure of talent. His ''density,'' at least, had frequently been remarked in other, less flattering terms: Charles Lamb famously wished to resuscitate both Greville and Thomas Browne in order ''to ask them the meaning of what no mortal but themselves, I should suppose, can fathom,'' and in his edition of *The Life of Sidney*, Nowell Smith inadvertently described what every enthusiastic interpreter of Greville must, at least part of the time, possess when he spoke of his own ''zest even in tracking his meaning through his devious syntax.''

As for Greville's cropped rhetoric, Richard Waswo's study exposes a wider range of styles in *Caelica* than either Winters or his student, Douglas Peterson, cared to admit. He concedes that Greville tended to prefer the plain to the ornate, but he grounds that concession in a historical account of the moral and religious beliefs that instructed Greville in this tendency. Prominent among those beliefs was a strong sense of both the depravity of human beings and their implacable desire to orchestrate their own remission. Greville's compressed language was, among other things, a stay against such a desire, an ascetic's attempt to speak the words of unaccommodated man.

BIBLIOGRAPHY

Works by Fulke Greville

Poems and Dramas. 2 vols. Ed. Geoffrey Bullough. New York, 1945.

The Prose Works of Fulke Greville, Lord Brooke. Ed. John Gouws. Oxford: Oxford University Press, 1986.

The Remains: Being Poems of Monarchy and Religion. Ed. G. A. Wilkes. Oxford, 1965.

Selected Poems of Fulke Greville. Chicago: University of Chicago Press, 1968.

The Works in Verse and Prose Complete. 4 vols. Ed. A. B. Grosart. London, 1870.

Studies of Fulke Greville

Bullough, Geoffrey. ''Fulke Greville, First Lord Brooke.'' *Modern Language Review* 28 (1933): 1–20.

Caldwell, Mark L. ''Sources and Analogues of the *Life of Sidney.*'' *Studies in Philology* 74 (1977): 279–300.

Croll, Morris W. *The Works of Fulke Greville.* Philadelphia: Haskell Bookseller's, Inc., 1903.

Ellis-Fermor, Una. ''Fulke Greville.'' In *The Jacobean Drama.* London: Methuen, 1958, 191–200.

Farmer, Norman, Jr. ''Fulke Greville and the Poetic of the Plain Style.'' *Texas Studies in Literature and Language* 11 (1969): 657–71.

Frost, William. *Fulke Greville's ''Caelica'': An Evaluation.* Brattleboro, VT: Privately by the Vermont Printing Co., 1942.

Ho, Elaine Y. L. ''Fulke Greville's *Caelica* and the Calvinist Self.'' *Studies in English Literature* 32 (1992): 35–57.

Litt, Gary. '' 'Images of Life': A Study of Narrative and Structure in Fulke Greville's *Caelica.*'' *Studies in Philology* 69 (1972): 217–30.

Maclean, Hugh N. ''Fulke Greville and E. K.'' *English Language Notes* 1 (1963): 90–109.

———. ''Fulke Greville on War.'' *Huntington Library Quarterly* 21 (1958): 95–109.

———. ''Greville's 'Poetic.' '' *Studies in Philology* 61 (1964): 1970–91.

Mahoney, John L. ''Donne and Greville: Two Christian Attitudes toward the Renaissance Idea of Mutability and Decay.'' *College Language Association Journal* 5 (1962): 203–12.

Morris, Ivor. ''The Tragic Vision of Fulke Greville.'' *Shakespeare Survey* 14 (1966): 66–75.

Newman, Franklin B. ''Sir Fulke Greville and Giordano Bruno: A Possible Echo.'' *Philological Quarterly* 29 (1950): 367–74.

Rebholz, Ronald A. *The Life of Fulke Greville, First Lord Brooke.* Oxford: Clarendon Press, 1971.

Rees, Joan. *Fulke Greville, Lord Brooke, 1554–1628: A Critical Biography.* Berkeley: University of California Press, 1971.

Roberts, David A. ''Fulke Greville's Aesthetic Reconsidered.'' *Studies in Philology* 74 (1977): 388–405.

Ure, Peter. ''Fulke Greville's Dramatic Characters.'' *Review of English Studies* n.s. 1 (1950): 308–23.

Waswo, Richard. *The Fatal Mirror: Themes and Techniques in the Poetry of Fulke Greville.* Charlottesville: University of Virginia Press, 1972.

Wilkes, G. A. "The Sequence of Writings of Fulke Greville, Lord Brooke." *Studies in Philology* 56 (1959): 489–503.

Winters, Ivor. "Aspects of the Short Poem in the English Renaissance." In *Forms of Discovery*. Chicago: Alan Swallow, 1967, 1–121.

LYELL ASHER

H

EDWARD HALL
(c. 1498–1547)

BIOGRAPHY

Edward Hall, a Londoner by birth and a lawyer by profession, came of age during the momentous reign of Henry VIII (1509–47). As a member of the House of Commons he witnessed and supported the first stages of the English Reformation. But we know relatively little of his life. He was of middle-class origins, his parents affluent enough to allow him to be educated at Eton, King's College, Cambridge, and Grey's Inn in London. He held the office of "common sergeant" (a judicial position) of the city of London, was a judge in the sheriff's court, and for a time represented Bridgnorth in the Commons. A loyal supporter of the king, Hall remained out of trouble, but his parents were not so fortunate. In 1555, in the Catholic reaction during the reign of Mary (1553–58), they were both jailed, and Hall's book was banned (Creighton, 947–48).

MAJOR WORKS AND THEMES

Hall's only work is his *Chronicle*, portions of which have been published separately. Its major theme is reflected in the full title: *The Union of the Two Noble and Ilustre Famelies of Lancastre and Yorke Beeyng Long in Continual Discension for the Crowne of this Noble Realme, with all the Actes Done in Bothe the Tymes of the Princes, bothe of the One Linage and of the Other,*

Beginnyng at the Tyme of Kyng Henry the Fowerth, the First Auchtor of this Devision, and So Successively Proceeding to the Reigne of the High and Prudent Prince Kyng Henry the Eight, the Undubitate Flower and Very Heire of Both the Sayd Linages, an 868-page political history of England from 1399, when Richard II was overthrown, to 1547, the death of Henry VIII. Another theme mentioned at the outset is to ''rescue from Oblivion the glory of English princes. Fame triumpheth upon death and renown upon Oblivion, and all by reason of writyng and historie'' (ii). Both themes, but especially the former, are sustained as the narrative proceeds reign by reign, year by year, chronicling the ''doyngs'' of the three Lancastrian kings, the three Yorkists, and the Tudors. The last portion of the book, dealing with events from about 1533 on, is written by Richard Grafton (c. 1513–73), a well-to-do London merchant, printer, and friend of Hall. Grafton writes in the introduction that Hall in the ''later tyme of his lyfe'' was ''not so painful and studious as he had been,'' and so Grafton completed the chronicle, dedicating it to King Edward VI, ''defender of the Catholicke [*sic*] Faith, and Under God Supreme Hed of the Church of England and Ireland'' (i).

Some attention is devoted to events in Scotland and France as they impinge on English politics. Occasionally, Hall describes a major European event, for example, the ''Great Schism'' in the church (he does not use the term) between 1378 and 1417, the fall of Constantinople, and the fall of Grenada. But there is no comment on Luther; the papal grant of the title ''Defender of the Faith'' is left unexplained. The words ''Protestant'' and ''Reformation'' do not appear. Nor is there mention of Columbus or Cabot; the word ''Renaissance'' is not used. Hall's work, essentially military-political history, is in some respects in the medieval tradition: annalistic, summaries of genealogies, reigns, battles, speeches, treaties, plots, revolts, executions. Again, in the medieval tradition, he interrupts his narrative to mention a plague, a storm, or a ''great feast.'' But unlike his medieval predecessors, he writes lengthy descriptions of pageants, ''iustes,'' ''bankettes'' with their ''delicate meates,'' processions, and masques with all the fine apparel of the participants. But reflecting a more critical Renaissance spirit, monsters and other ''marvels'' scarcely appear.

Hall's *Chronicle* (or *Union* as it is often called) is based on a thorough and impressive mastery of the available English, French, and Latin sources and especially on the work of ''Polydorus,'' Polydore Vergil* (1470?–1555). Vergil stemmed from a family of prominent scholars who had served the dukes of Urbino. After ordination in 1496 and entering papal service, he was dispatched to England in 1501. But he was already a humanist of considerable reputation and commissioned by Henry VII to write a history of England. The result was his multivolume *Historia Anglica* (in Latin, first published in 1534, and then revised), which told the story of England (with some attention to Scotland) from ancient times to Henry VIII. It has been pointed out that Hall's work, where it deals with the fifteenth century, is, for the most part, a translation of Vergil (Hay, *Polydor Vergil*, vii). But Hall—as he makes clear—also relies on Thomas

More* (1478–1535) for his account of Richard III, the *bête noire* of the Tudors and their supporters.

Both Hall and Vergil represent transition, as did the Renaissance itself. There is in Vergil a measure of skepticism, a disdain for the medieval annalist Geoffrey of Monmouth and for the Brutus and Arthurian fables. But with all his rationalism, Vergil still sees the hand of God in history, is impressed with portents and miracles. Holy Scripture, of course, is infallible. Some of this is apparent in Hall, some skepticism, but also a belief that God intervenes in history. But where Vergil is a bit dry and matter-of-fact, hostile to nationalism, Hall is the emotional partisan and patriotic Englishman (Hay, *Polydor Vergil*, 43–116; Hay, *Historia Anglica*).

In writing of the Lancaster–York feud, Hall is sometimes impartial, reproving members of both dynasties for lapses in judgment or misconduct. But he dispenses with impartiality as his story approaches his own time. This is blatantly apparent, to give one example, in his portrayal of Richard III, who emerges as a miscreant, "born fete forward," and murderer. His account, immortalized by Shakespeare,* makes wonderful theater but dubious history.

After describing the overthrow of the hapless Richard II in 1399, Hall relates the events of the reign of Henry IV (1399–1413), a story of plots, rebellions, executions, and murder—the murder of the deposed Richard II, a crime for which Hall believes the Lancaster dynasty would pay dearly. In 1413, Henry IV is succeeded by his son, the medieval paladin, the conquering Henry V (1413–1422), who resumes the war in France—the so-called Hundred Year's War, 1377–1453, a term coined in France in the early nineteenth century (Fowler, 1). The military events are well described, although modern scholarship arrives at different numbers for the battles. No matter, Hall's account of the Agincourt campaign of 1415 is still worth reading. Henry capped his stunning victory at Agincourt by marrying Catherine of Valois, daughter and heiress of the French king Charles VI ("the mad"). Their child, Henry VI (1422–61), inherited both kingdoms (and probably the mental illness of Charles). The union of the two kingdoms did not—and could not—last. Henry V was carried off with "camp fever" (dysentery), leaving Catherine and a child nine months of age. A long and disastrous minority ensued while a turbulent, lawless English nobility and a resurgent France overwhelmed the child king. Henry VI, ineffectual to the end of his reign, became a tool of overbearing relatives and favorites until his murder in 1461. Plots, counterplots, executions, and finally civil war, the so-called Wars of the Roses—a term not used by Hall and perhaps not current until the seventeenth century—rocked England from about 1455 to 1485. Edward IV of the House of York, emerging in 1461, ruled—with some interruption—until his death in 1483. Edward is rated by Hall as a "courageous captain" (257) who gave England a "prosperous reign" and who "loved well bothe to loke and fele faire dammsels" (265) but who committed a grievous sin when he broke his oath to the people of York who gave him succor when he was, for a brief time, ousted from power. He promised in return for admission to the city not to try to recover the Crown. Recover it he did, but for this Hall is convinced that "Edward's progeny . . . escaped not untouched by this open perjury" (291). Thus, on Edward's death in 1483, his son Edward V, a child of ten, was soon clapped into the Tower by his uncle the duke of Gloucester, who then seized the throne as Richard III, all in a series of breathtaking—and brutal—coups.

The reign of Richard ended at Bosworth field in 1485 at the hands of Henry Tudor, who personified—with dubious legality—the Lancastrian claim. Though Hall is a Tudor apologist, he is not blind to the skills of the Yorkist Edward IV or the ineptitude of Henry VI. Hall's first love is England, sharing its desperate wish for an end to dynastic strife, and an England secure and prosperous.

Hall's antipathy to the Scots, the French ("braggarts," with the "iyes of the waking serpent," 21), the Irish, and the pope (but not to the Italians) is apparent and is probably characteristically English at the time. His comments about Joan of Arc are particularly nasty, "a face so foul no man wanted her, a witch sent from Sathan, rather than God" (148); he seems to relish her fate, "brennt and consumed in the fire" (157). But to say that Hall hated the French would be to go too far. Rather than gloating over the victory of Agincourt, for example, he writes of the "dolorous and grievous slaughter" (71). In the context of his venting against Joan, he reveals a respect for the chivalry of France, writing "this wytch [Joan] or manly woman (called the maid of God) the Frenchemen greatly glorified and highly extolled, alledging that by her Orleaunce was revailled: by her Kyng Charles was sacred at Reynes, and by her the Englishmen wer often tymes put backe and overthrown. O Lorde, what dispraise is this to the nobilitie of Fraunce: what blotte is this to the Frenche nacion: what more rebuke can be imputed to a renowned region, then to affirm, write and confesse, that all notable victories and honourable conquetes . . . , were gotten and achieved by a shepherdes daughter, a chamberlin in a hostelrie, and a beggars brat" (157).

In another passage Hall reveals some unexpected compassion for the ordinary French people. Describing the siege of Rouen by Henry V, he writes how the people of Rouen "ate dogs, rats, mice [and] died dayly for lack of foode, and how yong infantes lay sucking in the streetes on their mothers' brestes lying dead. . . . You would abhorre the loathsome doyngs then reioise at their miserable mischance" (83). Describing the situation around 1435, during the final French resurgence, he describes the towns of France "vexed and tormented with the unreasonable men of warre: so that no region was more unquiete, more vexed, more poore, nor to be pitied then the country of France" (174).

Hall's account of the military events of the reign of Henry VII is well done. But there is little mention of the Court of Star Chamber, so hateful to the parliamentarians of the seventeenth century, nor much mention of the crucial commercial treaty with the Netherlands. Although Hall is at pains to extol the generosity of the king, he does offer criticism, albeit oblique, when he mentions the extortionate methods of two of Henry's henchmen, Richard Empson and

Edmund Dudley, who ''emptied any men's coffers'' and ''filled the Kynges and enriched themselves'' (499). Hall permits himself more direct criticism when he mentions the fate of Elizabeth Woodville, consort of Edward IV and mother-in-law to Henry, who shortly after Henry's accession was suddenly deprived of her lands, exiled to an abbey, and condemned to a ''wretched and miserable lyfe'' (431), a judgment too harsh, in Hall's view. Hall's statement here is somewhat surprising, given his well-known Tudor boosterism and the fact that Elizabeth Woodville was probably guilty of complicity in one of the plots against Henry (J. D. Mackie, 69). It is also surprising to read from a Tudor apologist a censure of Catherine of Valois, widow of Henry V, who after his death, ''beying yong and lusty, and folowyng her awne appetit, then friendly council and regarding more her private affection then her open honour, took to husband privily, a goodly gentleman . . . called Owen Teuther [Tudor]'' (184–85). This was the ancestor of Henry VII.

There is much in Hall, especially in his account of the reign of Henry VIII, that proves tedious to the modern reader: page after page of description of pageants, ''bankettes,'' ''iustes,'' descriptions of apparel, ''pleasaunt furres,'' page after page summarizing the legal opinions of various universities in support of Henry's contention that his marriage to Catherine was invalid. Some of Hall's comments on Henry are distasteful, if not embarrassing: Henry is ''a Kyng of such witte and wisedome that the like hath not reigned over this realme'' (759). This in light of Henry's fatuous foreign policy and squandering of the fortune created by his father. Henry, who begins his reign (in true Machiavellian* fashion) by executing Empson and Dudley and who goes on late in his reign to send wives, favorites, chancellors, and dissidents in a steady parade to the block, is described as the ''goodliest prince that ever reigned over the Realme of England'' (609) and a prince ''ever inclined to mercy'' (!) (584).

We hasten to concede that it would have been unusually courageous, if not rash, to level any direct criticism of the royal bluebeard, and—recalling the murderous paranoiac Georgian of our own century—quiet acquiescence perhaps was not sufficient. Loyalty had to be demonstrated and demonstrated effusively. (This was impossible for More,* but not for Hall.) In such a setting detailed discussion of religious differences carrying with it implicit criticism of current policy (which had an unnerving way of shifting) was unthinkable. But the military events, the wars against the French and Scots, and indeed the account of the entire reign of Henry VIII, with all its deficiencies, are still judged of ''first importance'' (Hunt and Poole, 490) and thus worth reading.

CRITICAL RECEPTION

It has been conceded that Hall's *Chronicle* is generally ''accurate'' (Hunt and Poole, 490). It has also been recognized as a major source for Shakespeare's history plays, but also that large portions are propagandistic and translations of *Polydor Vergil* (Kingsford, 261; Fussner, 255). Thus, one critic has judged that portions of Hall (probably those dealing with the fifteenth century) are "without independent value" (Creighton, 948) The description of Richard III, caricature that it is, has nonetheless been immortalized. Not quite immortal, but still of enormous longevity, again, is the Hall–Vergil picture of the fifteenth century, which has "remained undisturbed until a century ago [until about 1850] and his [Vergil's] evaluation of the reigns of Henry VII and Henry VIII has had an even longer currency" (Hay, *Polydor Vergil*, vii; Fussner, 255). One critic, a friendly one, has found "contradictions" and "misinterpretations of Vergil" in Hall (Trimble, 36). Another, also friendly, has found "distortions" (in connection with the reign of Henry VI) (Kingsford, 265). But Kingsford still rates Hall's account of the French wars between 1430 and 1438 of "exceptional value" (261).

Somewhat puzzling to this writer, in view of what we have shown about Hall's treatment of Henry VIII, is the generally favorable comment that those portions of the *Chronicles* have received. Two points explain this: (1) Hall's work is based, in part, on now lost sources; (2) Hall (as we have already noted) was an eyewitness to much of what he describes, capturing the zeitgeist of Tudor England and especially of its middle classes (Hunt and Poole, 490; Creighton, 948). To conclude, though Hall has been called "a creature of the crown" (Creighton, 947–48), it still may well be, as Trimble writes, that he was "the greatest of the native historians of this period" (Trimble, 36), who produced a work of literary merit of "a high order" (Kingsford, 261; Creighton, 948).

BIBLIOGRAPHY

Works by Edward Hall

Chronicle; Containing the History of England during the Reign of Henry the Fourth and the Succeeding Monarchs to the End of the Reign of Henry the Eighth in which are Particularly Described the manners and Customs of those Periods Carefully Collated with the Editions of 1548 and 1550. London: 1809.

The Triumphant Reigne of Kyng Henry VIII. 2 vols. Ed. C. Whibley. London: 1904.

Studies of Edward Hall

Breisach, Ernst. *Historiography: Ancient, Medieval and Modern*. Chicago: University of Chicago Press, 1983.

Campbell, Lily B. *Shakespeare's Histories; Mirrors of Elizabethan Policy*. San Marino, CA, 1947.

Castanien, Anne T. "Censorship and Historiography in Elizabethan England: The Expurgation of Holinshed's Chronicles." Diss., University of California, Davis, 1970.

Creighton, Mandell. "Edward Hall." In *Dictionary of National Biography*, ed. Leslie Stephen and Sidney Lee. Vol. 8. London: Oxford University Press, 1921–22, 947–48.

Fussner, F. Smith. *Tudor History and the Historian*. New York: Basic Books, 1970.

Hay, Denys, ed. *The Anglica Historia of Polydore Vergil AD 1485–1537*. London: Office of Royal Historical Society, 1950.

———. *Polydore Vergil: Renaissance Man of Letters*. Oxford: Clarendon Press, 1952.

Hunt, William, and Poole, Reginald L. eds. *The Political History of England.* 12 vols. Vol. 5, *The History of England from the Accession of Henry VII to the Death of Henry VIII.* London: Longman's, 1907, repr. 1969.

Kingsford, Charles L. *English Historical Literature in the Sixteenth Century.* Oxford: Clarendon Press, 1913.

Mackie, J. D. *The Earlier Tudors, 1485–1558.* Oxford: Clarendon Press, 1952.

Tillyard, E.M.W. *Shakespeare's History Plays.* New York: Macmillan, 1946.

Trimble, W. R. "Early Tudor Historiography 1485–1548." *Journal of the History of Ideas* 11 (1950): 30–41.

Other

Fowler, Kenneth, ed. *The Hundred Years War.* London: Macmillan, 1971.

LOUIS A. GEBHARD

SIR JOHN HARINGTON
(1560–1612)

BIOGRAPHY

Deserved or not, John Harington has always had the reputation of Elizabethan bad boy, as John Skelton* was known in the early Tudor era. Certainly, some of his behavior was refreshingly adolescent. Fortunately for Harington, his father was always in Princess and Queen Elizabeth's* good favor. The elder John Harington was imprisoned in the Tower in 1554, reportedly for nothing more than showing kindness to Elizabeth. The connection to Elizabeth was strengthened by Harington's marriage to her maid Isabelle Markham. Their son John was born in the summer of 1560, and Queen Elizabeth became his godmother. Though she did not give him steady employment at court, Elizabeth always forgave her godson for his quirky antics, one of which led to his famous translation of Ariosto's* *Orlando Furioso.*

Harington was educated at Eton and Cambridge. He enrolled in the law course at Lincoln's Inn after receiving his master's degree in 1581 but left the inn when he came into his inheritance upon his father's death in July 1582. Harington began by "Englishing" the twenty-eighth canto of Ariosto's masterpiece, which tells the story of a cuckolded knight named Jocundo, who concludes after his wanderings that women are by nature lascivious and unfaithful. This translation circulated at court. When the verses came to the notice of Elizabeth, she reprimanded him for rendering such an immoral portion of the work and apparently ordered him to translate the rest. Harington published the complete English *Orlando Furioso* in 1591.

Harington added to his reputation as a rebellious prankster when he wrote his treatise on a revolutionary new privy design entitled, *A New Discourse on a Stale subject, called the Metamorphosis of Ajax*, published in 1596. The Erasmian* spirit is also present in Harington's many epigrams, which were collected and published after his death. In addition to writing satire, Harington recorded his observations at historically interesting moments. For instance, he was with Robert Devereux, earl of Essex, during his infamous expedition in Ireland and was among those Essex inadvisedly knighted at Dublin in July 1599. Harington pleased Elizabeth by giving her the journal he had kept of Essex's Irish escapade.

Other of Harington's astute historical observations include remarks on the final days of Queen Elizabeth's life written at court in 1602; his "Tract on the Succession to the Crown," written in 1602 in support of James'* claim to the throne; his letter of application for the post of chancellor of Ireland written in 1605; and his notes appendixed to his copy of Bishop Godwin's *De Praesulibus Angliae*, given to Prince Henry. Between 1605 and his death in 1612, Harington set himself the task of instructing Prince Henry, James' heir, although he had no official charge. Note that over 100 years before, Skelton was tutor to the previous royal Henry. His association with the crown prince apparently gave Harington the impetus to translate the sixth book of Virgil's *Aeneid*, containing the trip to Hades and the prophecy with commentary for Henry's edification. Harington grew ill in May 1612 and died in November of the same year, only weeks before Prince Henry's own untimely death.

MAJOR WORKS AND THEMES

I cannot overemphasize the Erasmian stance of serious jester in Harington's life and work, and I believe it is beautifully exemplified by his gift to James VI* in 1602, when Elizabeth's death seemed imminent. He sent James a lantern, a symbol of the transmission of rulership from the waning light of Elizabeth's reign to the waxing brilliance of James'. On it was inscribed a picture of the Crucifixion of Christ and the words of the repentant thief, "Lord, remember me when thou comest into thy kingdom." That Harington was willing to cast himself in the role of thief while begging blessing from the future king reveals not only a fawning audacity but an admirable self-irony as well.

I argue that the satiric, yet sanguine, spirit of Harington's life and work is best captured in his translation of that "immoral" twenty-eighth canto of Ariosto's great work, which first earned Harington the charge of the entire translation. In this canto, a host tells a tale "to please the misogyny of the Saracen Rodomont" (193), and yet the main character ends up appreciating women more. In the story, the cuckolded knight Jocundo discovers that his friend King Astolfo is also betrayed by his beloved queen. The two set off together in quest of an honest woman and enjoyment of women in that quest: "Let us not spare our beauty, youth, and treasure / Till of a thousand we have had our pleasure" (205). Eventually, they decide to share a wife, reasoning, "Well might that woman think she had a treasure / That had us two her appetite to please; / And though to one man faithful none remain, / No doubt but faithful they would be to twain" (206). But even this woman manages to enjoy a third man while lying between these two. The two do not, however, give up on all women and become monks; instead they return happily to their wives, who, they realize, are no worse than any other women alive. They are, after all, ''as chaste and honest as the best'' (212).

As brutal as this implied assessment of women might be, Ariosto has the two knights assert an acceptance of life as it is and embrace it wholly rather than holding out for an ideal that, when lost, might be lamented. Adding to the depth of irony, immediately following the story of Jocundo, another character attempts to defend women, asking that while women may cheat, what husband among them has not also ''awry yet stepped?'' (213). Thus, Ariosto presents not only the view that women are unfaithful and we can forgive them, but also the view that perhaps women are blameless in their infidelity because men commit the same sin against them. While the tale pokes fun at the faults of both women and men in relationships, there is also a note of universal acceptance.

Harington's translation is para- rather than metaphrastic. He often takes liberties with the Italian, compressing two stanzas of Ariosto into one of his own. He even adds to the text, offering either religious commentary or moral witticisms such as, ''Be not in this sweet gulf of pleasure drowned; / The time will come and must, I tell you all, / When these your joys shall bitter seem as gall'' (160). In general, critics praise Harington for expressing the easy ironic tone of Ariosto better than other English translators. Perhaps because of the freedom he allowed himself in translation, he created a more Elizabethan *Orlando* than more recent word-for-word translations can provide.

The Metamorphosis of Ajax is clearly in the tradition of mock encomium. In his ''Prologue to the Reader,'' Harington explains how the term ''jakes'' for privy derived from Ajax. The body of Ajax, after his suicide, turned into hyacinth. Many years later, when a Frenchman plowed a field of hyacinth to build a privy, he was struck with St. Anthony's fire. In search of relief the offender must do penance to the ghost of such a great warrior. Thus, the man ''built a sumptuous privie, and in the most conspicuous place thereof, namely just over the doore; he erected a statue of AJAX, with so grim a countenance, that the aspect of it being full of terrour, was halfe as good as a suppositor'' (71). Thereafter, the privy was referred to as AJAX, although, through ''ill pronunciation,'' it is now just referred to as ''a Jakes'' (71). In addition to the mock-heroic, the treatise contains detailed directions on how to build a jakes with ventilation and a flush toilet. Harington is supposed to have built a replica at his own residence in Kelston. After philosophizing that most of our pleasures in life consist in avoiding sorrow, including that of wanting to rid ourselves of the stink of the privy, Harington goes on to assert that defecation can often be a more satisfying pursuit of pleasure than lust itself. So Joyce's Leopold Bloom was not the first to articulate this private joy. Although we may not yet know where he stands, if indeed where he sits, Harington raises questions about the modest nature of happiness.

CRITICAL RECEPTION

Harington's ''Englished'' *Orlando Furioso* enjoyed wide popularity. There are many exerpts from it in Robert Allot's *England's Parnassus*, and Beaumont* complimented the work. A second edition was published in 1607, and Harington's remained the only complete English translation of *Orlando* until 1755. Of his *Metamorphosis of Ajax*, Thomas Nashe* wrote that he couldn't understand ''what should move him to'' write it ''except he [m]eant to bid a turd in all gentle readers' teeth'' (Craig, 71). Apparently, Nashe later came to appreciate the *Metamorphosis*, complimenting Harington as one who ''disportes himself very schollarly and wittilie'' (Craig, 81). Although a pun on ''a jakes'' and ''Ajax'' appears in Shakespeare's* *Love's Labour's Lost* before *Metamorphosis* was published, Harington's work likely contributed to the popularity of the epithet. Shakespeare then took up the pun extensively in *Troilus and Cressida*. Perhaps *The Metaphorphosis*, as D. H. Craig writes, put the ''taint of the privy'' on Harington's own literary career (82). Several modern scholars, however, including T.G.A. Nelsen and John Leland, assert that the work has allegorical import. They argue that it contains a mystic current of religious commentary. Indeed, if it is true that the praise of the privy stuck with Harington more than his translation of Ariosto's masterpiece, we need only recall the wit with which Harington implies gravity and jest to esteem him highly.

BIBLIOGRAPHY

Works by Sir John Harington

Ariosto, Ludovico. *Ariosto's Orlando Furioso: Selections from the Translation of Sir John Harington*. Ed. Rudolf Gottfried. Bloomington: Indiana University Press, 1963. (All quotations are from this edition.)

———. *Ludovico Ariosto's Orlando Furioso: Translated into English Heroical Verse by Sir John Harington*. Ed. Robert McNulty. Oxford: Clarendon Press, 1972.

Harington, John. *Epigrams, 1618*. Yorkshire: Scolar Press, 1970.

———. *Nugae Antiquae*. 2 vols. Ed. Henry Harington and Thomas Park. London: Verner and Hood, 1804.

———. *The School of Salernum: Regimen Sanitatis Salernitanum*. Ed. Francis R. Packard and Fielding H. Garrison. 1920. Repr., New York: Kelley, 1970.

———. *A Short View of the State of Ireland* (1605). Ed William Dunn Macray. Oxford: Oxford University Press, 1879.

———. *Sir John Harington's A New Discourse of a Stale subject, called the Metamorphosis of Ajax*. Ed. Elizabeth Story Donno. New York: Columbia University Press, 1962.

———. *A Supplie or Addicion to the Catalogue of Bishops to the Yeare 1608*. Ed. R. H. Miller. Potomac, MD: José Porrúa Turanzas, 1979.

———. *A Tract on the Succession to the Crown* (1602). Ed. Clemens R. Markham. 1880. Repr., New York: Burt Franklin, 1969.

———. Virgil's *Aeneid*, Book 6. Translation and commentary. Unpublished manuscript. Berkshire Record Office. Trumball Additional MS 23.

Studies of Sir John Harington

Cauchi, Simon. "The 'Setting Foorth' of Harington's Ariosto." *Studies in Bibliography* 36 (1983): 137–68.

Craig, D. H. *Sir John Harington*. Boston: Twayne, 1985.

Engel, William E. "Was Sir John Harington the English Rabelais?" In *Rabelais in Context*, ed. Barbara C. Bowen. Birmingham, AL: Summa, 1993, 147–56.

"Harington, Sir John." *Dictionary of National Biography*. Vol. 7. Ed. Leslie Stephens and Sidney Lee. Oxford: Oxford University Press, 1917.

Lee, Judith. "The English Ariosto: The Elizabethan Poet and the Marvelous." *Studies in Philology* 80.3 (1983): 277–99.

Leland, John. "A Joyful Noise: *The Metamorphosis of Ajax* as Spiritual Tract." *South Atlantic Review* 47.2 (1982): 53–62.

Nelson, T.G.A. "Death, Dung, the Devil, and Worldly Delights: A Metaphysical Conceit in Harington, Donne, and Herbert." *Studies in Philology* 76 (1979): 272–87.

———. "Sir John Harington and the Renaissance Debate over Allegory." *Studies in Philology* 82.3 (1985): 359–79.

Rich, Townsend. *Harington and Ariosto: A Study in Elizabethan Verse Translation*. New Haven, CT: Yale University Press, 1940.

SARAH HILSMAN

GABRIEL HARVEY
(c. 1550–1631)

BIOGRAPHY

Gabriel Harvey's life spanned eight decades and breaks into two parts: the well-documented and eventful public career through the 1590s and the private era from the late 1590s until his death, a period of his life about which we know little. So often was Gabriel Harvey represented—often to his detriment—in literature during the first half of his life that versions of his life and works have often been unduly prejudiced. Coming to Harvey through the pages of literary history, we absorb with pleasure the satirical opinions of his great antagonist, Thomas Nashe,* and frequently are required to see Harvey the caricature rather than Harvey the person. Harvey himself, of course, contributed to this denigration through his thin-skinned ambition, pedantry, self-possession, and over-seriousness. Indeed, "Unhappy Harvey," as he once signed a letter to Burghley, bears much of the responsibility for this traditional caricature, for throughout his public life he possessed an uncanny ability to make others dislike him and to act on that dislike. Yet as G. M. Young argued as far back as 1930, the traditional definition of the man—"Harvey, G: pedant: tried to make Spenser* write the *Faerie Queene* in hexameters"—should more properly read: "Harvey, G: acute and independent critic; saved Spenser from wasting his time on classical metres."[1] Harvey was an indefatigable humanist whose energy and pride led the more pragmatic of his contemporaries to exaggerate his excesses. Only by resisting the appeal of such characterizations are we likely to gain a true picture of Harvey's life and that humanism in England he best represented.

Harvey was born, in all likelihood, in July 1550, the first of four sons of John and Ales Harvey, of Saffron-Walden, Essex. Harvey had two sisters, Alice and Marie (''Marcie''). His father was a prosperous rope maker, an occupation frequently jeered by Harvey's antagonists later in life. John Harvey the elder sent his four sons—Gabriel, Richard, John, and Thomas—to Walden's grammar school, which had been founded in 1525 upon the Etonian model. Everything would suggest that Harvey excelled there; Nashe writes of Harvey's precocious reading at this time and ascribes to the young Harvey both literary pretensions and an intellectual quarrelsomeness grounded in pride.

Harvey matriculated on 28 June 1566 at Christ's College, Cambridge. This university would prove central to the rest of his public career, as Harvey continually embraced new topics of learning (including law and medicine) and struggled (often unsuccessfully) with what seems to have been an unending supply of enemies. Having received his baccalaureate from Christ's in 1569/70, Harvey was elected in November 1570 to a fellowship at Pembroke College and was in 1573 appointed Greek lecturer. At Cambridge, Harvey became well known for his advocacy of the methods of the controversial Peter Ramus (Pierre de la Ramée) over and against Aristotle. During this time at Cambridge he became friends with Edmund Spenser and published letters with him in 1580. Frequently misread, these letters show Harvey ultimately relying on reason and common sense in his polite attempt to dissuade Spenser, Philip Sidney,* and Edward Dyer* from writing English poetry in classical verse forms. Although Harvey himself experimented with these forms, many of his verses seem to poke fun at the very principles that the mythology of literary history would see him as advocating, as in the folowing lines of ''Encomium Lauri'' from his letters to Spenser:

> What might I call this Tree? *A Laurel?* O bonny Laurel!
> Needs to thy bows will I bow this knee, and vail my bonnetto.

Harvey's connection at this time with Spenser and the ''areopagus'' of Sidney, Dyer, and others of the Leicester faction offers a clue to his Protestant, even Puritan politics, and to one source of the recurrent quarrels into which he would fall. The first of many such quarrels was occasioned by a poem in the *Three Proper... Letters* (1580) satirizing an Italianate Englishman, which was brought to the earl of Oxford's attention by John Lyly* as being a personal swipe—this in the year after Sidney had been insulted by Oxford in the 1579 tennis court encounter. Harvey would later trade barbs with not only Lyly but with Robert Greene* and Nashe, all of whom—along with Oxford—represented a political, social, and religious outlook opposite to that of Harvey and the left-leaning Protestants of the Leicester circle. Where Harvey's humanist faith in education led him to believe in self-empowerment based on reason and diligence, the Anglo-Catholic tendencies of writers like Lyly, Greene, Nashe—even

Shakespeare*—ensured that they saw Harvey as an overweening social climber; where Harvey championed the kingdom of knowledge and sought to be its sovereign, these writers realized the threat such a posture could pose to a state based on tradition and subordination.

This polarization of religious/cultural outlooks formed the ultimate source of Harvey's extended quarrel with Nashe, a quarrel for which Harvey is best remembered and that came to take on primarily personal overtones. When the Marprelate controversy broke out in the last years of the 1580s, Lyly intimated in his *Pap with a Hatchet* (1589) that Harvey might have been responsible for the scurrilous antiepiscopal remarks published under the pseudonym Martin Marprelate. Harvey responded in "Advertisement for Pap-hatchet and Martin Mar-prelate," written soon after Lyly's pamphlet but not published until 1593, when it was included in *Pierces Supererogation* (1593). Harvey's younger brother Richard entered the controversy in 1590, and when he criticized Nashe's "Preface" to Greene's *Menaphon* (1589), both Greene and Nashe retaliated with ad hominem attacks on Gabriel, Richard, and John Harvey. The nadir of this quarrel came with Nashe's *Have with You to Saffron-Walden, or Gabriel Harvey's Hunt is Up* (1596), a savage and witty mock biography of Harvey.

By 1599 the vogue of ad hominem writing that the Harvey–Nashe quarrel represents led the archbishop of Canterbury to issue a ban on certain satires and bawdy works; this ban also stipulated that "all Nashe's books and Doctor Harvey's books be taken wheresoever they may be found, and that none of their books be ever printed hereafter." With this act of state censorship and with the bonfire that consumed some extant copies of their writings, both Nashe and Harvey began to exit the public arena. Nashe would be dead within two years, and Harvey—who had last published in 1593—appears by this time to have retired to Saffron-Walden. Having lived away from the public view for over thirty years, he died on 7 February 1631.

MAJOR WORKS AND THEMES

Harvey's works are best thought of as including his unpublished marginalia—a voluminous amount of remarks on, responses to, summaries of, and other engagements with, what he read. Harvey often marked his books with an elaborate and idiosyncratic system of symbols (e.g., planetary and diagrammatic), cross-references, colored chalk marks, and captions. He also invented eight Latin and Greek personae through which he could both interpret texts and fashion his responses to them and the world: thus, "Angelus Furius" is angelic in action and speech, "Eutrapelus" (from the Greek for "turning well") persuasive and ingenious with language, and "Euscopus" ("of good vision") the sharp-sighted, rational man who sees the future as well as the past. These personae—in another writer, characters for a romance or play—suggest the deep divisions within Harvey's character and the tensions he felt in relating to the world. Harvey read much more than he wrote and wrote much more than he published, boasting in

1598 that he could, if he wished, ''publish more than any Englishman hath hitherto done.''[2] Nearly all Harvey's publications involve specific individuals and sometimes seem overfamiliar and even self-aggrandizing in their address of persons of worth. This humanism-of-personalities is present to his earliest published work, *Ode Natalitia* (1575), two Latin eclogues devoted to Ramus (who had died in the St. Bartholomew's massacre in 1572) and his influence as well as to *Ciceronianus* (1577), a celebratory exposition of Cicero's rhetorical philosophy. Following the death of Sir Thomas Smith, Harvey published a collection of Latin elegies eulogizing his friend and benefactor; published as *Smithus; vel musarum lachrymae* (Smith, or The Tears of the Muses) in 1578, this work features each of the Muses delivering a Latin verse lament. Spenser would replicate this pattern in his 1591 *The Teares of the Muses*. In 1578 Harvey published *Gratulationes Valdinenses* (Good Wishes from Walden), a compilation of elegiac verses in Latin that he had presented to Elizabeth* on one of her progresses through Essex earlier that year. Each of the four books included in this text is dedicated to persons of worth: Elizabeth, Leicester, Burghley, Oxford, Sidney, and Hatton. Likewise, Harvey's *Three Proper wittie familiar Letters* (1580), with its mix of literary criticism, poetry, and familiar remarks, brings his friendship with Spenser, recently known for the *Shepheardes Calendar* (1579), to the fore. In 1587 Harvey's Latin poems mourning the death of Sidney appeared anonymously in *Cantabrigiensis Lachrymae*. Harvey's quarrels with Greene and Nashe underlie his last three publications, *Four Letters* (1592), *Pierces Supererogation* (1593), and *A New Letter of Notable Contents* (1593). Perhaps the single exception to Harvey's thoroughly ''embodied'' writing is his two early lectures published under the title of *Rhetor* in 1577. Among the lost works is a manuscript entitled *Anticosmopolita*, a long and perhaps unfinished epic poem written ''in celebration of her majesty's most prosperous, & in truth glorious government.''[3]

CRITICAL RECEPTION

Harvey's earliest critics were his own contemporaries—students, friends, and antagonists who often represented his larger-than-life personality in their writings. Harvey appears, for instance, as Hobbinol in Spenser's *The Shepheardes Calendar* (1579), as Pedantius in the Cambridge comedy of that name (1581), and as Vanderhulke, the windy orator in Nashe's *The Unfortunate Traveler* (1593); he is perhaps a source for Rombus in Sidney's *Lady of May* (1578),[4] surely contributes to Holofernes in Shakespeare's *Love's Labour's Lost* (1595), and is represented in some speeches of Luxurioso in the Cambridge comedy *The Return from Parnassus, Part One* (1600). Since Harvey's time the caricature, rather than the person, has come to dominate his critical reception: he is seen as the overblown antagonist of Nashe, the clear loser in an entertaining battle of wits. Recently, however, a renewed interest in the reading practices of early modern subjects has found in Harvey's marginalia copious, if eccentric, material for study.

NOTES

1. G. M. Young, ''A Word for Gabriel Harvey,'' in *English Critical Essays: Twentieth Century*, ed. Phyllis M. Jones (Oxford: 1933), 285.
2. From a letter to Robert Cecil in 1598, quoted in Stern, *Gabriel Harvey*, 125.
3. Ibid., 51.
4. For this observation I am indebted to Alan Hager, who suggests (privately) that Harvey, rather than Ramus, formed the source for Sidney's Rombus. For a thorough description of this character see Hager, ''Rhomboid Logic: Anti-idealism and a Cure for Recusancy in Sidney's *Lady of May*,'' *ELH* 57 (1990): 485–502.

BIBLIOGRAPHY

Works by Gabriel Harvey

Contemporaneous Publications

Ode Natalitia (1575).

Rhetor (1577).

Ciceronianus (1577).

Smithus; vel musarum lachrymae (1578).

Gratulaniones Valdinenses (1578).

Three Proper wittie familiar Letters (1580).

Latin verses in *Cantabrigiensis Lachrymae* (1587).

Four Letters (1592).

Pierces Supererogation (1593).

A New Letter of Notable Contents (1593).

Modern Editions and Translations

For Harvey marginalia unnoticed by G. C. Moore Smith's 1913 collection, see the bibliography in Stern, *Gabriel Harvey*, Appendix E, 272–73.

Biller, Janet Elizabeth. ''Gabriel Harvey's *Foure Letters* (1592): A Critical Edition.'' Diss., Columbia University, 1969.

Chandler, Robert M., trans. ''*Rhetor*: The First Lecture by Gabriel Harvey.'' *Allegorica* 4 (1979): 146–290.

Grosart, A. B., ed. *The Works of Gabriel Harvey*. 3 vols. London: 1884–85.

Harvey, Gabriel. *A New Letter of Notable Contents*. New York: Walter J. Johnson, 1969.

Jameson, Thomas Hugh. ''The *Gratulationes Valdineness* of Gabriel Harvey.'' Diss., Yale University, 1938.

Scott, Edward John Long. *Letter-book of Gabriel Harvey, A.D. 1573–1580*. Camden Society n.s. 33 (1884).

Smith, G. Gregory, ed. *Elizabethan Critical Essays*. 2 vols. Oxford, 1971. (Vol. 1 contains the Harvey–Spenser correspondence of 1580; Smith, however, omits the important ''earthquake'' letter.)

Wilson, Harold S., ed. *Gabriel Harvey's ''Ciceronianus''* (with English translation by Clarence A. Forbes). Lincoln, NE, 1945.

Studies of Gabriel Harvey

Jardine, Lisa, and Anthony Grafton. '' 'Studied for Action': How Gabriel Harvey Read His Livy.'' *Past and Present* 129 (1990): 30–78.

Nielson, James. "Reading between the Lines: Manuscript Personality and Gabriel Harvey's Drafts." *Studies in English Literature* 33 (1993): 43–82.

Rogers, D. M. "Edmund Spenser and Gabriel Harvey: A New Find." *Bodleian Library Record* 12 (1987): 334–37.

Smith, G. C. Moore, ed. *Pedantius*. Louvain, 1905. (Introduction and notes.)

Stern, Virginia F. *Gabriel Harvey: His Life, Marginalia and Library*. Oxford: Clarendon Press, 1979.

Tobin, J.J.M. "Gabriel Harvey: 'Excellent Matter of Emulation.' " *Hamlet Studies* 7 (1985): 94–100.

Wilson, H. S. "The Cambridge Comedy *Pedantius* and Gabriel Harvey's *Ciceronianus*." *Studies in Philology* 45 (1948): 578–91.

DOUGLAS BRUSTER

WILLIAM HARVEY
(1578–1657)

BIOGRAPHY

William Harvey achieved the greatest feat in physiology, biology, and medicine in the first half of the seventeenth century with his discovery of the circulation of the blood. He was born to well-to-do yeoman stock in Folkstone, Kent, as the eldest son of nine children. From ten to fifteen he attended the King's School at Canterbury and then went to Cambridge. There he received the B.A., then moved on to Padua, where he received the best medical training Europe had to offer, studying with the comparative anatomist Fabricius of Aquapendente and his famous candlelit dissections in a theater hall that exists to this day. He earned his medical degree with special honors in 1602 and returned to England, where he soon began to practice under the College of Physicians in London.

Harvey's career was advanced by his marriage to the daughter of the king's physician, and his patients included such greats as Bacon* and Hobbes. By 1618, he was physician extraordinary to the king and attended him in his last illness, serving as personal physician to Charles until his removal to the Isle of Wight. The king was not only his patient but also his patron, providing much support.

Harvey was, of course, most familiar with Galen and the long line of medical authorities from classical times, but especially with Aristotle, whose suggestions about comparative anatomy and the combined studies of the physiology of animals and humans he took to heart in his meticulous evidencing of his famous theory. But he was also a scholar of Cicero and Virgil and other major classical authors. At the opening of his masterpiece, for example, he quotes Terence's *Andria* concerning the fact that he was only an aid to future scientists. This was the characteristic modesty he often employed in the face of the objections of his Continental opponents, most of whom accepted his theory well before his death on 3 June 1657. His final years were marked by the pain of gout—to relieve which he would stand in freezing water—and stone and the political opprobrium of Cromwell's government.

MAJOR WORKS AND THEMES

Like Copernicus,* Harvey may have been reticent to publish his findings. For example, although he lectured on the circulation of the blood at the College of Physicians as early as 1616, his major published work, *Exercitatio Anatomica de Motu Cordis et Sanguinis in Animalibus*, did not appear until 1628 at Frankfurt am Main. In this, he demonstrated the movement of blood from the heart through the arteries and the return through the veins. This slim volume created a great uproar and no little hostility, which did not abate until the middle of the century. His final experiments had to do with uterine diseases, and his final published work, *Exercitationes de Generatione Animalium* (1651), is a study of the fertilization of eggs that required the invention of the microscope for proof.

CRITICAL RECEPTION

Harvey met John Aubrey while Harvey was at Oxford after the King's Battle at Edgehill. Aubrey includes a vivid description of Harvey in his *Brief Lives*, which allows us to see his dedication to both the king and science. He lived an austere life and donated his library to the College of Physicians, with which he had a long association. He was a lucky man, as I have noted, in that he saw his scientific theories accepted within his own lifetime. Because of the precision of his proofs, with Gilbert,* Harvey can be seen as the founder of modern science.

BIBLIOGRAPHY

Works by William Harvey

Keynes, Geoffrey A. *A Bibliography of the Writings of William Harvey, 1578–1657*. 3d ed. Rev. by Gweneth Whitteridge and Christine English. Winchester, Hampshire, U.K.: St. Paul's Bibliographies, 1989.

The Works of William Harvey. Trans. Robert Willis. New York: Johnson Reprint, 1965.

Studies of William Harvey

Bylebyl, Jerome J., ed. *William Harvey and His Age: The Professional and Social Context of the Discovery of the Circulation of the Blood*. Baltimore: Johns Hopkins University Press, 1979.

Frank, R. G. *Harvey and the Oxford Physiologists: A Study of Scientific Ideas and Social Interaction*. Berkeley: University of California Press, 1980.

Keynes, Geoffrey A. *The Life of William Harvey*. Oxford: Clarendon Press, 1966, rev. 1978.

———. *The Portraiture of William Harvey*. New ed. London: Keynes Press, 1985, orig. 1948.

Whitteridge, Gweneth. *William Harvey and the Circulation of the Blood*. New York: Science History Publications, 1971.

FRANCIS R. CZERWINSKI

ROBERT HENRYSON
(c. 1420–before 1505)

BIOGRAPHY

Although there is much speculation about the life of Robert Henryson, what is known is limited to his residence in Dunfermline, approximate dates, and the esteem in which he was held by immediate successors. Dunbar's* *Lament for the Makaris*, printed in 1508, states ''In Dunfermelyne he hes done roune / With Maister Robert Henrisoun'' (81–82). A holograph gloss of the word ''Muse'' in Gavin Douglas'* translation of the *Aeneid* (c. 1522) notes: ''And of the ix Musis sum thing in my palys of honour and be Maistir robert hendirson in new orpheus.'' In *The Testament of the Papyngo* (c. 1530) Sir David Lindsay* includes Henryson among eight Scots poets who ''Thocht thay be deed, thar libells bene levand, / Quhilk to reheirs makeith redaris to rejoise.'' Henryson's first modern editor, David Laing, thought that the poet had studied abroad before an entry (10 September 1462) places him at Glasgow University ''vir Magister Robertus Henrisone in Artibus Licentiatus et in Decretis Bachalarius.'' Several printed editions of his poems, beginning in 1570, identify Henryson as a schoolmaster at Dunfermline, and his lyric *The Abbay Walk* suggests an association with the town's Benedictine Grammar and Song School. The Chartulary of Dunfermlime (1477–78) includes as witness ''Magister Robertus Henrison notarius publicus,'' a position there shared with schoolmaster. As with so many medieval writers, knowledge of Henryson comes most surely from his poems, which reveal an extraordinarily educated man, with traditional late-medieval Latin learning and a wide acquaintance with vernacular literatures. Henryson's works show both the indebtedness to Chaucer, for which he is well known, and the sophistication and internationalism of Scotland, which at the end of the fifteenth century went well beyond provincialism, especially through alliance with France. Of this Renaissance, he is the central literary figure.

MAJOR WORKS AND THEMES

The Fables is Henryson's largest and most distinctive work. ''The Prologue'' identifies ''This Nobill Clerk, Esope,'' universally read in schools, as the main source and explains that Henryson is translating from Latin (Gualterus Anglicus), ''In hamlie language and in termes rude.'' He shows great skill in telling Æsopian and Reynardian tales (available in Lydgate and Caxton*) and in making moral points. The play between ''ernest and game,'' a feature of Scottish sensibility and language, is one delight of the thirteen tales, which vary from fourteen to fifty stanzas, including *moralitas* of from three to ten stanzas. All (except two *moralitas*) are in rhyme royal.

The Preiching of the Swallow is overtly homiletic, a warning against the subtle snares of the devil and a reminder of mutability. It begins with praise of the wisdom and marvelous work of God and a celebration of the seasons and agricultural work. Then the poet hears a swallow warn the other birds that a sower of flax who tempts them with a possibility of ease will soon destroy them in nets made from the flax unless they destroy the seeds. Henryson enlivens this message through acute observations of the ordinary; flax suggests Dumferline's weaving. *The Preiching* is a good introduction to his learning, artistry, and morality.

Henryson begins *The Fables* with the perennial Western anxiety about the relation between truth and fiction, whether in Plato, Chaucer, or Sidney's* *Apologie for Poetry*. The sixth fable, *The Taill of the Sone and Air of the foresaid Foxe, callit Father wer: Alswa the Parliament of fourfuttit Beistis, haldin be the Lyoun*, notes that

> under ane Fabill figurall
> Sad sentence man may seik, and efter syne,
> As daylie dois the Doctouris of Devyne,
> That to our leving full weill can apply
> And paynt thair mater furth be Poetry. (1099–1103)

The Fox's bastard son hopes to exceed his father's evil but is caught out and tried before a parliament of animals, found guilty, and hanged. In the Moralitas each animal's allegorical quality underlines the theme, to avoid worldly entrapment. Bolder objection to the failures of Justice, a crucial dimension of contemporary life, comes in the next fable, *The Scheip and the Dog*. Like Boethius, the sheep, identified as the commons, is falsely accused and undefended; and the poet asks, "Quhilk dampnit hes the selie Innocent, / And Justifyit the wrangous Judgement?" A long Moralitas explores the religious question of why God allows such things to happen. The only explanation of suffering seems to be that God seeks to make people change. Since few amend their lives, the poet finishes with a brief prayer that "gude rest" may come in heaven; he relies on vertical faith, not a worldly community. But life is lived horizontally, and Henryson observes this more positively in most of *The Fables*.

The Lyõn & the Mous is the only fable told directly by the author. In a dream vision the poet meets Æsop, "Poet Lawriate" and "maister venerabill," writer of fables "full of prudence and moralitie." The Roman, schooled in civil law, hesitates to tell another tale; there are "richt few or nane / To Goddis word that has devotioun." The tale of forgiveness allays these anxieties. Mice run over the Lion, a sleeping king, until he wakes and angrily seizes one. The mouse admits negligence but argues her poverty against the King's Magnificence and asks for mercy. This eloquence wins over the prideful ruler, whose reason and mercy make him grant Remission. Later hunters capture and bind the Lion. The Mouse recognizes the Lion that "did hir grace" and requites his action by enlisting others to help gnaw the ropes to release him, showing that the mighty need the help of the lowly. Æsop's Moralitas details the allegory: the mice represent the commons, the Lion any ruler; the action shows a relation between justice and rebellion and that ''Pietie''—mitigating cruelty with mercy and remitting sentence for even great offenses—is the essential virtue for prudent lords.

The Uplondis Mous and the Burges Mous, a witty enactment of the beatitude ''Blessed be the poor,'' documents Scottish life, contrasting rural and urban living, riches and simplicity, and concludes that the dangers of luxury and attendant anxiety make indulgence a poor choice. All earthly joy is mingled with adversity, and the mice are two sisters who choose alternate ways, the elder basking in feasting and unmindful of the threats of city life, while the younger lives in the country making do with nuts, candle, and dried peas. The Burges mouse feels contempt for such poor fare—''My gude friday is better nor your pace''—and leads her younger sister to the town and a larder full of cheese, butter, meat and fish, sacks of meal and malt. They feast without washing or prayer. The Upland mouse soon asks how long such richness will last; she is disconcerted and frightened after ''Gib hunter, our Jolie Cat'' had seized her and played with her until she managed to escape. The sisters meet no more, their ways being incompatible; and the Moralitas praises ''Blyithnes in hart, with small possessioun.'' Wyatt's* *The Mean and Sure Estate* shows the poem's influence, and Robert Burns uses a mouse, originally, perhaps, Horatian, to echo Scottish sentiments of warning against vainglory.

Chaucer's *Nun's Priest's Tale* is the source for *Schir Chantecleir and the Foxe*, part of the *Roman de Reynart* tradition. The poor widow, a beguiling Lawrence (Scots Reynard), a Cok, his wife Pertok, and the dogs are the principals. In thirty-one rhyme royal stanzas Henryson cannot rival Chaucer's long and richly textured tale; he simplifies and highlights the moral argument. When the fox takes Chantecleir, Pertok laments the loss of watchman, singer, and lover. Sprutok consoles that he is not worth such grief and promises change; ''was never wedow sa gay!'' should be Pertok's song. Toppok judges Chantecleir's capture a ''verray vengeance from the hevin'' for his lechery, adultery, and pride. But the widow rises from her swoon and sends the dogs to rescue her noble cock, who, ''with sum gude Spirit inspyrit,'' tempts the fox to speak so that he can fly away. The Moralitas urges that under ''typis figurall,'' ''worthie folk'' can ''find ane sentence richt agreabill, / Under thir fenyeit termis textuall.''

A competition between fox and wolf is the center of another tale especially evocative of Scottish country life. *How this forsaid Tod maid his Confessioun to Freir Wolf Waitskaith* explores specific religious practice. After considering astronomy, which foretells his destiny, the fox confesses; but he lacks contrition and a wish to amend his life, agreeing only to a penance of not eating flesh until Easter. The wily fox, having killed a kid, baptizes it—''Ga doun, Schir Kid, cum up Schir Salmond agane!''—and gorges himself. Lying with full belly, he thinks of an arrow in it; the keeper shoots him so that ''ane word in play'' becomes ''ernist.'' The Moralitas affirms repentance because a sudden shot can catch man unready, and thus he forfeits "blis withouttin end." Humor makes the ordinary memorable, as does a highlighting of Scotland's natural resources and the poverty that encouraged poaching. *The Fables* are comparable to *The Canterbury Tales* for including all levels of Scotch life.

Henryson's best-known poem is *The Testament of Cresseid*, seventy-nine rhyme royal stanzas to provide an alternate ending to *Troilus and Criseyde*. Many have contrasted Chaucer's compassion and ambiguity with Henryson's making Cresseid a leper, unrecognized by Troilus, who gives her alms. Calchus, a good father who accepts the prodigal, is priest in a Temple, which for Cresseid is a "kirk." Ashamed because Diomeid abandoned her, she blasphemes by blaming Venus and Cupid for her plight. Swooning, Cresseid dreams that the planets/gods debate her situation. Later she acknowledges, "My blaspheming now have I bocht full deir" and laments the day that brought her to Saturn's sentence that the ugliness of leprosy replace her beauty. The issue is less false love than dishonoring God, Henryson's constant theme of spiritual waste. Cresseid, unlike the fox in *The Fables*, fulfilled the three points of Confession: admission of guilt, contrition, and satisfaction or penance. The last stanza, asking worthy women in Charity that their love not be deceitful, expands to the community. Henryson's literary critique renders pagan antiquity as medieval Christian. Its implied moralitas heavily influenced Shakespeare.*

Orpheus and Eurydice contains similar themes. The Moralitas, a third of the total and in couplets, while the story is rhyme royal, cites Boethius and Trivet's commentary on the *Consolation of Philosophy*, not the happy ending of *Sir Orfeo*. Henryson uses a thin narrative to explore man's arrogance in seeking God's role in knowing. Orpheus has an aristocratic heritage and a noble spirit; he learns much when he seeks help and journeys to hell. As intellectual understanding, Orpheus plays his harp and wins through by subduing sensual appetites and reaching toward the ideal of a contemplative life so that he is reunited with affection. His fatal glance is a return to sensuality with immediate results— "Quhat will ye moir? In short conclusion, / he blent bakwart, And pluto come annone, / And on to hell with hir agane is gone." In an encyclopedic pastiche of medieval commonplaces this poignant moment evokes the power of human love and a recognition that man cannot easily harmonize intellect and affections.

A lighter treatment of human misguided action is *Robene and Makyne*, in form like a French *pastourelle*, part of the tradition that leads to Spenser's* *The Shepheardes Calendar*. When the maid offers her love, the young shepherd displays blunt indifference to all but his sheep; later he must accept rejection with the pointed proverbial comment: "In gestis and storeis auld, / The man that will nocht quhen he may / sall haif nocht quhen he wald." There is no moral explanation, but stylistic devices and wit heighten brusqueness.

Several shorter poems present the same moral themes. *The Bludy Serk* tells of a princess saved from a giant, but the champion knight dies after asking her to remain loyal to his memory; the Moralitas identifies Christ as the lover/knight and urges constant love of God and prayer. *The Abbay Walk* offers consolation in adversity and recalls Job. Several lyrics are *memento mori*, and others emphasize that worldliness is not trustworthy. *Ane Prayer for the Pest* is a reminder of the breadth of catastrophe and of human dependence upon God's mercy. Henryson's admission of guilt, his view of plague as punishment for trespass, and urging of repentance are alien themes at the end of the twentieth century, as are his piety and exaltation in the soaring lyricism of *The Annunciation*, which proclaims the faith and joy that explain why sinning causes guilt and distress. These contrasting lyrics illustrate the two poles of religious argument; Henryson's storytelling characteristically balances them.

CRITICAL RECEPTION

Early praise of Henryson indicates a high reputation among Scottish writers during his lifetime, and survival of various manuscripts and printed texts suggests a broad audience. These show greatest interest in *The Fables*, for which there are two good manuscripts (B. L. Harleian MS 3865 and [Bannatyne] Nat. Library of Scotland 1.1.6), dated 1571 and 1568, and four printed editions, three in Edinburgh and one in London, 1570, 1571, 1621, and 1577, which suggest a middle-class professional audience. Thynne's inclusion of *The Testament of Cresseid* in his 1532 edition of Chaucer initiated Henryson's role as a ''Scots Chaucerian,'' and this has only just ceased to be the focus of attention, albeit modernizations continue. Henryson was not generally known in the seventeenth century, and the eighteenth-century antiquarians favored Gavin Douglas.* In the nineteenth century Henryson's poetry became accessible with reprints of separate poems and David Laing's complete edition in 1865, followed by an edition in the Scottish Text Society in 1906–14. The poet's reputation in Scotland has always been high, and recent scholarship has established the range of his learning and verbal and metrical skill. But Henryson is Scots, and his narrative poems are too long for anthologies. His traditional and insistent Christian morality—the great theme is the tragedy of sin—and quiet contemplation are antimodern, less compatible interests than Dunbar's* incisive social protest. Henryson asserts his moral imperatives with humor and compassion, and his learning is offset by a refreshing colloquialism. An engaging storyteller, he relies on tradition even back to Horace, Plato's Socrates, and Æsop, but his virtuosity and dynamism make familiar tale and allegory compelling. The ''Scots Chaucerian'' is increasingly recognized as a major medieval poet with a Shakespearean range of tragedy and comedy, praised for a plain style and the humanist learning to make him the first of the University Wits.

BIBLIOGRAPHY

Works by Robert Henryson

The Moral Fables of Æsop. Ed. George Gopen. Notre Dame: University of Notre Dame Press, 1987.

The Poems and Fables of Robert Henryson: Schoolmaster of Dunfermline. 2nd ed. Ed. H. Harvey Wood. Edinburgh: Oliver and Boyd, 1958.

The Poems of Robert Henryson. Ed. Denton Fox. Oxford: Clarendon Press, 1981.

Studies of Robert Henryson

Clark, G. "Henryson and Aesop: The Fable Transformed," *ELH* 43 (1976): 1–18.

Gopen, George. "The Essential Seriousness of Robert Henryson's Moral Fables: A Study in Structure." *Studies in Philology* 82.1 (1985): 42–59.

Gray, Douglas. *Robert Henryson*. Leiden: E. J. Brill, 1979.

Jack, R.D.S., ed. *The History of Scottish Literature*. Vol. 1. Aberdeen: Aberdeen University Press, 1988, 55–71.

Kindrick, Robert L. *Robert Henryson*. Boston: Twayne, 1979.

Ridley, Florence H. "Henryson." In *A Manual of the Writings in Middle English 1050–1500*. Vol. 4. New Haven: Connecticut Academy of Arts and Sciences, 1973, 965–88.

VELMA BOURGEOIS RICHMOND

PHILIP HENSLOWE
(155?–1616)

BIOGRAPHY

Though Philip Henslowe is the author of the most important document in the history of British theater, he was not a man of letters. He was, in fact, a successful businessman and entrepreneur, a dyer, pawnbroker, real estate investor, and landlord, but his most famous role was as theater owner/manager and, from 1592 to 1603, keeper of an account book/ ledger/ commonplace book known as *Henslowe's Diary*.

Henslowe's father was a gamekeeper in the Ashdown Forest in Sussex. By 1577, Henslowe was apprenticed to a dyer, but in the 1580s his master died, and two years later he married his master's widow. Her money enabled him to make a number of shrewd investments. In 1584 he leased a plot of land in Southwark and in 1587, in partnership with a grocer (who was to have the food concession and half the box office), built the Rose Theater, the first Bankside theater and the only one until the Swan of 1595.

The year 1592 was perhaps the most important year in Henslowe's colorful life. In that year, he inherited his brother's account book and began keeping his own accounts. Among the earliest expenditures recorded is an investment of £105 for renovations, probably to enlarge the theater and roof the stage. That year also saw the beginning of his long business and personal relationship with Edward Alleyn, the leading actor of the day, who created the roles of Orlando Furioso, Barabas, Tamburlaine, Dr. Faustus, and perhaps Titus Andronicus. In 1592 Alleyn brought his company, the Lord Admiral's Men, to the Rose and in October of that year married Henslowe's stepdaughter Joan, consolidating a partnership that was to last until Henslowe's death. Also noteworthy among the Rose performances in 1592 was the premiere of Shakespeare's* *I Henry VI.*

That year was also a typical one for an Elizabethan theater in its disruptions. Puritan authorities, particularly the mayor of London, were quick to seize upon any excuse to shut down the playhouses. In June, theaters were closed, ostensibly because of a civil disturbance, and Alleyn took the company on tour. The theaters remained closed through the fall, this time ostensibly because of the plague. Closure by the authorities was a threat throughout Henslowe's career; other problems besetting his theater management were the murder of his leading playwright Marlowe* in 1593 and the ascendancy of Shakespeare, the ''upstart crow.'' Competition with the Lord Chamberlain's Men, Shakespeare's company, culminated with the erection of the Globe Theater a block away from the Rose in 1599.

The lack of a Marlowe (Kyd,* another Rose playwright, also died in 1593) and a theater-hungry public's insatiable demand for new plays led to the practice of commissioning collaborative teams of authors to write plays. Sometimes a play had five coauthors. A frequent member of those teams was Dekker.* Carson has calculated that 82 percent of the spring-summer 1598 productions were collaborations. The collaborative approach to playwriting was enough of a success for Henslowe and Alleyn to build both the Fortune Theater in 1600 and the Hope in 1613. Diversification in investments by the two men also helped their finances. In 1593, perhaps because of the long forced closures of the Rose the previous year, Henslowe had begun pawnbroking (although it has been suggested that the pawn operation may have been an effort to set up a nephew in business). In 1604, he and Alleyn began sharing the mastership of the Royal Game, a post that gave them control over bull- and bear-baiting events. Henslowe may have used the 1587 Rose for bear-baiting as well as plays; a bear femur and skull were unearthed during the 1989 excavation. His last theater, the Hope, was also a multipurpose arena that could be used for plays or for animal-baiting.

Henslowe died in 1616. His papers passed to Edward Alleyn, who gave them to Dulwich College. Perhaps motivated by a desire to show the Puritans that even a player could do good works and enabled to do so by his considerable financial success as an actor, Alleyn had founded the institution in 1614. Henslowe's papers were first brought to public attention by Edmund Malone in 1790.

Remains of the Rose Theater were discovered in 1989 on the site of a proposed office block. A large protest against the developers led by theater superstars and academics drew worldwide media attention but failed to halt the building of the office complex and gained only a ''compromise'' of putting the high-rise on massive stilts, supposedly allowing archaeologists and later visitors access to the site. Before being re-covered, excavations revealed two stages and two back walls, evidence that the theater was enlarged in 1592, as suggested by the *Diary* expenses for that year. A temporary exhibition was opened for the summer of 1996, with a permanent exhibit to follow, but the failure to better protect the Rose Theater foundations is all the more regrettable since the remains of the Globe, with 40 percent lying under the Southwark Bridge Road and 30 percent under an eighteenth-century building, will quite possibly never be completely excavated.

MAJOR WORKS AND THEMES

Because the *Diary* first belonged to Philip Henslowe's brother John, the beginning is filled with accounts relating to mining, smelting, and logging operations in the Ashdown Forest. Philip's accounts begin in 1592 and include not only theatrical entries but also matters such as records of loans, rent payments, the management of his late brother's estate, details about outfitting a soldier whom Henslowe sponsored, cures for illness and wounds, surefire ways to locate stolen goods, details about a farm he contemplated buying, a memo about putting his horse to grass, and pawn accounts. The pawn accounts shed an especially rich light on Elizabethan daily life.

Theatrical records in the *Diary* have furnished scholars with information about play titles—280 different plays are mentioned, reminding us of how much is lost—performance dates, box office receipts for each play, authors, how much an author was paid for a finished play, costumes and their materials and cost, and actors' names and are the source for biographical information about authors like Dekker.* Such routine expenses in the running of an Elizabethan theater as the price of a flagstaff, of the bribe to a minor clerk in order to obtain the company's salary for performing at court, of taking a boy actor to the hospital, and of bailing insolvent authors like Dekker and Chettle out of debtor's prison are recorded.

Still extant in addition to the *Diary* are numerous miscellaneous documents, such as the deed of partnership between Henslowe and the grocer Cholmley for construction and profit sharing of the Rose Theater and the 1599/1600 contract for the building of the Fortune. The latter includes the most detailed available account of playhouse construction and dimensions for the period. The collection of Henslowe/Alleyn papers also contains affectionate letters among members of Henslowe's immediate family and extended family of actors during tours, such as a letter from one of the child actors to Henslowe's stepdaughter Joan. Several petitions exist, among them a 1592 letter from Thames watermen asking for the reopening of the theaters and reminding the government of the plight of the out-of-work watermen's wives and children. Also among Henslowe's papers are six dramatic "plots," outlines of plays for the prompters with lists of participating actors.

Some of the most interesting documents in the collection of Henslowe-Alleyn papers are now lost but were fortunately transcribed by Malone: the inventories of goods belonging to the Lord Admiral's Men, which include such items as (among the costumes) "a robe for to goo invisibell" (used in Act III of *Dr.*

Faustus) and the prop list, which includes "1 rocke, 1 cage, 1 tomb, 1 Hell mought . . . 1 tome of Dido, 1 gowlden flece, the sittie of Rome." Listed along with "Tantelouse tre" is the "tree of gowlden apelles" probably used in Act IV of Dekker's *Old Fortunatus*.

CRITICAL RECEPTION

Henslowe's papers were first put to scholarly use by Edmond Malone, who published extracts in an edition of Shakespeare's works in 1790. In 1845, John Payne Collier published an edition marred by forgeries. The first complete edition was Greg's, listed in the bibliography.

The value of the *Diary* as a historical document has never been disputed, but the author has been subjected to personal attack. Collier thought Henslowe ignorant and the ledger disorganized. In 1890, F. G. Fleay described Henslowe as an illiterate, money-grubbing philistine who was ignorant of literature and who exploited others for his own gain. Criticism of the man led to criticism of the plays produced at his theater as potboilers, as opposed to the works of lasting artistic merit being shown down the street at the Globe. Even company organization is supposed to have contributed to artistic success or failure; Shakespeare's company, with artists as shareholders, supposedly ensured a better product. Recently, Henslowe has been given a more sympathetic reading by Foakes and Rickert, Carson, Rhodes, and Eccles, who have found him patient, even generous, in his business dealings. In an era before lending institutions, Henslowe was a banker to his company members. The potboiler accusation seems especially unfair. With Henslowe as impresario, after all, his theater produced *The Spanish Tragedy, The Jew of Malta, Dr. Faustus, Tamburlaine*, and *Shoemakers' Holiday* and gave Shakespeare his start.

The 1989 demonstrations to save the remains of the Rose Theater focused media attention on Henslowe and sparked an interest in the man, his theater, and his contribution to English theater in his own right, not merely as an appendage to studies of Shakespeare.

Henslowe's papers are the chief source for Elizabethan theater history, their worth summed up by John Barton of the Royal Shakespeare Company when he said the *Diary* is "my Bible."

BIBLIOGRAPHY

Works by Philip Henslowe

Collier, John Payne. *Henslowe's Diary*. London: 1845.

Foakes, R. A. *The Henslowe Papers*. London: Scolar Press, 1977.

Foakes, R. A., and R. T. Rickert. *Henslowe's Diary*. Cambridge: Cambridge University Press, 1961.

Greg, Walter. *Henslowe's Diary*. 2 vols. London: A. H. Bullen, 1904–8.

———. *Henslowe's Papers*. London: A. H. Bullen, 1907.

Studies of Philip Henslowe
Carson, Neil. *A Companion to Henslowe's Diary*. Cambridge: Cambridge University Press, 1988.
Eccles, Christine. *The Rose Theatre*. London: Walker Books, 1990.
Rhodes, Ernest L. *Henslowe's Rose: The Stage and The Staging*. Lexington: University of Kentucky Press, 1976.
Rutter, Carol Chillingworth. *Documents of the Rose Playhouse*. Manchester: Manchester University Press, 1984.

JANET WOLF

JOHN HEYWOOD
(c. 1496–1578)

BIOGRAPHY

Because of John Heywood's intimate forty-year affiliation with the Tudor court and the Sir Thomas More* Circle and because of his sophisticated literary and musical creativity and wit, he is a highly important figure in the history of Tudor drama. Named "the father of English comedy" by the Renaissance scholar Alfred W. Pollard, John Heywood, dramatist, entertainer, and faithful Catholic, lived over eighty years during the central years of the Tudor monarchy. His skill as an entertainer brought him favor in the courts of King Henry VIII and his son King Edward VI, true friendship with Catholic Queen Mary, and even success in the court of Protestant Queen Elizabeth.* But his loyalty to Roman Catholicism led to intermittent persecution, arrest, near-execution, and finally exile and poverty in Belgium.

He was born sometime between 19 April 1496 and 18 April 1497 and died probably during the summer of 1578. His birthplace seems to have been outside London, possibly in Coventry in Warwickshire. As a child he may have served as a chorister for Cardinal Wolsey, and between the ages of eleven and fourteen he was matriculated at Broadgate's (now Pembroke College) at Oxford, although he did not graduate.

By 1519 he was serving as a musician in the court of Henry VIII, possibly as a result of the influence of his friends and neighbors, the Rastells and the Mores. Court records and accounts show that he was paid quarterly as a singer and player of the virginals until 1528, when he was named steward of the Royal Chamber and received a regular income of ten pounds while he continued to perform at court. He held this position for thirty years, and by the time of Queen Mary's death, the income had risen to fifty pounds.

Possibly because of earlier alliances during his youth or obvious shared interests, Heywood became a popular member of the Sir Thomas More Circle, a group of creative and influential individuals in King Henry's court, almost all of whom were Catholic and who were led by More and highly influenced by the Flemish writer and philosopher Desiderius Erasmus.* Sir Thomas More himself became the king's chancellor but was executed in 1535 because he refused to sign the Act of Supremacy. Other members of the circle include Margaret More Roper, More's scholarly daughter; William Roper, her husband; Margaret Giggs, the artistic adopted daughter of More; Dr. John Clement, her husband; Elizabeth More Rastell, More's sister; her husband, John Rastell, an attorney and dramatist and the only member of the group who converted to Protestantism; their son John; their other son, William, an attorney and printer of Heywood's works; and finally, their daughter Eliza Rastell, who married John Heywood in 1529. This marriage ensured Heywood an intimate position in this brilliant and politically vocal group.

Heywood's entertainments won him great favor. In 1533 William Rastell published four of Heywood's plays, which were reprinted several times during the sixteenth century and were often performed both at court and at entertainments at private houses. During his early career, however, Heywood was more respected for his skill as a musician. He survived difficult political situations such as Archbishop Cranmer's* pronouncement of divorce between Henry and Katherine and the execution of Sir Thomas More in 1535 while still maintaining and nurturing a friendship with Katherine's officially disdained daughter Mary. When Anne Boleyn was executed in 1536, however, Mary was gradually able to regain her father's favor, clearly a beneficial circumstance for Heywood. While Heywood's dramatic career is considered to have been at its peak between 1523 and 1533, records show court payments for a number of his entertainments during the following years, 1534 to 1558, especially from Queen Mary. Heywood amassed a considerable income from the court and from several properties during these years.

Yet Heywood's was not a smooth career. He apparently was plagued by a court rivalry with Will Somer, the highly favored court fool to Henry. Much more serious were the consequences of his active participation in plots to halt the spread of Protestantism. In 1543 he was involved in a plot against the Protestant archbishop Cranmer, which, when discovered, resulted in an indictment against Heywood and others, including the son of Sir Thomas More, John More. After a public recantation and confession in 1544, however, Heywood received a general pardon and even lived to see Cranmer fall from favor and suffer execution.

The next twenty-five years were more peaceful and clearly successful for Heywood, especially the years of the reign of the Catholic Queen Mary from 1553 to 1558. Heywood had become her friend, even attending her faithfully during her final illness. Her half-sister Queen Elizabeth's ascendance to the throne did not terminate Heywood's entertainments at court. But during her reign, his Catholicism grew troublesome, and he was forced into exile in Belgium with his son sometime after 1562. This exile was made more painful by the removal of his incomes from properties in England granted by Queen Mary and her predecessors. Heywood was comforted, however, by the loyalty of his children both to him and to the Roman Catholic faith. His daughter, Elizabeth

Donne, had married John Donne, an ironmonger, in 1563 and for the ninety-two years of her life, remained a faithful Catholic in England. She survived three husbands and was the mother of six children, including John Donne the poet. Heywood had two other daughters for whom few records exist; but his two sons, Jasper and Ellis, are known as the most notable Jesuits during the Elizabethan period. Both were themselves finally exiled, and Ellis, living at the Jesuit College in Antwerp, was allowed to have his father live nearby. Here in 1578 John Heywood died in poverty but with the love and respect of his family and friends.

MAJOR WORKS AND THEMES

A chronology of the plays attributed to Heywood is not possible because no dates of authorship exist. But the first is probably a nearly complete, signed manuscript, *Wytty and Wyttles* (WW), an interlude of about 850 lines, missing its opening section. In the form of a *debat*, it is a disputation or witty argument among the characters, each of whom represents a position in the debate. In this play, John argues for the wise man's life, and James, for the foolish man's. Finally Jerome, the schoolmaster, enters and successfully concludes that a life lived in wisdom is in all ways superior to one lived in foolishness. While the play is largely without plot, and some modern critics find it dull, it incorporates the university wit and wordplay so popular in the More Circle. The play reflects the central theme of Erasmus'* *Encomium Moriae*. It also contains an interesting attack on Will Somer, Heywood's rival in the court of Henry VIII, whose foolishness and slothfulness, Heywood believed, received excessive rewards. Jerome remarks, "Thynk yow the nombere / Standth as Somers dothe all day yn slomber / Nay Somers ys a sot; folle for a kyng" (WW).

The probable subsequent play is *The Play of Love*, since it too follows the *debat* structure, but more elaborately, more successfully, and in twice as many lines. It was printed at least four times during Heywood's lifetime. A double argument develops among four allegorical characters: "The Louer not Beloued and The Woman Beloued not Louing, and then The Louer Loued and Neither Louer nor Loued." The latter, along with Merry Report in *The Play of the Wether*, is first identified as a vice in the dramatis personae in a printed drama. The play's first two characters argue over who suffers more in love, while the second pair argues over who enjoys the greater pleasure. Toward the end of the disputation, Neither Louer nor Loued presents the only stage business of the play when he runs among the audience with squids of fire burning in his head-piece. He cries falsely that the home of the Lover's beloved is on fire. When this false news sends the Lover into a panicky exit from the stage, the Vice claims he has proven that love brings great pain. The play concludes with the bromide that all people suffer both joy and pain; an unusual amalgam of literary genres, it includes the Vice of the English morality play, medieval university disputation, the wit and wordplay typical of the interludes of the More Circle, and conventions of Continental courtly love literature. Thus, in both its structure and content, *The Play of Loue* represents the turmoil and change in the arts in Henry VIII's court of the 1520s and the attendant questioning of wisdom, foolishness, and language itself.

First printed in 1533 by William Rastell, Heywood's 1250-line *Play of the Wether* contains, like the other two, both disputation and comic drama. Jupiter and his agent, the Vice Merry Report, listen to the complaints of various characters about the weather. At the end, these characters are soothed by the great god's promise to bring enough variety of weather to satisfy everyone. Throughout the play, Merry Report mocks the petitioners, pairs of whom engage in separate debates about the weather—the gentleman and the merchant, the two millers, and the Gentlewoman and the Laundress. Each is self-important and of limited vision. Merry Report is most boastful, however, describing his own feats and his disinterest in weather, but he is sufficiently observant to mock Jupiter's elegant but empty rhyme royal solutions, which offer no actual solutions at all.

In all three plays, Heywood puts a debate into dramatic form for the first time. But he moves beyond the genre's obvious didactic function. With the wordplay of the Vice and the self-serving arguments of the petitioners, he mocks the forms of debate and reason themselves and the very language from which they are shaped. This questioning of whether words adequately convey reality is one of Heywood's major dramatic innovations.

The second important genre Heywood used in his interludes is farce, in which humor and comedy are the central concern. *The Foure PP's*, printed between 1543 and 1547 with Heywood's name on the title page, was probably written before the death of Sir Thomas More and was presented at court before the king. It is about a Pardoner, a Pedlar, a Palmer, and a Pothecary, who meet, degrade one another mercilessly, realize that they are all merry rascals who might enjoy and benefit from the fellowship of one another, and set off to determine who should be the leader of them all by resolving who can tell the greatest lie. The contest is finally won by the Pedlar, who claims, "Of all the women that I haue sene / I neuer sawe nor knewe in my consyens / Any one woman out of paciens" (4PP). The play ends with a disclaimer, apologetic in tone, that these corrupted characters are not representative of the Catholic church. The Palmer asks, "[O]ur lorde to prosper you all / In the fayth of hys churche uniuersall" (4PP). These are clearly Chaucerian characters, both as bawdy, self-serving knaves and corrupters of the church. That Heywood, the faithful Catholic, used such character types reveals just how conventional corrupt churchmen remained in literature.

The fifth play, *The Pardoner and the Friar*, is a farce of 1,000 lines printed by William Rastell in 1533 with no title page or author's name. But its attribution to Heywood is sound since it bears striking similarities to the previously discussed plays. Additionally, it was Rastell's custom to exclude the author's name when only a head title was included. Again the play is framed as a *debat*, but it quickly evolves into a simple name-calling argument that sinks to physical attacks. It is considered early because of its relative simplicity, but it includes characteristic wordplay and strong Chaucerian influences on the conventions of character.

The final play, *John, Tyb, and Sir John,* is a 700-line farce printed without authorship but with many echoes of Heywood's other works. The greatest objections to his authorship are based on the play's satire of Catholic churchmen. Criticism of the church, however, was common during this period and was practiced by such devout Catholics as Geoffrey Chaucer, Alexander Barclay, John Skelton,* and many conservative Catholics in France. The play is inspired by the popular contemporary French *sottie*, a burlesque of a religious drama. This form was apparently unknown in England before Heywood. But he went even further; he combined the burlesque elements of the *sottie* and the story of a secular fabliau and developed a drama that was quite new in England.

Other plays attributed to Heywood include *Thersites, Calisto and Meliboea,* and, most likely, *Gentilnesse and Nobility*, a *debat* printed without date by John Rastell, William's father. But because the colophon ambiguously reads, in translation, ''John Rastell caused me to be printed,'' it is unclear whether Rastell merely printed the text or whether he wrote it as well.

During Heywood's lifetime, he was most famous and respected as a writer of nondramatic works. In fact, in 1562, when his *Works* were printed, no interludes were included. This nondramatic part of his extant canon is three times longer than his interludes and consists of songs and other lyric poetry, proverbs and epigrams, and the lengthy poem *The Spider and the Fly.* Since Heywood considered himself, first of all, a musician, his songs show great skill. One of them, ''A Description of a Most Noble Lady,'' is included anonymously in Tottel's *Miscellany* in 1557, minus the final two stanzas containing somewhat familiar lines that identify the lady as the current queen, Mary, at the age of eighteen.

Most famous were Heywood's epigrams, some of which were printed at least five times during his lifetime. In the *Works* are included *Dialog of Proverbs concerning Marriage, Three Hundred Epigrams upon Prouerbs*, and *Three Hundred Epigrams*, all of which are short, clever, sometimes pithy narratives or jokes.

The final work of Heywood, twenty-five years in composing, is *The Spider and the Fly* (SF), a religious allegorical poem of 7,600 lines first published in 1556 but written, according to Heywood in the conclusion, ''[a]fter old beginning newly brought to end. The thing, years more than twenty since it begun, / To the thing years more than nineteen, nothing done'' (SF). Since the poem is an allegory and was begun around 1535 or 1536, the Tudor politics that form the framework of this allegory are enticing. The simple plot describes a fly who is caught in a spider web spun at the base of a window in the home of a lord. The spider seeks to kill the fly, an elaborate trial is held, and just as the fly is about to be executed, a maid in the household arrives, chastises the spider for building a web in the lower portion of the window, and kills him, allowing the other spiders and the fly to escape. While Heywood identifies the maid as Queen Mary serving Christ and his universal church, the identity of the remaining characters is unclear. But the spider may be Archbishop Cranmer, executed in 1556, and the flies may be the poor Catholics led by Sir Thomas More, who was indeed caught in the web illegally placed by Henry VIII and Anne Boleyn. Whatever the specific points of the allegory, its comments on the turbulent twenty years of Tudor rule between 1535 and 1556 are extremely useful to an understanding of the period.

CRITICAL RECEPTION

John Heywood's reputation as an early Tudor dramatist has been solid throughout the twentieth century. He is not forgotten as a significant step on the road to Shakespearean grandeur; he is called "the father of modern comedy"; and he may be remembered by some as the first dramatist to introduce a character called the Vice. John Heywood has, however, a more important literary legacy.

First, his work reveals the political, social, and philosophical atmosphere of the Sir Thomas More Circle and the Tudor court during its middle years. It was energetic, volatile, often brilliant, but divided so powerfully that Heywood's intimacy with the court combined with his survival for more than eighty years is remarkable. Heywood's life and works provide a close view of those times.

Second, Heywood's works show a sophistication and breadth of vision that are often overlooked. Rather, he is often superficially assessed almost as if he were a Cro-Magnon man—an extinct link—the fascination of whom lies only in those elements that he connects. Heywood's works raise questions of social order, the possibility of objective, rational thought, the nature of love, and the manifestation of religion. But most of all, Heywood examines the nature of language, displaying its strengths in maintaining social order and its weaknesses in representing the so-called actual world. In this, Heywood's timeless sophistication must be recognized.

BIBLIOGRAPHY

Works by John Heywood

Bevington, David. *Medieval Drama*. Boston: Houghton Mifflin, 1975.

de la Bere, R. *John Heywood: Entertainer*. London: George Allen and Unwin, 1937.

Farmer, John, ed. *Early English Dramatists: The Dramatic Writings of John Heywood*. 1905. New York: Barnes and Noble, 1966.

———. *Early English Dramatists: The Proverbs, Epigrams, and Miscellanies of John Heywood*. 1906. New York: Barnes and Noble, 1966.

———. *Early English Dramatists: The Spider and the Fly*. 1908. New York: Barnes and Noble, 1966.

Heywood, John. *The Foure P.P.* In *John Heywood Entertainer*, by R. de la Bere. London: George Allen and Unwin, 1937, 185–232.

———. *Johan Johan*. In *Medieval Drama*, by David Bevington. Boston: Houghton Mifflin, 1975.

———. *Johan Johan*. In *John Heywood: Entertainer*, by R. de la Bere. London: George Allen and Unwin, 1937, 233–67.

———. *The Pardoner and the Frere*. In *John Heywood: Entertainer*, by R. de la Bere. London: George Allen and Unwin, 1937, 147–84.

———. *The Play of the Wether*. In *Medieval Drama*, by David Bevington. Boston: Houghton Mifflin, 1975.

———. *A Play of Wytty and Wyttles*. In *John Heywood: Entertainer*, by R. de la Bere. London: George Allen and Unwin, 1937, 117–46.

Milligan, Burton A., ed. *John Heywood's "Works" and Miscellaneous Short Poems*. Urbana: University of Illinois Press, 1956.

Studies of John Heywood

Bolwell, Robert W. *The Life and Works of John Heywood*. 1926. New York: AMS Press, 1966.

de la Bere, R. *John Heywood: Entertainer*. London: George Allen and Unwin, 1937.

Hogrefe, Pearl. *The Sir Thomas More Circle*. Urbana: University of Illinois Press, 1959.

Johnson, Robert Carl. *John Heywood*. New York: Twayne, 1970.

Maxwell, Ian. *French Farce and John Heywood*. Melbourne: Melbourne University Press, 1946.

Phy, Wesley. "The Chronology of Heywood's Plays." *E Studien* 74 (1940): 27–41.

Reed, A. W. *Early Tudor Drama: Medwall, The Rastells, Heywood, and the Sir Thomas More Circle*. London: Methuen, 1926.

VICKI JANIK

THOMAS HOBY
(1530–1566)

BIOGRAPHY

Thomas Hoby, traveler, translator, and finally ambassador, died at the advent of the courtly life he had always emulated. Born in 1530 to William Hoby and Katherine Fordan Hoby, in 1545 he entered St. John's College of Cambridge, where both John Cheke and Roger Ascham were teaching. In pursuit of a diplomatic career, in 1547 he traveled to Europe to fortify his knowledge of languages and culture. He studied for one year in Strasbourg with the Lutheran Martin Bucer, whose "Gratulation unto the church of England" Hoby later translated. Scholars have often speculated that this year with Bucer was urged upon Hoby to strengthen his Protestantism before the young man continued on to Italy in the spring of 1548. Hoby remained in Italy until December 1550, when he returned to England and was introduced at the court of Edward VI.

Appropriate to the courtier of Baldassare Castiglione's* description, Hoby first took up the task of translating *Il Cortegiano* at the request of a woman—the wife of his employer the marquis of Northampton. In his journal entitled *Book of the Travaile and Lief of Me* Hoby explains that when he reached Paris in 1552, "the first thing [he] did was to translate into Englishe the third booke of the *Cowrtisan*, which [his] Ladie Marquess had often willed [him] to do" (78). In Hoby's translation we read the words of Castiglione's Lord Cesar Gonzaga:

> [N]o Court, how great ever it be, can have any sightlinesse, or brightnesse in it, or mirth without women, nor anie Courtier can be gratious, pleasant or hardye, nor at anye time undertake any galant enterprise of Chivalrye onlesse he be stirred wyth the conversacion and wyth the love and contentacion of women, even so in like case the Courtiers talke is most unperfect ever more, if the entercourse of women give them not a part of the grace wherwithall they make perfect and decke out their playing the Courtier. (3:3)

Hoby translated the other three books of Castiglione's masterpiece between 1553 and 1555 in Italy, where he fled from London after Mary's accession.

In 1558, when his brother Sir Philip Hoby died and bequeathed the family estate to Thomas, the rising diplomat married Elizabeth Cooke, daughter of Sir Anthony Cooke (whom Hoby met while in exile in Italy). He lived quietly on his estate until the last months of his life, when he reached the apex of his diplomatic career. One week after dubbing him knight, in March 1566, Queen Elizabeth* appointed Hoby ambassador to the court of the French king. Tragically, in July 1566, after only three months in office, Hoby died suddenly from an unexplained fever. Perhaps even this image of unblemished promise and early death is apposite for the translator of *The Book of the Courtier*.

MAJOR WORKS AND THEMES

Hoby's major contribution to literature, his vernacular and readable English translation of Castiglione's *Il Cortegiano*, was first published in 1561. *The Book of the Courtier* rapidly became a guidebook of behavior for young men with courtly aspirations during Queen Elizabeth's reign. Castiglione's work, a dialogue between ladies and gentlemen in the Italian court of the duke of Urbino, advises in piecemeal that the ideal courtier should be a skilled soldier, an accomplished scholar, an able musician, a charming guest, as well as a generous host and a wise and ethical counselor. Above all, these achievements should be born with "*sprezzatura*," or a nonchalance (Hoby translates the term, sometimes aptly, as "recklessness"), which allows the aspirant, without being flippant, to display all noble virtues with a graceful and unlabored ease. In the paradoxical final book of the work the Neoplatonist Pietro Bembo* explains the courtier's ultimate goal. This speech and its goal have been a locus for much critical debate in recent years. Throughout the work, Castiglione draws on Plato, Aristotle, and Cicero in presenting the ideal courtier who is a combination of the medieval chivalric knight and the scholar/gentleman knight of the sixteenth century.

Hoby's approach to language accords with that of John Cheke, who advises Hoby in a letter published with the book "that our own tung shold be written cleane and pure, unmixt and unmangeled with borowing of other tunges, wherin if we take not heed by tijm, ever borowing and never payeng, she shall be fain to keep her house as bankrupt'' (12). Accordingly, Hoby uses Anglo-Saxon rather than Latinate words wherever possible, and his prose is rich with native idiom and sometimes native metaphor. For instance, Hoby writes that the courtier should not carry his head ''so like a malthorse for feare of ruffling his hear'' (60). His aversion to taking liberties in translation led him sometimes to stick literally to a word-for-word translation or metaphrase, resulting in some distinctive, if slightly awkward, moments. Hoby's translation of ''twincklinges and sperkeles'' for what some would rather translate as ''lightning and thunderbolts'' may not be idiomatically astute, but it certainly adds color to Castiglione's prose. F. O. Matthiessen points out that many characteristics of Hoby's prose later became the vogue on the Elizabethan stage, including such phrases as having a ''faint heart'' for cowardice and ''stomacke'' for spirit or courage (41).

Hoby receives the most adverse criticism from scholars who note that for terms crucial to Castiglione such as *sprezzatura* and *affetazione* Hoby's translations ''recklessness'' and ''curiosity'' (respectively) do not render the full nuance required for a fruitful understanding of Castiglione's philosophy. I would argue that even these idiosyncrasies of Hoby's translation contribute to the overall effect of importing seminal ideas of the Italian Renaissance wholly into England, much as Sir Philip Sidney* later advises adapters of other cultures to ''by attentive translation (as it were) devour them whole, and make them wholly theirs'' (138). In a period when the anti-Italian sentiments expressed by Ascham* in his *Scholemaster* might have held sway, Hoby's naturalization of *Il Cortegiano* provided access to a masterpiece of Italian culture in the early years of Elizabeth's reign that would later find its way to the London stage.

Hoby's journal, *Book of the Travaile and Lief of Me*, was not published until 1902. Recently, Steven Masello argues that Hoby's *Lief* is a revealing sociohistorical document reflecting the values of his generation. Masello asserts as well that Hoby's penchant for travel influenced more people to try European travel, arguing that because he was the *Courtier*'s translator his tastes would have carried currency.

CRITICAL RECEPTION

In addition to Ascham's favorable notice of Hoby's translation, the work was embraced by Gabriel Harvey,* who filled his copy of Hoby's translation with enthusiastic, if sometimes cryptic, marginalia, often providing names of his contemporaries as examples of Castiglione's descriptions. For example, Harvey wrote ''Sir Thomas More''* next to the passage referring to the courtier's ''certaine sweetnesse'' in jesting and laughing (Matthiessen, 14). In his introduction to his 1901 edition of Hoby's translation, Walter A. Raleigh suggests that Edmund Spenser's* ''Of Heavenly Love'' and ''Of Heavenly Beauty'' are based on the Bembo orations in the fourth book of *The Courtier* and that Christopher

Marlowe's* famous lines "It lies not in our power to love or hate, / For will in us is over-rul'd by fate . . . / Who ever loved, who loved not at first sight?" (from *Hero and Leander*) were inspired by Hoby's "Forsomuch as our mindes are very apte to love and to hate . . . it is seene that the lookers on many times beare affecion without any manifest cause why" (48). Mary A. Scott asserts further that the witty repartee between Shakespeare's* Beatrice and Benedick of *Much Ado about Nothing* reflects Castiglione's representation of Lady Emilia Pia and Lord Gaspare Pallavicino. It would indeed be odd in this list of those influenced by *The Courtier* to overlook Sir Philip Sidney,* of whom Thomas Nashe* could write when discussing the ideal courtier in the dedicatory epistle of his *Anatomy of Absurdity*, "England . . . never saw any thing more singuler then worthy Sir Philip Sidney, of whom it might truely be saide, 'arma virumque cano' " (7). Sidney, however, may have taken "*sprezzatura*" to another level, one of true self-irony.

While recent attention to Castiglione continues to be great, Hoby is often ignored. Steven Masello tried to generate interest in Hoby's journal, completing a new, abundantly annotated edition as his dissertation. However, his work has not yet been published. In the twentieth century it seems Hoby's achievement has suffered from the faint praise of F. O. Matthiessen, and teachers have often thus looked to other translations. More recently than Matthiessen, Julius Molinaro asserts that even with its shortcomings Hoby's is the only English translation that "has acquired a measure of universal acclaim" and that it "does possess an authentic English flavor" (262). In his *Italian Influence in English Poetry*, A. Lytton Sells writes that Hoby's background and travel make him "the perfect translator and interpreter of Castiglione*" (86), an accolade attributable to no later translator.

BIBLIOGRAPHY

Works by Thomas Hoby

Bucer, M. Martin. *The Gratulation of . . . M. Martin Bucer . . . unto the Churche of England for the restitution of Christes religion, and hys Answere unto the two raylinge epistles of Steve, Bishop of Winchester*. Trans. Thomas Hoby. London, 1549.

Castiglione, Baldassare. *The Book of the Courtier of Count Baldassare Castiglione*. Trans. Thomas Hoby. Ed. Walter Raleigh. 1900. New York: AMS, 1967. (All quotes are from this edition.)

Hoby, Thomas. *A Book of the Travaile and Lief of Me Thomas Hoby*. London: Royal Historical Society, 1902.

The Tragedie of Free Will. Trans. Thomas Hoby, 1550. (An Italian morality play.)

Studies of Thomas Hoby

Bartlett, Kenneth. "*The Courtyer of Count Baldessar Castilio*: Italian Manners and the English Court in the Sixteenth Century." *Quaderni d'Itlaianistica* 6.2 (1985): 249–58.

Burke, Peter. *The Fortunes of "The Courtier."* Cambridge: Polity Press, 1996.

Cox, Virginia. "Introduction." In *The Book of the Courtier*, trans. Thomas Hoby. London: Everyman, 1994, xvii–xxxi.

''Hoby, Sir Thomas.'' In *Dictionary of National Biography*, ed. Leslie Stephen and Sidney Lee. 66 vols. London: Oxford University Press, 1921; vol. 9, 949–50.

Masello, S. J. ''Book of the Travaile and Lief of Me Thomas Hoby.'' Diss., Loyola University of Chicago, 1979.

———. ''Thomas Hoby: A Protestant Traveler to Circe's Court.'' *Cahiers Elisabethains* 27 (1985): 67–81.

Matthiessen, F. O. *Translation: An Elizabethan Art*. Cambridge: Harvard University Press, 1931.

Molinaro, Julius A. ''Castiglione and His English Translators.'' *Italica* 36 (1959): 262–78.

Nocera-Avila, Carmela. *Tradurre il 'Cortegiano': The Courtyer di Sir Thomas Hoby*. Bari: Adriatica Editrice, 1992.

Powell, Edgar. ''Preface.'' *Book of the Travaile and Lief of Me Thomas Hoby*. London: Royal Historical Society, 1902, v–xvi.

Raleigh, Walter Alexander. ''Introduction.'' In *The Book of the Courtier of Count Baldassare Castiglione*, trans. Thomas Hoby. 1900. New York: AMS, 1967, vii–lxxxviii; orig. London: D. Nutt, 1900.

Scott, Mary A. ''*The Book of the Courtyer*: A Possible Source of Benedick and Beatrice.'' *PMLA* 16 (1901): 475–502.

Sells, A. Lytton. *The Italian Influence in English Poetry*. Bloomington: Indiana University Press, 1955.

SARAH HILSMAN

RAPHAEL HOLINSHED
(c. 1525–1580)

BIOGRAPHY

Little is known of Holinshed's life. Born in Cheshire, probably the son of Ralph Holinshed, possibly a landowner in the region, he was educated at Oxford and perhaps, too, at Cambridge. At some time, probably afterward, he was ordained as a minister. By the late 1550s he was working as an editorial assistant and translator for Reginald (or Reynier) Wolfe, a former Rhinelander and printer. Wolfe, using the notes gathered by the ''King's antiquary,'' John Leland (1506–52), and other materials, was engaged in the production of a universal ''cosmographie,'' an encyclopedia representing the various nations. On Wolfe's death in 1573, the project was curtailed, limited to a ''cosmographie'' of the British Isles. Support for the project was assumed by several backers, Holinshed acting as editor and major contributor to the *Chronicles*, as they came to be called. In 1578, after the purchase of an expensive license, the first edition appeared. License or no license, the authorities were annoyed. At issue were the references to events in Ireland during the reign of Henry VIII. Printing was halted, the offending pages were excised, and publication resumed—with considerable commercial success (Lee, ''Holinshed,'' 1024–26).

Holinshed died in 1580. Of his views we know little. He has been called ''patriotic'' (Lee, ''Holinshed,'' 1024–26), and this is borne out by his work. Although a Protestant, he is said to have been ''an old fashioned conservative'' who ''disliked the Puritans'' (Thompson, vol. I, 607). But it has been ably argued by Annabel Patterson that he was a ''proto-liberal'' (ix–xiii, 7), concerned with justice, freedom of conscience, and, indeed, justice for the underprivileged (xv). To this point we return as we discuss his great work.

After Holinshed's death the publishers decided to prepare a new edition and enlist John Hooker (1526–1601) and the antiquarian John Stow (1525–1605) as contributors. Hooker, who signed his name ''John Hooker, alias Vowell, Gentleman,'' uncle of the ''judicious'' Richard Hooker, author of *The Laws of Ecclesiastical Polity*, was a son of a mayor of Exeter and educated in Cornwall and at Oxford. A lawyer, a ''Marian exile'' (a Protestant who lived abroad during the reign of Queen Mary), he was active in city government and in both the English and Irish Parliaments (Cooper, ''Hooker,'' 1185). Along with Abraham Fleming (1552?–1607) and Francis Thynne (1545?–1608) he completed volume 4 of the English history, translated Giraldus Cambrensis' portion of the Irish history, and wrote the last portion of that volume. Stow, another Londoner, was of humble origin, a tailor. His religious views brought him under suspicion, his house was searched, and he was interrogated but then released (Lee, ''Stow,'' 3–6). His contribution was that of writer and assistant editor to volume 4 on England.

Fleming, Londoner, Protestant clergyman, translator, poet, and antiquarian, acted as general editor after Holinshed's death (Castanien, 131; Patterson, 5, 9) and contributed miscellaneous pieces to the English history. Fleming also seems to be the author of the Latin and Greek epigrams and poems used to decorate the text (Patterson, 50). Another major contributor to both the English and Scottish histories was Francis Thynne, son of William Thynne, one of the editors of Chaucer. Trained in the law but preferring literature and history, he had a penchant for compilation (Cooper, ''Hooker,'' 843–45). Again and again the narrative is interrupted by a seemingly irrelevant disquisition in the form of a list or catalog of ''Constables,'' ''Protectors,'' ''Dukes,'' ''Treasurers,'' or ''Archbishops,'' usually without explanation of their significance.

The second edition appeared in 1586–87 in three volumes. This edition caused ire, not only on the part of their lordships of the Privy Council but on the part of Her Majesty herself. At issue (among other things) was the discussion of high politics, especially as it touched on negotiations with the Scots. (The judicial murder of the Scottish queen made matters more tense, apparently.) Large excisions this time were necessary (Castanien, 127–90). The excisions were restored when the *Chronicles* were reorganized and reissued about two centuries later, in 1807–8, now in six quarto volumes. This edition, reprinted in 1965, is discussed here.

MAJOR WORKS AND THEMES

Like the King James Bible, Holinshed's *Chronicles* (his only work), six volumes, over 5,000 pages, are the work of a committee, or "syndicate" (Kingsford, 271), some of whom have been introduced. As mentioned, Holinshed worked as editor for the entire set (for the first edition) and wrote the second portion of volumes 1–3 and portions of volumes 4 and 5 and a short portion of volume 6. Volume 2 tells the story of England from 1066 to 1399, the overthrow of Richard II; volume 3 tells the story of England from Henry IV (1399) to the death of Mary Tudor (1553); volume 4 relates events in England from 1533 to 1587 almost to the time of the execution of Mary Stuart. Volume 5 is devoted to Scotland; 6 to Ireland.

Volume 1 is divided into two sections. The first is a description of contemporary England by William Harrison (1534–93). Harrison, Londoner and clergyman, was a cousin of Thomas Wyatt, whose rebellion and execution in 1553 are described in volume 4 (Patterson, 26–27; Lee, ix, 46). Using Leland's notes, Harrison gives us a well-written description of the topography, rivers, soils, cities, roads, fairs, markets, society, government, food, and so on of Elizabethan England. Highly quotable, with all its prejudices and stereotypes, it is a proverbial mine of information and indispensable to the student of the period.

But Harrison feels it necessary to discuss origins. The result is a curious (for the modern reader) blend of ancient history, mythology, legend, and Scripture. Thus, Noah, Hercules, Neptune, Caesar, Christ, and Arthur all put in appearances in precise chronological order (as Harrison determined it). Such attempts at synchronization were traditional in medieval historiography, indeed almost de rigueur. Thus, Brute (a Trojan prince, of course) arrived in England in 1116 B.C., 2850 years "after the creation of the world" (vol. 1, 7). Whatever doubts Harrison may have about some of his sources, they did not extend to Scripture, "[t]he most sure and certain of all knowledge" (vol. 1, 15).

The second section of volume 1 is a traditional chronicle, relating the story of England "from the time it was first inhabited" (vol. 1, 423) until 1066. Written by Holinshed and then edited by Fleming, it repeats some of the legends related by Harrison and, again, attempts to amalgamate and synchronize Scripture, myths, legends, and material from medieval sources, although Holinshed does express a skeptical remark about one of the stories he mentions (vol. 1, 436).

Volumes 2–4 are the work of Holinshed, Fleming, Thynne, Stowe, and Richard Grafton. Volume 2 by Holinshed begins with the Norman Conquest, and the treatment, reflecting Elizabethan nationalism, is hostile. William and the Normans, he writes, are oppressors, hating the English people (vol. 2, 12). But Holinshed gives William his due: he acknowledges his courage, "wit" (intelligence), and ruthless effectiveness in creating law and order (rapists are castrated). For Holinshed the last Norman king was Henry II (1154–89). For

Holinshed Richard I, his son and successor, is an ''English'' king—because he was born in England (2, 122).

Reflecting English antipapal sentiments, Holinshed takes the side of Henry II in his struggle with Beckett. The archbishop is guilty of ''insolencie'' and ''presumption'' (vol. 2, 136), albeit a man of ''courage,'' and his murder is condemned. King John (1119–1216) receives surprisingly sympathetic treatment; the baronial opposition is guilty of ''shameful apostasie'' (vol. 2, 337). The beloved ''Magna Charta'' is not reproduced nor even summarized; it is mentioned some five times in volume 2. But Holinshed is no royal absolutist, as Patterson has contended. For example, in his account of the reign of Edward I (1272–1307), he quotes with approval the defiance of one landowner to the statute of *quo warranto* (which required proof of title to landed property) who reportedly pointed to his sword as his ''warrant'' (vol. 2, 483).

Kings are seen with their deficiencies. For example, Edward II (1307–27) is described as ''corrupt'' (vol. 2, 547), but not deserving his terrible fate. He is also highly critical of Richard II (1377–99) but partly exculpates him because of the ''frailtie of wanton youth'' (vol. 2, 868). Holinshed condemns Henry IV (1399–1413) for Richard's murder, noting that ''his [Henry's] lineall race [the Lancasters] were scourged afterwards'' but also remarks that the scourging was ''due punishment for rebellious subjects'' (vol. 2, 869).

There are careful description of the battles in France, and the claim of Edward III (1327–77) to the French throne is defended, but without the vehemence of Edward Hall. Following Hall, Henry V (1413–22) emerges as a paragon of knightly virtue, ''without a spot,'' ''a prince whom all men loved'' (vol. 3, 133). But Holinshed does describe the ill effects of the war on England, the high taxes, for example. But the war (any war) is not condemned, despite an occasional sigh for the benefits of peace. The great catastrophe of the fourteenth century, the Black Death, is mentioned, but not highlighted. Nor does the Lollard movement get much attention. The great popular uprising during the reign of Richard II is graphically described and, as Patterson has pointed out (190–92), with some sympathy for the rebels.

The attitude toward Joan of Arc is hostile: she was a ''devilish witch'' who broke the ''law of armes'' (by murdering a prisoner, says Holinshed), and, accusing her of homosexuality, he writes that she was guilty of ''shamefullie reiecting her sex in acts and apparell'' (vol. 3, 171). But he admits her courage (vol. 3, 163) and mentions, as Hall does not, her posthumous trial and exoneration.

The fifteenth century was a century of war in France (to about 1453) and then civil war, to 1485. This is all exhaustively recounted. In his story of the ''Wars of the Roses'' (he does not use the term) he offers verbatim a number of the letters exchanged between the opponents. Although it is mostly ''political'' history (kings, nobles, plots, speeches, battles, treaties), there is much information on prices, weather, plagues, and, occasionally, lists of writers. Chaucer, for example, is given credit for "reducing our English toong to a perfect conformitie" (vol. 2, 58), although *The Canterbury Tales* is not mentioned.

Events outside England receive relatively little attention. The capture of Grenada, in 1492, following Hall, is described. But no mention is made of the voyage of Columbus. As far as the Tudors are concerned, the *Chronicles* is on the whole, sympathetic. Richard III, following Thomas More, is demonized, and there are panegyrics to Henry VII and Henry VIII. But the avarice of Henry VII, "covetous in his old age" (vol. 3, 531), is acknowledged. Although the treatment of Henry VIII—and even his daughter Mary—is generally deferential, a gentle reproof (or a sense of embarrassment?) might be read into the comments on Henry's pamphlet of 1521 against Luther: "[O]f which booke published by the King, I will not (for reverence of his roialtie) though I durst, report what I have read: because we are to judge honourablie of our rulers, and so speake nothing but good of the princes of the people" (vol. 3, 675). There is also implicit criticism of Henry in the description of the execution of Ann Boleyn (vol. 3, 797). The death of John Fisher, too, is related in a tone of regret, but also with a dash of barbaric irony: "[D]octor John Fisher, Bishop of Rochester, was beheaded for denieng the [King's] supremacie [over the Church]. . . . This bishop was of manie sore lamented, for he was reported to be a man of great learning and of a verie good life. The pope elected him a cardinal, and sent his hat as far as Calis [Calais], but his head was off before his hat was on: so that they met not" (vol. 3, 793).

The treatment of Queen Mary (1553–58) is fair and balanced. "She was ioifully saluted by all the people" (vol. 4, 2) on her accession but arouses a rebellion by her marriage to Philip II. There then follows an apparent (and lengthy) digression containing a verbatim account of the trial and eventual acquittal of Sir Nicholas Throckmorton, who was accused of treason. Patterson has argued persuasively that Holinshed was seizing on the opportunity to make a statement—using Throckmorton's articulate and spirited defense—of the individual's right to justice. Holinshed goes on to condemn Mary's religious policies, though the appellation "Bloody Mary" is not used. Not only is she spared the vilification heaped on Richard III, but she is treated with respect and compassion. Her "stout courage," for example, is extolled (vol. 4, 20); her patriotism and her efforts to save Calais are recognized. Among her last words were, "[W]hen I am dead and opened, you shall find Calis lieng in my heart" (vol. 4, 37). Left desolate by Philip's treatment of her, she died after a short reign because "God did not permit [her] to reign long" (vol. 4, 138).

There is a remarkable passage buried in the discussion of Elizabeth's reign that places Holinshed far ahead of his time. After describing the great victory (of "Christendome") over the Turks at Lepanto in 1572, he proceeds to bemoan the wars between Christians and, wonder of wonders, calls for freedom of conscience (vol. 4, 264). Consistent with this sentiment, he describes the awful fate of a group of "anabaptists" who were "burned in Smithfield, [and] who died in great horror with roring and crieng" (vol. 4, 326).

The English story from 1576 to 1586 is told by Fleming and Hooker. It probably needs to be seen against a backdrop of serious threats to the regime: plots, uprisings, and the growing menace of Spain. Executions are approvingly described (sometimes in grisly detail), including that of Edmund Campion, one of the contributors to volume 6 (Ireland). The execution of Mary Stuart is not mentioned. Instead, the volume ends with some strange miscellany, including a description of the construction of the harbor works at Dover along with one of a bear-baiting.

Volume 5, Scotland, is ''gathered'' (Holinshed's phrase) and written by Holinshed, who carries the story from ancient beginnings to 1571. From then to 1586 it is told by Francis Thynne ''and others.'' Holinshed's history is preceded by a brief twenty-eight-page description of the country by ''the ignorant but inventive'' (Mitchison, 14) Hector Boethius (c. 1465–1536). Similar to the description of England, it relates an occasional monster fable and a lament (repeated occasionally in the history) of the decadence (although the word is not used) of Scotland. Boethius seems particularly concerned about gluttony.

Following Boethius and other Scottish chroniclers, Holinshed from time to time reminds the reader that he is relating the Scots' version of their history. Thus, at the outset he writes, ''Scotish men according to the maner of other nations, esteeming it a glorie to fetch their beginning of great anciencie, say their original descent came from Greeks and Aegyptians: for there was (as the historiographers have left in writing) a certaine noble man among the Greeks, named an Gathelus [actually a Gaelic name], the sonne of Cecrops, who builded the city of Athens.'' Gathelus married Scota (the origin of the name Scotland) and arrived in Scotland 4,617 years after the Creation (vol. 5, 33). Holinshed, following the chroniclers, then continues the story, listing a little over forty kings until he mentions ''Fergus,'' dating him A.D. 424. Then, using a paragraph symbol, he makes the comment, ''For I can neither persuade my selfe nor wish others to believe, that there was anie such continuance in successione of Kings, as their histories do make mention; and as we have here set downe in following the same histories, because we will not willinglie seem to offer iniurie to their nation'' (vol. 5, 122).

Holinshed continues to relate what he reads in the Scottish chronicles but is not always so tactful. Thus, after discussing the trouble in Scotland created by one of the innumerable rogue nobles, he writes, ''Such have been the unquiet nature of Scotishmen, even from the beginning never to live contented anie long time either with peace or warre . . . [and in peace] to raise some commotion among themselves'' (vol. 5, 213).

As the story approaches the tenth century, the marginal comments, probably by Thynne, occasionally offer a corrective to the text, but sometimes further on in the text, a sharp, even angry, rejoinder. The Scots writers, for example, are accused of ''malice'' toward Edward I (vol. 5, 323). Actually, this portion—devoted to Edward I, Robert Bruce, and William Wallace—is quite colorful and even moving.

The story of Mary Stuart—except for a flattering description of her person (vol. 5, 608)—is a bare recital of the facts. Knox and the Calvinists are mentioned; the religious tensions are apparent, but the dramatic confrontations between Mary and the doughty Reformer are not related. Mary's escape to England and confinement there are described, but the story is terminated just before her execution.

Volume 6, Ireland, comprises some 450 pages with the remainder of the volume devoted to a cumulative index for the whole set. Holinshed, in "despaire" (vol. 6, b) of dealing with the subject was assisted—through Reginald Wolfe—by Richard Stanyhurst (1547–1618), a prominent Anglo-Irishman (to use a modern term) and former student of Edmund Campion. After completing his contributions to the *Chronicles*, Stanyhurst left Ireland (in 1579), converted to Catholicism, and joined in emigré plotting against Elizabeth. But his contribution to *Chronicles*, whatever its merit, seems neutral on the religious issue. Following the format of the English and Scottish histories, the first section, written by Stanyhurst (using the notes of Edmund Campion), is a description of Ireland in the 1570s. Stanyhurst expresses "affection" (vol. 6, dedication) for Ireland, but not for the "meere Irish," also called the "wild Irish," or Gaelic population, a "savage people become degenerat" (vol. 6, 66–69) "by lawful conquest brought under subjection of England" (vol. 6, 5), a people "who need good English government" (vol. 6, 69).

The second section summarizes events—again, in the traditional manner—from Creation to 1167, the year of the Norman invasion. Also written by Stanyhurst, it is a mix of myth, legend, scriptural figures, and history. Thus, some of Noah's descendants arrived in Ireland, "about three hundred years after the general flood immediatlie upon the confusion of toongs" (vol. 6, 73). After some additional folklore *cum* history, Stanyhurst gets on firmer ground when he mentions "Turgesius" (Thorgest) and his Norsemen in the ninth century. But, to the disappointment of Holinshed for "feeling upon so blunt a conclusion," Stanyhurst ends his chapter, without, by the way, any mention of the Celtic culture that flourished from the sixth to the eighth centuries.

The next portion, dealing with the Norman Conquest (or attempted conquest) is devoted to the years 1167 to 1186 and is written by Giraldus Cambrensis (c. 1146–c. 1223), a member of one of the aristocratic families (the Fitzgeralds) who led the invasion, bishop, loyal servant of Henry II and John, and respected chronicler. He visited Ireland, considers it a "wicked nation" (vol. 6, 197), summarizes the campaign, mentions an occasional "marvel," and offers some refreshing—if not always convincing—analysis of events. The account is well translated and enhanced by the sometimes polemical remarks (against "papists" or "rebels") by Hooker.

Holinshed's contribution (using Campion's notes) covering the period from 1186 to 1509 is lamentable, both in content and execution: lists of appointments, deaths, murders, burials, fires, wars, invasion (the Bruce invasion of 1315), plagues, famines. But Holinshed was unaware of the fundamental trend: a Gaelic resurgence as more and more of the island is retaken from the English. There is only brief mention of such key landmarks as the Statutes of Kilkenny (1366) and Drogheda (1494).

The last portion, written with reluctance by Hooker (vol. 6, 322) is a readable but depressing story: more feuds and tragic rebellions; one by Shane O'Neill; the other by the Desmonds. Citing Romans XII on the need for obedience (vol. 6, 105 ff.), Hooker condemns both rebellions, the Irish, and the pope. He is appalled at the consequences of the rebellions, but not apparently by Sir Walter Ralegh when he massacres Spanish prisoners of war (vol. 6, 438). Here, as elsewhere in the work, protoliberalism is set aside. But Hooker goes beyond a summons to obedience and gives way to a hysterical outburst against Rome, that ''mightie Babylon, the mother of all wickedness and abhomination on earth.'' The pope is a ''sonne of Sathan, a man of sinne whose ravening guts be never satisfied but with the death of such as do serve the lord'' (vol. 6, 468).

CRITICAL RECEPTION

The *Chronicles* have received varied comment. They have been called a ''compilation,'' ''crude and naive'' (Castanien, 5; Patterson, 3). In the seventeenth century one critic referred to them as ''vast vulgar tomes'' and ''*ex faeces plebis*'' (Patterson, 3). One modern critic has said that they are significant only because ''Shakespeare read them'' (Patterson, 3).

The authors have been praised (faintly?) for their ''industry'' (Lee, ix, 1024–26). Yet C. L. Kingsford in 1913 pointed out that they created the first complete history of England of ''an authoritative character, composed in English and in a continuous narrative'' (271). James Westfall Thompson in his two-volume survey of Western historiography gives them three pages of appreciative discussion (vol. 1, 603–5). Ernst Breisach, writing in the early 1980s, notes the popularity of the *Chronicles* in their own time and their rapid eclipse afterward. But he is impressed with ''their rich and appealing mixture of materials'' and considers them ''a treasure house of information'' ''for a long time'' (174).

The most recent and most appreciative assessment is that of Annabel Patterson, who along with a resumé of the reception of the *Chronicles* (from which I have drawn), describes them as a ''giant interdisciplinary project'' (vii) of ''cultural history,'' with a ''proto-liberal'' agenda. There are, as she demonstrates, several examples of protoliberalism, but there are also, as I have shown, summonses to obedience, condemnations of rebellion, and expressions of great reverence for rulers not altogether consistent with liberalism. It is possible that the expressions of reverence for rulers are mostly ritualistic. As for the somewhat contradictory views expressed in the text, it is fairly certain that Holinshed and his collaborators were less concerned with maintaining a consistent political outlook than they were with producing their great ''cultural history.''

There is much that is depressing in the *Chronicles*: battles, rebellions, murders, executions, atrocities, sickening cruelty. There is, from time to time, comic relief in the form of a tall tale, ''a marvel,'' all told in pungent archaic English with its quaint orthography. But this is probably insufficient for most general readers. These six volumes, today, are for the scholar.

BIBLIOGRAPHY

Works by Raphael Holinshed

Holinshed, Raphael. *The Chronicles of England, Ireland and Scotland.* 6 vols. Ed. Henry Ellis. London, 1807–8.

Studies of Raphael Holinshed

Breisach, Ernst. *Historiography: Ancient, Medieval and Modern.* Chicago: University of Chicago Press, 1983.

Castanien, Anne T. "Censorship and Historiography in Elizabethan England: The Expurgation of Holinshed's Chronicles." Diss., University of California, Davis, 1970.

———. "Thynne, Francis." In *Dictionary of National Biography*, vol. 19, ed. Leslie Stephen and Sidney Lee. London: Oxford University Press, 1917, 843–45.

Cooper, Thompson. "Hooker, John." In *Dictionary of National Biography*, vol. 9, ed. Leslie Stephen and Sidney Lee. London: Oxford University Press, 1917, 1181–85.

Dean, L. *Tudor Theories of Historical Writing.* Ann Arbor, MI: University of Michigan Press, 1947.

Fussner, F. S. *The Historical Revolution, English Historical Thought and Writing, 1580–1640.* London: Routledge and Paul, 1962.

———. *Tudor History and the Historian.* New York: Basic Book, 1970.

Kingsford, C. L. *English Historical Literature in the Fifteenth Century.* Oxford: Clarendon Press, 1913.

Lee, Sidney. "Holinshed, Raphael." In *Dictionary of National Biography*, vol. 9, ed. Leslie Stephen and Sidney Lee. London: Oxford University Press, 1917, 1024–26.

———. "Stanyhurst, Richard." In *Dictionary of National Biography*, vol. 18, ed. Leslie Stephen and Sidney Lee. London: Oxford University Press, 1917, 975–79.

———. "Stow, John." In *Dictionary of National Biography*, vol. 19, ed. Leslie Stephen and Sidney Lee. London: Oxford University Press, 1917, 3–6.

Levy, F. *Tudor Historical Thought.* San Marino, CA, 1967.

Patterson, Annabel. *Reading Holinshed's Chronicles.* Chicago: University of Chicago Press, 1994.

Thompson, James Westfall. *A History of Historical Writing.* 2 vols. New York: Macmillan, 1942.

Other

Barnes, Harry Elmer. *A History of Historical Writing.* 2d rev. ed. New York: Dover, 1962.

Mitchison, Rosalind. *A History of Scotland.* London: Methuen, 1970.

LOUIS A. GEBHARD

RICHARD HOOKER
(1554–1600)

BIOGRAPHY

Richard Hooker, Christian humanist and apologist for the Church of England, was born in or near Exeter in early April 1554. Although his great-grandfather and grandfather had served as mayors of Exeter, his family was of modest means. Of his early childhood little is known. Most of the biographical information available is from Isaak Walton's pious and biased biography first published in 1665, which must be read with caution. Subsequent scholarship has either corroborated or corrected information in Walton's book. Based on contemporary documents, Hooker's father, Roger, was an absentee parent. From October 1562 to April 1565, Roger Hooker was in Spain serving as a steward to the ambassador Sir Thomas Chaloner. Several years later, he served as Sir Peter Carew's steward at Leighlin, Ireland, and died in Ireland in 1591. Hooker's uncle John Hooker became a kind of surrogate parent and benefactor. After completing grammar school in Exeter, where Hooker enjoyed the reputation of being an excellent student, he entered Corpus Christi College, Oxford, probably in the fall of 1569. He received the B.A. degree in January 1574 and the M.A. on 29 March 1577. Corpus Christi College's curriculum stressed the study of Greek, rhetoric, and early church fathers, subjects that Hooker mastered, as evidenced in his sermons and in the *Laws of Ecclesiastical Polity*. One of Hooker's probable tutors was John Rainolds. Rainolds, a fellow of the college and reader in Greek, was an ardent supporter of Calvinism and the Puritan cause. Probably, it was under his influence that Hooker became familiar with the works of Calvin* and other Continental Reformers. While at Corpus Christi, Hooker became tutor to Edwin Sandys, son of Edwin Sandys, bishop of London (later archbishop of York), and George Cranmer, a great-nephew of Archbishop Thomas Cranmer.* Both of these young men became lifelong friends and advocates of Hooker. In July 1579, his reputation for learning, especially his command of biblical languages, resulted in his appointment as deputy professor of Hebrew, due to the illness of Regius Professor Thomas Kingsmill. On 14 August of that same year, he was ordained a deacon by John Aylmer, bishop of London. There appears to be no documentary evidence of his ordination to priesthood, but references to his celebration of the Communion service in the Temple Church would confirm Walton's statement that he was a priest. In spite of his scholarly reputation and position as a fellow of the college, Hooker, John Rainolds, and three others were expelled from Corpus Christi in October 1580 but were reinstated early in the following month. In the fall of 1584, he was appointed vicar of St. Mary's Drayton-Beauchamp. By early December 1584, Hooker was living in London at the home of John Churchman, a wealthy merchant, where he met his future wife, Joan, Churchman's daughter.

The year 1585 brought an event that played a major role in the future direction of Hooker's life. The tranquil life of a scholar came to end on 17 March with Hooker's formal appointment by the queen as master of the Temple Church. In the political and religious climate of the times, the choice of a master who supported the established church was imperative, since the congregation was made up of the students of the law schools called the Inner and Middle Temples. In 1581, Walter Travers, a fervent Puritan who had been ordained abroad by Protestant ministers rather than by a bishop of the established church, had been appointed assistant to Richard Alvey, master of Temple Church. Upon Alvey's death, William Cecil advocated Traver's candidacy for the master's post. Archbishop Whitgift, however, opposed Traver's appointment and suggested Dr. Bond, one of the queen's chaplains, whom she rejected. Edwin Sandys, now the archbishop of York, suggested Hooker. Travers remained as assistant and preached the afternoon sermon. Trouble between the two men began almost immediately. Before delivering his first sermon, Hooker was asked by Travers to submit to congregational ratification. Hooker refused. Shortly thereafter, Hooker preached a series of sermons on salvation and justification. Travers quickly attacked the sermons as heretical. Initially, the theological controversy between the two men was conducted privately. However, during an afternoon sermon, Travers openly attacked Hooker's ideas, for which he was quickly silenced by Archbishop Whitgift. In response, Travers wrote a pamphlet entitled *A Supplication Made to the Privy Council*, in which he outlined Hooker's errors. Hooker replied by writing to Whitgift *The Answer of Mr. Hooker to a Supplication Preferred by Mr. Walter Travers*. This dispute was the probable catalyst for the writing of the *Laws*. Although he did not enjoy great popularity as a preacher, Hooker remained master of Temple Church until 1591. During this ministry, he married Joan Churchman on 13 February 1588 in the parish church of St. Augustine. He had six children, four daughters and two sons, both of whom died in infancy.

On 21 June 1591 he was made subdean of Salisbury and rector of Boscombe. It is doubtful, however, that he spent any time at Boscombe, but rather continued to live with his in-laws while he worked on the *Laws*. On 7 January 1595 he was presented the living of Bishopbourne by the queen. Unlike his appointment to Boscombe, Hooker resided in the rectory and dutifully carried out his pastoral duties while preparing the publication of Book V of the *Laws*.

Hooker died on 2 November 1600, and was buried in the chancel of the church at Bishopbourne. As remembered by his contemporaries, he was a humble, modest, and learned man. His spirit of charity and pleasant disposition attracted loyal friends and the patronage of important ecclesiastical and political figures of his day.

MAJOR WORKS AND THEMES

Hooker's principal themes are derived from three concepts: church polity, church doctrine, and church ceremony. Present to some degree in his sermons and other minor works, the following themes are more fully developed in his principal work, *Of the Laws of Ecclesiastical Polity*: the role of law human and divine in society and the church, God's work of salvation, justification by faith, the authority of Scripture, and the role of tradition in the formulation of church ritual and polity.

Of the Laws of Ecclesiastical Polity is a defense of the Elizabethan settlement of the English church against the Puritan Reformers, with particular reference throughout the text to Thomas Cartwright. The first four books were published in 1593 and contain the general principles used to refute Puritan objections to the ceremonies and polity of the Church of England. Book V, a lengthy defense of the *Book of Common Prayer* was published in 1597. Books VI–VIII were published posthumously; Books VI and VIII in 1648; Book VII in 1662.

In the opening paragraphs of the preface, Hooker addresses the Puritans, who want to bring the Church of England into conformity with the Reformed faith modeled on John Calvin's view of church, Scripture, and worship. The opening remarks are followed by a brief overview of Calvin, the Puritans' hero, in which Hooker begins to address one of the major themes of the *Laws*—the authority of Scripture. The Puritans espoused the principle of *sola scriptura*, which stated that any aspect of religion or worship that was not expressly commanded in Scripture was unlawful and to be rejected. This view precluded the argument of "things indifferent," which permitted those aspects of religion, particularly liturgy and church governance, even though they were not expressly found in Scripture, as long as they were not contrary to the Word of God. Hooker then outlines the issues that he discusses in the eight books. He defends the episcopal form of church polity against the Puritans' rule by elders. Scripture is the basis of authority for all thing pertaining to salvation, but the use of reason also plays an important role in religion. Based on the dual appeal to revelation and reason, Hooker seeks to persuade the Puritans to accept the established church. Their continued refusal to obey the realm's ecclesiastical laws will lead to anarchy and chaos. He begins to formulate the dominant theme of the *Laws*: Law, whose ultimate source is God, is the foundation of the civil and ecclesiastical structure of society and is to be obeyed. The preface concludes with a plea for peace and harmony in the church and reconciliation.

In Book I, Hooker elaborates his notion of law, its nature and various divisions. After giving a working definition, he discusses the twofold nature of eternal law. It is, first, God's own being, a law unto himself and beyond human understanding, and second, it is the law that governs all creation in heaven and on earth, which further subdivides into natural law, celestial law, the law of reason, law of revelation (Scripture), and human law. Crucial to the arguments of Book I is that some laws are immutable, while others, even some that are to be found in the Scriptures, are not. This axiom implicitly rejects the Puritans' argument of *sola scriptura* and is applied throughout the *Laws*. In Hooker's view, the church has the right and authority to determine its rules concerning worship and government. Those rules, once established, are to be obeyed. Here and throughout the *Laws*, Hooker cites Scripture, the early church fathers, classical writers, Thomas Aquinas, and Roman law, among other sources.

Book II addresses the issue of *sola scriptura* used by the Puritans to argue against the ceremonies and polity of the established church. Hooker rejects the notion that all aspects of human life and behavior must be based on expressly biblical commands. He returns to his theme that God has established a variety of laws to regulate human affairs, not just the law of Scripture. The law of reason also helps to guide human endeavor. Further, what is not clearly forbidden in Scripture is permitted. Hooker argues a balance between the Roman Catholic position that Scripture is not sufficient but needs tradition added to it, and the Puritan view, which states that not only does Scripture contain everything necessary for salvation, but to follow any other law is contrary to salvation and a sin.

Book III continues the discussion of the authority of Scripture as it pertains to church polity. First, he defines the nature of the church. The church is both invisible (the mystical body of Christ) and visible (the institutional church), distinguished by that unity described in Ephesians 4:5—"one Lord, one faith, one baptism." All professing Christians belong to the visible church, even if some members are in sin or error. Even the Church of Rome, considered by the Puritans to be the Antichrist, although in need of reform, is still part of the church of Christ. Following his excursus on the nature of the church, Hooker turns his attention to the Puritan contention that the English church's episcopal form of government has no biblical basis. Church government is a necessary part of the visible church, but no one form of church polity is required of the church universal. Hooker challenges the Puritans to show that a single form of polity is commanded in Scripture and to demonstrate a biblical basis for their rule by elders. He returns to the distinction between things necessary for salvation and "things indifferent." For the former, Scripture is the sole authority; for the latter, what Scripture does not forbid is permitted, thereby rejecting the Puritans' insistence that polity and ceremonies must be expressly justified by Scripture.

In Book IV Hooker responds to the Puritan claim that the rites and ecclesiastical orders of the English church are still too similar to those of Rome and should be rejected. Throughout this book Hooker responds to the objections posed by Thomas Cartwright. Hooker argues against the Puritans' static view of the church derived from their insistence on *sola scriptura*, particularly regarding ceremonies and polity, in favor of a dynamic view of church that permits change. He supports his argument by citing scriptural examples of change such as the ceremonies of the Jews before and after their bondage in Egypt as well as the opinion of St. Augustine. Within the context of a discussion of sacramentology, Hooker emphasizes the importance of ceremonies in aiding the faithful to benefit more deeply from their reception of the Sacraments. Hooker reminds the Puritans that they are not always strictly following New Testament tradition in their rites. There is no need in Hooker's view to abandon ceremonies hallowed by tradition and not contrary to the Word of God simply because they resemble those of Rome. Even the church in Geneva follows some of the rites of Rome accepted by the Church of England, such as those pertaining to godparents, supporting his statement by citing Calvin. He concludes by reminding his opponents that such things as ceremonies belong to positive law, and positive law allows for change, if the church deems it necessary. Having established his basic principles, Hooker applies them to the specific areas of Puritan dissent:

Book of Common Prayer, the episcopacy, and the sovereign as head of the church.

Book V is a detailed defense of the *Prayer Book*. With some exceptions, Hooker's defense follows the order of the *Prayer Book*. In its defense, he brings to bear the principles that he had previously established—positive law permitting change, the church's authority, and the role of tradition. Beginning with the basic concept that religion as the source of virtuous living is important for the well-being of the state, Hooker enunciates four propositions used in defense of the official worship of the church as mandated by the *Prayer Book*. He adds a fifth rule: the individual is to conform to the common liturgy in order to have peace and harmony in the church. Hooker addresses the four areas of particular concern to the Puritans: preaching, prayer, the Sacraments, and the ordained ministry.

Although Hooker recognizes the value of the sermon as a means to salvation, he defends the public reading of Scripture as yet another form of preaching. Drawing on the ancient tradition of liturgies in the church's history, Hooker argues for the practice of formal communal prayer such as collects, litanies, and so on as part of the worship service. In his discussion of the Sacraments as means for union with God, Hooker is not willing to enter into the theological fray concerning Christ's presence in the Eucharist, although he does reject transubstantiation and consubstantiation. The book ends with a discussion of the nature and purpose of the ordained ministry. For religion to continue, that is, for the gospel to be preached and the Sacraments to be administered, ordained ministers are needed. The rite of ordination, although not a Sacrament, has biblical foundation and permanently sets apart individuals for service to God and the church. There is a clear distinction between clergy and laity, which has its foundation in the teaching of St. Paul. Scripture and the ancient practice of the church permit ranks within the clergy. Presbyters (Hooker is willing to use this term instead of "priest"), deacons, and bishops are ranks founded on Scripture and tradition. Hooker continues to address other concerns raised by the Puritans such as clergy education, nonresident clergy, organization of parishes, and so on.

The final three books of the *Laws* deal with the issues of authority and jurisdiction. Book VI's intended purpose is a refutation of the Puritans' polity of lay elders. However, the text that has survived devotes only a small portion to the issue of lay elders. Hooker's basic argument against lay elders is founded on the spiritual role and jurisdiction of the ministry in the area of repentance. Through his ordination, it is the duty and right of the minister to help the people understand sin and call them to repentance, a function that cannot be performed by the lay elder. Book VII focuses on the Puritans' rejection of the episcopacy. Using an anecdote about a Reformer who urged that nobles, lawyers, and bishops be removed in order to establish true religion, Hooker begins his defense of bishops in the Church of England. Using Scripture and the early church fathers, especially Cyprian, Ignatius, and Jerome, Hooker justifies the authority and jurisdiction of bishops by tracing the development of the episcopacy within the dynamic history of the church. Although the office of bishop is apostolic in origin, it is not expressly commanded in Scripture, but rather it is part of positive law and therefore could be abolished in favor of another form of polity if the church so decided. However, at the present time, the Church of England, as a political society with the right to make laws, has chosen to retain episcopal polity, and as faithful subjects of the realm, all are obliged to accept that decision. In the final chapter of the book, Hooker defends the civil authority of the bishops as well as the honors and privileges due them.

Book VIII refutes the Puritans' objection to the sovereign's title "head of the church." Using biblical examples of kings as religious leaders of the Jews, Hooker begins his defense of the monarch's authority and jurisdiction in ecclesiastical affairs. To counter the Puritans' position that only Christ is the head of the church, Hooker asserts that the monarch is the head of the institutional church and is limited in that role by divine and human law. The king's role does not include the administration of the Sacraments nor the right to ordain. He can select bishops and assign them to a diocese, but he cannot consecrate them. Hooker reminds his opponents that although there is no biblical command regarding the sovereign as head of the church, that role has been established by law and must be obeyed.

CRITICAL RECEPTION

Criticism of Hooker's work, especially *Of the Laws of Ecclesiastical Polity*, emanates from a wide area of academic interests. Political scientists have examined his ideas on government as well as his theory of law. Earlier critics, as Cargill Thompson points out, considered Hooker one of the greatest political thinkers of the sixteenth century (3). However, recent scholarship has modified that superlative by placing Hooker within his own historical context and challenging the conventional view of Hooker as "the forerunner of Locke and one of the originators of the doctrine of the social contract" (Thompson, 6). Trying to put Hooker in his proper place in the history of political thought is made more difficult because Hooker's evolutionary process preceding the writing of the *Laws* is not known. This lacuna, Hill asserts, "accounts for the ambiguity of his position even today and for the uncertainty with which recent scholarship has viewed the significance of this work" ("The Evolution," 117).

Although the *Laws* was intended as a defense of the Elizabethan church settlement, it is also a source for theological study. Marshall asserts that the *Laws* "is one of the most brilliant expositions of the character of Christianity to be found in the whole history of thought . . . an organic scheme of both theology and philosophy" ("Hooker's Doctrine of God," 81). Hooker's ecclesiology with its apparent contradiction vis-à-vis the episcopacy is also the object of scholarly inquiry. Sommerville gives an excellent overview of the scholarly debate regarding Hooker's position on the office of bishop and concludes that

"Hooker adopted and applied a subtle distinction between scriptural recommendation of a form of church government and its immutable prescription. It was this distinction which made Books II and VII of the *Laws of Ecclesiastical Polity* compatible" (187). Critics also examine the sources of Hooker's theology. Studies have discussed his indebtedness to medieval theologians, particularly St. Thomas Aquinas, and to John Calvin. As for Hooker's earlier grounding in Calvinist thought, Grislis wryly observes that "Hooker's Calvinistic roots have been proclaimed with rather more enthusiasm than investigation" (161). Within the context of the received tradition of Hooker's respect for Calvin, Hooker's attempt to both praise and criticize the Puritans's icon in the *Laws* is achieved, according to Avis, by treating "Calvin's doctrine on its merits as a human construction and Calvin himself as a great but fallible human being" (27). Hooker's method of scriptural interpretation, particularly its countering his opponents' demands for *sola scriptura*, has received favorable critical attention from scholars. Grislis notes that "although he [Hooker] wrote no commentaries on the Scripture . . . he interpreted Scripture with notable skill" (183). Although Hooker's role in the development of Anglican theology has been discussed, Booty states that "there is, admittedly, very much that remains to be done in tracing Hooker's relationship to and influence upon Anglicanism as it developed and was transformed in the seventeenth century and beyond" (204).

Although Hooker's claim to fame in English literature rests upon his prose style, Brian Vickers observes that "there are surprisingly few studies of his writing" (41). More than a decade after Vickers' essay, Archer adds the judgment that "analyses of Hooker's style to date have been limited, though valuable, and much work remains to be done" (118). A recent search of the *MLA Bibliography*—1981 through 2 February 1995—for articles on Hooker's prose style confirms Vickers' and Archer's observation. All scholars have noted the principal characteristic of Hooker's prose, namely, long and hypotactic sentences. Hooker does use shorter sentences, even parataxis, when, according to Edelen, he wants "to enunciate the axioms of his philosophical system . . . to emphasize the logical force of his reasoning" (243). Modern readers may find his Ciceronian periods tiresome, if not boring, but in view of the apologetic purpose of the *Laws*, Edelen argues that "the period is a natural vehicle for the mind that insists that no conclusion can be validly reached prior to a discursive and open-minded examination of all the relevant premises, causes, evidence, arguments, distinctions or effects" (257). For Steuber, Hooker's use of the compound/complex sentence "reflects the universal and teleological design of the hierarchy of being and laws" (819). Breaking ranks with the critics who tend to view Hooker's prose within the context of the author's traditional image—due in no small part to Isaac Walton's biography—as a mild-mannered, ironic, scholarly clergyman, Vickers emphasizes Hooker's "emotional energy" (44) when dealing with his adversaries by pointing out stylistic devices such as "to summarize, or quote from their verbose writings and to follow with a sharp question or a challenging comment" (44). Another technique Vickers cites is

Hooker's ability to have the text read ''like a transcript of a trial, for Hooker also invents notional answers by the defendants which are either parodied internally or subjected to sarcasm'' (44). Hooker's use of imagery, metaphor, and rhetorical devices is also grist for the stylistic critic's mill. Of special interest to the student of Shakespeare is Cohen's thesis that ''Shakespeare's acquaintance with this treatise (*Laws*) is markedly apparent in *Richard II* and the ensuing Henry plays'' (181). Teachers of Shakespeare will find Young's technique for teaching *King Lear* an interesting pedagogical strategy: he places passages from the *Laws* ''alongside passages from *Lear*, with the aim of helping students to become aware of ideas, attitudes, and thematic patterns the works have in common. At the same time, I point to differences in the treatment the writers give to similar themes'' (98).

Hooker scholars in all disciplines now have, with the completion of *The Folger Library Edition of the Works of Richard Hooker*, not only an excellent critical text but also an important source of information concerning the publication history of the *Laws*, the provenance of manuscripts, the debates regarding the authenticity and content of Books VI–VIII, Hooker's sources, and the discovery of three incomplete sermons originally thought to be those of Archbishop Ussher.

BIBLIOGRAPHY

Works by Richard Hooker

The Folger Library Edition of the Works of Richard Hooker. Ed. W. Speed Hill. Cambridge: Belknap Press of Harvard University Press, 1977–93.

The Works of That Learned and Judicious Divine Mr. Richard Hooker: With an Account of His Life and Death by Isaac Walton. 7th ed. 3 vols. Ed. John Keble, revised by R. W. Church and F. Paget. New York: Butt Franklin, 1970.

Studies of Richard Hooker

Archer, Stanley. *Richard Hooker*. Boston: Twayne, 1983.

Avis, P.D.L. ''Richard Hooker and John Calvin.'' *Journal of Ecclesiastical History* 32 (1981): 19–28.

Booty, John E. ''Hooker and Anglicanism.'' In *Studies in Richard Hooker: Essays Preliminary to an Edition of His Works*, ed. W. Speed Hill. Cleveland: Case Western Reserve University Press, 1972, 207–39.

Cohen, Eileen Z. ''The Visible Solemnity: Ceremony and Order in Shakespeare and Hooker.'' *Texas Studies in Literature and Language* 12 (1970): 328–38.

Edelen, Georges. ''Hooker's Style.'' In *Studies in Richard Hooker: Essays Preliminary to an Edition of His Works*, ed. W. Speed Hill. Cleveland: Case Western Reserve University Press, 1972, 241–77.

Faulkner, Robert K. *Richard Hooker and the Politics of Christian England*. Berkeley: University of California Press, 1981.

Gibbs, Lee W. ''The Source of the Most Famous Quotation from Richard Hooker's *Laws of Ecclesiastical Polity*.'' *Sixteenth Century Journal* 21.1 (1990): 77–86.

Grislis, Egil. ''The Hermeneutical Problem in Richard Hooker.'' In *Studies in Richard Hooker: Essays Preliminary to an Edition of His Works*, ed. W. Speed Hill. Cleveland: Case Western Reserve University Press, 1972.

Hill, W. Speed. ''The Authority of Hooker's Style.'' *Studies in Philology* 67 (1970): 328–38.

———. ''The Evolution of Hooker's *Laws of Ecclesiastical Polity.*'' In *Studies in Richard Hooker: Essays Preliminary to an Edition of His Works*, ed. W. Speed Hill. Cleveland: Case Western Reserve University Press, 1972, 117–58.

McGrade, Arthur S. ''The Coherence of Hooker's Polity: The Books on Power.'' *Journal of the History of Ideas* 24 (1963): 162–82.

———. ''Repentance and Spiritual Power: Book VI of Richard Hooker's *Of the Laws of Ecclesiastical Polity.*'' *Journal of Ecclesiastical History* 29.2 (April 1978): 163–76.

Mahon, Vincent. ''The Christian Letter: Some Puritan Objections to Hooker's Work and Hooker's 'Undressed' Comments.'' *Review of English Studies* 24 (1963): 163–82.

Marshall, John S. *Hooker and the Anglican Tradition: An Historical and Theological Study of Hooker's Ecclesiastical Polity*. Sewanee: University Press at the University of the South, 1963.

———. ''Hooker's Doctrine of God.'' *Anglican Theological Review* 29 (1947): 81–89.

Munz, Peter. *The Place of Hooker in the History of Thought*. London: Routledge and Kegan Paul, 1952.

Pollard, Arthur. ''Richard Hooker.'' In *British Writers*, vol. 1, ed. under the auspices of the British Council. New York: Charles Scribner's Sons, 1979, 176–90.

Sisson, C. J. *The Judicious Marriage of Mr. Hooker and the Birth of the Laws of Ecclesiastical Polity*. Cambridge: Cambridge University Press, 1940.

Sommerville, M. R. ''Richard Hooker and His Contemporaries on Episcopacy: An Elizabethan Consensus.'' *Journal of Ecclesiastical History* 35.2 (April 1984): 177–87.

Standwood, P. G., and Laetitia Yeandle. ''Richard Hooker's Use of Thomas More.'' *Moreana* 18 (1974): 38–42.

Steuber, M. Stephanie. ''The Balanced Diction of Hooker's Polity.'' *PMLA* 71 (1956): 808–26.

Thompson, E.N.S. ''Richard Hooker among the Controversalists.'' *Philological Quarterly* 20 (1941): 454–64.

Thompson, W. D. Cargill. ''The Philosopher of the 'Politic Society': Richard Hooker as a Political Thinker.'' In *Studies in Richard Hooker: Essays Preliminary to an Edition of His Works*. Cleveland: Case Western Reserve University Press, 1972, 3–76.

Vickers, Brian. ''Hooker's Prose Style.'' In *Richard Hooker. Of the Laws of Ecclesiastical Polity*, ed. A. S. McGrade and Brian Vickers. New York: St. Martin's Press, 1975, 41–59.

Young, Bruce W. ''Shakespeare's Tragedy in Renaissance Context: *King Lear* and Hooker's *Of the Laws of Ecclesiastical Polity.*'' In *Approaches to Teaching Shakespeare's King Lear*, ed. Robert H. Ray. New York: Modern Language Association of America, 1986, 98–104.

TERRENCE J. McGOVERN

JOHN HOSKYNS
(1566–1638)

BIOGRAPHY

Born near the beginning of Elizabeth I's* reign, witnessing the reign of James I,* dying eleven years before the beheading of Charles I, John Hoskyns' life and career can be measured against the spirit of each reign. He was admitted to the Middle Temple in 1593 and thus began his law career; he joined Parliament in 1604 and was elevated to sergeant-at-law in 1624. Having received a thorough rhetorical education, Hoskyns was prepared for public service and exemplifies the function and purpose of a humanist education. Having opposed James I in the second Parliament, he was imprisoned in the Tower for a year. Although Hoskyns was not a radical Puritan, his opposition to the king and advocacy for an independent Parliament anticipate the civil wars that were to divide the country at midcentury.

MAJOR WORKS AND THEMES

Hoskyns' writings include family letters and Latin and English verses, but, most notably, a rhetorical treatise, *Directions for Speech and Style*, composed sometime between 1598 and 1603. As suggested by Hoskyns' dedication, the most immediate audience for the *Directions* was a young man in the temple. He writes, "To the forwardness of many virtuous hopes in a gent of the Temple by the Author." Hoskyns' description of his work, "[c]ontaining all the figures of rhetoric and the art of the best English," illustrates the age's fondness for figurative style; however, as Hoskyns indicates, an eloquent style is not to be considered mere ornamentation. Instead, style is an indication of character. "The shame of speaking unskillfully were small if the tongue were only disgraced by it. But as the image of the King in a seal of wax ill represented, is not so much a blemish to the wax or the signet, that seals it, as to the king whom it resembles." Further, style is not separate from substance: "Careless speech does not only discredit the personage of the speaker, but it discredits the opinion of his reason and judgment. It discredits the truth, force and uniformity of the matter and substance."

Hoskyns catalogs the figures of speech and illustrates their use with examples drawn from Sidney's* prose romance *Arcadia.* As such, Hoskyns emphasizes only one (style) of the five parts of rhetorical art invented by the Greeks and solidified by the Romans: invention, arrangement, style, memory, and delivery. Since Hoskyns' treatise concerns the composition of letters, treatment of memory and delivery would not be necessary. Hoskyns handles matters of invention quickly and alludes to arrangement. On invention, he says that the topic depends not only on the circumstances that would occasion a particular letter but also on a practical knowledge of human affairs. In this manner, Hoskyns suggests the Aristotelian idea of invention as finding the available means of persuasion in any situation; however, he does not elaborate on the logical, emotional, or ethical arguments that can be constructed out of any situation. "[F]or the invention that arises upon your business whereof there can be no rules of more certainty or precepts of better direction given you than conjecture can lay down of all the several occasions of all particular men's lives and vocations." Concerning the arrangement of parts, Hoskyns offers two guidelines that do suggest ethical, pathetic, and logical persuasion. "One is the understanding of the person to whom you write, the other is the coherence of the sentences for men's capacity and delight."

Before Hoskyns proceeds to name, describe, and offer examples of the various figures and tropes, he offers four desired qualities of style: brevity, perspicuity, plainness, and respect. Brevity concerns the length of the letter ("letters must not be treatises") but also pertains to a fitting of expression to substance. "[B]revity is attained but the matter in avoiding idle complements, . . . superfluous and wanton circuits of figures and digressions." Perspicuity is a desired clarity of thought. "[L]et them [thoughts] . . . come forth to light and judgment of your outward senses, as the censure of other men's ears." Hoskyns likens an obfuscating letter writer to a merchant who cannot readily bring forth the goods that are desired. Plainness, far from indicating an unadorned style, indicates the desired effect of unpracticed art, "diligent negligence." Finally, respect requires that one recognize the full rhetorical context. "Last is respect to discern what fits yourself, him to whom you write and that which you handle."

CRITICAL RECEPTION

Although Hoskyns' works were not published in his lifetime, they had influence. Grund notes that with the discovery in 1930 by Louise Osborn that passages of Ben Jonson's* commonplace book, *Discoveries*, were indebted to Hoskyns' *Directions*, scholars began to explore Hoskyns' influence on the development of English prose. Hoskyns may now be seen as a rhetorician who helped direct the move to a simpler, less artificial style. Although Hoskyns' own style and his extensive treatment of the figures and tropes may appear to us ornamental and superfluous, we should position him against the excesses of a euphuistic prose style. As Grund notes, Hoskyns, in his description of the figures, incorporates warnings against excessive or inappropriate use. Rather than see style as an end in itself, Hoskyns always sets it within the larger rhetorical framework, which must account not only for audience but for substance as well.

Recent scholarship has shown an increasing interest in all aspects of rhetoric: its history, its theoretical foundations, and its applications. The publication of scholarship such as *Renaissance Eloquence: Studies in the Theory and Practice of Renaissance Rhetoric* indicates a renewed interest in this subject and its influence on poetic and prose composition. Certainly, Hoskyns' treatise has a place within this tradition. Moreover, the treatise gives insight into the social/linguistic world of men trained to use language persuasively in the public realm.

BIBLIOGRAPHY

Works by John Hoskyns

Osborn, Louise Brown. *The Life, Letters, and Writings of John Hoskyns*. Hamden: Archon Books, 1973. (Contains ''Directions for Speech and Style'' and is a reprint of a 1937 Yale University Press publication.)

Studies of John Hoskyns

Croll, Morris W. *Style, Rhetoric, and Rhythm*. Princeton: Princeton University Press, 1945, 153–74.

Grund, Gary R. ''John Hoskyns.'' *Elizabethan Rhetoric and the Development of English Prose*. New York: Garland, 1987. (First presented to Harvard University as doctoral dissertation in 1972.)

Whitlock, Baird W. *John Hoskyns, Sergeant-at-Law*. Washington, DC: University Press of America, 1982.

Williamson, George. *The Senecan Amble*. London: Faber and Faber, 1951, 175–217.

ANITA DELLARIA

J

KING JAMES VI AND I
(1566–1625)

BIOGRAPHY

Mary, Queen of Scots* gave birth to James on 19 June 1566; upon her escape to England slightly more than thirteen months later, he was crowned King James VI of Scotland. Thus, in July 1567, the infant James might have lost his mother, but he gained one kingdom and, through the Tudor antecedents of both parents, the possibility of another. Initially, as the pawn in Scotland's turbulent religious and political struggles, James was used, by several factions, to extirp his Catholic mother's claim during her remaining life, the first twenty, formative years of his own.

James could be regarded as the last humanist king of the Renaissance, and his education during those early years certainly substantiates that claim. In common with other Christian princes of Europe, James' education in the classics and theology was of primary political importance. To rule an increasingly anti-Catholic Scotland, this son of a Catholic mother especially needed sound Protestant theological upbringing. Accordingly, James' tutor was one of the most brilliant, Protestant men of letters in Scotland, George Buchanan. In his late teens, James made deliberate attempts to create an intellectual and literary court, publishing a collection of verse that included his *Ane Short Treatise conteining some Reulis and Cautelis to be obserrvit and eschewit in Scottis Poesie* (1584); the poet/king attracted the best contemporary Scotch poets to his court to form a ''Castalian Band'' to promote Scotch vernacular literature.

Gradually assuming control over rival factions in Scotland, James married Anne of Denmark in 1589 and, through both secret negotiations and publications such as *Trew Law of Free Monarchies* (1598) and *Basilikon Doron* (1599), launched a campaign to be named heir to the throne of England. After succeeding to the throne upon Elizabeth's death in 1603, James transferred his court to London and followed a policy of negotiated peace in foreign and religious affairs, which he promulgated in several treatises published between 1604 and 1620. Although his reign was marked by economic and constitutional difficulties, James avoided involving England in the Thirty Years' War and bequeathed a kingdom at peace to his less able son, Charles, in 1625.

Although there have been many biographical studies of James' reigns (particularly in England), for the past thirty-five years scholarly consensus has been that David Willson's biography, *King James VI and I*, is the most comprehensive account of the monarch. Nevertheless, Willson yokes his scholarly consideration of James to a thinly veiled dislike for his subject; Willson's unsympathetic attitude toward James is, one hopes, the last influential account of the king and his life to foster moralistic censure. As Maurice Lee, Jr., Marc Schwarz, and Jenny Wormald have shown, negative versions of James' character and policies have persisted for more than 350 years, the product of several generations of parliamentary historians who have condemned James' ideas of kingship and perpetuated the idea of James' political incompetence in dealing with Parliament. Thus, the view that James caused the civil war by creating an opposition between the Stuart monarchy and the Commons has persisted. That this construct is a misleading oversimplification is immediately apparent to anyone who has consulted earlier parliamentary records in which Elizabeth's head-on confrontations with the Commons are documented.

MAJOR WORKS AND THEMES

As a self-consciously intellectual monarch inculcated in violent theological debate, James' publications reflect his ongoing concerns with the nature, identity, and practice of kingship and the centrality of interpretation in the understanding of Christianity. James' presentation of himself as a practicing Christian and king persistently oscillates between images of absolute clarity, and the twin mysteries of God's elusive presence among sinners and a king's unavoidable distance from his subjects. Like other seventeenth-century European monarchs, James seems to have been acutely aware of the theatrical nature of both his particular political role and the increasingly necessary display of monarchical power as a means to perpetuate it. This preoccupation with theatrical display can be seen as part of a larger and older concept of the world as the "theater of God's judgement" and the playing out of his providential script.

CRITICAL RECEPTION

Literary analysis of James' writing can be primarily divided into three unequal parts; curiously, the smallest body of traditional literary criticism is the most important to the ongoing study of texts authored by James. A large and influential new historicist canon analyzes James' cultural influence, while a group of critics argues that contemporary authors used James as a dramatic source.

G.P.V. Akrigg gives a useful overview of the critical tradition regarding ''The Literary Achievement of King James I'' and has issued a call, so far largely unanswered, for a positive reevaluation of James' writing. The traditionally pejorative view is expressed by Willson, who accuses James of plagiarism during his English reign: ''[H]is writing had an ulterior motive to defend himself and promote his material interests'' (''James I and His Literary Assistants,'' 57). Jenny Wormald, a determined champion for a Scottish perspective on James, has extrapolated from her historical and biographical research the literary theory that James ''turned to writing to clarify his thought'' (''James VI and I, Basilikon,'' 37). On the contrary, R.D.S. Jack, another apologist for James, has repeatedly argued, in general, for the uniqueness of Scottish poetry with its Continental flavor and for James' poetic ambitions in particular. James' influence on the Castalian group of poets is assessed by several critics; J. Derrick McClure analyzes James' sonnets and longer poems and his patronage of the ''Castalian band'' of Scottish poets. A. Walter Bernhart concludes that James' emphasis on the musical basis of meter reflected his humanist concerns to promote '' 'harmonious' political conditions in his state'' (455). As does Jack, Murray F. Markland and Richard M. Clewett contend that English poets had much less impact on James' poetic theory that did the poets of the Castalian band.

Leeds Barroll helpfully questions the theoretical foundations of new historicism's interest in James and suggests that it is patriarchally skewed and issues a call for new discourses. Jonathan Goldberg has written extensively on the cultural influence that James' use of theatrical metaphors in his writing and the connections of his authorship with royal authority exerted over contemporary English authors. Stephen Orgel has illuminated political acts of theater at James' court in several valuable contributions. Similarly, Kevin Sharpe has collected and written divers analyses of the frequently intersecting tropes of politics and the culture of James' court.

The most sustained interrogation of James' character and interests as a source for Jacobean dramatists can be found in book-length treatments. Leah Marcus highlights James' overriding political concerns about the nature of kingship and his cherished plan to unify his two kingdoms in Shakespeare's* plays. Similarly, the third and fourth chapters of Leonard Tennenhouse, *Power on Display: The Politics of Shakespeare's Genres* (1986) assess James' strategies for the display of monarchical and patriarchal power and ally them with genre characteristics of Jacobean plays. David Bergeron has explored James' familial and political roles both in general and as a source for Shakespeare's late plays. Aspects of other Shakespeare plays (*Measure for Measure, Macbeth, Othello, The Tempest* and *Henry VIII*) have been illuminated by the comparison of James' known characteristics and interests, as have plays by Chapman,* Middleton, and Barnes.

James has been a prime subject of two influential schools of thought. Until very recently he and his career have been regarded in the most pejorative terms by parliamentary historians and biographers. In the past two decades, however, serious considerations have animated new historicist consideration of the politics of his court's culture and its influence on literary history. Now it seems, with the work of scholars such as Craigie, Lee, Akrigg and Wormald, a revitalized and validated appreciation of James is emerging. This is a most propitious opportunity for reevaluating his literary output.

BIBLIOGRAPHY

Works by King James VI and I

Basilicon Doron. Edinburgh: Blackwood, 1944. Scottish Text Society 16. 3d ser. 2 vols. Ed. James Craigie. 1944–50.

Basilicon Doron: 1599 Facsimile Reprint. Menston, England: Scolar Press, 1969.

Daemonologie: 1597 Facsimile Reprint. New York: Barnes and Noble, 1966.

Daemonologie, Trew Lawe of Free Monarchies, A Counterblaste to Tobacco, and *A Declaration of Sports*. In *Minor Prose Works of King James VI and I*. Scottish Text Society, 14. 4th ser. Ed. James Craigie. Prepared for Press by Alexander Law. Edinburgh: Scottish Text Society, 1982.

Essays of a Prentise and *Poetical Extracts at Vacant Hours*. Edinburgh: Blackwood, 1955. In *The Poems of James VI of Scotland*. Scottish Text Society 22. 3d ser. 2 vols. Ed. James Craigie.

Letters of King James VI and I. Ed. G.P.V. Akrigg. Berkeley: University of California Press, 1984.

The Political Works of James I. Ed. Charles Howard McIlwain. 1918. New York: Russell and Russell, 1965.

Unpublished and Uncollected Poems. Edinburgh: Blackwood, 1958. In *The Poems of James VI of Scotland*. Scottish Text Society 26. 3d ser. 2 vols. Ed. James Craigie. 1955–58.

The Works of James: 1616 Facsimile Reprint. Ed. Marvin Spevak. Anglistica and Americana 85. Hildesheim: Georg Olms, 1971.

Studies of King James VI and I

Biography

Ashton, Robert, comp. *James I by His Contemporaries: An Account of His Career and Character as Seen by Some of His Contemporaries*. London: Hutchinson, 1969.

Bergeron, David. *Royal Family, Royal Lovers: King James of England and Scotland*. Columbia: University of Missouri Press, 1991.

Durston, Christopher. *James I*. London: Routledge, 1993.

Fraser, Antonia P. *King James VI of Scotland, I of England*. New York: Knopf, 1975.

Houston, S. J. *James I*. London: Longman, 1973.

Lee, Maurice, Jr. *Great Britain's Solomon: James VI and I in His Three Kingdoms*. Urbana: University of Illinois Press, 1990.

———. ''James I and the Historians: Not a Bad King After All?'' *Albion* 16 (1984): 151–63.

McElwee, William. *The Wisest Fool in Christendom: The Reign of King James I and VI*. New York: Harcourt, Brace, 1958.

Mathew, David. *James I*. Tuscaloosa, AL: University of Alabama Press, 1968.

Schwarz, Marc. ''James I and the Historians: Towards a Reconsideration.'' *Journal of British Studies* 13.2 (1974): 114–34.

Willson, David Harris. *King James VI and I*. London: Jonathan Cope, 1956.

Wormald, Jenny. ''James VI and I: Two Kings or One?'' *History* 68 (1983): 187–209.

Critical Reception of the Works

Akrigg, G.P.V. ''The Literary Achievement of King James I.'' *University of Toronto Quarterly* 44 (1975): 115–29.

Bernhart, A. Walter. ''Castalian Poetics and the 'verie Twichestane Musique.' '' *Scottish Studies* 4 (1984): 451–58.

Clark, Stuart. ''King James's *Daemonologie*: Witchcraft and Kingship.'' In *The Damned Art: Essays in Literature of Witchcraft*, ed. Sidney Anglo. London: Routledge and Paul, 1977.

Clewett, Richard M. ''James VI of Scotland and His Literary Circle.'' *Aevum* 47.5–6 (1973): 441–54.

Doelman, James. ''The Accession of King James I and English Religious Poetry.'' *Studies in English Literature* 34 (1994): 19–40.

———. ''George Wither, The Stationers Company and the English Psalter.'' *Studies in Philology* 90 (1993): 74–82.

———. '' 'A King of Thine Own Heart': The English Reception of King James VI and I's *Basilikon Doron*.'' *The Seventeenth Century* 9 (1994): 1–9.

Dunlap, Rhodes. ''King James' Own Masque.'' *Philological Quarterly* 41 (1962): 249–56.

Enright, Michael J. ''King James and His Island: An Archaic Kingship Belief?'' *Scottish Historical Review* 55 (1976): 29–40.

Jack, R.D.S. *The Italian Influence in Scottish Literature*. Edinburgh: Edinburgh University Press, 1972.

———. ''James VI and Renaissance Poetic Theory.'' *English* 16 (1967): 208–11.

McClure, J. Derrick. '' 'O Phoenix Escossois': James VI as Poet.'' In *A Day Estivall: Essays on Music, Poetry and History of Scotland and England and Poems Previously Unpublished in Honour of Helena Minnie Shire*, ed. Alsoun Gardner-Medwin and Janet Hadley Williams. Aberdeen: Aberdeen University Press, 1990, 96–111.

Markland, Murray F. ''A Note on Spenser and the Scottish Sonneteers.'' *Studies in Scottish Literature* 1 (1963): 136–40.

Sharpe, Kevin. ''Private Conscience and Public Duty in the Writings of James VI and I.'' In *Public Duty and Private Conscience in Seventeenth Century England*, ed. John Morrill, Paul Slack, and Daniel Woolf. Oxford: Clarendon, 1993.

Sisson, C. J. ''King James the First of England as Poet and Political Writer.'' *Seventeenth Century Studies Presented to Sir Herbert Grierson*. Oxford: Oxford University Press, 1938.

Skrine, Peter. ''James VI and I and German Literature.'' *Daphnis* 18 (1989): 1–57.

Willson, D. H. "James I and His Literary Assistants." *Huntington Library Quarterly* 8 (1945): 35–57.

Wormald, Jenny. "James VI and I, Baslilcon Doron and the Trew Law of Free Monarchies: The Scottish Context and the English Translation." In *The Mental World of the Jacobean Court*, ed. Linda Levy Peck. Cambridge: Cambridge University Press, 1991.

Textual Studies

Craigie, James. "*The Basilicon Doron* of King James I." *Library* (5th series) 3 (1948): 22–32.

———. "*Philotus*: A Late Middle Scots Comedy." *Scottish Literary Journal* 6 (1979): 19–33.

Dunlap, Rhodes. "King James and Some Witches: The Date and Text of the *Daemonologie*." *Philogical Quarterly* 54 (1975): 40–45.

Elliot, Alistair, ed. *Poems by James I and Others from a Manuscript Miscellany in Newcastle University Library*. Newcastle upon Tyne: Eagle University Press Library, 1970.

Rypins, Stanley. "The Printing of *Basilikòn Dôron*, 1603." *Papers of the Bibliographical Society of America* 64 (1970): 393–417.

Yamada, Akihiro. "The Printing of King James I's *The True Law of Free Monarchies*." *Poetica* 23 (1986): 74–80.

Zimmerman, Susan. "Popular vs. Scholarly Editions of Renaissance Letters: Review Article." *Medieval and Renaissance Drama in England* 3 (1986): 231–43.

Cultural Studies

Akrigg, G.P.V. *Jacobean Pageant or The Court of King James I*. Cambridge: Harvard University Press, 1962.

Barroll, Leeds. "A New History of Shakespeare and His Time." *Shakespeare Quarterly* 39 (1988): 441–64.

Germano, William Paul. "The Literary Icon of James I." Diss., Indiana University, 1981.

Goldberg, Jonathan. "Fatherly Authority: The Politics of Stuart Family Images." In *Rewriting the Renaissance*, ed. Margaret W. Ferguson, Maureen Quilligan, and Nancy J. Vickers. Chicago: University of Chicago Press, 1986.

———. *James I and the Politics of Literature: Jonson, Shakespeare, Donne and Their Contemporaries*. Baltimore: Johns Hopkins University Press, 1983.

———. "James and the Theater of Conscience." *English Literary History* 46 (1979): 379–98.

———. " 'Up a Publick Stage': The Royal Gaze and Jacobean Theatre." *Research Opportunities in Renaissance Drama* 24 (1981): 17–21.

Limon, Jerzy. *The Masque of Stuart Culture*. Newark, Delaware: University of Delaware Press, 1990.

Orgel, Stephen. "The Royal Theatre and the Role of King." In *Patronage in the Renaissance*, ed. Guy Fitch Lytle and Stephen Orgel. Princeton: Princeton University Press, 1981.

———, ed. *The Illusion of Power: Political Theater in the English Renaissance*. Berkeley: University of California Press, 1975.

Parry, Graham. *The Golden Age Restor'd: The Culture of the Stuart Court, 1603–42*. New York: St. Martin's Press, 1981.

Sharpe, Kevin, and Steven Zwicker. *Politics of Discourse: The Literature and History of Seventeenth Century England*. Berkeley: University of California Press, 1987.

Dramatic Influence

Barroll, Leeds. *Politics, Plague and Shakespeare's Theater: The Stuart Years*. Ithaca, NY: Cornell University Press, 1991.

Bergeron, David. *Shakespeare's Romances and the Royal Family*. Lawrence: University Press of Kansas, 1985.

Jones, Emrys. ''*Othello*, 'Lepanto' and the Cyprus Wars.'' *Shakespeare Survey* 21 (1968): 47–52.

Kennedy, Edward D. ''James I and Chapman's Byron Plays.'' *Journal of English and Germanic Philology* 64 (1965): 677–90.

Kinney, Arthur. ''Scottish History, the Union of the Crowns and the Issue of Right Rule: The Case of Shakespeare's *Macbeth*.'' In *Renaissance Culture in Context: Theory and Practice*, ed. Jean R. Brink and William F. Gentup. Aldershot: Scolar, 1993.

Kurland, Stuart M. '' 'A Beggar's Book Outworths a Noble's Blood': The Politics of Faction in *Henry VIII*.'' *Comparative Drama* 26 (1992): 237–54.

———. ''*Hamlet* and the Scottish Succession.'' *Studies in English Literature* 34 (1994): 279–300.

———. ''*Henry VIII* and James I: Shakespeare and Jacobean Politics.'' *Shakespeare Studies* 19 (1987): 203–17.

Latham, Jacqueline E. *The Tempest* and King James's *Daemonologie*.'' *Shakespeare Survey* 28 (1975): 117–23.

Marcus, Leah. *Puzzling Shakespeare: Local Reading and Its Discontents*. Berkeley: University of California Press, 1989.

Sinfield, Alan. ''*Macbeth*: History, Ideology and Intellectuals.'' *Critical Quarterly* 28 (1986): 63–77.

Stevenson, David L. ''The Role of James in Shakespeare's *Measure for Measure*.'' *English Literary History* 26 (1959): 188–208.

Tebbetts, Terrell L. ''Talking Back to the King: *Measure for Measure* and *Basilicon Doron*.'' *College Literature* 12 (1985): 122–34.

Tennenhouse, Leonard. *Power on Display: The Politics of Shakespeare's Genres*. London: Methuen, 1986.

SUSANNE COLLIER

JOHN JEWEL
(1522–1571)

BIOGRAPHY

John Jewel, bishop of Salisbury and apologist of the Church of England, was born on 24 May 1522 at Buden in Devonshire. In 1535, he entered Merton College, Oxford, where he came under the direction of John Parkhurst, humanist and later one of the early Elizabethan bishops, who introduced the young Jewel to humanist studies and biblical criticism. Jewel later transferred to Corpus Christi College, from which he received the bachelor of arts in 1540. In 1542 he became a probationary fellow and upon obtaining the M.A. in 1545 was appointed a permanent fellow at Corpus Christi. He was made reader in humanity and rhetoric in 1548 and in the same year met the Continental Reformer and regius professor of divinity, Peter Martyr Vermigli, with whom he developed a close and lifelong friendship. During the years 1551–52, Jewel was ordained and licensed to preach and earned a bachelor of divinity.

Because of his friendship with Parkhurst and Peter Martyr, Jewel was identified with the Reform group at Oxford. Further, in order to receive financial aid for his studies, he had subscribed to articles of religion that opposed several basic Roman Catholic tenets and practices. Unfortunately for Jewel and his fellow Reformers, Edward VI died, and in July 1553, the staunchly Roman Catholic Mary was crowned queen. Peter Martyr and Parkhurst left for the Continent, while Jewel opted to remain at Oxford. However, within months of Mary's accession, he was deprived of his fellowship. Despite having subscribed to articles that supported Roman Catholic dogmas, Jewel fled to the Continent and appeared in Frankfurt in March 1555. He was initially viewed with suspicion by the English exiles because of his signature to the articles. After a public confession and plea for forgiveness he aligned himself with the party of Richard Cox and became involved in the argument with the followers of John Knox* over the liturgy. During the years 1555 to 1558 he lived and studied with Peter Martyr, first at Strasbourg and later in Zurich, where Martyr was professor of Hebrew.

With the accession of Elizabeth in November 1558, Jewel returned to England, arriving in London in March 1559. He immediately became involved in the Reform movement and the government's efforts to enforce the Elizabethan settlement. Although Elizabeth was not moving as quickly as Jewel and the other Reformers had hoped, during the year 1559–60 the Marian bishops, deprived of their sees, were being replaced by Reformers, Jewel among them. He was consecrated bishop of Salisbury at Lambeth 21 January 1560 by Archbishop Parker. At Salisbury he devoted his time to the administration of the diocese and the defense of the English church. Jewel became famous for his generosity, especially toward students preparing for the ministry, among whom was Richard Hooker.*

Jewel's role as apologist of the Church of England began to take shape shortly before his consecration. On 26 November 1559, he delivered a sermon at Paul's Cross defending the established church and issued a challenge to Roman Catholic divines to prove him wrong. In 1562, he published the *Apologia Ecclesiae Anglicanae* as a reply to the Roman Catholic attacks on the Church of England. The challenge sermon together with the *Apologia* sparked a theological debate between Jewel and Thomas Harding, an English recusant living at Louvain. Harding took up Jewel's challenge by publishing *An Answere To Maister Iuelles Chalenge* (1564). Jewel responded with *A Replie unto M. Hardinges answeare* (1565). No sooner had Jewel finished the *Replie* than Harding published *A Confutation of a Booke intituled An Apologie of the Church of England* (1565). The lengthy *Defence of the Apology* (1567) served as Jewel's rebuttal to Harding's

Confutation. In addition to attacks from the recusants, Jewel became involved in the vestiarian controversy that arose among those Reformers who wished to rid the Church of England of any remaining vestiges of the Roman Church. Although privately against vestments, he upheld the regulation requiring their use during public worship services and other rites of the church.

Jewel died on 23 September 1571 while on a visitation of his diocese and was buried in Salisbury Cathedral.

MAJOR WORKS AND THEMES

The principal themes of Jewel found in the *Challenge Sermon*, the *Apologia*, and the *Defence of the Apology* derive from his attempt to explain and defend the Church of England's separation from Rome, as well as the 1559 Elizabethan settlement—a theological compromise between the conservative Anglo-Catholic party and the Reformers, who wanted all traces of the Roman Catholic Church removed, especially in the area of liturgy and popular devotions.

The *Challenge Sermon* serves as an introduction to the themes Jewel developed more fully in the *Apologia* and *A Defence*. He preached this sermon on three occasions: at Paul's Cross on 26 November 1559; on 17 March 1560 at court; and again on 31 March 1560 at Paul's Cross. Based on I Corinthians 11: 23, Jewel enunciated one of his principal themes, namely, that in order to correct an abuse, in this case the Mass, it is necessary to return to the original intent of the Sacrament or doctrine in question. It is necessary to consult the testimony of Scripture, the writings of the early church fathers, and the decrees of the early church councils. This trinity of authorities forms both the fundamental theme and argument of Jewel's apologetic works. Other themes that receive attention in the sermon and later works are papal supremacy, private masses, Communion under one kind, Christ's presence in the Eucharist, and Latin versus the vernacular in the liturgy and in the public and private reading of Scripture. Jewel challenges his opponents to find any statement of Scripture, the church fathers, and the early councils to prove him wrong on any of the articles discussed in the sermon. If proved wrong, Jewel will be "content to yield unto him and to subscribe" (*Works* I, 21).

Jewel's principal work is the *Apologia Ecclesiae Anglicanae*. Published in 1562 and translated into English by Lady Bacon* in 1664, the *Apologia* became the official defense of the Church of England against Rome. The Latin version was widely distributed on the Continent and received praise from the Continental Reformers but was quickly attacked by the English recusants at Louvain. Composed of six parts, Jewel begins the work with a catalog of the accusations leveled against the English church by the Roman church: heresy, internal division and strife, abrogation of liturgical rites, and so on. Appealing to Scripture, the patristic writers, and the early church, Jewel argues that the accusations are false, and if anyone is guilty of such charges it is the church of Rome "who to maintain their own traditions have defaced, corrupted, now these many hundred years, the ordinances of Christ and the apostles'' (*Works* III, 58). Using the formulas ''we believe,'' ''we say,'' ''we acknowledge,'' ''we allow,'' Jewel then plainly and clearly sets forth the basic dogmas held by the English church—all of which have their authority from Scripture, the early fathers, and the credal statements of the early councils such as those of Nicea and Carthage. In the remaining sections of the work Jewel refutes more completely the accusation of heresy and internal strife, attacks the papacy and its claims to universal supremacy in both the spiritual and temporal realms, demonstrates that the abuses present in the Roman church justify the separation of the Church of England, and defends the right of the English church to reform itself, rejecting the authority of the Council of Trent. He concludes with a recapitulation of his argument, confidently declaring that ''we are sure all is true that we teach, and we may not either go against our conscience or bear any witness against God'' (*Works* III, 107).

A Defence of the Apologie of the Churche of Englande forms part of the controversy between Jewel and Thomas Harding. First published in 1567, the work is essentially an amplification and further explanation of the *Apologia*. Jewel first cites a section from Lady Bacon's translation of the *Apologia* together with Harding's response to that particular section, which is then followed by Jewel's rebuttal. When Harding attacked the *Defence* in his *A Detection of sundrie foule errours, lies, sclaunders, corruptions, and other matters, uttered and practized by M. Iewel in a Booke lately by him set forth entituled, A Defence of the Apologie, etc* (1568), Jewel replied by issuing a new edition of the *Defence* in 1570, in which he added Harding's objections to the first edition of the *Defence* followed by his refutation of Harding.

CRITICAL RECEPTION

Studies on Jewel are scant and scattered. John E. Booty and W. M. Southgate have written major studies on Jewel's role in the evolution and history of the Church of England. According to Southgate a possible reason for this neglect is Jewel's ''extremely voluminous and unsystematic work [which], unlike the beautifully ordered treatise of Hooker, does not attract the modern reader'' (viii). However, Southgate insists that the study of Jewel's writings is especially important to the historian because Jewel's ''experience as apologist and as bishop during the formative and crucial first decade of the reign presents a significant and extremely valuable case study of Anglicanism'' (viii).

Jewel's ideas on the presence of Christ in the Eucharist within the broader context of the Protestant Reformers' rejection of transubstantiation have received scholarly attention as well as his method of scriptural exegesis in his sermons. However, the latter study again does not focus solely on Jewel but rather on the similarity and dissimilarity of his method to that of Latimer, Hooker, and Andrewes. As for Jewel's preaching, in an article on Jewel and Elizabeth I, Booty comments that Jewel's sermons are ''much neglected by scholars'' (Booty 215).

Literary studies of Jewel are also few in number. David K. Weiser has written a detailed study of Jewel's prose style, focusing on his sermons. Other critiques of Jewel's style are contained in general studies on the development of English prose. Booty in *John Jewel as Apologist* makes passing mention of Jewel's style as "often tedious to read" (123). This view echoes the earlier judgment by Creighton who, speaking of the *Defence*, states that the style is not only tedious but that it also "robbed his book as a whole of literary charm" (817). Creighton further states that Jewel's works have "an air of cold and mechanical precision . . . they are strictly logical, and make no appeal to the emotions" (818). However, Weiser asserts that when speaking of Jewel's sermons and treatises, Creighton's judgment is no longer acceptable (189). Jewel's writings and those of the English recusants that were spawned as a result of Jewel's apologetic works still await full critical analysis. Southern in his study on the English recusants' prose emphasizes the importance of these writings in the study of English literature. Jewel and his opponents provide "a considerable body of prose work, the outstanding marks of which are . . . clarity and naturalness of expression. . . . It may be held that they fill or help to fill a significant gap in the general history of our English prose" (66). This view is echoed by Weiser, who states that "Jewel's importance to the history of English prose is two-fold. First, he is significant for having written a perfectly clear style that can easily be understood by the modern reader. This fact will have to be considered by those scholars who place the beginnings of modern prose at much later dates. Secondly, his sermons succeed quite frequently in merging clear thought with strong feelings" (190).

BIBLIOGRAPHY

Works by John Jewel

An Apology of the Church of England. Ed. J. E. Booty. Ithaca, NY: Cornell University Press, 1963.

Works. 4 vols. Ed. J. Ayre. Cambridge: Cambridge University Press, 1845–50.

Studies of John Jewel

Booty, J. E. "The Bishop Confronts the Queen." In *Continuity and Discontinuity in Church History: Essays Presented to George Huntston Williams on the Occasion of His 65th Birthday*. Leiden: E. J. Brill, 1979, 215–31.

———. *John Jewel as Apologist of the Church of England*. London: SPCK, 1963.

Chavasse, Ruth. "The Reception of Humanist Historiography in Northern Europe: M. A. Sabellico and John Jewel." *Renaissance Studies* 2.2 (1988): 327–38.

Creighton, Mandell. "John Jewel." *The Dictionary of National Biography* 10, 815–19.

Crofts, Richard A. "The Defence of the Elizabethan Church: Jewel, Hooker, and James I." *Anglican Theological Review* 54 (1972): 20–31.

Gane, Erwin R. "The Exegetical Methods of Some Sixteenth-Century Anglican Preachers: Latimer, Jewel, Hooker, and Andrewes." *Andrews University Seminary Studies* 17 (1979): 23–28, 169–88.

Ker, Neil. "The Library of John Jewel." *The Bodleian Library Record* 9.5 (1977): 256–65.

Pruett, Gordon E. ''A Protestant Doctrine of the Eucharistic Presence.'' *Calvin Theological Journal* 10 (1975): 142–47.

Southern, A. C. *Elizabethan Recusant Prose 1559–1582*. Folcroft, PA: Folcroft Library Editions, 1975.

Southgate, W. M. *John Jewel and the Problem of Doctrinal Authority*. Cambridge: Harvard University Press, 1962.

Weiser, David K. *The Prose Style of John Jewel*. Salzburg: Institut fur Englische Sprache und Literatur, 1973.

TERRENCE J. McGOVERN

BEN JONSON
(c. 1572–1637)

BIOGRAPHY

Ben Jonson was born in London around 1572, one month after his father's death. The following year, his mother married a bricklayer, a profession Jonson also followed intermittently, though apparently viewing it with contempt. With a patron's help, he attended Westminster School and studied with William Camden, but he did not finish school or go on to university. He married Anne Lewis in 1594, a marriage that seems not to have been very happy and that was characterized by long separations. They had several children together, none of whom survived childhood.

By 1597, after a brief stint with the army in Flanders and a few years as a bricklayer's apprentice, Jonson had become involved with the acting profession, first as an actor, then as a playwright. One of his earliest writing efforts, his collaboration on *The Isle of Dogs* (no longer extant), led to his imprisonment for sedition. He was arrested again the following year for killing Gabriel Spencer, a fellow actor. Since he could read, he was allowed to plead the benefit of clergy and was released, although he was branded on the thumb and had all his goods seized. While in prison, Jonson converted to Catholicism, an act that later created problems for him, although he apparently escaped major repercussions professionally.

In fact, no aspect of these imprisonments seems to have impeded his writing career substantially. Starting in 1598 with *The Case is Altered*, closely followed by *Every Man in His Humor, Every Man Out of His Humor, Cynthia's Revels*, and *Poetaster*, Jonson made a name for himself as a popular playwright. At the same time, however, he became engaged in the so-called War of the Theatres, wherein Jonson, John Marston, and Thomas Dekker* traded insults through their literary endeavors, a skirmish that continued until 1601. In 1602, Jonson made major changes in his life. He abandoned stage comedies and left his wife, to reside first with Sir Robert Townsend, then with Esme Stuart, Seigneur D'Aubigny, patrons who supported him into the next phase of his literary career.

Jonson flourished during the reign of James I, despite further encounters with the law. He was imprisoned in 1605 with John Marston and George Chapman* after being accused of satirizing the Scots in *Eastward Ho!* He then returned to court in 1606, when he and his wife were charged with recusancy (he returned to the Church of England in 1610). There was also some suspicion that he had been involved in the Gunpowder Plot in 1604.

Nevertheless, Jonson remained in the good graces of the king and entered a period of rich theatrical production. Not only did he produce numerous masques and other court entertainments, but he also wrote several of the plays for which he is most remembered, including *Volpone, Epicoene, The Alchemist, Bartholomew Fair*, and *The Devil is an Ass*. Furthermore, in 1616, he published a folio edition of his *Works*, was granted a royal pension, and began a decade's reign in London taverns as head of the ''Tribe of Ben.'' However, despite the accolade of an honorary M.A. from Oxford in 1619 and a notable walking tour of Scotland in 1618 with William Drummond, who recorded their conversations, Jonson's fortunes began to decline into the 1620s. His house and books were destroyed by a fire in 1623, and the king's death in 1625 left him without his key supporter. Charles I increased Jonson's pension in 1630, but the new king did not continue his parents' avid patronage of theatrical entertainments. Consequently, despite Jonson's continuing literary efforts, he never regained his prominence, although he was appointed Thomas Middleton's* successor as chronologer of the city of London in 1628, the same year he suffered a debilitating stroke. Jonson died on 6 August 1637 at the age of sixty-five. He was buried in Westminster Abbey, with the famous epitaph ''O rare Ben Jonson.''

MAJOR WORKS AND THEMES

Ben Jonson's literary output was prodigious and varied. He wrote successful comedies and derided tragedies for the stage, as well as masques and entertainments for the Jacobean and Caroline courts. But he was a poet also, making it difficult to fit his work neatly into our traditional ''dramatic''/''nondramatic'' generic categories. Scholars approaching the writings of Jonson face a formidable task; his multiple talents produced an unwieldy, yet rich variety of artistic creations. His reputed friendships with both Shakespeare* and Donne* are reflective of his role within literary circles of the time and of his place in the subsequent study of English literature and early modern culture. Jonson's affinity with classical themes and influences and with theories of dramatic and literary production keep him appealing to scholars with related interests today. Similarly, his attention to economic issues, gender roles, social concerns, and concepts of race guarantees his work a central position in the studies of current early modern scholars. Now, as then, Jonson reaches a diverse audience and provides a dense body of material for literary and cultural study.

Jonson is probably best known for his comedies. Witty and satiric, his urban comedies emphasize personal and societal foibles. Today, students are most likely to be familiar with *The Alchemist, Volpone, Bartholomew Fair, Epicoene*, and *Every Man in His Humor*, but these represent only a few of Jonson's extant comedies. Although several of his individual and collaborative efforts are lost to us, over a dozen plays still exist, displaying the diversity that characterizes Jonson as a writer.

His earliest comedies roughly coincide with the "War of the Theatres" (c. 1596–1601) period, and many contain text written as part of that conflict. *Every Man in His Humor* (1598), *Every Man Out of His Humor* (1599), *Cynthia's Revels* (1600), and *Poetaster* (1600) were included in Jonson's 1616 collection of his works, but these years also included the composition of more amateur efforts, such as *The Case is Altered* (1598) and the collaborative *Isle of Dogs* (1597), which led, as we have seen, to his imprisonment for sedition.

Every Man in His Humor, which was first performed by the Lord Chamberlain's Men in 1598, displays many of the qualities that marked later Jonsonian comedy. Though originally set in Italy, Jonson revised the play several years later to include a distinctively English urban setting and characters. When he refashioned the figures in his drama, he used names that helped characterize them, such as Kitely and Wellborn, a technique that reappears in his later works. He also borrowed aspects of Roman comedy, which he skilfully interweaves with elements from Elizabethan rogue literature, humoral theory, and classical structure. Potentially a chaotic mix of event and character, *Every Man in His Humor*'s ultimate coherence demonstrates Jonson's remarkable ability to synthesize. Since both the Italianate and English versions of the play still survive, this play offers scholars an unusual opportunity to trace Jonson's development as a dramatist.

After *Poetaster* in 1600, Jonson shifted his dramatic energies to tragedy. When he returned his attentions to the comic form, his first composition remains notable as one of his best. *Volpone* was initially performed at the Globe Theatre by the King's Men (Shakespeare's company), c. 1606. In *Volpone*, Jonson transforms figures from the medieval Bestiaries into performers in a commentary upon the greed of a big-city society. Good and evil are replaced in the play by gulled and guller. The audience is presented with a tale where none of the characters warrant undue sympathy; instead, they view a story of one-upsmanship, where everyone's foolishness is eventually revealed as such. *Volpone* presents a world where personal and legal culpability intersect. A brilliant exposition of human greed, duplicity, and buffoonery, *Volpone* rightly claims a space as one of the great world comedies.

Jonson's next comic masterwork, *Epicoene, or The Silent Woman*, was first performed by the Children of Her Majesty's Revels at Whitefriars Theatre in 1609/10, then suppressed due to an allusion to Lady Arbella Stuart, whose place in line to the throne kept her a politically sensitive figure. *Epicoene* has enjoyed renewed interest among scholars since gender issues came to the fore in the 1980s and 1990s. The title of the drama refers to the disguised boy offered as a wife to the aptly named Morose. Morose has foresworn matrimony because of his aversion to noise, but when the play opens, he expresses his desire for a silent wife who can produce an heir. As part of a plot to ensure the transmission of the older man's fortune to his nephew Dauphine, Morose is married to Epicoene, who first becomes talkative and opiniated, then is disclosed to be a boy. This plot device is particularly noteworthy because it is revealed neither to the majority of the characters nor to the audience until the end of the play.

The production of *Epicoene* was followed closely by *The Alchemist*, which was performed originally by the King's Men at the Globe Theatre in 1610. Although the drama takes place in a confined setting within a limited time frame, it bustles with characters and activity representative of the plague-ridden London it reflects. Like his previous comedies, Jonson's *The Alchemist* is imbued with commentary on human greed and foolishness. Its structural characteristics are drawn from a panoply of sources, which are brought together masterfully. The classic desire to transform common elements into gold is paralleled by the characters' efforts to change themselves and their situations. Jonson's representation of the perils and pleasures of personal and material commodification makes *The Alchemist* and its comedic predecessors valuable texts for scholars grappling with the economic and social changes that pervaded the early modern period.

Bartholomew Fair appeared in 1614, following Jonson's four-year hiatus from comedic writing. Premiering at the Hope Theatre on Halloween and performed by Lady Elizabeth's Men, the play was presented at court the following day. Like the earlier comedies, *Bartholomew Fair* includes a large cast and chaotic array of actions. In fact, it is often difficult to isolate individual themes or plot lines. By setting this drama in the holiday world of a fair, Jonson is able to bring together characters from a broad cross-section of society, which exuberantly defies clear moral judgments.

Jonson's tragedies were received much less favorably than his comedies. *Sejanus*, which was first acted in 1603, was forced off the stage. *Cataline*, which was produced by the King's Men in 1611, fared similarly. Although *Sejanus* shares several dramatic elements with Jonson's more successful works, his efforts at producing Roman plays did not win favor during his lifetime. *Cataline*, however, was popular during the Restoration, and *Sejanus* has garnered its share of critical attention.

Despite Jonson's lasting reputation as a dramatist, much of his professional success came from the series of masques he produced at the Jacobean and Caroline courts. He began creating masques in 1603 and continued almost until his death. The masques contained elaborate costumes, settings, and music and were designed as spectacular events at court. Although professional performers generally received the singing and speaking parts, the monarch took his place at the center of these works, and the masquers were nobles. While these entertainments lacked dramatic situations, they were complicated, often allegorical, ritualized performances, often created for specific occasions. Jonson's entertainments in this genre have much more substance than one would normally expect to find, a fact Jonson acknowledged by publishing the text of his masques. Jonson used the masques to explore social and ethical issues and helped transform this genre from a frivolous endeavor into a literary form warranting serious study.

Remarkably, Jonson's accomplishments as the writer of drama and court entertainments represent only part of his acclaimed literary achievements. When King James granted him a pension in 1616, he became the first of what would later be called the poets laureate of England. Though his contemporary John Donne now receives more attention in studies of seventeenth-century poetry, Jonson's fame at the time was considerable, and he still rightly attracts much scholarly regard for his nondramatic writings.

Like his drama, Jonson's poetry evinces his classical learning and his interest in social and moral commentary. In addition, the poems dedicated to his deceased children reveal a more personal side than his drama tends to allow. A wide-ranging stylist who wrote odes, epigrams, and verse epistles, among other forms, Jonson also began the tradition of English country-house poems with "To Penshurst." Notably, given our renewed attention to women writers, he addresses Lady Mary Wroth* in his *Epigrams*.

The breadth of Jonson's literary range and his incisive presentation of contemporary urban and courtly practices keep his work alive as a major source of information about early modern literary and social concerns.

CRITICAL RECEPTION

As the texts remaining from the War of the Theatres period indicate, we have commentary on Jonson's literary output virtually from the start of his career. Charles Fitsgeffrey, for example, wrote in 1601 that Jonson was "guilty of stealing and of wicked thieving, / All the nine Muses sitting by in circle" (Craig, 86). Similarly, the anonymous *Returne from Pernassus: Or the Scourge of Simony* (1606), a play produced by the students at Cambridge in 1601–2, announces that Jonson was "so slow an Inventor, that he were better betake himselfe to his old trade of Bricklaying" (Craig, 87). A few years later, an anonymous attack on his Epigrams of 1615 suggests to readers that although they may "[p]eruse his [Jonson's] booke, thou shalt not find a dram of witt, befitting a true Epigram" (Craig, 122). Clearly, Jonson's popularity as a writer demonstrates that not everyone shared such views during this era; still, his prominence and his outspoken personality made him the target of many attacks as well as much praise throughout his lifetime. In his commendation, a notable collection of commemorative verses, *Jonsonus Virbius*, was published to honor him in 1638, followed shortly by Sir Kenelm Digby's two-volume folio edition of Jonson's *Works*.

Much of the criticism of Jonson after his death emphasizes areas of comparison with Shakespeare. The reputed personal feud between Shakespeare and Jonson seems largely to have been fabricated, but beginning in the 1630s, numerous critics have engaged in battles disputing the relative merits of the famous friends and contemporaries. Jonson has often been considered the inferior writer when the two are compared; nevertheless, many writers emphasize his unique contributions to literary history. When the comparison is set aside, the value of Jonson's writings becomes indisputable.

John Dryden's extensive criticism provides the most prominent seventeenth-century response to Jonson (Craig, 9), but many other writers also debated the merits of Jonson's canon, including Aphra Behn in 1673, who apparently favored the works of Shakespeare (Behn, 123). Thomas Shadwell, in contrast, announced in 1668 that Jonson "is the man, of all the World, I most passionately admire for his Excellency in Drammatick-*Poetry*" (Shadwell, 11), while Samuel Pepys alternately pronounces *Epicoene* "an excellent play" (Pepys, 109) and "[not] so good [a] play as I formerly thought" (Pepys, 390).

Alexander Pope, Samuel Johnson, and Henry Fielding are among those in the eighteenth century who commented upon Jonson's writing. Pope famously, if unfairly, declared, "What trashe are his [Jonson's] works, taken all together!" (Craig, 381), although in deference to Jonson, he apparently demurred from a plan to mark his dog's grave "O Rare Bounce!" (Spence, 269). Dr. Johnson, on the other hand, remarked that Jonson, "like Egypt's Kings," left a "lasting Tomb" (Craig, 314), and Henry Fielding praises Jonson at some length in his preface to *Joseph Andrews*.

Nineteenth-century writers prepared the way for the criticism that predominated in the early part of the twentieth century. A. C. Swinburne and others posed, once again, the contrast between Jonson and Shakespeare. They also devoted significant attention to Jonson's classicism and his theories of poetry and drama. Subsequently, Jonsonian studies were profoundly influenced by T. S. Eliot's essay on the playwright in 1919 and by the publication of the Herford and Simpson edition of Jonson's collected works, which began appearing in 1925. Over the next few decades, critics, including Douglas Bush, Cleanth Brooks, and L. C. Knights, debated topics such as Jonson's social realism, his originality, his classicism, the nature of his dramatic and poetic art, and his didacticism (Brock and Welsh, 16–18).

Among the book-length studies of Jonson in the 1960s and 1970s, Jonson's drama was central. Jonas Barish, for example, offered an important account of Jonson's prose in the comedies (1960); Stephen Orgel offered a study of Jonson's masques (1965); Gabriele Bernhard Jackson explored *Vision and Judgment in Ben Jonson's Drama* (1968); and Alan Dessen examined *Jonson's Moral Comedy* (1971). During the same period, scholars such as L. A. Beaurline, G. R. Hibbard, Hugh Maclean, and Arthur Marotti added to our understanding of Jonson's poetry.

The proliferation of new approaches to early modern texts that has occurred since 1980 is reflected in Jonsonian criticism. While essays continue to be written on familiar themes such as Jonson's classicism and comparisons between Shakespeare and Jonson, current books and articles display diverse interests, ranging from topics concerned with race and gender to proposed connections between Jonsonian comedy and MTV or, in Douglas Bruster's work, to the plays of David Mamet. Gail Kern Paster, for example, discusses *The Alchemist* and *Bartholomew Fair* in her study of early modern drama and humoral medical theory (1993). Also in 1993, Katharine Eisaman Maus included Jonson in her essay on gender "A Womb of His Own: Male Renaissance Poets in the Female Body." Several critics, including Kim F. Hall, Hardin Aasand, and Joyce Green MacDonald, published articles in the early 1990s that focus on the *Masque of Blackness*, a dramatic text that is helping scholars conceptualize the theories of race that were germane during the early modern period.

At the same time, critics such as Richard Helgerson, Jonathan Goldberg, Richard Burt, and Joseph Lowenstein have been considering Jonson in the light of questions of literary production, literary patronage, and censorship during this period. Similarly, numerous critics, including Kathleen McLuskie, Katharine Maus, and Karen Newman discuss Jonson and his works in relation to the economic imperatives operative while Jonson was writing.

Although Jonson's plays are performed less often than those of Shakespeare, critical interest in his drama and in his poetry remains deservedly high. As our knowledge of the Jacobean court continues to grow, Jonson will undoubtedly become even more significant for students of early modern literature and culture.

BIBLIOGRAPHY

Works by Ben Jonson

The Complete Poems. Ed. George Parfitt. New Haven, CT: Yale University Press, 1982.

Complete Poetry. Ed. William B. Hunter Jr. Garden City, NY: Archer Books, 1963.

Studies of Ben Jonson

Aasand, Hardin. " 'To Blanch and Ethiop, and Revive a Corse': Queene Anne and *The Masque of Blackness*." *Studies in English Literature* (1992): 271–85.

Barish, Jonas A. *Ben Jonson and the Language of Prose Comedy*. Cambridge: Harvard University Press, 1960.

Barton, Anne. *Ben Jonson, Dramatist*. Cambridge: Cambridge University Press, 1984.

Beaurline, L. A. "The Selective Principle in Jonson's Shorter Poems." *Criticism* (1966): 4–74.

Behn, Aphra. *The Selected Writings of the Ingenious Mrs. Aphra Behn*. New York: Grove Press, 1950.

Boehrer, Bruce Thomas. "Great Prince's Donatives: MTV Video and the Jacobean Court Masque." *Studies in Popular Culture* (1988): 1–21.

Brady, Jennifer, and W. H. Herendeen, eds. *Ben Jonson's 1616 Folio*. Newark: University of Delaware Press, 1991.

Brock, D. Heyward, and James M. Welsh. *Ben Jonson: A Quadricentennial Bibliography, 1947–1972*. Metuchen, NJ: Scarecrow Press, 1974.

Bruster, Douglas. "David Mamet and Ben Jonson: City Comedy Past and Present." *Modern Drama* (1990): 333–45.

Burt, Richard. *Licensed by Authority: Ben Jonson and the Discourses of Censorship*. Ithaca, NY: Cornell University Press, 1993.

Butler, Martin. "Ben Jonson's *Pan's Anniversary* and the Politics of the Early Stuart Pastoral." *English Literary Renaissance* (1992): 369–404.

Craig, D. H. *Ben Jonson: The Critical Heritage: 1599–1798*. New York: Routledge, 1990.

Dessen, Alan C. *Jonson's Moral Comedy*. Evanston, IL: Northwestern University Press, 1971.

Dryden, John. *Essays of John Dryden*. Ed. W. P. Ker. Oxford: Clarendon Press, 1926.

Fielding, Henry. *Joseph Andrews*. Ed. Martin Battesin. Middlebury, CT: Wesleyan University Press, 1967.

Goldberg, Jonathan. *James I and the Politics of Literature: Jonson, Shakespeare, Donne and Their Contemporaries*. Baltimore: Johns Hopkins University Press, 1983.

Hall, Kim F. "Sexual Politics and Cultural Identity in *The Masque of Blackness*." In *The Performance of Power: Theatrical Discourse and Politics*, ed. Sue-Ellen Case and Janelle Reinelt. Iowa City: University of Iowa Press, 1991, 3–18.

Helgerson, Richard. *Self-Crowned Laureates: Spenser, Jonson, Milton and the Literary System*. Berkeley: University of California Press, 1983.

Hibbard, G. R. "The Country House Poem of the Seventeenth Century." *Journal of the Warburg and Courtauld Institutes* (1956): 159–74.

Jackson, Gabriele B. *Vision and Judgment in Ben Jonson's Drama*. New Haven, CT: Yale University Press, 1968.

Knapp, Peggy. "Ben Jonson and the Publicke Riot: Ben Jonson's Comedies." In *Staging the Renaissance: Reinterpretations of Elizabethan and Jacobean Drama*, ed. David Scott Kastan and Peter Stallybrass. New York: Routledge, 1991, 164–80.

Lehrman, Walter D., Dolores J. Sarafinski, and Elizabeth Savage. *The Plays of Ben Jonson: A Reference Guide*. Boston: G. K. Hall, 1980.

MacDonald, Joyce Green. " 'The Force of Imagination': The Subject of Blackness in Shakespeare, Jonson, and Ravenscroft." *Renaissance Papers* (1991): 53–74.

Maclean, Hugh. "Ben Jonson's Poems: Notes on the Ordered Society." In *Essays in English Literature from the Renaissance to the Victorian Age. Presented to A.S.P. Woodhouse*, ed. Millar MacLure and F. W. Watt. Toronto: University of Toronto Press, 1964, 43–68.

McLuskie, Kathleen. "The Poets' Royal Exchange: Patronage and Commerce in Early Modern Drama." *Yearbook of English Studies* (1991): 53–62.

Marcus, Leah. "Pastimes and the Purging of Theater, *Bartholomew Fair*." In *Staging the Renaissance: Reinterpretations of Elizabethan and Jacobean Drama*, ed. David Scott Kastan and Peter Stallybrass. New York: Routledge, 1991, 196–209.

———. *The Politics of Mirth: Jonson, Herrick, Milton, Marvell, and the Defense of Old Holiday Pastimes*. Chicago: University of Chicago Press, 1989.

Marotti, Arthur F. "All about Jonson's Poetry." *ELH* (1972): 208–37.

Maus, Katharine Eisaman. "Satiric and Ideal Economies in the Jonsonian Imagination." *English Literary Renaissance* (1989): 42–64.

———. "A Womb of His Own: Male Renaissance Poets in the Female Body." *In Sexuality and Gender in Early Modern Europe: Institutions, Texts, Images*, ed. James Grantham Turner. Cambridge: Cambridge University Press, 1993, 266–88.

Newman, Karen. "City Talk: Women and Commodification, *Epicoene*." In *Staging the Renaissance: Reinterpretations of Elizabethan and Jacobean Drama*, ed. David Scott Kastan and Peter Stallybrass. New York: Routledge, 1991, 181–95.

Orgel, Stephen. "Jonson and the Amazons." In *Soliciting Interpretation: Literary Theory and Seventeenth-Century English Poetry*, ed. Elizabeth D. Harvey and Katharine Eisaman Maus. Chicago: University of Chicago Press, 1990, 119–42.

———. *The Jonsonian Masque*. Cambridge: Harvard University Press, 1965.

Paster, Gail Kern. *The Body Embarrassed: Drama and the Disciplines of Shame in Early Modern England*. Ithaca, NY: Cornell University Press, 1993.

Shadwell, Thomas. *Complete Works of Thomas Shadwell*. Ed. Montague Summers. London: Fortune Press, 1927.

Shapiro, James. *Rival Playwrights: Marlowe, Jonson, Shakespeare*. New York: Columbia University Press, 1991.

Spence, Joseph. *Anecdotes, Observations, and Characters*. London: W. H. Carpenter, 1820.

Wayne, Don E. *Penshurst: The Semiotics of Place and the Poetics of History*. Madison: University of Wisconsin Press, 1984.

SHEILA T. CAVANAGH

K

JOHN KNOX
(c. 1514–1572)

BIOGRAPHY

John Knox, the fiery Protestant Reformer of the Church of Scotland and self-styled prophet of God, was born between 1513 and 1515 in or near Haddington, East Lothian. Details concerning his family and early life are few. His father, whose exact profession is unknown, was William, and his mother was a Sinclair. He had an older brother named William, who became a businessman in England. His education most likely began at the local school in Haddington. Although a student named ''John Knox'' appears in the records of the University of Glasgow, there is no other evidence that this was the Reformer. Knox studied with John Major, professor of logic and theology at the University of St. Andrews. However, there is no documentary proof that Knox attended or graduated from St. Andrews. His writings indicate that he studied Latin, but he does not seem to have the scholarly preparation enjoyed by other Reformers such as John Calvin* and Martin Luther. At some point in his education, he studied law and theology, since in 1540 he was acting as a notary and was named in documents as Sir John Knox, a title used in that era for priests. From 1540 to 1543, he served as notary, and by 1544, he had become tutor to the sons of two prominent Scottish families who had become Protestants.

Knox gives no date of his conversion to the Reformed faith nor the circumstances that led to it. However, once convinced of the rightness of Protestantism, he became one of its most ardent champions and defenders. In 1546, Knox served as a bodyguard to George Wishart, a Protestant preacher, during the latter's preaching tour in East Lothian. Wishart was soon arrested, tried as a heretic, and executed on 1 March 1546. Knox's association with Wishart identified him as a Protestant sympathizer, making him liable to Wishart's fate. Wishart's death no doubt contributed to Knox's commitment to the Reform movement while at the same time it intensified his hatred of the Roman Catholic hierarchy, a hatred that pervades his sermons and writing. In May of the same year, Cardinal Beaton, who had ordered the trial and execution of Wishart, was murdered by a group of disgruntled lairds who, with their followers, took possession of the cardinal's Castle of St. Andrews.

On 10 April 1547, in order to escape possible arrest as a heretic, Knox and his students entered the Castle of St. Andrews, where he continued his teaching duties. Within a few weeks of Knox's arrival in the castle, the leaders of the rebel group, at the suggestion of their minister John Rough, invited Knox to be Rough's associate. Insisting on a public call to ministry, during a service conducted by Rough, Knox was formally called by the congregation to be a minister. His first sermon, based on Daniel 7:24–25, was an attack on the Roman Catholic Church and its doctrine of justification. He challenged his hearers to a debate if they did not agree with his interpretation of Scripture. A public debate followed in which Knox bested his challengers: his career as the prophet and preacher of the Reformed faith in Scotland had begun.

On 31 July 1547, the garrison at the castle surrendered to the French, and Knox was condemned to the galleys. During his time as a galley slave, his masters attempted without success to force Knox and his fellow Scots to abandon the Reformed faith. Released from the galleys in 1549, Knox went to England, where he became rector of the parish at Berwick. As pastor he considered preaching his primary responsibility and consequently did not use the Book of Common Prayer but rather a Communion service of his own devising that had the sermon as its focus. His sermons reflected his growing antagonism toward the Roman Catholic Mass. As a result of his preaching, Knox was summoned by the bishop of Durham to defend his views. While at Berwick, Knox became friends with Elizabeth Bowes, his future mother-in-law. His letters to her and to her daughter Marjory, his future wife, give a glimpse of the gentler and more pastoral side of his personality.

In the summer of 1551, Knox was transferred to St. Nicholas Church, Newcastle. A year later as a protégé of the duke of Northumberland, he went to London, where he was appointed one of the royal chaplains to Edward VI. By this date, Knox had identified totally with the radical Reform group, which sought to establish the Reformed faith as taught by the Swiss Reformers, most notably John Calvin.* Knox thought that the Reformed church of England was still too close to Roman Catholicism, especially in the liturgy. Thus, in October 1552, preaching before the king and Privy Council, Knox attacked the rubric of kneeling to receive Communion, which had been inserted in the revised and supposedly more Protestant version of the Book of Common Prayer. According to Knox, kneeling was adoration of the Sacrament, an act that had no scriptural foundation, and was, therefore, a form of idolatry. As a result of Knox's condemnation, a declaration later known as the "black rubric" was added to the Prayer Book that asserted that kneeling was not adoration but simply a sign of reverence. In spite of his strongly held views, he was offered the bishopric of Rochester. He refused, preferring to remain an evangelist of the Reform movement. In July 1553, Edward died, and Mary Tudor, a staunch Catholic, became queen. Realizing that Mary was planning to reestablish Catholicism, Knox left England for the Continent.

From 1554 to 1559, with the exception of a year in Scotland, Knox lived in exile. Arriving in Dieppe, Knox went on to Geneva to meet with Calvin and others. With them he discussed some politically sensitive theological issues dealing with allegiance to a sovereign who was both female and Catholic. After a brief trip to Dieppe to get an update on the fate of the Reform movement in England under Mary Tudor, Knox returned to Geneva to study Hebrew and Greek as tools for a deeper understanding of the Scriptures. This period of study was interrupted in 1554, when Knox was called by the English congregation in Frankfurt am Main to be their minister. At the urging of Calvin, Knox accepted. Upon his arrival in Frankfurt, Knox became involved in a controversy over the congregation's form of worship. At the heart of the debate was the majority's insistence on changes to the Prayer Book to bring it more in conformity with the practice of the Swiss Reformers and the minority's desire to retain the Prayer Book without any deletions. At the suggestion of Calvin, a service was drawn up to be used until April of the following year. In March 1555, Richard Cox, former chancellor of Oxford University, and a group of exiles asked to join the congregation but insisted on the use of the Prayer Book. To help solve the dispute Knox, who at this point in his career appeared more flexible and tolerant, persuaded the congregation to allow Cox and his followers to participate in a congregational meeting, a decision that was to be Knox's undoing as pastor. The Coxians joined forces with the minority group, who wanted to maintain the Prayer Book, to form a new majority. Knox was forbidden to preach and eventually was forced to leave the city. He returned to Geneva, where he was defended by Calvin. The Frankfurt congregation responded to Calvin's reprimand by accusing Knox of contributing to the Marian persecution by the publication of his *Admonition to the Professors of God's Truth in England.*

From September 1555 until the following late summer, Knox was in Scotland preaching and encouraging the people to remain true to the Reformed faith. Mary of Guise, the queen regent who, for her own political reasons, had appeared to tolerate the Protestant faith, was now advancing the Catholic cause. Having been charged with heresy by the bishops, Knox accepted a call from the English congregation in Geneva to be its minister and arrived there with his wife and mother-in-law. For the next three years, Knox was busy with his pastoral duties, publishing several tracts that dealt with the problems of the Reformed church in Scotland and England. During this time in Geneva his two sons were born.

Upon the accession of Queen Elizabeth I, the congregation in Geneva returned home, and Knox decided to return to Scotland. Leaving his family in Geneva, Knox arrived in Leith in May 1559. Although the Reform movement was growing in Scotland, a Catholic monarch still ruled, creating a dangerous political situation for the Protestant party. Knox immediately began his battle to ensure the ultimate victory of the Reformed faith in Scotland. Although by royal decree he was an outlaw, Knox preached throughout the country and urged the nobility to request aid from Elizabeth. He was elected minister of Edinburgh and was a member of a diplomatic mission to England to request aid from Elizabeth against the queen regent and her French troops. At the beginning of 1560 English warships were sent by Elizabeth to contain the French troops. In June of that year, the queen regent died. At the request of Parliament, Knox and several other ministers drew up a Confession of Faith, which was ratified on 17 August 1560.

Knox returned to his pastoral duties and continued to work on his *History of the Reformation in Scotland.* In December 1560 his wife died, and three years later he married seventeen-year-old Margaret Stuart, by whom he had three daughters. From the pulpit, Knox exhorted the nobles and others to continue to hold firm against what he perceived to be a weakening on their part in the face of strong pressure by the new queen, Mary Stuart,* to maintain Catholicism. In December 1566, the General Assembly gave Knox permission to travel to England to visit his sons. During his absence, events in Scotland were moving against Mary Stuart. She was forced to abdicate in favor of her son James and to make the earl of Moray regent. Upon his return, Knox continued to write and preach. In October 1570, Knox suffered a stroke but recovered sufficiently to continue preaching. Two years later on 24 November 1572, he died.

MAJOR WORKS AND THEMES

The corpus of Knox's writings consists of tracts reminiscent of the Pauline letters, letters to individuals, a treatise on predestination, and a history of the Reformation in Scotland. Of his sermons only two survive. A variety of theological and political themes—justification by faith, the nature of God, providence, mediation of Christ, covenant, sin, persecution, church polity, women and their role in society, allegiance to rulers, civil disobedience—pervades all his writings to a greater or lesser degree, depending on the event or events that occasioned a particular work. All these motifs, however, flow from the two major themes that dominate Knox's work. The first is *sola scriptura* with a special emphasis on the Old Testament and its literal interpretation. Knox viewed Scripture as the infallible source of knowledge about God, the history of salvation, true religion, and the conduct of individuals and nations. The authority of Scripture took precedence over civil and ecclesiastical authority. What was not found in the Word of God could not be approved of. Scripture was, like God himself, immutable and consequently allowed for no exceptions. Knox submitted all doctrines and forms of worship to this criterion. His stance did not allow for the concept of ''things indifferent,'' a practical principle used by some Reform theologians to allow for divergent theological opinions, especially in the area of worship and church polity. The second, flowing from the theme of *sola scriptura* and dominating Knox's writings, is idolatry. Throughout his writings, idolatry is synonymous with the Roman Catholic Church. Its doctrines, its ceremonies, especially the Mass, for which Knox had an intense hatred, and its use of extrabiblical sources (the church fathers, councils, tradition) as sources of authority were all variant forms of idolatry.

In 1558, Knox wrote four tracts, all of which dealt with the political situation of the day. Still in exile and living in Geneva, Knox became increasingly concerned with the survival of the Reformed faith in England and Scotland, where Catholic monarchs were attempting to keep Catholicism as the state religion. Of these tracts, the most famous and the one that would haunt Knox for the better part of his life was *The First Blast of the Trumpet Against the Monstrous Regiment of Women*, published in the spring of 1558. The central theme of the tract is that it is against natural and divine law for a woman to rule a kingdom. Knox castigates the English for permitting a sovereign who is not only a woman but also a Catholic and therefore in Knox's opinion an idolater. Invoking the prophetic tradition of the Old Testament, Knox considered himself a kind of Jeremiah who would call England to repent of its sin of idolatry or risk divine wrath and punishment. To defend his thesis, Knox invoked the authority of Scripture, especially the Pauline passages that assert that women should be subordinate to men and that their chief role is to serve and obey them. It is interesting to note that in this tract, he also cites extrabiblical sources—Roman and canon law, Aristotle, and several of the early church fathers—to bolster his argument. He also appealed to natural law, drawing examples from the animal kingdom. The foundation and core of his argument, however, were the immutability of God's Word and law as given in the Bible. As part of his argument, Knox returned to his second major theme, idolatry. Mary's Catholicism made her guilty of idolatry. Since Scripture plainly states that women are subordinate to men and that idolatry is a capital offense, Mary Tudor must be removed as sovereign on both accounts and be executed together with her followers as required by Mosaic law. Not to rebel against a ruler guilty of idolatry was itself a sin meriting divine punishment to England.

On Predestination, In Answer to the Cavillations of an Anabaptist was published in 1560 to refute the anonymous *Confutation of the Errors of the Careless by Necessity*. Before this treatise, Knox had not been greatly occupied with the doctrine of predestination, although he had discussed it from a pastoral perspective in his letters to Elizabeth Bowes (1553–54). Predestination for Knox was linked intimately to God's immutable nature as discerned in a reading of the Old Testament. Before the beginning of time God chose those who would be the elect and those who would be the reprobate. In view of this premise,

Knox considered God's love to be limited only to the elect, thereby denying the Anabaptists' universalist view of divine love and ultimately of salvation. Predestination is a necessary component of salvation. True faith flows from God's election, which, in turn, leads to good works. Having been chosen, the elect cannot be lost even if they commit sin. As Knox proceeds to refute the Anabaptists, he returns to the theme of *sola scriptura* and idolatry. Although Knox often cites Calvin, the authoritative basis of his argument is grounded in the canonical books of Scripture. Knox discusses at length the concept of God's Word, stressing its infallibility and immutability. All that is found in the Scriptures is to be believed literally. There is also a reprise of the theme of idolatry. Since God's laws are unchangeable, heresy, which is a form of idolatry, is rightly punished by death. Knox cites the example of Servetus, who, having denied the Trinity, was found guilty of blasphemy and thus was justly executed, based on Deuteronomy 13. The theme of idolatry is further developed by Knox's apocalyptic view that the elect and the reprobate are incarnated in two distinct camps. The elect constitute the true Church of God; the reprobate are the followers of Satan, whose chief lieutenant is the pope. The two groups are locked in a battle that will continue until the Parousia, at which time the elect will be victorious.

In 1559, Knox returned to Scotland, where Mary of Guise, the queen regent, was attempting to contain the spread of the Reformed faith. In addition to preaching the Reformed faith and ensuring its establishment throughout Scotland, Knox began *The History of the Reformation in Scotland*. The *History*, divided into four books, amplifies and summarizes the author's principal themes. Book I covers the years 1494–1558; Book II, 1558–59; Book III, 1559–61; Book IV, 1561–64. The work was not published until after Knox's death. In 1587, the first three books were published. An edition was published in 1664 with a fifth book, which was not written by Knox.

Although much of what we know about the Scotch Reformer comes from the *History*, it is not an autobiography, but a description of an apocalyptic struggle between good and evil, focusing on the Protestant struggle in Scotland to purify religion by ridding it of the idolatry introduced and maintained by the Roman Catholic Church. Beyond the themes of idolatry and *sola scriptura*, the fundamental view that informs the entire *History* is God's active involvement in the affairs of mankind. God has sovereign control of history.

Books I–III trace the trials of the Protestant movement from its early martyrs, such as Patrick Hamilton, to the writer's contemporaries. Persecution has been from the earliest Christian era the fate of the elect. In those early days, the faithful suffered at the hands of idolaters. So, too, the faithful of Scotland are suffering persecution at the hands of idolaters (the Catholic Church and a Catholic sovereign). But if the elect persevere, they will be victorious. In Book III, Knox tells his readers that victory has been achieved by Parliament's ratification in 1560 of the Confession of Faith, making Scotland a Protestant country.

Book IV chronicles what Knox perceives to be a serious erosion of the Protestant movement by the backsliding of some of the nobles. Mary Stuart has returned as queen and is insisting on her right to have the Mass said in her chapel. Knox totally opposed this reversion. He had several meetings with Mary, none of which were successful in convincing the queen of his opinions on faith, Scripture, and the duties of ruler and subjects to practice true religion, that is, the Reformed faith, and refrain from idolatry. At the end of the book, Knox recounts his lengthy debate in June 1564 with William Maitland of Lethington in which the Reformer tries to convince his opponent of the necessity of requiring the conversion of the queen from idolatry to true religion and of keeping Scotland Protestant in order to avoid divine wrath and punishment.

CRITICAL RECEPTION

Contemporary criticism of Knox's works divides into three major areas, theology, politics/history, and literature/linguistics.

In the area of theology, critics debate the sources of Knox's views of predestination, Sacraments, soteriology, and church polity, among others. Of special interest to scholars is the influence of John Calvin and other Continental Reformers on Knox's theological perspective. Kyle's study is an excellent bibliographic source for the major scholarly debates on Knox's theological sources and influences.

Criticism of Knox's political/historical writings tends to focus on two major topics. The first is the origins and development of Knox's resistance theory with a special emphasis on armed rebellion against a ruler. Kyle devotes a lengthy chapter to the scholarly debate on this issue. Dawson, departing from the traditional criticism of the political writings, offers a different interpretation of the so-called political tracts of 1558, which include *The First Blast*. Dawson argues that the tracts must be viewed within the context that "by 1558 there were two Knoxes: Knox the Scotsman by birth and Knox the Englishman by adoption" (556). *The First Blast* is written by Knox the Englishman and is directed to a specific audience, the English nation, which is exhorted to depose and execute Mary Tudor. The remaining three tracts (*Letter to the Queen Regent [Augmented], The Appellation, The Letter to the Commonality of Scotland*) are written by Knox the Scotsman to a specific audience, the Scottish nation, which is exhorted to press for the Reformation of the church without recourse to rebellion against the sovereign.

The History of the Reformation in Scotland has received much critical attention. Although scholars agree that Knox is a biased historian, they disagree, according to Kyle, over the "degree and depth" (13) of Knox's lack of impartiality. The role of women in society, especially as rulers, is the second major topic addressed by critics. Although Knox's basic attitudes toward women reflect those of other theologians of the era, his views, particularly in *The First Blast*, move beyond those of Calvin and others. Healey analyzes Knox's application of *sola scriptura* and the sixteenth century's views of women (a debate not unlike our own in the twentieth century regarding women in society, especially their ordination to the ministry). In spite of his denunciations in *The First Blast*, some critics do not think that Knox's reputation as a misogynist is justified. Kyle observes that ''out of Knox's surviving letters, more than half were written to women and many of them showed a high regard for the female sex'' (267). This view is echoed by Healey, who states that ''in all his dealings with Mary Stuart, Knox never demeaned her as a woman'' (385).

Literary/linguistic scholars have had only minimal interest in Knox's prose. C. S. Lewis opined that Knox is a minor author who is ''about as important a literary figure as More would have been if he had written neither the *Utopia* nor the *Comfort against Tribulation*'' (197). In his assessment of Knox's corpus, Lewis acknowledges that at times Knox ''writes a good level prose'' (197), but in a critique of the *History*, he asserts that Knox's use of ''original documents, a popular poem, large passages from Foxe and other authors . . . spoil the narrative flow'' (201). More recent scholars have taken issue with Lewis' judgments. For Lydall, Knox is the ''most original and most important Protestant prose writer'' (177). Lydall's study is also of particular interest to philologists, since it addresses in some detail Knox's Scots/English bilingualism and its influence on his writings. R. D. S. Jack also discusses Knox's bilingualism, asserting that Knox is ''a master of Scots and English, knowing when to move from one to the other and employing his 'bilingual' inheritance to marked effect'' (239). According to Jack, *The History* contains ''the thickest Scots employed by Knox'' (242). Both Kenneth D. Farrow and Jack discuss Knox's use of humor, particularly in *The History*, where, according to Farrow, it is often ''scathing and highly derisory'' (159). Recent criticism has addressed Knox's use of rhetoric, imagery, metaphor, and simile. However, more literary criticism of Knox remains to be done. Students of literature would do well to distance themselves from C. S. Lewis' opinion of Knox's literary worth and instead take up Farrow's challenge that ''it is perhaps time that literary critics stop just reacting to him [Knox], or writing him off to save themselves some effort, and start thinking about him'' (195). He is, however, no Calvin.

BIBLIOGRAPHY

Works by John Knox

''Epistle to the Congregation of Berwick.'' *John Knox and the Church of England.* Collected by Peter Lorimer. London: Henry S. King, 1875, 251–67.

''Memorial or Confession to the Privy Council of Edward VI, 1552.'' *John Knox and the Church of England.* Collected by Peter Lorimer. London: Henry S. King, 1875, 267–74.

''The Practice of the Lord's Supper Used in Berwick by John Knox, 1550.'' *John Knox and the Church of England.* Collected by Peter Lorimer. London: Henry S. King, 1875, 290–92.

The Works of John Knox. 6 vols. Ed. David Laing. Edinburgh: Printed for the Bannatyne Club, 1846–64.

Studies of John Knox

D'Assonville, V. E. *John Knox and the Institutes of Calvin: A Few Points of Contact in Their Theology*. Durban: Drahensburg Press, 1968.

Dawson, Jane E. A. ''The Two Knoxes: England, Scotland and the 1558 Tracts.'' *Journal of Ecclesiastical History* 42.4 (October 1991): 555–75.

Dickinson, William Croft. *Andrew Lang, John Knox, and Scottish Presbyterianism*. Edinburgh: Thomas Nelson and Sons, 1952.

Farrow, Kenneth D. ''Humor, Logic, Imagery and Sources in the Prose Writings of John Knox.'' *Studies in Scottish Literature* 25 (1990): 154–75.

Hazlett, Ian. ''A Working Bibliography of Writings of John Knox.'' *In Calviniana: Ideas of Influence of John Calvin*, ed. Robert V. Schnucker. Kirksville, MO: Sixteenth Century Journal Publications, 1988, 185–93.

Healey, Robert M. ''John Knox's 'History': A 'Compleat' Sermon on Christian Duty.'' *Church History* 61.3 (September 1992): 319.

———. ''Waiting for Deborah: John Knox and Four Ruling Queens.'' *The Sixteenth Century Studies Journal* 25.2 (Summer 1994): 371–86.

Jack, R.D.S. ''The Prose of John Knox: A Re-assessment.'' *Prose Studies* 4.3 (December 1981): 239–51.

Janton, Pierre. *John Knox: L'homme et l'oeuvre*. Didier, 1967.

Kyle, Richard G. *The Mind of Knox*. Lawrence, KS: Coronado Press, 1984.

Lewis, C. S. *English Literature in the Sixteenth Century, excluding Drama*. Oxford: Clarendon Press, 1962.

Lydall, R. J. ''Vernacular Prose before the Reformation.'' In *The History of Scottish Literature: Origins to 1600 (Medieval and Renaissance*. Ed. R.D.S. Jack. Aberdeen: The University Press, 1988, 163–81.

Reid, W. Stanford. ''John Knox's Theology of Political Government.'' *The Sixteenth Century Studies Journal* 19.4 (Winter 1988): 529–40.

———. *Trumpeter of God: A Biography of John Knox*. New York: Charles Scribner's Sons, 1974.

TERRENCE J. McGOVERN

THOMAS KYD
(1558–1594)

BIOGRAPHY

Thomas Kyd led an ironic existence. He lived only thirty-six years and produced a very small canon; yet it contained one of the most influential dramatic works of the Tudor period, *The Spanish Tragedy (ST)*. This work serves as the most significant extant model for the greatest revenge tragedies of Tudor and Jacobean drama and was perhaps the most famous play of its time. Kyd's other known works include only two translations. Even attributions are few in number and include plays that are no longer extant. Yet his literary importance is undeniable.

Ironically, his personal life was as dismal and nearly as tragic as that of his famous hero Hieronymo. Thomas Kyd was baptized in London on 6 November 1558 the son of Anna and Francis Kyd, a successful freeman of the Company of Scriveners. Scriveners, often disdained, were ancient tradespeople who served as scribes, letter writers, notaries, and later, moneylenders. Records reveal that Kyd had a sister and brother, that the family had at least one servant, and that they lived in a prosperous area of London near the western end of Lombard Street.

When Thomas was seven years old, the Kyds were sufficiently successful to enroll him in the four-year-old Merchant Taylor's School, a competitive school directed by the famous scholar Richard Mulcaster, who also instructed Edmund Spenser,* Lancelot Andrewes, and Thomas Lodge.* No documents record Kyd's activities until 1583; therefore, the number of years he studied at the school or his further study elsewhere is unknown. He mastered his studies well, given his relatively meager formal educational background. His extant writings show that he was fluent in Latin, French, Italian, and possibly Greek; but his understanding of history and geography was not thorough, and it is unlikely that he traveled outside England. The extent of his education and his highly formal handwriting suggest that he may have served as an apprentice for some years to his father.

Evidence also points to Kyd's work as a dramatist before 1585. In 1607 Thomas Dekker* refers to Kyd's pen, along with the pens of Thomas Achelley and Thomas Watson, "molding" the actor John Bentley, who died in 1585. These three men were associated with the Queen's Company, a popular acting company newly formed in 1583 from among the members of the Earl of Leicester's Men and other successful companies. These actors included the well-known comic actors Richard Tarlton, Robert Wilson, John Singer, and John Adams. That the performances of this company were in great demand suggests that the group required many new scripts. Dekker's comments imply that some of these were created by Kyd, at least those performed before 1585.

Thus, by 1585 Kyd was a working dramatist. In 1587 or 1588 he entered into service as a tutor or secretary for a patron, possibly the earl of Sussex. His greatest work, *The Spanish Tragedy*, was likely written by 1587, and its first recorded performance was on 14 March 1592, the year of publication of *Soliman and Perseda* and possibly when Kyd and the radical Christopher Marlowe* were working together, perhaps even sharing rooms.

The single document recording the events of Thomas Kyd's life during the period after 1585 is dated 12 May 1593. It identifies Kyd as a prisoner arrested for "lewd and malicious libels" against Dutch nationals living in London and for "vile hereticall Conceiptes denynge the deity of Jheses Christe or Savior" found among his papers. In a letter to Sir John Puckering, keeper of the Great Seal of England, Kyd denied vehemently the authorship of the latter statements and attributed them to the recently killed Christopher Marlowe. Kyd claimed that two years previously they had worked for the same patron, and their papers had inadvertently become mixed. The explanation may have merit. Unfortunately, even though he was freed in May 1593, the tortures that Kyd underwent during his imprisonment probably injured him severely enough that he was unable to regain his health. He died, poor, no doubt wrongfully accused, and alone in August 1594.

MAJOR WORKS AND THEMES

Kyd's canon is dominated by a single historically and aesthetically significant work, *The Spanish Tragedy*, ironically not attributed to him until 1773. The first record of performance is in 1592, when Lord Strange's Men presented it at the Rose Theater. First printed in 1592 also, it was subsequently printed nine times before 1633. None of the editions include significant alterations to the text except the edition of 1602, which has additions probably written by an anonymous author. But while the play was very popular, no attribution to Kyd was included in these early editions. Finally, in 1773, the historian Thomas Hawkins revealed in *The Origins of the English Drama* that in 1612 Thomas Heywood referred to "M. Kyd, in his Spanish Tragedy" in a comment on theater in *Apology for Actors*. Nearly 200 years after its completion, Kyd finally received credit for his masterpiece.

The Spanish Tragedy is remarkable for its originality as well as its considerable artistry and its enormous influence on later plays of the period. It is a prototype for the greatest works of Christopher Marlowe, William Shakespeare,* John Webster, Cyril Tourneur, Thomas Heywood, Thomas Middleton, and John Ford. Assuming Kyd wrote the play between 1585 and 1587, a hypothesis that will be examined later, he may be credited with the first English creation of a Machiavellian* villain, a play-within-play, a revenge tragedy, even a modern tragedy. Additionally, he incorporated popular Senecan dramatic elements into the plot, euphuisms into the language, and a clever interweaving of contemporary history into the script.

Unusually, historians have been unable to identify a clear source for the play. While it may be generically categorized as an Elizabethan romantic tale with a complex plot, Kyd must be given credit for the creativity and artistry required in blending the features previously named with a main plot seemingly developed solely from the inspiration of his muse.

Only a general source can be identified for the work, the third history of Henry Wotton's translation of Jacques Yver's *A courtlie controversie of Cupids Cautels*. This work provides first, the source for the Soliman and Persieda tale, which is the story used in the play-within-play, and second, many of the elements of the main plot's exposition.

Kyd's first innovation in this play is the character of Lorenzo, the English archetypal Machiavellian villain. He is the first such character extant and may be differentiated from tyrants or so-called pure villains like Iago or Tambourlaine. Machiavellian villains possess sly, devious, and self-promoting minds with which they contrive elaborate strategies to achieve their own goals. They experience at least as much pleasure in their cunning and cruel means as in their self-serving ends.

Politic Machiavellian villains became popular in Elizabethan drama, possibly because such characters seemed to permeate the actual world as well as the dramatic landscape. In *The Spanish Tragedy*, for example, the particular trap Lorenzo devises to ensnare Pedringano, allowing him confidently to expect a pardon that does not come—he is summarily hanged—is a clear example of a Machiavellian act. But this may have as a source a parallel story enacted by a possibly real-life Machiavellian politician, the earl of Leicester, and his victim, a thief named Gates, who, like Pedringano, was hanged while the plotter, Leicester, remained unscathed for his treachery.

Like the Machiavellian villain, the play-within-a-play is a second device introduced into English drama by Kyd. His use of a frame play in which a speaker or speakers introduce a story that becomes the main action is not a prototype, but Kyd's weaving of the frame exposition with the framed story is new. Beyond this, Kyd takes the convention even further when he introduces Hieronymo's play, an extra layer of fiction. Andrea's ghost and Revenge introduce the main action of the framed story, which focuses on Hieronymo, who then introduces his own play—a play in a play in a play. This latter device is thought to have its origin in Italian *intermedii*, short playlets, perhaps comic dumb shows, placed at the ends of acts, originally functioning as summaries of previous action but later providing extraneous, comic material. Hieronymo's playlet, however, is relevant to, and reflective of, the main plot, much like Hamlet's *Murder of Gonzago*.

While the Machiavellian villain and the play-within-a-play are innovations, Kyd also used popular Senecan conventions—a ghost as a character, a revenge theme, direct Senecan language, and Senecan rhetorical devices. Kyd's ghost of Andreas and the theme of revenge are altered from the prototypes, beginning with Euripides, because Andreas' revenge does not suddenly appear full-blown. Rather, his desire for revenge evolves gradually, mirroring a similar growth of revenge in the mind of Hieronymo. Senecan language and stylistic qualities are striking and include, most notably, strict stichomythic dialogue and the obvious example of Hieronymo's reading aloud from Seneca's work itself. Kyd also employs on occasion a euphuistic style, characterized by antitheses and overly extended figures, but not without purpose. He uses it to show artifice and falseness in the dialogue of Balthazar.

Contemporary history, too, is revealed in the script. Spain was the rival of England when this play was written, even if the play is dated after 1588, the year of the English defeat of the Spanish Armada. The play refers to Spain's defeat of Portugal and the institution of a viceroy, Don Balthazar, "the warlike prince of Portingale" (*ST*), who goes to battle with Spain and is defeated in a one-on-one battle with Horatio, Hieronymo's son. The Spanish king refers to the enemy as "our Portingales," a people who already had been defeated by the Spanish but were presently engaged in ongoing rebellion. They were to pay "tribute and wonted homage" (*ST*) as a result of Horatio's bravery. This element of the plot suggests that Portugal was under Spanish rule in the play, as it had been in the real world since 1580, and it further suggests that Portugal was rebelling, a laudable activity to any English audience during the 1580s.

It would be unfortunate, however, to value *The Spanish Tragedy* for its historical significance alone. Kyd was an artist as well as an innovator. His use of language, particularly blank verse, could be very moving, like that in the often parodied Prologue of Andreas. It is simpler than that of his contemporary, Christopher Marlowe, with its shorter words, dearth of passive voice, consistent use of the verb ''to be,'' and only mildly hyperbolic epithets. Both playwrights move away from the more direct translations of Senecan tragedies by George Gascoigne and Jasper Heywood with their noun-adjective order, emphatic verbs, and lengthy alliterations.

Kyd also uses few sententia or aphorisms, so the play acquires a certain realism with its more direct speech and lack of homilies. The homilies Kyd does include are often ironic or used for character development, such as those found in the sententious speeches of Hieronymo's wife, Isabella.

Kyd's magnificent caesural pauses and exclamations are innovatively used for alterations in tempo, particularly in moments of intensity. When Bel-Imperia discovers Horatio's body, she wails, ''Murder! Murder! Help, Hieronymo, help!'' (*ST*). Likewise, Hieronymo pleads to the king for the death of his son, ''Justice, O justice! O my son, my son'' (*ST*).

Finally, Kyd shows unusual interest in stagecraft. He refers to stage areas such as a window or a place above and directs certain actions within the lines such as kissing, closing of eyelids, leaning, or falling. He directs the placement of characters on the stage, perhaps a seating of the court in hierarchical order or Balthazar's being led prisoner between his two victors, Horatio and Lorenzo. The naturalistic violence in the play is inventive during the Tudor period and includes hanging, stabbing, struggling, ranting of a supposed madman, and a biting out of the tongue.

Finally, the dating of *The Spanish Tragedy* is important if it is to be recognized as a prototype. Its terminus ad quo is 1582, the date of the publication of Watson's *Hectatompathia*, from which Kyd plagiarized seven lines (II.i. 3–10). Its terminus ad quem is 1592, the year of its publication. Other evidence used in setting the date may include the *Copie of a Leter* describing the Leicester–Gates affair published in 1584 and the influence of the Spanish defeat in 1588. A reasonable interpretation of the play suggests that when the play was written, Spain was a current rival of England, not a vanquished, powerless victim as it gradually became after the defeat. In Hieronymo's masque, three ancient defeats of Spain by England are mentioned. Commenting on the masque, the Spanish king remembers one such defeat from the distant past, ''[w]hen it by little England hath been yok'd'' (*ST*). Such a reference to England seems to identify England as an underdog that has the potential to strike successfully. This is not the tone of a confident post-1588 victor but rather of a smaller, wary rival. Consequently, a hypothetical date for the play is often given as between 1584 and 1588.

Kyd may have written many other plays, poems, and prose works, but they are either lost or not clearly attributable to him. He was the playwright of the highly praised but poorly received *Cornelia*, a translation of Robert Garnier's tragedy, *Cornelie*. Printed in January 1594, only seven months before he died, it was reprinted the following year to great acclaim. It is praised by W. Covell in *Polimanteia* in 1595 as "excellently done," although underappreciated. It is quoted twenty-one times each in *England's Parnassus* and *Bel-vedere*, printed in 1600. A second, strongly probable attribution is *The Householder's Philosophy*, a 1588 translation from the Italian writer Torquato Tasso's* original work of 1583, *Il Padre di Famiglia*. Finally, we have *Soliman and Perseda*, first attributed to Kyd in 1773 because of substantial internal evidence. It is based on the same story as the play-within-a-play in *The Spanish Tragedy*, the tale I have mentioned of Soliman and Perseda written in 1578 in *A courtlie Controversy* by Henry Wotton. It has similarities of dramatic technique, such as changing the scene of the action, similar melodramatic and ironic characteristics, and similarities in versification, language, and terminology.

Additionally, Thomas Kyd is credited with historically significant, probably popular, but lost plays, alluded to by Thomas Nashe and several subsequent writers. Most important are an *ur-Hamlet* and an *ur-Titus Andronicus*, which are normally considered in Shakespeare studies. Another lost play to which there are many contemporary references is a comedy about Hieronymo, "spanes commodye donne oracioe," which portrays the action that had apparently taken place before the events of the popular tragedy. This comedy was performed at least six times in 1592 and is a probable source for the surviving drama of 1602 obviously by another playwright, *The First Part of Jeronimo*.

Literary historians have attempted to identify the creators of the many plays of the period labeled anonymous. Since Kyd's death, these historians have sought to include eight anonymous plays (along with a news pamphlet) in the otherwise meager canon of Kyd. Among these are *Arden of Feversham* and the prose pamphlet *The Murder of John Brewen*. Because an extant copy of the latter contains the name of the printer, John Kyd, in manuscript on the title and final pages of the publication, mistaken identities are inevitable. *Arden* was included in the canon because of its parallel passages with *John Brewen*; obviously, such evidence is useless. The remaining attributions that have been presented are *Edward II, Taming of a Shrew, The Rare Triumphs of Love and Fortune, King Leire, Selimus, 2 and 3 Henry VI, Richard III*, and *Titus Andronicus*.

A final attribution to Kyd is a poem entitled "Hendecasyllabon," printed in 1586 in a five-poem pamphlet, *Verses of Prayse and Joye written vpon Her Majesties preservation wherevnto is annexed Tychbornes lamentation written in the towre with his owne hand and an avnswere to the same*. This mediocre poem is an elegy responding to another elegy attributed to Chidiock Tychborne. The poem is printed with the initials T. K., and only one other poet, Timothy

Kendall, shared these initials. Since Kendall's work is stylistically unlike this poem, the chances are fair to good for Kyd's authorship.

CRITICAL RECEPTION

The canon of Thomas Kyd clearly survives because of one play, *The Spanish Tragedy*. The play was a huge success in its day, remarkably inventive and serving as the model for most subsequent tragedies. Because it was well known and popular among playgoers, playwrights were eager to imitate it, as much for its marketability as for its innovation and artistry. Sadly, the play itself is referred to far more frequently than Kyd himself, another irony of his unhappy life. Among the few direct references to Kyd himself, Thomas Nashe broadly criticizes him in the introduction to *Menaphon*, but he is praised by Francis Meres in *Palladis Tamia* as "our best for Tragedie" and, over the following thirty-five years, by the likes of Thomas Dekker, Thomas Heywood, and Ben Jonson,* who called him "sporting Kyd."

Today, after over two hundred years of scholarly respect for Thomas Kyd's originality, his artistry as well as his innovation make him, along with Christopher Marlowe, one of the two most important tragic playwrights preceding Shakespeare in Tudor England.

BIBLIOGRAPHY

Works by Thomas Kyd

Boas, Frederick S., ed. *The Works of Thomas Kyd*. Oxford: Clarendon Press, 1901.

Kyd, Thomas. *The Spanish Tragedy*. Ed. Philip Edwards. 1959. London: Methuen, 1965.

Studies of Thomas Kyd

Ardolino, Frank R. *Thomas Kyd's Mystery Play: Myth and Ritual in* The Spanish Tragedy. New York: Peter Lang, 1985.

Barish, Jonas. "*The Spanish Tragedy*, or *The Pleasures and Perils of Rhetoric*." *Elizabethan Theatre* 9 (1966): 59–85.

Edwards, Philip. *Thomas Kyd and Early Elizabethan Tragedy*. London: Longmans, Green, 1966.

Freeman, Arthur. *Thomas Kyd: Facts and Problems*. Oxford: Clarendon Press, 1967.

Hunter, G. K. "Ironies of Justice in *The Spanish Tragedy*." *Renaissance Drama* 8 (1965): 89–104.

Murray, Peter, B. *Thomas Kyd*. New York: Twayne, 1969.

Smith, Molly. "The Theatre and the Scaffold: Death as Spectacle in *The Spanish Tragedy*." *Studies in English Literature* 32.2 (Spring 1992): 217–37.

Talbert, Ernest W. *Eizabethan Drama and Shakespeare's Early Plays*. Chapel Hill: University of North Carolina Press, 1963.

VICKI JANIK

L

AEMILIA LANYER
(1569–1645)

BIOGRAPHY

Aemilia Lanyer's biography has been long confounded with Shakespearean* mythology since A. L. Rowse confidently identified her as the Dark Lady of Shakespeare's sonnets, a woman of dark complexion and bad reputation. Recently, Susanne Woods provides the most reliable account of her life. She was born in London in January 1569, the daughter of Baptist Bassano, a native of Venice and court musician to Queen Elizabeth, and his common-law wife, Margaret Johnson. As a young girl, she served, and was educated in, the household of Susan Wingfield, the countess of Kent. Early in the 1600s, she spent time at the country estate of Margaret, countess of Cumberland, whom she credits with fostering her poetry. Around 1587, at age eighteen, Aemilia became the mistress of Henry Cary, Lord Hunsdon, the queen's lord chamberlain, a man forty-five years her senior. Apparently upon becoming pregnant by him, she was hastily married to Alphonso Lanyer in October 1592 and early in 1593 she bore a son. Much of our knowledge about Lanyer during these years comes from the diary of Simon Forman, an astrologer whom she consulted several times in 1597. Forman indicates a growing sexual interest in Lanyer, which she declined to reciprocate, and thus the doubtfulness of his accounts of her character (''she was a hore and delt evill with him after'' [cited Woods, xxiii]). Rowse, however, used them to substantiate her immorality and hence, her suitability as a candidate for the Dark Lady. In 1598 Lanyer bore—and buried—an infant daughter, Odillya, and Woods suggests that its "name derives from combining 'ode' with her own name, 'Aemilia,' perhaps reflecting her developing identity as a poet" (xxv). Lanyer's only published work, *Salve Deus Rex Judaeorum* (1611), despite its wide net of dedicatory poems, apparently did not succeed in gaining Lanyer needed patrons, and she remained a marginal figure in court circles. Her husband's death in 1613 resulted in further financial hardship; for the next twenty years, Lanyer was involved in litigation with Alphonso's relatives over the control of his hay and grain monopoly. In 1617, she founded a school in St. Giles in the Field, a wealthy suburb of London. Unfortunately, we know nothing about the curriculum or her clientele, only that the enterprise was plagued by legal disputes with the landlord and discontinued in 1619. Lanyer outlived her son (who, like Alphonso, became a court musician) and died in 1645, at the venerable age of seventy-six.

MAJOR WORKS AND THEMES

Lanyer's only published work, *Salve Deus Rex Judaeorum*, is prefaced by eleven dedications addressed to women, including Queen Anne, the countess of Kent, Margaret, countess of Cumberland, and her daughter, and the countess of Pembroke, whose poetic heir Lanyer aspires to be. The epistle "To the vertuous Reader," addressed to women and men, is a defense of women's godly virtue and Lanyer's own authorship. The title poem, an 1,840–line meditation on the suffering and death of Christ, compliments the countess of Cumberland by imagining her as the primary devotee of Christ, the "Husband of [her] Soule" who "dying made her Dowager of all" (253, 257). Throughout Lanyer praises a God who favors the weak and powerless of this world ("unto the Meane he makes the Mightie bow, / And raiseth up the Poore out of the dust" [123–24]), including, of course, women. In her telling of the Passion, Lanyer expounds the faithlessness of Christ's male followers and depicts the wicked high priests and elders ranged "Against one siely, weake, unarmed man, / Who no resistance makes" (551–52). The emotional climax of the poem occurs as Pilate's wife intercedes for Christ. Lanyer places in her mouth a powerful defense of women, relieving them of the lion's share of blame for original sin:

> Till now your indiscretion sets us free,
> And makes our former fault much lesse appeare;
> Our Mother *Eve*, who tasted of the Tree,
> Giving to *Adam* what shee held most deare,
> Was simply good, and had no power to see,
> The after-comming harme did not appeare. (761–66)

This crime against Christ, springing from men's malice, is far worse than Eve's sin, she contends, for Eve was tricked. Moreover, Eve erred for love of Adam and "for knowledge sake" (797), while Adam compounded his wrong by stealing that knowledge: ''Yet Men will boast of Knowledge, which he tooke / From *Eves* faire hand, as from a learned Booke'' (807–8). On behalf of all women, she pleads

> Then let us have our Libertie againe,
> And challendge to your selves no Sov'raigntie;
> You came not in the world without our paine,
> Make that a barre against your crueltie. . . .
> If one weake woman simply did offend,
> This sinne of yours, hath no excuse, nor end. (825–32)

Like Christ himself, Pilate's wife, whose voice blends with that of Lanyer, emerges as the champion of the weak and oppressed. Next, the evil men are superseded by virtuous women: the daughters of Jerusalem, the Virgin Mary, the faithful women at the foot of the cross, and the Marys who find the empty tomb. Among them, Lanyer places the countess. Inviting her to meditate upon and even embrace the body of her divine spouse—''His lips like skarlet threeds, yet much more sweet / Than is the sweetest hony dropping dew'' (1314–15)—Lanyer strikingly applies the erotic imagery of Canticles (Song of Songs, Song of Solomon) to Christ. She then represents the countess in her many works of Christian mercy, as she becomes a figure for the true spouse of Christ, the church in the world, and a model of devotion who surpasses even Old Testament heroines such as Hester, Susanna, and the queen of Sheba.

Lanyer's volume concludes with ''The Description of Cookeham,'' which may predate Jonson's* ''To Penshurst,'' long considered the first country-house poem. This poem completes the volume's emphasis on female community as Lanyer laments the loss of a paradise of three women called away from Cookeham by the events of the countess' widowhood and her daughter's marriage; the poet, too, is forced to abandon an idyllic setting associated with the flourishing of her own poetry.

CRITICAL RECEPTION

Only within the last ten years has Lanyer's poetry received any serious critical attention. Rowse, committed to the fantasy that Lanyer was the Dark Lady, disavowed any interest in her as a poet. Barbara K. Lewalski has done the most to reclaim Lanyer and to place her work in the context of Protestant poetics, patronage, and feminist criticism. Though Lanyer's ''feminist perceptions can be rendered only in terms of the discourse of Scripture, . . . they force a radical imaginative rewriting of its patriarchal norms to place women at the center'' (*Writing Women*, 219). For Wall, Lanyer writes both ''within and against an ideologically problematic discourse'' (53). Specifically, she refashions Petrarchism and empowers herself as a female poet by presenting the ''spritualized and eroticized body of Christ'' (64) as the object of the female gaze. On the other hand, Beilin, though she emphasizes Lanyer's ''quintessentially feminine poetic consciousness'' (179), emphasizes the work's conventional devotional contexts, within which Lanyer presents women as the epitome of Christian virtue. Differing from Beilin, McGrath finds Lanyer's devotional stance a ''coded cover'' for her writing project, one purpose of which is to claim for women active subjectivity in their experiences of religion and writing.

Lanyer's poetry clearly foregrounds women's virtuous relationships and claims for them a privileged place in the Christian community, while offering alternative, even subversive, interpretations of Scripture and tradition. Further research would situate Lanyer with regard to the emerging tradition of women's writing in the seventeenth century, uncovering possible references to her work, voices echoing hers, or similar treatment of biblical material. Especially fruitful might be the writings of women involved in sectarian religious activity. Even readers of *Paradise Lost* have wondered if Milton's account of Adam's and Eve's responsibilities for the Fall in Book IX is in part a response to a subversive exegesis like Lanyer's. Surely Lanyer's work participates in—or even inaugurates—a tradition of revisionist, protofeminine scriptural exegesis in the seventeenth century, as well as engaging the centuries-old *querelle des femmes*.

BIBLIOGRAPHY

Works by Aemilia Lanyer

The Poems of Aemilia Lanyer: Salve Deus Rex Judaeorum. Ed. Susanne Woods. Oxford: Oxford University Press, 1993.

The Poems of Shakespeare's Dark Lady: Salve Deus Rex Judaeorum, by Emilia Lanier. Introduction by A. L. Rowse. London: Jonathan Cape, 1978.

Studies of Aemilia Lanyer

Beilin, Elaine V. ''The Feminization of Praise: Aemilia Lanyer.'' In *Redeeming Eve: Women Writers of the English Renaissance.* Princeton: Princeton University Press, 1987, 177–207.

Lewalski, Barbara K. ''Imagining Female Community: Aemilia Lanyer's Poems.'' *Writing Women in Jacobean England.* Cambridge: Harvard University Press, 1993.

———. ''Of God and Good Women: The Poems of Aemilia Lanyer.'' In *Silent but for the Word: Tudor Women as Patrons, Translators, and Writers of Religious Works*, ed. Margaret P. Hannay. Kent, OH: Kent State University Press, 1985, 203–24.

———. ''Rewriting Patriarchy and Patronage: Margaret Clifford, Anne Clifford, and Aemilia Lanyer.'' *Yearbook of English Studies* 21 (1991): 87–106.

McGrath, Lynette. '' 'Let Us Have Our Libertie Againe': Aemilia Lanier's 17th-Century Feminist Voice.'' *Women's Studies* 20 (1992): 331–48.

Wall, Wendy. ''Our Bodies/Our Texts?: Renaissance Women and the Trials of Authorship.'' In *Anxious Power: Reading, Writing, and Ambivalence in Narrative by Women*, ed. Carol J. Singley and Susan Elizabeth Sweeney. Albany: State University of New York Press, 1993, 51–71.

LISA MARY KLEIN

SIR DAVID LINDSAY OF THE MOUNT
(1490–1555)

BIOGRAPHY

Sir David Lindsay of the Mount was closely connected to the Scottish royal court for most of his life. Evidence suggests that he may have been employed there as early as 1508, but his intimacy with the royal family was established by 1512, when he was made usher to the prince. At fifteen months, in September 1513, James V acceded to the throne, and Lindsay later addressed many of his poems to this monarch. Between 1512 and 1523, in the sometimes stormy period of James' minority rule, Lindsay is described as ''Keeper of the King's Grace, Usher, Master Usher, and Gentleman of the Bedchamber or Household of the king'' (Edington, 17). As a member of the court, Lindsay was close to the center of power, which was at this time precarious. A notable instance of this was his sudden dismissal from court in 1524, when Margaret Tudor, in an attempt to isolate her son from his former companions, gave the position of master usher to Andrew, Lord Avondale, later to become her brother-in-law. The record of Lindsay's activity in the next few years is slight. He is twice referred to as the previous usher, and in 1526 he received a gown and velvet for a doublet (Edington, 22). In *The Complaint* (1530), Lindsay refers to himself in this period as being trampled down into the dust and not daring to be seen in open court (256, 289–90).

When James' personal rule began in 1529, Lindsay was back in favor, employed first as a herald, then, sometime in the 1530s, knighted and made Lyon king of arms. The Lyon king, Scotland's chief heraldic officer, governed the royal officers of arms and was responsible for the court's heraldry, as well as its entertainment and spectacle, its tournaments, marriages, plays, and pageants. Lindsay also performed diplomatic functions for James, at various times traveling to Flanders, France, England, Denmark, and perhaps Italy. For two decades, armed with considerable power and responsibility, Lindsay was in the midst of the practical workings of kingship and chivalry, in a notable position to assess their strengths and failings. The poetry and the drama that he produced so prolifically from 1528 onward suggest that he observed carefully and that he both enriched and was enriched by the Scottish court's humanist milieu in the early sixteenth century.

Though Lindsay was less closely attached to the court after James' death in 1542 and spent more time at the Mount near Cupar, he was more than once called upon for special missions and for his council. He attended Parliament in 1544 and 1545. In 1548, while on a mission in Denmark, he was detained by weather for at least a month. It is possible that as a vocal critic of the Scottish church, he would have met exiled religious dissidents, including John MacAlpine and John Gau, and experienced firsthand Denmark's Lutheranism

(Edington, 64). On 7 June 1552, *The Cupar Banns* announced a performance of Lindsay's *Ane Satyre of the Thrie Estatis*. His death was recorded in the Register of the Privy Seal in April 1555.

MAJOR WORKS AND THEMES

Lindsay's major works (with their abbreviated titles) are *The Dreme* (1528), *The Complaynt* (1530), *The Testament of the Papyngo* (1530), *The Complaint of Bagsche* (1530–42), *The Flyting* (1537), *The Deploratioun* (1537), *The Iusting* (1538–40), *The Tragedie of the Cardinal* (after 1547), *The Historie of Squyer Meldrum* (1550), *Ane Satyre of the Thrie Estatis* (1552), and *The Monarche* (1553).

Lindsay's early years at court, in a formative period of his life, may account for the fact that however satirical as a poet and dramatist, he remained loyal to the ideal of kingship and to the human qualities that constituted its effective realization. The official records, especially the *Accounts of the Lord High Treasurer of Scotland*, supply the dates and descriptions of Sir David Lindsay's association with the court. His poetry, however, gives us the rare glimpses of his person, his day-to-day relationship with the young king, and the habits of the court that employs him. Unlike the other court poets, Dunbar and Douglas, Lindsay portrays the courtly experience with personal directness, verging on intimacy:

> Quhen thow wes young, I bure the in myne arme
> Full tenderlie, tyll thow begouth to gang,
> And in thy bed oft happit the full warme,
> With lute in hand, syne, sweitlie to the sang:
> Sometyme, in dansing, feiralie I flang;
> And, sumtyme, playand fairsis on the flure.

(*The Dreme*, 8–13)

Elsewhere, Lindsay observes the implications to the young king and thus to Scotland of the political upheaval surrounding the departure of Albany, the ruler of Scotland during a period of the king's minority (1515–17, 1521, and 1523–24):

> The kyng was bot twelf yeiris of aige,
> Quhen new rewlaris come, in thare raige,
> For commoun weill makand no care
> Bot for thare proffeit singulair,
> Imprudentlie, lyk wytles fullis,
> Thay tuke that young Prince from the sculis,
> Quhare he, vnder obedience
> Was lernand vertew and science,
> And haistelie plat in his hand
> The gouernance of all Scotland.

(*The Complaynt*, 127–36)

Or he gives us more generally a sense of the sudden changes implicit in court life:

> The courte cheangeith, sumtyme, with sic outrage,
> That few or none may makyng resistance,
> And sparis nocht the price more than the paige,
> As weill apperith be experience.
>
> (*The Testament of the Papyngo*, 409–12)

This is poetry rich in historical detail, in the particulars of a given monarch's reign, but it has broader appeal as well. Lindsay is interested in the commonweal, in enlightened leadership, in education, and his poems (see especially *The Dreme* and *The Monarche*) move freely from the individual to eternity and back. Informed by the secular and spiritual traditions of governance described by Aristotle and St. Augustine, his work—especially his play, *Ane Satyre of the Thrie Estatis*—is remarkably frank in its criticism of abuses both ecclesiastical and secular. Lindsay repeatedly addresses those human failings, including laziness, greed, ambition, sensuality, and pride, in the court and outside it, that weaken the body politic. Kings, clerics, court flatterers, and commoners are all subject to his satiric pen. His poetry, but especially his satire, seeks to effect moral reform in the individual and in the commonwealth.

As herald and then as Lyon king of arms in the court of James V, Lindsay had an unusual outlet for his versatile talent. The socially relevant themes of his poetry and its breadth of style and genre suggest that he found a ready and sophisticated audience for his poetry both in the court and beyond it. He is at ease in a serious mode, as well as in a comic one, and in genres including the dream vision, beast fable, complaint, tragedy, debate, and dramatic allegory. Many of Lindsay's works—in addition to *Ane Satyre of the Thrie Estatis*, which is explicitly dramatic, performed both at the court and in Cupar—give the sense of the conflict essential to drama. His work is rich in dialogue and gives its audience characters, whether allegorical or not, generating discussion and probing the sources of society's shortcomings. To this purpose, Lindsay, like Langland, mixes allegory and vivid, realistic detail. John the Common Weal, who appears in both *The Dreme* and *Ane Satyre of the Thrie Estatis*, recalls Langland's *Piers the Plowman*; in *The Dreme*, he departs Scotland, vowing not to return "tyll that I see the cuntre gydit / Be wysedome of ane gude and prudent king" (1004–5). As with Langland, the objects of Lindsay's concern are wide-ranging and move easily from the personal level, to the spiritual, from "wantoun wyffis," to "Memento Mori" (*The Monarche*, 2693, 6271).

Like Gavin Douglas, whom he admired exceedingly (see especially *The Papyngo*, 24–36), Lindsay was aware of educating his readers, of exposing them in the vernacular to material that was until recently available only to the scholar:

> Quhowbeit that diuers deuote cunnyng Clerkis
> In Latyne toung hes wryttin syndrie bukis,

Our vnlernit knawis lytill of thare werkis,
More than thay do the rauying of the Rukis.
Quharefore to Colyearis, Cairtaris & to Cukis,—
To Iok and Thome,—my Ryme sall be diractit,
With cunnyng men quhowbeit it wylbe lactit.

(*The Monarche*, 545–51)

CRITICAL RECEPTION

David Lindsay could not have anticipated what a household word his name would become. After the Scottish Reformation of 1560, he was more read than any other poet of his period, his works in the library of cottage and castle. Indeed, what was not worth knowing was dismissed with the proverbial, "Ye'll nae find that in Davie Lyndsay." "Out o'Davie Lyndsay into *Wallace*," came to describe a student's promotion, and as late as 1792, Robert Herson remembers Lindsay being "esteemed little less necessary in every family than the Bible" and writes that it was "common to have, by memory, great part of his poetry." Lindsay's popularity shows up in Walter Scott's novels as well (Murison, ix–x). In *Redgauntlet*, for example,

> . . . the carles sat ower a stoup of brandy, and Hutcheon, who was something of a clerk, would have read a chapter of the Bible; but Dougal wad hear naething but a blaud of Davie Lindsay, whilk was the waur preparation.

As late as 1800, printed editions of Lindsay's work were far more numerous than those of Henryson and Dunbar. Indeed, so pervasive was Lindsay's influence on Scottish language and culture that we might abandon the term "Scottish Chaucerian" and call him instead the Scot's Chaucer.

In the nineteenth century both the Early English Text Society and the Scottish Text Society brought out Lindsay's complete works, but he is less admired than in his own age. In the twentieth century, C. S. Lewis found Lindsay lacking "the originality of Henryson and the brilliance of Dunbar and Douglas" but added, that "what there is of him is good all through" (*English Literature in the Sixteenth Century*, 100). Since then, when not neglected, Lindsay has often been faulted for precisely that historical presence and popular appeal that make him so fascinating.

The recent publication of Carol Edington's excellent and wide-ranging *Court and Culture in Renaissance Scotland: Sir David Lindsay of the Mount* sets Lindsay scholarship on a new footing. This book is sure to encourage further study of Lindsay. It is not insignificant that the expression "Scottish Chaucerian" simply does not occur in Edington's study, which focuses on the courtier and poet, Sir David Lindsay, in the intellectually rich milieu of sixteenth-century Scotland.

BIBLIOGRAPHY

Works by Sir David Lindsay of the Mount

For editions of Lindsay's poetry and his play printed up to 1602, see bibliography in Edington.

Ane Satyre of the Thrie Estatis. Ed. J. Kinsley. London, 1954.

The Poetical Works of Sir David Lyndsay. 3 vols. Ed. David Laing. Edinburgh, 1879. (This includes facsimilies of the title pages of chief previous editions.)

The Poetical Works of Sir David Lyndsay of the Mount. 3 vols. Ed. George Chalmers. London, 1806.

Sir David Lindsay of the Mount: Ane Satyre of the Thrie Estatis. Ed. R. J. Lyall. Edinburgh, 1989.

The Works of Sir David Lindsay. 5 vols. Ed. J. H. Murray. London: Early English Text Society, 1865–71.

The Works of Sir David Lindsay of the Mount. 4 vols. Ed. Douglas Hamer. Edinburgh: Scottish Text Society, 1931–36.

Studies of Sir David Lindsay of the Mount

Edington, Carol. *Court and Culture in Renaissance Scotland: Sir David Lindsay of the Mount*. Amherst: University of Massachusetts Press 1994.

Fox, Denton. "The Scottish Chaucerians." In *Chaucer and Chaucerians: Critical Studies in Middle English Literature*, ed. D. S. Brewer. Tuscaloosa, AL: University of Alabama Press, 1966.

Graf, Claude. "Theatre and Politics: Lindsay's *Satyre of the Thrie Estaitis* in *Bards and Makars*." Glasgow: University of Glasgow Press 1977, 143–55.

Kantrowitz, Joanne Spencer. *Dramatic Allegory: Lindsay's "Ane Satyre of the Thrie Estaitis."* Lincoln: University of Nebraska Press, 1975.

Lewis, C. S. *English Literature in the Sixteenth Century, excluding Drama*. Oxford: Clarendon Press, 1954.

Murison, J. *Sir David Lyndsay: Poet and Satirist of the Old Church in Scotland*. Cambridge: Cambridge University Press, 1938.

MICHAELA PAASCHE GRUDIN

THOMAS LODGE
(1558–1625)

BIOGRAPHY

Thomas Lodge, best known for his euphuistic prose romance *Rosalynd*, was born in 1558 in London into a family of London mayors. His father, Sir Thomas Lodge, would serve as lord mayor of London for the 1562–63 term, and his mother, Lady Anne Lodge, was the stepdaughter of William Laxton, who had been lord mayor of London from 1544 to 1545. This eminent social status was admittedly weakened by Sir Thomas Lodge's bankruptcy following his mayoralty in 1564, and this may have contributed to young Thomas Lodge's later belief that "virtue is not measured by birth but by action," as he states at the conclusion of *Rosalynd* (139). This may be his central theme. Despite his father's financial straits, Lodge's early education was rich in classics and brought him into contact with major literary figures of the time. As a boy, Lodge was a page in the home of Henry Stanley, earl of Derby, where he undoubtedly received an introduction to the classics and to the Roman Catholicism he later embraced. In 1571 he began his formal education at the Merchant Taylor's school, where Thomas Kyd* was also enrolled and where Edmund Spenser* had attended only a few years prior. After two years at Merchant Taylor's, Lodge left for Trinity College, Oxford, where he studied under Edward Hoby (son of Thomas Hoby*) and must have known John Lyly,* whose prose style known as euphuism he later emulated.

After earning a bachelor of arts degree in 1577, Lodge returned to London and was admitted to Lincoln's Inn as a law student. He apparently gave up the study of law before earning a degree. However, he did make important literary connections there. Lodge first gained literary notice in 1580 for his "Defence of Plays" (sometimes called "Honest Excuses"), which was refused for publication but circulated privately by Lodge himself. He wrote this defense of the theater in answer to the Puritan sentiments of Stephen Gosson, who had published an attack on drama and music entitled "The School of Abuse," also, apparently, answered by Philip Sidney.* Gosson responded to Lodge with a further treatise entitled "Plays Confuted in Five Actions," in which he personally slanders Lodge. Lodge closed the public rivalry with his first published work, entitled "An Alarum for Usurers," in which he departs from the personal attacks in which he and Gosson had both indulged. During these early years in London, Lodge developed a friendship with Robert Greene,* with whom he later collaborated in writing the play *A Looking Glass for London*, in 1587. Additionally, he was at least acquainted with Barnabe Rich,* whose romance entitled *The Stronge and Wonderful Adventures of Don Simonides* he revised while imprisoned for heresy (for his Catholic leanings) in 1581. To Rich's romance Lodge prefixed dolorous verse bemoaning his muse's desertion of him: "long distresse hath laied [my] Muse to rest." In addition to suffering accusations of heresy, by 1584, Lodge was in financial difficulties. Perhaps to alleviate these stresses, he entered the army for a brief stint in 1586 and went on a sea voyage with Captain Clarke to the Canaries and the Azores in 1586, which continued into 1587. In apparent repossession of his errant muse, he published two plays, a major collection of poetry, the euphuistic pastoral romance *Rosalynd*, and over ten other literary works in the succeeding decade (1587–97). At the end of this prodigious period, Lodge renounced his literary career and entered the University of Avignon to study medicine.

In his later life, Lodge practiced medicine and translated works by Luis of Granada (a Catholic writer), Josephus, and Seneca. Although he was given license to practice medicine by Oxford in 1602, he was denied license in London in 1604, probably on the basis of his Catholicism. It is likely that the authorities could not condone the combination of the Catholic sentiments in Lodge's 1596 pamphlet *Prosopopeia*, his translation of Granada, and the known Catholic connections of his recent bride, Joan Aldred. He therefore returned to Belgium, where he worked as a physician until he was finally granted license to practice in London in 1610, where he lived and worked until he died of plague in 1625. In addition to his translations, Lodge published two medical works, *A Treatise on the Plague* in 1603 and a collection of medical cures entitled *The Poore Mans Talentt* in 1621.

MAJOR WORKS AND THEMES

As is apparent in *Rosalynd*, Lodge's work is often concerned with appropriate outward expressions of inward virtue. The actions of the virtuous person are done not for fame but for the good of others. Lodge dedicated his first published work, "An Alarum for Usurers," to Sir Philip Sidney, and in the opening words of this dedication Lodge clearly values virtuous actions above noble lineage. He writes, "It is not (noble Gentleman) the titles of Honour that allureth me, nor the nobilitie of your Parents that induceth me, but the admiration of your vertues that perswadeth me, to publish my pore travailes under your undoubted protection" (3). Lodge repeats this ideal in the dying words of the character Sir John in the opening pages of the romance: "Let your country's care be your heart's content, and think that you are not born for yourselves, but to level your thoughts to be loyal to your prince, careful to the common weal, and faithful to your friends" (11). In *Rosalynd*, the sons of Sir John of Bordeaux must prove themselves worthy of the duke's dying admonitions. Youngest son, Rosader, while steadfast, must yet perform acts to match his noble character, and Saladyne, errant from gentlemanly comport, must be reformed by Dame Fortune.

The euphuistic style and pastoral idealism of the work may give some readers cause to underestimate *Rosalynd*, rife as it is with humorous and typically alliterative euphuistic puns; for example, Sir John tells his sons that "women are wantons, and yet men cannot want one" (12). However, Lodge intentionally sets up a hall of mirrors in introducing the work that produces a narrative stance broad enough to contend with any voices of dissent. First Lodge dedicates the work, which he calls "the work of a soldier and a scholar," to Lord Hunsdon, so that he might be "under the favour of so martial and learned a patron" (5). After thus arraying himself with both the "launce and the bay," he offers an address to the gentlemen readers in which he further hedges his bets (7). He begins, "[L]ook not here to find any sprigs of Pallas' bay tree" because "they be matters above my capacity" (7). He claims to be "a soldier and a sailor" bursting with passion whose labors were "wrought in the ocean, when every line was wet with a surge" (7). Furthermore, he asserts that those who find the work perhaps too wet (highly emotional) might be a Momus or a Midas who may "find fault with the tackling, when he knows not the shrowdes" (8). In other words, Lodge is saying that if you find it beyond your taste for passions, you are not playing the game in earnest—only those with a serious sense of humor need apply. The message is profound if you accept the messenger in the spirit in which it is written.

The mirrors do not end there. The full title of the work is *Rosalynde. Euphues Golden Legacy: found after his death in his Cell at Silexedra*, and following his epistle to the gentlemen readers Lodge includes a dedication supposedly written by John Lyly's fictional character Euphues himself, to his friend Philautus. In his dedicatory letter, Euphues explains that the book *Rosalynd* is for the sons of his friend in order to teach them that "virtue is the king of labours, opinion the mistress of fools" (Shakespeare Classics, edition xxx). Euphues ends his dedication by advising his friend "that instead of worldly goods [he] leave [his] sons virtue and glory" (xxx). Thus, having attributed the book to a soldier and a scholar, then disclaiming the scholar and claiming the passion of the sailor and of the sea and further espousing earned rather than inherited gentility or refinement, Lodge begins the work in "earnest," which, as we know, begins with Sir John's admonitions to his sons regarding the same earned gentility. Thus, Lodge presents an ideal model wrapped in layers of disguises for his narrative voice. The effect is as if he were saying to us, "Here is the ideal; I know it is high flown, but it is nonetheless crucial to aim for it." If Lodge had simply presented the euphuistic pastoral ideal without narrative distance, as it were, readers may have more easily laughed off his Arden. Lodge's layers of dedication say to the reader, "I know you know I know, so let's agree to suspend our cynicism" perhaps in the spirit of earnest game or serious jesting. This spirit of serious jest permeates the work since Rosalynd herself takes on layers of disguise by playing Ganymede, who then pretends to be Rosalynd. Shakespeare* certainly saw this potential in *Rosalynd.*

While the plot of the dying father and his three sons was provided to Lodge by the medieval tale of Gamylen, this source contains neither Rosalynde nor the romance theme. Often people study Lodge's romance today because it is the main source for Shakespeare's *As You Like It.* To *Rosalynd*, Shakespeare added Touchstone and Jacques (who may be based on Lodge himself) and streamlined the plot. Where Lodge presents the story in the euphuistic style of Lyly, Shakespeare's quick-witted dialogue extends the irony that Lodge more subtly provides through his dedicatory devices.

In *Alarum against Usurers*, his first published work, Lodge realistically describes the practices of London usurers to whom he had himself fallen victim. At the time that he was writing *Alarum*, Lodge was in financial difficulties, having spent what inheritance was left him through an extravagant lifestyle made possible by the financing of such usurers. Thus, in his *Alarum*, in typically euphuistic simile, Lodge warns those who might "become meate for [usurers'] mouths . . . to shunne the Scorpion ere she devoureth" (3). This attempt to expose depravity through realistic depiction of lowlife in London in *Alarum* is an early example of the style that came to fruition in the work of Robert Greene, Thomas Dekker,* and Ben Jonson.* Furthermore this "realistic" element probably led to Lodge's later satirical mode. In his *Defence of Plays*, Lodge voices the need for a satirist who will "discypher the abuses of the worlde" and thus "ryd our assemblies" of such "notorious offenders" (39). Perhaps this was an announcement of his intention to write what later appeared as *A Fig for Momus*, a collection of satirical poems and epistles. While John Skelton,* Thomas Wyatt,* George Gascoigne,* and Edward Hake preceded Lodge in writing Tudor satire, Lodge was among the first (with John Donne and Bishop Hall) to publish satire in English that follows the classical model of formal epistle in verse (in Horace's and Juvenal's mode) in heroic couplets—the form that appears in *A Fig for Momus*—to match Latin hexameters.

Lodge wrote two plays, *A Looking Glass for London* (in collaboration with Robert Greene) and *Wounds of Civill War. Wounds*, which depicts the events of the civil wars in Rome during 88 to 78 B.C. in chronological fashion, is one of the earliest extant plays that attempt an accurate sequence of historical events. *A Looking Glass for London* is better crafted than *Wounds*, but it is often assigned the dubious accolade of being the last medieval morality play complete with Heywood's traditional Vice character. Unlike *Wounds, Looking Glass* enjoyed some popularity in its own time. It was performed repeatedly in 1592 and reprinted four times, in 1598, 1602, 1605, and 1617.

Debate over the transmission of influence between Lodge and Christopher Marlowe arises here because of similarities between *Wounds* and *Tamburlaine* and between *Looking Glass* and *Dr. Faustus.* Doubts regarding the dates of composition of all four plays feed this controversy. There is a triumph scene in *Wounds* in which Sylla enters sitting in a chariot drawn by people he has conquered. Similarly, in *Tamburlaine*, after his wife, Zenocrate, has died, Tamburlaine enters in a chariot drawn by kings he has recently conquered. Many critics assert that this shows Lodge was influenced by Marlowe. However, Marlowe uses the device much more dramatically. The kings have bits in their mouths, and Tamburlaine has "reins in his left hand, and in his right hand a whip." It seems to me more likely that Marlowe enlarged the idea from Lodge and unlikely that Lodge would use such a dramatic scene from Marlowe in a weakened form.

There may be a similar transmission between *Looking Glass* and *Faustus*. The repentance scenes of Lodge's Usurer and Marlowe's Faustus contain obvious parallels. In the words of Lodge's Usurer:

> Hell gapes for me, heaven will not hold my soule.
> You mountains shroude me from the God of truth.
> Mee-thinkes I see him sit to judge the earth. . . .
> Cover me hilles, and shroude me from the lord. (61)

In the words of Faustus:

> And see where God
> Stretcheth out his arm and bends his ireful brows.
> Mountains and hills, come, come, and fall on me,
> And hide me from the heavy wrath of God. . . .

Earth, gape! O no, It will not harbor me! . . .
Ugly hell, gape not! (5.2. 147–87)

Since recent scholars tend to date *Looking Glass* at 1587 or 1588 and *Dr. Faustus* as perhaps as late as 1592, it is likely that Marlowe again developed this material from Lodge.

CRITICAL RECEPTION

In the words of one of Lodge's biographers, N. B. Paradise, "Lodge seems to have been always on the doorstep of Parnassus, but never to have quite succeeded in entering the company of the elect" (180). His contemporary Francis Meres mentions Lodge among those who were "best for comedy." Some critics argue that Greene's praise of the "young Juvenal, that biting satirist" in his *A Groatsworth of Wit* refers to Lodge. Thomas Nashe* may have described Lodge in his portrait of the "Prodigall Young Master" in *Pierce Penilesse.* Lodge may also have provided the basis for Shakespeare's *Venus and Adonis* in his *Glaucus and Scilla.* Although the only complete works of Lodge were not published until 1893, Lodge has received significant critical attention in the twentieth century. In addition to the several biographical works produced in the 1930s, bibliographies are complete through 1990. Among recent scholars to comment on Lodge are Arthur Kinney, who analyzes Lodge's contribution to a literature of humanism in the 1590s, and the new historicist Richard Helgerson, who examines Lodge's struggle to define a stable literary identity amid ethical and artistic conflicts. Most important to Lodge, I argue, was that he fulfill his own definition of success as expressed at the conclusion of *Rosalynd* that "virtue is not measured by birth but by action . . . [and] concord is the sweetest conclusion" (139). In this light I would say that Lodge succeeded in reaching his own Arden and did not find it apt to pursue Parnassus.

BIBLIOGRAPHY

Works by Thomas Lodge

The Complete Works of Thomas Lodge. 4 vols. Ed. Sir Edmund Gosse. London: Hunterian Club, 1883. (All references to this edition unless noted.)

Rosalynd. Euphues Golden Legacy. Ed. W. W. Greg. London: Chatto and Windus, 1907.

Studies of Thomas Lodge

Cuvelier, Eliane. *Thomas Lodge, Temoin de son Temps.* Paris: Didier Erudition, 1984.

Gosse, Sir Edmund. "Introduction." In *The Complete Works of Thomas Lodge,* ed. Edmund Gosse. 4 vols. London: Hunterian Club, 1883.

Kinney, Arthur. " 'O vita! misero longa, foelici brevis': Thomas Lodge's Struggle for Felicity." In *Humanist Poetics.* Amherst: University of Massachusetts Press, 1986, 363–423.

Lee, Sidney. "Thomas Lodge." In *Dictionary of National Biography,* vol. 12, ed. Leslie Stephen and Sidney Lee. London: Oxford University Press, 1921, 60–66.

Paradise, N. Burton. *Thomas Lodge, History of an Elizabethan.* New Haven, CT: Yale University Press, 1931.

Rae, Wesley D. *Thomas Lodge*. New York: Twayne, 1967.
Ryan, Pat M., Jr. *Thomas Lodge, Gentleman*. Hamden: Shoe String Press, 1958.
Sisson, Charles J. "Thomas Lodge and His Family." In *Thomas Lodge and Other Elizabethans*, ed. Charles J. Sisson. Cambridge: Harvard University Press, 1933, 1–163.
Tenney, Edward Andrews. *Thomas Lodge*. Ithaca, NY: Cornell University Press, 1935.
Walker, Alice. "Life of Thomas Lodge." *Review of English Studies* 9.36 (1933): 410–432.
———. "Life of Thomas Lodge (continued)." *Review of English Studies* 10.37 (1934): 46–54.
———. "Reading of an Elizabethan: Some Sources of the Prose Pamphlets of Thomas Lodge." *Review of English Studies* 8.31 (1932): 264–81.
Whitsworth, Charles W. "The Plays of Thomas Lodge." *Cahiers Elisabethan* 4 (1973): 3–14.

Bibliographies of Thomas Lodge

Donovan, Kevin. "Recent Studies in Thomas Lodge 1969–1990." *English Literary Renaissance* 23.1 (1993): 201–11.
Harner, James L. "Thomas Lodge." *English Renaissance Prose Fiction 1500–1660.* Boston: G. K. Hall, 1978, 266–86.
Houppert, Joseph. "Thomas Lodge." *Predecessors of Shakespeare: A Survey and Bibliography of Recent Studies in Renaissance Drama.* Lincoln: University of Nebraska Press, 1973, 153–60.
Johnson, Robert C. "Thomas Lodge, 1939–1965." In *Elizabethan Bibliographies Supplements, V: Robert Greene, 1945–1965; Thomas Lodge, 1939–1965; John Lyly, 1939–1965; Thomas Nashe, 1941–1965; George Peele, 1939–1965*, comp. Robert C. Johnson. London: Nether Press, 1968, 27–34.
Tannenbaum, Samuel A. *Elizabethan Bibliographies No. 2: Thomas Lodge*. New York: Samuel A. Tannenbaum, 1940.

SARAH HILSMAN

JOHN LYLY
(c. 1554–1606)

BIOGRAPHY

John Lyly was born in Kent around 1554. Grandfather William Lyly, who published a famous Latin grammar, was the first high master of St. Paul's School and a friend of Thomas More* and John Colet.* His father, Peter, was a minor ecclesiastical official. Lyly took M.A. degrees at both Oxford and Cambridge. In the late 1570s, he went to London to seek a place at court, hoping that his academic and literary abilities would serve to commend him.

Lyly's early success as a prose writer brought celebrity but no serious courtly recognition. His two narratives, *Euphues: The Anatomy of Wit* (1579) and *Euphues and His England* (1580), were very popular, the first being reprinted five times and the second four times by 1581. Their success brought Lyly to the attention of Lord Burghley, who offered some work; however, not until writing plays for the boys' acting companies of the Chapel Royal and St. Paul's cathedral did Lyly gain a notable, if not important, position. The plays were performed at Blackfriars Theater and at court before the queen, and Lyly was appointed "vice-master" of the St. Paul's company. He remained set on becoming the master of revels, and during the 1590s, as time passed, and he did not get the position, he directly petitioned Elizabeth, declaring his faithful service and unrewarded merit. The letters have a shrill, almost desperate tone and were ignored.

Lyly served in Parliament from 1589. He married and had three children. He died in relative obscurity, not having realized the courtly career he had wanted, his literary and dramatic style superseded and at times a target of parody.

MAJOR WORKS AND THEMES

Lyly's writing falls into two phases, the initial prose period, when the two parts of *Euphues* appeared, and the period after 1581, when he wrote eight plays—first *Campaspe*, then *Sapho and Phao, Endimion, Gallathea, Mydas, Mother Bombie, The Woman in the Moon*, and *Love's Metamorphosis*. He is also known to have written some Latin verses in praise of the queen (1597) and an anti-Puritan tract, "Pappe with an Hatchet" (1589).

There are stylistic and thematic continuities through the two phases of Lyly's work. He uses prose in all of the plays except *The Woman in the Moon*, written in blank verse. The main stylistic link is the rhetorical pattern known as euphuism—series of short clauses, using similar syntax and figures of speech, including antithesis, alliteration, and similes drawn from natural history and classical mythology. These sequences are first used in *Euphues* but reappear in the mouths of many of the dramatic characters. Euphues' perception of his queen's glory employs the repetitive pattern of like clauses: "[A]n other sight there is in my glass, which maketh me sigh for grief I cannot show it . . . the more I go about to express the brightness, the more I find my eyes bleared, the nearer I desire to come to it, the farther I seem from it" (2:203–4). Hephestion's misogynist denunciation in *Campaspe* shows this patterning along with the use of natural similes: "I, but she is beautiful; yea, but not therefore chaste; I, but she is comely in all parts of the body: yea, but she may be crooked in some part of the mind. . . . Beauty is like the blackberry, which seemeth red, when it is not ripe, resembling precious stones that are polished with honey, which the smoother they look, the sooner they break. . . . Hermyns have fair skins, but foul livers; sepulchres fresh colors, but rotten bones, women fair faces, but false hearts" (2.2.45–57). This style became very popular, its witty and ornate tone, wide range of allusions and maxims, repetitive rhythm, and flamboyant finish animating readers and audiences.

Euphuism is meant to be heard and read; it is a sign of the sixteenth-century transition from oral to written culture. The striking parts of both *Euphues* texts are set speeches, usually delivered as advice or counsel by one character to another. The declamatory style of these passages anticipates the plays. Though the narrator is not strongly present, the ornate rhetoric allows for degrees of narrative irony that may relativize or undercut the characters' viewpoints. Lyly's work in both genres shows the important influence of rhetorical models and concepts in humanist education and literature during the Elizabethan period (Altman, Kinney).

There are various thematic links between the prose and dramatic works. *Euphues* tells of a bright youth's experiences of love, friendship, and social intrigue. The protagonist undergoes lessons on youthful arrogance, impetuous romance, superficial social style, moral and patriotic integrity. The didactic motives continue in the drama, with the virtues of male solidarity and patriotism extolled in *Campaspe* and *Endimion* and the pitfalls of romance revealed there and in *Sapho and Phao, Love's Metamorphosis*, and *The Woman in the Moon*. In contrast to *Euphues*, the plays develop a sustained and at times complex depiction of court politics, with issues such as submission and resistance to power being raised in these plays and also in *Midas*. That the plays were performed before the queen suggests that Lyly was tactfully presenting demands for patronage along with views on court affairs, which sometimes included specific events such as the mooted marriage of Elizabeth to the Duc d'Alençon in the early 1580s (Berry, Bevington). The prevailing system of Petrarchan politics and service to the queen, mingling questions of sexuality and power, is also intimated in plays such as *Gallathea, Campaspe, Endimion*, and *Sapho and Phao*.

Just as *Euphues* has been seen as important for the development of narrative method, so Lyly's plays are significant in the development of drama. The genre of allegorical romance enables subtle depictions of various themes at once, often inviting an active interpretive response from the audience (Gohlke). The issues are presented from different angles, with characters' views weighed against one another. A key structural element aiding thematic debate is a comic subplot, often questioning or parodying the major characters' preoccupations. Thus, in *Campaspe* rebellious servants reflect the main plot's thoughts on the limits of loyal service, while in *Endimion* a burlesque romance gently mocks the selfless devotion of the hero to his queen.

The plays are noteworthy for their theatricality and staging. The key techniques are multiple staging and allegorical characterization. Multiple staging uses three ''houses'' to represent key locations. They are on stage at all times, possibly curtained off when not in use. In *Sapho and Phao*, for example, the three houses are Sapho's chamber, Sybilla's cave, and Vulcan's forge; in *Endimion*, they are Endimion's lunary bank, Corsites' castle, and Geron's fountain. In front of these locations is a kind of free space, used for general action and movement. With the houses juxtaposed, visual comparisons can be prolonged throughout the play, sustaining points of conflict between the characters and their perspectives (Saccio).

These viewpoints are amplified through trios of central characters—Alexander, Apelles, and Campaspe; Sapho, Phao, and Venus; Cynthia, Endimion, and Tellus—who represent different ideas of love, loyal service, and earthly desire. As dramatic personae and abstractions (Cynthia is a queen in the action and an archetype of chaste majesty; Endimion, a courtier and an ideal of loyal service; Tellus, a lady-in-waiting and an image of desire), the characters and their locations articulate contesting principles of subjection and sovereignty. With their simple but effective staging and structure, Lyly's plays form an interesting midpoint between the first Tudor revels under Henry VII and the elaborate Stuart masques of Ben Jonson* and Inigo Jones.

CRITICAL RECEPTION

The immediate popularity of *Euphues* saw Lyly become a topic of critical judgment and opinion. In his 1586 *Discourse of English Poetrie*, William Webbe rates Lyly as the rhetorical peer of Demosthenes and Cicero. In *Palladis Tamia* (1598), Francis Meres praises him as one of the most eloquent comic writers. A number of authors, including Robert Greene* and Thomas Lodge,* wrote euphuistic sequels, and in publishing six of his comedies in 1632 Edward Blount declared that Lyly had reinvented English. On the other hand, Philip Sidney* in *Astrophil and Stella* and *The Defence of Poetry*, Thomas Nashe* in *Summer's Last Will and Testament*, and Ben Jonson in *Every Man out of His Humor* and *Cynthia's Revels* criticize or caricature Lyly's work. Shakespeare* echoes Lyly in early romantic comedies such as *Love's Labor's Lost* and *A Midsummer Night's Dream* but also parodies his stylistic excesses in those plays and has Falstaff voice some satiric versions of euphuistic maxims in *1 Henry IV* (2.5.401–22) as excessively courtly.

C. S. Lewis considers Lyly a writer of poetic genius, delicate touch, and stylistic flexibility who marks the shift from "drab" to "golden" literature. Subsequent criticism tends to fall into two camps: one focusing on the potential for romantic and moral complexity realized by Lyly's generic and rhetorical modes (e.g., Barish, Gannon, Houppert, Meyer, White), and the other considering the texts' effects and functions in Elizabethan court discourse and politics (e.g., Axton, Bates, Caldwell, Lancashire, Margolies). Extended studies of Lyly's work such as Hunter's *John Lyly: The Humanist as Courtier* and Saccio's *Court Comedies* combine these perspectives to examine ways in which Lyly's conscious artistry figures and participates in court relations.

In concluding a bibliography of criticism on Lyly since 1969, Kevin J. Donovan notes "the prominence . . . of questions of authority and gender" in his work (446). A number of recent studies focus on these topics, especially in the plays, where issues including submission and resistance, gender and identity, and sexual politics are often raised but not decisively resolved. The lack of finality that surrounds Endimion's and Phao's unrequited desires or seems glossed over in reconciling Gallathea's and Phillida's same-sex passion is considered a sign of complex notions of selfhood and desire at the end of the Elizabethan period (Bevington, Davis, Rackin, Rose).

BIBLIOGRAPHY

Works by John Lyly

An Anthology of Elizabethan Prose Fiction. In *Euphes: The Anatomy of Wit*. Ed. Paul Salzman. Oxford: Oxford University Press, 1987.

Campaspe and Sapho and Phao. Ed. David Bevington and G. K. Hunter. Manchester: Manchester University Press, 1991.

The Complete Works of John Lyly. 3 vols. Ed. R. Warwick Bond. Oxford: Clarendon, 1902. (Quotations are from this edition.)

The Dramatic Works of John Lyly. 2 vols. Ed. F. W. Fairholt. London: John Russell Smith, 1858.

Elizabethan Prose Fiction. In *Euphues: The Anatomy of Wit*. Ed. Merritt E. Lawliss. New York: Odyssey Press, 1967.

Euphues: The Anatomy of Wit. Ed. Morris W. Croll and Harry Clemons. London: Routledge, 1916.

Four Tudor Comedies. In *Mother Bombie*. Ed. William Tydeman. Harmondsworth: Penguin, 1984.

Gallathea. Drama of the English Renaissance. Ed. Russell A. Fraser and Norman Rabkin. New York: Macmillan, 1976.

Mother Bombie. Ed. Harriette Andreadis. Salzburg: Salzburg Studies in English Literature, 1975.

Studies of John Lyly

Altman, Joel B. *The Tudor Play of Mind: Rhetorical Inquiry and the Development of Elizabethan Drama*. Berkeley: University of California Press, 1978.

Axton, Marie. ''The Tudor Mask and Elizabethan Court Drama.'' *English Drama: Forms and Development*. Ed. Marie Axton and Raymond Williams. Cambridge: Cambridge University Press, 1977, 24–47.

Barish, Jonas. ''The Prose Style of John Lyly.'' *ELH* 23 (1956): 14–35.

Bates, Catherine. *The Rhetoric of Courtship in Elizabethan Language and Literature*. Cambridge: Cambridge University Press, 1992.

Bergeron, David M. ''The Education of Rafe in Lyly's *Gallathea*.'' *Studies in English Literature* 23 (1983): 197–206.

Berry, Philippa. *Of Chastity and Power: Elizabethan Literature and the Unmarried Queen*. London: Routledge, 1989.

Bevington, David. '' 'Jack hath not Jill': Failed Courtship in Lyly and Shakespeare.'' *Shakespeare Survey* 42 (1989): 1–13.

———. *Tudor Drama and Politics: A Critical Approach to Topical Meaning*. Cambridge: Harvard University Press, 1968.

Caldwell, Ellen M. ''John Lyly's *Gallathea*: A New Rhetoric of Love for the Virgin Queen.'' *English Literary Renaissance* 17 (1988): 22–40.

Davis, Lloyd. *Guise and Disguise: Rhetoric and Characterization in the English Renaissance*. Toronto: University of Toronto Press, 1993.

Donovan, Kevin J. ''Recent Studies in John Lyly (1969–1990).'' *English Literary Renaissance* 22 (1992): 435–50.

Gannon, C. C. "Lyly's *Endimion*: From Myth to Allegory." *English Literary Renaissance* 6 (1976): 220–43.

Gohlke, Madelon. "Reading *Euphues*." *Criticism* 19 (1977): 3–21.

Henderson, Judith Rice. "Euphues and His Erasmus." *English Literary Renaissance* 12 (1982): 135–61.

Hilliard, Stephen S. "Lyly's *Midas* as an Allegory of Tyranny." *Studies in English Literature* 12 (1972): 243–58.

Hodges, Devon L. *Renaissance Fictions of Anatomy*. Amherst: University of Massachusetts Press, 1985.

Houppert, Joseph W. *John Lyly*. Boston: Twayne, 1975.

Hunter, G. K. *John Lyly: The Humanist as Courtier*. Cambridge: Harvard University Press, 1962.

Jankowski, Theodora A. "The Subversion of Flattery: The Queen's Body in John Lyly's *Sapho and Phao*." *Medieval and Renaissance Drama in England* 5 (1991): 69–86.

Kinney, Arthur F. *Humanist Poetics: Thought, Rhetoric, and Fiction in Sixteenth-Century England*. Amherst: University of Massachusetts Press, 1986.

Lancashire, Anne. "John Lyly and Pastoral Entertainment." In *The Elizabethan Theatre, VIII*, ed. G. R. Hibbard. Port Credit, Ont.: Meany, 1982, 22–50.

Lenz, Carolyn Ruth Swift. "The Allegory of Wisdom in Lyly's *Endimion*." *Comparative Drama* 10 (1976): 235–57.

MacCabe, Richard A. "Wit, Eloquence, and Wisdom in *Euphues and the Anatomy of Wit*." *Studies in Philology* 81 (1984): 299–324.

Margolies, David. *Novel and Society in Elizabethan England*. London: Croom Helm, 1985.

Meyer, Robert J. " 'Pleasure Reconciled to Virtue': The Mystery of Love in Lyly's *Gallathea*." *Studies in English Literature* 21 (1981): 193–208.

Mittermann, Harald, and Herbert Schendl. *A Complete Concordance to the Novels of John Lyly*. Olms: Hildesheim, 1986.

Peterson, Douglas L. "Lyly, Greene, and Shakespeare and the Recreations of Princes." *Shakespeare Survey* 20 (1988): 67–88.

Rackin, Phyllis. "Androgyny, Mimesis, and the Marriage of the Boy Heroine on the English Renaissance Stage." *PMLA* 102 (1987): 29–41.

Roosador, Kurt Tetzeli von. "The Power of Magic: From *Endimion* to *The Tempest*." *Shakespeare Survey* 43 (1991): 1–13.

Rose, Mary Beth. *The Expense of Spirit: Love and Sexuality in English Renaissance Drama*. Ithaca, NY: Cornell University Press, 1988.

Saccio, Peter. *The Court Comedies of John Lyly: A Study in Allegorical Dramaturgy*. Princeton: Princeton University Press, 1969.

Salzman, Paul. *English Prose Fiction, 1558–1700: A Critical History*. Oxford: Clarendon, 1985.

Scragg, Leah. "John Lyly." In *Elizabethan Dramatists*, ed. Fredson Bowers. In *Dictionary of Literary Biography* 62 (1987): 196–211.

———. *The Metamorphosis of "Gallathea": A Study in Creative Adaptation*. Washington, DC: University of America Press, 1982.

Shulman, Jeff. "Ovidian Myth in Lyly's Courtship Comedies." *Studies in English Literature* 25 (1985): 249–69.

Steinberg, Theodore L. "The Anatomy of *Euphues*." *Studies in English Literature* 17 (1977): 27–38.

Stephanson, Raymond. "John Lyly's Prose Fiction: Irony, Humor and Anti-Humanism." *English Literary Renaissance* 11 (1981): 3–21.

Thomas, Susan D. "*Endimion* and Its Sources." *Comparative Literature* 30 (1978): 35–52.

Truchet, Sybil. "*Campaspe*: A Brave New World?" *Cahiers Elisabethains* 15 (1979): 17–28.

Weimann, Robert. "History and the Issue of Authority in Representation: The Elizabethan Theater and the Reformation." *New Literary History* 17 (1986): 449–76.

Weld, John. *Meaning in Comedy: Studies in Elizabethan Romantic Comedy*. Albany: State University of New York Press, 1975.

Westlund, Joseph. "The Theme of Tact in *Campaspe*." *Studies in English Literature* 16 (1976): 213–21.

White, R. S. "Metamorphosis by Love in Elizabethan Romance, Romantic Comedy, and Shakespeare's Early Comedies." *Review of English Studies* 35 (1984): 14–44.

LLOYD DAVIS

M

NICCOLÒ MACHIAVELLI (1469–1527)

BIOGRAPHY

Machiavelli, like any genius, is a man of many questions, many quite funny. He was born in Florence on 3 May 1469. That same year, Piero de' Medici, who had followed Cosimo as de facto ruler of republican Florence, died leaving two sons, Lorenzo and Giuliano. Having survived the 1478 Pazzi conspiracy and murder of Giuliano, Lorenzo "Il Magnifico" effectively governed Florence during the formative years of Machiavelli's youth. Niccolò began the study of Latin at age twelve, and five years later his father acquired Livy's *Decades*, a book that was to prove central to Machiavelli's thinking. In his early twenties he would have witnessed the death of Lorenzo, the rise of the preacher Girolamo Savonarola, the 1494 invasion of Italy by Charles VIII of France, who took Italy with no more effort than was required to chalk the houses where his troops were to be billeted (*Principe*, XII), the flight of Piero de Lorenzo and the fall of the Medici, and the brief ascendancy of Savonarola (*Decennale primo*, 1504, 11.11–12).

In 1498, the same year that Savonarola was executed, the republic's Grand Council elected Machiavelli secretary of the Second Chancery and later secretary of the Ten (*Dieci*) of Liberty and Peace. Though Machiavelli, unlike his father, never became a member of the lawyer's guild, his study of Roman law, history, and literature provided the kind of education that allowed him to function for the next fourteen years of his life as an observer and analyst of internal and external affairs, as a writer of reports and dispatches, and as a representative of the Florentine republic who set the groundwork for its ambassadors. Until the fall of the republic in 1512, when he was forty-three years of age, Machiavelli was, as he describes himself, a man whose only "arte" or profession was statecraft (letter to Vettori, 9 April 1513). An exile from contemporary state affairs, Machiavelli entered the courts of the ancients, not ashamed to converse with those who, unlike the Medici, welcomed him kindly (*amorevolemente*). To them he posed questions that explored the reason (*ragione*) for their actions (letter to Vettori, 10 December 1513). The very potential for such a dialogue with the ancients was based upon the assumption of an essential unity in human experience, and that dialogue Machiavelli extended to his contemporaries via his "opuscolo *De principatibus*." In his dedication of that work to Lorenzo de' Medici, Machiavelli draws attention to the two voices of this dialogue—his long experience of modern affairs and his continual reading of the ancients.

In 1513, when Machiavelli embarked on an extremely prolific period of writing, he was still attempting to persuade the Medici to reopen the doors to the political world that had so absorbed his energies. During his years as secretary, Machiavelli had worked within a republican government, negotiated with the leaders of an emerging nation-state in France and a loosely organized empire in Germany, observed the charismatic new prince Cesare Borgia, organized a militia in 1506, and composed reports and lengthy dispatches for the Ten on a variety of subjects ("L'ordinanza fiorentina" and "L'esperienza di Alemagna"). The depth and complexity of his firsthand experience of the political world shaped the kinds of questions he would ask about politics and the way he would ask them.

The dispatches of 1502–3 recording the dramatic rise and fall of Cesare Borgia show us what it was like for Machiavelli to question and be questioned by a contemporary who did not always treat him as humanely as he claims those ancient writers did (Legations X, XI, XII). Amid the dramatic, violent, often confusing events of that year, Machiavelli was obliged to respond to his superiors, to avoid some of the pointed questions Borgia posed regarding the support he desired of the Florentine republic, to summarize dialogues and monologues, and even to interpret gestures, while always attempting to get at the reasons behind words and actions.

A dispatch recounting the execution of Borgia's lieutenant Rimirro de Orco (an event described vividly in his *Principe* VII) is dated 26 December. When addressing the Ten, Machiavelli would not be expected to raise questions about the state of Borgia's soul that Christmas Day in 1502. The "most secret" Borgia must be studied in other ways by the Florentine secretary. However, moral questions are often conspicuous by their absence from works that recast Machiavelli's diplomatic experience for the edification of his contemporaries or future generations, as was the case with his *Del modo di trattare i popoli della Valdichiana ribellati (1503)*, noteworthy for its use of Livy as a framework for the questioning of contemporary policy. Similarly, in 1506 Machiavelli reported on Pope Julius II's daring, if foolhardy, expedition to Perugia, an event that he reshaped in *Discorsi* I, 27 with particular emphasis on Giovampagolo Baglioni's failure to trap the pope within the city's walls. Questions regarding individual *virtù*, the opportunities presented by *occasione*, and the complexities of *fortuna* replace the queries that might have formed part of a Christian mirror for princes.

If Bentivogli had seized the occasion offered by fortune and treated Pope Julius in a way that accorded more with Machiavellian *virtù* than with Christian goodness, things might have gone differently for the Florentine republic. Julius II's support of the Spanish led to the defeat of the Florentine militia at Prato, which, in turn, caused Soderini to resign as Gonfaloniere in August 1512. Giuliano de' Medici took control of Florence in September, and Machiavelli was implicated in the anti-Medicean Boscoli conspiracy and arrested in February 1513 and freed only when Giovanni de' Medici became Pope Leo X in March 1513. After Giuliano's death in 1518 Machiavelli dedicated his *Principe* to Lorenzo di Piero (d. 1519).

The final eighth of Machiavelli's life was devoted to the *History of Florence (Storia fiorentino)*, delivered in sections to the new popes; *Clizia*, a comedy based on Plautus' *Cosina* (1525) and possibly the author's own lachrimose fling with a singer named Barbara; and several minor works. He died on 21 June 1527, after the signal disappointment of being virtually ignored by the free republic that reigned in Florence after ousting the Medici early in the same year.

MAJOR WORKS AND THEMES

The letter of 10 December 1513 to Francesco Vettori shows us a Machiavelli who has already embarked on the serious examination of statecraft that is his "arte." We know that he frequented the discussions at the Orti Oricellari, a setting mirrored in his *Arte della Guerra* (1521). It is now generally agreed that Machiavelli had begun his reflections on the first ten books of Livy's *History* when he turned to that "opuscolo *De principatibus*" that he offers to Lorenzo as the fruit of his varied experience and continual study of those states, like postrepublican Florence, that can be considered *principato nuovo*. Machiavelli composes the work in an unadorned style befitting the gravity of its subject and in keeping with the practical training of its author. It is a work offered to the new prince, who will be faced with complex questions and who needs explicit answers.

While Machiavelli distances his *Principe* from utopian treatments of imagined republics (XV), the effective reality of "the thing" he turns to includes everything from vile actions to the highest examples of political leadership represented by founders such as Moses, Cyrus, Romulus, and Theseus (VI). The questions he asks are posed with reference to the effective reality of success for the prince and security for the state and are weighted by Machiavelli's years of day-to-day experience in the chancery. To explore the consequences of a given line of action, such as whether to colonize a newly acquired state, Machiavelli tests solutions or cures for what ails the body politic by drawing on his experience and his teaching, for the organic processes of the body politic remain the same from ancient to modern times, beyond or within the confines of the Alps (VI). For Machiavelli memory is an analytical faculty—to recollect events or ancient texts is to pose questions from which answers are born (*nacque*) and conclusions can be drawn, such as, for example, that a prophet ought to be armed, and the arms ought to be one's own (VII). Though the complex variables that make up what Machiavelli calls *fortuna* do not admit of easy answers (XXV), he does not hesitate to grasp the most nettlesome questions. How do we understand the relationship between *virtù*, that heroic capacity for effective action, and *scelleratezze*, those admittedly criminal actions that may nonetheless prove politically efficacious? The very willingness to think of the criminal act as capable of being well or poorly used forces difficult problems of definition on the reader, pushing the dialogue into those unexplored regions that Machiavelli refers to in the Proem to Book I of his *Discorsi*. His is a daring quest for "the reason" that can be discovered behind actions, an exploration of the body politic that would understand the workings of those appetites and humors that create civic health or distemper (IX).

One can argue, as many students of Machiavelli do, that the kinds of questions he asks reflect his particular training and experience, the preoccupations of his age, or the orientation of his education. When looking for an answer to the overriding question of why most new princes in Italy have failed (XXIV), Machiavelli focuses on the lack of military *virtù* and political daring, qualities represented by Cesare Borgia (VII) and Borgia's nemesis Pope Julius II (XI). His rejection of mercenaries (XII–XIII) and tendency to equate the art of governing with the art of war (XIV) can be studied in the context of those very real questions Machiavelli was forced to leave unanswered in his diplomatic legations precisely because the Florentine republic lacked arms of its own (or because his own attempts to build an effective militia never succeeded). But that military emphasis and the questions born from it follow the philosophical shift from the imagined or ideal to the parameters of necessity, that "verità effetuale della cosa" that shapes his discussion of the character of the new prince (XV). If one must ask how "good" qualities are to be used in a world of those who are not good, the question itself begins a dialectical process of redefining what it means to be good. One must appear good to achieve success among those who judge by appearances alone, but *only* appear good, because the capacity to respond effectively to the many questions posed by fortune requires that a prince be capable of adopting the quality that best fits the time. Thus, questions about character are not posed with reference to an ideal or defined in terms of a fixed principle of being; rather, they are born from a desire to explore a ruler's capacity to respond to the infinite variety of questions presented by fortune. He asks whether it is advantageous to combine the nature of man and of the beast or whether it is possible to alternate between the deception of the fox and the aggression of the lion, thereby transforming fortune into occasion. The questions Machiavelli raises about the nature of counsel and flattery seem to mirror the role his work will play in the courts of princes who attempt to achieve the success that has eluded Italians in their struggles with fortune, success they may achieve by responding to his examination of the very nature of political inquiry. Students of his work continue to question whether Machiavelli provides the kinds of answers that would direct a new prince toward the successful liberation of Italy or whether he addresses those who like to think about such answers rather than act them out. Some would argue that the complexities can be managed only rhetorically or with the sense of unresolved contradiction and irony that comes through in his epistolary exchanges with Vettori and Guicciardini (letters to Vettori, 31 January 1515 and to Guicciardini, 17 May 1521). The tone of ironic mockery predominates in his comedies *Mandragola* (1518) and *Clizia* (1525), as well as in his poem *Asino* and the narrative *Favola (Belfagor arcidiavolo)* (1520).

A more serious tone emerges from the dedication of his *Discorsi* to Zanobi Buondelmonti and Cosimo Rucellai when Machiavelli asserts that the commentaries on the first ten books of Livy's *History* express everything he has learned from his extensive practical experience and continual study. Machiavelli brings that experience and study to bear on a fundamental question that is examined from many points of view: Why do some states, like Rome, enjoy a long and robust existence, while others, like Florence, are short-lived? Political bodies, like all things of this world, follow a natural cycle of birth, growth, and decline (I, 3), but some are made stronger by conflict, internal and external, while others languish in what Machiavelli will call the ''*viltà*'' of the modern Florentine state. In a world that is constantly in motion (*Discorsi* Proem II) the malignancy of fortune can be overcome only by good laws, education, and religion. These *ordini* can be used to impose an order that will, for a time, counter the inherent drift of human nature toward disorder. The state is literally founded on the necessary assumption that men are bad, that the malignant nature of the human soul will inevitably manifest itself, and, therefore, that conflict, between individuals, classes, or states, is the fundamental *verità* that will be brought forth by time.

As opposed to the Christian vision of an original state of perfection from which mortals fall and to which they aspire to return, Machiavelli's questions presuppose an original state of disorder or bestiality from which humans emerge by necessity, gathering together for protection under a strong, just leader. This instinct for preservation generates a consciousness of good and evil and the potential for civic life, though the enjoyment of justice and liberty never escapes the fundamental presupposition that states, like human bodies and like consciousness itself, must eventually expire. What combination of accidents and conscious choices, of fortune and *virtù*, or of subjugation and conquest makes some states expand while others decline? What creates the state in which the various forces are balanced as opposed to one in which they fly apart?

As he sets out to answer these difficult questions, Machiavelli presents himself as a sixteenth-century discoverer of unexplored intellectual realms, while his veneration for the past places him squarely within the Renaissance-humanist tradition (*Discorsi* Proem I). The Machiavellian variation on humanist optimism looks for the good generated by disorder, as represented by the class conflict within Rome, which produced good education, good laws, civic freedom, military *virtù*, and, eventually, the expansion of the Roman republic. The fundamental question for Machiavelli is not how to avoid, but how to bring something good from, the necessary condition of conflict and acquisitiveness that constitutes the human condition.

How can political *ordini* (which would include the constitution, written laws, unwritten mores and education, and religion) control or channel the disruptive humors that threaten the state (*Discorsi* I, 7)? Given the inevitability of decline, how does periodic reform serve to prolong the life of the state (III, 1)? While the questions confronted in *Principe* revolve around the central issue of how to maintain what a particular ruler has acquired, his *Discorsi* examine the institutional life of the state itself. The individual founder, reformer, or military leader is no more important to the continued strength of the republic than the character of its laws, education, and civic values. According to Machiavelli, we must be clear about two points: the ancients did have the right answers to many of the questions that moderns face, and we need not be inhibited in our search for answers by a tendency to idealize the past and demean the present. Conflict and competition are constants within human experience (III, 37), and the ways particular societies resolve internal conflict and meet external threats (III, 39) can be understood and either imitated or rejected. Since the same passions and humors that drive human behavior in the modern world were at work in the ancient, Machiavelli develops what one might call laws for social/political behavior.

The potential for expansion based on good military orders balances his critical assessment of the vile condition of political life in contemporary Italy. Extraordinary individuals may still emerge, as Machiavelli demonstrates with his *Vita di Castruccio Castracani* (1520). In his comic view of the human condition, represented by *Mandragola, Clizia, Asino*, and *Belfagor*, Machiavelli explores the potential for humans (if not devils) to learn and for society to be renewed. Despite the malignant power of fortune, the difficulty of coordinating *virtù* with the ever-shifting conditions of this world, and the ineluctable dysfunction of human nature, Machiavelli discovers laws for human behavior in his search for the reason behind the actions of ancients and moderns.

CRITICAL RECEPTION

The questions Machiavelli posed and the way he answered them influenced those in England who considered him a serious, if mistaken, thinker, as well as those who reacted to the popular image of the duplicitous machiavel (Raab, Kahn). The critical assessment of Machiavelli has always been complicated by the fact that he produced many aphoristic statements that pop easily from the very different genres in which he worked.

The question of deceit has in many ways dominated the response to his work, from the English Renaissance to the present. Preoccupation with this question attaches to the deceptive political practices Machiavelli describes and/or espouses and to the real or assumed duplicity of his writing. The stage Machiavel, as in Marlowe's *The Jew of Malta*, was perceived as a proponent of deceptive power politics, and Machiavelli himself as one who teaches this new brand of politics in a deceptively seductive manner.

The assessment of what is new in Machiavelli led Leo Strauss to portray the political philosophy of the Florentine secretary as a watershed between the classical tradition and a modern age in which the concern for justice and the opposition to tyranny give way to a philosophy that is normative even in its supposed scientific objectivity. For Strauss and those who follow his approach (H. Mansfield), the deceptive character of Machiavelli's writing is the result of a rhetorical strategy designed carefully to conceal unorthodox views from the uninitiated reader, while revealing them to those who are alert to meaningful ironies and contradictions.

For others the Machiavelli who is a servant of princes is the Machiavelli not to be trusted, especially by princes, because the true Florentine is a loyal servant of the republic whose commentaries on Livy represent his most important contribution to political philosophy (Pocock). From this critical perspective, the questions raised by Machiavelli's problematical relationship to princes and, particularly, to the Medici must be answered in the context of his abiding republicanism.

Whether Machiavelli is seen as a student of the classical tradition who subverts its values or as a follower of the ancients, many important questions about the character of his work and its place in intellectual history have focused on Machiavelli as Renaissance humanist (Chabod, Allan H. Gilbert). More recently, Machiavelli has attracted the attention of commentators for whom the way he poses questions is more important than how he answers them. For these scholars Machiavelli emerges as either a tragic figure whose verbal strategies never achieve the promised control of political reality (McCanles, Squarotti) or as an intellectual gamester who plays adroitly or is himself played upon by his wily contemporaries (Najemy, Rebhorn).

There is, certainly, a dark or tragic side of Machiavelli where the *verità* of the thing questioned reveals ever more variables, contradictions, and unpredictable shifts of fortune that elude analysis and regulation (Pitkin). But whether dressed in his somber curial robes commenting on all things ancient and modern or joking in the garb of a boon companion, Machiavelli never relents in his aggressive pursuit of those serious political questions that drive his discourse. A sense of that drive is what brought a smile to the lips of Nietzsche. Speaking of the tempo of Machiavelli's prose, he remarks that in his *Principe* Machiavelli "lets us breathe the dry, refined air of Florence and cannot help presenting the most serious matters in a boisterous *allegrissimo*, perhaps not without a malicious artistic sense of the contrast he risks—long, difficult, hard, dangerous thoughts and the *tempo* of the gallop and the very best, most capricious humor'' (*Beyond Good and Evil*, 28). What might constitute the malicious or capricious humor of Machiavelli? One might consider Machiavelli's advice that the prince leave citizens their possessions (*Principe* XVII) ''because men sooner forget the death of their father than the loss of their inheritance'' as a good example of an assessment that brings a smile to the lips of anyone who is ready to ask hard questions about the effective reality of human behavior.

Chapter 17 offers an excellent example of Machiavelli's tempo. The opening thesis that a prince should desire to be considered merciful (*pietoso*) rather than cruel is immediately qualified—mercy can be poorly used, and cruelty, under certain conditions, may contribute to the greater civic good. This opening, in turn, leads to the question (*disputa*) of whether it is better for a prince to be loved or feared, which is quickly answered—one should be loved and feared, but if one has to choose (and one does), it is better to be feared. This choice rests on a generally negative assessment of human beings, creatures who are essentially untrustworthy (*tristi*), driven by self-interest, and held in check only by fear. Machiavelli moves on to a further qualification, which is that the prince should avoid hatred by respecting the goods of those sorry citizens who care more for property than paternity. Now in full stride, he takes up the question of love and fear with reference to the military commander who may either be severe, like Hannibal, or more humane, like Scipio. The brief conclusion is that fear depends less on the will of others and is to be preferred.

In a chapter of some 970 words, Machiavelli moves quickly from one topic to the next without slighting the grave implications of his discourses; what Nietzsche calls Machiavelli's malicious sense of humor derives from the clear light his unadorned prose throws on the discussion. The questions are certainly complex, and the rhetorical strategies challenging. From the Renaissance to the present, artists and philosophers have found this unique combination of the *allegro* style and the *grave* content both engaging and disturbing. As was the case for writers as diverse as Ascham, Sidney* Greville,* Ralegh*, Marlowe,* Shakespeare,* and Bacon,* the questions raised by Machiavelli and the rich human contexts in which he raised them will continue to make us think and, as we think, smile.

BIBLIOGRAPHY

Works by Niccolò Machiavelli

The Chief Works and Others. 3 vols. Trans. Allan Gilbert. Durham, NC: Duke University Press, 1965.

The Discourses. 2 Vols. Trans. Leslie J. Walker. Boston: Routledge, 1950.

Florentine Histories. Ed. and trans. Laura F. Banfield and Harvey C. Mansfield Jr. Princeton: Princeton University Press, 1968.

Le grande opere politiche. Vol. 2. *Discorsi sopra la prima Deca di Tito Livio*. Turin: Bollati Boringhieri, 1993.

Mandragola. Trans. Mera J. Flaumenhaft. Prospect Heights, IL: Waveland Press, 1981.

Opere. 8 vols. Ed. Sergio Bertelli and Franco Gaeta. Milan: Feltrinelli, 1960, 65.

The Prince. Trans. Harvey C. Mansfield, Jr. Chicago: University of Chicago Press, 1985.

Tutte le opere storiche e letterrarie di Niccolò Machiavelli. Ed. Guido Mazzoni and Mario Casella. Florence: Barbera, 1929.

Studies of Niccolò Machiavelli

Baron, Hans. "Machiavelli: The Republican Citizen and the Author of *The Prince*." *English Historical Review* 76 (1961): 217–53.

Berlin, Isaiah. "The Originality of Machiavelli." In *Against the Current*, by Isaiah Berlin. New York: Viking Press, 1980, 25–79.

Bock, Gisela, ed. *Machiavelli and Republicanism*. New York: Cambridge University Press, 1990.

Chabod, Federico. *Machiavelli and the Renaissance*. London: Bowes and Bowes, 1958.

de Grazia, Sebastian. *Machiavelli in Hell*. Princeton: Princeton University Press, 1989.

Geerken, John H. "Machiavelli Studies since 1969." *Journal of the History of Ideas* 37 (1976): 351–68.

Gilbert, Allan H. *Machiavelli's Prince and Its Forerunners: The Prince as a Typical Book de Regimine Principum*. Durham, NC: Duke University Press, 1938.

Gilbert, Felix. *Machiavelli and Guicciardini: Politics and History in Sixteenth-Century Florence*. Princeton: Princeton University Press, 1965.

Hulliung, Mark. *Citizen Machiavelli*. Princeton: Princeton University Press, 1983.

Mansfield, Harvey C., Jr. *Machiavelli's New Modes and Orders: A Study of the Discourses on Livy*. Ithaca, NY: Cornell University Press, 1979.

McCanles, Michael. *The Discourse of 'Il Principe.'* Malibu, CA: Undena Publications, 1983.

Najemy, John M. *Between Friends: Discourses of Power and Desire in the Machiavelli-Vettori Letters of 1513–1515*. Princeton: Princeton University Press, 1993.

Pitkin, Hanna Fenichel. *Fortune Is a Woman: Gender and Politics in the Thought of Niccolò Machiavelli*. Berkeley: University of California Press, 1984.

Pocock, J.G.A. *The Machiavellian Moment*. Princeton: Princeton University Press, 1975.

Raab, Felix. *The English Face of Machiavelli: A Changing Interpretation 1500–1700*. Toronto: University of Toronto Press, 1964.

Rebhorn, Wayne A. *Foxes and Lions: Machiavelli's Confidence Men*. Ithaca, NY: Cornell University Press, 1988.

Ridolfi, Roberto. *The Life of Niccolò Machiavelli*. Trans. Cecil Grayson. Chicago: Chicago University Press, 1963.

Ruffo-Fiore, Silvia. *Niccolò Machiavelli: An Annotated Bibliography of Modern Criticism and Scholarship 1935–1988*. New York: Greenwood Press, 1990.

Squarotti, Giorgio Barberi. *La Forma Tragica del Principe*. Florence: Olschki, 1966.

Strauss, Leo. *Thoughts on Machiavelli*. Glencoe, IL: Free Press, 1958.

Whitfield, J. H. *Discourses on Machiavelli*. Cambridge: Heffer, 1969.

JACK D'AMICO

SIR THOMAS MALORY
(140?–1471)

BIOGRAPHY

Thomas Malory was the author, translator, editor, compiler, and genius behind *Le Morte Darthur*. His work, which has had a considerable impact on the cultural history of English-speaking countries since 1485, represents the best of the synthetic, creative tradition of late medieval England. The facts of his life in many ways remain a mystery. The text of his work solicits prayers on the author's behalf from his readers, and the Malory manuscript tells us that he was a "knyght presonere." All else remains speculation.

While several Thomas Malorys have been identified, the scholarly world has generally settled on the so-called Kittredge-Hicks Malory, Sir Thomas Malory of Newbold Revel. Nagging doubts have persisted, however, because of aspects of his character. This Sir Thomas Malory was born sometime between 1400 and 1410, the son of Sir John Malory of Newbold Revel in Warwickshire. In 1434 Sir John died, and Thomas Malory inherited the family estates. In 1436 he fought at the siege of Calais in the retinue of Richard Beauchamp, earl of Warwick. Clearly, Malory's family was of some consequence in Warwickshire. However, criminal records on the man himself intermingle with his military career. In 1443, he was apparently indicted for theft in the substantial amount of forty pounds. The charge was not proved, for Malory and his apparent accomplice, Eustace Burnaby, did not appear in court to deal with the charges. Sometime around this period he married a woman named Elizabeth, who bore him two sons, Robert, who died in his youth, and Nicholas, who survived.

Malory was undoubtedly popular in Warwickshire, for, in 1445, he was chosen as one of the two knights of the shire and served in Parliament at Westminster for the year. Despite his popularity, he was back in trouble virtually immediately. During the period 1450–51, he was putatively involved in attempted murder, robbery, cattle raids, rape, and extortion. He was imprisoned at Coleshill and escaped. After his escape he was alleged to have robbed a Cistercian monastery. He was arrested in 1452 and imprisoned. In 1454, he was released on bail and went on a cattle raid. He also stole personal property and was imprisoned in Colechester. Through a series of legal manipulations, he was released from Marshalsea through a royal pardon and sent to Ludgate, which was ordinarily a debtor's prison. On 13 October 1457, he was released on bail until 28 December, with heavy penalties pending if he did not return. On 28 December he was recommitted to Marshalsea. He was imprisoned again in 1460 at Newgate. His career during this period can only be described as marked by rapine and violence. For the next ten years, the Newbold Revel Malory drops out of sight generally. It appears that he was excluded from two general pardons granted by Edward IV in 1468. It is speculated that he was in prison when he finished *Le Morte Darthur* between 1469 and 1470. He apparently died on 14 March 1471, likely due to plague and while still in prison. In *The Indian Summer of English Chivalry*, Arthur B. Ferguson notes that the late medieval interest in romance in England was sparked by a craving for traditional, old-fashioned values. The career of the Newbold Revel Malory hardly presents a portrait of a very true and perfect knight. It is not surprising, then, that the search has continued for other candidates.

In 1966, William Matthews reviewed the evidence for all previous candidates for the authorship and suggested a new one. Basing his arguments on the text of *Le Morte Darthur*, Matthews suggests that the real author is "another man of the same name." Matthews suggests that the predominance of northern linguistic elements in the text and the availability of sources and other material point to Sir Thomas Malory of Hutton and Studley. While very little information is available on this candidate, Matthews builds a case that seems logical on its surface. It will have to stand the test of time and further investigation by historians and literary scholars of the sort the Newbold Revel Malory has previously attracted. Until Matthews' arguments are elaborated by further investigation or until additional candidates come forth, the Newbold Revel Malory, with all his warts, remains the most likely candidate for authorship.

MAJOR THEMES AND WORKS

Malory's *Le Morte Darthur* has attracted critics, readers, and imitators through the ages. It is the only work attributed to Sir Thomas Malory, but it has been the basis for other literary, musical, and artistic works, musicals, and cinema. Its influence extends today to electronic games and all aspects of popular culture. The work includes tales of valor and chivalry, themes that still capture the imagination in defining "nobility" and judging political and social conduct. Malory's understanding of the tension between loyalty and love remains a basic measure of modern tragedy. His exploration of the nature of justice, mercy, duty, and the concept of general welfare speaks to the modern political conscience.

The work, however, has had its detractors. During the Renaissance, Roger Ascham (*The Scholemaster* [London, 1570] 27–28) commented that the work was awash with "bold bawdry and open manslaughter." In the Protestant age, it has also been criticized for its emphasis on the story of the Grail. Yet it has found major adherents, and most literary evaluations that focus on its merits reveal the work to be a masterpiece. Until 1934, only one text was known, that printed by Caxton in 1485. In his preface, Caxton notes it can certainly be read with pleasure as a narrative, but he also notes that it contains "noble & renomed actes of humanyte / gentylnesse and chyualrye." He goes on to elaborate the moral nature of the work by saying, "Doo after the good and leue the euyll / and it shal brynge you to good fame and renommee." The pleasure to be derived from *Le Morte Darthur* has never been in doubt. That, perhaps, is the reason for its widespread popularity through the ages. Similarly, generations of readers have taken to heart Caxton's admonition to use the work as a moral guidebook. Certainly, Tennyson found the tales appropriate for the Victorians with their emphasis on good works, duty, and moral conduct.

In 1934, however, when Walter Oakeshott discovered the Malory manuscript, a number of other critical issues emerged for consideration. The manuscript contained a different structure, lacking Caxton's *explicits* and *incipits*. Moreover, there were significant differences in the text, especially in Book V, dealing with the battle between Arthur and the Emperor Lucius. When Eugène Vinaver published his edition of the manuscript in 1947, he also attacked William Caxton for manipulating Malory's text. He further argued that Caxton had likely tried to impress his own moral sense on the work in an effort, perhaps, to make it more attractive to the fifteenth-century audience seeking tales of romance and chivalry. These charges have been answered by Robert Lumiansky and others in *Malory's Originality* and more recently by William Matthews (*Arthuriana*). The question of ''best text'' is a critical one, for it involves not only the intention of the author but the basic structure of the tale.

Caxton's edition of *Le Morte Darthur* is divided into twenty-one books, with each book chaptered. It traces the history of King Arthur from his birth and his magical acquisition of Excalibur, through his death. It provides, perhaps, the most complete exposition of all of Arthurian romances, including the betrayal of Lancelot and Guinevere and the quest of the Holy Grail. It is, as Charles and Ruth Moorman have described it (*An Arthurian Dictionary*, 85), ''the culmination of the medieval Arthurian tradition.'' The Malory manuscript provides the same comprehensive view of the adventures of King Arthur and his knights. It offers, however, significant differences in structure and possibly intent.

Questions about the authenticity of the text of *Le Morte Darthur* remain to be decided. Robert L. Kindrick has argued elsewhere that both the Caxton version and the Malory manuscript deserve independent attention. He strongly believes that the Malory manuscript is an earlier version, likely modified by Malory himself prior to publication. If that assumption is correct, then Caxton is also correct in his interpretation of the work as providing both pleasure and instruction, a Horatian rhetorical goal. Whether the tales of romance and chivalry are interpreted as dealing with bawdy and manslaughter or in terms of a return to traditional mores, Malory's accomplishment is masterful. Malory's work has provided generations of readers entertainment and useful lessons.

CRITICAL RECEPTION

As previously noted, throughout the last 500 years, Malory has had his detractors, but they have always been eventually shouted down by his proponents. Besides those who challenge the work on moral grounds, others have raised questions about its unity because Malory worked from a complicated and diverse set of English and French sources. Eugéne Vinaver, Robert H. Wilson, and C. S. Lewis, among others, all dealt with the question of unity. Lewis' perspective is perhaps the most useful. He indicates that in one sense it does not matter whether Malory had ''any intention either of writing a 'single work' or of writing may 'works.' '' He goes on to suggest that the unifying feature is Arthur and his knights and their character consistency. D. S. Brewer has suggested that *Le Morte Darthur* is sui generis and that it has qualities of older cyclical romances.

In similar fashion, the nature of the romance tradition in *Le Morte Darthur* has come under scrutiny. Larry D. Benson has argued for the ''realism'' of the romance. Typically, readers have seen the work as the epitome of romance and romance traditions. Discussions about Malory's sources continue. A major event in source studies occurred in the earlier part of the twentieth century, when H. Oskar Sommer published the *Vulgate Version of the Arthurian Romances* and made readily available some of the sources that Malory had used. Sommer, Wilson, Vinaver, Benson, and numerous other later critics have helped us to understand Malory's creative process as he constructed *Le Morte Darthur*. Other questions relating to social ethics abound. What is the tension between courtly love and chivalry? Is chivalry itself a benevolent or outmoded aspect of society? Questions involving characterization in the work have also recently been raised. Did the characters actually evolve, or are they static? As early as 1934, Robert H. Wilson attempted to resolve questions about characterization in the work, but more remains to be done.

A particularly noteworthy aspect of Malory's appeal is his prose style. Working from diverse sources, he integrated plot and character through a distinctive rhetorical voice. Field has noted Malory's tendency to use ''narrative without description'' (see *Romance and Chronicle*, 36–38) as one of his most important techniques in adapting his sources. He also softened the epic violence of some sources, as well as deleting prolix descriptions from others, in forging a unified compendium of Arthurian romance.

All of these matters relate to the single most important question now current among Arthurian scholars with regard to *Le Morte Darthur*. Is it properly titled *Le Morte Darthur* or more properly titled *Works?* Matthews argues that the Caxton version is the ''best text,'' and his arguments are persuasive. Despite the efforts of new critics and others to eliminate authorial intention from consideration, Malory's design for *Le Morte Darthur* remains at the forefront of critical debate.

BIBLIOGRAPHY

Works by Sir Thomas Malory

Ker, N. R. *Introduction. The Winchester Malory: A Facsimile*. London: Oxford University Press, 1976. Early English Text Society, s.s. 4.

Needham, Paul. Introduction. *Le Morte D'Arthur*. London: Scolar Press, 1976. (Caxton Facsimile.)

Sommer, H. Oskar, ed. *Le Morte Darthur*. London: David Nutt, 1889.

Spisak, James, and William Matthews, eds. *Caxton's Malory: Le Morte Darthur*. Berkeley: University of California Press, 1983.

Vinaver, Eugène, ed. *The Works of Sir Thomas Malory*. Oxford: Clarendon Press, 1947; rev. and rpt., 1967; rev. and rpt., ed. P.J.C. Field, 1990.

Studies of Sir Thomas Malory

Benson, Larry D. *Malory's Morte Darthur*. Cambridge: Harvard University Press, 1976.

Field, P.J.C. *The Life and Times of Sir Thomas Malory*. New York: D. S. Brewer, 1993.

———. *Romance and Chronicle*. Bloomington: Indiana University Press, 1971.

Hanks, D. Thomas, Jr. *Sir Thomas Malory: Views and Reviews*. New York: AMS, 1992.

Hellinga, Lotte, and Hilton Kelliher. ''The Malory Manuscript.'' *The British Library Journal* 3.2 (Autumn 1977): 97–113.
Hicks, Edward. *Sir Thomas Malory, His Turbulent Career*. Cambridge: Harvard University Press, 1928.
Kennedy, Beverly. *Knighthood in the Morte Darthur*. Woodbridge, Suffolk: D. S. Brewer, 1985.
Kindrick, Robert L., ed., with the assistance of Michele R. Crepeau. ''William Matthews: On Caxton and Malory.'' *Arthuriana* 6 (1996).
Kittredge, George Lyman. ''Who Was Sir Thomas Malory?'' *Harvard Studies and Notes in Philology and Literature* 5 (1987).
Lambert, Mark. *Style and Vision in Le Morte Darthur*. New Haven, CT: Yale University Press, 1975.
Life, Page West. *Sir Thomas Malory and the Morte Darthur: A Survey of Scholarship and Annotated Bibliography*. Charlottesville: University Press of Virginia, 1980.
Lumiansky, Robert, ed. *Malory's Originality*. Baltimore: Johns Hopkins University Press, 1964.
Matthews, William. ''The Ill-Framed Knight.'' In *A Skeptical Inquiry into the Identity of Sir Thomas Malory*. Berkeley: University of California Press, 1966.
Parins, Marylyn Jackson. *Malory, The Critical Heritage*. London: Routledge, 1988.
Reiss, Edmund. *Sir Thomas Malory*. New York: Twayne, 1966.
Spisak, James W., ed. *Studies in Malory*. Kalamazoo: Medieval Institute Press, 1985.
Vinaver, Eugéne. *Malory*. Oxford: Clarendon Press, 1929, rpt. 1970.
Wilson, Robert H. *Characterization in Malory: A Comparison with His Sources*. Chicago: University of Chicago Libraries, 1934.
———. ''Malory and Caxton.'' In *A Manual of the Writings in Middle English*, ed. Albert E. Hartung. New Haven, CT: Connecticut Academy of Arts and Sciences, 1972, 909–60.

ROBERT L. KINDRICK AND RUTH E. HAMILTON

CHRISTOPHER MARLOWE
(1564–1593)

BIOGRAPHY

Christopher Marlowe is news that stays news. Both the man and his writings continue to intrigue us because Marlowe was and is a brilliant mischief-maker, a trickster, a crosser of boundaries. His was a life and is a corpus that are pertinent by being impertinent.

''Christofer the sonne of John Marlow'' was baptized in Canterbury on 26 February 1564. After attending the King's School in Canterbury, he was admitted to Corpus Christi College, Cambridge. He received his B.A., but excessive absence, apparently spent abroad at Rheims, delayed his M.A., and thus begins the Marlowe mystery. The degree was finally granted in 1587, after the Privy Council explained that he had been employed ''in matters touching the benefitt of his Countrie.'' Presumably, Marlowe was spying on recusant English Catholics and potential plotters against the Anglican queen.

During his student days he wrote translations, poems, and his earliest play, *Dido, Queen of Carthage*, which was performed by a boys' company. *Tamburlaine the Great* also belongs to this period and was followed shortly by *Tamburlaine, Part II, The Jew of Malta, Doctor Faustus*, and *The Massacre at Paris*. All except *Edward II* were produced by Philip Henslowe,* and Edward Alleyn played Tamburlaine, Barabas, and Faustus. The chronology is almost impossible to determine; none of Marlowe's writings, except for the two parts of *Tamburlaine*, were published during his lifetime, and even they appeared anonymously. The 1657 first edition of the play *Lust's Dominion* claims Marlowe as its author; more recent critics have attributed to him parts of Shakespeare's *Henry VI* and the whole of *Arden of Feversham*; and some, given to fantasy, imagine a Marlowe who survived his official death and wrote most or all of Shakespeare.*

Marlowe spent most of his six postgraduate years in London or at the home of his patron, Sir Thomas Walsingham, to whom *Hero and Leander* was posthumously dedicated. Marlowe managed to get into a fair amount of trouble: he was briefly imprisoned in 1589 in connection with a killing, bound by constables to keep the peace in 1592, and deported from the Netherlands that same year. He was connected with what has been called the ''School of Night,'' a group of innovative thinkers—at whose center were the earl of Northumberland, Baron Cobham, and Sir Walter Ralegh*—who took literally a line from Terence, ''I hold nothing human alien to me,'' and who dared to investigate and speculate about all matters on earth, above and below. That connection, as well as Marlowe's plays, may have led Robert Greene* to allude to Marlowe as the ''famous gracer of Tragedians'' who has studied ''pestilent Machiavelian pollicy'' and says, ''There is no God.''

A different playwright, Thomas Kyd,* precipitated Marlowe's—and perhaps his own—downfall. Kyd claimed that a religiously controversial tract found in his room belonged to Marlowe. On 20 May 1593, Marlowe was required to appear daily before the Star Chamber. Ten days later he was dead, stabbed over his right eye by Ingram Frizer with a dagger. The inquest found that Marlowe had started the fight over a tavern debt. Some contemporaries thought the fight was about a woman; others followed the lead of Thomas Beard, who saw in Marlowe's death ''a manifest signe of Gods judgement'' for Marlowe's ''Atheisme & impiety.'' The late twentieth century believes Marlowe's death was a political cover-up, perhaps to protect Walsingham and members of the School of Night, perhaps in a court intrigue aimed by Essex against Ralegh. This same Ralegh mourned (or anticipated) Marlowe's death in his ''Nymph's Reply'' to Marlowe's ''Passionate Shepherd,'' which laments how, through time, flowers fade, and the nightingale, the voice of the poet, ''Philomel becometh dumb.''

MAJOR WORKS AND THEMES

Even in his Cambridge writings based on classical sources, Marlowe determined to do something new. He translated *All Ovids Elegies* and the first book of Lucan's *Pharsalia*, neither of which had been rendered before into English. His *Dido, Queen of Carthage* is the earliest English dramatization of Book IV of *The Aeneid*. The brief epic *Hero and Leander*, if written during his college days, is the earliest English epyllion; because Musaeus, whose Greek poem provides Marlowe with much of his story, was thought to be a student of Orpheus, Marlowe based his own originality on the supposed origin of Western literature.

From the beginning, Marlowe's works raise problems of indeterminacy, uncertainty, and incompleteness that seem appropriate to Marlowe as trickster. The first edition of *Hero and Leander* ends with the words *Desunt nonnulla*, "several [lines? portions?] are missing," which led George Chapman* to "complete" a poem that now seems quite sufficient unto itself. The title page of *Dido* claims Thomas Nashe* as coauthor and so problematizes Marlowe's authorship. The printer of *Tamburlaine* informs readers that he deliberately "omitted . . . some fond and frivolous gestures" included in the play's performance. *The Tragicall History of [the Life and Death of] Doctor Faustus* is replete with farcical interludes and suspended between the substantially different texts of 1604 and 1616. Another kind of problem is presented by the tone of *The Jew of Malta*, by what T. S. Eliot in 1919 labeled "the farce of the old English humour, the terribly serious, even savage comic humour," so disturbing to post-Holocaust readers (Greenblatt). *The Massacre at Paris* survives in a poor memorial reconstruction only half as long as Marlowe's other plays.

Dido is of interest largely for what it anticipates. Written in heroic couplets, the play shows Marlowe's nod to tradition via Virgil and his early interest in invention, notably in a subplot about the tragic loves of Dido's sister Anna and Iarbus. The violence of war is vividly depicted when Aeneas relates the destruction of Troy, when Hecuba's fingernails reached the eyes of Neoptolemus until "the soldiers pull'd her by the heels, / And swung her howling in the empty air." The play also evidences Marlowe's fascination with the homoerotic; *Dido* begins with Jupiter's "dandling" Ganymede on his knee, and Venus soon rebukes him for "toying there / And playing with that female wanton boy."

Hero and Leander displays Marlowe again as transgressor. It is an Ovidian, erotic, narrative, comical, satirical poem, derivative and wholly original, complete, though it tells only part of a story. Leander falls in love with Hero, the virginal—and so oxymoronic—nun of Venus, swims the Hellespont to be with her, proves at least as sexually inexperienced as she, and finally completes their intercourse. Offering a witty and frequently shifting narrator and including a tale to explain why "to this day is every scholar poor," the poem is most fascinating as a study in the complexities of sexual desire; description of the nude body is reserved for Leander, whereas Hero is as elaborately clad as Oscar

Wilde's Salome envisaged by Aubrey Beardsley. As Hero is desired by Leander, so is Leander by Neptune, who nearly drowns him when the lusting god attempts to embrace the swimming man.

In *Tamburlaine the Great*, Marlowe emerges as graduate student in his consultation of numerous scholarly sources. Nevertheless, as its prologue announces, *Tamburlaine* did indeed lead its original audience "[f]rom jigging veins of rhyming mother wits" to the "high astounding terms" of what Ben Jonson* later dubbed "Marlowe's mighty line." Algernon Swinburne overstated Marlowe's accomplishment only slightly when, in 1910, he credited Marlowe with beginning "his career by a double and incomparable achievement; the invention of English blank verse, and the creation of English tragedy." Though both the verse and the dramatic form precede Marlowe, in Surrey* and Kyd,* everyone who follows him is directly or indirectly in his debt.

The protagonist of *Tamburlaine* begins as a shepherd, enacts his belief that Nature "[d]oth teach us all to have aspiring minds," and concludes as conqueror of empires and incipient beloved husband of Egyptian Zenocrate, whom he had captured in Act I. Marlowe proved a genius at conceiving dramatic spectacles: crowns pass from hand to hand, the coloration of the stage changes from white to red to black on successive days of a siege, and a captured emperor dashes his brains out on the bars of his cage. Marlowe not only masters dramatic language but makes it a major motif of the play. A weak king is "insufficient to express" his grief; when a strong king is told he will "ride in triumph through Persepolis," the phrase inspires Tamburlaine to overthrow that king; a brave enemy is converted to a loyal ally by Tamburlaine's "working words"; and the offstage battle of two armies has its onstage correlative in an exchange of insults by the women of the leaders.

Tamburlaine the Great was so successful that it generated imitations, allusions, and eventually a sequel by Marlowe. In *Part II* the death of the wife of Tamburlaine and the cowardice of one of their sons—whom Tamburlaine kills as unworthy—anticipate his own death at the end. What is striking about both parts and is a hallmark of Marlowe's work is the extent to which he keeps the audience off-balance. A long soliloquy in *Part I*, in which Tamburlaine expresses sympathy for Zenocrate and creates a sonnet in praise of beauty, is immediately preceded by his ordering the death of four weeping maidens, and it is followed by his treading on the back of a captive emperor. Even more disorienting is the treatment of religion in *Part II*, which shows Christians breaking a vow and Muslims keeping one made to their respective deities. At play's end, as soon as Tamburlaine commands that "the Turkish Alcoran" be burned and dares "Mahomet" to revenge the deed, he is stricken by the disease that kills him. One might suspect religious syncretism, except that the plays never maintain anything but an elusive and tricky point of view.

The Jew of Malta is an often farcical study in cause and effect. Barabas, the title character, has his home and wealth confiscated by the Maltese Christians. In revenge, he sets up a duel between his daughter's fiancé and the governor's son, in which both are killed. His grieving daughter joins a nunnery, which leads Barabas to poison all the nuns, aided by a slave, who then blackmails his master. With his crimes coming to light, Barabas feigns death and is thrown over the city wall, whence he is able to lead invading Turks into the city by a secret passage. Insecure about his position among the triumphant Turks, Barabas offers to betray them to the Maltese Christians, who in turn doublecross Barabas and make him plunge into a boiling cauldron he has prepared for the Turkish leader.

Though the prologue by ''Machiavel'' speaks of ''the tragedy of a Jew,'' the tone is impossible to determine, and the play invites production by puppets. The modern term ''black humor'' best describes the conversation in which the ''bottle-nosed'' Jew and his Muslim slave try to outdo one another with stories of villainy or the moment when one friar ''kills'' another by knocking over a propped-up corpse or the way the pathetic last words of Barabas' daughter—''Witness that I die a Christian''—are undermined by her confessor's response, ''Ay, and a virgin too; that grieves me most.'' Every time we feel comfortable with a given stance, Marlowe pulls the rug out from under us.

Both the A (1604) and the B (1616) texts of *Doctor Faustus* have their critical champions. About each some claim that the scenes of low comedy interspersed along Faustus' path to damnation are extraneous or are integral; the drama is a heroic tragedy and/or a morality play; its theology is orthodox or heretical; and there is debate about when and even whether Faustus is damned. Beyond doubt, the play is powerful because of the richness of the poetry and the tension created when the tragic protagonist faces not just death but eternal damnation. Faustus' verse soliloquies constitute a character more complex than any predecessor on the English stage. Faustus is an individual trapped in a system, blind and insightful, timid and daring, torn between medieval and modern, confounding ''hell in Elysium.''

Edward II, a chronicle history that employs emblematic staging appropriate to its medieval setting, shows the king heaping titles and treasure on his lover, Piers Gaveston, alienating his nobles so much that they execute Gaveston. When Edward replaces Gaveston with another male lover, his queen leaves Edward for the love of Mortimer. They conquer Edward and have him killed, but young Edward III, who knows his authentic place is beside his nobles, puts a quick end to Mortimer's reign.

Edward Alleyn did not act in *Edward II*, and there is certainly a correlation between the absence of this titanic performer and the lack of a dominating protagonist. Marlowe's focus on several characters enables him to study causality via their rise and fall on the Boethian wheel of Fortune. Not only do the characters change their loyalties, but Marlowe makes the audience adjust our perspective when the incompetent king, cruelly imprisoned at the end, wins our sympathy because of his underdog status. The shifting loyalties of Edward's brother, Kent, serve to orient the audience, as Shakespeare's duke of York does later in *Richard II*.

Although the only text of *The Massacre at Paris* has all the limitations of memorial reconstruction, it reveals Marlowe characteristically turning in a new direction, to events that occurred in his own lifetime. In his portrayal of the Saint Bartholomew's Day massacre, he continues his macabre humor, still explores the many forms taken by the union of power and duplicity, and is again fascinated by the clash of religions. What surprises most, if written by this master of cutting irony, is the repeated praise of "the Queen of England specially, / Whom God hath bless'd for hating papistry."

CRITICAL RECEPTION

After his death, Marlowe was castigated as a blasphemer and atheist but was equally praised and imitated as a poet and dramatist. The view of his contemporaries is summarized in *The Second Part of the Return from Parnassus* (c. 1600):

> *Marlowe* was happy in his buskined muse,
> Alas unhappy in his life and end.
> Pity it is that wit so ill should dwell,
> Wit lent from heaven, but vices sent from hell.

Among the best-known tributes to Marlowe are Ralegh's response to "The Passionate Shepherd," one of dozens, and Chapman's continuation of *Hero and Leander*. Shakespeare's *As You Like It* echoes *Hero*'s "Who ever loved, that loved not at first sight?" and *2 Henry IV* mockingly refers to Tamburlaine's king-drawn chariot.

Largely ignored in the eighteenth century, Marlowe's texts were revived in the nineteenth, and some productions were staged, notably Edmund Kean's *Jew of Malta* in 1818 and William Poel's 1896 *Doctor Faustus*. Nevertheless, that period tended to see Marlowe more as a poet than a playwright and to view him much as the preceding century had looked at Shakespeare, as a native genius unrestrained by decorum and unfortunately limited by his audience. By the 1920s and 1930s, Marlowe and his works were thought to exemplify the splendors and contradictions of the Renaissance: aspiring beyond what society and its system of beliefs could permit, gloriously but dangerously overreaching the limits of what could be tolerated.

Recent critics have stopped arguing about Marlowe's iconoclasm or orthodoxy or worrying about his seeming inconsistency; instead, they appreciate the boldness of his clashing concepts. Increasingly frequent production of his plays has created greater understanding of their theatricality and how they affect their audience. The subtleties of Marlowe's rhetoric have received fresh study. His influence on Shakespeare and even on Jonson has been explored anew.

Marlowe's fascination with the outsider or "other" has been fruitfully correlated with Renaissance England's growing exploration of the non-European world. Several contemporary scholars examine Marlowe's presentation of the human body, especially its sexual potential. In his own day, Marlowe supposedly claimed that Christ and John the Baptist were lovers and "that all they that love not Tobacco & Boies were fooles." These assertions, together with the number of men or gods in his works who are strongly attracted to other males, have made Marlowe a major figure in the burgeoning fields of gay and gender studies; Derek Jarman's recent film adaptation of *Edward II* is one reflection of this work. The nexus of homoerotic author and characters has, in turn, generated many psychological explorations of both Marlowe and his creations. Finally, recent criticism and historical study about Marlowe's experiences as an intriguer, spy, or double agent have opened up promising inquiries into the significance of observation and duplicity—indeed trickery—in his work.

My remarks here are merely suggestive. More detailed surveys can be found in the books by Friedenreich and by MacLure. The more one looks, the more one finds that Marlowe slyly resists definition. There can be no closure for a crosser of boundaries, no final word about a trickster.

BIBLIOGRAPHY

Works by Christopher Marlowe

Complete Works

Bevington, David, and Eric Rasmussen, eds. *Christopher Marlowe: "Doctor Faustus" and Other Plays*. Oxford: Oxford University Press, 1995.

Bowers, Fredson, ed. *The Complete Works of Christopher Marlowe*. 2d ed. 2 vols. Cambridge: Cambridge University Press, 1981.

Gill, Roma, ed. *The Complete Works of Christopher Marlowe. I: Translations, II: Doctor Faustus, III: Edward II, IV: The Jew of Malta*. Oxford: Oxford University Press, 1987–95.

Kirschbaum, Leo, ed. *The Plays of Christopher Marlowe*. Cleveland: Meridian, 1962.

Ribner, Irving, ed. *The Complete Plays of Christopher Marlowe*. New York: Odyssey, 1963.

Steane, J. B., ed. *Christopher Marlowe: The Complete Plays*. Harmondsworth: Penguin, 1969.

Individual Works

Bawcutt, N. W., ed. *The Jew of Malta*. Manchester: Manchester University Press, 1978.

Bevington, David, and Eric Rasmussen, eds. *Doctor Faustus: A- and B-texts (1604, 1616)*. Manchester: Manchester University Press, 1993.

Cunningham, J. S., ed. *Tamburlaine the Great*. Manchester: Manchester University Press, 1981.

Keefer, Michael, ed. *Doctor Faustus. A 1604-Version Edition*. Peterborough, Ontario: Broadview, 1991.

Orgel, Stephen, ed. *Christopher Marlowe: The Complete Poems and Translations*. London: Penguin, 1971.

Studies of Christopher Marlowe

Bibliographies

Brandt, Bruce E. *Christopher Marlowe in the Eighties: An Annotated Bibliography of Marlowe Criticism from 1978 through 1989*. West Cornwall, CT: Locust Hill, 1992.

Chan, Lois Mai. *Marlowe Criticism: A Bibliography*. Boston: G. K. Hall, 1978.

Friedenreich, Kenneth. *Christopher Marlowe: An Annotated Bibliography of Criticism since 1950*. Metuchen, NJ: Scarecrow, 1979.

Kimbrough, Robert. "Christopher Marlowe." In *The Predecessors of Shakespeare: A Survey and Bibliography*, ed. Terence P. Logan and Denzell S. Smith. Lincoln: University of Nebraska Press, 1973, 3–55.

Levao, Ronald. "Recent Studies in Marlowe (1977–1986)." *English Literary Renaissance* 18 (1988): 329–42.

Concordances

Fehrenbach, Robert J., L. A. Boone, and M. A. Di Cesare, eds. *A Concordance to the Plays, Poems, and Translations of Christopher Marlowe*. Ithaca, NY: Cornell University Press, 1982.

Ule, Louis. *A Concordance to the Works of Christopher Marlowe*. Hildesheim: George Olms, 1979.

Sources

Christopher Marlowe: The Major Sources. Ed. Vivien Thomas and William Tydemen. London: Routledge, 1994.

The English Faust Book: A Critical Edition, Based on the Text of 1592. Ed. John Henry Jones. Cambridge: Cambridge University Press, 1994.

Biographies

Bakeless, John. *The Tragicall History of Christopher Marlowe*. 2 vols. Cambridge: Harvard University Press, 1942.

Nicholl, Charles. *The Reckoning: The Murder of Christopher*. London: Jonathan Cape, 1992.

Wraight, A. D. *In Search of Christopher Marlowe: A Pictorial Biography*. London: Macdonald, 1965.

Criticism

Bartels, Emily C. *Spectacles of Strangeness: Imperialism, Alienation, and Marlowe*. Philadelphia: University of Pennsylvania Press, 1993.

Friedenreich, Kenneth, R. Gill, and C. B. Kuriyama, eds. *"A Poet and a filthy Playmaker": New Essays on Christopher Marlowe*. New York: AMS Press, 1988.

Greenhlatt, Stephen. "Marlowe and the Will to Absolute Play." *Renaissance Self-Fashioning: From More to Shakespeare*. Chicago: University of Chicago Press, 1980, 193–221.

———. "Marlowe, Marx, and Anti-Semitism." *Critical Inquiry* 5 (1978): 291–307.

Healy, Thomas. *Christopher Marlowe*. Plymouth: Northcote House, 1994.

Levin, Harry. *The Overreacher: A Study of Christopher Marlowe*. Cambridge: Harvard University Press, 1952.

MacLure, Millar. *Marlowe: The Critical Heritage, 1588–1896*. London: Routledge and Kegan Paul, 1979.

Miller, David Lee. "The Death of the Modern: Gender and Desire in Marlowe's 'Hero and Leander.'" *South Atlantic Quarterly* 88 (1989): 757–87.

Tydeman, William, and Vivien Thomas. *Christopher Marlowe: A Guide through the Critical Maze*. Bristol: Bristol Press, 1989.

MATHEW WINSTON

MARY, QUEEN OF SCOTS
(1542–1587)

BIOGRAPHY

Six days after her birth, Mary Stuart, the only surviving child of James V and Mary of Guise, became queen of the Scots. At the age of five, she was sent to be raised at the French court as the betrothed of the dauphin. Contemporary reports indicate that, in addition to her exalted royal status as both queen of Scotland and future queen of France, Mary's considerable charm and polish made her most admired and popular in the most cultivated court in Europe. Her education included both classical languages in addition to English, Italian, and Spanish, although French remained her primary written language. Throughout her education in France, her most enduring literary influence was the court poet, Pierre de Ronsard, to whom she later dedicated poetry.

She married Francis in 1558 and became his queen in the next year upon the death of Henry II. Her reign in France was brief: Francis II died in late 1560, and Mary became a widow, three days before her eighteenth birthday. Returning to her throne in Scotland, Mary faced profound political and religious conflicts, which only intensified after her marriage to the ambitious and insolent Henry, Lord Darnley. After giving birth to their son, James, Mary's position was seriously destabilized by Darnley's murder. Compounding her difficulties, Mary brought suspicion of complicity on herself by forming an alliance with the prime suspect, the earl of Bothwell, whom she married in 1567. A month after the wedding, the couple was separated by Bothwell's defeat at the hands of rival Scotch nobles; Mary was imprisoned and forced to abdicate in favor of her son, James VI. Escaping in 1568, Mary unfortunately chose rather to cross the border to England than to go to her relatives in France. She remained under house arrest in England, gradually becoming more of a political danger to her cousin Queen Elizabeth. After aborted attempts by Mary's supporters to invade England, assassinate Elizabeth or both, Mary was brought to trial and convicted of conspiracy. Elizabeth eventually overcame her moral qualms and obliquely authorized Mary's execution in 1587, when the queen of Scots was forty-four.

There are two exhaustively researched and highly regarded biographies of Mary. Lady Antonia Fraser's detailed account quite self-consciously focuses more upon what the legendary "Queen of Scots must have been like as a person." In complement, Jenny Wormald's book, part of a series on monarchs and monarchy, deliberately entitles Mary's reign as a "failure" and treats "this monarch as other monarchs are treated, . . . to ask what effect her sex and her personal relationships and actions had on her subjects and kingdom" (18). These modern biographies contrast sharply with an overwhelming amount of lurid and frequently contradictory historiographies and romantic depictions of her life and loves that preoccupied nineteenth- and early twentieth-century biographers.

MAJOR WORKS AND THEMES

The reconciliation of conflicting claims of passion and moral duty pervades Mary's letters and poems. Her awareness of her royal position, from her happy teenage years in France until the eve of her death, when she wrote to her French relatives, is palpable in her letters. In her poems, her knowledge of duties as a queen and as a Catholic is frequently juxtaposed against her passion and its effects, producing concerns that her true character should be clearly understood. Mary's anxiety to be read truly in her letters—particularly in her two verse epistles to Elizabeth*—foreshadows the rhetoric of her son James, whose utilization of the opposing tropes of kingly mystery and crystal clarity has been well documented by new historicist critics.

CRITICAL RECEPTION

Although Mary's biographers have established her reputation of artistic intelligence, surprisingly little critical attention has been paid to the queen of Scots' literary output. The preponderance of research into her letters has mainly perpetuated the arguments about her participation in two criminal conspiracies: first, whether she did—or conversely did not—knowingly participate in Bothwell's plot to murder her second husband and, second, whether she instigated those attempts against Elizabeth that her letters so damningly supported. These arguments are based upon the only complete edition of Mary's letters in their original French, the seven-volume collection made by Prince Alexander Labanoff in 1844. An English translation of excerpts from that edition was published the following year by William Turnbull.

Although collections of some of Mary's poems have been published, the first complete edition did not appear until 1992, in which Robin Bell prints the French and Latin originals in parallel columns with an English verse translation. Bell champions Mary as having "a freshness and urgency that rank with the best writers of her day," analyzing her "fine ear for the rhythms of speech and sound grasp of metre and rhyme" and highlighting Mary's sophisticated word-play, so typical of her schoolmaster, Ronsard.

BIBLIOGRAPHY

Works by Mary, Queen of Scots

Bittersweet Within My Heart: The Love Poems of Mary Queen of Scots. Trans and ed. Robin Bell. San Francisco: Chronicle Books, 1992.

Letters of Mary Stuart, Queen of Scotland. Trans. William Turnbull. London: Charles Dolman, 1845.

The Poems of Mary Queen of Scots to the Earl of Bothwell. Ed. John Enschede en Zonen. Haarlem, 1932.

Queen Mary's Book. Ed. P. Arbuthnott. London, 1907.

Receuil des Lettres de Marie Stuart. 7 vols. Comp. Alexander Labanoff. London: Charles Dolmon, 1844.

The Silver Casket. Ed. and trans. Clifford Box. London, 1946.

Stuart, May. *Latin Themes of Mary Stuart, Queen of Scots*. Ed. Anatole de Montaiglon. London: Warburton Club, 1855.

Studies of Mary, Queen of Scots

Cowan, I. B. *The Enigma of Mary Stuart*. London, 1971.

Davison, M. H. Armstrong. *The Casket Letters*. London, 1965.

Donaldson, Gordon. *The First Trial of Mary, Queen of Scots*. New York: Stein and Day, 1969.

———. *Mary, Queen of Scots*. London, 1974.

Fleming, D. Hay. *Mary, Queen of Scots*. London: Hodder and Stoughton, 1897.

Fraser, Antonia. *Mary, Queen of Scots*. London: Weidenfeld and Nicholson, 1969.

Phillips, James Emerson. *Images of a Queen: Mary Stuart in Sixteenth Century Literature*. Los Angeles: University of California Press, 1964.

Plowden, Alison. *Two Queens in One Isle: The Deadly Relationship of Elizabeth I and Mary, Queen of Scots*. Brighton: Harvester, 1984.

Wormald, Jenny. *Mary: Queen of Scots: A Study in Failure*. London: George Philip, 1988.

SUSANNE COLLIER

MICHEL DE MONTAIGNE
(1533–1592)

BIOGRAPHY

Michel de Montaigne was born in the Dordogne region of France into a family recently elevated to the minor nobility. The infant was put out to nurse with a peasant woman and, upon his return to the family chateau, was placed in the care of a tutor. As Montaigne recounts, this German doctor spoke to him in Latin only, according to the dictates of the elder Montaigne, who had strong yet apparently kind views about his son's upbringing (essai I:26). At the age of six, Michel was sent off to pursue a more standardized education at the College de Guyenne in Bordeaux, where, as a native speaker of Latin, he caused some consternation among the Latin masters. Almost nothing is known about his young adulthood; he may have attended law school in Toulouse; he may have spent some time in Paris.

It is likely, though not certain, that in 1554 Michel assumed a post in a local tax court. Three years later, when the tax court had merged with the Parlement of Bordeaux, Michel is documented on the role of counselors; he would serve in the Parlement for some thirteen years. Here he met Etienne de La Boétie, with whom he formed perhaps the closest emotional attachment of his life. During this time, too, Michel married Françoise de la Chassaigne. In 1568 the elder Montaigne died, and Michel, as the oldest male child, inherited the title. Two years later, Michel, now "de Montaigne," left his position in the Parlement and went to Paris, where he published sonnets written by La Boétie, who had died in 1563. Whatever may have been Montaigne's aims in going to Paris to publish these works under dedications to influential people, after a year at court he went home and declared his retirement to a life of quiet reflection and study.

Anticipating tranquility, he experienced instead a disturbingly mobile and disorderly mental state. In order to come to terms with, or at least take account of, the unquiet products of his mind, he began to ''keep a register'' of his thoughts (I:8 trans. Florio). This ''register'' would evolve into the *Essays*, the first two volumes of which were published in 1580. Three months later, Montaigne set out on his first and only international journey, the journal of which would be published after his death. In 1581 Montaigne returned to France in order to take up the mayoralty of Bordeaux, an office he held for two terms and a total of four years. Although his first impulse had been to decline the office, he later wrote that the responsibilities he faced as mayor ''suited [his] disposition'' (III: 10).

The last years of Montaigne's retirement continued to be relatively active. In 1588 Catholic extremists succeeded in having him briefly confined in the Bastille. This year, too, he traveled with the court of Henri III. He later corresponded with Henri IV from his chateau and twice received him as a visitor. During these later years, too, he became acquainted with Marie de Gournay, who would become his adopted daughter and literary executor.

Montaigne was a moderate in times of violent religious and political strife. He deplored the brutalities of the Wars of Religion, whether perpetrated by Protestant or Catholic, and ''took beatings,'' as he put it, from extremists on both sides (III:12). The extent of the role he played in affairs of state has not been established in detail, but his importance as a negotiator between Henri III and Henri de Navarre is known. Privately, he observed the rites of the Catholic religion, while actively seeking to understand Protestant beliefs. Privately, too, he may have aspired to some more formal position at court, but he was not called, as far as we know, until Navarre came to the Crown, when Montaigne was obliged, perhaps because of ill health, to decline. The essayist died at home in September 1592, not—as he had feared—in the agony of a kidney stone attack, but of a throat infection.

MAJOR WORKS AND THEMES

The *Essays*, the sole work both authored and published by Montaigne, comprise three books, the first two having appeared at Simon Millanges in Bordeaux in 1580, the third in 1588 at Angelier in Paris; they amounted in all to four authorized editions during the author's lifetime. Two years after his death the first annotated edition was prepared by Marie de Gournay.

Physically, the *Essays* present themselves as a collection of commentaries of varying lengths gathered together in three ''books.'' The 107 essays contain reflections on a wide range of ponderables, such as cannibals, Cicero, desire, discomforts of high rank, faces, and friendship. Many chapter titles, such as ''On Sadness,'' ''On Names,'' or ''On Coaches,'' seemingly point to a clear, fairly concrete topic. Other titles appear to promise reflections on complex social or philosophical issues. Among these are ''We Should Meddle Soberly With Judging Divine Ordinances'' and ''How the Mind Hinders Itself'' (Frame trans.). One of the first things a reader is likely to notice, however, is that Montaigne's titles often do not point directly to his topic, which may itself be difficult to determine. In fact, the *Essays* distinguish themselves sharply from preceding works of similar vein, such as Cicero's ''On Friendship'' or ''On Old Age,'' Seneca's moral essays (or letters about mores), Plutarch's *Morals*, or sixteenth-century collections of lessons and sayings—all of which were probably meant to be read as improving and entertaining assemblages of widely accepted verities. Montaigne's text deflects this sort of reading with a claim to both the unity and the particularity of a consciously individual point of view. The text sees itself as internally consistent in that it springs from one intellect, and for the same reason, it avoids any appearance of setting forth universal truths. To this unity and particularity is added a crucial third characteristic: the essayist's awareness of the ways in which his own actions, emotions, judgments, and reflections fail to add up to a stable, internally consistent identity, even as they represent his individuality.

Perhaps the best-known aspect of the *Essays* is the author's claim that he writes in order to ''paint'' himself (II:18). This evocation of self-portraiture has been read variously as yet another in a long line of responses to the ancient injunction ''know thyself'' and as the establishing moment of the modern literary subject. As a transitional text, the *Essays* permit both interpretations but are constrained by neither. This combination of textual malleability and elusiveness, in part, accounts for the essays' durability and generosity as objects of literary study. One hesitates, consequently, to limit them with a thematic summary. Broadly, though, the concerns of the text return repeatedly to the capabilities and especially the limits of human judgment; to the interplay of reason and emotion, body and mind; and to the impact of this interplay on belief, opinion, and action. In this regard, if Montaigne observes and documents the contents and conditions of his own mind and body, he aims, in part, to collect data touching the large questions of life from a source appropriate and accessible to his human perceptions and understanding. Partly, too, his insistence on self-portrayal demonstrates the conviction that the humble details of the human condition and the ''ordinary'' life are worthy of consideration and expression.

Montaigne did not, as far as I know, consider publishing the journal of his 1580–81 trip to Rome. The manuscript, written in Montaigne's own hand as well as that of another person whose identity is unknown, was discovered in the late eighteenth century and was first published in 1774 by Meusnier Querlon.

The *Travel Journal* documents the daily progress of a company of five noblemen on horseback and an uncertain number of their serving people as they traveled through Germany and Switzerland to Italy. The ''secretary,'' as the second writer of the journal is known, records in particular the availability, price, and quality of food, rooms, bed linens, and washing water. This writer also notes technological wonders, such as an ingenious timepiece, city gate, or fountain. Montaigne is by no means silent on such matters, but the parts of the journal he penned are perhaps most striking as documents of the scientific interest he took in his health. His record of the many treatments he took for kidney stones shows patience, precision, and persistence in the face of the frightening and painful ailment that had killed his father. Notably, too, the traveler's reflections on the mingling of his conception of ancient Rome with his perception of the sixteenth-century city before him mark the journal as a source for students of the Rome topos in Renaissance humanism.

CRITICAL RECEPTION

The *Essays* were generally well thought of when they appeared. They were variously approved as imitating Plutarch, as being unlike anything else, as coupling elegant style with freedom of expression, and as displaying wisdom untrammeled by pedanticism. In her preface to the 1595 edition Marie de Gournay complains of the cold reception accorded the *Essays*, but Maurice Rat places the first significant negative reaction to Montaigne's text near the end of the reign of Louis XIII, when both literary and religious purists began to look disapprovingly at the essayist's "portrait." Not least among these critics was the pope, who banned the *Essays* in 1676. Accordingly, the Pléiade *Oeuvres Completes* bibliography lists no editions of the work from 1636 to 1723. Appreciative readers were not lacking during this time, however, as the support of Madame de Sévigné and La Bruyère indicates. Donald Frame points to Montaigne's pertinence to the discourse of the late seventeenth century in Europe when he writes, "In the great line of French *Moralistes*, he is the first and the greatest." Similarly, the importance of the *Essays* for the French Enlightenment is suggested by Pierre Villey, for whom the essayist's "great originality is to have offered . . . a model of human wisdom organized solely according to the light of reason" (Villey, XXXII, my trans.).

Contemporary readings of the *Essays* fall into four interrelated categories. The best-established of these is the psychological reading, which, while it allows for a range of interpretations, invariably depends on the organizing and validating principle of a particular individual subjectivity. Such criticism often incorporates the idea of a historical Montaigne, the development of whose opinions and personality may be tracked through the essays (see Frame, Greene).

Recent critical work has branched out to include gender-related, socioeconomic, and textual concerns. The gender-related approach explores the cultural significance of references to, and silences about, women (see Bauschatz, Charpentier, Parker), while socioeconomic studies focus on the text as a response to, and an account of, a specific historical moment (see Desan). Textually oriented criticism often relies on close readings that may not be so much concerned with Montaigne's message as with the sparks of significance that fly when a modern sensibility comes into contact with the Renaissance text (Regosin). The twofold effect of this diversification has been to complicate the venerable view of the essays as a "mirror" for the reader and to demonstrate the availability of this early modern text for readings that are based in postmodern literary theory.

The *Travel Journal* has, to date, held a decidedly minor place in Montaigne studies. It has been, with very few exceptions, valued not as a text in its own right but rather as a source of information about the *Essays*, their author, and their time.

BIBLIOGRAPHY

Works by Michel de Montaigne (in the original French)

Le Journal de voyage. Ed. Fausta Garavini. Paris: Gallimard, 1983.

Le Journal de voyage. Ed. François Rigolot. Paris: PUF, 1992.

Les Essais. Ed. V. L. Saulnier and Pierre Villey. Paris: PUF, 1978.

Oeuvres Completes. Ed. Maurice Rat and Albert Thibaudet. Paris: Gallimard (Bibliothèque de la Pléiade), 1967.

Works by Michel de Montaigne (in translation)

The Complete Works of Montaigne. Trans. Donald M. Frame. Stanford, CA: Stanford University Press, 1957.

The Essays of Michel de Montaigne. Trans. M. A. Screech. London: Penguin Books, 1991.

The Essays of Montaigne. Trans. John Florio. New York: AMS Press, 1967.

Montaigne's Travel Journal. Trans. Donald M. Frame. San Francisco: North Point Press, 1983.

Studies of Michel de Montaigne

The Essays

Bauschatz, Cathleen M. " 'Leur plus universelle qualité, c'est la diversité': Women as Ideal Readers in Montaigne's *Essais*." *Journal of Medieval and Renaissance Studies* 19 (1989): 83–101.

Bowen, Barbara. "Speech and Writing in the 1580 Text of 'Du parler prompt ou tardif.' " In *Montaigne (1580–1980)*, ed. Marcel Tetel. Paris: Nizet, 1983.

Brody, Jules. *Lectures de Montaigne*. Lexington: French Forum, 1982.

Brush, Craig, B. *From the Perspective of the Self: Montaigne's Self Portrait*. New York: Fordham University Press, 1994.

Calder, Ruth. " 'Une marqueterie mal jointe': Montaigne and Lucilian Satire." *Bibliothèque d'Humanisme et Renaissance* 54 (1991): 385–93.

Cave, Terence. "Problems of Reading in the Essais." In *Montaigne: Essays in Memory of Richard Sayce*, ed. I. D. McFarlane and Ian Maclean. Oxford: Clarendon Press, 1982.

Charpentier, Françoise. "L'absente des *Essais*: quelques questions autour de l'essai 2:8, 'de l'affection des peres aux enfans.' " *Bulletin de la Société des Amis de Montaigne* 17–18 (1984): 7–16.

Clark, Carol. "Talking about Souls: Montaigne on Human Psychology." In *Montaigne: Essays in Memory of Richard Sayce*, ed. I. D. McFarlane and Ian Maclean. Oxford: Clarendon Press, 1982.

Compagnon, Antoine. "A Long Short Story: Montaigne's Brevity." *Yale French Studies* 64 (1983): 24–50.

Conley, Tom. "An 'Allegory of Prudence': Text and Icon of 'De la phisionomie.' " *Montaigne Studies* 4 (1992): 156–79.

Cottrell, Robert. *Sexuality/Textuality: A Study of the Fabric of Montaigne's Essais*. Columbus: Ohio State University Press, 1981.

Defaux, Gerard. "Readings of Montaigne." *Yale French Studies* 64 (1983): 73–92.

Desan, Philippe. "Quand le discours social passe par le discours économique: les *Essais* de Montaigne." *Sociocriticism* 4 (1988): 59–86.

Engel, William. "Cites and Stones: Montaigne's Patrimony." *Montaigne Studies* 4 (1992): 180–99.

Farquhar, Sue W. "From Venus to Venality: Legal Hermeneutics and Montaigne's Use of the Example in I:21–23." In *Montaigne and the Gods: The Mythological Key to the Essays*, ed. Daniel Martin. Amherst, MA: Hestia, 1993.

Frame, Donald M. "Specific Motivation for Montaigne's Self Portrait." In *Columbia Montaigne Conference Papers*. Lexington: French Forum, 1981.

Freccero, Carla. "Cannibalism, Homophobia, Women: Montaigne's 'Des Cannibales' and 'De l'amitié.' " In *Women, 'Race,' and Writing in the Early Modern Period*, ed. Margo Hendricks and Patricia Parker. London: Routledge, 1994.

Garces, Maria Antonia. "Coaches, Litters, and Chariots of War: Montaigne and Atahualpa." *Journal of Hispanic Philology* 16 (1992): 155–83.

Glidden, Hope. "The Face in the Text: Montaigne's Emblematic Self-Portrait (Essais III: 12)." *Renaissance Quarterly* 46 (1993): 71–97.

Gray, Floyd. *Montaigne bilingue: le Latin des Essais*. Paris: Champion, 1991.

Greenberg, Mitchell. "Montaigne at the Crossroads: Textual Conundrums in the *Essais*." *Stanford French Review* 6 (1982): 21–34.

Greene, Thomas M. "Dangerous Parleys—Essais I:5 and 6." *Yale French Studies* 64 (1983): 3–23.

Henry, Patrick. "Montaigne and Heraclitus: Pattern and Flux, Continuity and Change in 'Du Repentir.' " *Montaigne Studies* 4 (1992): 7–18.

Hoffmann, George. "The Montaigne Monopoly: Revising the *Essais* under the French Privilege System." *PMLA* 108 (1993): 308–19.

Johnson, Eric Aaron. *Knowledge and Society: A Social Epistemology of Montaigne's Essais*. Charlottesville, VA: Rookwood Press, 1994.

Kritzman, Lawrence D. "Montaigne's Fantastic Monsters and the Construction of Gender." *Writing the Renaissance: Essays on Sixteenth-Century French Literature in Honor of Floyd Gray*. Lexington: French Forum, 1992.

La Charité, Raymond C. "Montaigne's Silenic Text: 'De la phisionomie.' " In *Le Parcours des Essais Montaigne 1580–1980*, ed. Marcel Tetel and G. Mallary Masters. Paris: Aux Amateurs de Livres, 1989.

McGowan, Margaret. "Contradictory Impulses in Montaigne's Vision of Rome." *Renaissance Studies* 4 (1990): 392–409.

McKinley, Mary B. *Words in a Corner: Studies in Montaigne's Latin Quotations*. Lexington: French Forum, 1981.

Martin, Daniel. *L'architecture des Essais de Montaigne: mémoire artificielle et mythologie*. Paris: Nizet, 1992.

Mathieu-Castellani, Gisèle. "Dire, Signifier: la figure de la significatio dans les *Essais*." *Montaigne Studies* 3 (1991): 68–81.

Meijer, Marianne S. ''The Significance of 'de la diversion' in Montaigne's Third Book.'' *Romance Notes* 32 (1991): 11–17.

Nakam, Geralde. *Montaigne et son temps: les événements et les Essais*. Paris: Nizet, 1982.

Parker, Patricia. ''Gender Ideology, Gender Change: The Case of Marie Germain.'' *Critical Inquiry* 19 (1993): 337–64.

Polachek, Dora E. ''Imagination, Idleness, and Self-Discovery: Montaigne's Early Voyage Inward.'' In *Reconsidering the Renaissance: Papers from the Twenty-First Annual Conference*, ed. Mario DiCesare. Binghamton: Medieval and Renaissance Texts and Studies, 1992.

Regosin, Richard L. ''Recent Trends in Montaigne Scholarship: A Poststructuralist Perspective.'' *Renaissance Quarterly* 37 (1984): 34–54.

Reiss, Timothy. ''Montaigne and the Subject of Polity.'' In *Literary Theory/Renaissance Texts*, ed. Patricia Parker and David Quint. Baltimore: Johns Hopkins University Press, 1986.

Rendall, Steven. *Distinguo: Reading Montaigne Differently*. New York: Oxford University Press, 1992.

Rigolot, François. *Les métamorphoses de Montaigne*. Paris: PUF, 1988.

Starobinski, Jean. *Montaigne in Motion*. Chicago: University of Chicago Press, 1985.

Tetel, Marcel. *Montaigne*. Boston: Twayne, 1990.

Tournon, André. ''Self-Interpretation in Montaigne's Essais.'' *Yale French Studies* 64 (1983): 51–74.

Journal de Voyage

Autour du Journal de voyage de Montaigne, 1580–1980, ed. René Bernoulli and François Moureau. Genève-Paris: Editions Statkine, 1982.

Coats, Catharine Randall. ''Writing Like a Woman: Gender Transformations in Montaigne's *Journal de Voyage*.'' *Montaigne Studies* 5 (1993): 207–18.

Rigolot, François. ''La situation énonciative dans le *Journal de Voyage* de Montaigne.'' In *Poétique et narration: Mélanges offerts à Guy Demerson*, ed. Jacques-Philippe Saint-Gerand. Paris: Champion, 1993.

CARLA BOYER

THOMAS MORE
(1478–1535)

BIOGRAPHY

More lived the first English life that has become a field of study in itself. Versions of the man have ranged from William Roper's saint, to Froude's fanatic anti-Protestant (in the *Dictionary of National Biography*), to R. W. Chambers' hero of conscience, to the ambitious, self-divided man of Richard Marius. Born 7 February 1478 in London, More was one of six children of John More, a prominent lawyer who would rise to the King's Bench. He learned his Latin at St. Anthony's School, London, entered Oxford for two years (college unknown), then read for the law at New Inn and Lincoln's Inn, where he was called to the bar in 1501. His first wife, Jane Colt, died in 1511, leaving him with three small daughters and a son. More's parish priest later recalled that a month after her death More came to him late one night with a dispensation permitting marriage the next day without reading of banns. Alice More, then an uneducated widow six years More's senior, learned, says Erasmus,* to sing and play the lute and virginals; she also managed the household and family expertly.

More's life seemingly divides into the periods of the humanist, public servant, and suffering saint; but all three roles were lived simultaneously. Even while preparing for a career in law, More was considering life in the priesthood; after 1501 he even went to live with the monks at Charterhouse, the home of the austere Carthusians in London. He also gave an arresting series of lectures (now lost) on Augustine's *City of God.* Probably the combined influence of his father and John Colet,* his spiritual adviser, led him to settle for marriage and secular life. Yet even after his rise in the world, his habits remained ascetic. More the humanist remains linked with Erasmus, whom he met during the elder scholar's first visit to England in 1499 and his second in 1505. In 1509, Erasmus enjoyed More's hospitality and at his urging undertook *The Praise of Folly.*

More's commitment to the new learning is evident in his study of Greek with William Grocyn, his support of Colet's new grammar school at St. Paul's, and his correspondence. His household acquired a reputation as a center of learning, with children, wife, wards, servants, and grandchildren engaged in instruction and discussion. He harbored visiting statesmen and scholars; he employed musicians; interest in nature led him to gather a small animal menagerie. His prize student, his eldest daughter Margaret (1505–44), testifies to an interest in the education of women shared with other humanists like Juan Luis Vives. At sixteen, Margaret married a sometime Lutheran William Roper, barely obtaining her father's blessing; she retained her scholarly interests and is responsible for preserving (partly through her husband's biography) much that we know of More.

The continuity between humanist and public servant is most evident in his writing of *Utopia* during an embassy to the Netherlands in 1515. Two years later he joined Henry VIII's Privy Council; he also helped quell a public riot on May Day that year. Historians do not now believe that More went into royal service unwillingly. Erasmus says that Cardinal Wolsey, even while disliking More, thought him the most capable successor to the chancellorship; by that time More had been knighted (1521), had served as speaker in Parliament (1523), and had risen to the posts of undertreasurer and chancellor of the duchy of Lancaster. As chancellor (1529–32) he was less effective than his great enemy and successor Thomas Cromwell, partly because of the king's consuming interest in obtaining a divorce, partly because of his own single-minded devotion to hunting heretics. His record in this role is hardly monstrous, however. He was directly involved in three out of the six cases of heresy that led to execution during his chancellorship—though he was supported in this by both the council and an anticlerical but orthodox Parliament. He seems also to have been unusually keen in his censorship of the press. However, Guy finds that a significant contribution of More while in office was to "rejuvenate the ancient theory that judges had a personal duty in conscience to see right done by all whose business was entertained in the courts they directed." In 1534 More found himself in the Tower of London, having refused to take the oath affirming the validity of Henry's second marriage. He was beheaded 6 July 1535 and declared a saint by the Catholic Church 400 years later.

For recusant Catholics More became a model of faith under trial, commemorated in the Tudor biographies of Roper, Nicholas Harpsfield, Thomas Stapleton, and "Ro. Ba." A more secular hero—defender of the poor and teller of merry tales—survives in the Elizabethan play *Sir Thomas More*, perhaps written, in part or whole, by Shakespeare.* Jean Anouilh and Robert Bolt brought More to the modern stage as an existential hero confronting totalitarianism. *Utopia* has given more than a word to the West: the Spanish colonial government embodied some Utopian practices in sixteenth-century Mexico, while modern communists like Karl Kautsky (Engels' secretary) saw in Utopia a primitive blueprint for the socialist state.

MAJOR WORKS AND THEMES

The English poems, both comic and religious, are an acquired taste, like tripe sausage. More's sense of irony and human absurdity finds early expression in his and Erasmus' first collaboration, their translation from Greek to Latin of some of Lucian's comic dialogues (Paris, 1506). *Utopia* (Louvain, 1516) is, in many respects, a Lucianic dialogue-cum-fabulous voyage. More, a character in Book 1, addresses serious concerns of his day: unemployment, cruel rents, the enclosure of English common land for the benefit of the wool industry. England, he remarks, is a country where the sheep eat the men. His practicality contrasts with the idealism of a traveler he meets, Raphael Hythloday, who recounts his visit to Utopia in Book 2 (written before Book 1, Hexter shows). The debate whether to enter service as a royal councillor affords some glimpse into More's self-doubts in choosing his profession. Hythloday voices high-minded disgust with political affairs, while More urges that if one cannot make things perfect, he might at least make them less bad. Clues throughout encourage an ironic distancing from both positions. Utopia is *eu topos* in Greek, a good place, but also *ou topos*, no place. The traveler's name is probably from *hythlos*, idle talk, and *audē*, voice. Morus, More's Latin name, means "foolish," a pun that More and Erasmus enjoyed in the *Praise of Folly*, dedicated to More as *Encomium Moriae*. The fashion of *serio ludere*, playing seriously, lost currency with readers in later centuries, who usually took the proposals of Book 2 in earnest.

The capacity for wisdom of state exists in More's portrait of Bishop (later, cardinal archbishop of Canterbury) John Morton, his actual boyhood patron. But vain, self-serving courtiers surround Morton, and a sense of the futility of counsel remains when wise words dissipate in a spat between a proud friar and a fool. The enfolded ironies of Book 1 often carry over to Book 2, as, for example, when More the lawyer has his ''nonsense-speaker'' praise the Utopian contempt for lawyers. There are, certainly, notes of conviction: enthusiasm for gardens, music, dark churches, and especially for a moral philosophy grounded in reason, nature, and the pursuit of happiness. At the end, Hythloday's description terminates in a burst of rage against human pride—though he himself in his solipsism is scarcely innocent on this score. It has remained for recent scholars (Logan, Skinner) to sort out the authentic political philosophy from the irony in *Utopia* and to show both its reliance on, and critical detachment from, contemporary thought. The growing awareness of More's complexity has led to reexamination of his Latin and dissatisfaction with English translations. When one modern translation reads ''serious controversy'' and ''well-established cities,'' instead of (to quote a closer translation of these phrases) ''some differences of no slight import'' and ''commonwealths not badly governed,'' it conceals More's frequent technique of litotes, a trope crucial to both the man and the work (McCutcheon). Even the favored translation in the Yale edition has not found unqualified acceptance.

A widely circulated early edition put *Utopia* with More's Latin *Epigrams*, written between 1509 and 1519. These touch on many subjects, but I am especially drawn to the political verses, which often touch on the matter of kingship. One, ''De Rege et Rustico'' (On the King and the Rustic), shows with delicate ambiguity that to the untutored man of nature there is no difference between a king and an ordinary mortal except for the ''painted clothes.'' Tyranny is a principal theme of several of these poems, though More can be fulsome in his praise of the future tyrant Henry VIII. *The History of Richard III*, perhaps begun simultaneously with *Utopia*, shows the consequences of a demonic power-lust when the tyrant enjoys a vain, ambitious, or cowardly aristocracy. Written in different English and Latin versions (a manuscript discovered after the Yale edition was published in volume 15), the history remains all but finished. It was substantial enough to furnish Edward Hall,* and through him Shakespeare, with both the details of the reign and their interpretation. It shares with other humanist histories a frequency of Thucididean invented speeches (these constitute a third of the text) and character studies (of Edward IV, his mistress Jane Shore, Elizabeth Woodville, Buckingham, and others), not to mention dutiful citation of sources (some directly from his father, who witnessed several events). The old claim that More was writing Tudor propaganda seems now to hold little water.

More's sense of irony shapes several political scenes to show the difference between actions and words on the public stage. Theater is a root metaphor in the *History*, and at certain points More virtually does Shakespeare's work for him. More's account of King Edward's deathbed speech, Shakespeare's Act 2, scene 1, shows a similarly pious-sounding king making peace among an apparently sincere nobility, but the scene grimly concludes: ''[T]hese in his presence (as by their words appeared) each forgave other, and joined hands together, when (as it after appeared by their deeds) their hearts were far asunder.'' Although Edward had enjoyed respect from earlier chroniclers, More lumps him with his brothers Richard and Clarence as equally ''greedy and ambitious of authority, and impatient of partners.'' Richard outdoes everyone in hypocrisy, and I sense More, as much as Shakespeare, enjoying the usurper's staged shows of public support. On one hand, the narrative acquires its shape from the author's belief in divine justice, and the approaching closure of the narrative is perceptible despite its unfinished state. On the other, the *History* affirms the devil's existence as much as God's, suggesting at every turn the dark forces that so preoccupied More and his melancholy century.

Reading More's religious, controversial works has few rewards for those who lack my interest in the art of polemics, the relation of faith to reason, or the political implications of worship. Scholars have seen these debates as inexorably drawing the jocular humanist into the vortex of Reformation-era obsession and vindictiveness. The evidence is that More swam there on his own.

First, in 1523, came the *Responsio ad Lutherum*, answering Luther's answer to Henry VIII's defense of the seven Sacraments (which More probably helped write). An important theme emerging here is More's objection to the idea of an ''invisible church,'' the collection of saved souls with identities known only to God. More's belief in the unity of flesh and spirit made him especially hostile to Luther's belief ''not in this palpable and perceptible church, but in some other multitude of Christians, somehow imperceptible and mathematical—like Platonic ideas—which is both in some place and in no place, is in the flesh and is out of the flesh, which is wholly involved in sin and yet does not sin at all.'' With William Tyndale's* activity on behalf of Lutheran ideas in England, More's polemics grow strident. *The Dialogue concerning Heresies* (1529) is not without humor, though More's ridiculing of Luther's marriage to an ex-nun becomes rather tedious. At about this time More supposedly said that if Luther had restricted himself to attacking clerical abuses in the church, he would have supported him. In the dialogue the speaker More sometimes does give an appearance of accommodating the Lutheran messenger, as when he says that while widespread Bible reading is dangerous, bishops might lend Bibles to approved people, though they would have to get them back once the reader died.

More wrote *The Confutation of Tyndale's Answer* (1523–33), an enormous mass of vituperation, sometimes funny, mostly tiresome, when he must have known that his time on earth and his church's time in England were dwindling. Like polemicists for centuries to come, he constructs his argument as a passage-by-passage rebuttal of his opponent. Again he hammers away at his enemies' distortion of the meaning of ''church.'' This has always meant several things: ''that part of the church that in synods and councils do represent the whole church''; ''rulers or heads of the church''; finally, all Christians ''throughout the whole world.'' It becomes increasingly apparent that More objected to Tyndale's closure of doctrinal discussion almost as much as the doctrine itself. God, he says, deliberately left much unexplained in order to draw us to inquire, to ''find out good and fruitful things, allegories and other, not affirming those to be the very things there intended, but things that devoutly and fruitfully may be thereon taken and turn men to devotion, and this as well in the ceremonies as in the hard and not intelligible texts.'' He especially defends allegorizing of Scripture, contrasting the literalism of Tyndale and Luther with Christ's allegorical language in his sermons and parables. Tyndale's insistence on a Christianity of understanding and reason rather than ''superstition'' anticipates many long and bloody arguments of the next two centuries. Although no weak logician, More often counters Tyndale's logic with a humor that is heavy-handed and visual—perhaps because of Tyndale's stress on the ''invisible.'' At one point he mockingly envisions Tyndale drunk with Lutheranism, falling into a vat, being pulverized with the grapes and eaten by hogs. In extenuation, More's editors say that the audience for this work was the wide range of common, literate Englishmen not yet won over to Lutheranism, a readership that demanded, in More's mind, a humor less subtle, less dependent on irony, than he had known in the past.

I think More's well-placed fear of social disorder, as well as the intellectual's contempt for misguided opinions, lies behind much of his anti-Protestant writing. In his *Apology* (1533) he links, as some historians still do, the Lutheran and the medieval Lollard movements. In the time of Henry V, he says, heretics ''conspired among them, not only the abolition of the faith, and spoiling of the spirituality, but also the destruction of the king and all his nobility, with a plain subversion and overturning of the state of his whole realm.'' This reading of religious reform as a subterfuge for political rebellion continues throughout the century, again showing how much is augured in the More–Tyndale debate. There is evidence, however, of a weariness with public life in these later polemics. Take, as a benchmark of the distance More had come since *Utopia*, his response to Tyndale's charge that in earlier days More and his ''darling'' Erasmus had attacked some of the same ecclesiastical abuses as he and Luther. More snaps back, ''[I]n these days in which men by their own default misconstrue and take harm of the very scripture of God, until men better amend, if any man would now translate *Moria* [i.e., *The Praise of Folly*] into English, or some works, either that I have myself written ere this, albeit there be none harm therein, folk yet being (as they may) given to take harm of that that is good, I would not only my darling's books but mine own also, help to burn them both with mine own hands, rather than folk should (though their own fault) take any harm of them, seeing that I see them likely in these days to do so.'' Willful misreading, in other words, had put learning in cold storage.

While imprisoned in the Tower, More experienced a final surge of creativity. It is manifest in the English letters, especially those to Margaret, as well as in several books of spiritual meditation. These ''Tower works'' begin with *A Treatise upon the Passion* (actually written a little before his imprisonment), which shows More reading the Scriptures with regard both for the letter and for the ''allegories'' he mentioned in the *Confutation*—such as the ancient identification of Pharaoh with ''the prince of this dark world, the devil.'' His reflections on the Sacraments and the mystical body of Christ anticipate the matter of *A Treatise to Receive the Blessed Body of Our Lord.* These two books, linking the mysteries of the Passion and Eucharist, lead directly to *De Tristitia Christi* (On Christ's Sadness, that is, in the Garden of Gethsemane), a fuller and more absorbing book, partly because it centers on one short episode in the gospel. Again, More finds allegories prompted by the spirit. The brook Cedron is so named from ''sadness'' or ''blackness,'' evidence of ''a secret plan of the Holy Spirit, who concealed in these names a store of sacred mysteries to be ferreted out sometime later,'' says his editor. The name of Malchus, servant of the high priest who had his ear cut off, means ''king,'' which in the human soul is reason; but reason has gone over to the high priest, who represents superstition (More follows Augustine and Jerome in his reading).

CRITICAL RECEPTION

Many rank *A Dialogue of Comfort against Tribulation* as an achievement equal to *Utopia.* At one level the participants in this dialogue, an uncle and his nephew in Hungary awaiting disaster at the hands of the invading Turks, represent the condition of faithful Catholics in More's own country. In the polemical works More sometimes compared Luther with Mohammed and spoke of ''heretics worse than Turks.'' The Turk now symbolizes the great satanic force of unbelief, the armies of Antichrist threatening faith from within as well as without. This last of More's dialogues serves to remind us how aptly this form suits a mind that both affirms belief and resists closure. Of special value, too, are the wit and charm that return to his writing, displayed in the older speaker's reminiscences about politics and churchmen, husbands and wives, including a number of the ''merry tales'' for which More was known. *The Dialogue of Comfort* belongs to the long tradition of preparations for death, confronting and analyzing human fears and the temptations of despair. Transcending the narrowness of polemics to meditate on the larger question of evil in the world, it is a great work of theodicy.

BIBLIOGRAPHY

Works by Thomas More

The Complete Works of Saint Thomas More. 15 vols. Ed. Richard S. Sylvester, Clarence H. Miller, et al. New Haven, CT: Yale University Press, 1963–86.

The Correspondence of Sir Thomas More. Ed. Elizabeth F. Rogers. Princeton: Princeton University Press, 1947.

Selected Letters. Ed. Elizabeth F. Rogers. New Haven, CT: Yale University Press, 1961.

Utopia. Trans. and ed. Robert M. Adams and George M. Logan. Cambridge: Cambridge University Press, 1989.

Studies of Thomas More

Adams, R. P. *The Better Part of Valor: More, Erasmus, Colet, and Vives on Humanism, War, and Peace.* Seattle: University of Washington Press, 1962.

Baker-Smith, Dominic. *More's* Utopia. New York: HarperCollins Academic, 1991.

Chambers, R. W. *Thomas More*. London: Cape, 1935.

Duncan, Douglas. *Ben Jonson and the Lucianic Tradition*. Cambridge: Cambridge University Press, 1979.

Elliott, Robert C. *The Shape of Utopia: Studies in a Literary Genre*. Chicago: University of Chicago Press, 1970.

Essential Articles for the Study of Thomas More. Ed. Germain Marc'hadour and Richard S. Sylvester. Hamden, CT: Archon, 1977.

Fox, Alistair. *Thomas More: History and Providence*. New Haven, CT: Yale University Press, 1983.

Gairdner, James. "A Letter concerning Bishop Fisher and Sir Thomas More." *English Historical Review* 7 (1892): 712–15.

Geritz, Albert J. "Recent Studies in More (1977–1990)." *English Literary Renaissance* 22 (1992): 112–40.

Gibson, R. W. *St. Thomas More: A Preliminary Bibliography of His Works and of Moreana to the Year 1750*. New Haven, CT: Yale University Press, 1961.

Greenblatt, Stephen J. *Renaissance Self-Fashioning*. Chicago: University of Chicago Press, 1980.

Guy, J. A. *The Public Career of Sir Thomas More*. New Haven, CT: Yale University Press, 1980.

Hexter, J. H. *More's Utopia: The Biography of an Idea*. Princeton: Princeton University Press, 1952.

Logan, George M. *The Meaning of More's* Utopia. Princeton: Princeton University Press, 1983.

McCutcheon, Elizabeth. "Denying the Contrary: More's Use of Litotes in the *Utopia*." *Moreana*, nos. 31–32 (1971): 107–21.

Marius, Richard. *Thomas More: A Biography*. New York: Knopf, 1984.

Mueller, Janel. " 'The Whole Island like a Single Family': Positioning Women in Utopian Patriarchy." In *Rethinking the Henrician Era*, ed. Peter C. Herman. Urbana: University of Illinois Press, 1994, 93–122.

O'Brien, Brian. "J. H. Hexter and the Text of *Utopia*: A Reappraisal." *Moreana* 29.110 (1992): 19–32.

Roper, William. *The Lyfe of Sir Thomas Moore, Knighte*. Ed. E. V. Hitchcock. Early English Text Society. London, 1935.

Skinner, Quentin. "Sir Thomas More's *Utopia* and the Language of Renaissance Humanism." In *The Languages of Political Theory in Early-Modern Europe*, ed. Anthony Pagden. Cambridge: Cambridge University Press, 1987, 123–57.

Sullivan, Frank, and Majie Padberg. *Moreana: Materials for the Study of Saint Thomas More*. 5 vols. and supplement. Los Angeles: Loyola University of Los Angeles, 1964–77.

Surtz, Edward. *The Praise of Pleasure*. Cambridge: Harvard University Press, 1957.

"Thomas More and the Classics." Ed. Ralph Keen and Daniel Kinney. *Moreana*, no. 86 (1985).

White, Thomas I. "Index Verborum to *Utopia*." *Moreana*, no. 52 (1976): 5–17.

Wilson, K. J. *Incomplete Fictions: The Formation of English Renaissance Dialogue*. Washington: Catholic University of America Press, 1985.

RICHARD F. HARDIN

N

THOMAS NASHE
(1567–c. 1600)

BIOGRAPHY

Thomas Nashe was born in Lowestoft in November 1567, son of William Nashe, a minor clergyman. He attended St. Johns College at Cambridge from 1582 to 1588, taking his B.A. in March 1586. His father, who had been supporting his education, died in 1587, which may explain why Nashe left before taking his M.A. From Cambridge, Nashe went to London, where he quickly became a member of the literary scene, his first published work being a rather lengthy (and self-serving) preface to Robert Greene's* *Menaphon* (1589). Also in 1589 Nashe entered the Marprelate controversy (which may be how he met Greene, as well as John Lyly,* both of whom wrote for the Established Church position). Because the Marprelate pamphlets were all published anonymously, it is impossible to be certain which of them Nashe wrote, but the most likely candidate is *An Almond for a Parrat.*

Nashe's first full-length work, *Anatomie of Absurdities*, was published in 1589 but was probably written while Nashe was still a student at Cambridge. It exhibits none of the boisterous style for which Nashe was to become famous (and which he probably developed through his engagement in the Marprelate controversy). Perhaps the primary point of interest in the *Anatomie* is the fact that Nashe first mentions Gabriel Harvey* in it. The comment on Harvey, while not exactly generous, is also not really critical, but it may nevertheless have initiated

Nashe's long quarrel with the Harvey family, which McKerrow identifies as "by far the most important event in Nashe's life as a man of letters" (I.65). Nashe would ultimately publish two lengthy attacks on Gabriel Harvey—*Strange Newes* (1592) and *Have with You to Saffron-Walden* (1596).

It is difficult to tell how Nashe supported himself from 1589 to 1592, but he may have been writing occasional pieces for manuscript circulation like his pornographic *The Choice of Valentines*, known popularly as *Nashe's Dildo* (c. 1592). He would later declare, "I have written in all sorts of humors privately, I am persuaded, more than any young man of my age in England" (i.320). In 1592, Nashe published the work for which he was best known during his lifetime, *Pierce Penilesse His Supplication to the Devil*, which was printed five times by 1595. Nashe was generally identified with his protagonist Pierce (probably pronounced "purse"), and he apparently adopted him as his own persona.

In the summer of 1592, to escape the plague raging in London, Nashe stayed at Archbishop Whitgift's castle at Croyden, where he composed his only surviving play, *Summers Last Will and Testament*, which contains the justifiably famous and often-anthologized song "Adieu, farewell earths blisse." During the following winter, he resided on the Isle of Wight with Sir George Carey, where he presumably composed *Strange Newes* and *The Terrors of the Night* (though Nicholl believes the latter was written at Robert Cotton's Conington Manor). Sometime during the spring or summer of 1593, Nashe composed the work most appreciated by modern audiences, *The Unfortunate Traveler*, as well as the work least appreciated by modern readers, *Christs Teares Over Jerusalem*. Nicholl believes that *Christs Teares* was the product of "an actual nervous breakdown" (169) and offers as partial evidence the fact that Nashe apparently wrote nothing else until *Have with You* in 1596, but I would argue that if a breakdown occurred, it occurred during the final pages of *The Unfortunate Traveler*, and *Christs Teares* was a deliberate attempt to recover a God-centered universe.

In 1597, Nashe was forced to flee London because of his part in the composition of the scandalous play, with Ben Jonson,* *Isle of Dogs* (no copy of which survived the government's suppression). He settled for a time in Yarmouth, where he apparently was received with genuine hospitality. In gratitude for the town's welcome, he celebrated Yarmouth and its chief industry, the herring fishery, in his final work, *Nashes Lenten Stuffe* (1599). It was apparently published just prior to the order of 1 June 1599, prohibiting the publication of all works by Nashe or Gabriel Harvey (although *Summers Last Will* was published in 1600). Nashe apparently died shortly after this official censorship, though the date and cause of death are unknown. He is referred to as deceased in 1601.

MAJOR WORKS AND THEMES

Nashe was a remarkable prose stylist. Unfortunately, many readers have used that fact to dismiss his work as "mere style" or "mere rhetoric." It is not surprising, however, that most readers emphasize style over content, since Nashe self-reflexively calls attention to the importance of style in his works, most famously perhaps in *Pierce Penilesse*: ''I haue tearmes (if I be vext) laid in steepe in *Aquafortis*, & Gunpowder, that shall rattle through the Skyes, and make an Earthquake in a Pesants eares'' (i.195) or in *Strange Newes* when he says of Gabriel Harvey's style, ''[H]e hath some good words, but he cannot writhe them and tosse them to and fro nimbly, or so bring them about, that hee maye make one straight thrust at his enemies face'' (i.282). This use of language as a physical weapon is characteristic of Nashe's style, especially at times when he seems to care less for the precision of single words than for the cumulative effect of tone and vocabulary. At the same time, Nashe achieves a degree of intimacy through his direct address of the reader and his constant self-reflexiveness that few, if any, of his contemporaries managed to achieve.

It is true that Nashe rarely stays focused on any idea or theme long enough to develop it in a coherent, logical fashion; his writing is a kind of guerrilla warfare. In fact, the most common ''theme'' in Nashe's works may be said to be language itself—its fullness, its fertility. Some of the most compelling passages in Nashe's works are ones in which he almost compulsively rings changes on a phrase or a single word, as he does on Richard Lichfield's name in the Epistle Dedicatory of *Have With You* (iii.5–6) or on the word ''stone'' in *Christs Teares* (ii.24–25), the word ''page'' in ''The Induction to the dapper Mounsier Pages of the Court'' in *The Unfortunate Traveler* (ii.207–08), or in the mythic treatment of the red herring in *Lenten Stuffe* (iii.185–90). This linguistic extravagance is explicitly affirmed as Nashe's personal style in his epistle to the readers in *Lenten Stuffe*, where he declares that he does not care for

> this demure soft *mediocre genus*, that is like water and wine mixt together; but giue me pure wine of it self, & that begets good bloud, and heates the brain thorowly: I had as lieue haue no sunne, as haue it shine faintly, no fire, as a smothering fire of small coales, no cloathes, rather then weare linsey wolsey. (iii.152)

Nevertheless, there are a few consistent themes in Nashe's work, although they are really mentioned only in passing, as it were, rather than developed coherently and at length. Not surprisingly, the ideas most frequently alluded to have direct or indirect connections to Nashe's career as a writer—the issue of patronage (and other related economic concerns), literary criticism, and the question of interpretation (or, more accurately, misinterpretation).

As with so much else in his writings, Nashe is clearly self-conscious about his vulnerability as an artist in need of a patron, and, as a result, he constantly plays with the idea of patronage, both as a social and economic ideal and as a source of frustration. His ambivalence about his relationship with patrons and potential patrons is most clearly traced in his dedicatory epistles. For instance, the dedication to Charles Blount that introduces *Anatomie of Absurdities* is relatively conventional except that the lengthy praise of the dead Philip Sidney risks lumping Sir Charles in with the ''many mediocrities'' in England since

Sidney's death. The dedication in Nashe's next work, *Pierce Penilesse*, is conventional in its lavish praise of the "thrice noble *Amyntas*," but it is totally unconventional in its placement. Instead of beginning his book with the deferential gesture of dedication to a patron, Nashe ends with it, as if it were an afterthought. Not only that, but it follows immediately after a long diatribe against stingy courtiers, in which the economic ground of patronage is explicitly stipulated: "[W]hat reason haue I to bestow any of my wit vpon him, that wil bestow none of his wealth vpon me?" (i.241).

In the dedications for *Terrors of the Night* and *Christs Teares* the economics of patronage is again unapologetically foregrounded. In the first, Elizabeth Carey is described as one "whose purse is so open to her poore beadsmens distresses" (i.342), and in the second, Nashe promises to "memorize" her, "for you recompense learning extraordinarilie" (ii.11). Increasingly, however, Nashe uses comic dedicatory epistles to mock the whole idea of patronage. *Strange Newes* is dedicated to the "famous pottle-pot Patron" Master Apis Lapis (William Beeston) (I.255); *Have With You* is dedicated to Richard Lichfield, barber of Trinity College; and *Lenten Stuffe* is dedicated to the "most unlearned louer of Poetry," "lustie" Humphrey King (iii.147). For all his mockery, however, Nashe clearly regarded financial support of learning as a critical social issue:

> Can Common weales florish where learning decaies? shall not felicitie haue a fall when as knowledge failes? yea, peace must needes perrish from amongst vs, when as we rather seeke to choke then cherrish, to famish then feede, the Nurses of it. (i.36)

The dynamics of patronage colored Nashe's larger perspective on social issues in contradictory ways. His respect for the power and obligations of patrons encouraged in Nashe a strong commitment to hierarchical politics, which he first expresses in the *Anatomie*:

> To prescribe rules of life, belongeth not to the ruder sort; to condemne those callings which are approoued by publique authoritie, argueth a proude contempt of ye Magistrates superiority. (i.21).

Nashe encourages every man to "endure the destinie whereto he was borne" (i.176). On the other hand, his personal experience of the limitations and failures of patronage and his consequent poverty simultaneously sensitized him to the economic plight of England's underclass: "Our dogges are fedde with the crumbes that fall from our Tables. Our Christian bretheren are famisht for want of the crumbes that fall from our Tables" (ii.161). This sensitivity to economic injustice finds frequent expression in Nashe's endorsement of almsgiving and "good works." Speaking of Roman Catholics in *The Unfortunate Traveler*, the narrator (Jack Wilton) says, "[T]his I must saie to the shame of vs protestants; if good workes may merite heauen, they doe them, we talke of them" (ii.285).

Nashe's repeated call for "good works" has led some readers (including his biographer Nicholl) to suspect that he was a recusant, but that seems unlikely to me. Nashe's emphasis on almsgiving and good works has an economic rationale, not a spiritual one. His treatment of Catholicism as ''superstition'' leaves little doubt where his sympathies lie. Throughout his works he is consistently anti-Catholic, from *Pierce Penilesse*, where he condemns Catholicism as ''a wrong Faith'' (I.204), to *Lenten Stuffe* with its brilliant satire on the pope (iii.206–11).

The other face of patronage is censorship, and, just as Nashe was never really at ease in a patron–client relationship, he was equally anxious about how his works were interpreted. As Lorna Hutson says, Nashe's pamphlets are ''relentlessly topical'' (116), and, justifiably or not, contemporary readers sought to apply allegorical interpretations to his works. In his prefaces and in the body of his pamphlets as well Nashe tries consistently to defuse the dangers of misinterpretation, condemning ''this moralizing age, wherein euery one seeks to shew himselfe a Polititian by mis-interpreting'' (i.154); explicitly disclaiming any topical application in his satires: ''[N]o man in thys Treatise I will particulerly tutch, none I will semouedly allude to, but onely attaint vice in generall'' (ii.80); and even composing a mock allegory in *Lenten Stuffe* in order to challenge misreading: ''O, for a legion of mice-eyed decipherers and calculaters vppon characters, now to augurate what I mean by this: the diuell, if it stood vpon his saluation, cannot do it'' (iii.218). Such a challenge is characteristic of Nashe (or at least of Nashe's literary persona). Despite his many disclaimers of innocence, Nashe's pamphlets are filled with exuberant attacks on pettiness, hypocrisy, stupidity, and avarice, which Nashe engages in with a charming sense of impunity. For all his satirical wit, however, there is something finally superficial about his outrage. Despite his admiration for Aretino,* who was famous for his satirical attacks on princes and aristocrats, Nashe was finally too conservative socially to confront the class origins of many of the injustices he saw and experienced. His writing was not particularly thoughtful; it was simply reactive and often blustering. As a result, there are both a powerful immediacy in his tone and subject matter as well as an occasionally appalling devotion to the superficial and the ephemeral. While the astonishing time and energy Nashe devoted to his feud with Gabriel Harvey, for instance, often strike modern readers as a regrettable waste of talents, he simultaneously offers us an almost unmediated access to the feel and flavor of life in the London of the 1590s.

CRITICAL RECEPTION

The critical reception of Nashe's works can reasonably be said to begin with Gabriel Harvey, but the context of their feud effectively disqualifies Harvey as a reader. Other contemporaries were generally more favorable in their assessments, which characteristically praised Nashe for his ''wit.'' The anonymous *Parnassus Plays* portrays Nashe warmly in the figure of ''Ingenioso,'' and Shakespeare,* apparently recognizing the dramatic qualities of Nashe's characterizations (or perhaps Nashe's own self-dramatization), adopts recognizable elements from his works for his own plays.

For his contemporaries, as for modern readers, Nashe's distinction was as a stylist. His long harangues, his flurries of alliteration, his remarkable neologisms provoked both approval and exasperation among his contemporaries, as they do for us. We are, however, more suspicious of style or rhetoric today than the Renaissance was, so appreciation of Nashe's works tends to require more justification and hence sometimes sounds rather defensive. Nashe's biographer Charles Nicholl, for instance, offers a sympathetic insight into the conditions of Nashe's life to explain why his work strikes us as superficial: ''Championing Nashe as a pioneer journalist we must remember the 'deadlines'—poverty, hunger, sickness, imprisonment. If his writings sometimes seem two-dimensional, these are a kind of third dimension'' (47). Nicholl finally sees Nashe's engagement with the surface of life as partaking of the power of innocence: ''He never quite lost that child's eye: its magnifications, its sense of suddenness, its fascination slipping into fear'' (260). For G. R. Hibbard, on the other hand, Nashe's inability to see below the surface left him with nothing really to say, which is why style replaced substance in his work: ''The way he says a thing counts for more with him than the thing said. It is for this reason that he is, and always has been, a minor writer'' (64). Neil Rhodes also sees a discrepancy in Nashe's work between childish energy and artistic control: ''Like the Sorcerer's Apprentice he activates the world around him with a reckless energy, but he cannot bring it under control'' (52).

More recently, critics have begun to demonstrate how Nashe's works are constructed not out of a discrepancy between surface and depth but out of the identity between surface and depth by historicizing the overlap of immediate, impersonal social pressures and the private formulation of a life lived within them. Looking primarily at the pressures of patronage and censorship, Reid Barbour sees Nashe's work arising from ''a knot where the commissioned and autonomous Nashe are bound together'' (70). Lorna Hutson, dismissing as inadequate ''any purely aesthetic or purely rhetorical approach'' to Nashe's writings, offers a detailed analysis of the broad economic realities that inspire or underwrite Nashe's pamphlets in order to expose the transactional quality of Nashe's writing, in which wit equals wealth in a festive economy of expenditure and consumption.

Perhaps more than most writers, Nashe profits from such extensive historical contextualization. He was a child of his time, ''in many ways the most Elizabethan of all our writers,'' as Hibbard says (ix), and to read him well, we must learn to read him within his historical moment.

BIBLIOGRAPHY

Works by Thomas Nashe

The Works of Thomas Nashe. 5 vols. Ed. Ronald B. McKerrow. 1904–10; rpt. Oxford: B. Blackwell, 1958.

Studies of Thomas Nashe

Barbour, Reid. *Deciphering Elizabethan Fiction*. Newark: University of Delaware Press, 1993.

Crewe, Jonathan V. *Unredeemed Rhetoric: Thomas Nashe and the Scandal of Authorship*. Baltimore: Johns Hopkins University Press, 1982.

Hibbard, G. R. *Thomas Nashe: A Critical Introduction*. Cambridge: Harvard University Press, 1962.

Hilliard, Stephen S. *The Singularity of Thomas Nashe*. Lincoln: University of Nebraska Press, 1986.

Hodges, Devon L. *Renaissance Fictions of Anatomy*. Amherst: University of Massachusetts Press, 1985.

Holbrook, Peter. *Literature and Degree in Renaissance England*. Newark: University of Delaware Press, 1994.

Hutson, Lorna. *Thomas Nashe in Context*. Oxford: Clarendon, 1989.

Kinney, Arthur. *Humanist Poetics*. Amherst: University of Massachusetts Press, 1986.

Margolies, David. *Novel and Society in Elizabethan England*. Totowa, NJ: Barnes and Noble, 1985.

Nicholl, Charles. *A Cup of News: The Life of Thomas Nashe*. London: Routledge, 1984.

Rhodes, Neil. *Elizabethan Grotesque*. London: Routledge, 1980.

DEREK ALWES

P

RICHARD PACE
(c. 1482–1536)

BIOGRAPHY

Richard Pace is best known for his failed diplomatic missions on behalf of the court of Henry VIII and for his role as a member of the scholarly circle of Erasmus* and Thomas More.* Pace's name appears more often than any other in the extant letters of Erasmus, who considered Pace a "dear friend." He once wrote to More of Pace, "I seem to have lost half of my second self by his absence" (Routh, 60).

Pace was born near Winchester in or about 1482. His patron, Bishop Thomas Langton, sent him to study in Padua, and from there he traveled to Ferrara, where he met Erasmus, later returning to England to attend Queen's College, Oxford. In 1509, Pace accompanied Cardinal Bainbridge, archbishop of York, to Rome. The cardinal's sudden death in 1514 at the papal court caused Pace to suspect poisoning at the behest of Bainbridge's chief rival, Silvestro Gigli. Pace's tireless exertions to unmask the murderer provoked controversy but were ultimately unsuccessful in bringing a suspect to justice.

Pace's loyalty in Rome to his deceased master combined with his enviable Italian education made him attractive in England to both the royal court and the humanist community. Hence, his career as courtier and man of letters developed concurrently during the 1510s and 1520s. Both the king and Cardinal Wolsey entrusted him with delicate and sometimes urgent diplomatic missions across the Channel. Pace thereby developed a network of scores of scholarly correspondents and often enjoyed their hospitality while abroad. He became famous among his friends for his good character and learned, amusing conversations.

As Henry VIII's secretary, Pace was sent to Switzerland in October 1515 to attempt to exacerbate belligerent relations between France and the Holy Roman Empire. Emperor Maximilian of Hapsburg had employed Swiss mercenaries in an attempt to wrest Milan from Francis I of France. Pace was commissioned to employ a limited volume of English gold and unlimited amount of talk to press the Swiss to continue the fight. What was from the beginning a bad idea took on the color of farce as Pace fell out with England's permanent ambassador to Maximilian's court, Sir Richard Wingfield, whom Pace referred to as ''summer-will-be-green'' for his penchant for mistaking his own obvious statements for diplomatic tact (Bowle, 75).

For the first of several times in his life, Pace drove himself into sickbed with overwork. The Swiss mission came to nothing except for the production of Pace's most ambitious work, *de Fructu*, a satire written ostensibly during visits to a public bath in Constance.

Relations improved between England and France soon thereafter, and at a splendid banquet at St. Paul's Cathedral in 1518, Pace delivered a sermon on peace to commemorate the betrothal of two infants, Princess Mary and the heir to the French throne. As Pace grew more valuable to Henry and Wolsey, he accrued further honors and titles. In 1519 he became dean of St. Paul's and the following year, a reader of Greek at Cambridge University. The year 1519 also found Pace in Frankfurt trying to influence electors to make Henry VIII the new emperor instead of Charles Hapsburg, grandson of Ferdinand and Isabella of Spain. He was dispatched twice to Rome in 1521 and 1523, at the deaths of Leo X and Adrian VI, to promote Wolsey's candidacy for the papal see, failing both times in what were nearly impossible tasks. Meanwhile, he had been made ambassador to Venice, charged with persuading the Venetians away from the French camp. He was immensely popular at the doge's court to the point of accepting Venetian honors for his diplomatic endeavors.

Pace was passed over as Henry's principal adviser at the cardinal's fall in 1527, due in part to his stress-induced ill health. Like most of the humanists of his day, Pace feared the potential explosive effects of religious Reformation on social life. His opposition to Henry's divorce from Queen Catherine may have resulted in his trial at Star Chamber and brief imprisonment in the Tower of London. At any rate, the divorce crisis caused Pace so much anxiety that Thomas Cromwell suspected he had lost his grip on reality for a time. In a state of broken health and deflated fame, Pace quietly withdrew to the countryside in 1529 and died in retirement in 1536.

MAJOR WORKS AND THEMES

Richard Pace's value as a politician declined as he moved from giving advice and doing paperwork for Henry and Wolsey to operating in an international field of action. Like Erasmus, Pace's reputation as a humanist resulted in part from his mobility. His many diplomatic missions made him available to a remarkable international network of scholars. His public and scholarly lives were thereby tightly linked. Like other humanists who took up politics, Pace became caught up in early modern European statecraft, which combined Machiavellian diplomacy and power politics with a cruel medieval disregard for the value of individual human life. Pace's career reflects a central tension in Renaissance humanism that extolled the virtues of classically educated heroes such as young prince Henry only to watch these leaders succumb to the political ruthlessness demanded by the times. As early as 1521, in a letter to Pace, Erasmus voiced concern for the corrosive dangers connected with Thomas More's increased involvement in politics. Ironically, Pace's fall from the king's grace came before More's.

Pace drove himself to illness attempting to succeed as a man of action. Similarly, his attempts at becoming an active scholar, namely, a published one, caused his star to fall as a humanist. Pace began work on *de Fructu qui ex Doctrina Percipitur* in 1515. The book, along with his 1504 oration in favor of studying Greek, was printed in 1517 in Basil by Froben, Erasmus' publisher. Although dedicated to John Colet,* Pace meant for *de Fructu* to impress Erasmus with its erudition. It failed as a satire because, unlike *Praise of Folly* or *Utopia*, its humor depended almost entirely on specific contemporary situations—such as complaints about the mean-spirited drunkenness of the Swiss—rather than explorations of universal ironies, paradoxes, and absurdities inherent in the human condition. Erasmus called *de Fructu* ''a very feeble little book. I know all his friends will deplore it with me sincerely'' (Wegg, 118). The book proved to Erasmus that Pace was lacking in sound scholarly judgment, a flaw that his affable and witty conversations and letters had hidden. Under such devastating criticism, Pace could only argue that the work was extemporaneous, being written while he was away from his books.

Erasmus fell out with Pace for a time over a passage in *de Fructu* extolling the virtues of an impoverished scholarly life, using Erasmus as the prime example. While Erasmus often spoke of a lack of funds, he did not like Pace's reminding his readers of the scarce monetary value placed on his work. Erasmus' anger soon dissipated, however, and he later suggested tactfully that Pace's real talent was as a translator. Pace's translations into Latin of some of Plutarch's treatises and Bishop Fisher's sermon against Luther were admired, even by humanists, like Thomas Elyot,* who were outside his circle.

His *Oratio Richardi Pacei in Pace* argued, in part, that war is the worst of evils and that human nature can find its virtues only in times of peace (Adams, 176–77). His insistence that war transforms humans into calamitous, unreasoning beasts is a theme often encountered in twentieth-century war novels and memoirs. Scholars at Pace's oration on peace found the speech admirable. The political leaders present apparently thought it elegantly naive. At any rate, it was published in 1518, with French translations. Rumors regarding the true authorship of Henry VIII's anti-Lutheran tract sometimes settled upon Pace.

These suspicions were no doubt compounded by the pope's having sent the bull making Henry "Defender of the Faith" to Pace (Anglo, 171).

CRITICAL RECEPTION

Richard Pace is of interest today mainly to historians and biographers. His work and career as a politician are found in most modern biographies of Henry VIII and in treatments of early Tudor diplomatic histories. Pace also appears in many biographies of the more famous humanists of his times. Pace represents part of a group of second-rank humanists whose avid study of the works of classical antiquity failed to spark originality on their part. Pace also helps prove the observation that the learned are best left out of public office. Like Thomas More, his public career eventually caused both his scholarship and his physical self to suffer immeasurably.

BIBLIOGRAPHY

Works by Richard Pace

De Fructu qui ex Doctrina Percipitur. Also called *de Fructu Studiorum*, 1517.

Epistolae Antiquot Eruditorum Virorum, 1520. (Letters written to and by Thomas More.)

Oratio Richardi Pacei in Pace, 1517.

Translations by Richard Pace

Bishop John Fisher's "Sermon against Luther" into Latin, 1521.

Plutarch's "Treatises" into Latin, 1521.

"Psalms" into Latin, 1520–21.

Studies of Richard Pace

Adams, Robert P. *The Better Part of Valor.* Seattle: University of Washington Press, 1962.

Anglo, Sydney. *Spectacle, Pageantry, and Early Tudor Policy.* Oxford: Oxford University Press, 1969.

Bowle, John. *Henry VIII.* London: Allen and Unwin, 1964.

Guy, John A. *The Public Career of Sir Thomas More.* New Haven, CT: Yale University Press, 1980.

Reynolds, E. E. *Thomas More and Erasmus.* London: Burns and Oates, 1965.

Ridley, Jasper. *Statesman and Saint: Cardinal Wolsey, Thomas More, and the Politics of Henry VIII.* New York: Viking Press, 1983.

Routh, Enid. *Sir Thomas More and His Friends.* New York: Russell and Russell, 1963.

Scarisbrick, J. J. *Henry VIII.* Berkeley: University of California Press, 1968.

Wegg, Jervis. *Richard Pace, a Tudor Diplomatist.* New York: Barnes and Noble, 1971 (orig. 1932).

JOHN A. SHEDD

PARACELSUS
(1493–1541)

BIOGRAPHY

The name "Paracelsus" was probably coined by friends and intended as an implication of going "beyond" (Gr. *para*) the then-authoritative work of Celsus, an ancient medical encyclopedist. The official name was Philippus Aureolus Theophrastus Bombastus von Hohenheim, and the child was born in a village near Zurich in 1493. As a boy he apprenticed at the nearby Fueger mines, where he had direct contact with the use of chemicals; he would later write a book on miners' diseases. Between 1513 and 1516 he studied medicine in Italy. After that he traveled widely, employed as an army surgeon. The rest of his life, devoted to lecturing, writing, private practice, and religious preaching, was divided into a series of brief stays—at Basel, Colmar, Nuremberg, St. Gall, Innsbruck, Ulm, Vienna, and other locations—sojourns both initiated and terminated by his restless nature. He died in Salzburg in 1541.

Records of Paracelsus' actions, as well as the testimony of his own discourse, portray him as a bumptious iconoclast, aggressive, absolute, pugnacious, vindictive. This character is apparent in his choice of a student riot as the occasion to burn the work of Avicenna in Basel. Oporinus, his "famulus" who would later become well known as a professor of Greek at Basel, had opportunity to observe his habits closely and confirms his reputation as a thoroughgoing eccentric. Paracelsus never undressed, except to put on a brand-new outfit (he tried to give his old clothes away but could not because they were too filthy). He would lie down on his bed still girt with his longsword, sleep for a spell, and then leap up, either to write, to labor at his furnace or, when the fit was upon him, to pull out the sword and madly flail it about in the air. He drank heavily and sometimes on a dare, yet what he dictated in his cups had all the clarity and coherence of his sober productions. Oporinus (Pagel, 30) is the more credible for showing no rancor at these excesses. He describes Paracelsus the way one might describe some colossal act of nature, like a hurricane or earthquake, that had come and tormented history and passed away.

MAJOR WORKS AND THEMES

Paracelsus is the least known and least acknowledged of all the major Renaissance thinkers. His obscurity, though unmerited, is easily enough explained. His opinions were so dangerously unorthodox that many sixteenth- and seventeenth-century writers conveyed his ideas without mentioning his name. His thought is so interdisciplinary that few historians have the breadth to appreciate it. His writing (in German and Latin) is dense and oracular enough to defy all but the most highly motivated readers. Yet his influence was broad and so thoroughly identified with the "new" in science, philosophy, and spirituality that John Donne* pays him the negative compliment of placing him, together with Copernicus* and Machiavelli,* at the center of his imaginary Hell (*Ignatius His Conclave*).

Donne's grouping is especially pertinent. Just as Machiavelli and Copernicus labored to cut inquiry loose from classical and Christian premises about society and nature, Paracelsus strove to establish natural science as an entity free from Galenic blueprints and Christian assumptions. To sustain such a radical project during the Inquisition required his use of the ''double truth'': an Averroistic verbal strategy that simultaneously asserted religious faith and allowed for scientific autonomy.

Yet Paracelsus walked dangerously close to the edge. He clearly had no use for the doctrine of original sin, believing instead that human beings were born with elements of God inside them. His notion that many diseases were, in fact, *living things* (he rightly held that contagion resulted from invisible germs or ''seeds'') flew in the face of the dogma that all created nature was ''good.'' His foundation and practice of homeopathy (''*similia similibus curantur*'') were a medical heresy whose moral implications were strangely similar to Machiavellian politics. He was a consistent opponent of religious dogma, whether in the hands of Catholic or Protestant. These doctrinal elements combined in a comprehensive image of nature, humanity, and God that differed from established Christianity in almost every particular.

CRITICAL RECEPTION

Both practically and conceptually, Paracelsus made major contributions to early modernity. Practically, by applying alchemical methods to the preparation of remedies, he not only laid the foundation for modern medicine but invented the science of chemistry (which he also named). His treatments (including his improvements in the use of mercury against syphilis) were often sensationally effective. Erasmus himself heartily congratulates him on a successful cure. For all its unorthodoxy, Paracelsian influence spread rapidly through Europe. The Holy Roman Emperor Rudolf II of Prague (reigned 1576–1612) was an enthusiastic patron of Paracelsians. James I* of England had a Paracelsian court physician. Shakespeare's* son-in-law, the noted Warwickshire physician John Hall, availed himself of Paracelsian authorities, and I have suggested that Shakespeare himself adumbrated Paracelsus' doctrine of free will and developed the moral equivalent of the homeopathic cure (Grudin). In the seventeenth century Paracelsus influenced the Royal Society and the Puritans alike (Webster). In the twentieth century his ideas were advanced by Carl Jung.

Conceptually, Paracelsus was important in developing what T. S. Eliot would characterize as the unified sensibility: the reciprocating, mutually allusive frames of reference that were typical of Renaissance thought. This holistic, endlessly suggestive style of thinking, which owes its existence as well to Erasmian *copia*, was adopted by Montaigne* and Shakespeare and radicalized by the metaphysical poets. But for Paracelsus, experience was also troubled by dynamic conflicts. Michel Foucault, who labels Paracelsus a champion of analogies, unaccountably ignores that he was also a notable dualist. This subtle vision, with its warp of profound analogy and its weft of violent opposition, led to startling insights into nature and humanity.

Though Paracelsus was a notable figure for writers of the nineteenth century, including Browning and Hawthorne (see Browning, Bensick, and, more generally, Pagel, 34), he has since drifted into the eddies of intellectual history and is currently of interest chiefly to historians of early modern science. In large measure this fate is shared by two other heroes of early modernity, Bruno* and Bacon*. That figures of such stature should be ignored by their cultural beneficiaries constitutes another testament to faulty graduate education and disciplinary blindness.

BIBLIOGRAPHY

Works by Paracelsus

Samtliche Werke. Wiesbaden: Franz Steiner, 1955, 1961; Leipzig: 1977, 1982; Anger Verlag Eick, 1993.

Selected Writings. Trans. Norbert Guterman and ed. Jolande Jacobi. Princeton: Princeton University Press, 1951.

Studies of Paracelsus

Bensick, Carol. *La Nouvelle Beatrice: Renaissance and Romance in Rappaccini's Daughter*. New Brunswick: Rutgers University Press, 1985.

Browning, Robert. ''Paracelsus.'' In *The Complete Works of Robert Browning*, ed. Roma A. King Jr. and others. Athens: Ohio University Press, 1969–. (A poem.)

Debus, Allan. *The Chemical Philosophy*. New York: Science History Publications, 1977.

———. *The English Paracelsians*. New York: F. Watt, 1966.

———. *The French Paracelsians*. Cambridge: Cambridge University Press, 1991.

———, with Ingrid Merkel. *Hermeticism and the Renaissance*. Washington, DC: Folger Shakespeare Library, 1988.

Donne, John. *Ignatius His Conclave* (1611).

Foucault, Michel. *The Order of Things*. New York: Vintage Books, 1973.

Grudin, Robert. *Mighty Opposites*. Berkeley: University of California Press, 1979.

Jung, Carl. *Psychology and Alchemy*. 2d ed., rev. Trans. R.C.F. Hull. Princeton: Princeton University Press, 1968.

Pagel, Walter. *Paracelsus*. Basel: S. Karger, 1958.

Webster, Charles. *The Great Instauration*. London: Duckworth, 1975.

ROBERT GRUDIN

CATHERINE PARR (Catharine, Katharine, Kateryn) (c. 1512–1548)

BIOGRAPHY

Catherine Parr's life is poorly documented. Eldest daughter of Sir Thomas Parr and Maud Greene, Catherine Parr was born around the year 1512 in either Kendal, Westmoreland, at her father's castle or in his London house in Blackfriars. At the age of five her father died, leaving her mother to raise three children alone. The mother saw to her children's education, through the appointment of humanist Juan Luis Vives as their tutor. Parr received an education unusual for women of her age, and later in life she was to ensure that King Henry's daughters received an equally strong education. When Parr came of age, her mother, selecting among the various suitors, chose Edward Borough, son of Thomas, Lord Borough. In 1527 Parr moved with her husband to his family home in Gainsborough, a home visited by two kings: Richard III in 1485 and Henry VIII in 1509. The marriage was short-lived, however, for only two years later, Lord Borough died.

With her mother's death the year before, Parr was left alone until her marriage to the Catholic Lord Latimer, which occurred sometime before 1533. Lord Latimer, considerably older than Parr, had failing health by 1542. Catherine began to receive attention both from the ambitious Thomas Seymour, brother of the late Queen Jane, and from Henry VIII, who sent her a gift of "pleats and sleeves." It is clear from later correspondence that Catherine Parr's heart lay with the younger and more attractive Seymour. Years later, after Henry's death, she was to write to Seymour of this time, "[A]s truly as God is God, my mind was fully bent, the other time I was at liberty, to marry you before any man I know." In 1542, though, Henry VIII witnessed their growing affection and intervened by sending Seymour on permanent embassy to Brussels. Not long after Seymour's departure, Parr received an offer of marriage from the king, and despite her lack of enthusiasm, she could not refuse. They were married on 12 July 1543.

Suffering from health problems and ill temper, Henry found a sympathetic and competent mate in Catherine, a woman who took as her motto "To be useful in all I do." She brought together Henry's family as no previous wife had done, uniting Mary, Edward, and Elizabeth* within her household. Not only did Parr secure education for the children under the leading humanist scholars, just as her own mother had done for her, but she also can take credit for restoring Mary and Elizabeth to succession rights to the Crown. In addition to these notable achievements, she received the highest praise at court for her virtue and intellect. Henry himself praised and relied on these traits, making Parr regent during his absence in 1544, an honor granted on only one other occasion, to Catharine of Aragon.

Despite the affection and trust shared by the king and his wife, Henry suspected her, as he had his other wives. Specifically, Henry distrusted Parr's religious allegiance. If her intellect initially seemed a virtue, it proved a liability by 1546, when Henry, suffering from both physical pain and pressure of ministers, disciplined his wife for her outspokenness. According to John Foxe, who provides the primary record of the events, Parr, in speaking with her husband on the subject of religion, had "in the heat of discourse gone very far." Her outspokenness, made much of by those courtiers such as Lord Chancellor Wriothesley, who had suspicions about her Lutheranism, led the king to bring charges against her. Informed of the charges through an anonymous source, Parr reassured the king of her own subordination to him, claiming that through her discourse on religion she had hoped merely to divert him from his pain. Back in favor, she tended to Henry during his increasingly ill health. On 28 January 1547 the king died, leaving Parr a widow for the third time.

Less than four months after the king's death, Thomas Seymour had regained enough of Parr's affections to sign a letter to her as "him whom you have bound to honor, love, and all things obey." While the exact date of their marriage is unknown, the fact that it occurred, unconventionally, within a year after Henry's death, is certain. That they married for love seems clear. Parr continued to provide for Henry's children, and Elizabeth lived with Catherine and Thomas Seymour until Seymour's flirtations with the young girl resulted in her relocation. Shortly after Elizabeth's move from the Seymour home, Parr bore her first and only child, a girl. As a result of the labor, she contracted puerperal fever, dying six days later, on 5 September 1548.

MAJOR WORKS AND THEMES

Testament to Parr's intellect and faith are her two books published during her years as queen. The first, probably written during her year as queen regent in 1544, is entitled *Prayers or Meditations*. This popular volume collects prayers from various sources, the bulk of them from Whitford's translation of Thomas a Kempis' *Imitatio Christi*. Scholars debate the religious affiliation revealed in the text. Yet *Prayers or Meditations* focuses on universals, such as affirmations of sin, frailty, and dependence upon God: "Teache me lorde, to fulfyll thy wyll, to live meekely, and worthilye before the, for thou arte all my wysedom and cunnyng, thou art he, that knowest me as I am, that knewest me before the worlde was made, and before I was borne or brought into this lyfe." Parr emphasizes the singular soul in its private relation to God, yet she does so, as Janel Meuller argues, in such a way that "the connotations of spirituality are wrenched from the perceptibly Catholic to those of an emergent Protestantism" (1990). Yet this emergent Protestantism manifests itself not through doctrinal assertions. Instead, it is hinted at in the sensibility of the prayers, which stress the individual's relation to God in personal and immediate terms more typical of Lutheranism than Henry's Catholicism. Noted for her role in furthering Protestant faith, at this early date, Parr's allegiance here is balanced between its Protestant elements and Henrician-Catholic faith.

Parr's second book leaves little question of her Protestantism. In her *Lamentations of a Sinner*, written during Henry's life but not published until after his death, Parr shows her Reformist allegiance. One of the few confessional narratives by an Englishwoman, *Lamentations* expresses Parr's efforts, as William Cecil claims in the preface, "to lerne the simplicitie of the gospel." One of the major supporters of vernacular translation, Parr demonstrates her engagement with Scripture through reference and quotation on every page. She juxtaposes the darkness of the sinner's world to the grace of God: "I am, partely by the hate I owe to sinne, who hathe reygned in me, partely by the love I owe to all Christians, whom I am contente to edifye, even with the example of mine owne shame, forced and constrayned with my harte and wordes, to confesse . . . how ingrate, negligent, unkynde, and stubberne, I have bene to God my Creator." Her critical eye, turned inward to examine the state of her own soul, anticipates the poetics that will emerge nearly a century later. Still indebted to Erasmian models, Parr's *Lamentations* nevertheless reveals a distinctly Protestant voice, what Janel Meuller calls "an alternative model, wholly English but eclectic, that builds on Tyndalian foundations with local resources derived from Thomas Cranmer and . . . Hugh Latimer" (1988). Certainly, her religious allegiance to Protestant Cranmer and Latimer earned her enemies, and only through her skillful preservation of Henry's affection did Parr remain free from the persecution suffered by her friend and contemporary Anne Askew.* Perhaps her self-effacement, evident throughout the *Lamentations*, in part, preserved her: "God knoweth of what intent and minde I have lamented mine owne sinnes, and autes to the worlde. I trust no bodye will judge I have doon it for prayse."

In addition to writing two books, Parr was also a patron of the arts. Through Parr's support, many of the leading Protestant humanists received appointments as tutors to noble families. In addition, she oversaw the translation of Erasmus'* *Paraphrases of the New Testament* into English. Nicholas Udall, one of the translators engaged for the project, wrote in the dedication prefacing the Gospel of Saint Luke that "by procuring the whole paraphrase of Erasmus to be diligently translated into English, [Queen Catherine] ha[s] minced it and made it ever English man's meat, though his stomach be never so weak and tender." As Udall's claim suggests, Parr's involvement with the world of letters, both through her patronage and through her celebrated management of her stepchildren's education, proved influential in fostering the growth of Protestant humanist thought in England

CRITICAL RECEPTION

"Lorde, Jesu, I praye the grant me grace, that I never sette my herte on the thynges of this worlde, but that all worldly and carnall affeccions maie utterlye dye and be mortified in me." Parr may pray for release from the material world in her *Prayers or Meditations*, but much of the critical attention she has received results from her quite substantial earthly power. Inheriting the estates of her first two husbands, Parr came to Henry VIII a wealthy woman. At the head of a group of powerful court women, Parr wielded considerable influence during some of Henry VIII's most difficult and reactionary years. In her position as queen and especially as regent, her piety created suspicion among the Catholic faction at court. Balanced between Henry's Catholicism and the emergent Protestantism, Parr steered a delicate and ultimately successful course that brought her increasing commendation from the time of Elizabeth's reign. Foxe celebrated her as a great Reformist. Her *Prayers or Meditations* went through ten editions in the sixteenth century alone. Praised by contemporaries for her patronage, Parr has been celebrated recently for her position as an early modern woman writer. Recent work addresses the issues of Parr's authorship, her female friendships, and her religion, rather than focusing solely on Parr's relation to Henry. While Parr's biographers, such as Martienssen and Fraser, trace Parr's life in political and personal, rather than literary, terms, Janel Meuller and John King are among the recent scholars who focus on Parr as a writer and patron.

BIBLIOGRAPHY

Works by Catherine Parr

The Lamentations of a Sinner, Made by ye Most Vertuous Ladie, Quene Caterine, Bewayling the Ignorance of Her Blind Life. London: Edward Whitchurche, 1547.

Prayers or Meditacions, Wherin the Mynde Is Styrred Paciently to Suffre all Afflications Here. London: Thomas Berthelet, 1545.

Studies of Catherine Parr

Foxe, John. *Acts and Monuments*. Vol. 5. London: Seeley, Burnside, and Seeley, 1843–49.

Fraser, Antonia. *The Wives of Henry VIII*. New York: Vintage Books, 1994.

Haugaard, William P. ''Katherine Parr: The Religious Convictions of a Renaissance Queen.'' *Renaissance Quarterly* 22 (1969).

James, Susan E. ''The Devotional Writings of Queen Catherine Parr.'' *Transactions* 82 (1982).

———. ''Queen Kateryn Parr. 1512–1548.'' *Transactions of the Cumberland and Westmorland Antiquarian and Archaeological Society* 88 (1988).

King, John N. ''Patronage and Piety: The Influence of Catherine Parr.'' In *Silent but for the Word: Tudor Women as Patrons, Translators, and Writers of Religious Works*, ed. Margaret Patterson Hannay. Kent, OH: Kent State University Press, 1985, 43–60.

Martienssen, Anthony. *Queen Katherine Parr*. New York: McGraw-Hill, 1973.

Meuller, Janel. ''Devotion as Difference: Intertextuality in Queen Katherine Parr's Prayers or Meditations (1545).'' *Huntington Library Quarterly* 53.3 (1990): 171–97.

———. ''A Tudor Queen Finds Voice: Katherine Parr's Lamentations of a Sinner.'' In *The Historical Renaissance: New Essays on Tudor and Stuart Literature and Culture*, ed. Heather Dubrow and Richard Strier. Chicago: University of Chicago Press, 1988, 15–47.

Weir, Alison. *The Six Wives of Henry VIII*. New York: Grove Weidenfeld, 1991.

REBECCA LEMON

GEORGE PEELE
(c. 1556–c. 1596)

BIOGRAPHY

As with a number of Tudor authors, there is a degree of uncertainty regarding both the birth and death of George Peele. Citing as evidence the 1556 baptismal register for the St. James Garlickhithe parish—''The 25 Iulye, George peele''—Leonard Ashley surmises that this indeed refers to the dramatist, while other critics suggest Peele may have been born as late as 1558. What is certain, however, is that Peele was born in London and was one of at least five children born to James Peele and his first wife, Anne. Peele's father proved to be a man of some learning and notoriety in his own right: he was a salter and citizen of London, he published two books on bookkeeping (constituting the first known book in English on double-ledger accounting), he arranged (and probably wrote) material for the annual lord mayor's pageants, and he became clerk of a London charity home and school, Christ's Hospital.

In 1565, young George Peele entered grammar school at Christ's Hospital, where his father was employed, after which he moved to Oxford, matriculating at Broadgates Hall (now Pembroke College) in 1571, becoming a student at Christ Church by 1574, and in turn earning a B.A. in 1577 and an M.A. in 1579. Little is known of Peele's university days, except that he translated Euripides' *Iphigenia*, the translation of which was commended by fellow student and Latin dramatist William Gager. Though Peele's translation is lost, its very existence underlines Peele's long-standing interest in classical antiquity, which was to permeate so much of his literary production throughout his career. A by-product of Peele's school years is that he received the notorious/glorious appellation of being a ''university wit'' (other figures in the crowd included Thomas Nashe,* John Lyly,* Robert Greene,* and Thomas Lodge*).

In 1580 Peele married Anne Cooke (aged sixteen), the only child of a prosperous London merchant who died the same year, leaving Peele and his new bride a legacy of £250, along with sundry lawsuits that accompanied the sum. The following year Peele moved from Oxford to London (whether or not Anne joined him is a matter of conjecture), where he was to remain, probably beginning his professional literary career at that time. In 1583 Peele was given a rather ponderous sum of £23 by his former college, in all likelihood for his contribution to an entertainment honoring Albert Alesco, the count Palatine of Siradia (Poland). However, making a decent living by the pen, as numerous other Elizabethan writers were to discover, was exceedingly difficult, and indeed Peele was dogged by Grub Street financial hardship virtually to his dying day. Perhaps the most heartbreaking and pitiable anecdote of Peele's life is his sending, by means of his ten-year-old daughter, a pathetic letter to Lord Burghley, along with a copy of his ''olde poem,'' *A Tale of Troy*, begging his lordship for financial relief, saying amid billows of flattery, ''Longe sickness hauing so enfeebled me maketh bashfullness allmost become impudency''; Burghley's response was to file Peele's desperate plea with other crank letters. Peele died that same year (1596), Francis Meres averring, probably inaccurately, ''As Anacreon died by the pot; so George Peele by the pox.'' Whether deservedly or not, after his death, Peele earned the reputation of a dissolute and debauched bohemian who was a stranger to clean living. A weighty portion of this undesirable notoriety was garnered from the at times very funny but most certainly apocryphal *Merrie and Conceited Jests of George Peele*; but that Peele's name would even be a hanger on which to pin such jests has been for some critics in itself telling evidence of Peele's profligacy. As for other contemporary references to Peele, Thomas Nashe, in his preface to Robert Greene's *Menaphon*, referred to Peele as ''the *Atlas* of poetrie, & *primus verborum artifex*.''

MAJOR WORKS AND THEMES

Though Peele is known today chiefly as a pioneering (though minor) dramatist and forerunner to the Elizabethan heavyweights, there are actually three literary genres of writing for which Peele is known: his poems (of which there are less than ten), his pageants for the lord mayor of London (of which Peele wrote at least three, though probably more, only two of which survive—*The Device of the Pageant Borne before Wolstan Dixi* [1585] and *Descensus Astraeae* [1591]), and his plays (of which five remain, while at least two—*The Hunting of Cupid* and *The Turkish Mahomet and Hiren the Fair Greek*—have been lost).

Peele's first literary endeavors were thoroughly classical in their subject matter. Though not published until 1589, *A Tale of Troy* was probably written early. This poem of nearly 500 lines in heroic couplets offers a reader's digest version of the fall of Troy from before Paris' birth to Aeneas' landing in Carthage. Thus, *A Tale of Troy* is, in many ways, a rather characteristic piece not only because of the subject matter; here Peele presents to the reader the golden apple, the rape of Helen, the gathering of the Greek forces, the sacrificing of Iphigenia, Cassandra, the deaths of Patroclus, Hector, Achilles, the fight for Achilles' armor, the suicide of Ajax, the wooden horse, Sinon, Pyrrhus slaying Priam, the mourning of Hecuba, the flight of Acneas—it's all there. One often notices when reading Peele (and this is especially true of his three lesser plays) that he simply tries too hard to get everything in, the result often being episodic and disunified plots, little depth in characterization, and a static and elliptical feel to the entire piece. Such a mélange has led some critics to complain (I think justly) that one gets the sense they are viewing pageants or a slide show rather than plays.

Also written in the early years of the 1580s was *The Arraignment of Paris*, a far more successful effort because of both his varying of verse forms and his varying from the official mythological account of a hard-line classical purist. The variation for which he is most noted is the enormous piece of flattery wherein Diana gives the golden apple and paeans of hyperbolic praise to none other than Queen Elizabeth.* Peele's next effort, *The Battle of Alcazar* (1589), has both the feel of a patriotic, post-Armada piece with the addition of all the exotic background, Senecan rant, and blood and thunder, which fittingly place it chronologically amid *The Spanish Tragedy, The Jew of Malta, Tamburlaine*, and *Titus Andronicus*—plays with which it has numerous affinities. Like *The Battle of Alcazar, Edward I* (p. 1593) and *David and Bethsabe* (c. 1592–94) have affinities with the chronicle history play, and these three are the least favored of Peele's five extant plays. *Edward I* will forever be unpopular, for it is simply a bad play: the plot was madly conceived, full of discontinuity and confusion: the characterization is poor; and the best that can be said of the poetry is that some of it is not bad; it is truly torturous to read and is, all in all, a play that cannot help but make the judicious grieve. Although *David and Bethsabe* is not a great play, a few would argue it is a better effort than *Edward I*. Though it is episodic and, arguably, follows the biblical source too assiduously, there are nevertheless flashes of sonorous lyric beauty rarely found in the dramas that antedate it. Very little has been written about these, the lesser plays of Peele's and his minor works (though many seem to see these as one and the same).

CRITICAL RECEPTION

Most of the critical attention on Peele has concentrated on *The Old Wives Tale* and, to a lesser extent, on *The Arraignment of Paris*. Beyond the individual glories of each of these two plays, they exhibit two characteristics endemic to Peele's literary career: his use of classical mythology and his tireless experimentation. Concerning the former, Peele is forever drawing allusions from Olympus (as with *The Arraignment of Paris* and some of his poems) or treating the myths and legends of the classical world as his subject. As for experimentation, for better or for worse, Peele was original to the core, not only with metrical forms—in Peele they are legion—but in subject matter and in trying different genres and even mixing them together, Peele was constantly going in different directions and trying new things. Thus, he was a remarkable innovator.

BIBLIOGRAPHY

Works by George Peele

The Arraignment of Paris. C. 1581–84; pub. 1584.

The Battle of Alcazar. C. 1589; pub. 1594.

The Famous Chronicle of King Edward I. Pub. 1593; rpt. 1599.

A Farewell. 1589.

The Honour of the Garter. 1593.

The Life and Works of George Peele. 3 vols. Gen. ed. Charles Tyler Prouty. New Haven, CT: Yale University Press, 1952–70. (The standard edition.)

The Love of King David and Fair Bethsabe. C. 1592–94; pub. 1599.

The Old Wives Tale. C. 1590–94; pub. 1595.

The Praise of Chastity. 1593.

A Tale of Troy. Pub. 1589; rpt. 1604.

Studies of George Peele

For further bibliographical material, see also Ashley (229–41), Braunmuller (151–58), Donovan, and Prouty (vol 1., 283–94).

Ashley, Leonard R. N. *George Peele*. New York: Twayne, 1970.

Berek, Peter. "*Tamburlaine*'s Weak Sons: Imitation as Interpretation before 1593." *Renaissance Drama* 13 (1982): 55–82.

Bergeron, David M. *English Civic Pageantry 1558–1642*. London: Arnold Press, 1971.

Bradbrook, Muriel C. "Peele's *Old Wives Tale*: A Play of Enchantment." *English Studies* 43 (1962): 323–30.

Bradley, David. *From Text to Performance in the Elizabethan Theatre*. Cambridge: Cambridge University Press, 1992.

Braunmuller, A. R. *George Peele*. Boston: Twayne, 1983.

Candido, Joseph. "Captain Thomas Stukeley: The Man, the Theatrical Record, and the Origins of Tudor 'Biographical' Drama." *Anglia* 105 (1987): 50–68.

Cope, Jackson. "Peele's *Old Wives Tale*: Folk Stuff into Ritual Form." *Journal of English Literary History* 49 (1982): 326–88.

Cox, John D. "Homely Matter and Multiple Plots in Peele's *Old Wives Tale*." *Texas Studies in Literature and Language* 20 (1978): 330–46.

Doebler, Joan. "The Tone of George Peele's *Old Wives Tale*." *English Studies* 53 (1972): 412–21.

Donovan, Kevin J. "Recent Studies in George Peele (1969–1990)." *English Literary Renaissance* 23.1 (1993): 212–20.

Edwards, Philip. " 'Seeing Is Believing': Action and Narration in *The Old Wives Tale* and *The Winter's Tale*." In *Shakespeare and His Contemporaries: Essays in Comparison*, ed. E.A.J. Honigmann. Manchester: Manchester University Press, 1986, 79–93.

Ewbank, Inga-Stina. "The House of David in Renaissance Drama: A Comparative Study." *Renaissance Drama* 8 (1965): 3–40.

———. " 'What words, what looks, what wonders?': Language and Spectacle in the Theatre of George Peele." In *The Elizabethan Theatre V*, ed. G. R. Hibbard. Toronto: Macmillan, 1975, 124–54.

Free, Mary. "Audience within Audience in *The Old Wives Tale*." *Renaissance Papers* (1983): 53–61.

Greenfield, Thelma. *The Induction in Elizabethan Drama*. Eugene: University of Oregon Press, 1969.

Greg, Walter. *Pastoral Poetry and Pastoral Drama*. London: Bullen, 1906.

Hunter, George K. *John Lyly: The Humanist as Courtier*. London: Routledge, 1962.

Jenkins, Ron. "*The Old Wives Tale*: A Study in Folklore Narrative." *Journal of the Society of English and American Literature* 36.1 (1991): 1–24.

Jones, Gwenan. "The Intention of Peele's *Old Wives' Tale*." *Aberystwyth Studies* 7 (1925): 79–93.

Lensick, Henry G. "The Structural Significance of Myth and Flattery in Peele's *Arraignment of Paris*." *Studies in Philology* 65 (1968): 163–70.

Marx, Joan C. " 'Soft, Who Have We Here?': The Dramatic Technique of *The Old Wives Tale*." *Renaissance Drama* 12 (1981): 117–43.

Moffett, A. S. "Process and Structure Shared: Similarities between the Commedia dell' Arte and *The Old Wives Tale*." *New England Theatre Journal* 4 (1993): 97–105.

Montrose, Louis Adrian. "Gifts and Reasons: The Contexts of Peele's *Arraygnment of Paris*." *Journal of English Literary History* 47 (1980): 433–61.

Nellis, Marilyn K. "Peele's *Edward I*." *Explicator* 44.2 (1986): 5–8.

Senn, Werner. *Studies in the Dramatic Construction of Robert Greene and George Peele*. Bern: Francke, 1973.

Stilling, Roger. *Love and Death in Renaissance Tragedy*. Baton Rouge: Louisiana State University Press, 1976, 56–66.

Viguers, Susan T. "The Hearth and the Cell: Art in *The Old Wives Tale*." *Studies in English Literature* 21 (1981): 209–21.

———. "Peele's *Battle of Alcazar*." *Explicator* 43.2 (1985): 9–12.

Von Hendy, Andrew. "The Triumph of Chastity: Form and Meaning in *The Arraignment of Paris*." *Renaissance Drama* n.s. 1 (1968): 87–101.

Weil, Judith. "George Peele's Singing School: *David and Bethsabe* and the English History Play." *Themes in Drama* 8 (1986): 51–66.

Wells, R. Headlam. "Elizabethan Epideictic Drama: Praise and Blame in the Plays of Peele and Lyly." *Cahiers Elisabethains* 23 (1983): 15–33.

JOHN WILSON

MARY SIDNEY HERBERT, COUNTESS OF PEMBROKE (1561–1621)

BIOGRAPHY

Mary Sidney was born in 1561, the second of four children who survived infancy. Her grandfather was the duke of Northumberland, her uncles the earls of Leicester and Warwick, yet as the daughter of their sister Mary Dudley and of Sir Henry Sidney, the queen's deputy in Ireland and Wales, she belonged to the gentry. While this fact dogged the careers of her brothers, Philip Sidney* and Robert Sidney,* Mary's marriage in April 1577 to Henry Herbert, 2d earl of Pembroke, would have represented for her parents their most conspicuous success. She received a fairly broad humanist education at home (for languages she learned, at the least, Latin, French, and Italian), as well as training in such expected accomplishments as music and needlework, but in 1575, after the death of her younger sister Ambrosia, she attracted the attention of the queen, who took her under her wing at court. Her marriage to Pembroke was primarily a political match, cementing the loose Protestant faction formed by the collective interests of her father, uncles, and new husband. Yet it seems to have been a happy marriage, perhaps because of the prompt appearance of healthy male heirs, and to have allowed her a measure of freedom. In 1586, she lost first her parents and then her brother Philip, but in the years between her marriage and this turning point, she and Philip Sidney seem to have spent much time together at Wilton, Pembroke's main country residence. To this period belongs all of Sidney's surviving writing, and it is likely that it was done, as Sidney describes his writing of the *Arcadia*, "most of it in your presence, the rest, by sheetes, sent unto you, as fast as they were done."

After her husband's death in 1601 her public profile was substantially reduced, and less is known of her activities. She seems to have expended much energy administering her properties and dependencies and late in life to have traveled on the Continent, staying at Spa. She died in 1621 and did not live to see the publication that year of the *Urania* of her niece Mary Wroth.* But between 1586 and 1601 she rose to an unprecedented position as a patron, as writers who might have looked to Sidney for reward learned to offer their works to his sister. It is likely that, to some extent, she encouraged her depiction in works dedicated to, or mentioning, her as the "learned" sister of Sidney and inheritor of his muse. She received a stream of dedications from the likes of Abraham Fraunce, Nicholas Breton, and other actual or would-be clients of her husband, as well as more speculative addresses from writers with no personal connection to her. Some authors spent time at Wilton, though in most cases they were employed by the family in some other capacity—as tutor or secretary. She may have had some close dealings with Spenser. More important, she seems to have taken Samuel Daniel under her protection after the publication of his

Delia (1592) and to have had some direct involvement in his play *Cleopatra* (1594). Daniel moved on to other patrons but returned finally to the countess and addressed the last book (1609) of his *Civil Wars* directly to her.

The countess of Pembroke is primarily remembered for her role in the publication of Sidney's works. She conceived the composite 1593 *Arcadia*, which succeeded Greville's unfinished 1590 edition; she probably acted to suppress a pirated edition of *Astrophil and Stella*; and in the 1598 folio she assembled texts of all his works, including the *Defence of Poetry* and the unpublished *Certaine Sonnets*. While these editorial labors are seen as encouraging and legitimating her own writing—the completion of the *Arcadia* ''out of the author's own writings'' forms an obvious analogy to her own completion of Sidney's *Psalmes*—it is worth remembering that her only substantial printed work appeared in 1592, before the appearance of those editions of Sidney for which she was responsible.

MAJOR WORKS AND THEMES

Her works are a translation of Garnier's play *Marc Antoine* (to which Daniel's *Cleopatra* is a companion piece); a translation of Du Plessis Mornay's *Discours de la vie et de la Mort* (published together: *A Discourse of Life and Death . . . Antonius*, 1592); a completion of Philip Sidney's metaphrase of the Psalms; two poems prefaced to a single manuscript copy of this, addressed in turn to the queen and to Sidney's soul (''Even now that Care''; ''To thee pure sprite''); a short poem in praise of the queen (''A Dialogue . . . in praise of Astraea,'' printed in Francis Davison's *Poetical Rhapsody*, 1602); and a translation of Petrarch's *Trionfo della Morte* (''The Triumph of Death,'' which survives in a single manuscript copy, itself a copy of the text sent by Sir John Harington to his cousin Lucy, countess of Bedford, in 1600); in addition, the ''Dolefull Lay of Clorinda,'' part of Spenser's collection of elegies for Sidney (''Astrophel,'' printed as part of *Colin Clouts Come Home Againe*, 1595) may be by her, or by Spenser; other works that do not survive may be alluded to in her correspondence.

Setting aside her major work, the *Psalmes*, her three other translations treat the question of dying and the good death, from the stoic heroism of suicide to the Christianized *ars moriendi*; read together, they may go some way to investigating the possibilities for female heroism. The countess is a sensitive but conservative translator, and more can be said about her style than her convictions when her texts are compared to their originals; the *Triumph*, for instance, is most impressive for being written in fluent pentameter *terza rima*. Within the narrow scope of the translator, however, she manages in her works from the French to add life and warmth to what can seem cool moral exposition. Although both the translation of Mornay and the dedication to Elizabeth of the *Psalmes* confirm her connection to the ideals of Continental Protestantism, it is difficult to claim that they actually intend or achieve any political objective.

Style and form are the main points of entrance to the *Psalmes*, too, although here analysis of deviation and embellishment in translation proves more fruitful. Sidney left at his death an unfinished metaphrase of the Psalms, which his sister completed, perhaps largely by 1594, certainly by 1599. She translated Psalms 44–150, and if we count rejected variant versions and the twenty-two sections of Psalm 119, we have 154 different poems. She follows Sidney in aiming for an overwhelming metrical variety, adjusting every possible metrical and stanzaic variable so that in the entire *Psalmes*, with only a few exceptions, no two Psalms have the same form. Where Sidney borrows some forms from the French Marot-Bèze psalter, the countess seems less interested in fitting her meters to existing tunes. While often her construction of forms is more of a mathematical game than a careful suiting of form to sense, she becomes, if anything, a lesser experimenter and a better poet as her work progresses. Her later translations show a return to particular models from Sidney—several forms are borrowed from the songs in *Astrophil and Stella* and *Certaine Sonnets*—and her Psalm 150 uses Sidney's favorite sonnet scheme. The *Psalmes* were circulated widely in manuscript but not printed; of about twenty complete copies made at the time (not including other selections) fifteen survive, as well as two much later ones. Their devotional purpose is private, and while Donne pointed to their improvement on current metrical psalters (primarily the old version of Sternhold and Hopkins), they set a wider formal agenda for poetry in general. Responding in their metrical variety to French and Dutch examples and to current interest in the likely metrics of the Hebrew original, the powerful lyrics of the *Psalmes* exerted a particular influence on such devotional poets as Herbert.

In her three later poems, all probably written around 1599 and representing her only certain original work, the countess attains the sort of direct and euphonious, yet slidingly ambiguous, assertions of the best poets of her own—and not her brother's—generation. The poem to Sidney returns the compliment of his dedication to the *Arcadia*—"onelie for you, onely to you"—and in a language that is not unerotic. The dedication of the *Psalmes* to Elizabeth that precedes this—and is qualified by it—lectures the queen on her duties as godly monarch, while the "Dialogue" (possibly a direct response to Sir John Davies' less subtle *Astraea*) praises Elizabeth while interrogating dialectically the language of panegyric. Whatever can be said of these last two poems as political gesture, however, is mitigated by the likelihood that they never reached their ailing addressee, for the queen's projected visit to Wilton in 1599 was canceled, and the *Psalmes* and "Dialogue" were probably never delivered to her.

CRITICAL RECEPTION

Criticism of the countess of Pembroke has always been dominated by the myth of her brother. During her life she was seen primarily as a patron and praised as Sidney's heir; the *Psalmes*, on which her contemporaries said her fame would rest, were known only to those with access to a manuscript copy. Since then, her writings have been dismissed as a minor contribution to the plan credited to her of reforming English letters through careful patronage; in addition, that most of her works existed only in manuscript made serious attention unlikely. Since Rathmell (1963) and Waller (1977) a more considered assessment has been possible, but the terms of this remain problematic. For earlier literary historians, the countess' literary endeavors, as author, editor, and patron, were entirely a memorial to her brother. Elements shared by her works and those dedicated to her were traced back to Sidney's writings. She was seen as basing her perceived tastes on a simplistic reading of Sidney's agenda as presented in the *Defence* and of upsetting the natural evolution of English letters by prescriptiveness. The most stubborn version of this approach found evidence—in Daniel's* dedication to his *Cleopatra* and in references in Breton, Sweeper, and, later, Aubrey—that she attempted to set up at Wilton a kind of college of writers, all busy writing neo-stoic closet dramas and quantitative verse. Her influence was imagined as extending to most major Elizabethan writers, but the result of this inflation of her aims was the myth of a consequently splendid failure to halt the golden age of English literature in its tracks. She may be the second most popular nonroyal female patron in the late Elizabethan and early Jacobean period, but to receive a dedication is not to commission a work. Writers she may or may not have known dedicated to her the sort of works they thought she would, or should, reward; the connection to her own writings is, with one exception, tenuous. From the endless hexameters of Abraham Fraunce to the penitent meditations ventriloquized by Nicholas Breton, writers constructed an image of her—conventional and exaggerated—that critics have perhaps still not escaped.

While accepting that she would not, and probably could not, have written without the model of Sidney (the *Psalmes* are frequently described as a process of self-education), many recent critics have nevertheless found him a stumbling block. Where literary history had circumscribed the countess by the more substantial political and literary successes of her brother and sons—seeing her as the misguided and obsessive literary executor of Sidney and the fading mother of Jacobean England's most important patron—modern critics have tried to discover a character and a writer who can be understood in her own terms. These efforts are hampered by the fact that it was possible for her to act in the public sphere only precisely by espousing the limiting view of her as dutiful sister and mother. Where the focus is on the dynamics of early-modern womanhood, this paradox is precisely the interest, but recent studies of the countess have tried to combine such a perspective with more traditional author-centered readings, and here it is a hindrance. A case in point is the authorship of the ''Dolefull Lay.'' Either she wrote a Spenserian poem because decorum allowed her no other way to print an elegy for her brother; or Spenser wrote a piece of ventriloquy; or, again, they collaborated. We cannot know which is the case because the result is the same: a woman's voice failing to ring true in a male setting. It is quite likely that she was a capable politician in a man's world and a brilliant creator of tapestries in a woman's world, but history has limited her visibility and hence her perceived value in both. Biographies accordingly can find what they expect and approve in a woman of the period—be it piety or feistiness—yet the only substantial traces of her are her works, and most of these are translations. Attention has been paid to the significance of her achievement in the *Psalmes* primarily in formal terms—for in this overall ''fore-conceit'' (her brother's term) one sees a vision that is hers alone—but most recently attempts have been made to prize from the choices she made, when translating or imitating the words of others, some essence—or voice—that can be called independent or self-assertive, personally and politically. The recognition of the bounds of this endeavor leads to the subtlest criticism of the writings and image of the countess. But inevitably, her critics reach a point of frustration that her response to the limits imposed on her is not the same as ours. As is not the case with her niece, Mary Wroth,* she created a space for herself as a literary figure by managing never to challenge the decorum of gender. The construction of the countess of Pembroke in the image of her reader that went on in the 1590s continues to this day.

BIBLIOGRAPHY

Works by Mary Sidney Herbert, Countess of Pembroke

Antonius. In *Narrative and Dramatic Sources of Shakespeare*, ed. Geoffrey Bullough. Vol. 5. New York: Columbia University Press, 1966.

Collected Works. Ed. Michael G. Brennan, Margaret P. Hannay, and Noel J. Kinnamon. Oxford: Oxford University Press, forthcoming.

Discourse of Life and Death. Ed. Diane Bornstein. Detroit: Michigan Consortium, 1983.

The Psalms of Sir Philip Sidney and the Countess of Pembroke. Ed. J.C.A. Rathmell. New York: New York University Press, 1963.

The Triumph of Death and other Unpublished and Uncollected Poems. Ed. G. F. Waller. Salzburg: University of Salzburg, 1977.

Studies of Mary Sidney Herbert, Countess of Pembroke

General

A comprehensive, annotated bibliography is to be found in Josephine A. Roberts, ''Recent Studies in Women Writers of Tudor England, Part II: Mary Sidney, Countess of Pembroke,'' *English Literary Renaissance* 14 (1984): 426–39. References to works mentioned in Roberts' article are not, for the most part, included here.

Beilin, Elaine. *Redeeming Eve: Women Writers of the English Renaissance*. Princeton: Princeton University Press, 1987.

Brennan, Michael G. *Literary Patronage in the English Renaissance: The Pembroke Family*. London: Routledge, 1988.

Buxton, John. *Sir Philip Sidney and the English Renaissance*. London: Macmillan, 1954.

Hannay, Margaret P. *Philip's Phoenix: Mary Sidney, Countess of Pembroke*. New York: Oxford University Press, 1990.

Lamb, Mary Ellen. ''The Countess of Pembroke's Patronage.'' *English Literary Renaissance* 12 (1982): 162–79.

———. *Gender and Authorship in the Sidney Circle*. Madison: University of Wisconsin Press, 1990.

———. ''The Myth of the Countess of Pembroke: The Dramatic Circle.'' *Yearbook of English Studies* 11 (1981): 194–202.

Waller, G. F. ''The Countess of Pembroke and Gendered Reading.'' In *The Renaissance*

Englishwoman in Print, ed. Anne M. Haselkorn and Betty S. Travitsky. Amherst: University of Massachusetts Press, 1990, 327–45.

———. *Mary Sidney: A Critical Study of Her Writings and Literary Milieu*. Salzburg: University of Salzburg, 1979.

Young, Frances Berkeley. *Mary Sidney, Countess of Pembroke*. London: David Nutt, 1912.

Particular

Erler, Mary C. "Davies's *Astraea* and Other Contexts of the Countess of Pembroke's 'A Dialogue.' " *Studies in English Literature* 30 (1990): 41–61.

Fisken, Beth Wynne. " 'To the Angell Spirit . . . ': Mary Sidney's Entry into the 'World of Words.' " In *The Renaissance Englishwoman in Print*, ed. Anne M. Haselkorn and Betty S. Travitsky. Amherst: University of Massachusetts Press, 1990, 263–75.

Freer, Coburn. *"Music for a King": George Herbert's Style and the Metrical Psalms*. Baltimore: Johns Hopkins University Press, 1972.

Hannay, Margaret P. " 'House-confinèd maids': The Presentation of Woman's Role in the *Psalmes* of the Countess of Pembroke." *English Literary Renaissance* 24 (1994): 44–71.

———, ed. *Silent but for the Word: Tudor Women as Patrons, Translators, and Writers of Religious Works*. Kent, OH: Kent State University Press, 1985.

Todd, Richard, "Humanist Prosodic Theory, Dutch Synods, and the Poetics of the Sidney-Pembroke Psalter." *Huntington Library Quarterly* 52 (1989): 273–93.

Woods, Suzanne. *Natural Emphasis: English Versification from Chaucer to Dryden*. San Marino, CA: Huntington Library, 1984.

Zim, Rivkah. *English Metrical Psalms: Poetry as Praise and Prayer, 1535–1601*. Cambridge: Cambridge University Press, 1987.

GAVIN ALEXANDER

GEORGE PUTTENHAM
(c. 1529–1590)

BIOGRAPHY

George Puttenham has been accepted as the author of the important Elizabethan critical work *The Arte of English Poesie*, since the 1936 edition of Willcock and Walker. Until then, opinion tended to view Puttenham's elder brother Richard as author. Both brothers led relatively insignificant lives, though at times each became embroiled in legal controversies.

The Puttenhams were landowning gentry from southern England. The brothers' father married Margery Elyot, sister of Sir Thomas Elyot,* author of *The Governor* (1531). Elyot alludes to his nephews in the dedication to *The Education or Bringing up of Children* (1535). The author of the *Arte* refers to studying at Oxford (though no Puttenham is listed in the university registers), growing up among courtiers and diplomats, and visiting various Continental courts.

George married Elizabeth Coudray. A poor reputation prompted the bishop of Winchester to describe him to the Privy Council as dissolute and ungodly. In the late 1570s and 1580s, Puttenham fought bitterly with his wife's family. He was summoned before the council and imprisoned for a period, before finally receiving a cash grant for injustices suffered. His will left all his property to his servant, Mary Symes.

MAJOR WORKS AND THEMES

The single extant text that identifies Puttenham as its author is a handwritten 1590 pamphlet, *An Apologie or True Defens of her Majesties Honorable and Good Renowne*, defending Elizabeth's treatment of Mary Stuart. The author of the *Arte* describes other works he has written, but only one survives—*Partheniades*, poems presented to the queen. The lost texts include a comedy, *Ginecocratia*; two interludes, *Lusty London* and *Woer*; a hymn dedicated to the queen; and some prose treatises on rhetorical decorum, ornament, and the history of English. The main concerns of these works are praise of the sovereign and rhetoric. They also form the focus of *The Arte of English Poesie*.

In many ways the *Arte* is the most comprehensive early-modern piece of English literary criticism. It surveys the history of poetry and compares English poetry to classical and European traditions. It provides a detailed glossary of tropes and figures. Perhaps most interestingly, it reflects on the social and political stakes of poetry and the position of the ''courtly maker'' or poet. Like other writers at Elizabeth's court such as John Lyly,* Philip Sidney,* Edmund Spenser,* and George Peele,* Puttenham is sharply conscious of the need to balance submission and service against hopes of promotion, reward, and self-assertion. More directly than many, however, Puttenham discusses the ways that texts and symbolism represent and inform these relationships.

The *Arte* is divided into three books: ''Of Poets and Poesie,'' ''Of Proportion Poetical,'' and ''Of Ornament.'' The first offers various definitions of poetry and poets, reiterating traditional accounts of their development and considering their position in sixteenth-century England. The opening chapters make similar points to Sidney's* *Defence of Poesie*, such as poets' descent from ancient seers and makers and their pivotal role in the development of civilized society, as ''the first law-makers to the people, and the first politicians, devising all expedient means for th' establishment of Common wealth, to hold and contain the people in order and duty'' (7). The poet imitates and creates, ''both a maker and a counterfeiter'' (3). The natural purpose of language is to persuade others and benefit oneself, and because poetry is pleasing, it can be highly persuasive. Appropriate subject matter includes praise of gods, kings, and virtue, condemnation of vice, and moral instruction. These thematic goals determine its various forms, including the heroic, lyric, elegiac, tragic, and satirical. Puttenham maintains that poetry and poets are not properly appreciated and supported in present times. This is despite the excellence of contemporary English poetry, its quality fostered earlier in the sixteenth century by Thomas Wyatt* and the earl of Surrey.*

The second book of the *Arte* focuses on poetry's formal elements and variations. Puttenham details rules for technical aspects such as placement of the caesura and various rhyme schemes. He emphasizes the interrelation between visual and aural responses to poetry—the shape of the verse should be linked to its meaning. Square poems, for example, capture the solidity and materiality of earthly topics, while spherical poems reflect heavenly ideas. Similar kinds of visual effects are created by having emblems or devices accompany poems, "the words so aptly corresponding to the subtlety of the figure, that as well the eye is therewith recreated as the ear or the mind" (102). Puttenham's notion of poetry is of a form read as much as heard.

The third book, "Of Ornament," is the longest. It contains much detail on tropes and figures, taken from classical rhetoric but enlivened by English names and examples from contemporary poetry and life, notably Ralegh's.* Puttenham considers that figures affect the mind, not the senses; hence ornament is central to the persuasive functions of language. A text's style should suit its subject matter; but style is also an index of the poet's mind, "for man is but his mind, and as his mind is tempered and qualified, so are his speeches and language at large, and his inward conceits be the metal of his mind" (148). Textual style becomes the arena where an author's motives and reader's responses interact.

Tropes and figures deviate from normal usage and are "occupied of purpose to deceive the ear and also the mind, drawing it from plainness and simplicity to a certain doubleness, whereby our talk is the more guileful & abusing" (154). There are three kinds of figures. The "auricular" strikes the ear; an example is a suggestive midsentence pause, what the Greeks called *Aposiopesis* but what Puttenham Englishes as the figure of Silence or Interruption (166). The "sensible" strikes the imagination and includes metaphor and metonymy, renamed Transport and the Misnamer. The key sensible figure is "the Courtly figure *Allegoria* . . . the figure of *false semblant* or *dissimulation*," which comes into play "when we speak one thing and think another, and that our words and our meanings meet not" (186). For Puttenham, this figure is so central that it crosses over to the next category, "sententious" figures, which strike the ear and imagination, such as the trope "*Amphibologia* . . . the *ambiguous*, or figure of sense uncertain" (260).

All figures should realize "decency" or decorum, a kind of natural conformity between "sense and the sensible" (261–62). A lack of "decency" risks losing poets their audience's good opinion. The key to sustaining decorum and opinion is to simulate the natural through practice and training in the figurative. The rhetorical concepts start to supply models for ways of constructing identity, especially amid the court's social rivalries and political complexities.

Here Puttenham returns to the figure of *Allegoria*, which he sees as highly relevant to the courtly poet's position. As courtier, the poet must "cunningly . . . be able to dissemble . . . his conceits as well as his countenances, so as he never speak as he thinks, or think as he speaks . . . the figure *Allegoria* . . . therefore not impertinently we call the Courtier or figure of fair semblant'' (299). Through careful monitoring of self and others, the poet shall ''be more commended for his natural eloquence then for his artificial, and more for his artificial well dissembled, than for the same overmuch affected and grossly or undiscreetly bewrayed'' (307). The *Arte* closes with an appeal to the queen's recognition of the author's talent and ''ability to any better or greater service'' (308).

CRITICAL RECEPTION

Puttenham's emphasis on rhetorical and personal dissimulation has been studied in detail in recent criticism. The *Arte* is now considered a central Elizabethan account of the social and political stakes of literature and representation, while its concern with courtly identity raises issues of selfhood as cultural process.

Prior to this reading, the *Arte* was recognized as a significant handbook on rhetoric and poetics. It was cited and commended by various contemporaries, including John Harington,* William Camden, Francis Meres, Ben Jonson,* and Henry Peacham. The focus on courtiership raises ideas related to Castiglione's* *The Courtier*, especially on naturalized performance of actions and speech. The *Arte* was reprinted twice during the nineteenth century. Its pre–World War II editors, Willcock and Walker, see in it ''an urbane and flexible temperament, shrewd and critical in its judgments'' (c), not taken in by ideological excesses but holding to an Elizabethan and an English *via media* (xcvi). Similarly, C. S. Lewis considers Puttenham's views highly sensible, marking a civilized and disinterested critical intelligence.

Recent interpretations have reviewed these responses to the *Arte*. The author's humanism is deemed a strategic negotiation of the court's Petrarchan submission and service to the queen. Allegorical dissemblance is seen as resisting this rhetoric of obedience, enabling the courtier to exercise some individuality and agency within it (Davis, Javitch, Montrose, Plett). Other critics have questioned whether Puttenham's ideas can be seen as ideologically resistant, since they remain focused on the fate of the male courtier and reinforce existing class and gender hierarchies (Lezra, Kegl; also David Norbrook and Annabel Patterson). All these discussions underline the *Arte*'s depictions of selfhood as social and discursive process (Whigham).

A further critical development has been to read Puttenham's rhetoric in deconstructive terms, with its emphasis on the power of tropes to subvert premises of natural linguistic order and meaning (Galyon, Attridge, Parker).

BIBLIOGRAPHY

Works by George Puttenham

An Apologie or True Defens of her Majesties Honorable and Good Renowne. British Library Harleian Manuscript 831, 1590.

The Arte of English Poesie. London, 1589.

Partheniades. 1579. Cotton Manuscript Vesp. E. viii. 169–78. Rpt. with *Arte* in *Ancient Critical Essays*. 2 vols. Ed. Joseph Haslewood. London, 1811–16; and in *Ballads from MSS*. Ed. W. R. Morfill. London, 1873.

Reprints of the Arte

Ed. Edward Arber. London, 1869.

Elizabethan Critical Essays. 2 vols. Ed. G. G. Smith. Oxford: Clarendon Press, 1904.

Ed. Gladys Doidge Willcock and Alice Walker. Cambridge: Cambridge University Press, 1936. (Quotations are from this edition.)

Ed. R. C. Alston. Menston: Scolar Press, 1968.

Studies of George Puttenham

Attridge, Derek. ''Puttenham's Perplexity: Nature, Art, and the Supplement in Renaissance Poetic Theory.'' In *Literary Theory/Renaissance Texts*, ed. Patricia Parker and David Quint. Baltimore: Johns Hopkins University Press, 1986, 257–79.

Davis, Lloyd. ''Passing, Subjection, and the Elizabethan Rhetoric of Obedience.'' *Southern Review* (Australia) 24 (1991): 244–58.

Galyon, Linda. ''Puttenham's *Enargeia* and *Energeia*: New Twists for Old Terms.'' *Philological Quarterly* 60 (1981): 29–40.

Javitch, Daniel. *Poetry and Courtliness in Renaissance England*. Princeton: Princeton University Press, 1978.

Kegl, Rosemary. '' 'Those Terrible Aproches': Sexuality, Social Mobility, and Resisting the Courtliness of Puttenham's *The Arte of English Poesie*.'' *English Literary Renaissance* 20 (1990): 179–208.

Lezra, Jacques. '' 'The Lady Was a Little Peruerse': The 'Gender' of Persuasion in Puttenham's *Arte of English Poesie*.'' In *Engendering Men: The Question of Male Feminist Criticism*, ed. Joseph A. Boone and Michael Cadden. New York: Routledge, 1990, 53–65.

Montrose, Louis. ''Of Gentlemen and Shepherds: The Politics of Elizabethan Pastoral Form.'' *ELH* 50 (1983): 415–59.

Norbrook, David. *Poetry and Politics in the English Renaissance*. London: Routledge, 1984.

Parker, Patricia. *Literary Fat Ladies: Rhetoric, Gender, Property*. New York: Methuen, 1987.

Patterson, Annabel. *Shakespeare and the Popular Voice*. Oxford: Basil Blackwell, 1989.

Plett, Heinrich F. ''Aesthetic Constituents in the Courtly Culture of Renaissance England.'' *New Literary History* 14 (1983): 597–621.

Whigham, Frank. *Ambition and Privilege: The Social Tropes of Elizabethan Courtesy Theory*. Berkeley: University of California Press, 1984.

LLOYD DAVIS

R

SIR WALTER RALEGH
(c. 1552–1618)

BIOGRAPHY

Sir Walter Ralegh, a courtier, explorer, planter, and prisoner who also wrote, was born at Hayes, Devonshire (1552?), the youngest son of Walter and Katherine Champernowne Ralegh. While his extended family connections (Ralegh, Champernown, Drake, Carew) no doubt opened doors for him, his rise to power and his subsequent fall were of his own making. After spending his teen years in France fighting for the Huguenot cause (1568–72), Ralegh spent time in residence at Oriel College, Oxford (1572), and the Middle Temple (1575) before going to Munster (1580) to fight against Irish rebels. There, his outspoken criticism of England's Irish policies brought him to the attention of Queen Elizabeth.

Returning to London in late 1581, Ralegh quickly established himself in Queen Elizabeth's court, both as an expert on Irish affairs and as a royal favorite. The queen's favor brought Ralegh rapid social and economic advancement, in the form of estates in Munster, monopolies of wine licenses (1583) and broadcloth exports, (1584) and even new colonies; the queen knighted him in 1585 and made him warden of the Stannaries, lieutenant of Cornwall, vice admiral of Devon and Cornwall, and, in 1587, captain of the Queen's Guard. When Ralegh's secret marriage to Elizabeth Throckmorton (1588) became known by the birth of a son in 1592, the queen had both husband and wife imprisoned in the Tower of London. Subsequently, in 1593, a commission called by Ralegh's enemies at court investigated him for unorthodox religious thought, but without success. Although Ralegh was released from the Tower after several months and continued to work in the queen's service, the two were not reconciled until 1597. In 1601 Ralegh helped to put down the Essex rebellion. Ralegh's service at court ended shortly after the death of Queen Elizabeth in 1603; King James stripped him of his offices and monopolies, then had him tried and convicted of treason.

Ralegh is perhaps best known as an explorer and adventurer, activities that engaged him before and during his years at court and even after his imprisonment on the treason conviction. Between 1584 and 1589 Ralegh unsuccessfully attempted to establish a colony of English settlers at Roanoke Island (also known as the Virginia colony, in present-day North Carolina). But it was as privateer that Ralegh made his name. In 1578 Ralegh captained a ship in Sir Humphery Gilbert's search for a Northwest Passage to the Indies, a failed expedition that evolved into a privateering voyage. Ralegh proved himself adept at the extremely profitable art of raiding Spanish ships, an exercise he practiced and sponsored for the rest of his life. In 1595 Ralegh led an expedition into Guyana, in South America, in search of El Dorado, the fabled city of gold reported in Spanish documents and Indian stories. *The Discoverie of Guiana* (1596) recounts the failed expedition up the Orinoco River, through the heart of the Spanish colonies. In 1596 Ralegh accompanied the earl of Essex on the Cadiz raid and in 1597 on the expedition to the Spanish-held Azores Islands.

Leasing cheap land in Ireland, Ralegh styled himself a planter. From about 1583 through 1602, he expended great time, energy, and resources in an unsuccessful attempt to colonize Ireland. When the English, led by Lord Grey of Wilton, quashed the Desmond rebellion in Southern Ireland in 1583, they decimated the population and devastated the land. Ralegh saw this as an opportunity for the English finally to convert Ireland into a friendly and prosperous extension of the British homeland. To this end, Ralegh personally took possession of vast tracts of land in counties Cork, Waterford, and Tipperary and encouraged others, including Edmund Spenser, to do the same. The plan failed politically and financially, as the English planters were continually besieged by Irish rebellions. By 1602 Ralegh had sold most of his Irish holdings and turned his attention to more pressing matters.

Ralegh's raids on Spanish shipping and his generally anti-Spanish political views, while encouraged by Elizabeth's governments, did not sit well with King James and his policies of appeasement. At the urging of the Spanish ambassador, in 1603, James had Ralegh arrested and tried on trumped-up charges of treason. In a rigged trial, Ralegh was convicted of betraying England to Spain, no less, and sentenced to death. Public outcry led James to defer execution of sentence and leave Ralegh imprisoned in the Tower of London. Ralegh spent his years in prison productively, despite several strokes and periods of extended illness. While he invested in several expeditions to the Americas, his primary occupation was as tutor to Prince Henry, heir to the throne. In this role he wrote most of his prose tracts, instructing the teenaged Henry on a wide range of topics, all tending toward radical Reform Protestant and anti-Spanish ends. The best known of these works is the monumental *History of the World*, left unfinished after Henry's death in 1612. In 1616 Ralegh persuaded King James, by then deeply in debt, to permit him to establish a gold mine in Guyana; the expedition failed, and Ralegh returned to England, where the French ambassador convinced him to escape to France rather than return to the Tower. Betrayal by a friend led to his capture and subsequent beheading, on 29 October 1618, on the trumped-up 1603 treason conviction.

MAJOR WORKS AND THEMES

Ralegh's literary works, like his life, are diverse and, by and large, occasional pieces, written for specific purposes. In this respect, it is important to note that the roles of courtier, planter, and explorer were in no way distinct from his role as poet.

Ralegh's reputation as an esteemed poet makes me rue the fact that relatively few of his poems still exist. Establishing the canon of Ralegh's lyric poems is a major critical problem: during his lifetime few poems were published under his name; while scores of anonymous poems were attributed to him in Renaissance collections (both printed and in manuscript), only five poems are in his own handwriting. Many poems traditionally attributed to Ralegh have been excluded from the canon by recent scholars, Michael Rudick and Steven May being among the most severe. The excluded poems include some of the best-known "Ralegh" poems: "Like to a Hermite poore in place obscure" (*The Phoenix Nest*, 1593), a melancholy sonnet that became the lyrics to one of the most popular songs of the seventeenth century, and "The Nimphs reply to the Sheepheard," a companion poem to Christopher Marlowe's "The passionate Sheepheard to his love" (both printed in *England's Helicon*, 1600). "Ralegh's" nymph, playing the part of the Petrarchan lady, responds stoically to the seduction speech of Marlowe's Petrarchan shepherd, literalizing the shepherd's idealistic love metaphor and making the seducer's appeal seem faintly silly. In so doing, "Ralegh" suggests that love (or at least the possibility for love) lies outside the realm of the Petrarchan ideal.

The sober tone of "Ralegh's" reply to Marlowe's poem lies under much of his verse: as Yvor Winters observed, Ralegh is a serious poet. The point becomes clear in "What is our life?" The short poem, probably written during imprisonment, builds on the world-as-stage conceit, describing human life as "this short Comedy." Yet Ralegh makes literal the conceit when he carries human life into death, the grave being the final curtain. Doing so, he reveals the shortcoming of the conceit, concluding that, unlike the stage, life's final curtain is forever. "To praise thy life," an elegy on Sir Philip Sidney,* a political ally, if not a friend, also employs the stage conceit to emphasize the limits of mortality. Here Ralegh finds consolation in the belief that Sidney's ''soule and spright enrich the heauens aboue.''

Ralegh wrote two very different commendatory poems to Edmund Spenser's* *The Faerie Queene*. The first places Spenser's poem in the context of literary history; the other, in the context of Elizabethan court politics. ''Methought I saw the graue, where *Laura* lay'' is one of the finest sonnets in the English language and promotes Spenser and *The Faerie Queene* as the world's ultimate literary achievement. Ralegh's sonnet presents a dream allegory, which, in turn, introduces the person of ''the Faery Queene: / At whose approach the soule of *Petrarke* wept.'' The speaker suggests that Spenser at once overgoes both Petrarch and Homer and brings together the traditions of love poetry and heroic poetry that they, respectively, represent. Steven May argues that Ralegh's second commendatory poem, ''The prayse of meaner wits this worke like profit brings,'' much less well wrought, was written in response to a poem by the earl of Essex, as part of a feud between the two men.

A group of four poems, often referred to as the Cynthia poems, exists in Ralegh's own handwriting: ''If Synthia be a Qveene, a princes, and svpreame,'' ''My boddy in the walls captived,'' ''Sufficeth it to yow my ioyes interred'' (entitled ''The 11th: and last booke of the Ocean to Scinthia''), and ''My dayes delights'' (entitled ''The end of the bookes, of the Oceans love to Scinthia, and the beginninge of the 12 Boock, entreatinge of Sorrow''). The poems are undoubtedly parts of Ralegh's poems to Queen Elizabeth, to which Edmund Spenser alludes in both *The Faerie Queene* and *Colin Clouts Come Home Again*. The third and fourth poems, at least, were likely written during Ralegh's 1592 imprisonment. Whether Ralegh ever wrote, or even intended to write, other Cynthia poems is a matter of debate. ''The 11th: and last booke of the Ocean to Scinthia'' is the most important of the group and Ralegh's longest poem (520 lines). Yet the poem is not narrative, despite the frequent use of epic simile, but lyric, a Petrarchan complaint addressed to Cynthia, who has absented herself from her faithful lover. The poem often is read as a thinly veiled complaint by Ralegh to Elizabeth about her mistreatment of him during his period of disfavor caused by the discovery of his marriage to Elizabeth Throckmorton. Indeed, employing the Petrarchan metaphor of amorous combat with a female warrior, Ralegh writes,

> Twelue yeares intire I wasted in this warr
> twelue yeares of my most happy younger dayes,
> butt I in them, and they now wasted ar
> of all which past the sorrow only stayes. (120–23)

Yet Ralegh's speaker, for all the pain his error has caused (imprisonment and disgrace), still feels compelled to seek forgiveness in order to continue his pursuit of power and glory.

Ralegh records his quest for power and glory much more explicitly in the Guyana tracts and in accounts of his expedition up the Orinoco River, through the heart of the Spanish colonial empire, in search of the fabled El Dorado. *The Discoverie of the Large, Rich and Bewtiful Empyre of Guiana* (1596) was Ralegh's most popular work, seeing numerous editions and translations into other languages during his lifetime. *Discoverie* opens with a lengthy description of Guyana, overviewing its location and the customs of its people, telling of its wealth and of the history of Spanish colonial exploitation. The middle part of the book is an account of the expedition itself, detailing the actual voyage up the Orinoco. Ralegh closes the book by calling for the English to colonize Guyana, noting that it would be an easy position to defend against the Spanish, while permitting the Spanish to get it first would be disastrous. Ralegh positions Guyana rhetorically as the place where England must take its stand in the New World against the Spanish colonizers, an elaboration of Ralegh's anti-Spanish views. The book was popular in Ralegh's lifetime due to his vivid descriptions of an Edenic paradise, on the brink of being ruined by the Spanish. Today the book is seen to exhibit the exuberance of the English colonial enterprise as it set into gear in the later sixteenth century. The failure of the voyage itself seems not to have bothered sixteenth- and seventeenth-century readers anymore than it does modern readers.

Ultimate human failure forms the theme of Ralegh's mammoth, magisterial, and uncompleted *History of the World*, which attempts to marry Christian and classical traditions in an account of the rise and fall of great empires, from the world's beginning (Genesis, naturally) through the establishment of the Roman Empire. The stories follow the pattern of a ruler's rise to power through divine providence and fall through human folly. Written during Ralegh's imprisonment, after his 1603 treason conviction, as an educational treatise for Prince Henry, King James' son and heir, the *History* is perhaps the ultimate achievement in the genre of universal history; Ralegh's preface, which outlines the principles governing its writing, may be the finest statement of English historiography in the early Stuart period. Even while emphasizing divine providence as the first cause in human history and always subordinating the work of classical historians to the authority of the Bible, Ralegh displays a remarkable capacity to evaluate and choose among differing sources.

By the time of the English civil war, *The History of the World* came to be seen as a Puritan handbook, in part due to its providential interpretation of history but also due to its attention to the falls of tyrants, often read as an implicit critique of the autocratic Stuart monarchy, first King James and, by extension, his son, Charles I. The degree to which Ralegh intended and James read such critique is a matter of debate. While Ralegh repeatedly decries tyranny, and the book's first edition (1614) was printed anonymously, and copies were confiscated by the government, it is also clear that James later (1616) sold the confiscated books and retained the proceeds for himself. For his part, Ralegh claims not to address contemporary affairs, noting the dangers of so doing: "[W]hosoever in writing a modern History, shall follow truth too near its heels, it may happily strike out his teeth.'' Ralegh's express denial, of course, might well indicate that his aim was indeed directed at King James.

CRITICAL RECEPTION

Much Ralegh scholarship has emphasized and been dedicated to questions of canon, chronology, and text, questions to which any discussions or criticism of the poems is subject. For example, while Yvor Winters places Ralegh in the tradition of the ''plain style'' poets (with Gascoigne, Googe, and Turberville, as opposed to the Petrarchan school of Spenser and Drayton), two of the four poems upon which he bases his interpretation have been excluded from Ralegh's canon by some recent editors. Still, the trend of recent scholarship on Ralegh continues to focus on his role as a court poet, subordinating his roles as explorer, planter, prisoner, and general Protestant provocateur.

Greater critical attention has been paid recently to Ralegh's exploration writings, as means of understanding the roots of European (especially British) colonization and imperialism. Additionally, Ralegh's life and his relationships to Edmund Spenser have come under increasing scrutiny in the study of England's complex relationship to Ireland in the later sixteenth century. As with the poems, Ralegh's prose works seem read not so much for their intrinsic or artistic value so much as for what they say about a fascinating character who played a major role in a fascinating age.

BIBLIOGRAPHY

Works by Sir Walter Ralegh

No proper edition of Ralegh's poems exists. The best edition, not widely available, is contained in Michael Rudick's unpublished doctoral dissertation. The most readily available edition is Agnes Latham's.

Latham, Agnes M. C., ed. *The Poems of Sir Walter Ralegh.* London: Routledge and Kegan Paul, 1951.

Oldys, William, and Thomas Birch, eds. *The Works of Sir Walter Ralegh, Kt., Now First Collected; to Which are Prefixed The Lives of the Author.* 8 vols. London, 1829. Rpt. New York: Burt Franklin, 1965.

Patrides, C. A., ed. *The History of the World.* Philadelphia: Temple University Press, 1971.

Rudick, Michael. ''The Poems of Sir Walter Ralegh: An Edition.'' Diss., University of Chicago, 1970.

Studies of Sir Walter Ralegh

Armitage, Christopher M. *Sir Walter Ralegh, an Annotated Bibliography.* Chapel Hill: University of North Carolina Press, 1987.

Bednarz, James P. ''Ralegh in Spenser's Historical Allegory.'' *Spenser Studies* 4 (1983): 49–70.

Fuller, Mary C. ''Ralegh's Fugitive Gold: Reference and Deferral in *The Discoverie of Guiana.*'' *Representations* 33 (1991): 42–64.

Fussner, F. Smith. *The Historical Revolution: English Historical Writing and Thought, 1580–1640.* New York: Columbia University Press, 1962.

Greenblatt, Stephen J. *Sir Walter Ralegh: The Renaissance Man and His Roles*. New Haven, CT: Yale University Press, 1973.
Hill, Christopher. *The Intellectual Origins of the English Revolution*. Oxford: Clarendon Press, 1965.
Lefranc, Pierre. *Sir Walter Ralegh Écrivain: l'oeuvre et les idées*. Paris: Librairie Armand Colin, 1968.
Levy, F. J. *Tudor Historical Thought*. San Marino, CA: Huntington Library, 1967.
May, Steven W. "Companion Poems in the Ralegh Canon." *English Literary Renaissance* 13 (1983): 260–73.
———. *The Elizabethan Courtier Poets: The Poems and Their Contexts*. Columbia: University of Missouri Press, 1991.
———. *Sir Walter Ralegh*. Boston: Twayne, 1989.
Mills, Jerry Leath. "Recent Studies in Ralegh." *English Literary Renaissance* 15 (1985): 225–44.
———. *Sir Walter Ralegh: A Reference Guide*. Boston: G. K. Hall, 1986.
Oakeshott, Walter. *The Queen and the Poet*. London: Faber and Faber, 1960.
Racin, John. *Sir Walter Ralegh as Historian: An Analysis of* The History of the World. Salzburg: Institut für Englische Sprache und Literatur, Universität Salzburg, 1974.
Rudick, Michael. "The 'Ralegh Group' in *The Phoenix Nest*." *Studies in Bibliography* 24 (1971): 131–37.
Strathmann, Ernest A. *Sir Walter Ralegh, a Study in Elizabethan Skepticism*. New York: Columbia University Press, 1951.
Tennenhouse, Leonard. "Sir Walter Ralegh and the Literature of Patronage." In *Patronage and the Renaissance*, ed. Guy Fitch Lytle and Stephen Orgel. Princeton: Princeton University Press, 1981, 235–58.
Wallace, Willard M. *Sir Walter Raleigh*. Princeton: Princeton University Press, 1959.
Winters, Yvor. *Forms of Discovery: Critical and Historical Essays on the Forms of the Short Poem in England*. Chicago: Alan Swallow, 1967.

RONALD W. HARRIS

BARNABE RICHE
(1542–1617)

BIOGRAPHY

Barnabe Riche was a professional soldier and writer and a paid or, perhaps, voluntary informer. He served at Le Havre during 1562–63 and in the Netherlands briefly sometime between 1572 and 1576, but his primary service was in Ireland. He was there during most of the years 1570–82; he served under Sir Nicholas Malby in the suppression of Desmond's rebellion in 1581. In 1585, he had charge of 100 men at Colraine, but the command was of short duration because his men were ambushed and killed while he was absent. Riche was in Ireland again 1587–92 and from about 1608 until his death.

Riche's periods of military service alternated with periods of residence in London. There, he mixed with a literary crowd. For example, he returned to England in 1582 with Thomas North, the translator of Plutarch, he wrote a commendatory poem for Thomas Lodge's* *An Alarum against Usurers* (1584), and Thomas Churchyard acknowledged his indebtedness to Riche in his *True Discourse Historical of the Succeeding Governors in the Netherlands* (1602). In London in 1586, Riche married Katherine Easton, cousin of Sir Edward Aston. They had no children.

Riche's finances were not secure. He lost whatever land he had as the result of a privateering venture. In 1587, Queen Elizabeth granted him a pension of 2s.6d. a day to be paid out of the Irish treasury, but Riche frequently complained in letters that he had no small difficulty collecting it. At the time of his death he was receiving a smaller pension of 12d. per day.

Riche's avocation of informer made his life tumultuous. Having provided the Privy Council with information prejudicial to Adam Loftus, lord chancellor of Ireland, and to Thomas Jones, his brother and bishop of Meathe, Riche got into a brawl with Loftus' servant and then was attacked by six armed men in the employ of Loftus or some other person against whom Riche had informed. In London in 1592, Riche denounced Loftus to the Privy Council, accusing him of being tolerant of Catholics, but Loftus kept his office. In 1604, Riche informed against a fellow dinner guest who, he claimed, had spoken irreverently of King James' sex life to Riche's wife, but again the charges were dismissed.

MAJOR WORKS AND THEMES

A prolific author, Riche claimed to have written twenty-six works; twenty-two have survived. They fall into four large categories: military, fictions, social criticism and advice, and anti-Catholic and anti-Irish satires and tracts. The dialogue is one of Riche's favored forms. The military works often are very practical. *Allarme to England* criticizes the way the English raised troops, arguing that their method resulted in a ragtag army (I2–I2v), and *Faults* argues that military success depends on recognition of the financial need of the troops; "the want of pay is the original of all disorder" (51).

Riche's most influential work was the story anthology *His Farewell to Militarie Profession* (1581). Elaborate dedicatory letters position the author with regard to women and men readers. *Farewell* contains five pastiches of numerous Italian *novelle* and three translations of a single *novelle* by Giraldi Cinthio. Riche attributes these last to L. B., and they are generally accepted to be his revisions of translations done by Lodovick Bryskett, a friend of Edmund Spenser's.* The stories combine geographical range, cross-dressing, and magical potions of romance with detailed, realistic representation of middle-class life and worries, a combination that appealed to Shakespeare.*

Riche's social writings frequently mix the satiric with the straightforward. *Faults* includes a series of ludicrous portraits—the parasite, the malcontent, the fantasticke—but also the sage military advice quoted earlier. *The Excellency of good women* defends women with timeworn wit and then gives serious advice about choosing a wife and instructions about wifely behavior.

A Catholicke Conference and the other anti-Irish and anti-Catholic tracts represent Catholics as traitors and do not suggest any sort of accommodation of the Irish or any affection for their land.

Riche brags that he did not have a university education. His works betray the lack. In *Faults*, he refers to a tragedy by Aristophanes, and throughout his writings he misattributes classical quotations. This inaccuracy is generally taken as a sign that he was relying on a sloppily kept commonplace book rather than on his own reading.

CRITICAL RECEPTION

Contemporary references to his work suggest that Riche was popular in his own day. Gabriel Harvey,* in his *Pierces Supererogation* (1593), included Riche in a list of vulgar writers in whose works ''many things are commendable, divers things notable, somethings excellent'' (190–91), and in the dedicatory letter to *Have with you to Saffron-Walden*, Thomas Nashe* referred to his own hypothetical reader as well versed in Riche's works. James VI considered *Farewell* influential enough to make it worth his while to protest the work's conclusion; in it, in the first three editions of *Farewell*, there is a story in which a devil possesses the king of Scotland; in the fourth edition, the monarch in question is the Grand Turk.

The frequent use of his stories by dramatists also testifies to his popularity. Shakespeare drew heavily on *Farewell* for *Twelfth Night, or What You Will*. He based the main plot on ''Apolonius and Silla,'' Malvolio's imprisonment in the dark room on ''Two Brethren,'' and used several new words from ''Sappho, Duke of Mantua.'' Parts of *The Merry Wives of Windsor* are indebted to ''Two Brethren.'' ''Gonsales and Agatha'' is the source of the anonymous play *How a man may Choose a Good Wife from a Bad* and of the subplot of *The Old Law* by Middleton, Rowley, and Massinger.

Until recently, critics paid Riche scant attention except in source studies because he wrote in marginal genres, and his heavy borrowing led critics, especially Lievsay, to challenge his originality. Schlaugh, an early defender of Riche, asserted that comparison of Riche with his sources would show that ''in execution as well as style Rich shows greater independence than most of his peers. He stresses human frailties as mainsprings of action; he creates homely English environments despite his use of exotic proper names; he dwells occasionally on economic motives'' (151). So far, no one has substantiated these stylistic and economic claims, but recent critical theorists have provided other sympathetic perspectives. In his edition of *Farewell*, Beecher argues strenuously that Riche's assemblages of other people's parts are worthy of consideration as new works. The recent interest in feminism and gender studies has revived interest in *Farewell*, which makes a great show of being directed to the woman reader (though I find, on one occasion, an alarming obsession with the prefix ''con,'' suggesting subterfuge). Relihan offers the results of ''reading as a woman'' (100). Fleming uses Riche to exemplify her argument that "in displaying their fictions as products of a prodigal phase, Elizabeth's poets intended their writings first to explore, and then to reject, female power and its most alarming consequences" (178).

BIBLIOGRAPHY

Works by Barnabe Riche

Original Editions

A Right Exelent and Pleasaunt Dialogue, betwene Mercury and an English Souldier, 1574.

Allarme to England, 1578.

Riche his Farewell to Militarie Profession, written c. 1579; pub. 1581.

The Straunge and Wonderfull Adventures of Don Simonides, 1581.

The True Report of a Late Practise Enterprised by a Papist, with a Yong Maiden in Wales, 1582.

The Second Tome of the Travailes and Adventures of Don Simonides, 1584.

A Path-way to Military Practise, 1587.

The Adventures of Brusanus Prince of Hungaria, written c. 1585; pub. 1592.

A Martial Conference, 1598.

A Looking Glass for Ireland, 1599.

Captaine Pill his Humorous Fit. Captaine Skil his Temperate Judgement, issued with the titles *The Fruites of Long Experience*, 1604, and *A Souldiers Wishe to Britons Welfare*, 1604.

Faultes Faults, and Nothing Else but Faultes, 1606.

Roome for a Gentleman, 1609.

A Short Survey of Ireland, 1609.

A New Description of Ireland, 1610. Reissued as *A New Irish Prognostication*, 1624.

A Catholicke Conference, 1612.

A True and a Kinde Excuse Written in Defence of that Booke, Intituled A Newe Description of Irelande, 1612.

The Excellency of Good Women, 1613.

Opinion Diefied, 1613.

The Honestie of this Age, 1614.

My Ladies Looking Glasse, 1616.

The Irish Hubbub, 1617.

Modern Editions

"Anothomy of Ireland." Ed. E. M. Hinton. *PMLA* 55 (1940): 73–101.

Barnabe Riche His Farewell to Military Profession. Ed. Donald Beecher. Ottawa: Medieval and Renaissance Texts and Studies, 1992.

Don Simonides, Parts one and two. Ed. Norbert Kind. Cologne: Hundt Druck, 1989.

Faultes Faults and Nothing Else but Faultes. Ed. Melvin H. Wolf. Gainesville, FL: Scholars' Facsimiles and Reprints, 1965.

The Honestie of This Age. Ed. Peter Cunningham. *Early English Poetry, Ballads, and Popular Literature of the Middle Ages* 11.4. London: Percy Society, 1844.

"Remembrances of the State of Ireland." E.C.L. Falkiner, *Proceedings of the Royal Irish Academy* 26 (1906–7): 125–42.

Rich's Farewell to Military Profession. Ed. Thomas Mabry Cranfill. Austin: University of Texas Press, 1959.

Studies of Barnabe Riche

Beecher, Donald. "Determining Displacements in the *Farewell to Military Profession* of Barnabe Riche." *Cahiers-Elisabethains* 44 (1993): 1–8.

Bullough, Geoffrey. Introduction to *The Merry Wives of Windsor. Narrative and Dramatic Sources of Shakespeare. Vol. II.* London: Routledge and Kegan Paul, 1958, 3–19.

Caliumi, Grazia. *Studi e ricerche sulle fonti italiane del teatro elisabettiano.*—Vol. I: *Il Bandello.*" *Quaderni dell'istituto di lingue e letterature germaniche della facoltà di magistero*—Universita Di Parma 4. Rome: Bulzoni Editore.

Carroll, D. Allen. "Rich and Green: Elizabethan Beast Fables and Ireland." *Eire-Ireland: A Journal of Irish Studies* 25 (1990): 106–13.

Clements, Robert, and Joseph Gibaldi. *Anatomy of the Novella.* New York: New York University Press, 1977.

Craigie, James. "*Philotus*: A Late Middle Scots Comedy." *Scottish Literary Journal* 6 (1979): 19–33.

Cranfill, Thomas Mabry. "Barnaby Rich: An Elizabethan Reviser at Work." *Studies in Philology* 46 (1949): 411–18.

———. "Barnaby Rich and King James." *Journal of English Literary History* 16 (1949): 65–75.

———. "Barnaby Rich's 'Sappho' and *The Weakest Goeth to the Wall.*" *University of Texas Studies in English* (1945–46): 142–71.

Cranfill, Thomas Mabry, and Dorothy Hart Bruce. *Barnaby Rich: A Short Biography.* Austin: University of Texas Press, 1953.

Fleming, Juliet. "The Ladies' Man and the Age of Elizabeth." In *Sexuality and Gender in Early Modern Europe*, ed. James Grantham Turner. Cambridge: Cambridge University Press, 1993, 158–81.

Harrington, John P. "A Tudor Writer's Tracts on Ireland, His Rhetoric." *Eire-Ireland: A Journal of Irish Studies* 17 (1982): 92–103.

Jorgensen, Paul A. "Barnaby Rich: Soldierly Suitor and Honest Critic of Women." *Shakespeare Quarterly* 7 (1956): 183–88.

Krieger, Gottfried. " 'Barnaby Rich His Crafte of Fylching': A Reappraisal in the Light of the Interextuality Debate." In *Modes of Narrative: Approaches to American, Canadian and British Fiction*, ed. Reingard M. Nischick and Barbara Korte. Wurzburg: Konigshausen and Neumann, 1990, 203–17.

Levenson, Jill L. Introduction to *A Critical Edition of the Anonymous Elizabethan Play "The Weakest Goeth to the Wall."* New York: Garland, 1980, 21–27.

Lievsay, John Leon. "A Word about Barnaby Rich." *Journal of English and German Philology* 55 (1956): 381–92.

Lucas, Caroline. *Writing for Women: The Example of Woman as Reader in Elizabethan Romance.* Milton Keynes: Open University Press, 1989.

McDiarmid, M. P. "*Philotus*: A Play of the Scottish Renaissance." *Forum for Modern Language Studies* 3 (1967): 223–35.

Mariniello, Giuliana. "Vicende Biografiche e formazione ideologica di un letterato elisabettiano, Barnaby Rich." *Annali Istituto Universitario Orientali, Napoli, Sezione Germanica 17*, no. 3 (1974): 45–105.

Mill, Anna J. Introduction to *Philotas. Miscellany Volume.* Edinburgh: Blackwood for the Society, 1933, 83–96.

Muir, Kenneth. *The Sources of Shakespeare's Plays.* New Haven, CT: Yale University Press, 1978, 132–40.

Price, John Edward. " 'Because I Would Followe the Fashion': Rich's *Farewell to the Military Profession* and Shakepeare's *Twelfth Night.*" *Iowa State Journal of Research* 62 (1988): 397–406.

Relihan, Constance C. *Fashioning Authority: The Development of Elizabethan Novelistic Discourse.* Kent, OH: Kent State University Press, 1994.

Rice, Warner G. "The Moroccan Episode in Thomas Heywood's *The Fair Maid of the West.*" *PQ* 9 (April 1930): 131–40.

Rodax, Yvonne. *The Real and the Ideal in the Novella of Italy, France and England: Four Centuries of Change—the Boccaccian Tale.* Chapel Hill: University of North Carolina Press, 1968.

Schlaugh, Margaret. *Antecedents of the English Novel: 1400–1600 (from Chaucer to Deloney).* Warszawa: PWN—Polish Scientific Publishers, 1963.

Starnes, D. T. "Barnabe Riche's 'Sappho Duke of Mantona' A Study in Elizabethan Story-Making." *Studies in Philology* 30 (1993): 455–72.

PAMELA JOSEPH BENSON

JOHN ROSS
(1563–1607)

BIOGRAPHY

John Ross was scarcely known until I assembled his biography and edited some of his poems a few years ago. A Latin poet and lawyer with close ties to the Inner Temple, his claim as a "major author," if any, would lie in his nearly unique place at the intersection of several vital cultural paths. Ross was baptized at Waddesdon, Buckinghamshire, 26 June 1563. Like his younger brother Gabriel, he attended Westminster School, where he began a lifelong acquaintance with Camden, who perhaps aroused his interest in ancient Britain. Evidence suggests a stay at Trinity College, Cambridge, before entering the Inner Temple in 1584, where the admission book lists him as "late of Lyon's Inn." Poems written before his call to the bar in 1593 indicate a dislike of Puritans and Catholics on both theological and patriotic grounds. Friendships with Cambridge divines like John Overall and Benjamin Carier must have fueled his interest in religious controversy.

At this time or soon after, he came to know Edward Coke, in whose orbit he seems to have worked as a barrister. Other friends were members of the Manners family (earls of Rutland), Elizabeth Goodwin (daughter of Arthur Lord Grey, wife of the litigant in the famous case of Goodwin versus Fortescue), and Sir William Sackville (one of Lord Buckhurst's sons). Several acquaintances followed the earl of Essex: Roger Manners, the eccentric Sir Anthony Sherley, and Sir William Constable, later a signer of Charles I's death warrant, whom the Privy Council placed in Ross' custody following the Essex fiasco. Ross' long poem on the Gunpowder Plot emerges from a knowledge of both the prosecutor

Coke and one of the plotters, Sir Everard Digby. His will was probated in November 1607, the year his one printed book, *Britannica*, appeared in Frankfurt.

MAJOR WORKS AND THEMES

The most interesting of Ross' poems appear in the manuscript collection at the Folger Library entitled "Parerga," which are included with translations in my edition. These constitute an Elizabethan diary in verse, stretching from the 1580s (with a poem on Mary, Queen of Scots* and The Jesuit father Edmund Campion) to the new king's arrival in 1603. Insights of well-informed witnesses are rare at this period, and I for one enjoy hearing from a contemporary about Essex and Ralegh* (the people loved one and hated the other, says Ross, but both met catastrophe: so much for popular opinion) or about the many dry eyes at Elizabeth I's funeral. "Parerga" celebrates as leading events of the day episodes now scarcely mentioned in Tudor histories: the Battle of Nieupoort, the fall of the Hungarian city called Strigonium, the pretense of one Valentine Thomas that James hired him to murder Elizabeth, the pretense of one Sebastian to be king of Portugal. In sheer range of interest these 200 mostly short poems equal or surpass that of the best epigrammatists of the day, even John Owen, for whom Ross wrote a commendatory epigram in Owen's 1607 collection.

Britannica, sive de Regibus Veteris Britanniae (1607; the subtitle means, "or concerning the kings of ancient Britain") summarizes in elegiac couplets the lives of Geoffrey of Monmouth's kings from Brutus to Cadwallader. Although thin on Arthur, the collection is valuable on several counts. It represents the common lawyer's appropriation of an antiquity coinciding with that of the common law itself, supposedly originating at a date "time out of mind." Accordingly, the poem on Dunwallo Mulmutius praises English law, since that king was the first lawgiver. Another theme is the hoped-for return to a unified Britain under James I, the book's dedicatee. In a long poem on Constantine, Ross conveys an image of the ideal Erastian king in ways that would have delighted James, whom he frequently praises in "Parerga." (Seemingly intended for print, that manuscript, too, is dedicated to James.) The only poem from *Britannica* included in my edition is that on the Gunpowder Plot, the 439-line "Ad Praesens Tempus Apostrophe" (Apostrophe at the Present Time), so called because the shade of Cadwallader returns to find Britain's new king beset by worse evils than were ever known in the ruinous past. In dialogue with Cadwallader the nymph Alethia (Truth) reveals details of the scheme, depending on contemporary printed accounts of the conspiracy and trial, but partly on the author's observations. The poem ends with a scathing rebuke of the present age, the crime being symptomatic of moral and religious disintegration: "vile id genus est hominum, cum nil sapiat nisi quaestum" (It is a worthless breed of humanity that is wise in nothing but profit-making).

The pessimism here echoes that of much poetry by Ross, disenchanted with church, court, and his own profession. This mood explains the epigraph of *Britannica* from Horace's Odes (3.6): ''Aetas parentum peior avis'' (The age of the parents is worse than that of the grandparents). Some great doom, he felt, would soon afflict his countrymen as it had a thousand years earlier. A late poem on the western flooding of January 1607 envisions a second deluge because ''quod sustenavit egenos Crapula et ebrietas, et vana superbia vastat'' (Drunkenness and revelry and vain pride consume what supported the needy).

In 1592 Sir William Sackville perished during an attack on a French village as he led troops supporting Henry of Navarre. His death prompted Ross' one long English poem, surviving in a Bodleian manuscript, ''Th'Authors Teares upon the Death of Sir William Sackville.'' Ross and this third son of the distinguished Thomas Sackville Lord Buckhurst had entered the Inner Temple a year apart. Early in the poem are stanzas echoing Spenser's* *Ruins of Rome*.

Spenser, the subject of an epigram in ''Parerga,'' is a frequent presence in Ross. Despite his apparent preference for the short, epigrammatic poem, Ross held a high regard for the epic style and substance. A ''Poem Exhorting Poets'' in ''Parerga'' echoes Spenser's ''October'' in urging poets to celebrate the heroic deeds of Norris and Drake. Either his profession or his talents led him toward the brand of epigrammatic, topical, and occasional verse familiar in writers who belonged to the Inns of Court (''parerga'' means ''incidental works''), hence the linking of Ross with Robert Hayman (Lincoln's Inn) and John Owen (Inner Temple). Ross alludes to Hayman's verse collection *Quodlibets* in a ''Parerga'' poem of 1602, though this was unprinted until Hayman's old age; Hayman, for his part, translates Ross' poem to Owen from the latter's 1607 edition.

CRITICAL RECEPTION

Of interest to scholars of British antiquarianism is Ross' prose ''Tractatus Apologeticus,'' or apology defending the historicity of Geoffrey, ''De Fide et Antiquitate Huius Historiae'' (On the truth and antiquity of this history), published with *Britannica* (86–113). This essay marshals a variety of English and Continental authorities to argue for the actual existence of Brut and his legendary lineage. Noteworthy is Ross' outcry against ''opinio'' (opinion), which has cast all things in doubt in a world gone awry.

BIBLIOGRAPHY

Works by John Ross

Britannica, sive de Regibus Veteris Britanniae usque ad Exitium Gentis, & Saxonum Imperium. Frankfurt, 1607.

Poems on Events of the Day 1582–1607. Ed. Richard F. Hardin. Delmar, NY: Scholars' Facsimiles and Reprints, 1991.

Studies of John Ross

Hardin, Richard F. ''Geoffrey among the Lawyers: *Britannica* (1607) by John Ross of the Inner Temple.'' *Sixteenth Century Studies Journal* 23 (1992): 235–49.

RICHARD F. HARDIN

S

JAMES SANDFORD
(fl. 1567)

BIOGRAPHY

Because the reputation of James Sandford (Sanford, Sanforde) of Somerset is based almost entirely on his diligent translations—especially of Agrippa's* *De vanitate*—his biography comes down to us as a list of other writers' titles. This may be an appropriately Borgesian paradox for an age preoccupied with self-fashioning through imitation and eloquence, but there are also hints in his dedicatory epistles that Sandford had a more eventful life than he hoped for, as I will soon suggest.

Like many of his colleagues, Sandford occasionally translated translations (as did Sir Thomas North in his classic English translation of Amyot's French translation of Plutarch's *Lives*), but he also directly tackled substantial Latin (and less Greek) as well as Italian and French texts. He was probably tutor to William Herbert, third earl of Pembroke, nephew to Sir Philip Sidney* and a leading candidate in the modern hunt for "Mr. W. H." of Shakespeare's* *Sonnets*. As is often the case in Tudor translations, Sandford's dedicatory epistles are addressed to the great and near great—Queen Elizabeth,* Robert Dudley, earl of Leicester, Sir Hugh Paulet, Sir Christopher Hatton, and Thomas Howard, fourth duke of Norfolk—and reflect the Tudor view of translation as a patriotic act, making available classical and Continental wisdom to rulers and ruled. Indeed, while the epistles indulge some of the usual flattery of the former, that is subordinate to a didactic emphasis.

The epistles contain clues, however, of a tumultuous world beyond the reach of his instruction. In 1569 Sandford published his translation of Agrippa with an epistle reminding the duke of Norfolk that it is easier to shun overt evil than to choose between alternative goods, under which evil sometimes lurks. Norfolk was, in fact, receiving love letters from Mary, Queen of Scots,* and was a nervous and ambivalent partner in the plans to have Mary succeed Elizabeth. Norfolk did not heed Sandford's oblique warning: in 1571 the duke was part of the Ridolfi plot that involved a Spanish invasion of England, the arrest of Elizabeth, and the installation of Mary as queen of England. The plot was uncovered, and in 1572 he was beheaded for treason. The following year Sandford published an entertaining collection, *The Garden of Pleasure*, but with an urgent epistle to Leicester pleading for support, darkly lamenting some unstated adversity, and cherishing books as his consolation. Three years later this collection was enlarged and retitled, with an epistle to Hatton praising the cult of Elizabeth, comparing her to the Muses, classical poets, and the Virgin Mary. However closely Sandford may have brushed up against the dangerous events of the late 1560s and early 1570s—the marriage schemes, the Northern Rebellion, the Ridolfi plot—the deletion of the epistle to Norfolk in the second edition of *De incertitudine et vanitate* (1575) is mute testimony to the scholar's discretion within historical uncertainty.

MAJOR WORKS AND THEMES

The title page of one of Sandford's ''Englished'' volumes (*Houres of Recreation*) declares its contents to be ''no lesse delectable, than profitable.'' Between the poles of the Horatian dictum revolves the world of Tudor tastes and preoccupations. Sandford's texts and dedications are, by turns, pedantic, sensational, witty, pious, patriotic, defensive, and apocalyptic. His first two books appeared in 1567, both from the London printer Henry Bynneman. First was his translation of the Stoic wisdom of Epictetus, dedicated to the queen, but the second is more suggestive of Sandford's range: *The Amorous and Tragicall Tales of Plutarch, whereunto is annexed the Hystorie of Cariclea and Theagines and the sayings of the Greeke Philosophers*. It begins with a severe, moral epistle approving Draco's death sentence on idleness because idleness is the origin of mischief, engendering ''the lothsome luste of Carnall concupiscence.'' Its few, brief narratives, ostensibly negative *exempla*, are tales of rape, mayhem, and suicide, the first of a maid torn to pieces by rival lovers, the second of a young boy torn to pieces by his father and his abductors, and so on. Ascham's complaint (in *The Scholemaster*, 1570) about immoral translations (referring perhaps to Painter's and Fenton's *novelle*, both also published in 1567, Painter's also by Bynneman) might apply here, but Sandford blithely combines these sketches with an anthology of biographical introductions to, and sage maxims from, Solon, Socrates, Antisthenes, Bias, and others and with a partial translation of Heliodorus (soon displaced by Underdowne's). The year 1568 saw the publication of his poem praising George Turberville in the latter's own translation, *Plaine Path to Perfect Virtue*. Sandford's is an undistinguished poem notable for a historical irony: it praises scholars who follow Minerva even as its author was probably hard at work on his translation of Agrippa's *De vanitate* (1569), a massive assault on the vices of human learning. The Agrippa translation, by far Sandford's most enduring work, includes a characteristic caution "To the Reader," claiming that *De vanitate* attacks abuses only, that knowledge ought to be perfected, and that Agrippa intends the work to display "the excellencie of his wit." Anything troubling is attributed to Agrippa's human error and the corrupting influence of his Catholic and magical affiliations. (Sandford repeats the famed canine anecdote.) Sandford's other projects include *Houres of Recreation or Afterdinners* (the expansion of his *Garden of Pleasure*), with a new epistle that praises Elizabeth and all learned women, including Lady Ann Bacon,* and also provides a numerological explanation of why, if the world is not destroyed in 1588, at least the wicked will feel God's wrath (many English writers gloating over the fate of the Armada were to agree with him that year); *Mirror of Madnes* (1576), a minor but adroit mock encomium translated from French, sometimes compared to Erasmus'* *Praise of Folly*, and probably attractive to Sandford because of the success of his Agrippa translation; and *The Revelation S. Ihon, reueled, or a paraphrase written in Latine by Jame Brocard* (1582), a dense, lengthy commentary for those who find the Revelation of St. John too "darke & difficult." Sandford also earns some notice in Thomas More* studies by being the first to translate two of More's Latin epigrams—about an obtuse, cuckolded astrologer—which are conflated and quoted by Agrippa.

CRITICAL RECEPTION

Sandford has received little direct notice beyond his translation of Agrippa, which after 400 years is still the standard English version. He was proud of the work, informing the reader that he had consulted an Italian version as well as the Latin and discerned a pattern of censorship deleting attacks on "the Popes folowers," which he restored. Sandford himself, however, deleted a bitter passage about the inevitable corruption of all religions. This passage has been restored by the modern editor of Sandford's work, who has also noted and corrected a suggestive slip in the conclusion; Sandford's rendering had all knowledge "reueled" rather than concealed by the Fall.

BIBLIOGRAPHY

Works by James Sandford

Amorous and Tragicall Tales of Plutarch, whereunto is annexed the Hystorie of Cariclea and Theagines and the sayings of the Greeke Philosophers. London, 1567.

The Manuell of Epictetus, translated out of Greeke into French and now into English, conferred with two Latine translations. London, 1567.

Of the Vanitie and Vncertaintie of Artes and Sciences. London, 1569, Rpt. ed. Catherine M. Dunn. Northridge: California State University, 1974.

The Garden of Pleasure, contayninge most pleasante tales, worthy deeds, and witty sayings of noble Princes & learned Philosophers, Moralized. London, 1573.

Houres of Recreation, or Afterdinners, which may aptly be called the Garden of Pleasure. London, 1576.

Mirror of Madnes, or a Paradoxe, maintayning madnes to be most excellent, done out of French into English by Ja. San. Gent. London, 1576.

The Revelation of S. Ihon, reueled, or a paraphrase . . . written in Latine by James Brocard. London, 1582.

Studies of, or Relevant to, James Sandford

Amos, Flora Ross. *Early Theories of Translation.* New York: Columbia University Press, 1920.

Dean, William. ''Kendall's Translation of a Morean Epigram.'' *Moreana* 27. 101–2 (May 1990): 139–45.

Matthiessen, F. O. *Translation: An Elizabethan Art.* Cambridge: Harvard University Press, 1931.

''Sandford or Sanford, James.'' *The Dictionary of National Biography.* Vol. 17: 761–62, Ed. Leslie Stephen and Sidney Lee. Rpt. London: Oxford University Press, 1959–60, 761–62.

RONALD LEVAO

WILLIAM SHAKESPEARE
(1564–1616)

BIOGRAPHY

William Shakespeare was baptized on 26 April 1564 at Trinity Church Stratford-upon-Avon and was buried there on 25 April 1616 (his birth and death are often conjectured to be on 23 April, appropriate for a national poet, as it is St. George's or Red Cross Knight's Day). He was the son of John Shakespeare, a tradesman who married well into the minor gentry, to Mary Arden, mother of William, and became bailiff, or mayor, of Stratford, securing the coat of arms of a gentleman, though his last years seem to have been less successful. William is likely to have studied at the local grammar school, which was well endowed enough to secure excellent tutors from nearby Oxford University. In late November 1582, William contracted a precocious and hurried marriage with a much older woman, Anne Hathaway, for the first child was born soon after a marriage by special license. After the later birth of twins early in 1585, William disappears from records for several years, though recently E.A.J. Honigman has argued that he may have been employed by the Houghtons, a recusant family in Lancashire, to whom one of William's teachers may have recommended him because of shared Catholic sympathies (of which there are also some faint hints in other records of the Shakespeare family).

The Houghtons had both court and theatrical connections, perhaps leading to

Shakespeare's subsequent career in the theater, though he could have encountered traveling theater companies at Stratford, observed court players at aristocratic festivals at Kenilworth, and even seen the last medieval mystery cycles at nearby Coventry. By 1592 Shakespeare surfaces in London as a professional actor who is already a successful dramatist, noted for revising and adapting existing scripts, thereby inviting charges of plagiarism (1592) from rivals such as Robert Greene,* a graduate of Cambridge University like many dramatists of the time, such as John Lyly* and Christopher Marlowe.* Shakespeare often ridicules the pretensions of such graduates, as in *Love's Labour's Lost*, implying the possible competitiveness of a nongraduate. However, in apologizing later in 1592 for publishing Greene's slanders, Henry Chettle praised Shakespeare "because I have seen his demeanor no less civil than he excellent in the quality he professes [i.e., his profession]: Beside, divers of worship have reported his uprightness of dealing, which argues his honesty, and his facetious grace in writing, that approves his art."

Shakespeare early acquired the reputation of a talented author, not only for his first chronicle history plays, *Henry VI* and *Richard III*, but for neoclassical comedies (such as *The Comedy of Errors*), realistic farces (*The Taming of the Shrew*), and romantic comedies (*The Two Gentlemen of Verona*). He also wrote extravagant tragedies such as the exaggeratedly gruesome *Titus Andronicus* and the highly sentimental *Romeo and Juliet*. His claims as a serious poet were strengthened by his widely circulated *Sonnets* (about his friendship with a young aristocrat, which overlapped with an adulterous love affair with a Dark Lady) and by his publication of two narrative poems, *Venus and Adonis* and *The Rape of Lucrece* (probably written while the theaters were closed because of epidemics of the plague). The narrative poems' dedication to the youthful earl of Southampton (perhaps the friend of the *Sonnets*) indicates that Shakespeare was fashionable among the aristocracy frequenting the court of Queen Elizabeth.* He developed a close professional association with the talented theatrical family of the Burbages: the father, James, created London's first custom-built Theatre in Shoreditch and later rebuilt it as the Globe in Southwark. His son, Richard, was for long Shakespeare's leading actor. This invaluable association confirmed Shakespeare's success in the theater and ensured access at court, where his skills seem to have earned him the approval of Queen Elizabeth, if we believe the story of her commissioning *The Merry Wives of Windsor*. The company progressed from being official court performers, as the Lord Chamberlain's Company under Elizabeth, to more explicit royal status as the King's Men, under James I.*

The early success of Richard Burbage's performances of such intense characters as Richard III and Hamlet and other comic creations such as Falstaff made Shakespeare one of the most popular dramatists of the time, though his fortune was ensured chiefly through his share in the newly built outdoor Globe Theatre in Southwark (1599) and in the later use of the Blackfriars indoor theater (1608). After completing a series of successful comedies and histories, Shakespeare wrote his major tragedies during the early years of the reign of the new King James I, whose somber Scottish tastes were directly exploited in *Macbeth*. Increasingly in later years Shakespeare withdrew to Stratford, where he bought New Place, one of its principal houses, thus perhaps restoring his marriage after the adulterous episode of the Dark Lady commemorated in the *Sonnets*. His last plays show a turn to more fanciful, even mystical attitudes, with strong pastoral elements. He seems finally to have shared his writing with his successor as dramatist for the King's Men, John Fletcher, though the exact share of the latter in such works as *The Two Noble Kinsmen* and even (just possibly) in *Henry VIII* is still debated. Many of his works were rewritten for later revivals either by the author or his successors. Shakespeare's works were collected, in various states, by his two colleagues Hemminge and Condell and published in a folio edition introduced by his friend Ben Jonson* in 1623—though many of its contents had been previously published in single-play quarto editions.

Shakespeare's son Hamnet died early, in 1596; his father died in 1601, and his mother in 1608. Both his daughters married, but his direct line died out with their children, thus frustrating the apparent concern to establish a prosperous family line shown in Shakespeare's sustained financial efforts to the end of his life. However, the first of his Stratford homes, in Henley Street, and those of the families of his wife and daughter have survived.

MAJOR WORKS AND THEMES

Shakespeare inherited and echoed the powerful traditions of English medieval drama, stressing didactic biblical themes. These cycles evolved into the more allegorical mode of the morality plays, while later the more secular chronicle history plays succeeded the miracle plays covering ecclesiastical history. Shakespeare also learned how to offset the religious plays' relative seriousness by figures based on their comic vices and devils (e.g., Richard III, Falstaff, Iago) and to develop comic interludes by aid of classical precedents of Plautus and Terence as seen in Renaissance Italian comedy. The strong interest in drama at both Oxford and Cambridge Universities carried over into the sixteenth-century professional theater groups, above all in London, usually protected from the hostile civic authorities (often Puritan) by aristocratic patrons, including Queen Elizabeth herself. Shakespeare's company proved one of the strongest of these, though its origins overlap with those of several others. Shakespeare often found himself in bitter competition with such university wits as Greene and Lodge.* Shakespeare's greatest rival was another Cambridge graduate, Christopher Marlowe, who provided him with such models as the heroic militarism of *Tamburlaine* (for *Henry V*), the supernatural drama of *Dr. Faustus* (for the magic of Prospero), the Machiavel of *The Jew of Malta* (for Richard of Gloucester), and the chronicle histories of *The Massacre at Paris* and *Edward II* (for *Richard II*).

As a company playwright, Shakespeare was expected to be prolific enough to write numerous, equally lively plays on such popular themes as the wickedness of Richard III (the opponent of Queen Elizabeth's grandfather, Henry VII) or the victories in France of the hero King Henry V, matching current military successes in Normandy of a contemporary Elizabethan hero, the Huguenot king Henry IV of France, seen as the king of Navarre in *Love's Labor's Lost*. Shakespeare managed to combine popular interest in Anglo-French history with melodramatic episodes such as the witchcraft of Joan of Arc and Duchess Eleanor in *Henry VI* or the rape and mutilations of *Titus*. His early comedies add romantic touches to the comic formulas of Plautus and Terence, while his tragedies include comic characters such as Juliet's Nurse to provide relief from pathos. Many of his plays are not easily limited to the genres of comedy or tragedy, following the successful Italian precedents of tragicomedy popularized by authors such as Cinthio, from whom Shakespeare borrowed many precedents of plot and character, such as the melodramatic story of *Measure for Measure*. Cinthio also, perhaps, provided Shakespeare with a theory of romance or tragicomedy. Tragicomedy favored contemporary or realistic stories and characters, with highly bizarre effects involving suspense, discoveries, reversals, and sexually provocative situations, as seen in such comedies as *Much Ado* and *All's Well* and even in the tragedy of *Othello*. It encouraged variety. As Geoffrey Bullough has shown, in most of his scripts Shakespeare either revises existing plays or dramatizes popular fiction, usually translated from French or Italian. He rarely invents his stories and characters wholly by himself, so that his materials already have a proven popular interest. His tragedies are not clearly distinguished from his history plays and usually have a substantially historical base, derived from native chroniclers such as Holinshed* for British themes, even going as far back as *King Lear* and *Cymbeline*, or from Plutarch for classical ones.

However, Shakespeare often evokes stereoscopic depth of borrowed characters and plots by including contrasting ideas, data, and interpretations from other, conflicting sources, resulting in a layering of impressions that prevents simple moral and political judgments. Moreover, despite hints in these sources, some of his greatest characters, such as Falstaff and Hamlet, display uniquely Shakespearean twists given to established stereotypes (in these cases, the braggart soldier and the melancholy malcontent, both made dazzlingly witty and more sympathetic), thus creating ambivalences and paradoxes not readily rationalized by any simple code of interpretation. This elusiveness and openness to diverse points of view have been a major feature of his fascination for later ages, coupled with his actor's acute sense of provocative stage effects, including radical shifts of character. These startling dramatic strokes continue to fascinate modern directors, actors, and audiences—whether it be Richard of Gloucester's improbable courtship of the very woman whom he has just widowed or the ethnic and racial polarities of his two Venice plays, *The Merchant* and *Othello* or the gender tensions in *The Taming of the Shrew* and *All's Well*. In his lively treatment of women's roles, Shakespeare shows open concern with the presence of influential women in his audiences both in the public theater and at court. His plots often deal with the great social and political impact of energetic women: Joan of Arc, Queen Margaret, Portia, Olivia and Viola, Lady Macbeth, Cleopatra, Paulina, Marina, and many others. The virtuosity required of the boy actors who successfully played these parts on Elizabethan and Jacobean stages continues to astound modern Shakespeareans.

The physical stages for which Shakespeare wrote largely governed the priorities for his successful dramatic enactments. The stage lacked elaborate scenery, inviting stress on actors' skills in rhetoric (reflected in formal debates, trials, and political speeches) and in physical action such as battles, duels, dances, and rituals requiring elaborate costumes (such as coronations, festivals, processions, and marriages). The physical stage was a composite including a medieval platform, backed by a curtain. This stage could be set in any expedient enclosed but uncovered space such as an innyard with surrounding galleries or a college hall and might have spectators both in front and behind, if not all round it. When purpose-built structures such as Burbage's Theatre appeared, this form persisted with a stage enriched by a galleried facade to the Green Room, pierced by two or three doors, and protected by a roof supported on two pillars at its outer corners, with various traps and with mobile props to dress a permanent set (particularly a central curtain, a throne, and furniture such as beds, and so on). The limited stage scenery shifted emphasis from exact re-creation of historical locations and periods to accommodate elaborate, but largely contemporary, costumes, manners, and issues, so that Shakespeare's work transcends the context of its nominal sources.

The Globe audiences appear to have been large (up to 3,000), diverse, usually prosperous, even aristocratic, but not excluding the working class, who could stand round the stage as groundlings for a penny. With the option of performances at court or, later, in the more expensive indoor theater at the Blackfriars, Shakespeare wrote his plays to appeal to a wide range of social classes. This mixed audience encouraged the diversification of content and tone in Shakespeare's treatment of issues likely to appeal to popular tastes: often a serious or sentimental plot was diversified by comic, melodramatic, or violent interludes. The plays are fast-paced, full of variety of mood, with surprises and reversals of plot and character, intended to hold a restless, usually outdoor audience for two hours or more without interruption. Mere consistency and the calculated decorum apparently favored by neoclassical critics such as Sir Philip Sidney* had little relevance, though many of the plays approach neoclassical unity of time and place (from *The Comedy of Errors* and the last four acts of *Othello*, to *The Tempest*). While Shakespeare (and others) often rewrote his plays for revivals (hence the discrepancies between earlier single-play quarto editions and the later collected Folio version), playwrights had little control over the performance and publication of scripts once they were sold to the players. Modern editors wrestle with the resulting divergences between various texts (some perhaps crudely and inexactly pirated), often even of such major plays as *Hamlet* and *King Lear*, not to mention the drastically different versions of both *Merry Wives* and *The Taming*.

Shakespeare did not radically distinguish between the dramatic genres: his comedies often contain tragic elements as in the life-threatening ethnic tensions of *The Merchant of Venice* or the melodrama of *Much Ado*. His tragedies contain powerful comic strains such as the black humor of Iago in *Othello* or the salutary jibes of Lear's Fool. Nor, like most of his contemporaries, did Shakespeare distinguish among histories, comedies, and tragedies: early chronicle plays like *Richard III* are seen as tragedies, while *Henry IV* is dominated by the comic genius of Falstaff; a comedy like *Love's Labor's Lost* uses the names of living contemporaries for its characters, enacting recorded events, as matched by the historical Don John of *Much Ado* or the Orsino of *Twelfth Night*. Usually, in such cases, Shakespeare compresses and heightens, rather than wholly recasts, his sources in history, fiction, or previous stage successes such as Legge's *Richardus Tertius*, Kyd's *Hamlet, The Chronicle History of King Leir*, and so on.

The two great themes of Shakespeare are the psychological tensions of sexual relationships (as seen in the comedies and romantic tragedies) and the instabilities of political power (seen in the almost medieval cycles of sequential rises and falls of rulers, often in series of plays: *Henry VI–Richard III; Richard II–Henry IV–Henry V; Julius Caesar–Antony and Cleopatra–Cymbeline*). The two themes frequently intersect, almost always with tragic results, as with the Macbeths, Othello and Desdemona, and Antony and Cleopatra. In the comedies, tragic potentialities are usually avoided by the virtuosity of the heroines (Portia, Rosalind, Helena), who typically prove wiser, subtler, and more incisive than their enamored but incompetent admirers. Some later "comedies" achieve more problematic resolutions (*Measure for Measure*, not to mention *Troilus and Cressida*). In the late plays both the tragic potentialities and the amatory intensities are softened and resolved from a more mystical worldview, leading to their characterization as "romances"—though Shakespeare's last history play, *Henry VIII*, shares the same tendency to introduce divine interventions. Scholars still debate whether this shift is personal or reflects the influence of Shakespeare's late collaborator John Fletcher, King James and his court, or the more sophisticated indoor theater audience.

It has become customary to see Shakespeare as enshrining traditional values of patriotism and patriarchal authority, but he creates many powerful nonconforming male and female roles, by no means always tragic in their outcomes. He deliberately uses conflicting sources and interpretations of dominant figures such as Henry V, Octavius Caesar, not to mention the calculated ambiguities of Brutus, Hamlet, Coriolanus, and Henry VIII. These tensions indicate a systematic intent to allow a wide range of interpretation for actors and audiences. Indeed, there is a recurrent element of provocation matching similar challenging effects in Euripides, Molière, Ibsen, Shaw, Chekhov, Strindberg, and even Brecht (the moderns having all consciously followed Shakespearean precedents). Shakespeare's intellectual agility and psychological flexibility explain the accessibility of his scripts to the aesthetic, moral, and political vagaries of each later age, including the twentieth century, which has found Shakespeare readily adaptable to every variant of modern sensibility, so that he remains the most popular of all staged dramatists.

CRITICAL RECEPTION

Even during Shakespeare's lifetime his scripts were subject to casual revision by himself or by others for revivals and special occasions. While he was respected as a discreet personality (called "gentle Shakespeare") and as a deft artist, the seventeenth century did not accord him the modern adulation as a unique and authoritative master playwright. By the Restoration his plays were seen by such critics as Thomas Rhymer as incompatible with the neoclassical decorum imported from France and the scenic sophistication borrowed from the Italian theater by entrepreneurs such as William Davenant, who found it necessary to adapt and correct Shakespeare to suit Restoration tastes. Revisions multiplied by such writers as John Dryden (*Antony and Cleopatra*), Nahum Tate (*King Lear*), and Colley Cibber (*Richard III*), many of whose versions survived on stage into the nineteenth century and even influenced adaptations as late as Olivier's film of *Richard III*. Modern critics such as L. L. Schücking and Norman Rabkin still seem to prefer the smoother revisions to the hectic originals.

The eighteenth century saw the dawn of scholarly editing of Shakespeare by Nicholas Rowe, Alexander Pope, Lewis Theobald, Samuel Johnson, Edward Capell, and others, often with bold emendations that have survived to the present, including such misleading additions as overly descriptive cast lists and stage directions with questionable locations. From Dryden to Johnson the critical tone was one of genuine admiration tinged with serious reservations about Shakespeare's lack of discipline and decorum, as reflected in the adaptation of scripts to suit the eighteenth-century proscenium stages of Garrick and his successors. With the Romantics came a new enthusiasm for Shakespeare's freedom from Aristotelian discipline and emotional restraint, as in Coleridge's delight in Shakespeare's imagination, coupled with distaste for the difficulty of displaying it via the supposed limitations of current stage practices, as expressed by Charles Lamb. However, critics such as William Hazlitt approved the passionate interpretations of Romantic actors, particularly Edmund Keene.

In roles such as Lady Macbeth, Sarah Siddons had also confirmed the stage-worthiness and emotional power of many of Shakespeare's female roles, which continued to attract the interest of Victorian audiences and early feminist critics such as Mrs. Jameson. Charlotte Cushman even made fashionable the casting of actresses in such male roles as Romeo. However, from the time of Charles Kean historical realism was increasingly favored in Victorian staging, and by the end of the nineteenth century picturesque Shakespearean production reached a climax of extravagant local color in the historical detailing of Henry Irving and Beerbohm Tree, which looked forward to such historical epics of the modern cinema as Olivier's *Henry V.* These scenic elaborations required severely cut texts.

The dawn of the twentieth century saw an increasing revulsion from such divergence from Elizabethan practices. Both scholarship and staging began to move toward recovery of the original character of the scripts and their first conditions of performance, under the influence of scholars such as William Poel. Literary historians such as E. K. Chambers sought to establish objective documentation about Shakespeare and his theater, while editors such as W. W. Greg became ever more cautious and scrupulous about the history of scripts and their staging. Critics such as E. E. Stoll sought to recover the original concerns and expectations of Shakespeare's contemporary audiences. Lyly B. Campbell reestablished the cultural context of Shakespeare's composition of his histories provided by such works as *The Mirror for Magistrates.* Interest in Shakespeare's history plays increased under the influence of patriotic interpreters such as E.M.W. Tillyard. Many critics like M. M. Reese followed this affirmative lead, only to be increasingly countered by the more pessimistic political readings of Hugh Richmond, Michael Manheim, and David Riggs.

While artistic values had remained influential in the close verbal studies of the new criticism, Shakespeare critics like Caroline Spurgeon treated all scripts as lyric verse, whose imagery was ungoverned by conditions of performance or sustained dramatic structure. Context was ignored to an extent that provoked a vigorous reassertion recently of broader cultural values. As the disciplines of political science, sociology, and psychology evolved in the middle of the twentieth century, they impinged drastically on Shakespeare criticism. The application of psychoanalysis and Marxism increased, with subordination of literary considerations to psychiatric and sociological issues. Ernest Jones reinterpreted Hamlet as a victim of Freud's Oedipus complex. He was followed by a multitude of critics and scholars from T. S. Eliot down to Norman Holland and by neo-Freudians such as Janet Adelman. This subordination of the texts to psychiatric theory remains a major element of academic Shakespeare criticism even in such subtle appreciations of the therapeutic role of the "festive" comedies as Cesare Barber's.

The current polemical feminism of a Germaine Greer and a Lisa Jardine has sought divergence from aesthetic concerns to gender politics, which has defined a self-referential approach for most female academics. In America this deflection by preemptive considerations was increased recently by stress on nonliterary cultural contexts, following French theories of structuralism (in which Lévi-Strauss put art into a broader context of expression, following Saussure's study of the language of symbols) and of deconstruction (when Derrida questioned the concept of artistic consistency and coherence), which finally collapsed modern critics into postmodern skepticism about the coherence or even the referential value of all art.

However, Shakespeare studies were still superficially much affected by sociological deflections deriving from the interest in power and class authorized by Michel Foucault and Raymond Williams, combined diversely with other influences by such movements as cultural materialism (Jonathan Dollimore), new historicism (Stephen Greenblatt), and neo-Freudianism (Jacques Lacan). Freud and Marx remain favored authorities among fashionable academic Shakespeare critics fearful of postmodern anarchy, not to say nihilism.

Postmodern repudiation of all objective standards of history and recoverable truth currently fosters a Restoration-like indifference to Shakespeare's printed scripts in producers such as Charles Marowitz, whose questioning of all precedents and authority has facilitated the radical dismemberment and displacement of scripts via almost every available mode of staging and interpretation. Following the early radical experiments of Tyrone Guthrie, Orson Welles, Peter Brook, and others, such active modern directors have resited Shakespearean scripts in the India of the British raj, in medieval Japan, in a modern circus, and even in outer space. Sexes, races, and ethnicities are shuffled almost at random.

This flexibility of approach has achieved a feeling of freshness and contemporaneity for alien audiences even while often involving radical dislocation of Shakespeare's text and its specifications. Shakespeare is now probably performed more than ever, but his identity as an intelligible person and a conscious artist has largely disappeared in fashionable expression of his work, both in performance and in criticism. One local gesture of more traditional historical affirmation supported by scholars such as Andrew Gurr and John Orrell may be found in the rebuilding of an approximation of the original Globe Theatre near its site in Southwark to attempt some recovery of the historical conditions of Shakespearean performance. The work of A. C. Sprague, Charles Shattuck, and Marvin Rosenberg confirms that the study of performance is the one field of Shakespearean study where traditional historical scholarship remains active, since even editors no longer believe now in a stable text. Meanwhile, scholars such as Anthony Nuttal, Richard Levin, and Brian Vickers have initiated counterattacks on the fashionable anachronisms of partisan interpreters and nihilistic theorists. Such moves hint at a possible return to the more meaningful, referential interpretation of Shakespeare's own identifiable artistic intentions, which has always been endorsed by actors and audiences.

BIBLIOGRAPHY

Complete Works of William Shakespeare

The Riverside Shakespeare. Gen. ed. G. Blakemore Evans. Boston: Houghton Mifflin, 1974.

The Complete Works of Shakespeare. 4th ed. Gen. ed. David Bevington. New York: HarperCollins, 1992.

Single-Play Series

New Cambridge Shakespeare. Gen. ed. Philip Brockbank. Cambridge: Cambridge University Press.

Oxford Shakespeare. Gen. ed. Stanley Wells. Oxford: Oxford University Press.

Signet Classic Shakespeare. Gen. ed. Sylvan Barnet. New York: Harcourt Brace Jovanovich.

Studies of William Shakespeare

Barber, C. L. *Shakespeare's Festive Comedy: A Study of Dramatic Form and Its Relation to Social Custom.* Princeton: Princeton University Press, 1959.

Beckerman, Bernard. *Shakespeare at the Globe, 1599–1609.* New York: Macmillan, 1962.

Booth, Stephen, ed. *Shakespeare's Sonnets.* New Haven, CT: Yale, 1977.

Boyce, Charles. *Shakespeare A to Z.* New York: Roundtable Press, 1990.

Bradley, A. C. *Shakespearean Tragedy.* London: Macmillan, 1904.

Bullough, Geoffrey. *Narrative and Dramatic Sources of Shakespeare.* 8 vols. London: Routledge, Kegan Paul, 1957–75.

Campbell, Lily B. *Shakespeare's Tragic Heroes: Slaves of Passion.* Cambridge: Cambridge University Press, 1930.

Chambers, E. K. *William Shakespeare: A Study of Facts and Problems.* 2 vols. Oxford: Clarendon Press, 1930.

Chute, Marchette. *Shakespeare of London.* New York: Dutton, 1949.

Dollimore, Jonathan, and Alan Sinfield, eds. *Political Shakespeare: New Essays in Cultural Materialism.* Ithaca, NY: Cornell University Press, 1985.

Dusinberre, Juliet. *Shakespeare and the Nature of Women.* London: Macmillan, 1975.

Erickson, Peter. *Patriarchal Structures in Shakespeare's Drama.* Berkeley: University of California Press, 1985.

Farnham, Willard. *Shakespeare's Tragic Frontier.* Berkeley: University of California Press, 1950.

French, Marilyn. *Shakespeare's Division of Experience.* New York: Ballantine, 1981.

Goddard, Harold C. *The Meaning of Shakespeare.* Chicago: University of Chicago Press, 1951.

Greg, Walter W. *The Shakespeare First Folio: Its Bibliographical and Textual History.* Oxford: Clarendon Press 1954.

Gurr, Andrew. *Shakespeare's Stage 1574–1642.* Cambridge: Cambridge University Press, 1992.

———, with John Orrell. *Rebuilding Shakespeare's Globe.* New York: Routledge, 1989.

Hager, Alan. *Shakespeare's Political Animal: Schema and Schemata in the Canon.* Newark: University of Delaware Press, 1990.

Holland, Norman. *Psychoanalysis and Shakespeare.* New York: McGraw-Hill, 1966.

Knight, G. Wilson. *The Imperial Theme.* Oxford: Oxford University Press, 1931.

———. *The Wheel of Fire.* London: Methuen, 1930.

Odell, George C. D. *Shakespeare from Betterton to Irving.* 2 vols. New York: Charles Scribners, 1920.

Palmer, John. *Political and Comic Characters of Shakespeare.* London: Macmillan, 1962.

Peterson, Douglas L. *Tide, Time and Tempest: A Study of Shakespeare's Romances.* San Marino, CA: Huntington Library Press, 1973.

Rabkin, Norman. *Shakespeare and the Common Understanding.* New York: Free Press, 1967.

Ribner, Irving. *The English History Play in the Age of Shakespeare.* New York: Barnes and Noble, 1957.

Richmond, Hugh. *Shakespeare's Political Plays.* New York: Random House, 1967.

———. *Shakespeare's Sexual Comedy.* New York: Bobbs Merrill, 1971.

Righter, Anne. *Shakespeare and the Idea of the Play.* London: Chatto and Windus, 1962.

Schoenbaum, Samuel. *William Shakespeare: A Documentary Life*. Oxford: Clarendon Press, 1975.

Shakespeare Criticism. Detroit: Gale Research, 1984–.

Speaight, Robert. *Shakespeare on the Stage: An Illustrated History of Shakespearean Performance*. London: Collins, 1973.

Spevack, Maurice. *The Harvard Concordance to Shakespeare*. Cambridge: Harvard University Press, 1973.

Spivack, Bernard. *Shakespeare and the Allegory of Evil*. New York: Columbia University Press, 1958.

Spurgeon, Caroline. *Shakespeare's Imagery and What It Tells Us*. Cambridge: Cambridge University Press, 1935.

Tillyard, E.M.W. *Shakespeare's History Plays*. London: Chatto and Windus, 1944.

Traversi, Derek. *An Approach to Shakespeare*. New York: Doubleday, 1956.

Vickers, Brian. *Appropriating Shakespeare*. New Haven, CT: Yale University Press, 1993.

———, ed. *Shakespeare: The Critical Heritage 1623–1801*. 6 vols. London, 1974–81.

Wells, Stanley. *Shakespeare: A Bibliographical Guide*. Oxford: Oxford University Press, 1990.

HUGH RICHMOND

SIR PHILIP SIDNEY
(1554–1586)

BIOGRAPHY

Sidney's life and accomplishments were the stuff of myth and legend even in his own time, and often it is difficult to separate them. He was born at Penshurst, Kent, on 30 November, the eldest son of two distinguished families, of Henry Sidney and Mary Dudley Sidney. His father's family had, for several generations, been personal servants to the kings of England, and Henry Sidney had been elevated by the French king to a gentleman ordinary, ''considerans combien est grande la maison de Sydenay en Angleterre.'' The Dudleys were nobility, and since childhood Mary Dudley had been a friend and companion of Princess Elizabeth and was destined to spend her life as waiting lady to the queen. Such ancestry is good material for myth. But events contributed, too. The recent history of the Dudley family was stained by treason: Philip's great-grandfather was executed by Henry VIII for extortion; in 1553, his mother had helped his grandfather, John Dudley, duke of Northumberland, in his short-lived plot to put Philip's uncle Guilford and Lady Jane Grey on the throne, resulting in his grandfather's execution for treason that year and Guilford's execution the year Philip was born. The act to seize the throne from Mary Tudor was a Protestant act that failed; perhaps in reparation, the Sidneys named their son for Catholic King Philip of Spain and of England and made King Philip and the widowed duchess of Northumberland his godparents. What may have been a politic choice at the time, however, turned out to be ironic through most of

Philip's life, since the king of Spain became his arch political and religious enemy, and he lost his life fighting against Philip's troops when they invaded the Low Countries.

Moreover, the family was, from the start of Philip's life, victimized by poverty. The thirteenth-century castle of Penshurst had been given to Philip's grandfather, Sir William Sidney, by Edward VI in 1552, and Philip's father never had the financial means to support his estate adequately. Both of Philip's parents spent their lives in service to Elizabeth I*: Sir Henry was named lord deputy governor of Ireland three times and was also lord president of the Marches of Wales—service that was costly to perform and that kept him from tending his southern lands; once, when the queen awarded him a barony, he declined because he could not afford to maintain the title. Lady Mary attended the queen during the most serious epidemic of her reign, the smallpox outbreak in 1572, and while the queen escaped unharmed, Lady Mary's face was disfigured for life and, although she was kept at court, the queen declined to advance her because of her appearance. Philip Sidney, who also suffered from minor facial scars, probably based the disfigured Parthenia in the *Arcadia* on his mother, thus commenting on, and also memorializing, her suffering.

Despite such long shadows at the time of his birth, Philip was given the finest available humanist education, drawing on the recent legacy of John Colet,* William Lily, Thomas More,* Roger Ascham, and Thomas Wilson.* He received his first training at Penshurst; in September 1564, he entered grammar school at Shrewsbury, thirty miles from Sir Henry's headquarters in Ludlow, where he studied under Thomas Ashton, a Calvinist who taught from Calvin's Bible but who was reputed to be one of the country's best schoolmasters; in 1568 he began three years at Christ Church, Oxford, where, although with his family's movements he was not always in attendance, he began, among other things, a translation of Aristotle's *Rhetoric*. Then, from 1572 to 1575 he completed the customary humanist trivium of training by going on a grand tour among the countries on the Continent, studying most frequently national histories and governments. Extensive subsequent correspondence shows he was frequently tutored by Hubert Languet, a distinguished graduate of Padua who, converted to Protestantism by Melanchthon, represented the elector of Saxony at Paris, Vienna, and Prague. Philip arrived at Paris in June 1572 and stayed with Languet's friend, Sir Francis Walsingham, who would later be Elizabeth I's lord treasurer, Philip's father-in-law, and, following his death, the man who would bankrupt himself to give Sidney the funeral of state he deserved. There he probably met the dowager Catherine de' Medici, the duke of Anjou (and later Henri III); the duke of Alençon (whose proposed marriage to Elizabeth I he would later challenge); Phillippe du Plessis Mornay, the philosopher and theologian whose daughter would be his godchild (in London in 1578) and whose *Truth of Religion* he would begin to translate as one of his last literary tasks; and Peter Ramus, the rhetorician whose sense of style as strings of binaries Sidney would use occasionally in his sonnet sequence, poetic treatise, and novel, but always in subordination to the classical Aristotelian rhetoric Ramus opposed. In Paris, too, Sidney witnessed the forced marriage of Henry of Navarre in August 1572 and the subsequent slaughter on St. Bartholomew's Day—the St. Bartholomew's Day massacre—which took the life of the Huguenot leader Admiral de Coligny and which served as the source for the carnage described as the Helot rebellion in *Arcadia I* and the various tortures and bloodshed in *New Arcadia II*.

Sidney fled Paris as quickly as he could following the Catholic uprising, visiting Europe's finest humanist scholars and printers, Henri Estienne in Heidelberg and Johan Strum in Strasbourg. He visited Vienna briefly, staying once more with Languet, and then traveled through Italy with a companion whom Edmund Spenser* would honor, Lodowick Bryskett. In Venice, he commissioned Veronese to paint his portrait (now lost) and returned home by way of Vienna and Poland.

For the next three years, from 1576 through 1579, Sidney sought unsuccessfully to win a significant position at court. He had every reason, given his ancestry, parentage, and education, to expect something from the queen, but she gave him only a minor office, that of cupbearer, in 1576. Still, he is reported—whether fact or partly myth is now difficult to determine—to be the very perfection of courtliness and honor, known for his skill at horsemanship and in tournaments and for his skill at writing such royal entertainments as *The Lady of May*. Contemporaries again and again credit him with *sprezzatura*—talents and artful behavior executed with apparent ease and naturalness, a term coined and urged at court by Castiglione.* He is now often compared with Hamlet, based on Ophelia's description of him as the glass of fashion and the mold of form; and it is certainly the case that he attracted the earl of Essex in the summer of 1576 when he accompanied the earl to Ireland to visit Sir Henry, and Essex began to arrange Philip's marriage to his eleven-year-old daughter Penelope. Essex died, however, before the marriage contract was completed, and Penelope Devereux grew up to marry Robert Lord Rich; whether this loss inspired Sidney's sonnet sequence or he simply found it a convenient fictional frame is now also beyond the realm of certainty.

In December 1576, Elizabeth I sent Sidney as head of an embassy to the Holy Roman Empire to express her sympathies for the recent death of Maximilian and to congratulate his son Rudolph on his succession, by election, to the imperial throne; she added the additional duty of paying similar respects to Louis, newly elected to head the Palatinate upon his father's death; and finally, by a late dispatch, she approved his uncle's request to stand in as godfather to the new daughter of William of Orange. The journey was quite possibly the turning point of his life: while the queen was keeping him busy with minor tasks, he was learning firsthand the fervor of the Protestant League in Europe and was extending his popularity abroad—both because European leaders thought him a more powerful representative for the queen than he was and because he was personally so charming and intellectually so accomplished. Such popularity only soured him at home, increasing his frustrations over lack of advancement at Whitehall. His lack of progress can be seen in the angry defense of his uncle Robert Dudley, earl of Leicester; in his increasing endorsement of the Protestant League (which the queen saw as a rival center of power); in his agreement to write, on behalf of the liberal Puritan wing of the Privy Council, a letter to the queen opposing her projected marriage to Anjou; and, finally, in a quarrel with the earl of Oxford during a tennis match in 1579. When he refused to apologize, the queen rebuked him, noting that a gentleman was always beholden to an earl. As a direct consequence, he left the court—voluntarily, I think, although myth has it at the sentence of the queen—for his sister Mary's house at Wilton.

For the next five years—from 1580 to 1585—Sidney and his father continued their pleas with the queen for more financial support and for better positions in service to the state, and for the next five years she continued either to ignore or to deny them. I think this is partly because she was so accustomed to Sir Henry's and Lady Mary's devoted service at such little cost that she saw no reason to reward them with more; I think it is also because Philip's growing popularity at home—where in 1583 Walsingham gave him his daughter—and abroad was potentially threatening: she was, after all, a single monarch who kept her nearly absolute authority by playing one faction against another in her court so that no one faction (nor any single family) would be too strong but would instead remain dependent on her. Nevertheless, these five years were, as matters turned out, Sidney's best years. He was not only happily married but in 1583 knighted when his friend Prince Casimir (not the queen) asked him to stand proxy when he was installed as a knight of the Order of the Garter at Windsor.

Moreover, the country house and great park at Wilton were sufficiently pastoral and idyllic to give Sidney ample time to read, meditate, and write. He had already set out his principles in his *Defense of Poesie* in 1579, and at Wilton he put them into practice with the *Arcadia*, a great-house romance that he wrote for his sister and, I think, for long winter evenings when it was the custom of nobility to sit about the fire and read aloud the various parts of long works of fiction. At Wilton he wrote *Certaine Sonnets*, testing quantitative meter, and the Petrarchan sonnet sequence *Astrophil and Stella*, both initially composed in 1581–82. In 1583 he began a lengthy revision of the *Arcadia*, transforming it into a serious analysis of politics and governance, using this as a substitution for the court life he now saw beyond his grasp. Around 1584 he began translating the *Psalms* with his sister, exploiting his interest in Calvinist thought, and beginning his incomplete translation of Du Plessis Mornay's treatise on *The Truth of the Christian Religion*. Both of these religious works, it has been argued, remained unfinished because he was called to war in the Low Countries, but I think it is likelier that the portions of Mornay that he completed—the parts dealing with the proofs of the existence of God and on the immortality of the soul—were the only parts that interested him: philosophy rather than straight theology of the sort that also informs the most significant speeches in the *New*

Arcadia. A strong Protestant at court, fiery and partisan, according to observers, I think Sidney turned more reflective during the years at Wilton.

Still, his yearning for adventure and travel did not desert him entirely, and in September 1584 he secretly signed on with Sir Francis Drake to explore the New World. The queen interrupted his plans and appointed him governor of Flushing. He arrived at his new post in November, preceding his uncle, the earl of Leicester. From the outset, he was surprised and concerned with the decayed state of the English garrisons. The troops were largely volunteers and mercenaries—unwanted rogues who had not received pay because of graft and corruption in the armed forces and who managed to live by pillaging the countryside. Sidney urged Leicester to arrive, take command, and bring order to the English soldiers, but when he came he, too, began squandering the queen's money, keeping much of it for himself. When the leaders of the Low Countries offered Leicester the position of governor-general—disobeying his queen by becoming a foreign ruler himself—Sidney distanced himself by fighting battles alongside his own soldiers. In addition to the garrison at Flushing and a company of horse he had recruited from England, he took command of a regiment from Zeeland. He established his military leadership in a successful assault on Spanish troops at Axel; the antiquarian John Stow records that Sidney addressed his men before the battle with such stirring words that they chose to die in service to their country rather than to live by avoiding battle. In the battle, not one English soldier was killed. One of them, George Whetstone, noted that Sidney was a special favorer of the common soldier.

On 22 September 1586, Sidney again led his troops in battle against the Spanish at Zutphen, attempting to block a major supply route. The skirmish—thought to be a minor one—was crucial strategically, but in the course of fighting he was wounded in the thigh, fell from his horse, and was taken off the field to receive medical care at Arnheim. Initially, he improved, but then gangrene set in, and on 17 October he died, at the age of thirty-one. He was not buried, however, until 16 February 1587, in a lavish public ceremony at St. Paul's Cathedral, London. The Dutch had offered to bury him in their own country, but Walsingham, who insisted on the ceremony, could not raise the money until early the following year, and the queen refused to contribute to the costs of the funeral.

Sidney's first biographer, Fulke Greville, a classmate at Shrewsbury School, reported that Sidney took off his thigh-armor to give to a soldier who had none and thus exposed himself to the fatal wound through his own personal sacrifice. He was also asked for water by a dying soldier and offered his own canteen in a gesture that combined battleground companionship with noblesse oblige. It now seems reasonably clear that the first is wholly myth; Sidney was much too professional and skilled a soldier to fight without armor; the second, while it may be factual, is thus open to a range of interpretation. His youthful death on a foreign battlefield, defending Protestantism as much as England, was also the stuff of myth and legend—and Greville, who was attempting to rewrite Sidney's life as an educational sermon, may have embroidered it. What is factually beyond dispute, however, is that he became, in the 1590s, the most influential poet in England, and his uniquely popular novel *Arcadia* remained a best-seller in England for nearly a century and a half, surpassing the sales of Spenser's epic and even of Shakespeare's* plays.

MAJOR WORKS AND THEMES

Renewed activity concerning Sidney's work in the past thirty years has assured his reputation as the most important English writer of the sixteenth century since Thomas More. Geoffrey Shepherd has noted that the statements in his *Defense of Poesie* "are moments of European self-consciousness," recovering for English poetics the best classical and Continental thought. His sonnet sequence *Astrophil and Stella*, making him the English Petrarch, imported into England the cycle initiated by Petrarch's *Rime* and initiated a full decade of imitations, through the 1590s, by all the significant English poets, including Daniel,* Drayton, Spenser, and Shakespeare. C. S. Lewis sees the *Arcadia* as a touchstone that "gathers up what a whole generation wanted to say," and, perhaps nearer the mark, Virginia Woolf saw the work "as in some luminous globe, all the seeds of English fiction" lying latent within it. It was not replaced in the history of the English novel until Samuel Richardson's *Pamela* (1740), which takes its themes and the name of its protagonist from the *Arcadia*.

The extraordinary strength and richness of Sidney's work derive from many sources. He was a thoughtful reader of the ancients—of Aristotle, Plato, and Cicero; of Ovid, Horace, Vergil, Xenophon, Plutarch, and Seneca. He knew the Bible and the commentary of Buchanan and others. He knew the older romance of Heliodorus and the new ones of Sannazaro and Montemayor as well as the French *Amadis de Gaul*. His critical theory absorbed antiquity alongside Scaliger and Landino. He knew Continental poetry, especially revering Petrarch. His understanding of these works, especially his memory of them, is vivid and usually infallible in accuracy and understanding, but his contemplative mind had the ability to synthesize them, to make writers of the past and present the silent collaborators of his own work. Yet, as absorbed as he was in the tradition of the past and the currents of his time, he kept his distance, too: flashes of wit are everywhere. His most serious and explicit statement of poetics begins with a parody of Stephen Gosson's respect of horsemanship and the military; it ends with a joke on the reader who is foolish enough to ignore his or her own epitaph. Finally, his mind is restless, and his approach experimental: he is always searching to make old forms and ideas newly formed and newly alive; his sonnet sequence, following the general lines laid down by Petrarch, nevertheless makes nearly every sonnet different in tone or form, with the customary caesura of sound and thought moving to various positions throughout what had been a staid, fixed sonnet form.

His *Defense of Poesie* remains the best in the English language, the wellspring of the work of those to follow, such as Jonson, Shelley, and Eliot. Taking poetry to mean any creative literary act, Sidney sees three kinds: religious (such as David, Orpheus, or Homer in his ''Hymns''), philosophical (such as Lucretius, Vergil, or Lucan), and ''right poets,'' those who combine Platonic idealization with Aristotelian *mimesis* by understanding poetry as an act of imitation so as to teach virtuous behavior through examples but to teach ideal behavior by inventing ideal exemplars that are, nevertheless, recognizably human. To do this, the poet needs to rummage through the zodiac of his own wit, his imaginary world where many Cyruses lead to an ideal concept of Cyrus, far transcending and modifying the historical Cyrus and making such Cyruses of his readers. At the same time that poets begin with history but then leave it behind for an improved, imaginary version, they do not become mere philosophers, lost in abstractions: to do so, he says, alluding to a classical example, so fixes the poet's eyes on the stars that the same poet will lose his earthly bearing and fall into a ditch. Rather, poetry is anchored in a concrete image. Such a practice—teaching virtuous behavior—has religious overtones and is meant to for Sidney: he sees the poet as a second God creating a second nature that, like God's first nature, is crowded with poetic lessons but, with the poet, more forceful through metaphor, rhetoric, and meter or style and thus more memorable and forceful. This key idea—the representative ideal—is the ''*idea* [of a perfect man] which is manifest, by delivering [him] forth in such excellency as [the poet] had imagined him''—the objective correlative that is the foreconceit, or starting-place, of all poetry. But Sidney does not see such a high calling, if an unelected vocation for himself, as any easy task: man's ''infected will,'' he remarks, keeps us from realizing the best we can contemplate, the results of our ''erected wit.'' Thus, the poet is always contending in a battle of wills with fallen human nature, and it is the glory of poetry that, like the inspired Word of God, it, too, can inspire and elevate mankind. It does so not merely by teaching and inspiring but by guaranteeing its worth in daily human actions. It does so through delight as well as instruction. Poetry has had no more articulate champion.

Sidney's *Astrophil and Stella* (or *star-lover* and *star*) shows both the possibility and danger of such a poetics. To love a distant star, as Astrophil does—that is, to yearn for the impossible, the general state of the Petrarchan lover—is absurd; rather, Astrophil must take sterner measure of himself, just as Sidney the poet must. This poetics is repeated in the first sonnet of the sequence: he catalogs the conventional forms of poetry to find all of them insufficient to the occasion and determines, at the close of the poem, the true source of poetry: '' 'Fool,' said my muse to me, 'look in thy heart and write.' '' Astrophil's heart is full of conflicting thoughts and emotions, realized by Sidney in an unmatched number of experiments in poetical form and perspective. All are partial, and therefore all are inadequate. In the end, Astrophil has so imprisoned his idea of Stella in his own series of shortsighted observations that he loses her, but this testing of the hope of humanity opposed to its achievement underscores Sidney's belief that an ideal must be carefully constructed, by poet and reader alike. It must remain ideal and yet, somehow, be sufficiently mimetic to be exemplary and useful. Wit, he says elsewhere, must always be exercised—and by exercise, he means the exercise of thought (look in thy heart) and the exercise of action (and write).

If *Astrophil and Stella* is for Sidney an example of how poetry can instruct daily living, then his great prose romance, England's first novel, the *Arcadia*, illustrates how daily living impinges on poetry and reshapes it. Taking his view of a full poetic world from Heliodorus, whose tangled threads of several plots played private life against public and love alongside governance, Sidney argues that any leadership—such as that of Basilius or Pyrocles and Musidorus—must take into account private desire and public citizenship. All three characters suffer from imbalance, and their partial views again and again erupt into dialectic, into debates of words and actions about the right and proper courses of life. Behind all the events and speeches lie Aristotle's two great virtues—magnanimity of soul and justice for society. They are combined, in the end, in the great trial scene of Book V, when Euarchus fails to allow exceptions to case law, to precedent, and thus would condemn to death his own son and his nephew for crimes that did not, in fact, exist. The young men are saved when Basilius arises from the dead—on the face of it, wondrous and miraculous. Sidney's point is that poetry (like religion) must always have room for the wondrous and miraculous, as strict law never does. Put in legal terms, justice must always make allowance for mercy, and precedent for extenuating circumstances. What might seem both poetic in its happy ending and philosophic in its debate of love and justice as necessarily both private and public concerns was also politically pointed in Sidney's time: he used *Arcadia*, in part, to mount an argument against common-law courts revered by Tudor governments in favor of chancery courts, which took each case on its own terms, as a poet would.

This intervention into political affairs is part of the design of *Arcadia*, and when Sidney began an exhaustive revision of the work in 1583, he concentrated on matters of governments and politics in far more complicated ways. What is clear is that he had found a new way to enter into the queen's service—by commenting on her rule and her society if he was otherwise not to be a participant in it. It was not merely compensatory; it was his unelected vocation, the task he was born to. What is so clear in what is now called the *New Arcadia*, however, had been true before. The *Defense of Poesie* and *Astrophil and Stella* also teach by showing how we must govern human behavior by governing ourselves. The difference is that they are essentially private works where the poet addresses the reader. The *Arcadia*, on the other hand, was designed not merely to instruct the individual but to instruct society as well. The ancient exemplars for Sidney's *Arcadia* are Aristotle (for its ideas on politics and ethics) and Cicero (for its beliefs in, and techniques of, persuasive rhetoric). Both, like Sidney, were essentially public men. Whether or not Elizabeth I ever admitted Sidney to the inner circles of her court, he nevertheless captured the attention of both the queen and her people through his writing.

CRITICAL RECEPTION

Sidney lived in a time when poetry circulated among friends and court circles in manuscript, and none of his works were published until the 1590s, some time after his death. The writer Thomas Nashe* was employed to write a preface supporting *Astrophil and Stella*, and an unauthorized edition of the *Defense of Poetrie* caused Sidney's sister, the countess of Pembroke,* to publish her more authentic text. Not until 1598, however, did she publish all of Sidney's main works in a folio collection as *The Countess of Pembroke's Arcadia*. I have already remarked that the sonnet sequence created a literary fashion throughout the 1590s, but *Arcadia*, too, unfinished in its revised form, was added to by others. In 1616 William Alexander attempted to round out Book III; his text was incorporated in all editions beginning in 1621. Later printings also included Richard Beling's additions as Book VI and James Johnstoun's to Book III. The work was also popular abroad, with two French translations appearing in 1624 and 1625; a German translation in 1629 augmented in 1638; and a Dutch edition that went through three different printings beginning in 1639. In the century following Sidney's death, the *Defense of Poetrie* was translated into German and Dutch, and *Astrophil and Stella* into Italian. Anna Weamys published a "continuation" in which she completed some of the subplots in the *Arcadia* and concluded with the death of Philisides, Sidney's own nominal counterpart. Sidney's sister completed their translation of the *Psalmes*, and in 1587 Arthur Golding completed and published Sidney's partial translation of de Mornay.

Acclaim was not universal. Ben Jonson* scoffed at Sidney's style in *Every Man Out of His Humor* and *Timber*, and, after it was said that Charles I read Pamela's prayer from the *Arcadia* just before his execution, Milton scoffed at the king's "impiety." The reputation of the *Arcadia* suffered under the neoclassical interests of the eighteenth century, but the *Defense of Poetrie* continued to have influence. The general revival began in the early nineteenth century with Thomas Zouch's *Memoir of Sir Philip Sidney*, followed in 1862 with H. R. Fox Bourne's biographical works based on extant primary documents. Editions of the *Defense* edited by Albert Cook and Evelyn Shuckburgh began appearing in the 1880s and 1890s, and in 1909 Bertram Dobell announced his discovery of the *Old Arcadia*, leading to R. W. Zandvoort's comparison of the two versions in 1929. Not until the late 1950s, however, did Sidney begin to attain the prominence he now enjoys, as one of the three major writers of the sixteenth century. This came about partly because of the Oxford edition of Sidney's *Works* and partly because two major schools of literary study—the new criticism and the new historicism—both saw in Sidney's texts the careful artistic ability and the cultural pressures that for them were central to any important literary achievement. Recent studies comparing Sidney to Spenser, often to Sidney's advantage, now seem to guarantee his significant position for the foreseeable future.

BIBLIOGRAPHY

Works by Sir Philip Sidney

An Apology for Poetry. Ed. Geoffrey Shepherd. New York: Harper and Row, 1973.

Astrophil and Stella. Ed. Max Putzel. Garden City, NY: Anchor Books, 1967.

The Countess of Pembroke's Arcadia (The Old Arcadia). Ed. Jean Robertson. Oxford: Clarendon Press, 1973.

The Countess of Pembroke's Arcadia (The New Arcadia). Ed. Victor Skretkowicz. Oxford: Clarendon Press 1987.

The Countess of Pembroke's Arcadia. Ed. Maurice Evans. London: Penguin, 1977. (The composite text modernized.)

Miscellaneous Prose of Sir Philip Sidney (including *The Lady of May* and *A Defence of Poetry*). Ed. Katherine Duncan-Jones and Jan Van Dorsten. Oxford: Clarendon Press 1973.

The Poems of Sir Philip Sidney. Ed. William A. Ringler Jr. Oxford: Clarendon Press, 1962.

Sir Philip Sidney: Selected Prose and Poetry. 2d ed. Ed. Robert Kimbrough. Madison: University of Wisconsin Press, 1983.

Studies of Sir Philip Sidney

Buxton, John. *Sir Philip Sidney and the English Renaissance*. London: Macmillan, 1954.

Connell, Dorothy. *Sir Philip Sidney: The Maker's Mind*. Oxford: Clarendon Press, 1977.

Craft, William. *Labyrinth of Desire: Invention and Culture in the Work of Sir Philip Sidney*. Newark: University of Delaware Press, 1994.

Duncan-Jones, Katherine. *Sir Philip Sidney Courtier Poet*. London: Clarendon Press, 1991.

Greenfield, Thelma N. *The Eye of Judgment: Reading the "New Arcadia."* Lewisburg, PA: Bucknell University Press, 1982.

Hager, Alan. *Dazzling Images: The Masks of Sir Philip Sidney*. Newark: University of Delaware Press, 1991.

Hamilton, A. C. *Sir Philip Sidney: A Study of His Life and Works*. Cambridge: Cambridge University Press, 1977.

Kalstone, David. *Sidney's Poetry: Contexts and Interpretations*. Cambridge: Harvard University Press, 1965.

Kay, Dennis, ed. *Sir Philip Sidney: An Anthology of Modern Criticism*. Oxford: Clarendon Press, 1987.

Kimbrough, Robert. *Sir Philip Sidney*. New York: Twayne, 1971.

Kinney, Arthur F., ed. *Essential Articles for the Study of Sir Philip Sidney*. Hamden, CT: Anchor Press, 1986.

———. *Humanist Poetics: Thought, Rhetoric, and Fiction in Sixteenth-Century England*. Amherst: University of Massachusetts Press, 1986, 230–91.

Lindheim, Nancy. *The Structures of Sidney's "Arcadia."* Toronto: University of Toronto Press, 1982.

McCoy, Richard C. *Sir Philip Sidney: Rebellion in Arcadia*. New Brunswick: Rutgers University Press, 1979.

Myrick, Kenneth. *Sir Philip Sidney as a Literary Craftsman*. Cambridge: Harvard University Press, 1935.

Osborn, James M. *Young Philip Sidney 1572–1577*. New Haven, CT: Yale University Press, 1972.

Raitiere, Martin N. *Faire Bitts: Sir Philip Sidney and Renaissance Political Theory*. Pittsburgh: Duquesue University Press, 1984.

Robinson, Forrest G. *The Shape of Things Known: Sidney's "Apology" in Its Philosophical Tradition*. Cambridge: Harvard University Press, 1972.

Rudenstine, Neil L. *Sidney's Poetic Development*. Cambridge: Harvard University Press, 1967.

Stillman, Robert E. *Sidney's Poetic Justice: "The Old Arcadia," Its Eclogues, and Renaissance Pastoral Traditions*. Lewisburg, PA: Bucknell University Press, 1986.

Stump, Donald V., Jerome S. Dees, and C. Stuart Hunter. *Sir Philip Sidney: An Annotated Bibliography of Texts and Criticism (1554–1984)*. New York, 1994.

Van Dorsten, Jan, Dominic Baker-Smith, and Arthur F. Kinney, eds. *Sir Philip Sidney: 1586 and the Creation of a Legend*. Leiden: Leiden University Press, 1986.

Wallace, Malcolm William. *The Life of Sir Philip Sidney*. Cambridge: Cambridge University Press, 1915.

ARTHUR F. KINNEY

ROBERT SIDNEY
(1563–1626)

BIOGRAPHY

Although he wrote poetry and was intimately involved with the affairs of his age, Robert Sidney is better known for his relatives than for his own accomplishments. Brother to Philip Sidney,* the renowned writer and courtier, and Mary Sidney Herbert, the writer, patron, and editor, Sidney was also the father to Mary Wroth,* who wrote a prose romance, sonnet sequence, and play during the seventeenth century. In many ways, Sidney was the prototypical younger brother; overshadowed by his more glamorous siblings, he quietly set about improving the always shaky family fortunes during the late Elizabethan and early Jacobean era.

Robert Sidney was born to Sir Henry and Lady Mary Sidney on 19 November 1563 at the family seat of Penshurst Place. Lady Mary, whose maiden name was Dudley, sister to Robert Dudley, earl of Leicester, for whom Robert was named, was well connected, and Sir Henry had been brought up with the young Prince Edward. When Elizabeth took the throne, Sir Henry was able to establish his service to the queen, first in Ireland and then in Wales, as the lord president of the Marches of Wales. Younger than his brother Philip by nine years, Robert was often compared to his brother—his father urged him in one letter to "imitate" his elder brother, who was "a rare Ornament of thys Age." After the required education and Continental trip, Robert Sidney was more than willing to enter the courtier life that his brother had been exploring with mixed success.

In an attempt to improve his standing at court by stressing his connection with his famous Protestant uncle, Leicester, Robert Sidney went over to the Low

Countries to fight in the wars. Not long after he arrived, his brother Philip received his famous fatal wound at the Battle of Zutphen in 1586. After his brother's death, he assumed the role of head of the family (their father had died six months earlier) and was also given his brother's position as governor of Flushing in the Low Countries. Unfortunately, neither position gave him much satisfaction. The Sidney family had always been strapped for money, and Robert Sidney had to maneuver to try to pay off the family's debts. To do so required a visible and strong court presence to procure some preferment from the queen. Unfortunately, the situation at Flushing forced him to be on the Continent for long periods of time, away from the court, which could have provided him solvency and notice. The Low Country situation dragged on interminably, hindered by corruption, ineptitude, and greed, and Sidney's position as colonial governor often forced him to make unpopular decisions.

Under Elizabeth, Robert Sidney was generally unnoticed since the Queen thought of Sidney as too immature and flighty for the responsibilities of court. As a colonial governor, he could be used but needed to remain out of sight. He returned to England more frequently during the end of her reign and was actually one of the small group of men who captured the rebellious earl of Essex at his house in London in 1600. Despite this service to the Queen, not until James came to the throne was Sidney released from service in Flushing and able to try to repair his fortunes at home. Eventually, under James, he was made Viscount Lisle in 1605 before becoming earl of Leicester in 1618.

One of the pleasures of his life was the steadiness of his domestic arrangements; Ben Jonson* rightly celebrated the joys of Penshurst as run by Sidney and his capable wife, Barbara. He had married Barbara Gamage in 1584 in a wedding that was conducted as quickly as possible to assure her hand. Despite the speed of what would seem to be an arranged nuptial, they were quite happy together and produced eleven children, six of whom grew into adulthood. Lady Barbara died in 1621; Sidney married once again to a younger woman, Sarah Smythe, shortly before his own death in 1626.

MAJOR WORKS AND THEMES

Sidney's major literary contribution is a collection of sonnets and songs that was only recently published and was actually first attributed to him in the early 1970s, after it was sold by Sotheby's to the British Library. This is thought by many to be his working copy of his poetry that was presumably written during the 1590s while he was at Zutphen. His level of experimentation in the structural components of the verse, although not as extreme as his brother's, still produced an unfinished crown of sonnets and a variant on the Walsingham ballad, the traditional song between a lady and a pilgrim.

In terms of topic and treatment, Sidney remains fairly well entrenched within the Petrarchan sonnet craze of the 1590s. In the beginning of the sequence, through sonnet 20, the poetic persona speaks of his great love for a highly abstract Neoplatonic lady. After that point, the tone becomes progressively more bitter and melancholic as he describes his rejection in more graphic terms than he describes the lady: ''Sick past all helpe or hope, or kills or dies; / While all the blood it [his love] sheds my heart doth bleed / And with my bowels I his cancers feed'' (26.12–14). Throughout the sequence he uses images of the sea and martial endeavor to suggest the struggles of love; in addition, he toys with the Petrarchan paradox of concomitant absence and presence to describe his helplessness. This emphasis suggests a particularly biographical reading of the sonnets since Sidney himself was so upset about his continuing presence in Flushing and what that would mean for his success at court. Although some critics have tried to suggest that the ''Lysa'' and ''Charys'' that he refers to in the poem have some biographical standing, given the faddishness of sonnet writing, this may not be the case.

Robert Sidney's collection of his letters, often ignored, proves intriguing. Written primarily to his secretary, Rowland Whyte, from Flushing, they provide a fascinating picture of an aspiring courtier during the turn of the century. Part of the problem with these letters is that we do not have a highly accurate and well-edited collection; the two collections of letters we do have, however, suggest all the ups and downs that were part and parcel for a man of Sidney's standing. In addition, they provide a unique glimpse into the English viewpoint on the Low Country wars and occupation.

CRITICAL RECEPTION

Aside from an initial flurry of interest when Sidney's collection of poetry was found and published, there actually is very little critical mention of Robert Sidney. Most of it, like Waller's, tends to find Sidney's worth either in his influence on his daughter, Mary Wroth, or through his literary relationship with his brother, Philip Sidney. All three wrote sonnet and song miscellanies that show similar patterns of experimentation and phrasing as well as images and subject matter. For instance, all three wrote crowns of sonnets; however, Mary Wroth was the only one to complete hers. Robert Sidney's oeuvre is considerably smaller and less developed than his brother's and daughter's and as a result gets considerably less attention.

As I mentioned, a potentially profitable area for exploration for Robert Sidney scholars would be some combination of the poetry and the letters. If the sonnet sequence is the expression of individual desire in a literary form, the letters of Sidney take these expressions of desire and ambition even further by revealing the machinations and despair behind the Elizabethan system of preferment. The additional revelations of the sheer ineptitude this system fostered when taken abroad provide a potent correction to notions of the fortunate Sidneys. Ironically, Robert Sidney's position as a writer in the current canon reflects his position as a dutiful younger son in a family of achievers: no matter what he does, he is rarely recognized.

BIBLIOGRAPHY

Works by Robert Sidney

The Poems of Robert Sidney. Ed. P. J. Croft. Oxford: Clarendon Press, 1983.

Studies of Robert Sidney

Brennan, Michael. "Sir Robert Sidney and Sir John Harington of Kelston." *Notes and Queries* 232 (1987): 233–37.

Collins, Arthur, ed. *Letters and Memorials of State, Vol. II.* 1746 edition. New York: AMS, 1973.

Duncan-Jones, Katherine. "The Poems of Sir Robert Sidney." *English* 30 (1981): 3–72.

———. " 'Rosis and Lysa': Selections from the Poems of Sir Robert Sidney." *English Literary Renaissance* 9 (1979): 240–63.

Hay, Millicent V. *The Life of Robert Sidney, Earl of Leicester (1563–1626).* Washington, DC: Folger Shakespeare Library, 1984.

Kelleher, Hilton, and Katherine Duncan-Jones. "A Manuscript of Poems by Sir Robert Sidney: Some Early Impressions." *British Library Journal* 1 (1975): 107–44.

Kingford, C. L. *Historical Manuscripts Commission: Report on the Manuscripts of Lord De L'Isle and Dudley Preserved at Penshurst Place, Vol. II.* London: His Majesty's Stationery Office, 1934.

Waller, Gary. " 'My wants and yowr perfections': Elizabethan England's Newest Poet." *Ariel* 8 (1977): 3–14.

———. "The 'Sad Pilgrim': The Poetry of Sir Robert Sidney." *Dalhousie Review* 56 (1975): 689–705.

Wright, Deborah Kempf. "Modern-Spelling Text of Robert Sidney's Poems Proves Disappointing." *Sidney Newsletter* 3 (1982): 12–16.

IRENE S. BURGESS

JOHN SKELTON
(c. 1463–1529)

BIOGRAPHY

A caveat: what little we know of John Skelton's life often comes from the Scylla and Charybdis of overreading what might be internal evidence in his varied works and accepting apocryphal data that collected around him in alarmingly rapid fashion in his life and afterward in ballads and broadsides and other popular narrative accounts, mostly from the famous jest-books.

In several ways, Skelton, probably born in Norfolk, probably on 2 May 1463 (Brownlow, 92–93), was, with George Cavendish,* the last great medieval figure in the Renaissance court of Henry VIII. More akin to Scotch poets, such as Dunbar* and Douglas* and even Lindsay* than to, say, Wyatt the Elder* or Surrey,* Skelton was well educated in rhetoric and poetry in Latin ultimately at Oxford, Cambridge, and at Louvain in the Low Countries, at all of which he received the advanced degree of rhetoric, the laureate. He was also an expert, like the Scotch poets, in contemporary French literature and at least a student of Italian. Thanks to his early production of a sequence of encomiastic poems on royalty and court nobility, he secured the position of tutor to Henry VII's second son Henry, then duke of York, whom he claims to have taught spelling—so anomalous, at least in English of the time—and, more likely, the nine Muses. For his poetical services at a court in London that always made him uneasy, Henry VII, we hear, presented Skelton with a white and green dress to wear in court embroidered in gold with the name ''Calliope,'' the Muse of epic poetry.

Admitted to Holy Orders in 1498, Skelton held the post of parson of Diss in Norfolk until his death, and gradually he saw less time in a court that struck him more and more as vainglorious and deceitful. He remained, however, for the most part, a Londoner. While his early verse was panegyric, his later was pointed satire in the vein of Scotch ''flyting'' poems of Dunbar and others. Some of his biting derision was mock-satire designed to produce answers in kind—thus, to some degree, self-ironic—but some was apparently vitriolic in essence, some directed at his close contemporary cleric and courtier, Thomas Wolsey. Although he lost some friends at court, in the church, and among the church laity with his satirical turn, he also had powerful supporters to the end, including Elizabeth Stafford, the countess of Surrey, mother of Surrey the poet and sister-in-law to Queen Catherine Howard.

Skelton's career, thus, was centrally marked by one ambiguous success and one disastrous confrontation. His prize was to be considered poet laureate of England. Caxton* announced that he is the ''late created poet laureate in the University of Oxenford,'' and Erasmus* spoke of him as ''the incomparable light and glory of English letters.'' This capacity, which went with the green and white dress and various crowns of bay leaves from the universities and other institutions, carried no stipend. Furthermore, it went unrecorded except in the author's own ambiguous dream vision, *The Garlande of Laurell*, which enumerated his forebears and his own works in Chaucerian rhyme royal and in a mass of ribald anecdotes that gathered around this unorthodox and highly theatrical poet/preacher. But the epithet ''laureate'' stuck. Even though a cleric, Skelton also reveled in a quasi marriage and his several offspring. One apocryphal story has him holding up a newborn son to his congregation saying, in part, ''How say you, neighbors all? Is not this child as fair as the best of all yours?''

Skelton's disaster followed his several satirical attacks in 1521 and part of 1522 on Cardinal Wolsey, whose career reached its apogee around the time of Skelton's death at Westminster on 21 June 1529. He is credited with satiric verse on Wolsey's bullying of the archbishop of Canterbury as early as 1521 and 1522 by the chronicler Hall,* and his most famous work after *The Boke of Phylyp Sparowe*, *Colyn Cloute*, contains satire of Wolsey's extravagant lifestyle at Hampton Court in Molesey, as does *Speake Parrot* and *Why Come Ye Not to Court?*, both in rhyme royal. The dates of Skelton's open attacks on Wolsey run, in my estimation, less than a year, but their effects lasted on and off the rest of Skelton's life. Covert attacks, furthermore, perhaps encouraged by the

Howard family, may go back to 1516. Apparently, he was imprisoned briefly on Wolsey's instigation, finally forcing him, after that disagreeable experience, to seek sanctuary several times in Westminster Cathedral, where he probably died four months before Wolsey's catastrophic fall, so ably chronicled in the medieval tragical mode of Chaucer's *Monk's Tale* and a bit of *Troilus and Criseyde* by George Cavendish. Like Ovid's appeals to Augustus from exile near the Black Sea, Skelton's final works, including *The Garland of Laurel* and the *Replication* against the Cambridge radicals, were all dedicated to Wolsey. The latter work may even have been commissioned by the cardinal.

MAJOR WORKS AND THEMES

John Skelton was, in O. B. Hardison's terms, an epideictic poet, that is, a master of the rhetoric of praise and blame. Early, as we have seen, he solidified an enviable position in Henry VII's court with elegies and eulogies, mostly lost, beginning with an English poem on the death of Edward IV and an elegy on the death of Henry Percy, fourth earl of Northumberland, killed in a civil disturbance in Yorkshire on 28 April 1489. In the second half of his career, he became, as we have seen, a formidable satirist, but not without relief, even within the works themselves. His is a complex and, as I argue, a medieval mind.

Beyond the strict encomia and satire already mentioned, Skelton produced four remarkably original works, all difficult to date exactly. The first is the morality play, *Magnificence*, whose title suggests his sarcasm about court life and which best features a group of fools exposing themselves in Chaucerian hubristic poses. *The Garland of Laurel*, as I have mentioned, is a dream vision whose frame and allegorical center are baffling in their irony and self-irony, especially in mysterious *locae* that come from the mythographers from Servius and Boccaccio forward and in Skelton's own list of his major accomplishments. One is a mock elegy on the death of a girl's pet sparrow, *Philip Sparrow*. The bird is ambiguous, coming from Catullus, and the delicious satire is partly directed at the liturgical office for the dead. The most remarkable may be *The Tunning of Elinour Rumming*, a detailed portrait of a B-girl in an alehouse, most remarkable for its "skeltonics," the three-beat short line alliterated and rhymed for comic effect. All these works have a medieval message of *vanitas vanitorum* of the court—that is, the venal life with some sympathy. The imminence of death is what Skelton preaches universally. As Colin Clout says,

> It is wrong with each degree
> For the temporality
> Accuseth the spirituality.

CRITICAL RECEPTION

No poet, to my knowledge, has suffered the extremes of praise and denigration over the centuries—often simultaneous—as John Skelton did. While his reputation evolved nicely in the courts of Edward IV, Richard III, and Henry VII, in Henry VIII's court his habit of flyting by means of satirical skeltonics came under severe opprobrium, and he lost many supporters, as we have seen, outside the powerful Howard family and Europe at large. While Erasmus praised Skelton to the skies, Alexander Barclay, perhaps offended by his attacks on the Scots before and after Flodden, produced several vitriolic attacks on him, including *Contra Skeltonium*, some of which personal invective found a friendly audience in the jest-books. In the next generation, practically simultaneous to Sidney's* toying with the idea of an alter ego, Philip Sparrow in *Astrophil and Stella*, Spenser's* adopting his pseudonym Colin Clout for both *The Shepheardes Calendar* and the sixth book of *The Faerie Queene*, and Shakespeare's* giving some of his lines to Hamlet, Puttenham* mocked him with the skeltonoic epithet, "rude railing rhymer." Alexander Pope lent him the epithet "beastly" in 1737, the same year the brilliant and charming Elizabeth Cooper praised his "very rich vein of Wit, Humour, and Poetry." Thomas Walton called him "a fool in any language" a generation before the Romantic poets, especially Southey and Wordsworth, proclaimed him a "genius." Only after World War I and especially after Robert Graves' and W. H. Auden's various appreciations of him has Skelton's reputation remained relatively secure. This history of appreciation and rejection brings us back, I think, to a notion of a poet who could be smooth in his roughness and could contain praise in his apparent blame. One of the anomalies of Skelton criticism lies in the fact that two brilliant contemporary students of the seventeenth century and of Milton in particular, Stanley Fish and David Loewenstein, have contributed to our knowledge of Skelton's rhetorical complexity, notably, his use of irony in, above all, his pseudocompliments to the ladies of the Howard coterie in *Garland of Laurel*.

BIBLIOGRAPHY

Works by John Skelton

The Book of the Laurel. Ed. F. W. Brownlow. Newark: University of Delaware Press, 1990.

Magnificence. Ed. Paula Neuss. Manchester: Manchester University Press, 1980.

Magniyfycence: A Moral Play. Ed. Robert Lee Ramsay. Millwood, NY: Kraus Reprint, 1981 (orig. Early English Text Society no. 98). Oxford: Oxford University Press, 1908.

The Poetical Works of John Skelton. 2 vols. Ed. Alexander Dyce. New York: AMS, 1965 (orig. 1843).

Studies of John Skelton

Edwards, Anthony S. G. *Skelton: The Critical Heritage*. Boston: Routledge and Kegan Paul, 1981.

Edwards, H.L.R. *Skelton: The Life and Times of an Early Tudor Poet*. London: Cape, 1949.

Fish, Stanley Eugene. *The Poetry of John Skelton*. New Haven, CT: Yale University Press, 1965.

Kinney, Arthur F. *John Skelton, Priest as Poet: Seasons of Discovery.* Chapel Hill: University of North Carolina Press, 1987.
Loewenstein, David. ''Skeleton's Triumph: *The Garland of Laurel* and Literary Fame.'' *Neophilologus* 68 (1984): 611–22.
Nelson, William. *John Skelton, Laureate.* New York: Columbia University Press, 1939.

ALAN HAGER

ROBERT SOUTHWELL
(1561–1595)

BIOGRAPHY

Robert Southwell, perhaps the most important recusant poet of the latter sixteenth century, was born to a noble Catholic family, though his grandfather, Sir Richard Southwell, had been an efficient courtier in the service of Henry VIII, responsible for the downfall of his companion Henry Howard, earl of Surrey,* and for the confiscation and ruination of many Catholic monasteries, including the ruined Priory of Horsham St. Faith in Norfolk, where Robert was born in 1561. At age fifteen, he was sent to Flanders to study at the University of Douay and was received into the Jesuit-run Anchin College. After six months, he was ''evacuated'' with his fellow students to the College of Clermont in Paris, where he studied for perhaps one year before traveling to the English College in Rome with the intention of joining the Jesuits. After what he regarded as insufferable delay, he was admitted as a novice to the Society of Jesus on 17 October 1578 at the age of sixteen. Two years later he took first vows, and beginning in 1582 he served as ''repetitor,'' responsible for tutorial work. He was ordained in 1584, and by early that summer ''Padre Roberto Southwello'' had become prefect of studies at the English College.

On 8 May 1586 he set forth with Father Henry Garnet for England, where his fellow Jesuit Edmund Campion had been executed soon after arriving from Rome in 1580. Southwell had expressed more than once his willingness, even desire, to follow Campion and other English martyrs ''to the desired port.'' So, after a ten-year stay upon the Continent, he set foot on the terrestrial port of England on the Feast of St. Thomas Becket, 17 July 1586, one month before the failed Babbington Plot.

Soon after his arrival, his new superior, Father Weston, was executed, and Southwell took his place as chaplain and confessor in the house of Sir Philip Howard, earl of Arundel. Since he left the household only in disguise, his residence at Arundel may be regarded as a rather luxurious house arrest, affording him long hours for literary and nonliterary work. Eventually, he rented private quarters in London, where he housed and operated a secret printing press, in lieu of a public pulpit. He remained at large for six years, writing, attending to the spiritual needs of the Catholic nobility, and fostering literary connections with his cousin Anthony Copley and his friend Thomas Lodge, as well as with an impressive litany of literary descendants within the houses of the nobility.

In January 1592 he was captured by the infamous Topcliffe "the priest-hunter," who reported to the queen that he "did never tayke so weightye a man." At the Gatehouse Prison Southwell was tortured and interrogated by, among others, his kinsman Sir Robert Cecil, who was impressed by the young priest's heroic endurance, having been thirteen times put to "a new kind of torture no less cruel than the rack." In July, having come forth with no information, he was removed to the Tower, where he remained until 1595, when he was finally brought to trial. The outcome was predictable, but the proceedings, recorded in some detail, are testament to Southwell's eloquence, patience, and wit, though most memorable is his plain response to Topcliffe's defense of the use of torture: "Thou art a bad man." On Friday, 4 March, Southwell was drawn through the streets of London, and, after making a stirring avowal of his loyalty to the queen, his priesthood, and the Catholic Church, he was hanged and quartered according to the sentence handed down by the court.

MAJOR WORKS AND THEMES

Robert Southwell is the literary embodiment of the English Counter Reformation, a fact that itself accounts for his relative obscurity. He ardently believed and openly professed that the reforming of English literature was an intricate and vital part of his spiritual mission. Eloquently conversant with the Christian classicism of the European Renaissance, Southwell sought to propagate in England the sort of religious literary rebirth that was occurring on the Continent. That the divine art of poetry should be put to frivolous and immoral use by his countrymen and that poets should spend their time in making "idle fancies" were abhorrent to Southwell. He wrote to his cousin, "Poets by abusing their talent, and making the follies and fayninges of love, the customary subject of their base endeavors, have so discredited this facultie, that a Poet, a Lover, and a Liar, are by many reckoned but three words of one signification." Southwell urged his fellow poets to embrace sacred themes, to lift poetry from the pagan mire into which it had been dragged.

The extraordinary footnote to this one-man literary Reformation is its unpredictable, unlikely, and uncanny success. That the likes of Ben Jonson* and Shakespeare's* patron, Southampton, gave ear to this young Jesuit's pleas for divine poetry is interesting, but of far greater significance is the recognition that in the person of Robert Southwell one finds the unintentional and unconsecrated father of English metaphysical poetry. Southwell's intimacy with, and reliance upon, Ignatius' *Spiritual Exercises*, which prescribes imaginative narrative and an engagement of the five senses to the art of mediation, gave birth in English to the meditative verse that would characterize so much of the poetry of the early seventeenth century. Those characteristics by which we now describe metaphysical poetry—the dramatic opening, the argued metaphor, the eccentric conceit, self-introspection and spiritual ascent—are all to be found in the poetry of Robert Southwell.

Since all of these metaphysical qualities are found in "The Burning Babe," I should not object to its frequent anthologization. The poem, after all, should not be blamed for reducing Southwell's place in the literary canon to an eccentric one-hit wonder. But, though representative, it is neither his finest nor his fullest work. In the sustained excellence of the sequence from which that poem is taken, "The Sequence on the Virgin Mary and Christ," or in the 792–line "Saint Peter's Complaint," one recognizes, I think, Southwell's full poetic power. Here, as in the ethereal splendor of "A Vale of Tears" and the personal drama of "Looke Home" or "What Joy to Live?" one sees and hears in Southwell what Donne,* Herbert, Crashaw, Vaughn, and Traherne all clearly saw and heard.

CRITICAL RECEPTION

Collected and published immediately after his execution, Southwell's poetry served primarily to influence poets in the seventeenth century and occasionally poets during later ages such as Hopkins, for whom Southwell was his only important Jesuit literary ancestor. Southwell's literary canonization, however, occurred with fitting simultaneity with his religious canonization at the beginning of the twentieth century.

The Complete Poems of Robert Southwell was published for the first time in 1872 by Alexander B. Grosart. The first evaluation of Southwell as an important literary figure was accomplished in two articles by Father Hurston in *The Month* in 1895. In 1935 Pierre Janelle published *Robert Southwell the Writer*, a thorough consideration of the poet's development, which includes a studied biography. This book's remarkable contribution to an understanding of Southwell remains undiminished by time. Louis Martz's treatment of Southwell in his book *The Poetry of Meditation* (1954) and his placement of Southwell as the first poet in *English Seventeenth Century Verse v. 1* (1963) did much to exhibit the connection among religious mediation, Robert Southwell, and seventeenth-century religious poets. Christopher Delvin's *Life of Robert Southwell* (1956) presents in one chapter a compelling, if not wholly convincing, case for Southwell's influence upon William Shakespeare.* James McDonald and Nancy Pollard Brown's edition of *The Poems of Robert Southwell* (1967) offered readers a reliable critical edition of the poet's works, and the past two decades have seen a small explosion of interest in Southwell, both as a recusant poet and as an early metaphysical poet. Interest in Southwell is greater now than it has ever been, and while provocative readings of his poems will and should continue, a reevaluation of the scope of his influence upon his own and later centuries will remain at the center of "Southwell studies."

BIBLIOGRAPHY

Works by Robert Southwell

An Epistle of Comfort. Ilkley: Scholar Press, 1974.

The Poems of Robert Southwell, S.J. Ed. James H. McDonald and Nancy Pollard Brown. Oxford: Clarendon Press, 1967.

The Triumphs Over Death. London: Manresa Press, 1914.

Studies of Robert Southwell

Brownlaw, Frank. "Southwell and Shakespeare." *KM80: A Birthday Album for Kenneth Muir.* Liverpool: Liverpool University Press, 1987.

King, John N. "Recent Studies in Southwell." *English Literary Renaissance* 13.2 (1983): 221–27.

Scallon, Joseph D. "The Poetry of Robert Southwell, S.J." *Elizabethan and Renaissance Studies.* 11th ser. Salzburg: University of Salzburg Press, 1975.

Schweers, Gregory. "Bernard of Clairvaux's Influence on English Recusant Letters: The Case of Robert Southwell, S.J." *American Benedictine Review* 41.2 (June 1990): 157–66.

GARY M. BOUCHARD

EDMUND SPENSER
(c. 1552–1599)

BIOGRAPHY

Edmund Spenser's life is comparatively well documented. He was born, we conjecture from *Amoretti* 60, in 1552 or shortly thereafter in London. His parents were poor but remotely connected, or so Spenser claimed, with the noble Spencers [*sic*] of Althorp, from whom in due time descended Princess Diana of England. Spenser's father may have been a free journeyman in the Merchant Taylors' Company, that is, a cloth maker. From 1561 to 1569, Spenser attended the renowned Merchant Taylors' School in London as a "poor scholar." In 1569, he was admitted to Pembroke Hall, Cambridge, as a sizar—a poor scholar given servant's duties such as kitchen work and waiting on tables. While there, in 1570, he began a friendship with Gabriel Harvey,* then a new fellow, subsequently represented in Spenser's pastorals as Hobbinol. In 1573 he earned his B.A. and in 1576, his M.A., but he failed to win a fellowship.

Forced to make his own way in the world, he served as secretary to John Young, bishop of Rochester. In 1579, he published under the pseudonym Immerito his first significant literary effort, *The Shepheardes Calender*. It was an instant success. His patron at the time was the earl of Leicester, a champion of militant international Protestantism, at whose house he sometimes resided. The dedicatee was Sidney,* with whom Spenser claimed to be on friendly terms—a big step up the social ladder; at any rate, Spenser, Harvey, and Sidney all belonged to the Areopagus, apparently a literary group of some sort; and some of Sidney's theories about literature are reflected in Spenser's famous "Letter to Ralegh.'' In 1580, someone, not Harvey, arranged for the publication of *Three Proper . . . Letters* between Spenser and Harvey, thus revealing valuable biographical information: some of *The Faerie Queene* (henceforth *FQ*) was already circulating in manuscript; and Harvey thought it too fanciful and insufficiently classical. Harvey also satirizes the Calvinism at Cambridge and refers to many recent French and Italian belletristic writers, feelings and tastes we may presume Spenser shared. In this same year, after working briefly as a secretary for John Young, bishop of Rochester, Spenser became private secretary to Arthur Lord Grey de Wilton, newly appointed lord deputy of Ireland with orders to quell the Desmond rebellion. This ruthless colonialist is allegorized as Artegall in *FQ* V.xii and praised in *The View of the Present State of Ireland* (henceforth *The View*). Spenser settled in Dublin. In 1582, he was accorded the rank of a landed gentleman. In 1588 or a little later, he occupied the ruined castle of Kilcolman, County Cork, a property that had been confiscated from the Irish ''rebel'' Sir John of Desmond. In 1589 Spenser met his third role model: Sir Walter Ralegh,* a neighbor, visited Spenser; they critiqued each other's poetry; and Spenser accompanied him back to England and read some of the *FQ* to Queen Elizabeth,* an event later allegorized in *Colin Clouts Come Home Againe*. Spenser mentions Ralegh in the proem to *FQ* 3 and allegorizes him as Timias and perhaps Marinell, in books 3 and 4. In 1590 came the most important event of Spenser's career, the publication of *FQ* 1–3, dedicated to Queen Elizabeth with an appended explanation of the entire poem's genesis and allegory addressed to Ralegh (Letter to Ralegh). Elizabeth is mentioned in the proem to every book of the *FQ* and is typified by at least three female characters—Queen Gloriana of Faeryland, Belphoebe, and Queen Mercilla; if not also Britomort, Florimell, and Amoret. Elizabeth disliked war; she was a moderate in religion, and in the *FQ*, Spenser's religious coloration pretty much matches hers. In 1591 Spenser published a miscellany of shorter poems he had lying around, *Complaints: Containing Sundrie Small Poems of the Worlds Vanitie*—nine poems, including *Muiopotmos: or the Fate of the Butterflie* (dated 1590) and *Prosopopoia: or Mother Hubberds Tale*. In the latter, the passage where the fox acts like the Lord Treasurer, William Cecil, Lord Burghley, caused the volume to be ''called in.'' On the brighter side, in this year, Spenser was granted a life pension of fifty pounds a year by the queen, presumably in recognition of the *FQ*. He returned to Ireland.

In 1594 Spenser married his second wife (nothing certain is known about his first wife except that she bore him a son and heir, Sylvanus); she outranked him, being a kinswoman to Sir Richard Boyle, afterward first earl of Cork. In 1595, Spenser published a little volume, *Amoretti and Epithalamion*, which purported to record Spenser's own recent courtship and marriage. He also published *Colin Clouts Come Home Againe*, on which see earlier, bound in with his elegy on the death of Sidney (died 1586) and those of six others. In 1596, he published the second edition of *FQ* Books 1–3 (with the old happy ending of Book 3 canceled and replaced by an open-ended one) together with the first edition of

Books 4–6. In the same year, he published *Fowre Hymnes* and *Prothalamion.* King James of Scotland complained that his mother, Mary, is slandered as Duessa in *FQ* 5.9, but nothing was done about it. In 1598, *The View* was entered in the Stationer's Register anonymously by Matthew Lownes; it circulated in many manuscripts and was eventually attributed to Spenser but was not published until 1633, long after his death. Certainly the worst event of Spenser's life occurred in the autumn of 1598, when Kilcolman was sacked and burned in the course of Tyrone's rebellion. With his wife he fled to Cork; then he alone went to England on political business. In 1599, while still in England, he fell sick, died, and was buried in Westminster Abbey; at his funeral, poets filed past his grave, throwing into it poems and their pens. In 1609, Lownes brought out the first folio edition of *FQ* Books 1–6, together with the first edition of the newly discovered ''Cantos of Mutabilitie'' (henceforth *The Mutability Cantoes*), apparently part of an uncompleted Book 7. These facts reveal something both of Spenser's enemies and of his intellectual community of friends and patrons. Spenser's indebtedness, friendship, admiration, ambition, and desire to please raised his patrons almost to the status of coauthors.

MAJOR WORKS AND THEMES

We start with the most utilitarian and autobiographical works. Spenser's life, like that of many other English poets, was bound up with Ireland; while exact dates are sometimes in doubt, it is there that Spenser wrote most of his work and achieved his social goals. In all his works, while Spenser celebrates the Irish landscape and some aspects of the Irish language, literature, and folkways, he praises native Irish individuals rarely. Current interest in *The View* runs high but must be tempered by awareness of the unrevised state of the work and the paucity of external evidence for its authorship. The Anglo-Norman conquest under ''Strongbow'' (Richard de Clare), reaffirmed by a pope's gift of Ireland to King Henry II, supposedly gave the English the right to exploit Ireland as a colony. The major theme of *The View* is that the native Irish must be brought under control. This political tract is in the form of a dialogue: Spenser's spokesman is the knowledgeable but repressive Irenius; his interlocutor Eudoxus, while equally colonialist, is both argumentative toward Irenius and pacific toward the Irish. While impressed by some elements of Irish culture such as the status of poets, Irenius wants to eliminate three central elements: the native Irish or ''Brehon'' law, most Irish social and political customs, and Catholicism. All the native Irish and some of the Anglo-Irish were either Catholics or crypto-Catholics. Religion merged with national security in that (1) the pope had excommunicated the queen and absolved in advance anyone who would assassinate her and (2) the Catholic nations had already sent not only missionaries but mercenaries to Ireland, making it a potential staging area for attacks on England. Spenser's program, while unethical by present standards, is not quite genocide because it offers an alternative—total submission. The harshness toward Ireland that we sense both here and implicitly in Book 5 of the *FQ* must be motivated in part by Spenser's Protestantism and by his desire to "make something of himself."

It is a relief to turn to Spenser's poetry, which is multivocal and variously related to life. *Amoretti, Epithalamion*, and *Colin Clouts Come Home Againe* purport to be autobiographical. The last has captured the attention of social and materialistic critics. In this pastoral dialogue, Spenser, under the mask of Colin, weighs with insightful ambivalence the drawbacks and virtues of court life, equated with England, and of country life under the name of Ireland. He decides to remain in Ireland.

Amoretti and *Epithalamion* intrigue the learned by their generic experimentation and by their numerological dimension: *Epithalamion* has twenty-four stanzas and 365 long lines; *Amoretti* contains, among several sonnets on particular days, an Ash-Wednesday Sonnet (22) and an Easter Sonnet (68); the number of sonnets between them equals the number of days between Ash Wednesday and Easter. It appeals to laymen by its occasional air of biographical authenticity, by its relatively conspicuous story line, and by its unified yet comprehensive ethos, reconciling *eros* with *agape*. Although the sonnets are graceful rather than colloquial, some are vapid and overexpanded, and others, such as 54, 58, 59, 65, and 68, are as fresh and as seemingly authentic as are the best of Shakespeare's* and are without his contorted metaphors. Spenser was the first poet in English to cap a sonnet sequence with an epithalamion to the same lady, thus giving it, instead of the usual sad ending, one that is both happy and Christian. In a mood of affirmation, the poet describes an entire universe that is almost completely harmonious with itself and with his wishes. Although it has always been recognized as one of the greatest lyrics in the language, in isolation, the *Epithalamion* may seem saccharine to modern tastes because it lacks tension; nevertheless, in its volume it stands as a resolution to those sharp conflicts between mercy and cruelty in the mistress, between flesh and spirit in the lover, between male and female dominance, and between the lovers and spiteful outsiders that made the *Amoretti* a typical sonnet sequence.

The *Epithalamion, Muiopotmos, Mother Hubberds Tale*, and *The Mutability Cantoes* (which can be considered as a minor poem for this purpose) are Spenser's best minor poems and should be chosen over *FQ* or *The Shepheardes Calendar* (a tour de force, often stylistically gauche) to represent Spenser in anthologies and survey courses. *Mother Hubberds Tale* is a versified picaresque novella in the form of a beast fable satirizing all levels of Elizabethan society from the point of view of two upstarts, a Fox and an Ape. Mock-epic and mock-tragic in genre, *Muiopotmos* is Spenser's most accessible poem—Keatsian in its sensuousness and in some of its sentiments, like the vulnerability of youth and beauty before the envious.

The *Mutability Cantoes*, while allusive, are not only appealing to students but philosophical in scope, a worthy coda to the *FQ*. As lively, richly varied in its materials, and masterly in its verse as is the *Epithalamion*, it takes a harder look at things. It concludes, first, that change is cyclical and therefore not so bad, but finally that only a static eternity with God can satisfy the individual.

The *Fowre Hymnes*, little read today, are interesting for their Platonism, syncretism, seemingly straightforward confession of what Spenser at that moment believed, and palinodic structure embodying a dialogue between earthly and heavenly love. The *Prothalamion*, celebrating English scenery and a double betrothal, contains the quintessentially Spenserian refrain that T. S. Eliot quoted in *The Wasteland*, "Sweete Themmes runne softly, till I end my Song."

The Faerie Queene

Space allows a summary of only one central plot, that of Britomart. Book 3, the Book of Chastity, has for its hero a female knight; her quest is for her ideal man, whom she has seen in a magic mirror. This curious love story stitches together Books 3 to 5. In 4, she wins her man by jousting with him and eventually losing, and they become engaged. In 3 and 5 she has two visions of her future as wife, queen, mother, widow, and progenetrix of a dynasty climaxing in Elizabeth. In 5, she rescues her man when he is imprisoned by an embittered, man-hating version of herself. They do not marry in the poem as we have it.

The genre to which the *FQ* as a whole belongs—ignoring the inset or intermittent genres such as personification-allegory, pastoral (6.10), and lyric—is the then-popular hybrid known as romance-epic, like those produced by the Italians Ariosto* and Tasso.* Harvey* teased Spenser about trying "to overgo Ariosto." Despite epic trappings like invoking the Muses, glorifying a ruler, and beginning in medias res, the poem has less of the epic about it and more of the romance. The romance is a very loose genre, requiring only two story elements, love of a woman and combat with a man. The heroes and heroines are highly gendered role models; the villains are double-dyed. Combat is never massed, usually single, and often for no other purpose than to weigh the worth of the combatants, like an athletic contest. The loosely connected adventures are vividly described and often fantastic. The *FQ* exemplifies these characteristics with a few significant exceptions, such as the androgynous Britomart.

While epic entails high-mindedness, the genre romance, aiming at entertainment, had been charged with a laxity not only aesthetic but moral. Roger Ascham had criticized Malory* and certain unidentified "books written in Italy" (including Ariosto's *Orlando Furioso*?) and by implication the whole genre, saying that "the whole pleasure of [Malory's] book standeth in two special points, in open manslaughter and bold bawdry." As if in acknowledgment of Ascham's charges, Spenser has his spokesman Contemplation assert that "bloud can nought but sin and wars but sorrowes yield" (1.10.60); in heaven, "battailes none are to be fought"; and "as for loose loues, [they] are vaine, and vanish into nought" (62). Spenser strove in Book 1 to escape these limitations. The quest is to kill a dragon, not a man; the heroine is pure and religiously symbolic; and bawdry is painted in the blackest of terms. Spenser initially announced about his poem as a whole, ''Fierce warres and faithfull loues shall moralize my song,'' meaning presumably, ''My song shall moralize fierce warres and faithfull loues.'' At least in Book 1, he agrees with his external and internal critics that his materials are frivolous in themselves, but not if they are ''moralized.''

Spenser thus indicates that writers of romance can and should convey a moral by allegory. In the Letter to Ralegh, too, his generic classification of the *FQ* is not only ''historical poem'' but ''allegory.'' Strictly speaking, however, only Books 1 and 7, and perhaps also 2 and 5, are allegory. In Book 1, the Despair episode is so allegorical that the literal level constitutes the meaning, thus representing the extreme of abstraction, personification-allegory, the mark of allegory as a genre. Speaking as a compelling and insightful voice within the hero, Despair almost persuades him to commit suicide. Books 3, 4, and 6 have too few personifications to gain admittance to the genre allegory; they are, in the main, romance-epic. Spenser claims allegory pervades the poem because he includes in the term any story that has a moral.

Summarizing Spenser's plots makes him sound banal and repetitious. These tales of knights and ladies are interspersed with allegorical tableaux or ''loci of recognition.'' Summarizing the five tableaux dealing with sexual love and art—two gardens, two temples, and a mountaintop—conveys the flavor of the poem. The beautiful seductress Acrasia traps young men in her carefully constructed pleasure-garden, the Bower of Bliss (2.12). Venus, Adonis, Cupid, Psyche, and Pleasure preside over the Garden of Adonis, where sex is natural—uninhibited yet spontaneously monogamous (3.6). As everyone now knows, the Garden of Adonis stands as a correction to the Bower of Bliss. But it is not Spenser's last word, as C. S. Lewis believed, for while it rehabilitates sexuality, it does so only at the expense of art. The evil Bower slathers art over nature (gold ivy and jeweled grapevines), and the good Garden banishes it. The conciliatory Temple of Venus (4.10) sets art up as a supplement or complement to Nature (4.10.21). The fourth locus of recognition, the House of Busyrane, is really a Temple of Cupid. Free of plant and animal life, it is a palace of art, having objets d'art on the walls, mounting an interactive masque every night, owned by a master of the ''black arts,'' and allegorizing a sadistic style of lovemaking that is nothing if not artful. In contrast to the artful lust in the Bower of Bliss, which errs by producing pleasure ''more than natural'' (Genius), this artful love is bad because it produces and accepts only pain (3.11–12). Amoret also turns up in the Temple of Venus; her abduction from there by the masterful Scudamour is also more cruel than is necessary; her resulting fear of male dominance leads to her imprisonment at Busyrane's, so that at one stage of her life or another, she inhabits three of these places. Aside from the abduction, however, the Temple of Venus represents an attainable ideal love; like an Aristotelian mean, it shows how much pain is simply natural and inevitable. A fifth locus of recognition, Mount Acidale (6.10), provides a resolution on the subject of art: Calidore's vision of Colin and the Graces there announces like Polyxenes that ''the art itself is nature''; like the highest courtesy (6.2.2), art must be spontaneous, and it must spring from inspiration (the Graces and their understudies), a quality that Calidore's own poetry lacks (6.9.35).

The variety of Spenser's work as a whole illustrates what can also be inferred from his life: whatever his source of income, he considered himself a professional poet. He spans medieval and Renaissance period styles: *Mother Hubberds Tale* is self-consciously medieval, an imitation of Chaucer; the *FQ* is largely medieval in its many personifications and in its romance genre; the sonnet sequence is a Renaissance form; and the *Shepheardes Calendar, Epithalamion, Prothalamion, Muiopotmos*, and *Colin Clouts Come Home Againe* are all in good Renaissance fashion conspicuously classical; even the occasional Christianity of the first two is of the syncretic, Christian-humanist variety.

CRITICAL RECEPTION

As noted earlier, two of Spenser's poems, *Mother Hubberds Tale* and *FQ* 5, got him into political trouble. While *The Shepheardes Calender* was understood and appreciated right away, the *FQ* was seldom interpreted analytically, just respected as a ''classic'' and a model for imitation (starting with Barnfield, Drayton, and the Fletchers) until the mid-eighteenth century, when Spenser scholarship got going in earnest with Upton, Warton, Hurd, and Hughes. Spenser has always been part of the canon, receiving at times more attention than Shakespeare. The Romantics—even Burns—all apprenticed themselves to him at one point or another in their development, most memorably Keats in the ''Eve of St. Agnes''; they valued him for his music, passion, and sensuousness; as for the allegory, Hazlitt warned not to meddle with it. The Victorian debt is epitomized in Tennyson's ''Lotos Eaters.'' Spenser earned Lamb's sobriquet ''the poet's poet,'' implying that poets learn from him; and they do so, I believe, not only because his opulent stanza combines interwovenness (the unexpected return of the b rhyme in line 5) with closure (the final couplet with alexandrine), but because his entire style is more workmanlike, his effects more analyzable, than those of other poets. To the first two-thirds of the twentieth century, he epitomized Christian humanism and the hierarchical unity of the Renaissance world-view of Lovejoy and Tillyard. The new critics, themselves disdainful of his gushiness, led some of us to see that the *FQ* is formally stitched together by repeated images. Genre criticism has always been a lively topic; in the *FQ*, current interest centers on modulations between romance and epic. One of the enduring achievements of the more recent Spenser scholarship is discovery and reinterpretation of sociopolitical matrices, meanings, and inflections in Spenser, bringing *The View* into prominence for the first time. Previous biographical critics swept his social goals under the rug, partly to protect their bard, partly because they privileged the poetry, which is mostly of an idealistic bent, over *The View* and the life-records, which are predictably utilitarian. Now that material conditions of cultural production claim the spotlight, now that genius is demystified, and any document merits literary analysis, critics have started to reason the other way round. In the *FQ*, another achievement is the recognition of the diversity of Spenser's meanings and attitudes not only between one passage and another but even within a given passage. Women feel a particular fondness for the *FQ* and the *Amoretti and Epithalamion*, especially now in the days of feminism, though some feminists find him mired in patriarchy. The vogue for fantastic narrative, especially chivalric romance, makes the *FQ* popular with today's undergraduates, while maturer scholars admire its intertextuality, its interlaced plots, its symbolism, and its political cunning. While Sidney wrote individual passages that are more powerful, Spenser's scope is more comprehensive; he gets more things into his poetry.

BIBLIOGRAPHY

Works by Edmund Spenser

The Faerie Queene. Ed. A. C. Hamilton. London: Longman, 1977.

Poetical Works. Ed. J. C. Smith and E. de Selincourt. Oxford: Oxford University Press, 1991.

Works: A Variorum Edition. 11 vols. Ed. Edwin Greenlaw et al. Baltimore: Johns Hopkins University Press, 1932–57.

The Yale Edition of the Shorter Poems. Ed. William A. Oram, Einar Bjorvand, Ronald Bond, Thomas H. Cain, Alexander Dunlop, and Richard Schell. New Haven, CT: Yale University Press, 1989.

Studies of Edmund Spenser

Alpers, Paul. *The Poetry of The Faerie Queene*. Princeton: Princeton University Press, 1967.

Anderson, Judith H., Donald Cheney, and David Richardson, eds. *Spenser's Life and the Subject of Biography*. Amherst: University of Massachusetts Press, 1996.

Berger, Harry. *Revisionary Play: Studies in the Spenserian Dynamics*. Berkeley: University of California Press, 1988.

Brink, Jean R. "Constructing the *View of the Present State of Ireland*." *Spenser Studies* (1990): 203–28.

Cummings, R. M. *Spenser: The Critical Heritage*. New York: Barnes and Noble, 1971.

Frye, Northrop. "The Structure of Imagery in *The Faerie Queene*." *University of Toronto Quarterly* 30 (1961): 109–27. Rpt. in *Essential Articles*, ed. A. C. Hamilton. Hamden, CT: Archon Press, 1972, hereafter *EA*, 153–70.

Hamilton, A. C. *The Structure of Allegory in the "Faerie Queene."* Oxford: Oxford University Press, 1961.

Hamilton, A. C., et al., eds. *Spenser Encyclopedia*. Toronto: University of Toronto Press, 1990.

Helgerson, Richard. *Self-Crowned Laureates: Spenser, Jonson, Milton, and the Literary System*. Berkeley: University of California Press, 1983.

Hieatt, A. Kent. *Chaucer, Spenser, Milton: Mythopoeic Continuities and Transformations*. Montreal: McGill University Press, 1975.

———. *Short Time's Endlesse Monument: The Symbolism of Numbers in Spenser's "Epithalamion."* New York: Columbia University Press, 1960.

Hoopes, Robert. " 'God Guide Thee, Guyon': Nature and Grace Reconciled in *The Faerie Queene*, Book II." *Review of English Studies* n.s. 5 (1954): 14–24.

Kaske, Carol. "How Spenser Really Used Stephen Hawes." In *Unfolded Tales*, ed.

George Logan and Gordon Teskey. Ithaca, NY: Cornell University Press, 1990, 119–36.

———. ''Spenser's *Amoretti and Epithalamion* of 1595.'' *ELR* 8.3 (1978): 271–95.

———. ''Spenser's Pluralistic Universe: The View from the Mount of Contemplation (*Faerie Queene* I.x).'' In *Contemporary Thought on Spenser*, ed. Richard Frushell and Bernard Vondersmith. Carbondale: University of Southern Illinois Press, 1975, 121–49, 230–33.

Lewis, C. S. *The Allegory of Love*. Oxford: Oxford University Press, 1936.

Maley, Willy. *A Spenser Chronology*. Lanham, MD: Barnes and Noble, 1994.

Norbrook, David. *Poetry and Politics in the English Renaissance*. London: Boston: Routledge and Kegan Paul, 1984.

Roche, Thomas P. *The Kindly Flame: A Study of ''The Faerie Queene'' III and IV*. Princeton: Princeton University Press, 1964.

Williams, Kathleen. ''Eterne in Mutabilitie: The Unified World of *The Faerie Queene*.'' *ELH* 19.2 (1952): 115–30. Rpt. in *Critical Essays on Spenser from ELH*. Baltimore, 1970, 59–74.

———. ''Romance Tradition in *The Faerie Queene*.'' *Research Studies* 32 (1964): 147–60.

———. *Spenser's World of Glass*. Berkeley: University of California Press, 1966.

CAROL V. KASKE

HENRY HOWARD, EARL OF SURREY
(1517–1547)

BIOGRAPHY

Surrey's short, spectacular life is the stuff of romantic legend. He was born Henry Howard in 1517, the eldest son and heir of Thomas Howard, earl of Surrey, and Elizabeth Stafford. His grandfather Thomas Howard, second duke of Norfolk, was England's finest military commander and had just four years earlier destroyed an invading Scottish army at Flodden, killing the Scottish king. Upon his grandfather's death in 1524, Surrey's father succeeded as third duke of Norfolk, and Surrey succeeded to his father's title as earl. The third duke was one of the most powerful councillors throughout the remainder of Henry VIII's reign, and two of his nieces (Anne Boleyn and Catherine Howard) sat on the throne. Surrey's mother was daughter of the duke of Buckingham and a direct descendant of King Edward III.

Surrey received a nobleman's education, that is, heavy on outdoor sports, music, dance, and religious forms that would make him a soldier, courtier, and councillor. He would have had a private tutor to teach him Latin grammar, literature, and history. We do not know who that tutor was, but by some stroke of luck he seems to have been a good one, and by age twelve Surrey was showing notable signs of learning. In the Renaissance patronage system, children of elite families were frequently brought up in the households of allied families, creating a crisscross system of godparentage. In 1530, at age fourteen, Surrey was placed at Windsor Castle as companion to the twelve-year-old Henry Fitzroy, bastard son of Henry VIII. Surrey and Fitzroy then spent the years 1532–33 in the retinue of king François Ier of France at his palace at Fontainebleau. There Surrey would have seen the spectacular styles of architecture, painting, and sculpture that François was importing from Renaissance Italy, under the influence of Leonardo and the Mannerists. Shortly after their return, Fitzroy was married to Surrey's sister Mary Howard.

In 1536, when Surrey was nineteen, the charm that had been cast over his life was dispelled. His cousin Anne Boleyn was tried for treason and executed in May. Two months later, his friend Fitzroy died. It is impossible to probe Surrey's psyche from a distance of over 450 years, but William Sessions is surely right to say that "Surrey's grief marked a clear change in his social personality." Had Anne survived, or had Fitzroy come to the throne—a possibility for which Henry VIII always kept his illegitimate son in reserve—Surrey would have been guaranteed a permanent place of honor. Instead, he found his and his family's position imperiled and the closely woven threads of his social and emotional life ripped apart.

The remaining ten years of Surrey's brief life are marked by sharp swings between reckless violence and politic calm. Three times he was imprisoned for brawling. With each occurrence, the Privy Council considered his behavior more threatening and less excusable as youthful indiscretion. In between, he lived ostentatiously, held positions of high command in Henry's army, and took his place at court as the scion of one of the kingdom's most powerful families. In 1541 he was created a knight of the Order of the Garter. In 1545 he was made governor of the English outpost at Boulogne, named "Lieutenant General of the King on Sea and Land," and given an army to command against the French.

While Surrey seems to have had a genuine talent for battlefield command, he suffered losses in the French campaign and was recalled under a cloud. His father attempted to form an alliance with the Seymour family, the main enemies of the Howards and the in-laws of the heir-apparent, the future Edward VI. Surrey, who seems to have grown increasingly isolated from his own family as well as from the subtleties of court politics, objected violently to the proposed marriage of his sister to Edward Seymour, duke of Somerset. She was, after all, the widow of his friend Henry Fitzroy, and Surrey seems to have taken the proposed match as a betrayal of Fitzroy and of himself. He changed his coat of arms to emphasize his royal forebears—an insignificant matter to modern eyes, but one that threw the aging Henry VIII into a rage. In Henry's eyes, it was clear evidence that Surrey intended to dominate the boy Edward when he came to the throne, or, indeed, to grab the throne for himself. In December 1546, Surrey was arrested and charged with treason for his use of royal arms. On 19 January 1547, still shy of his thirtieth birthday, he was beheaded. Eight days later, Henry VIII died.

One of the enduring mysteries of Surrey's biography is the origin of his friendship with Sir Thomas Wyatt.* Both had connections to Anne Boleyn, but

Surrey was only nineteen when she died. Wyatt was fourteen years older than Surrey and a client of Sir Thomas Cromwell,* one of the most bitter enemies of the Howards. He acknowledged an inclination toward Lutheranism, while the Howards were staunchly Catholic (though Surrey's own religious attitudes are hard to pin down). The link between them is usually ascribed to a natural affinity between poets. It is equally possible that they were brought together by Wyatt's son, who was in Surrey's service. All that is certain is that, by 1541, Wyatt wrote poetry addressed to the young earl and that after Wyatt's death a year later Surrey wrote some of his best verse in Wyatt's praise and imbibed elements of Wyatt's style.

MAJOR WORKS AND THEMES

Surrey is celebrated for four distinct bodies of poetry, amorous lyrics, translations, lyrics lamenting his imprisonments, and epitaphs on the deaths of others. At least one amorous lyric, "From Tuscan cam my ladies worthi race," is addressed to "Geraldine," or Lady Elizabeth Fitzgerald, whom Surrey encountered at the royal court in 1541. Surrey travels through a landscape of Petrarchan language toward his conclusion that "happy ys he that may obtaine her love." It is possible, even likely, that a good number of Surrey's other lyrics, several of which are direct translations of Petrarch, are indeed part of a real or playful attempt to "obtaine her love." The emphasis of the amorous lyrics, however, is not on love attained but on love denied. Though the love that masters him may betray him, the poet proclaims in "Love that doth reign and live within my heart" that he will remain faithful to the end, for "[s]weet is the death that taketh end by love."

William Sessions and others have argued persuasively that Surrey's lyrics are best understood as a humanist poetry of translation, not in a narrow sense of changing a poem from one language into another, but in the broadest sense of "trans-latio," the "bringing across" of its meaning from one place, time, or situation to another. Conversely, one may think of "translation" as a way that a poet reaches into another time, place, and language to find a way of rendering his own thought and feeling. Hence the Latin-derived word "translation" is close in meaning to the Greek-derived word "metaphor."

If Surrey's lyrics are "translated," using Petrarchan style, imagery, and verse form to create a vehicle within which his meaning is carried, they must also be understood as "occasional," that is, closely adjusted to an immediate situation. If a "translation" carries a meaning from someplace, it also carries it to someplace. Surrey's "translations" carefully register his own position, in terms of gender and social status and in terms of incidents in his life and the lives of those around him. These references are more hinting than direct in the amorous poems, placing the modern reader in the position of an outsider in a love game where Surrey's own friends would alone know who loves whom.

The personal resonances are most difficult to trace in Surrey's direct translations from the Bible and from Vergil's *Aeneid.* His biblical translations are principally from the *Penitential Psalms* and from *Ecclesiastes,* both texts that were widely used in his culture as vehicles for meditation. Hence the bringing across of their meaning into English is more a collective than a personal act. From the *Aeneid* Surrey chooses not the epic portions about the founding of Rome, but the tragic sections from books 2 and 4 in which Aeneas describes the destruction of Troy and the story of Aeneas and Dido, culminating in her suicide when he leaves her. Though stylistically different from the Petrarchan poems—partly indebted to Gavin Douglas*—they are alike in showing how historical action resonates as personal sorrow.

In the lyrics referring to Surrey's imprisonments, the biographical references are more overt, as in ''London, hast thou accused me / Of breach of laws, the root of strife?'' Exemplary is one of the poems from his 1537 imprisonment at Windsor:

So cruel prison how could betide, alas,
As proud Windsor, where I in lust and joy,
With a king's son, my childish years did pass
In greater feast than Priam's sons of Troy?

Here Surrey describes the sorrow of his immediate situation and contrasts it to a happier past at Windsor when he was the companion of Henry Fitzroy. He then links their situation to that of the Trojan princes before the fall of the city. Like Aeneas in Book 2 of Vergil's poem, Surrey finds himself in an emotional bondage where the ''remembrance of the greater grief'' overwhelms the present.

Surrey's masterworks are his epitaphs, especially those on Sir Thomas Wyatt. Surrey brings together all of the elements of his other verse—the language of classical military heroism, the language of sorrow from the *Psalms*, the language of loss from the Petrarchan sonnet—to praise Wyatt, analyze his own inner torment, and rage at the corruption of his society and his king himself. Jonathan Crewe has aptly found in these poems a ''suicidal poetics'' by which Surrey brought together all the psychological, social, and cultural elements that he could not control elsewhere and that in the end destroyed him.

CRITICAL RECEPTION

In the sixteenth century, Surrey was regarded as the finest poet in English after Chaucer and before Sidney. If his reputation stands not quite so high in the twentieth century, he nonetheless is clearly second only to Sir Thomas Wyatt among the poets of the age of Henry VIII. He published his work primarily through manuscript circulation rather than through the new technology of print, and most of his poems initially survived in a few manuscript collections assembled by his family and immediate friends. When Surrey's poems were printed in 1557 by Richard Tottel in his famous *Miscellany*, they were retitled and frequently rewritten in order to explain their occasions (sometimes invented occasions) to help a wider audience, and their meaning was often titled away from the particular toward the general. Tottel's reproduction of Surrey is best understood not as a piece of bad editing but as another ''translation,'' in which the poems are carried from the aristocratic milieu of the court to the milieu of the gentry and the commercial class of London.

Surrey was celebrated by the Elizabethans primarily as a lyricist and valued for the dignity that his social class gave to poetry itself. (Indeed, Surrey is the highest-ranking English aristocrat ever to be a significant literary figure.) In the *Defence of Poesy* (c. 1581), Sir Philip Sidney* praises ''in the Earl of Surrey's lyrics many things tasting of a noble birth, and worthy of a noble mind.'' Thomas Nashe* creates a fictional account of a journey through Europe as Surrey's servant in *The Unfortunate Traveler* (1594). Surrey is here an embodiment of courtly idealism in all its heroic extravagance and absurdity. He is too noble to actually seduce a willing lady and always ''more in love with his curious-forming fancy,'' for ''truth it is, many become passionate lovers only to win praise to their wits.''

In the nineteenth and twentieth centuries, Surrey's lyrics have been given a minor but important place in the perfecting of modern English verse forms. In a sort of nationalist poetic relay race, Chaucer runs the first leg in his supposed primitive but creative fashion. Wyatt moves us from middle English to modern English, though still in a ''rough,'' natural form. Surrey smooths out modern language, making it fit the sophisticated and polished forms of the Continental Renaissance. Wyatt is thus the poet of feeling, and Surrey the poet of form. The anchor leg is run by one's favorite Elizabethan: Shakespeare, Sidney, or Spenser, all of whom bring English lyric to perfection by creating a perfect balance of feeling and form. The poetic race is run on the same course where one can trace the development of the English language and the rise of the English nation-state to a position where they can bid for world domination.

Surrey's *Aeneid* had a similar reception. The translation of the classics into the vernacular languages of Northern and Western Europe in many ways corresponds to the transfer of power, from Rome to the nation-states of early modern Europe and finally to the world powers of the twentieth century. By his happy choice of unrhymed iambic pentameter to render the Latin dactylic hexameters of the *Aeneid*, Surrey translates the high poetic form of the Roman Empire into the form that Shakespeare will use. Hence Surrey, with his resounding blank verse, is unwitting grandfather to the national poet.

These nationalistic appropriations of Surrey's poetry have accounted for some of the features of his verse, but by no means all. Surrey's reputation as a formalist caused him to be held in low esteem by the new critics, who preferred Wyatt. The class and nationalist dimensions of his verse, however, are readily compatible with the themes of new historicism. But the lyrics and translations have generally received less attention in recent years than have the epitaphs, especially those on Wyatt. Their psychological brooding and scarcely concealed bitterness stand in stark contrast to the usual image of Surrey as a superficial versifier—they are, in effect, more like the works of Wyatt himself.

BIBLIOGRAPHY

Works by Henry Howard, Earl of Surrey

The Aeneid of Henry Howard Earl of Surrey. Ed. Florence H. Ridley, Berkeley: University of California Press, 1963.

The Arundel Harington Manuscript of Tudor Poetry. 2 vols. Ed. Ruth Hughey. Columbus: Ohio State University Press, 1960.

Henry Howard, Earl of Surrey: Poems. Ed. Emrys Jones. Oxford: Clarendon Press, 1964.

The Poems of Henry Howard Earl of Surrey. Ed. F. M. Padelford. Seattle: University of Washington Press, 1928.

Tottel's Miscellany (1557–1587). 2 vols. Ed. Hyder E. Rollins. Cambridge: Harvard University Press, 1929–30.

The Works of Henry Howard, Earl of Surrey, and of Sir Thomas Wyatt the Elder. 2 vols. Ed. G. F. Nott. London: Longman, 1815.

Studies of Henry Howard, Earl of Surrey

Casady, Edwin. *Henry Howard, Earl of Surrey*. New York: MLA, 1938.

Crewe, Jonathan. *Trials of Authorship: Anterior Forms and Poetic Reconstruction from Wyatt to Shakespeare*. Berkeley: University of California Press, 1990.

Jentoft, C. W. *Sir Thomas Wyatt and Henry Howard, Earl of Surrey: A Reference Guide*. Boston: G. K. Hall, 1980.

———. ''Surrey's Five Elegies: Rhetoric, Structure, and the Poetry of Praise.'' *PMLA* 91 (1976): 23–32.

Lever, J. W. *The Elizabethan Love Sonnet*. London: Methuen, 1956.

Lewis, C. S. *English Literature in the Sixteenth Century, excluding Drama*. Oxford: Clarendon Press, 1954.

Mason, H. A. *Humanism and Poetry in the Early Tudor Period*. London: Routledge, 1959.

Mumford, Ivy L. ''Petrarchism in Early Tudor England.'' *Italian Studies* 19 (1964): 56–63.

Peterson, Douglas. *The English Lyric from Wyatt to Donne*. Princeton: Princeton University Press, 1967.

Richardson, David A. ''Humanistic Intent in Surrey's *Aeneid*.'' *English Literary Renaissance* 6 (1976): 204–19.

Sessions, William A. *Henry Howard, Earl of Surrey*. Amherst: University of Massachusetts Press, 1986.

———. ''Surrey's Wyatt: Autumn 1542 and the New Poet.'' In *Reassessing the Henrician Era*, ed. Peter C. Herman. Urbana: University of Illinois Press, 1994.

Southall, Raymond. *The Courtly Maker: An Essay on the Poetry of Wyatt and His Contemporaries*. Oxford: Blackwell, 1964.

Stevens, J. E. *Music and Poetry in the Early Tudor Court*. London: Methuen, 1961.

Thompson, John. *The Founding of English Metre*. New York: Columbia University Press, 1961.

Thompson, Patricia. ''Wyatt and Surrey.'' In *English Poetry and Prose, 1540 to 1674*, ed. Christopher Ricks. London: Barrie and Jenkins, 1975.

Twombley, R. B. "Surrey's Fidelity to Wyatt." *Studies in Philology* 77 (1978): 376–87.

Zitner, S. P. "Truth and Mourning in a Sonnet by Surrey." *ELH* 50 (1983): 509–29.

CLARK HULSE

T

TORQUATO TASSO
(1544–1595)

BIOGRAPHY

Torquato Tasso, whose life was as troubled as it was glorious, was born in Sorrento in 1544. His father, Bernardo, an important poet in his own right, was secretary to the prince of Salerno, a great baron and leader of the opposition to Spanish rule in the kingdom of Naples. When Salerno was exiled in 1551, Bernardo followed, taking his son with him, but his patron's star was in decline, and Bernardo soon had to look elsewhere for support—first in Rome, then in Urbino, Venice, and finally in Mantua. The young Tasso went with him, acquiring an excellent education as well as the high literary and intellectual ambitions that were still fostered in those brilliant centers of Renaissance culture.

By 1560, when Tasso entered the University of Padua, he had already begun work on an epic about the first Crusade—a project that was ultimately to produce his masterpiece, *Jerusalem Delivered*—and in 1562 he published his first major poem: a chivalric romance, *Rinaldo*, which established him at the age of eighteen as a poet of promise. At Padua, Tasso first studied law, then changed to philosophy, a discipline for which he developed a taste that lasted the rest of his life, and it was probably at Padua that he wrote the *Discourses on the Art of Poetry*, his first effort to develop a coherent theory of literature, although the work was not published until 1587.

In 1565, Tasso left Padua without a degree and went to Ferrara to join the household of Cardinal Luigi d'Este, brother of Duke Alfonso. He had no regular duties except to bring honor to the Este by writing, and he did so copiously, producing numerous lyrics, orations for special occasions, a pastoral drama entitled *Aminta*, a prose account of a trip to France, the first two acts of a tragedy, and so forth. In 1575, moreover, he completed his great project, the *Jerusalem Delivered*, which was eagerly awaited by a large audience throughout Italy, especially by Duke Alfonso, whose service he had entered in 1572 and whose family the poem celebrated. Before he would publish, however, Tasso insisted on having the poem reviewed by five eminent critics, whose opinion he wanted not only about the poem's literary qualities but also about its theological and political orthodoxy.

It was a backbiting and hypercritical age, its tensions exacerbated by currents of severe piety promoted by the Counter Reformation, and the critics provided little reassurance. Tasso soon found himself embroiled in exhausting debates over a multitude of details. He responded to the criticisms in long and carefully argued letters, agreeing to some changes but resisting others, and he produced a prose "Allegory" to be published with the poem emphasizing its edifying and orthodox purposes; but the debates continued, and in the end, Tasso seems to have suffered a nervous breakdown. The facts remain obscure. What we know or can reasonably surmise is that he grew quarrelsome and suspicious at court, on one occasion even coming to blows, that he sought to prevent or counter his enemies' accusations by going to the Inquisition of his own accord to confess, and that in 1577 he tried to stab a servant whom he suspected of spying on him (an episode that gave rise to the legend, celebrated in Goethe's *Tasso*, of his love affair with Alfonso's sister, Lucrezia).

Diagnosed as suffering from melancholy after this last episode, Tasso was placed under guard, and although he managed to escape from Ferrara during the summer of 1577, he left the precious manuscript of *Jerusalem Delivered* behind. He spent the next two years wandering from one refuge to another, seeking in vain the return of his poem. In 1579 he visited Ferrara, hoping for a reconciliation with Alfonso, but the duke was preoccupied with the festivities surrounding his marriage to Margherita Gonzaga, and Tasso went neglected. Moreover, the manuscript was not forthcoming, and Tasso's morbid fears and anger overwhelmed him. He burst out in denunciations of Alfonso in the palace itself and had to be removed by force. Taken to the nearby hospital of Sant'Anna, he was chained as a madman. Although the chains were soon removed, his imprisonment lasted seven years.

The extraordinary length of this imprisonment has never been satisfactorily explained. Tasso continued to suffer periods of emotional instability in Sant'Anna, but the testimony of his many visitors and the evidence of his literary activity indicate that he was no mere madman. Perhaps the old notion that Alfonso was motivated by some hidden fear or animosity is true; given the current state of our knowledge, it is impossible to say. In any case, from prison Tasso conducted a voluminous and learned correspondence on many subjects;

he returned to revising the *Jerusalem Delivered*, which was restored to him and which he finally agreed to publish, together with the "Allegory," in 1581; he continued to write prolifically in shorter, lyric forms; he contributed two seriously argued pamphlets to the great literary quarrel of the mid-1580s over the relative merits of his own epic and Ariosto's *Orlando Furioso*; and he produced eighteen dialogues, many of them lengthy and complex, as well as a *Discourse on the Art of the Dialogue*. At last, in 1586, for reasons that remain as mysterious as the reasons for holding him, Alfonso released him into the custody of Vincenzo Gonzaga, heir apparent to the duchy of Mantua.

Tasso's last years were ones of continued productivity and restless wandering. Mantua, Florence, Rome, and Naples were the centers to which he gravitated without ever stopping for long. He finished the tragedy *Il Re Torrismondo* (King Torrismondo), which he had begun before his imprisonment in Ferarra, and composed a major new religious poem, *The Seven Days of the Created World*, as well as other works in verse and prose, more dialogues, and another theoretical treatise, the *Discourses on the Heroic Poem*. His major project, however, was a revision of the *Jerusalem Delivered* along lines that would make it more consistent with Tridentine theology, with history and geography, and with the epic practice of Homer and Virgil. The result, published in 1593 with a new title, *Jerusalem Conquered*, and dedicated to a new patron, Cinzio Aldobrandini, nephew of Pope Clement VIII, has never supplanted the earlier version in critical favor or in popularity. In 1595, Tasso died in the Monastery of Sant' Onofrio in Rome.

MAJOR WORKS AND THEMES

Tasso's work reflects in varying ways the two dominant elements of his artistic personality: intense, emotional sensuousness, on one hand, and equally intense moral and intellectual seriousness; on the other. The second of these elements has sometimes been neglected or underestimated, but his distinctive achievement cannot be grasped without due attention to both. In his greatest work, sensuousness, moral earnestness, and intellect combine in remarkable and interesting ways, often full of tension. On one hand, Tasso's art is informed by an impulse to impose coherence and order on the world; on the other hand, his overall vision is never simple. Subtle irony often colors the earnestness and melancholy that are his characteristic tones.

Public opinion since the sixteenth century has been right in judging *Jerusalem Delivered* to be Tasso's masterpiece. It is the work that gives fullest scope to his talent. In contrast—and in spite of what was apparently Tasso's own view—*Jerusalem Conquered* is a diminished thing. Love and war are *Jerusalem Delivered*'s great themes, and the poem presents as rich and complex an account of both as Tasso deemed consistent with epic dignity. In practice, this meant greatly expanding the range of his classical models, Homer and Virgil, while eliminating the grotesque, comic, and supposedly morally dubious elements of his sixteenth-century rival Ariosto and subjecting everything to the test of a higher, specifically Christian vision. So for Rinaldo, the poem's Achilles, love is not merely a brief prelude to heroic wrath but an extended escape from heroic virtue in the erotic paradise of the beautiful witch Armida, which is as beautifully and seductively described as any paradise in Ariosto. At the same time, Tasso firmly rejects the moral uncertainty that pervades the *Orlando Furioso*. Beautiful though it is, Armida's garden is evil because it distracts Rinaldo from heroic duty, specifically the heroic duty of Christian warfare, which is a higher thing than merely human desire. Thus, the Christian hero Tancredi can never consummate his love for the pagan heroine Clorinda. Rather, he must kill her (albeit unwittingly) in heroic combat and baptize her as she dies.

Jerusalem Delivered celebrates a Crusade, and its battle scenes include some of Tasso's finest writing. He is especially good at combining violent action with delicate psychological analysis. The combat between Tancredi and Clorinda with its profound mixture of eroticism, wrath, violence, and religion is famous, but there are many other heroic passages of comparable subtlety and force. The view expressed by some critics that Tasso's heart is not in the specifically heroic action is simplistic. Like Virgil, Tasso expresses the melancholy of warfare, but his celebration of Christian heroism, while certainly complex, is also sincere and poetically convincing. The last three cantos, describing the final battle for Jerusalem, are among the most exciting and successful in the genre.

Tasso composed *Jerusalem Delivered*—all twenty books—in the ottava rima stanzas prescribed by tradition for the sixteenth-century Italian heroic poem. In the *Aminta*, written in the early 1570s while he was working on his epic, he employed a much freer verse to celebrate the freer love of the fictive, pastoral world or the golden age—a pure, creative force of nature untrammeled by heroic duty or any other civilized constraints. That this love is as impossible as it is beautiful Tasso makes clear through the irony that throughout the poem balances the lyric enthusiasm. Against the young lovers, Aminta and Silvia, Tasso plays off the older Tirsi and Dafne, who remind us of the real world and the fact that young love provides at best a fleeting refuge from its sorrows.

Combining the fatalism of classical tragedy with the elaborate plot of a medieval romance, *Il Re Torrismondo*, which Tasso began in the 1570s but did not complete until after his release from Sant' Anna, offers a vision of love unredeemed by either pastoral imagination or higher Christian vision. Torrismondo and Alvida's incestuous love is an emblem of stark human misery, of a destructive fate that the lovers cannot understand and cannot resist. Although the play has never been popular, it contains some powerful poetry and, taken as a whole, constitutes a compellingly grim vision of a world with no exits, a world devoid of religious or heroic consolation.

By comparison with *Jerusalem Delivered, Aminta*, or *Torrismondo*, Tasso's lyrics may seem slight and artificial. With the exception of a few short autobiographical and religious poems, the lyrics ring the changes on the well-worn erotic themes of the Renaissance, offering little of substance that is original.

What makes them stand out from the mass of sonnets, madrigals, and other *rime* of the period is the consummate skill of their versification—especially their much admired verbal inventiveness and their musicality, qualities that have made them inspirations to composers looking for texts to turn into song and also to poets not only in Italy but throughout Europe.

The most ambitious poem of Tasso's final years, *The Seven Days of the Created World*, is a long meditation on God's creation in both its pristine and its fallen states, on nature, man, and God, and on God's ways to man and man's need for grace. Designed as a kind of *summa theologica* organizing Tasso's vast learning into a complex demonstration of piety, the poem impresses but fails to come to life except now and then in isolated passages of fanciful learning or religious feeling. The central themes of his great poetry—love and war—are absent, and the results seem more an intellectual exercise than an expression of his deepest imaginative impulses.

The works in which Tasso displays his strictly philosophical interests most impressively are his treatises on poetic theory and his dialogues. In the former—the *Discourses on the Poetic Art*, printed in 1587 but written much earlier, and the *Discourses on the Heroic Poem*, probably begun in the late 1580s and published in 1594—Tasso works out a theory of poetry that is both interesting in itself and a helpful guide to his own practice. The later treatise is essentially an expansion of the earlier, ampler in argument and illustration but also more qualified and more cautious, more questioning, evidence of his restless taste for philosophy in the root sense: pursuit of truth. The same questioning spirit informs the twenty-six dialogues, most of which were written in the sixteen years from his incarceration in Sant' Anna (1579) to his death (1595). On a wide variety of subjects—beauty, the court, fathers, emblems—they give broader scope than any of Tasso's other works to his capacity for intellectual play, humor, and irony.

CRITICAL RECEPTION

As early as the 1570s, as *Rinaldo, Aminta*, the early lyrics, and parts of *Jerusalem Delivered* circulating in manuscript become known, Tasso was recognized, not only in Italy but throughout Europe, as one of the foremost poets of the age. In the 1580s a fierce debate arose in Italy over the respective merits of Tasso's epic and Ariosto's *Orlando Furioso*, the latter being praised for its inventiveness and variety, its liveliness, its innovation, its modernity, and the former for its clear and unified structure, its moral and religious seriousness, its respect for tradition, its conformity to ancient models.

Outside Italy, the debate was less important than its clear implication that Tasso had already, in his own lifetime, been elevated to the status of a classic. In England, recognition of this status was immediate. Tradition has it that Queen Elizabeth* committed passages of *Jerusalem Delivered* to memory and expressed envy for the Este because they had such a poet to glorify their dynasty.

In *Defense of Poetry*, Sir Philip Sidney* makes use of Tasso's Rinaldo to exemplify the way in which an epic poet teaches virtue. Tasso's lyrics were well known and imitated by such poets as Edmund Spenser* and Samuel Daniel,* and Tasso is exalted to the company of Homer, Virgil, and Ariosto in the "Letter to Ralegh" that Spenser published with the first three books of *The Faerie Queene* in 1590. Richard Carew's translation of the first five cantos of *Jerusalem Delivered* appeared in 1594. Edward Fairfax's* complete version, a minor classic in its own right, appeared in 1600.

In the seventeenth century, the rise of neoclassicism, with its emphasis on rules and reason, produced a reaction against certain features of *Jerusalem Delivered*, for example, its use of the supernatural and its mingling of lyric and epic style. The poem's general popularity, however, endured. Poets like Milton and Dryden expressed their admiration. Tasso's fame, moreover, fortified in the late eighteenth century by romantic interest in him as a type of suffering genius, continued unshaken well into the nineteenth century.

Today, however, his reputation has diminished. Even in Italy, he is little read outside the universities, and there he has become primarily a subject for academic analysis, for erudite construction and deconstruction of various kinds, rather than a model of excellence and a source of inspiration. The ironic result is that while scholarship on him accumulates, serious interest in the things that he took seriously has been on the wane. His deepest theological, philosophical, moral, and artistic concerns—his celebration of Christian heroism, his subordination of eros to duty, the conservatism of his literary theory, and so on—are taken to be out-of-date. The modern and postmodern sensibility, with its skepticism and easy irony, finds Ariosto far more congenial than Tasso. In the late twentieth century, Tasso's view of the world runs against the grain, and even scholars who have studied him deeply tend to shy away from serious engagement with his weltanshauung. This neglect is understandable, but unfortunate, because as we moderns and postmoderns imply when we proclaim our love of diversity, we are often most in need of the things we find least congenial. Perhaps it could be said that Tasso reminds the modern world of an "other" that it wishes to forget but knows it should not.

BIBLIOGRAPHY

Works by Torquato Tasso

Aminta. 5th ed. Ed. Luigi Fasso. Florence: Samsoni, 1967.

Dialoghi. 3 vols. Ed. Ezio Raimondi. Florence: Samsoni, 1958.

Discorsi dell' arte poetica e del poema eroico. Ed. Luigi Poma. Bari: Laterza, 1964.

Gerusalemme conguistata. Ed. Luigi Bonfigli. Bari: Laterza, 1934.

Gerusalemme liberata. 2d ed. 2 vols. Ed. Bruno Maier. Milan: Biblioteca Universale Rizzoli, 1988.

Lettere. 5 vols. Ed. Cesare Guasti. Florence: Le Monnier, 1852–55.

Opere. 5 vols. Ed. Bruno Maier. Milan: Rizzoli, 1963.

Opere di Torquato Tasso. 33 vols. Ed. Giovanni Rosini. Pisa: Capurro, 1821–32.

Poesie. Ed. Francesco Flora. Milan: Ricciardi, 1952.
Prose. Ed. Ettore Mazzali. Milan: Ricciardi, 1959.
Rime. 4 vols. Ed. Angelo Solerti. Bologna: Romagnoli-dall'Acqua, 1898–1902.
Le sette qiornate del mondo creato. Ed. Giorgio Petrocchi. Florence: Le Monnier, 1951.

Selected Translations

Aminta. Trans. Augustine Mathews (seventeenth century). In *Three Renaissance Pastorals*, ed. Elizabeth Story Donno. Binghamton: Medieval and Renaissance Texts and Studies, 1993.
Creation of the World. Trans. Joseph Tusiani. Binghamton: Medieval and Renaissance Texts and Studies, 1982.
Discourses on the Heroic Poem. Trans. Mariella Cavalchini and Irene Samuel. Oxford: Oxford University Press, 1973.
Jerusalem Delivered. Trans. Edward Fairfax. New York: Capricorn Books, n.d.
Jerusalem Delivered. Trans. Ralph Nash. Detroit: Wayne State University Press, 1987.
Tasso's Dialogues. Trans. Carnes Lord and Dain A. Trafton. Berkeley: University of California Press, 1982.

Studies of Torquato Tasso

Brand, C. P. *Torquato Tasso*. Cambridge: Cambridge University Press, 1965.
Donadoni, Eugenio. *Torquato Tasso*. 1920–21. Florence: La Nuova Italia, 1936.
Getto, Giovanni. *Interpretazione del Tasso*. Naples: Edizione scientifiche italiane, 1951.
Leo, Ulrich. *Torquato Tasso: Studien sur Vorqeschichte des Secentismo*. Bern: Francke, 1951.
Pittorru, Fabio. *Torquato Tasso*. Milan: Bompiani, 1982.
Solerti, Angelo. *Vita di Torquato Tasso*. 2 vols. Turin: Loescher, 1895.
Torquato Tasso. Ed. Comitato ferrarese per le celebrazioni di Torquato Tasso. Milan: Marzorati, 1957.
Ulivi, Ferruccio. *Torquato Tasso: l'anima e l'avventura: romanzo*. Casale Monferrato: Edizioni Piemme, 1995.

DAIN A. TRAFTON

WILLIAM TYNDALE (William Tindall, William Hutchins, William Huchyns, William Hychyns)
(c. 1494–1536)

BIOGRAPHY

While his exact parentage is not known, it is known that William Tyndale belonged to that long line of Tyndales (a.k.a. Hutchins), merchants, cloth makers, and landowners who came out of the north and settled in Gloucestershire, a region well known for its associations with Lollardy and the suppressed Wycliffe Bible. He received his B.A. at Oxford on 4 July 1512 (as William Hychyns), was approved to acquire his M.A. on 26 June 1515, and finally received his M.A. on 2 July 1515, also at Oxford, all from Magdalen Hall. While at Oxford, he was scornful of the fact that one could not undertake the study of theology until both the B.A. and M.A. courses were completed, so that, as he would write later, ''armed with false principles . . . he is clean shut out of the understanding of scriptures'' (*The Practice of Prelates*). Whether his years at Oxford would have retained the spirit of John Colet's* call to the literal meaning of Scriptures is a matter of conjecture, as is the influence of the Lutherans during the 1520s at Cambridge, where Tyndale apparently spent the years 1517–21. Yet it is clear that during these years he became deeply affected by Erasmus'* *Novum Instrumentum*, the Greek New Testament with a facing Latin translation, and by 1524 sought support from the bishop of London, Cuthbert Tunstall, for a translation of Erasmus' text into English. During this time he translated Erasmus' *Enchiridion* (possibly the translation published by Wynkyn de Worde in 1533) as well as one or more orations by Isocrates, which he apparently used to establish his credentials as a translator from the Greek. Nonetheless, he could find no support for translating the Scriptures into English, and by the spring of 1524 he left for Europe.

In 1525, he was on the point of being arrested by the Cologne authorities in the midst of printing what is now known as the *Cologne Matthew* (largely a translation of Luther's *September Bible* with Tyndale's emendations) at Peter Quentell's and fled to Worms, where a revised *New Testament* based upon Erasmus' Greek text was published in 1526 at Peter Schoeffer's. Originally he did not append his name as translator because ''I followed the counsel of Christ, which exhorteth men (Matt. vi) to do their good deeds secretly, and to be content with the conscience of well-doing, and that God seeth us; and patiently to abide the reward of the last day, which Christ hath purchased for us.'' After he was falsely implicated in some scurrilous antipapist poetry written by his assistant William Roye, he dissociated himself from Roye, and, starting with *A Compendious Introduction to Romans* printed in 1526, he began to attach his name to his work. (For Tyndale's version of this incident, see his preface to *The Parable of the Wicked Mammom.*)

By 1528, he was in Antwerp, where, aside from short trips to Germany, he would remain until his betrayal at the hands of Henry Phillips in 1535. During this time he not only translated the *Pentateuch* (the first five books of the Old Testament) from Hebrew (1530) and a revised New Testament (1534, 1535) but also produced those works, such as *The Parable of the Wicked Mammom, The Obedience of a Christian Man*, and *The Answer to More*, upon which his reputation as a polemicist rests. A rapprochement between Tyndale and Henry VIII almost occurred after Anne Boleyn presented the king with Tyndale's *Obedience of a Christian Man.* With Cromwell* as go-between, Henry agreed to let Tyndale return to England if he would write no more; Tyndale agreed that if the king would allow an English translation of the Bible, he would write no more, regardless of who translated it; there was no further movement on either side during Tyndale's life. On or near 21 May 1535, he was arrested for heresy against the Court at Brussels (and as such against the Holy Roman Emperor himself) and was taken to Vilvorde Castle (between Brussels and Louvain), where he was kept prisoner for one year and 135 days. In his only surviving letter from prison, he asks only for a warmer coat for the winter and his Hebrew Bible, grammar, and dictionary. Whether he received them will never be known (his books were confiscated and used to pay for his stay in prison), but in August 1536 he was convicted of heresy and was degraded from the priesthood. In early October 1536 (commemorated the sixth) he was strangled at the stake and burned. His last words were, "Lord! Open the king of England's eyes!"

MAJOR WORKS AND THEMES

While Tyndale is today seen as a polemicist, propagandist, political reformer, moralist, theologian, historian, and enemy of the institutions of the church, it is clear that he saw himself as first and foremost a translator, so much so that his response to reports that his New Testament was being burned was reportedly, "Burn my books, burn me." A polyglot, Tyndale knew Latin, Greek, German, French, Hebrew, Spanish, Italian, and probably some other languages including Welsh, and his linguistic and rhetorical abilities shine through his translations. Throughout his life he endeavored to present an English Scripture that would more accurately represent the true voice of Christ and the apostles, a Scripture that would refer inwardly to itself and not outwardly to the secondary structures with which the medieval church had laden it. That he was conscious that he was undercutting a thousand years of church practice can hardly be denied, but his faith in the Greek testament (and later the Hebrew Old Testament) gave him the assurance that the church, not himself, was heretical. Tyndale's translations, which ultimately would supply most of the Matthew Bible as well as the Authorized (King James) Bible, established the linguistic and doctrinal base for English readers of the Bible for almost five centuries.

For Tyndale to reclaim the Bible as God's Word spoken to mankind, it was first necessary to silence the voices that had drowned out that word, and in *The Obedience of a Christian Man* (Antwerp, 1528), Tyndale attacked the kinds of readings that the "modern theologians" whom Erasmus so disliked had institutionalized over the past few centuries. In place of the traditional "four senses, the literal, tropological, allegorical, and anagogical," Tyndale wanted to return the literal sense to primacy: "The literal sense is become nothing at all, for the pope hath taken it clean away, and hath made it his possession. He hath partly locked it up with the false and counterfeited keys of his traditions, ceremonies, and feigned lies; and partly driveth men from it with violence of sword: for no man dare abide by the literal sense of the text, but under a protestation, 'If it shall please the pope' " (303). For Tyndale, the "four senses" are not four at all, but two (for "[t]ropological and anagogical are terms of their own feigning, and altogether unnecessary. For they are but allegories, both two of them, and this word allegory comprehendeth them both, and is enough" [303]), and of those two, only the literal is genuine: "Thou shalt understand . . . that the scripture hath but one sense, which is the literal sense. And that literal sense is the root and ground of all, and the anchor that never faileth, whereunto if thou cleave, thou canst never err or go out of the way. And if thou leave the literal sense thou canst not but go out of the way'' (303). For Tyndale, the literal sense is the sense that God intended, and all else is ''no sense of the scripture, but free things beside the scripture'' (304).

Tyndale is certainly not advocating a plain style here: for him, the literal sense comprehends all of the images used in the Bible, but their intended significance is central: ''[T]he scripture useth proverbs, similitudes, riddles, or allegories, as all other speeches do; but that which the proverb, similitude, riddle, or allegory signifieth, is ever the literal sense, which thou must seek out diligently'' (304). The literal sense comes from God; all others come from man. While aware of the rhetorical virtues of allegory, metaphor, and simile, Tyndale nevertheless makes it clear that we ought to be very careful in employing and interpreting them: ''The greatest cause of which captivity [under antichrist the pope] and the decay of faith, and this blindness wherein we now are, sprang first of allegories. For Origin and the doctors of his time drew all the scripture unto allegories: whose ensample they that came after followed so long, till that they at last forgot the order and process of the text, supposing that the scripture served but to feign allegories upon. . . . Then came our sophisters with their analogical and chopological sense, and with an antitheme of half an inch, out of which some of them will draw a thread of nine days long'' (307). For ''our sophisters,'' the Scripture serves merely as an occasion for them to spin out their chop-logic conclusions until all are trapped within their web of deceit; for Christ's true followers, the Scripture must serve as the means by which we hear Christ's voice.

In what we may take as a paradigmatic example of his own writing. Tyndale tried to convey what that voice was saying clearly yet powerfully, as when he suggests in his *Parable of the Wicked Mammon* that to have one's eye on a goal is to lose the reward one seeks: ''Christ's blood hath purchased life for us, and hath made us the heirs of God; so that heaven cometh by Christ's blood. If thou wouldst obtain heaven with the merits and deservings of thine own works, so didst thou wrong, yea, and shamedst, the blood of Christ; and unto thee were Christ dead in vain. Now is the true believer heir of God by Christ's deservings; yea, and in Christ was predestinate, and ordained unto eternal life, before the world began. And when the gospel is preached unto us, we believe the mercy of God; and in believing we receive the Spirit of God, which is the earnest of everlasting life, and we are in eternal life already, and feel already in our hearts the sweetness thereof, and are overcome with the kindness of God and Christ; and therefore love the will of God, and of love are ready to work freely; and not to obtain that which is given to us freely and whereof we are heirs already. . . . For they that look unto the reward, are slow, false, subtle and crafty workers, and love the reward more than the work, yea hate the labour; yea, hate God which commandeth the labour; and are weary both of the commandment, and also of the commander; and work with tediousness. But he that worketh of pure love, without seeking of reward, worketh truly'' (65). In this exposition of Luke 16, Tyndale succeeds in conveying what he takes to be the core of the gospel message—salvation is not by works but by Christ's blood, shed for those who are called to belief—in simple yet rhetorically powerful rhythms that are aimed at stirring the mind and emotions of the reader while they remind that reader of the meaning of the Christian faith.

What was radical about Tyndale can, in a sense, be easily overlooked for often it is as much for what he did not say as for what he said that his work is noteworthy. For example, the 1526 Worms New Testament presented in English for the first time the complete New Testament stripped bare of all allegorizing text, written in a language natural to the average Englishman or Englishwoman and in a format small enough to carry around and be read. In the expanded prologue to the Cologne Matthew, which Tyndale had separately printed in 1531 as *The Pathway to the Scriptures*, he affirmed three principles: that the law and the gospel may never be separate; that our nature is fallen, but through grace we are redeemed; and that the work of Christ is sufficient for our salvation. To those hundreds and thousands of Londoners and south and east Englanders who were able to possess one of Tyndale's New Testaments before they were confiscated and burned, the news would be transformative (as it clearly was for James Bainham; cf. Greenblatt, 74–84). For as Daniell writes, "If Tyndale is saying in print that the body of Christ is everyone, without distinction—no laity, no priests, no bishop, no pope, if everyone is equal in Christ—then the gathering of Christians together is a congregation of equals, not a church of divisions and hierarchies, where priest and bishop and pope are essential. So Tyndale translated the Greek New Testament word *eklesia* as 'congregation.' Philologically, he was correct: Erasmus, no less, had done the same before him. Theologically he was correct, too, as the New Testament understands the gathering of believers as a congregation of equals in the Kingdom of Heaven" (122).

CRITICAL RECEPTION

Tyndale wrote in the prologue to the Cologne Matthew: "I have here translated (brethren and sisters most dear and tenderly beloved in Christ) the New Testament for your spiritual edifying, consolation, and solace: Exhorting instantly and beseeching those that are better seen in the tongues than I, and that have higher gifts of grace to interpret the sense of the scripture and meaning of the spirit, than I, to consider and ponder my labour, and that with the spirit of meekness. And if they perceive in any places that I have not attained the very sense of the tongue, or meaning of the scripture, or have not given the right English word, that they put to their hands to amend it, remembering that so is their duty to do. For we have not received gifts of god for ourselves only, or for to hide them, but for to bestow them unto the honouring of god and christ, and edifying of the congregation, which is the body of christ."

As Daniell notes, it is difficult for a late twentieth-century audience to understand how such mild words could have been "countered by the most vicious burnings, of books and men and women'' (121). Yet the immediate reception of Tyndale's works was the extremes of faithful reception and attacks for heresy. Among the earliest who worked against Tyndale was Sir Thomas More,* who accused Tyndale of 5,000 heresies and whose initial ''answer'' filled four books. Wolsey and More together would see that hundreds of Tyndale's books were collected and burned. Henry VIII, while sidestepping the issue of an English Bible, recommended to all his fellow monarchs *The Obedience of a Christian Man* for Tyndale's argument in support of the divine right of monarchs (although he most likely ignored Tyndale's proviso in doing so: ''As God maketh the King head over his realm, even so giveth he him commandment to execute the laws upon all men indifferently. For the law is God's, and not the King's. The King is but a servant, to execute the law of God, and not to rule after his own imagination'' [334]). After his death it would take less than a year for Henry to authorize an English Bible for which Tyndale's translation would be the mainstay (as it would continue to be until the revisions in the latter part of the twentieth century).

Tyndale, of course, figures as one of Foxe's martyrs, but the best testimony to his reputation in the sixteenth century can be seen in the afterlives of his books. His complete works were republished in 1573; there were six posthumous editions of *The Obedience of a Christian Man* and six of *The Parable of the Wicked Mammon.* All told at least two dozen separate printings of various of his works were issued by various English printers between his death and the end of the sixteenth century. In the nineteenth century the Parker Society republished his works; these remain the most accessible source of his words. Throughout most of the twentieth century, Tyndale has been viewed as a minor polemicist, but with the quincentenary republication of both his Old and New Testaments and David Daniell's major new biography, his importance to Tudor Reformation history should be firmly reestablished.

BIBLIOGRAPHY

Works by William Tyndale

The Beginning of the New Testament Translated by William Tyndale 1525. Facsimile of the Unique Fragment of the Uncompleted Cologne Edition. Ed. A. W. Pollard. Oxford: Oxford University Press, 1926.

[*The New Testament.*] Worms, 1526.

A Compendius Introduction . . . unto the epistle of Paul to the Romans. Worms, 1526.

[*The Parable of the Wicked Mammon.*] Antwerp, 1528.

The Obedience of a Christian Man . . . Antwerp, 1528.

[*The Pentateuch.*] Antwerp, 1530.

The Practice of Prelates. Antwerp, 1530.

A Pathway to the Holy Scripture. Antwerp, 1530.

The Prophet Jonas . . . Antwerp, 1531.

An Answer to Sir Thomas More's Dialogue . . . Antwerp, 1531.

An Exposition of the First Epistle of St. John. Antwerp, 1531.

An Exposition upon the V, VI, VII Chapters of Matthew. Antwerp, 1533.

The New Testament. Antwerp, 1534.

The First Book of Moses called Genesis. Antwerp, 1534.

The New Testament. Antwerp, 1535.

The Testament of Master W. Tracie Esquire. Antwerp, 1535.

A Brief Declaration of the Sacraments. London, c. 1548.

Expositions and Notes on . . . The Holy Scriptures . . . together with The Practice of Prelates. Ed. H. Walker. Cambridge: Parker Society, 1848.

Doctrinal Treatises and Introduction to Different Portions of the Holy Scriptures. Ed. H. Walter. Cambridge: Parker Society, 1849.

An Answer to Sir Thomas More's Dialogue . . . Ed. H. Walker. Cambridge: Parker Society, 1850.

Tyndale's New Testament. Ed. David Daniell. New Haven, CT: Yale University Press, 1989. (Modern spelling edition.)

Tyndale's Old Testament. Ed. David Daniell. New Haven, CT: Yale University Press, 1992. (Modern spelling edition.)

Studies of William Tyndale

Daniell, David. *William Tyndale: A Biography*. New Haven, CT: Yale University Press, 1994.

Foxe, John. *The Actes and Monuments of John Foxe*. London: 1843–49.

Greenblatt, Stephen. *Renaissance Self-Fashioning: From More to Shakespeare*. Chicago: University of Chicago Press, 1980.

Lupton, L. *The History of the Geneva Bible, XVIIII, Part 1: Tyndale the Translator*. London, 1986.

———. *The History of the Geneva Bible, XIX, Part 2: Tyndale the Martyr*. London, 1987.

Mozley, J. F. *William Tyndale*. London, 1937.

O'Day, Rosemary. *The Debate on the English Reformation*. London: Methuen, 1986.

Smeeton, D. D. *Lollard Themes in the Reformation Theology of William Tyndale. Sixteenth Century Essays and Studies 6*. Ed. C. G. Nauert. Kirksville, MO: Sixteenth Century Journal Pubs., Inc., 1986.

SONJA HANSARD-WEINER AND ANDREW D. WEINER

V

POLYDORE VERGIL
(c. 1470–1555)

BIOGRAPHY

Polydore Vergil, Italian humanist and English historiographer, was born in Urbino around 1470 into a family with established ties to erudition and to the court of Urbino, patron of his father, Giorgio Virgilio. Although the details of Vergil's early life are few, we know that he was educated at Padua, possibly at Bologna. By the end of 1496 he had been ordained a priest, and soon after he entered the service of Pope Alexander VI. There his budding scholarly achievements—his edition of Perotti's *Cornucopiae latinae linguae* (1496), his *Proverbiorum libellus* (1498), and his *De inventoribus rerum* (1499)—likely drew the attention of Adriano Castellesi, for whom Vergil first traveled to England in 1502 as the subcollector of papal revenues. In England, Vergil was recognized at Henry VII's court, where he joined other learned Italians. Vergil mostly prospered in England, although he ran afoul of the exchange laws in 1504 and also had difficulties retaining his position as subcollector. He was rewarded with several preferments, receiving the living of Church Langston in 1503, prebends in Lincoln Cathedral, Hereford, and Oxgate in St. Paul's, and the archdeaconry of Wells in 1508. During these years he began researching the English past and, sometime before 1513, completed the first version of his *Anglica historia*. In 1515, however, he incurred Wolsey's ire and landed in the Tower, an act for which Wolsey would pay dearly in the historical portrait that Vergil handed down to generations of historians. Vergil was soon released, but he appears to have learned enough about the dangers of political involvement to avoid controversy, a lesson that enabled him to live in relative peace through the reigns of Henry VIII and his son and, most significantly, to weather the turbulence of the Reformation. Although he visited Italy several times in his life, he remained in England, unobtrusively bending with the political and religious winds, until his return to Urbino in 1553, where Vergil, scion of the Italian Renaissance and the ''Father of English History,'' as he has been called, died two years later.

MAJOR WORKS AND THEMES

While Vergil's role in Tudor historiography has now overshadowed his other accomplishments, his contemporary reputation was solidly grounded on two popular and largely original early works: *Proverbiorum libellus*, or *Adagia*, first published in 1498, which appeared in some twenty subsequent editions before 1550, and *De inventoribus rerum*, published in 1499, with an additional five books added in 1521 and over thirty editions printed by 1555. The *Proverbiorum libellus* was a didactic (literary and moral) collection of proverbs drawn from classical sources with commentary in good, sententious Latin. The book and the idea were immediately popular: Vergil engaged in a brief epistolary debate with Erasmus,* whose own *Adagia* appeared in 1500, over who originated the idea for such a collection. The *De inventoribus rerum*, described as one of the most popular books in the sixteenth century and used by Rabelais and Cervantes, offered scholars, writers, and the curious an encyclopedic, eclectic compilation of the origins of cultural productions drawn from an extensive body of medieval, contemporary, but chiefly classical sources. In it one might find the inventors of plays, books, magic, music, writing, mirrors, religious practices, and hair dying, which he attributes to Medea.

Vergil's most influential work in England, however, was his *Anglica historia*, a Latin narrative history begun at the instigation of Henry VII that recounted England's past from its origins, still wrapped in the myths handed down by Geoffrey of Monmouth, to the turbulent events of the fifteenth and early sixteenth century, which heralded the ascendance of the Tudor dynasty. First published in 1534 and wisely terminating with the events of Henry VII's reign, an edition expanded to include the years of Henry VIII's rule appeared in 1555. Vergil combined the perspective of an outsider with a humanist's critical awareness of sources, concern with causation, and emphasis on political biography to mold a wide range of sometimes conflicting sources into a national history of England. He is best remembered for daring to question the stories of Brutus and Arthur, cherished myths of the Tudors; yet he also laid the foundation for a dynastic view of history that often justifies, as much as describes, the rise of the Tudors. Although loosely ordered around the reigns of individual kings and eclectic in its treatment of causation, Vergil's history offered patterns of explanation and an argument to his more famous successors, Hall* and Holinshed,* who, like Vergil, sometimes used providence to explain the course of history. Vergil's moralizing resonates in the *Mirror for Magistrates* and in Tudor drama. While clearly breaking new ground in English historiography, in certain respects the *Anglica historia* advances historiography little beyond his *De inventoribus*, in which the origins of institutions and cultural practices are to be found in human, often mythological inventors. Vergil's classicism led him to focus primarily on the *res gestae*, the actions of influential men and their consequences, both practical and moral; but in so doing he created a history that was largely static: history always reflects the recurrent patterns of human behavior. Although Vergil's influence can be felt in the more sophisticated political histories of Hayward* and Bacon,* who eschewed his providentialism, the road to a modern English history begins in the work of antiquarians such as Camden and Selden and their successors in the seventeenth and eighteenth centuries.

CRITICAL RECEPTION

In *De inventoribus rerum*, Vergil argues that "the first office of an historiographer is to write no lye" and that the second is that "he shall conceal no truth for favour, displeasure or fear" (III.x), both difficult tasks for a historiographer subject to the pressures of the Tudor court. Although lately Vergil's reputation for being a "party hack" has been challenged, he did much to promote a Tudor view of history, vilifying Richard III and feeding Henry VIII's imperial dreams. Yet his sixteenth-century successors faulted him not for his bending slavishly to authority, but rather for his audacity in questioning England's national myths; as a papist and Italian, he was held in suspicion by patriots and Protestants such as Leland, Bale, and Foxe, who even accused him of covering his attack on Geoffrey by destroying historical evidence. But if he was criticized, his "most hostile detractors," Denys Hay argues, "found the *Anglica historia* indispensable." Hall and Holinshed often followed Vergil closely, and in Shakespeare's* intricate historical tapestries, one finds patterns originating with Vergil. His work continued to be viewed with suspicion by English historians until the nineteenth century, when he finally began to rise above the opprobrium of his critics and assume his proper role in the history of English historiography.

BIBLIOGRAPHY

Works by Polydore Vergil

Cornucopiae latinae linguae. Ed. Nicholas Perotti. Venice, 1496.

Proverbiorum libellus or *Adagia*. Venice, 1498.

De inventoribus rerum. Venice, 1499. Expanded edition, Basel, 1521.

Gildas . . . de calamitate, excidio et conquestu Britanniae. Antwerp, 1525.

Anglica historia. Basel, 1534, 1546, 1555 (includes events to 1538).

Studies of Polydore Vergil

Clough, C. H. "Federigo Veterani, Polydore Vergil's Anglica Historia, and Baldassare Castiglione's 'Epistola . . . ad Henricum Angliae regem,' " *English Historical Review* 82 (1967): 772–83.

Copenhaver, Brian P. "The Historiography of Discovery in the Renaissance: The Sources and Composition of Polydore Vergil's *De Inventoribus Rerum*, I–III." *Journal of the Warburg and Courtauld Institutes* 41 (1978): 192–214.

Ferguson, John. "Notes on the Work of Polydore Vergil, 'De inventoribus rerum.' " *Isis* 17 (1932): 71–93.

Freeman, Thomas, S. "From Catiline to Richard III: The Influence of Classical Histories on Polydore Vergil's *Anglica Historia*." In *Reconsidering the Renaissance: Papers from the Twenty-First Annual Conference*, ed. Mario Di Cesare. Binghamton: Medieval and Renaissance Texts and Studies, 1992.

Hanham, Alison. *Richard III and His Early Historians, 1483–1535*. Oxford: Clarendon Press, 1975.

Hay, Denys. *Polydore Vergil: Renaissance Historian and Man of Letters*. Oxford: Clarendon Press, 1952.

Koebner, Richard. " 'The Imperial Crown of the Realm': Henry VIII, Constantine the Great, and Polydore Vergil." *Bulletin of the Institute for Historical Research* 26 (1953): 29–52.

Levy, F. J. *Tudor Historical Thought*. San Marino, CA: Huntington Library, 1967.

Stegmann, Andre. "Le *De inventoribus rei christianae* de Polydore Vergil ou l'Erasmisme critique." *Colloquia Erasmiana Turonensia*. Ed. Jean-Claude Margolin. Toronto: University of Toronto Press, 1972. 2 vols. vol 1: 313–22.

ANDREW M. KIRK

W

THOMAS WILSON
(1523–1581)

BIOGRAPHY

Born poor in Lincolnshire, Thomas Wilson worked through Eton and Cambridge on charitable scholarship and work-study tutorials. In 1551 he published a treatise on dialectic, *The Rule of Reason*, dedicated to King Edward VI, and in 1553 *The Arte of Rhetoric*, dedicated to John Dudley, the young monarch's lord protector. Apparently seeking patronage among a nobility hostile to Mary Tudor, Wilson fled to the Continent when she became queen in 1553. After studying civil law at Padua and Ferrara, he returned to England upon Elizabeth's* coronation in 1558. He soon enjoyed a meteoric rise to high positions serving the Crown. In 1560 he published an augmented edition of *The Arte of Rhetoric*, which would undergo six more editions by 1585. Wilson was called to every session of Parliament from 1563 onward and was appointed ambassador to Portugal in 1567 and to the Netherlands in the 1570s. In 1572 he published a lengthy dialogue, *A Discourse upon Usury*, unfashionably condemning the widespread practice of lending money at high rates of interest. His oppositional stand cost him no royal support, for in 1577 he became secretary of the Privy Council, a post that he shared with Sir Francis Walsingham until his death in 1581.

MAJOR WORKS AND THEMES

The Rule of Reason, Conteinyng the Arte of Logique (1551) outlines a form of argumentation practiced in the schools since the twelfth century. Differing from systems of symbolic logic and syllogistic reasoning, it entails hair-splitting disputation and verbal controversy in which one speaker, the ''apposer,'' defends a proposition that another, the ''aunswerer,'' attacks. Unlike the broad public audience in rhetoric, the audience for this tightfisted logic consists of learned experts. Concerned with judgment and the invention of possible arguments, this art expresses the ''closed'' hand of truth, as opposed to rhetoric which expresses the ''open-hand'' of inquiry (see Howell).

The Arte of Rhetoric (1553, 1560) outlines more dynamic forms of argumentation calibrated for heterogeneous audiences. Teeming with illustrative examples, it surveys theories and practices explored by classical rhetoricians from Aristotle, Cicero, and Quintilian, to George of Trebizond, Melanchthon, and Erasmus* (see Conley, G. Kennedy, Vickers, and, for literary applications, W. Kennedy). Its usefulness superseded the earlier English rhetorics of Leonard Cox (*Art or Craft of Rhetoric*, 1524) and Richard Sherry (*Treatise of Schemes and Tropes*, 1550). Divided into three books, it systematically considers the processes of invention, or discovering topics for an argument; of disposition, or arranging it into a persuasive structure; and of elocution, or articulating it with stylistic flair.

Book 1 examines appropriate topics for three kinds of discourse: demonstrative rhetoric, which directs praise or blame toward specific persons or objects; deliberative rhetoric, which urges others to adopt a particular course of action; and judicial rhetoric, which seeks to prove or disprove charges brought against an individual. Here Wilson offers several examples for each type: an oration in praise of Henry Brandon, duke of Suffolk, one of the author's pupils (Medine ed., 57–59); another celebrating King David for defeating Goliath (61–64); a third commending royal justice (66–70); an exhortation for the aristocracy to study English law (72–79); an epistle, translated from Erasmus, offering comfort to Mary Brandon upon her son's death (103–20); and a legal brief accusing a soldier of civil offenses (126–28).

Book 2 examines the structure of a persuasive discourse, including the ''entrance'' or introduction; the ''narration,'' forecasting the dominant argument; the ''division,'' stating its major parts; the ''proposition,'' formulating its thesis in succinct terms; the ''confirmation,'' analyzing its argument in detail; the ''confutation,'' refuting opposing arguments; and the conclusion. Wilson then discusses procedures for ''amplification and copia,'' the former to expand the argument, and the latter to multiply it. Finally, Wilson offers his most original contribution to rhetorical pedagogy in a section on moving the audience's emotions through pity and laughter. To complement his advice that rhetoricians should spice their discourse with ''things wittily devised and pleasantly set forth'' (47), Wilson provides a short anthology of illustrative, humorous anecdotes (164–83).

A discourse will succeed if it ''use these lessons, whereof the first is to be short; the next to be plain; and the third is to speak likely and with reason'' (139). This practical advice dominates Part 3, which focuses upon ''exornation,'' or stylistic embellishment through figures and tropes. Its commendation of crisp, clear, concise usage advances the claim ''that we never affect any strange inkhorn terms but speak as is commonly received, neither seeking to be overfine nor yet living overcareless, using our speech as most men do, and ordering our wits as the fewest have done'' (188). Wilson's review of figures and tropes is the least inspired part of his treatise, but it still affords a useful compendium of conventionally received definitions. The book ends with a short treatment of the roles of memory and pronunciation in oral delivery.

CRITICAL RECEPTION

The spectacular contrast between Wilson's lower-class origins and his ultimate prominence at Elizabeth's court suggests a paradigm for the Elizabethan self-made man, an exemplar of upward mobility in an age that encouraged self-advancement. It also suggests the tensions that brace his work between compliance with authority and opposition to it (see Bushnell, Rebhorn, and especially Sloan). These tensions inform Wilson's discussion of rhetoric's usefulness and also his selection of examples. Wilson exalts the power of rhetoric to defend legitimate authority, affirm the status quo, and empower the ruling classes. Orators persuade resistant individuals to accept their lot in the name of a conventionally sanctioned social order. At the same time, Wilson suggests the power of rhetoric to change, if not the entire order, at least one's place within it. Verbal skills provide an entry into the commercial and bureaucratic world, permitting the user to work advantageously for, as well as against, the established institutions.

Rhetoric can also demystify the status quo, as Wilson suggests in frequent satirical anecdotes and in his repeated endorsement of skeptical insights by Socrates, Diogenes, Lucian, Erasmus, and Thomas More.* To exemplify the despised ''inkhorn'' style, Wilson concocts a hilarious parody of Latinate verbosity in a letter written by a Lincolnshire man, perhaps the man he would have been if he had not climbed to higher circles (189–91). Here we can discern the simultaneous self-acclamation and self-laceration of a man born into one level of society but striving to secure and defend his place in another. Few rhetoricians allow so candid a glimpse into the processes of psychic reaction formations.

BIBLIOGRAPHY

Works by Thomas Wilson

The Arte of Rhetorique. Ed. G. H. Mair. Oxford: Clarendon Press, 1909.

The Art of Rhetoric (1560). Ed. with notes and commentary Peter E. Medine. University Park: Pennsylvania State University Press, 1994.

A Discourse upon Usury by way of Dialogue and Orations. Ed. R. H. Tawney. New York: Harcourt, Brace, 1925.

The Rule of Reason, Conteinying the Arte of Logique. Ed. Richard S. Sprague. Northridge, CA: San Fernando Valley State College, 1972.

Studies of Thomas Wilson

Bushnell, Rebecca. *The Subject of Humanism: Rethinking Early-Modern Humanist Pedagogy*. Ithaca, NY: Cornell University Press, 1996.

Conley, Thomas M. *Rhetoric in the European Tradition*. White Plains, NY: Longman, 1990.

Howell, Wilbur S. *Logic and Rhetoric in England, 1500–1700*. Princeton: Princeton University Press, 1956.

Kennedy, George A. *Classical Rhetoric and Its Christian and Secular Tradition from Ancient to Modern Times*. Chapel Hill: University of North Carolina Press, 1980.

Kennedy, William J. *Rhetorical Norms in Renaissance Literature*. New Haven, CT: Yale University Press, 1978.

Medine, Peter E. *Thomas Wilson*. Boston: Twayne English Authors Series, 1986.

Rebhorn, Wayne A. *The Emperor of Men's Minds*. Ithaca, NY: Cornell University Press, 1995.

Sloan, Thomas. *On the Contrary: Studies in Rhetoric, Education, Erasmus, and Thomas Wilson*. Washington, DC: Catholic University Press of America, 1997.

Vickers, Brian. *In Defence of Rhetoric*. Oxford: Clarendon Press, 1988.

WILLIAM J. KENNEDY

LADY MARY WROTH
(c. 1584–1653)

BIOGRAPHY

Mary Wroth, born Mary Sidney, is known both for her family associations as well as for her literary accomplishments. Daughter of Barbara Gamage and Robert Sidney,* whose estate and hospitality are celebrated in Ben Jonson's* "To Penshurst," niece to Mary Sidney,* literary patron and translator of Psalms, and to Philip Sidney,* the renowned Elizabethan courtier and poet, Lady Mary was born into, and participated in, an aristocratic literary culture. As an author, Mary Wroth was the first Englishwoman to compose and publish a prose romance, *The Countess of Montgomery's Urania*, to which was appended her sonnet sequence *Pamphilia to Amphilanthus*. Mary Wroth was also the author of a play, *Love's Victorie*, and letters to family and members of the aristocracy and royalty, including Queen Anne. As a young woman in the Jacobean court,

Lady Mary participated in court entertainments, specifically as an Ethiopian nymph in Queen Anne's first masque, *The Masque of Blackness* (1605) and again in *The Masque of Beauty* (1608).

In 1604, Lady Mary was married to Robert Wroth, knighted in 1603, son of Sir Robert Wroth. Having acquired her husband's debts upon his death in 1614 and having lost control of the estate to her husband's uncle upon the death of their two-year-old son in 1616, Lady Mary's financial situation changed radically. Any hopes she might have had to gain financial independence through the sale of her romance proved fruitless, as the publication (1621) was revoked six months later.

Lady Mary also maintained a love affair with her first cousin, William Herbert, earl of Pembroke. After her husband's death, she bore two children by Herbert, a son, William, and a daughter, Catherine. Although little is known about these children, the Herbert papers establish that William died unmarried. Gary Waller cites a paper delivered by Sharon Valiant, who suggests that Catherine may have been the mother of Aphra Behn. After the revocation of the *Urania* in 1621 little is heard from or about Lady Mary save documents recording the transfer of land. As Waller further notes, "[H]er death is referred to in passing in a Chancery deposition of 1668" as having most likely occurred in 1653.

MAJOR WORKS AND THEMES

As the title of Lady Mary's romance and sonnet sequence suggests, Lady Mary establishes herself as a literary descendant of her uncle Philip Sidney, as indicated by their nominal similarities between her uncle's *Arcadia* and his sonnet sequence, later called *Astrophil and Stella*, and her *Urania* and *Pamphilia to Amphilanthus*. In the sonnet sequence, Lady Mary explores the language and structure of Petrarchism through the creation of her female persona, Pamphilia ("lover of all"?), and through her reversal of conventionally gendered roles of lover and beloved. Unlike the Elizabethan male sonneteers, Wroth does not catalog the physical attribute of the beloved and uses the language of praise more often in the service of ideal love. While she makes use of the language of the suffering lover, the figure of Amphilanthus, who would conventionally be the source of this suffering, is notably absent. The sonnet sequence's tour de force is a fourteen-sonnet cycle entitled "A crowne of Sonetts dedicated to Love." Using the corona structure, where the last line of each sonnet is the first line of the next, Wroth creates an architecture using both the image of the circle and the labyrinth.

Mary Ellen Lamb characterizes the *Urania* as "loosely structured upon . . . a series of enchantments, the relationship between Pamphilia and Amphilanthus, and the multiple refractions of events and issues encountered by Pamphilia through dozens of other plots and characters" (144). Wroth makes use of inset stories, inset lyrics, digression, and dialogue in a composition that merges narrative technique with themes of love, identity, and female rule. Throughout, Pamphilia's constancy is emphasized, as opposed to Amphilanthus' infidelity, as is the subject of women as authors of, and audience for, romances.

Roberts theorizes that Wroth's play *Love's Victorie* was composed in the 1620s, about the time when she was writing the second (and unpublished) half of the *Urania*. Roberts draws a parallel between the two, particularly in terms of plot, in which Cupid takes revenge on two lovers and uses pastoral conventions such as the disguised shepherd/poets. The play appears not to have been performed.

CRITICAL RECEPTION

As with many early female writers, the history of critical reception is brief and has been written primarily in the last quarter of this century. Modern critical studies of Wroth's lyric poetry were made possible by the archival and editorial work of the late 1970s and early 1980s. With the forthcoming edition of the *Urania* and the recent publication of *Loves Victory*, Lady Mary's work will be available to a larger audience for study and critique.

To say that Lady Mary was unrecognized as an author in her own time would be inaccurate. Ben Jonson* praises her gifts as a poet in a sonnet in which he claims to have been a better lover and poet. Perhaps the most notorious record of contemporary reception is contained in an exchange of letters between Lady Mary and Lord Edward Denny. Angered by what he believed to be references to family scandal in her *Urania*, Denny accuses Lady Mary, in verse, of being "hermaphrodite in show / In deed a monster." He also chastises her for her choice of genres and for not following the example of her aunt, who chose sacred over amorous subject matter.

Lady Mary Wroth's importance is not simply historical; it is literary as well. As one of the first women to compose, in English, a substantial and complex body of work, she invites us to challenge our ideas of female authorship, genre, and literary history.

BIBLIOGRAPHY

Works by Lady Mary Wroth

The Countess of Mountgomeries Urania. London: John Marriott and John Grismand, 1621.

Pamphilia to Amphilanthus. Ed. Gary Waller. Salzburg: Institut fur Anglistik und Amerikanstik, 1977.

The Poems of Lady Mary Wroth. Ed. Josephine A Roberts. Baton Rouge: Louisiana State University Press, 1983.

Lady Mary Wroth's Loves Victory: The Penshurst Manuscript. Ed. Michael Brennan. London: Roxburghe Club, 1988.

The First Part of The Countess of Montgomery's Urania. Ed. Josephine A. Roberts. Binghamton, NY: Center for Medieval and Early Renaissance Studies, State University of New York at Binghamton, 1995. The remainder forthcoming.

Studies of Lady Mary Wroth

Beilin, Elaine. *Redeeming Eve: Women Writers of the English Renaissance*. Princeton: Princeton University Press, 1987.

Carrell, Jennifer Lee. "A Pack of Lies in a Looking Glass: Lady Mary Wroth's *Urania* and the Magic Mirror of Romance." *Studies in English Literature* 34 (1994): 79–107.

Haselkorn, Anne M., and Betty Travitsky, eds. *The Renaissance Englishwoman in Print: Counterbalancing the Canon*. Amherst: University of Massachusetts Press, 1990.

Lamb, Mary Ellen. *Gender and Authorship in the Sidney Circle*. Madison: University of Wisconsin Press, 1990.

Lewalski, Barbara Kiefer. *Writing Women in Jacobean England*. Cambridge: Harvard University Press, 1993.

Miller, Naomi. " 'Not much to be marked': Narrative of the Woman's Part in Lady Mary Wroth's *Urania*." *Studies in English Literature* 29 (1989): 121–37.

Miller, Naomi, and Gary Waller, eds. *Reading Mary Wroth: Representing Alternatives in Early Modern England*. Knoxville: University of Tennessee Press, 1991.

Pauliessen, May Nelson. *The Love Sonnets of Lady Mary Wroth: A Critical Introduction*. Salzburg: Institut fur Anglistik und Amerikanistik, 1982.

Quilligan, Maureen. "Lady Mary Wroth: Female Authority and the Family Romance." In *Unfolded Tales: Essays on the Renaissance Romance*, ed. Gordon M. Logan and Gordon Teskey. Ithaca, NY: Cornell University Press, 1989.

Roberts, Josephine A. "The Biographical Problem of Pamphilia to Amphilanthus." *Tulsa Studies in Women's Literature* 1 (1983): 43–53.

———. "Lady Mary Wroth's Sonnets: A Labyrinth of the Mind." *Journal of Women's Studies in Literature* 1 (1979): 319–29.

———. "An Unpublished Literary Quarrel concerning the Suppression of Mary Wroth's 'Urania' (1621)." *Notes and Queries* 222 (December 1977): 532–35.

Swift, Carolyn Ruth. "Feminine Identity in Lady Mary Wroth's Romance *Urania*." *English Literary Renaissance* 14 (1984): 328–46.

Waller, Gary. *The Sidney Family Romance: Mary Wroth, William Herbert, and the Early Modern Construction of Gender*. Detroit: Wayne State University Press, 1993.

ANITA DELLARIA

THOMAS WYATT, THE ELDER
(1503–1542)

BIOGRAPHY

Sir Thomas Wyatt was born in 1503 at Allington Castle, the Wyatt family estate in Kent. His father, Sir Henry Wyatt, was a member of the Privy Council of Henry VII and later of Henry VIII. Henry, a man fabled for his loyalty, had been imprisoned and tortured by Richard III for his fidelity to the exiled earl of Richmond (later Henry VII). Wyatt's father was a dominant influence in his life, both as a model for what he valued and a measure of his own inability to match his father's rectitude and sternness of character, and Wyatt's poetry is haunted by the themes of loyalty and betrayal.

In 1515, Wyatt entered St. John's College, Cambridge, which was, in the words of Thomas Nashe,* "an university within itself, shining so far above all other houses . . . that no college in the town was able to compare." Wyatt was only twelve, but that was not an unusually early age of entrance for a young man of the upper gentry who was being prepared for a life at court. He would have been expected to learn some law and history and perfect his knowledge of languages. At St. John's, Wyatt clearly found all he needed, for in later life he showed himself proficient in Latin, French, Italian, and Spanish, with a fine humanistic sense of the interaction of history, literature, politics, and diplomacy. He also made and kept the acquaintance of learned men, such as the great historian John Leland.

By 1516 Wyatt was also making his first appearances at court, under the wing of his father. He was appointed Ewer extraordinary and later clerk of the king's jewels (both ceremonial posts) and became part of the retinue of gallants who surrounded the young and fun-loving Henry VIII. In 1520 Wyatt was married to Elizabeth Brooke, daughter of Thomas, Lord Cobham, who was also a member of the Privy Council and near neighbor to the Wyatt family in Kent. This was politically and socially an extremely advantageous marriage, but it was also a bitterly unhappy one. Both partners were continuously unfaithful to one another. In a letter to his son written in 1537, Wyatt acknowledges that the fault for the lack of "good agreement between the wife and husband . . . is both in your mother and me" and adds somewhat ungraciously, "but chiefly in her."

The central problem of Wyatt's biography is whether the number of his infidelities includes Anne Boleyn. A few years younger than Wyatt, Anne had been brought up at the courts of Margaret of Austria, regent of the Netherlands, and François Ier of France. She returned to England in 1521 as a polished and sophisticated young lady, already being shopped on the marriage market as a suitable bride for an earl. By 1529 she was openly marked out for Henry VIII himself. What happened in the eight-year interval is a subject for conjecture and surmise but not for proof, with the current evidence. Some of Wyatt's most important poems do not make much sense unless they allude to an attachment to Anne. In dismissing these allusions, historian Retha Warnicke admonishes that "caution must be used in reading historical facts into his poetry" and that "there is no surviving evidence except for his arrest in 1536 that his name was ever linked to hers." This view, of course, excludes literature as "evidence" and begs the fact that a liaison between Wyatt and Anne before 1527 would have been unremarkable, and reference to such a liaison between 1527 and 1536 would have been extremely dangerous. After her execution, stories of a connection between them were rife. They mostly emanate from sources friendly to the memory of Katharine of Aragon and hence are designed to defame Anne, but that does not mean they are untrue. Indeed, they may well originate in a campaign of slander against Anne in 1529–33, designed to scare off Henry from proceeding with the divorce.

It seems wisest to accept the allusions of the poems, to accept that a significant number of people who knew them both were prepared to believe they were linked, and to acknowledge that at the time of Anne's execution Wyatt was among those arrested, though not among those accused of committing adultery with her and executed. What they actually did or did not do does not really matter. What matters is that such passionate and dangerous possibilities float under, around, and through the poetry.

From the moment he came to the attention of Henry VIII, Wyatt—like Anne or like anyone else at the court—was launched on a perilous course between favor and mortal danger. In 1526 and 1527 he was member of ambassadorial parties sent to the king of France and the pope. In 1528 he held the office of Marshal of Calais, and in 1533 he served as chief ewer at the coronation of Anne Boleyn. In 1536 he was in prison and facing death; no reason, except his connection to Anne, has ever been alleged as the cause. He witnessed the execution of Anne and the others from the window of his cell in the Tower of London. Only the influence of his father and of Thomas Cromwell*—or perhaps some whim of Henry's—preserved his life.

Wyatt wrote that "these bloody days have broken my heart," and his near escape indeed seems to have changed him. He turned away from what he called his "folly and unthriftness" and turned increasingly toward the guidance of Cromwell, whom Wyatt's aging father had appointed as a sort of substitute parent. Under Cromwell's sponsorship, Wyatt was appointed ambassador to Charles V, Holy Roman Emperor. He distinguished himself in this office, winning the confidence of the emperor and serving as a valuable negotiator on Henry's behalf for the rest of his life.

Shortly after the fall of Cromwell in 1540, however, Wyatt found himself back in prison, along with others of Cromwell's party. His principal accuser was Edmund Bonner, bishop of London, who resented Wyatt's success and his own failure at the imperial court. Wyatt was accused of consorting with traitors. In the two surviving versions of Wyatt's defense to the council, Wyatt pleaded guilty to whatever the king chose to suspect him of but explained how he was only seeking intelligence about the king's enemies—that is, doing exactly what an ambassador should do. To the added accusation of favoring Catholicism, Wyatt acknowledged that he was actually more inclined toward Lutheranism. This time it took the intercession of Henry Howard, earl of Surrey, and his young cousin, Queen Catherine Howard, to win from Henry VIII a pardon for Wyatt.

The price that Henry VIII set for Wyatt's freedom was that he go back to his wife, from whom he had long been separated. The king's hypocrisy on the matter of wives must have cost Wyatt what chance he had left for personal happiness. In 1537 he had begun an affair with a gentlewoman named Elizabeth Darrell, and subsequently they lived together and had a son out of wedlock. Their forced separation in 1541 did not prevent Wyatt from providing for her and the child in his will.

Though Wyatt was a free man, restored to Henry's favor, and still only in his late thirties, his health and perhaps his spirit were broken by the nightmarish tensions of the court. On 3 October 1542 his diplomatic talents were again called upon when he was sent to escort the Spanish ambassador from Dorset to London. Wyatt rode post for several days on his mission but upon his arrival in Sherborne was overcome with exhaustion and fever. After an illness of three days, he died, and was buried there on 11 October.

Wyatt's likeness is preserved in a number of works by Hans Holbein the younger, who was commissioned around 1535 to produce portraits of several members of the Wyatt family. Holbein's painting of the poet's father, Sir Henry Wyatt, is now in the Louvre. Two nearly identical drawings of Wyatt, showing him with full beard, jaunty cap, and penetrating eyes, were probably done in preparation for a full-scale portrait, but no such painting survives. A woodcut likeness in profile, bareheaded, and with classical garb adorns the title page of Surrey's *Epitaph* and John Leland's *Naeniae* (both 1542) and is also attributed to Holbein. Finally, paintings of Wyatt's sister Margaret Lee (Metropolitan Museum, New York) and his son Sir Thomas Wyatt the younger (private collection), both done c. 1543, probably derive from Holbein's workshop or from a follower.

MAJOR WORKS AND THEMES

Wyatt's life was primarily occupied with the court and with diplomatic activities. Writing poetry was an incidental activity, a form of self-promotion, diversion, and reflection. His themes are those of the courtier; sexual flirtation and conquest, political advancement, friendship, and the morality of the social order. His forms are those of lyrical poetry: ballad, song, sonnet, psalm, epigram, and satire. He was particularly celebrated in his own time and forever since for his translations of Petrarch.

Above all, Wyatt's poetry is about the bitterness of sexual and political betrayal. In his most famous lyric, "They flee from me that sometime did me seek," he recalls numerous sexual liaisons ("twenty," but one in particular, "[w]hen her loose gown from her shoulders did fall / And she me caught in her arms"). Though now his partner tries to deny it ever happened, Wyatt knows better: "It was no dream: I lay broad waking." She has given him leave to end the relationship, as if breaking up were his idea, and so he ends in an angry outburst:

> But since that I so kindly am served
> I would fain know what she hath deserved.

His anger is directed not just at one, but at the whole "kind" of women who do not serve him as he has "served" them.

In his epigram "Lucks, my fair falcon," Wyatt laments a similar abandonment by friends: "Like lice away from dead bodies they crawl." The world of the court, like the erotic realm, is a realm with "chains of gold" whose joys have "bitter taste," a realm always haunted by the danger of sudden and devastating betrayal. In "Stand whoso list . . ." Wyatt contrasts the quiet life of obscurity with the dangers of the court and of high estate. He who, by climbing to a place of prominence, "is much known of other," concluded Wyatt, inevitably "of himself, alas, / Doth die unknown, dazed, with dreadful face." The death Wyatt speaks of is not—or is not exclusively—a metaphor. The executions of Anne Boleyn and Thomas Cromwell marked him and marked his poetry.

Wyatt's sexual bitterness and political bitterness are so nearly identical that it is often difficult—or superfluous—to distinguish which he means. In the sonnet "Whoso list to hunt, I know where is an hind," the two are masterfully intertwined. The poem is based on Petrarch's Rime 190, "Una candida cerva." Petrarch's sonnet metaphorically weaves together two different deer: the tame deer of Caesar, who wear jeweled collars protecting them, and a mystical deer with an image of Christ between its antlers that appears to St. Maurice while he is hunting. In Petrarch's poem, the deer is his beloved Laura, who, after her death, appears to him as a memory image that leads him toward Christ and the afterlife. In Wyatt's poem she is a far more physical lady whose love he is forbidden to seek:

> And graven with diamonds in letters plain
> There is written her fair neck round about:
> "*Noli me tangere* for Caesar's I am,
> And wild for to hold though I seem tame."

Most commentators identify the deer with Anne Boleyn and Caesar with Henry VIII. If, as skeptics assert, the identification is not certain, then we would have to invent a nearly identical situation involving some other lady or some other ruler. The beauty of the poem, however, lies not in the historical reference, but in the way Wyatt weaves his reference into the poetic and religious metaphors. By changing Petrarch's "Nessun mi tochi" in the next-to-last line back to the biblical "Noli me tangere," Wyatt recalls more forcefully the words of the risen Christ to the three Marys—or, indeed, to Thomas the doubter—and makes more pointed the ironic difference between himself and Petrarch, between his lady and Laura, and between Henry and either Caesar or Christ. There are no quest for redemption in Wyatt's poem, no conversion of earthly love into spiritual love, no substitution of a heavenly king for a worldly king, only Wyatt's irretrievable loss of the lady's love and perhaps of the king's as well.

The strain of social criticism in Wyatt's verse is most fully developed in "Mine owne John Poyntz," an epistolary satire closely based on a poem by a Florentine contemporary, Luigi Alamanni, and probably written shortly after Wyatt's release from prison in 1536. Wyatt draws for his fellow courtier Poyntz a contrast between life at court and life at his estate in Kent. It is a contrast between tyranny, hypocricy, lechery, sycophancy, and back-stabbing, on one hand, and freedom, honesty, truth, and learning, on the other. The conclusion evokes a humanism like that of Erasmus* or Thomas More* as the bulwark against the corruption of power:

But here I am in Kent and Christendom,
  Among the muses where I read and rhyme,
  Where, if thou list, my John Poyntz, for to come,
Thou shalt be judge how I do spend my time.

Probably at the time of Wyatt's second imprisonment, in 1541, he composed his final masterpiece, a translation of the Penitential Psalms. Wyatt based his work not on the Latin or Greek text, but on an Italian translation by Pietro Aretino* that placed the Psalms in a narrative framework, recounting David's adulterous desire for Bathsheba. This narrative setting reflects a widespread understanding of the Psalms, for medieval and early Renaissance books of hours routinely connected them to David at the time of his adultery. As in his poems on love and on courtship, Wyatt carefully modulates his voice and his imagery in order to interweave personal and historical references. His poem pleads to God for mercy and to the king as if he were a god and yet maintains its distance, always allowing that the king himself might, like David, be the adulterous source of vice and administrative murder.

Such subtle modulation of poetic voice is best understood in light of the circulation of Wyatt's poetry. Because poetry was a courtly avocation, and print was a new and not very reputable technology, only a few of Wyatt's poems were printed in his lifetime. His poems circulated in manuscript among friends and were recited on social occasions. Readers would copy the poems into their private collections of notable writings, known as commonplace books. Of these, the most important is the Egerton manuscript (British Library manuscript 2711), in which Wyatt's poems are recorded in his own hand and in that of a copyist, with corrections by Wyatt throughout. Later material was added by subsequent owners. Other manuscripts mix Wyatt's poetry with that of his predecessors and contemporaries, especially Chaucer and Surrey.*

Taken as a whole, the manuscripts show a poetry that underwent constant revision in response not only to aesthetic demands but also to shifting occasions. Some poems were distributed widely, and others seem to have been meant for only a few eyes. Historical and personal references are often stated in glancing form: those who are in the know will recognize them, and those who are not in the know are closed out. Hence, Wyatt's poetry in manuscript often seems more like a dramatic script than like poetry in print. It requires the poet's own voice and the presence of an audience, which together will fill out its ironies and allusions. Wyatt's first editor, Richard Tottel, recognized as much in 1557, when he fitted out Wyatt's poems with descriptive headnotes in order to re-create, or replace, the deadly intimacy of the Henrician court.

CRITICAL RECEPTION

Wyatt's reputation was secured immediately after his death in 1542 by his young admirer Henry Howard, earl of Surrey, who took the unusual step of printing *An excellent Epitaffe of syr Thomas Wyat* and supporting the publication of a book of elegies by Wyatt's old friend John Leland under the title *Naeniae in mortem Thomae Viati equitis incomparabilis* (Little poetic laments on the death of the incomparable Sir Thomas Wyatt). In these verses, Wyatt is celebrated as a bold thinker and person of strong moral character who "reft Chaucer the glory of his wit" and turned his eloquence to Britain's glory. Surrey's epitaphs give a twist to this portrait: Wyatt's honesty—especially in his translation of the *Penitential Psalms*—stands as a rebuke to the hypocrisy of the adulterous King Henry. In his *Miscellany* of 1557, Richard Tottel echoes the core of Surrey's and Leland's assessment when he invokes "the weightiness of the deepwitted Sir Thomas Wyatt the elder's verse." Characteristically, though, he overlooks any particular topical reference in Wyatt's verse and so pulls the fangs of any criticism of the late monarch that might still prove offensive to a daughter on the throne.

By the late sixteenth century, Wyatt was still celebrated by George Puttenham* as a leader of "a new company of courtly makers" who sprang up toward the end of the reign of Henry VIII, but his roughness of meter made him less attractive than Surrey. The assessment of Wyatt as Surrey's forerunner held sway through the seventeenth, eighteenth, and nineteenth centuries, so long as the primary focus was on their Petrarchan translations. In his *History of English Poetry* (1781), Thomas Warton wrote that "Wyatt, although sufficiently distinguished from the common versifiers of his age, is confessedly inferior to Surrey in harmony of numbers, perspicuity of expression, and facility of phraseology. Nor is he equal to Surrey in elegance of sentiment, in nature and sensibility. . . . He has too much art as a lover, and too little as a poet."

In the twentieth century, proponents of modernist aesthetics reversed this assessment of Wyatt. E.M.W. Tillyard reedited Wyatt's poetry in 1929, stressing his connection to Chaucer and medieval lyric. This freed Wyatt from the suspicion of being a mere imitator of foreign affectation and shifted the emphasis to those qualities that Surrey and Leland had praised: honesty, directness, and incisive wit. This native and plainspoken Wyatt thus seemed a better representative of the British national character than the affected and refined Surrey. Likewise, C. S. Lewis (1954) and H. A. Mason (1959) stressed Wyatt's ability to achieve a manly sincerity. The work of Mason, Kenneth Muir (1963), and Patricia Thomson (1964) restored the biographical and political context of Wyatt's verse, separating out likelihood from romantic legend and again underscoring the ways in which his poetic voice can be understood as a personal one. Wyatt's satires and non-Petrarchan lyrics became the locus of a dramatic and at times confessional poetic voice, a fit if distant precursor to Eliot, Yeats, and Auden.

The historicizing of Wyatt also opened the door to a new historicizing of the poet. Wyatt has a crucial place in Stephen Greenblatt's pivotal book *Renaissance Self-Fashioning* (1980), where he is linked to Thomas More and William Tyndale* as one of a trio of early Tudor writers negotiating a place for the self between the absolute power of God and the absolute power of the monarch. Of the three, Wyatt becomes the avatar of modernity—though of a rather different modernity than Tillyard's. Unlike Tyndale or More, Wyatt projects little sense of a being or identity derived from God. He is the creature and, at times, the prisoner of state power. Ironically, this analysis turns attention even more away from Wyatt's Petrarchan poetry and focuses on his translation of the *Penitential Psalms* as the site of the voice speaking in terror *de profundis*. Greenblatt's political reading of Wyatt hence returns to the very poems that Surrey had seen as most political 450 years earlier.

BIBLIOGRAPHY

Works by Thomas Wyatt, the Elder

The Arundel Harington Manuscript of Tudor Poetry. 2 vols. Ed. Ruth Hughey. Columbus: Ohio State University Press, 1960.

Tottel's Miscellany (1557–1587). 2 vols. Ed. Hyder E. Rollins. Cambridge: Harvard University Press, 1929–30.

The Works of Henry Howard, Earl of Surrey, and of Sir Thomas Wyatt the Elder. 2 vols. Ed. G. F. Nott. London: Longman, 1815.

Wyatt, Thomas. *Collected Poems*. Ed. Joost Daalder. Oxford: Oxford University Press, 1975.

———. *The Complete Poems*. Ed. R. A. Rebholz. New Haven, CT: Yale University Press, 1981.

Studies of Thomas Wyatt, the Elder

Crewe, Jonathan. *Trials of Authorship: Anterior Forms and Poetic Reconstruction from Wyatt to Shakespeare*. Berkeley: University of California Press, 1990.

Greenblatt, Stephen. *Renaissance Self-Fashioning: Wyatt to Shakespeare*. Chicago: University of Chicago Press, 1980.

Harrier, Richard. *The Canon of Sir Thomas Wyatt's Poetry*. Cambridge: Harvard University Press, 1975.

Herman, Peter C., ed. *Rethinking the Henrician Era: Essays on Early Tudor Texts and Contexts*. Urbana, 1994.

Jentoft, C. W. *Sir Thomas Wyatt and Henry Howard, Earl of Surrey: A Reference Guide*. Boston: G. K. Hall, 1980.

Lever, J. W. *The Elizabethan Love Sonnet*. London: Methuen, 1956.

Lewis, C. S. *English Literature in the Sixteenth Century, excluding Drama*. Oxford: Clarendon Press, 1954.

Mason, H. A. *Humanism and Poetry in the Early Tudor Period*. London: Routledge, 1959.

———. *Sir Thomas Wyatt: A Literary Portrait*. Bristol, 1986.

Muir, Kenneth. *The Life and Letters of Sir Thomas Wyatt*. Liverpool, 1963.

Peterson, Douglas. *The English Lyric from Wyatt to Donne*. Princeton: Princeton University Press, 1967.

Smith, Hallett. "The Art of Sir Thomas Wyatt." *Huntington Library Quarterly* 9 (1946): 323–55.

Southall, Raymond. *The Courtly Maker: An Essay on the Poetry of Wyatt and His Contemporaries*. Oxford: Blackwell, 1964.

Stevens, J. E. *Music and Poetry in the Early Tudor Court*. London: Methuen, 1961.

Thompson, John. *The Founding of English Metre*. New York: Columbia University Press, 1961.

Thomson, Patricia. *Sir Thomas Wyatt and His Background.* London: Routlegde and K. Paul, 1964.

———, ed. *Wyatt: The Critical Heritage*. London: Routledge and K. Paul, 1974.

Waddington, Raymond, and Thomas Sloan, eds. *The Rhetoric of Renaissance Poetry: From Wyatt to Milton.* Berkeley: The University of California Press,1974.

Warnicke, Retha. *The Rise and Fall of Anne Boleyn: Family Politics at the Court of Henry VIII.* Cambridge: Cambridge University Press, 1989.

Zagorin, Perez. ''Sir Thomas Wyatt and the Court of Henry VIII: The Courtier's Ambivalence.'' *Journal of Medieval and Renaissance Studies* 23 (1993): 113–41.

CLARK HULSE

SELECTED GENERAL BIBLIOGRAPHY

Burckhardt, Jacob. *The Civilization of Renaissance Italy*. 3d ed. Oxford: Phaidon, 1995.

Cassirer, Ernst. *The Individual and the Cosmos in Renaissance Philosophy*. Oxford: Blackwell Press, 1963.

Colie, Rosalie. *Paradoxia Epidemica: The Renaissance Tradition of Paradox*. Princeton: Princeton University Press, 1966.

Fish, Stanley Eugene. *Self-Consuming Artifacts: The Experience of Seventeenth Century Literature*. Berkeley: University of California Press, 1972.

Gombrich, Ernst Hans. *Gombrich on the Renaissance*. 3 vols. London: Phaidon Press, 1993.

Greenblatt, Stephen Jay. *Renaissance Self-Fashioning from More to Shakespeare*. Chicago: University of Chicago Press, 1980.

Hardison, O. B. *The Enduring Monument: A Study of the Idea of Praise in Renaissance Literary Theory and Practice*. Chapel Hill: University of North Carolina Press, 1962.

Hayden, Hiram Collins. *The Counter-Renaissance*. New York: Grove Press, 1960.

Helgerson, Richard. *Self-Crowned Laureates: Spenser, Jonson, Milton and the Literary System*. Berkeley: University of California Press, 1983.

Huizinga, Johan. *The Weaving of the Middle Ages*. Garden City, NY: Doubleday, 1954.

Kerrigan, William, and Gordon Braden. *The Ideas of the Renaissance*. Baltimore: Johns Hopkins University Press, 1989.

Lewis, C. S. *English Literature in the Sixteenth Century excluding Drama*. Oxford: Clarendon Press, 1954.

Lovejoy, Arthur O. *The Great Chain of Being: A Study of the History of an Idea*. Cambridge: Harvard University Press, 1933.

Montrose, Louis. ''Renaissance Literary Studies and the Subject of History.'' *English Literary Renaissance* 16 (1986): 5–12.

Panofsky, Erwin. *Renaissances and Renacences in Western Art*. 2d ed. London: Paladin, 1970.

Patterson, Annabel. *Censorship and Interpretation: The Condition of Writing and Reading in Early Modern England*. Madison: University of Wisconsin Press, 1984.

Pollard, A. F. *Wolsey*. London: Longmans, Green, 1929.

Raleigh, Walter. ''Introduction.'' *Book of the Courtier from the Italian of Count Baldassare Castiglione*. Trans. Thomas Hoby. London: David Nutt, 1900, vii–lxxxviii.

Stone, Lawrence. *Crisis in the Aristocracy: 1558–1641*. Oxford: Clarendon Press, 1965.

Tillyard, E.M.W. *The Elizabethan World Picture*. New York: Vintage, 1966.

Wind, Edgar. *Pagan Mysteries in the Renaissance*. New York: Norton, 1958, 1968.

Wolfflin, Heinrich. *The Art of the Italian Renaissance*. New York: Schochen, 1968.

Yates, Frances Amelia. *Astraea: The Imperial Theme in the Sixteenth Century*. London: Routledge and K. Paul, 1975.

INDEX

Page numbers in **bold type** refer to main entries in the sourcebook.

ABOUT THE CONTRIBUTORS

MELISSA D. AARON is a graduate student at the University of Wisconsin.

GAVIN ALEXANDER is a professor at Gonville and Caius College in Cambridge, England.

DEREK ALWES is a professor at Ohio State University, Newark Campus.

LYELL ASHER is a professor at Lewis and Clark College.

PAMELA JOSEPH BENSON is a professor at Rhode Island College.

DOUGLAS BIOW is a professor at the University of Texas at Austin.

GARY M. BOUCHARD is a professor at Saint Anselm College.

CARLA BOYER is a graduate student at Cornell University.

DOUGLAS BRUSTER is a professor at the University of Texas at San Antonio.

IRENE S. BURGESS is a professor at Wheeling Jesuit College.

SHEILA T. CAVANAGH is a professor at Emory University.

SUSANNE COLLIER is a professor at California State University in Northridge.

FRANCIS R. CZERWINSKI is a professor at SUNY Cortland.

JACK D'AMICO is a professor at Canisius College.

LLOYD DAVIS is a professor at the University of Queensland.

ANITA DELLARIA is a graduate student at the University of Illinois at Chicago.

MONICA DURANT is a graduate student at the University of Oregon.

LOUIS A. GEBHARD is professor emeritus at SUNY Cortland.

MICHAELA PAASCHE GRUDIN is a professor at Lewis and Clark College.

ROBERT GRUDIN is a professor at the University of Oregon.

ALAN HAGER is a professor at SUNY Cortland.

RUTH E. HAMILTON is the director of exhibitions at the Newberry Library.

SONJA HANSARD-WEINER is a professor at the University of Wisconsin.

RICHARD F. HARDIN is a professor at the University of Kansas.

RONALD W. HARRIS is a professor at Southeastern Louisiana University.

SARAH HILSMAN is a graduate student at the University of Chicago.

SEYMOUR BAKER HOUSE is a professor at Mount Angel Seminary.

CLARK HULSE is a professor at the University of Illinois at Chicago.

JOHN W. HUNTINGTON is a professor at the University of Illinois at Chicago.

VICKI JANIK is a professor at SUNY Farmington.

CAROL V. KASKE is a professor at Cornell University.

WILLIAM J. KENNEDY is a professor at Cornell University.

ROBERT L. KINDRICK is a provost and professor at the University of Montana.

ARTHUR F. KINNEY is a professor at the University of Massachusetts and New York University.

ANDREW M. KIRK is a professor at the University of California at Davis.

LISA MARY KLEIN is a professor at Ohio State University.

ROGER A. LADD is a graduate student at the University of Wisconsin.

CLAYTON D. LEIN is a professor at Purdue University.

REBECCA LEMON is a graduate student at the University of Wisconsin.

RONALD LEVAO is a professor at Rutgers University.

TERRENCE J. McGOVERN is a senior assistant librarian at the Memorial Library at SUNY Cortland.

SUSANNAH BRIETZ MONTA is a graduate student at the University of Wisconsin.

MARY A. PETERS is a graduate student at the University of Oregon.

HUGH RICHMOND is a professor at the University of California at Berkeley.

VELMA BOURGEOIS RICHMOND is a professor at Holy Names College.

JOHN A. SHEDD is a professor at SUNY Cortland.

DAIN A. TRAFTON is a professor at Rockford College.

JAMES GRANTHAM TURNER is a professor at the University of California at Berkeley.

RAYMOND BRUCE WADDINGTON, JR. is a professor at the University of California at Davis.

ANDREW D. WEINER is a professor at the University of Wisconsin.

JOHN WILSON is a graduate student at the University of Oregon.

MATHEW WINSTON is a professor at the University of Alabama.

JANET WOLF is a professor at SUNY Cortland.

KENNETH R. WRIGHT is a graduate student at the University of Oregon.

ISBN 0-313-29436-4
90000>
EAN
9 780313 294365
HARDCOVER BAR CODE